Operations Research and Cyber-Infrastructure

OPERATIONS RESEARCH/COMPUTER SCIENCE INTERFACES

Professor Ramesh Sharda   Prof. Dr. Stefan Voß
Oklahoma State University   *Universität Hamburg*

John W. Chinneck • Bjarni Kristjansson
Matthew J. Saltzman
Editors

Operations Research and Cyber-Infrastructure

 Springer

Editors

John W. Chinneck
Carleton University
Dept. Systems & Computer Engineering
Ottawa ON K1S 5B6
Canada
chinneck@sce.carleton.ca

Dr. Matthew J. Saltzman
Clemson University
Dept. of Mathematical Sciences
College of Engineering and Science
Clemson SC 29634
Box 340975
USA
mjs@clemson.edu

Bjarni Kristjansson
Maximal Software, Inc.
2111 Wilson Blvd.
Arlington VA 22201
USA
bjarni@maximalsoftware.com

ISSN: 1387-666X
ISBN: 978-1-4419-4702-4   e-ISBN: 978-0-387-88843-9
DOI: 10.1007/978-0-387-88843-9

Printed on acid-free paper

springer.com

Dedicated to the memory of Chester MacRae "Mac" Chinneck, 1926–2008. He was the kind of father everyone hopes for, but few are lucky enough to have.

Preface

This book is the companion volume to the Eleventh INFORMS Computing Society Conference (ICS 2009), held in Charleston, South Carolina, from January 11 to 13, 2009. It includes 24 high-quality refereed research papers.

The focus of interest for ICS is the interface between Operations Research and Computer Science, and the papers in this volume reflect that interest. This is naturally an evolving area as computational power increases rapidly while decreasing in cost even more quickly. The papers included here illustrate the wide range of topics at this interface. For convenience, they are grouped in broad categories and subcategories. There are three papers on modeling, reflecting the impact of recent development in computing on that area. Eight papers are on optimization (three on integer programming, two on heuristics, and three on general topics, of which two involve stochastic/probabilistic processes). Finally, there are thirteen papers on applications (three on the conference theme of cyber-infrastructure, four on routing, and six on other interesting topics). Several of the papers could be classified in more than one way, reflecting the interactions between these topic areas.

We thank the members of the program committee (listed below), local arrangements co-coordinator Chris Starr (College of Charleston) and the many authors, referees, and stream organizers who contributed their time and effort.

JOHN CHINNECK, BJARNI KRISTJANSSON, AND MATTHEW SALTZMAN

Program Committee:
Edward Baker, University of Miami
John Chinneck, Carleton University
Robert Fourer, Northwestern University
Bruce Golden, University of Maryland
Lou Hafer, Simon Fraser University
William Hart, Sandia National Laboratories
Allen Holder, Rose-Hulman Institute of Technology
Bjarni Kristjansson, Maximal Software
Manuel Laguna, University of Colorado at Boulder
Laurent Michel, University of Connecticut

Warren Powell, Princeton University
S. Raghu Raghavan, University of Maryland
Ted Ralphs, Lehigh University
Matthew Saltzman, Clemson University
Douglas Shier, Clemson University
Cole Smith, University of Florida
Michael Trick, Carnegie Mellon University
Pascal Van Hentenryck, Brown University
Edward Wasil, American University
David Woodruff, University of California, Davis

Contents

Part 3 Applications

Part 1
Modeling

Python Optimization Modeling Objects (Pyomo)

William E. Hart

Abstract We describe Pyomo, an open-source tool for modeling optimization applications in Python. Pyomo can be used to define abstract problems, create concrete problem instances, and solve these instances with standard solvers. Pyomo provides a capability that is commonly associated with algebraic modeling languages like AMPL and GAMS. Pyomo leverages the capabilities of the Coopr software, which integrates Python packages for defining optimizers, modeling optimization applications, and managing computational experiments.

Key words: Python, Modeling language, Optimization, Open Source Software

1 Introduction

Although high quality optimization solvers are commonly available, the effective integration of these tools with an application model is often a challenge for many users. Optimization solvers are typically written in low-level languages like Fortran or C/C++ because these languages offer the performance needed to solve large numerical problems. However, direct development of applications in these languages is quite challenging. Low-level languages like these can be difficult to program; they have complex syntax, enforce static typing, and require a compiler for development.

There are several ways that optimization technologies can be more effectively integrated with application models. For restricted problem domains, optimizers can be directly interfaced with application modeling tools. For example, modern spreadsheets like Excel integrate optimizers that can be applied to linear programming and simple nonlinear programming problems in a natural way. Similarly, engineering design frameworks like the Dakota toolkit (Eldred et al, 2006) can apply optimizers

William E. Hart
Sandia National Laboratories, Discrete Math and Complex Systems Department, PO Box 5800, Albuquerque, NM 87185 e-mail: wehart@sandia.gov

J.W. Chinneck et al. (eds.), *Operations Research and Cyber-Infrastructure*, Operations Research/Computer Science Interfaces Series 47, DOI: 10.1007/978-0-387-88843-9_1, © Springer Science+Business Media, LLC 2009

to nonlinear programming problems by executing separate application codes via a system call interface that use standardized file I/O.

Algebraic Modeling Languages (AMLs) are alternative approach that allows applications to be interfaced with optimizers that can exploit problem structure. AMLs are high-level programming languages for describing and solving mathematical problems, particularly optimization-related problems (Kallrath, 2004). AMLs like AIMMS (AIMMS, 2008), AMPL (AMPL, 2008; Fourer et al, 2003) and GAMS (GAMS, 2008) have programming languages with an intuitive mathematical syntax that supports concepts like sparse sets, indices, and algebraic expressions. AMLs provide a mechanism for defining variables and generating constraints with a concise mathematical representation, which is essential for large-scale, real-world problems that involve thousands of constraints and variables.

A related strategy is to use a standard programming language in conjunction with a software library that uses object-oriented design to support similar mathematical concepts. Although these modeling libraries sacrifice some of the intuitive mathematical syntax of an AML, they allow the user to leverage the greater flexibility of standard programming languages. For example, modeling tools like FlopC++ (FLOPC++, 2008), OPL (OPL, 2008) and OptimJ (OptimJ, 2008) enable the solution of large, complex problems with application models defined within a standard programming language.

The Python Optimization Modeling Objects (Pyomo) package described in this paper represents a fourth strategy, where a high level programming language is used to formulate a problem that can be solved by optimizers written in low-level languages. This two-language approach leverages the flexibility of the high-level language for formulating optimization problems and the efficiency of the low-level language for numerical computations. This approach is increasingly common in scientific computing tools, and the Matlab TOMLAB Optimization Environment (TOMLAB, 2008) is probably the most mature optimization software using this approach.

Pyomo supports the definition and solution of optimization applications using the Python scripting language. Python is a powerful dynamic programming language that has a very clear, readable syntax and intuitive object orientation. Pyomo was strongly influenced by the design of AMPL. It includes Python classes that can concisely represent mixed-integer linear programming (MILP) models. Pyomo is interated into Coopr, a COmmon Optimization Python Repository. The Coopr Opt package supports the execution of models developed with Pyomo using standard MILP solvers.

Section 2 describes the motivation and design philosophy behind Pyomo, including why Python was chosen for the design of Pyomo. Section 3 describes Pyomo and contrasts Pyomo with AMPL. Section 4 reviews other Python optimization packages that have been developed, and discusses the high-level design decisions that distinguish Coopr. Section 5 describes the Coopr Opt package and contrasts its capabilities with other Python optimization tools. Finally, Section 6 describes future Coopr developments that are planned.

2 Pyomo Motivation and Design Philosophy

The design of Pyomo is motivated by a variety of factors that have impacted applications at Sandia National Laboratories. Sandia's discrete mathematics group has successfully used AMPL to model and solve large-scale integer programs for many years. This application experience has highlighted the value of AMLs for real-world applications, which are now an integral part of operations research solutions at Sandia.

Pyomo was developed to provide an alternative platform for developing math programming models that facilitates the application and deployment of optimization capabilities. Consequently, Pyomo is not intended to perform modeling *better* than existing tools. Instead, it supports a different modeling approach for which the software is designed for flexibility, extensibility, portability, and maintainability.

2.1 Design Goals and Requirements

2.1.1 Open Source

A key goal of Pyomo is to provide an open-source math programming modeling capability. Although open-source optimization solvers are widely available in packages like COIN-OR, surprisingly few open-source tools have been developed to model optimization applications. An open-source capability for Pyomo is motivated by several factors:

- **Transparency and Reliability:** When managed well, open-source projects facilitate transparency in the software design and implementation. Since any developer can study and modify the software, bugs and performance limitations can be identified and resolved by a wide range of developers with diverse software experience. Consequently, there is growing evidence that managing software as open-source can improve its reliability.
- **Customizable Capability:** A key limitation of commercial modeling tools is the ability to customize the modeling or optimization process. An open-source project allows a diverse range of developers to prototype new capabilities. These extensions can customize the software for specific applications, and they can motivate capabilites that are integrated into future software releases.
- **Flexible Licensing:** A variety of significant operations research applications at Sandia National Laboratories have required the use of a modeling tool with a non-commercial license. Open-source license facilitate the free distribution of Pyomo within other open-source projects.

Of course, the use of an open-source model is not a panacea. Ensuring high reliability of the software requires careful software management and a commited developer community. However, flexible licensing appears to be a distinct feature of open-source software. The Coopr software, which contains Pyomo, is licensed under the BSD.

2.1.2 Flexible Modeling Language

Another goal of Pyomo is to directly use a modern programming language to support the definition of math programming models. In this manner, Pyomo is similar to tools like FlopC++ and OptimJ, which support modeling in C++ and Java respectively. The use of an existing programming language has several advantages:

- **Extensibility and Robustness:** A well-used modern programming language provides a robust foundation for developing and applying models, because the language has been well-tested in a wide variety of contexts. Further, extensions typically do not require changes to the language but instead involve additional classes and modeling routines that can be used in the modeling process. Thus, support of the modeling language is not a long-term factor when managing the software.
- **Documentation:** Modern programming languages are typically well-documented, and there is often a large on-line community to provide feedback to new users.
- **Standard Libraries:** Languages like Java and Python have a rich set of libraries for tackling just about every programming task. For example, standard libraries can support capabilities like data integration (e.g. working with spreadsheets), thereby avoiding the need to directly support this in a modeling tool.

An additional aspect of general-purpose programming languages is that they can support modern language features, like classes and first-class functions, that can be critical when defining complex models.

Pyomo is implemented in Python, a powerful dynamic programming language that has a very clear, readable syntax and intuitive object orientation. When compared with AMLs like AMPL, Pyomo has a more verbose and complex syntax. Thus, a key issue with this approach concerns the target user community and their level of comfort with standard programming concepts. Our examples in this paper compare and contrast AMPL and Pyomo models, which illustrate this trade-off.

2.1.3 Portability

A requirement of Pyomo's design is that it work on a diverse range of compute platforms. In particular, working well on both MS Windows and Linux platforms is a key requirement for many Sandia applications. The main impact of this requirement has been to limit the choice of programming languages. For example, the .Net languages were not considered for the design of Pyomo due to portability considerations.

2.1.4 Solver Integration

Modeling tools can be roughly categorized into two classes based on how they integrate with optimization solvers: *tightly coupled* modeling tools directly link in optimization solver libraries (including dynamic linking), and *loosely coupled* modeling tools apply external optimization executables (e.g. through system calls). Of course, these options are not exclusive, and a goal of Pyomo is to support both types of solver interfaces.

This design goal has led to a distinction in Pyomo between model formulation and optimization execution. Pyomo uses a high level programming language to formulate a problem that can be solved by optimizers written in low-level languages. This two-language approach leverages the flexibility of the high-level language for formulating optimization problems and the efficiency of the low-level language for numerical computations.

2.1.5 Abstract Models

A requirement of Pyomo's design is that it support the definition of abstract models in a manner similar to the AMPL. AMPL separates the declaration of a model from the data that generates a model instance. This is supports an extremely flexible modeling capability, which has been leveraged extensively in applications at Sandia.

To mimic this capability, Pyomo uses a symbolic representation of data, variables, constraints, etc. Model instances are then generated from external data sets using construction routines that are provided by the user when defining sets, parameters, etc. Further, Pyomo is designed to use data sets in the AMPL format to facilitate translation of models between AMPL and Pyomo.

2.2 Why Python?

Pyomo has been developed in Python for a variety of reasons. First, Python meets the criteria outlined in the previous section:

- **Open Source License:** Python is freely available, and its liberal open source license lets you modify and distribute a Python-based application with few restrictions.
- **Features:** Python has a rich set of datatypes, support for object oriented programming, namespaces, exceptions, and dynamic loading.
- **Support and Stability:** Python is highly stable, and it is well supported through newsgroups and special interest groups.
- **Documentation:** Users can learn about Python from extensive online documentation, and a number of excellent books that are commonly available.
- **Standard Library:** Python includes a large number of useful modules.
- **Extendability and Customization:** Python has a simple model for loading Python code developed by a user. Additionally, compiled code packages that optimize computational kernels can be easily used. Python includes support for shared libraries and dynamic loading, so new capabilities can be dynamically integrated into Python applications.

- **Portability:** Python is available on a wide range of compute platforms, so portability is typically not a limitation for Python-based applications.

Another factor, not to be overlooked, is the increasing acceptance of Python in the scientific community (Oliphant, 2007). Large Python projects like SciPy (Jones et al, 2001–) and SAGE (Stein, 2008) strongly leverage a diverse set of Python packages.

Finally, we note that several other popular programming languages were also considered for Pyomo. However, in most cases Python appears to have distinct advantages:

- **.Net:** As mentioned earlier, the .Net languages are not portable to Linux platforms, and thus they were not suitable for Pyomo.
- **Ruby:** At the moment, Python and Ruby appear to be the two most widely recommended scripting languages that are portable to Linux platforms, and comparisons suggest that their core functionality is similar. Our preference for Python is largely based on the fact that it has a nice syntax that does not require users to type weird symbols (e.g. $, %, @). Thus, we expect this will be a more natural language for expressing math programming models.
- **Java:** Java has a lot of the same strengths as Python, and it is arguably as good a choice for Pyomo. However, two aspects of Python recommended it for Pyomo instead of Java. First, Python has a powerful interactive interpreter that allows realtime code development and encourages experimentation with Python software. Thus, users can work interactively with Pyomo models to become familiar with these objects and to diagnose bugs. Second, it is widely acknowledged that Python's dynamic typing and compact, concise syntax makes software development quick and easy. Although some very interesting optimization modeling tools have been developed in languages like C++ and Java, there is anecdotal evidence that users will not be as productive in these languages as they will when using tools developed in languages like Python (PythonVSJava, 2008).
- **C++:** Models formulated with the FlopC++ package are similar to models developed with Pyomo. They are be specified in a declarative style using classes to represent model components (e.g. sets, variables and constraints). However, C++ requires explicit compilation to execute code, and it does not support an interactive interpreter. Thus, we believe that Python will provide a more flexible language for users.

3 Pyomo Overview

Pyomo can be used to define abstract problems, create concrete problem instances, and solve these instances with standard solvers. Pyomo can generate problem instances and apply optimization solvers with a fully expressive programming language. Python's clean syntax allows Pyomo to express mathematical concepts with a reasonably intuitive syntax. Further, Pyomo can be used within an interactive

Python shell, thereby allowing a user to interactively interrogate Pyomo-based models. Thus, Pyomo has many of the advantages of both AML interfaces and modeling libraries.

3.1 A Simple Example

In this section we illustrate Pyomo's syntax and capabilities by demonstrating how a simple AMPL example can be replicated with Pyomo Python code. Consider the AMPL model, `prod.mod`:

```
set P;

param a {j in P};
param b;
param c {j in P};
param u {j in P};

var X {j in P};

maximize Total_Profit: sum {j in P} c[j] * X[j];

subject to Time: sum {j in P} (1/a[j]) * X[j] <= b;

subject to Limit {j in P}: 0 <= X[j] <= u[j];
```

To translate this into Pyomo, the user must first import the Pyomo module and create a Pyomo **Model** object:

```
#
# Import Pyomo
#
from coopr.pyomo import *

#
# Create model
#
model = Model()
```

This import assumes that Pyomo is available on the users's Python path (see Python documentation for PYTHONPATH for further details). Next, we create the sets and parameters that correspond to the data used in the AMPL model. This can be done very intuitively using the **Set** and **Param** classes.

```
model.P = Set()

model.a = Param(model.P)
model.b = Param()
model.c = Param(model.P)
model.u = Param(model.P)
```

Note that parameter b is a scalar, while parameters a, c and u are arrays indexed by the set P.

Next, we define the decision variables in this model.

```
model.X = Var(model.P)
```

Decision variables and model parameters are used to define the objectives and constraints in the model. Parameters define constants and the variables are the values that are optimized. Parameter values are typically defined by a data file that is processed by Pyomo.

Objectives and constraints are explicitly defined expressions in Pyomo. The **Objective** and **Constraint** classes require a **rule** option that specifies how these expressions are constructed. This is a function that takes one or more arguments: the first arguments are indices into a set that defines the set of objectives or constraints that are being defined, and the last argument is the model that is used to define the expression.

```
def Objective_rule(model):
    ans = 0
    for j in model.P:
        ans = ans + model.c[j] * model.X[j]
    return ans
model.Total_Profit = Objective(rule=Objective_rule,
                               sense=maximize)

def Time_rule(model):
    ans = 0
    for j in model.P:
        ans = ans + (1.0/model.a[j]) * model.X[j]
    return ans < model.b
model.Time = Constraint(rule=Time_rule)

def Limit_rule(j, model):
    return (0, model.X[j], model.u[j])
model.Limit = Constraint(model.P, rule=Limit_rule)
```

The rules used to construct these objects use standard Python functions. The **Time_rule** function includes the use of $<$ and $>$ operators on the expression, which define upper and lower bounds on the constraints. The **Limit_rule** function illustrates another convention that is supported by Pyomo; a rule can return a tuple that defines the lower bound, body and upper bound for a constraint. The value 'None' can be returned for one of the limit values if a bound is not enforced.

Once an abstract model has been created, it can be printed as follows:

```
model.pprint()
```

This summarize the information in the Pyomo model, but it does not print out explicit expressions. This is due to the fact that an abstract model needs to be instanted with data to generate the model objectives and constraints:

```
instance = model.create("prod.dat")
instance.pprint()
```

Once a model instance has been constructed, an optimizer can be applied to it to find an optimal solution. For example, the PICO integer programming solver can be used within Pyomo as follows:

```
opt = solvers.SolverFactory("pico")
opt.keepFiles=True
results = opt.solve(instance)
```

This creates an optimizer object for the PICO executable, and it indicates that temporary files should be kept. The Pyomo model instance is optimized, and the optimizer returns an object that contains the solutions generated during optimization.

3.2 Pyomo Commandline Script

Appendix 7 provides a complete Python script for the model described in the previous section. Although this Python script can be executed directly, Coopr includes a pyomo script that can construct this model, apply an optimizer and summarize the results. For example, the following command line executes Pyomo using a data file in a format consistent with AMPL:

```
pyomo prod.py prod.dat
```

The pyomo script has a variety of command line options to provide information about the optimization process. Options can control how debugging information is printed, including logging information generated by the optimizer and a summary of the model generated by Pyomo. Further, Pyomo can be configured to keep all intermediate files used during optimization, which can support debugging of the model construction process.

4 Related Python Optimization Tools

A variety of related optimization packages have been developed in Python that are designed to support the formulation and solution of specific classes of structure optimization applications:

- **CVXOPT:** A Python package for convex optimization (CVXOPT, 2008).
- **PuLP:** A Python package that can be used to describe linear programming and mixed-integer linear programming optimization problems (PuLP, 2008).
- **POAMS:** A Python modeling tool for linear and mixed-integer linear programs that defines Python objects for abstract sets, constraints, objectives, decision variables, and solver interfaces.
- **OpenOpt:** A relatively new numerical optimization framework that is closely coupled with the SciPy scientific Python package (OpenOpt, 2008).
- **NLPy:** A Python optimization framework that leverages AMPL to create problem instances, which can then be processed in Python (NLPy, 2008).
- **Pyipopt:** A Python interface to the COIN-OR Ipopt solver (Pyipopt, 2008).

Pyomo is closely related to the modeling capabilities of PuLP and POAMS. Pyomo defines Python objects that can be used to express models, and like POAMS, Pyomo supports a clear distinction between abstract models and problem instances. The main distinguishing feature of Pyomo is support for an instance construction process that is automated by object properties. This is akin to the capabilities of AML's like AMPL and GAMS, and it provides a standardized technique for constructing model instances. Pyomo models can be initialized with a generic data object, which can be initialized with a variety of data sources (including AMPL *.dat files).

Like NLPy and OpenOpt, the goal of Coopr Opt is to support a diverse set of optimization methods and applications. Coopr Opt includes a facility for transforming problem formats, which allows optimizers to solve problems without the user worrying about solver-specific implementation details. Further, Coopr Opt supports mechanisms for reporting detailed information about optimization solutions, in a manner akin to the OSrL data format supported by the COIN-OR OS project (Fourer et al, 2008).

In the remainder of this section we use the following example to illustrate the differences between PuLP, POAMS and Pyomo:

$$
\begin{aligned}
\text{minimize} \quad & -4x_1 - 5x_2 \\
\text{subject to} \quad & 2x_1 + x_2 \leq 3 \\
& x_1 + 2x_2 \leq 3 \\
& x_1, x_2 \geq 0
\end{aligned}
\tag{1}
$$

4.1 PuLP

PuLP relies on overloading operators and commonly used mathematical functions to define expression objects that define objectives and constraints. A problem object is defined, and the objective and constraints are added using the += operator. Further, problem variables can be defined over index sets to enable compact specification of constraints and objectives.

The following PuLP example minimizes the LP (1):

```
from pulp import *
x1 = LpVariable("x1",0)
x2 = LpVariable("x2",0)
prob = LpProblem("Example", LpMinimize)
prob += -4*x1 - 5*x2
prob += 2*x1 + x2 <= 3
prob += x1 + 2*x2 <= 3
prob.solve()
```

4.2 POAMS

POAMS is a Python modeling tool for linear and mixed-integer linear programs that defines Python objects for abstract sets, constraints, objectives, decision variables, and solver interfaces. These objects can be used to compose an abstract model definition, which is then used to construct a concrete problem instance from a given data set. This separation of the problem instance from the data facilitates the definition of abstract models that can be populated from a diverse range of data sources.

POAMS models are managed by classes derived from the POAMS LP object. The following POAMS example minimizes the LP (1) by deriving a class, instantiating it, and then running the model:

```
from poams import *

class Example(LP):

    index = Set(1,2)
    x = Var(index)
    obj = Objective()
    c1 = Constraint()
    c2 = Constraint()

    def model(self):
        self.obj.min(-4*self.x[1] - 5*self.x[2])
        self.c1.load( 2*self.x[1] +   self.x[2] <= 3.0)
        self.c2.load(   self.x[1] + 2*self.x[2] <= 3.0)

prob = Example().model()
prob.solve()
```

4.3 Pyomo

The following Pyomo example minimizes LP (1) by instantiating an abstract model, populating the model with symbols, generating an instance, and then applying the PICO MIP optimizer:

```
from coopr.pyomo import *

model = Model()

model.index = Set(initialize =[1,2])
model.x = Var(model.index)

def obj_rule(model):
    return −4*model.x[1]−5*model.x[2]
model.obj = Objective(rule=obj_rule)

def c1_rule(model):
    ans = 2*model.x[1] + model.x[2]
    return ans < 3.0
model.c1 = Constraint(rule=c1_rule)

def c2_rule(model):
    ans = model.x[1] + 2*model.x[2]
    return ans < 3.0
model.c2 = Constraint(rule=c2_rule)


instance = model.create()
opt = solvers.SolverFactory("pico")
results = opt.solve(instance)
```

5 The Coopr Opt Package

The goal of the Coopr Opt package is to support the execution of optimizers in a generic manner. Although Pyomo uses this package, Coopr Opt is designed to support a wide range of optimizers. However, Coopr Opt is not as mature as the OpenOpt package; it currently only supports interfaces to a limited number of optimizers aside from the LP and MILP solvers used by Pyomo.

Coopr Opt is supports a simple strategy for setting up and executing an optimizer, which is illustrated by the following script:

```
opt = SolverFactory ( name )
opt . reset ()
results = opt . solve ( problem )
results . write ()
```

This script illustrates several design principles that Coopr follows:

- **Dynamic Registration of Optimizers:** Optimizers are registered via a plugin mechanism that provides an extensible architecture for developers of third-party optimizers. This plugin mechanism includes the specification of parameters that can be initialized from a configuration file.
- **Separation of Problems and Solvers:** Coopr Opt treats problems and solvers as separate entities. This promotes the development of tools like Pyomo that support flexible definition of optimization applications, and it enables automatic transformation of problem instances.
- **Problem Transformation:** A key challenge for optimization packages is the need to support a diverse set of problem formats. This is an issue even for LP and MILP solver packages, where MPS is the least common denominator for users. Coopr Opt supports an automatic problem transformation mechanism that enables the application of optimizers to problems with a wide range of formats.
- **Generic Representation of Optimizer Results:** Coopr Opt borrows and extends the representation used by the COIN-OR OS project to support a general representation of optimizer results. The *results* object returned by a Coopr optimizer includes information about the problem, the solver execution, and one or more solutions generated during optimization.

If the problem in Appendix 7 is being solved, this script would print the following information that is contained in the results object:

```
=========================================================
------   Solver   Results                         ------
=========================================================

----------   Problem   Information              ----------

name :  None
num_constraints :  5
num_nonzeros :  6
num_objectives :  1
num_variables :  2
sense :  maximize
upper_bound :  192000

----------   Solver   Information               ----------

error_rc :  0
nbounded :  None
```

```
ncreated : None
status : ok
systime : None
usrtime : None
```

─────── Solution 0

```
gap : 0.0
status : optimal
value : 192000
Primal Variables
        X_bands_            6000
        X_coils_            1400
Dual Variables
        c_u_Limit_1         4
        c_u_Time_0          4200
```

It is worth noting that Coopr Opt currently does not support direct library interfaces to optimizers, which is a feature that is strongly supported by Python. However, this is not a design limitation, but instead has been a matter of development priorities. Efforts are planned with the POAMS and PuLP developers to adapt the direct solver interfaces used in these packages for use within Coopr.

Although Coopr Opt development has focused on developing interfaces to LP and MILP solvers, we have recently begun developing interfaces to general-purpose nonlinear programming methods. One of the goals of this effort is to develop application interfaces that are consistent with the interfaces supported by Acro's COLIN optimization library (ACRO, 2008). COLIN has recently been extended to support a system call interface that uses standardized file I/O. An XML format has been developed that can be more rigorously checked than the file format used by the Dakota toolkit (Eldred et al, 2006), and this format can be readily extended to new application results. Coopr Opt supports applications defined using this system call interface, which will simplify the integration of COLIN optimizers into Coopr Opt.

6 Discussion

Coopr is being actively developed to support real-world applications at Sandia National Laboratories. This experience has validated our assessment that Python is an effective language for supporting the solution of optimization applications. Although it is clear that custom languages can support a much more mathematically intuitive syntax, Python's clean syntax and programming model make it a natural choice for optimization tools like Coopr.

Coopr will be publicly released as an open source project in 2008. Future development will focus on several key design issues:

- Interoperable with commonly available optimization solvers, and the relationship of Coopr and OpenOpt.
- Exploiting synergy with POAMS and PuLP. Developers of Coopr, POAMS and PuLP are assessing this intersection to identify where synergistic efforts can be leveraged. For example, the direct solver interface used by POAMS and PuLP can be adapted for use in Pyomo.
- Extending Pyomo to support the definition of general nonlinear models. Conceptually, this is straightforward, but the model generation and expression mechanisms need to be re-designed to support capabilities like automatic differentiation.

Acknowledgements We thank the ICS reviewers for their critical feedback. We also thank Jon Berry, Robert Carr and Cindy Phillips for their critical feedback on the design of Pyomo, and David Gay for developing the Coopr interface to AMPL NL and SOL files. Sandia is a multiprogram laboratory operated by Sandia Corporation, a Lockheed Martin Company, for the United States Department of Energy's National Nuclear Security Administration under Contract DE-AC04-94-AL85000.

References

ACRO (2008) ACRO optimization framework. `http://software.sandia.gov/acro`

AIMMS (2008) AIMMS home page. `http://www.aimms.com`

AMPL (2008) AMPL home page. `http://www.ampl.com/`

CVXOPT (2008) CVXOPT home page. `http://abel.ee.ucla.edu/cvxopt`

Eldred MS, Brown SL, Dunlavy DM, Gay DM, Swiler LP, Giunta AA, Hart WE, Watson JP, Eddy JP, Griffin JD, Hough PD, Kolda TG, Martinez-Canales ML, Williams PJ (2006) DAKOTA, a multilevel parallel object-oriented framework for design optimization, parameter estimation, uncertainty quantification, and sensitivity analysis: Version 4.0 users manual. Tech. Rep. SAND2006-6337, Sandia National Laboratories

FLOPC++ (2008) FLOPC++ home page. `https://projects.coin-or.org/FlopC++`

Fourer R, Gay DM, Kernighan BW (2003) AMPL: A Modeling Language for Mathematical Programming, 2nd Ed. Brooks/Cole–Thomson Learning, Pacific Grove, CA

Fourer R, Ma J, Martin K (2008) Optimization services: A framework for distributed optimization. Mathematical Programming (submitted)

GAMS (2008) GAMS home page. `http://www.gams.com`

Jones E, Oliphant T, Peterson P, et al (2001–) SciPy: Open source scientific tools for Python. URL http://www.scipy.org/

Kallrath J (2004) Modeling Languages in Mathematical Optimization. Kluwer Academic Publishers

NLPy (2008) NLPy home page. http://nlpy.sourceforge.net/

Oliphant TE (2007) Python for scientific computing. Computing in Science and Engineering pp 10–20

OpenOpt (2008) OpenOpt home page. http://scipy.org/scipy/scikits/wiki/OpenOpt

OPL (2008) OPL home page. http://www.ilog.com/products/oplstudio

OptimJ (2008) Ateji home page. http://www.ateji.com

PuLP (2008) PuLP: A python linear programming modeler. http://130.216.209.237/engsci392/pulp/FrontPage

Pyipopt (2008) Pyipopt home page. http://code.google.com/p/pyipopt/

PythonVSJava (2008) Python & java: A side-by-side comparison. http://www.ferg.org/projects/python_java_side-by-side.html

Stein W (2008) Sage: Open Source Mathematical Software (Version 2.10.2). The Sage Group, http://www.sagemath.org

TOMLAB (2008) TOMLAB optimization environment. http://www.tomopt.com/tomlab

7 A Complete Pyomo Example

```
#
# Imports
#
from coopr.pyomo import *

#
# Setup the model
#
model = Model()

model.P = Set()

model.a = Param(model.P)
model.b = Param()
model.c = Param(model.P)
model.u = Param(model.P)

model.X = Var(model.P)
```

```
def  Objective_rule (model ):
    ans  =  0
    for  j  in  model.P:
      ans  =  ans  +  model.c[j]  *  model.X[j]
    return  ans
model . Total_Profit  =  Objective (rule=Objective_rule ,
                                   sense=maximize )

def  Time_rule (model ):
    ans  =  0
    for  j  in  model.P:
      ans  =  ans  +  (1.0/ model.a[j])  *  model.X[j]
    return  ans  <  model.b
model . Time  =  Constraint (rule=Time_rule )

def  Limit_rule (j ,  model ):
    return  (0 ,  model.X[j],  model.u[j ])
model . Limit  =  Constraint (model.P,  rule=Limit_rule )
```

Object Oriented Modeling of Multistage Stochastic Linear Programs

Leo Lopes and Robert Fourer

Abstract We present a specialization of the Unified Modeling Language (UML) to help diverse stakeholders in an organization collaborate on the development of Stochastic Optimization Models. Our language describes, at an abstraction level distinct from that possible through algebraic notation, the relationships between decisions and parameters, the dynamics of information acquisition, and the requirements for model input and output. This paper describes the formal language and provides a few illustrative examples.

Key words: Optimization, Modeling, UML

1 Introduction

While Operations Research (OR) applications and software applications differ in fundamental ways, they also share some very important characteristics: complexity; cross-disciplinary nature; and non-expert customers. Furthermore, OR applications often include important software components, and usually reside inside Information Technology (IT) infrastructures. These observations motivated us to study how established Software Engineering (SE) techniques may be adapted to help create OR models. Our emphasis is on Multistage Stochastic Linear Programs with Recourse (MSPRs). Typical applications of MSPRs include asset and liability management

Leo Lopes

Systems and Industrial Engineering, University of Arizona, 1127 E James E Rogers Way Room 111, Tucson, AZ, 85721, e-mail: leo@sie.arizona.edu

Robert Fourer

Industrial Engineering and Management Sciences, Northwestern University, 2145 N. Sheridan Road Room C210, Evanston, IL, 60201 e-mail: 4er@iems.northwestern.edu

J.W. Chinneck et al. (eds.), *Operations Research and Cyber-Infrastructure*, Operations Research/Computer Science Interfaces Series 47, DOI: 10.1007/978-0-387-88843-9_2, © Springer Science+Business Media, LLC 2009

Yu et al (2003), energy production and distribution Sen et al (2006); Beraldi et al (2008), strategic supply chain design Alonso-Ayuso et al (2003), and natural resources management Heikkinen (2003).

SE techniques facilitate analysis and documentation and enhance maintainability and reliability. The object oriented (OO) paradigm and graphical modeling languages are important components of current SE techniques. This paper addresses the question of how to adapt these components to aid the development of Stochastic Optimization Models. We have two motivations. First, OO methodology has had great success in tackling very difficult but well structured problems similar in many ways to OR problems. Second, OO methodology is pervasive and still expanding in reach within the modern cyberinfrastructure.

The remainder of this paper proceeds as follows: In Section 2 we examine related OR research on model complexity and integration, as well as similar work in other fields. In Sections 3 and 4 we briefly summarize OO SE methods and Multistage Stochastic Programming. In Section 5, we introduce the major aspects of our language with an illustrative example. In Section 6 we apply our language in a few examples from the literature. Section 7 discusses some conclusions and possible extensions.

2 Graphical Modeling and Communication in Optimization

Previous research on formal treatment of OR modeling can be grouped roughly into two approaches: one whose goal is to produce more natural formulation environments for problems that are relatively precise; and one whose goal is to produce analysis techniques suitable for problems which are very "messy", where formality may not be possible or productive.

Structured Modeling Geoffrion (1987), the Intelligent Mathematical Programming System Greenberg (1996), and Jones' work on graph-based Modeling Systems Jones (1990, 1991), are representatives of the more formal approach. Ideas from those contributions have found their way into implementations like MODLER and ANALYZE Greenberg (1993), and into graphical systems like MIMI/G Jones (1996a), LPForm Ma et al (1996), and gLPS Collaud and Pasquier-Boltuck (1994). A commercial modeling system based on ideas developed in the research above is the Enterprise Optimizer (http://www.riverlogic.com). Some of the work in visualization applied to optimization is summarized in Jones (1996b).

Less formal approaches include Problem Structuring Methods (PSM) Rosenhead (1996) and Soft Systems Methodology (SSM) Checkland (2000). These approaches consider conflicting objectives by different actors, group dynamics, incomplete information, ill-defined measures, and other issues that can arise in complex business models.

Our language is designed to support a formal, well structured OR technique. At the same time, it is designed to be used starting at the early stages of the modeling process, at which time some of the conditions well addressed by PSM are still present. This is an important difference between our work and the existing literature, which focuses mostly on replacing Algebraic Modeling Languages (AMLs) like AMPL Fourer et al (2002) or GAMS Brooke et al (1988) with graphical languages Collaud and Pasquier-Boltuck (1994), or with creating detailed consistent multi-level models Geoffrion (1987). In particular, this research addresses the need to maintain a Problem Owner, usually not an OR specialist, involved as an Active Modeler Powell (1997) and to communicate with other stakeholders in the OR project, like IT professionals and operational managers. Our language does not attempt to replace the AML, but to augment and support it.

The UML has been used or extended in a variety of fields including engineering design Felfernig et al (2002), data warehousing Luján-Mora et al (2002, leading to the CWM OMG Standard), groupware Rubart and Dawabi (2002), and secure systems Jrjens (2002). No similar study applying OO to OR-centric systems is available, although a study of Entity Relationship Diagrams applied to optimization Choobineh (1991) exists. The new language SysML Bock (2006), also a specialization of the UML, is of particular interest, since it deals with requirements, constraints, performance measures, and other concepts distinct but similar to those used in OR.

Many important details of stochastic optimization problems are not explicit in our diagrams. This is intentional. *Elision*, modeling an element with certain characteristics hidden in a specific view, is a powerful abstraction mechanism used extensively in the UML. The primary intent of the graphical notation is to describe problems at a high level of abstraction, to encourage discussions between analysts at early stages of the modeling process, or to serve as complementary documentation to an existing precise mathematical model. We believe that customary mathematical notation is adequate to express the relationships in the model at more detailed levels. Algebraic notation is far more concise than any graphical notation can be when representing the same objects and relationships. The algebraic notation in use today is very stable Cajori (1993). For instance, Leibniz used $\int$ for summation of integers as well as integration. Later, Euler introduced $\sum$ to indicate integer summation. Variations in the use of $\sum$ exist in the work of Lagrange, Cauchy, Fourier, and Jacobi up to the 1820s, but except for specialized uses, the use of $\sum$ has remained stable since.

With additional assumptions, in specific application areas, it is possible to devise graphical notations that capture all the detail necessary to build precise models in a practical way. For example, the commercial package Enterprise Optimizer is capable of representing a variety of deterministic linear programs arising from supply chains using icons to represent resources and arcs to represent resource flows. Thus, we have built enough expressiveness and detail into our design so that it is *possible* to represent any linear expression using element diagrams, although we don't foresee this as the primary use case. A significant level of detail can be achieved in our diagrams by using *adornments*. Adornments are optional graphical markers added to an element that add semantic value to its representation. With the aid of adornments, a significant proper subset of algebraic expressions can be rendered in a simple way. An additional function of the adornments is to provide a convenient and intuitive link to access more detailed expressions within a software system.

3 Graphical Modeling and Software Engineering

SE is inherently dynamic and multidisciplinary. As systems became more complex, new methodologies for SE evolved, each with accompanying graphical notations to describe structural or dynamic aspects of systems. Structural aspects define how parts of the system relate to each other. Dynamic aspects describe operations step by step.

The first formal diagram language to find widespread use was the fluxogram or flowchart (Figure 1). Fluxograms use special icons to indicate printing, disk storage, tests, etc. and display control flow using edges. Fluxograms provided basic concepts that would be reused by all the other modeling diagrams that describe the dynamics of systems.

The use of redirections (*i.e.* goto statements), promoted by fluxograms, made large systems difficult to manage. In response, the structured paradigm gained popularity. Its main characteristic was continuous flow of control. Small structures were used for each iterative process, and within each structure systems were again described by a continuous flow of control. Fluxograms did not encourage structured thinking, and thus fell out of favor. Multiple graphical modeling languages like Jackson diagrams Jackson (1983) and data flow diagrams DeMarco (1979) were created to support structured SE and adopted widely. People who were trained to use one set of diagramming techniques were not always comfortable using another, even when both diagrams were used in fundamentally similar ways.

As systems continued to become more complex, the structured paradigm reached its own limits, and the OO paradigm became more popular. This brought to the forefront of the modeling process many concepts which were previously dealt with less formally, like: encapsulation, the notion that an object has a clear interface, but its implementation is hidden from view; and specialization, the concept of having a general class in charge of common functionality, and specialized subclasses for specific behavior. None of the above concepts were necessarily new, but now they were handled explicitly at the modeling level and enforced by development systems.

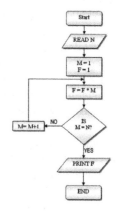

Fig. 1 A fluxogram for computing $N!$ (This image is from Wikipedia, and is in the public domain).

As with the structured paradigm, many modeling methodologies were proposed for the OO paradigm, each accompanied by a graphical notation. Three became particularly popular: the Booch method, by Grady Booch; OMT, by James Rumbaugh and associates; and OOSE by Ivar Jacobson. In the early nineties, at Rational Software Corporation, now part of IBM, they unified their methods. The result was the Unified Modeling Language. Subsequently, the language became an Object Management Group (OMG) standard, currently on version 2.1.

4 Multistage Stochastic Programming

For a more comprehensive introduction to stochastic programming, see Birge and Louveaux (1997, Chapter 1). Our main focus is on the MSPR. In the MSPR, we do not know all the data with certainty when some decisions are made. The data will only be observed at known points in the future. Unfortunately, our decisions need to be made *before* the uncertainty is resolved. Our objective is to make a decision now which minimizes its current (known) cost plus its expected future cost. In the future, there may be **recourse** decisions available *after* the uncertainty has been observed. Those decisions, in turn, may also have to be taken under uncertainty, in recursive fashion, as illustrated in Figure 2.

The periods between when portions of the uncertain data are revealed are called **stages**. To describe what information becomes available when, we created stochasticity diagrams (Section 5.2). Decisions available within a stage are typically dependent on decisions taken earlier and influence future decisions. Within a stage, there are constraints that describe what types of decisions are available and how decisions taken earlier affect the decisions available at this stage. Some of the costs associated with the decisions, the effects of previous decisions, and the limits on the available resources may be uncertain. Element diagrams (Section 5.3) help model these aspects of the MSPR.

Sets are central to practical modeling. Decisions often need to be made over sets of objects of the same kind. Input parameters are also provided over sets. The UML class models this situation. For example, in a facility location model each warehouse has a characteristics like fixed cost or maintenance cost. Each warehouse is an instance of the Warehouse class. A class is represented in UML by a box with compartments for different types of elements, as in Figure 3. UML class diagrams (Section 5.1) describe the sets in an MSPR.

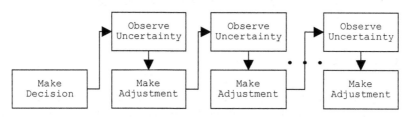

Fig. 2 A stochastic programming model.

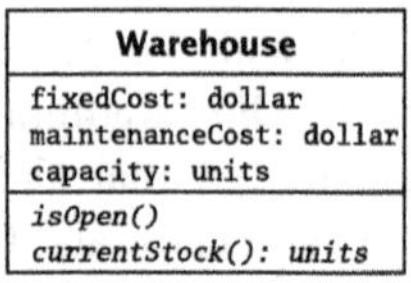

Fig. 3 A simple class.

Warehouse
fixedCost: dollar
maintenanceCost: dollar
capacity: units
isOpen()
currentStock(): units

5 A Meta-model for Multistage Stochastic Programming

The collection of definitions which include Objective, Constraint, Random Variable, etc... is part of the *Meta-model* for stochastic programming. Every problem is an instance of this Meta-model, in the same sense that *Knapsack* is an instance of a combinatorial optimization problem. A Meta-model is similar to a Graph Schema in Jones (1990, 1991).

There are three main types of diagrams in our meta-model: Class Diagrams, specialized from UML Class Diagrams; Stochasticity diagrams, specialized from UML Statechart Diagrams; and Element Diagrams, also specialized from UML Class Diagrams. In this section, we will explain each diagram and illustrate it using a stochastic location-routing problem (SLRP) with the following characteristics:

- The objective is to locate a number of facilities in order to maximize expected profit over a finite horizon.
- Facilities must be opened at one or more candidate locations *before* the demand is observed.
- At the start of each planning period, all orders to be served during that period are known. Orders are shipped in less-then-truckload quantities by a fixed number of trucks of limited capacity.
- Each truck services a number of areas, each of which has some demand associated with it. There is a limit to the time spent on each route, which includes travel time as well as service time.
- New routes can be devised at the beginning of each planning period, but a penalty is incurred for changing routes. A penalty is also incurred when a region that was served in the previous planning period is dropped, if that region's demand in the current planning period is greater than zero.
- Demand not served may be lost to a competitor.

Many formulations and solution approaches are plausible for this problem. For the purposes of this research, we will focus on devising a mechanism to communicate the essential information above to all interested parties, not only OR specialists, but also executive decision makers, IT specialists, or Floor Managers.

5.1 Class Diagrams

The function of a class diagram is to describe details of the classes in a system and the relationships between them. Classes are represented by a box with

Fig. 4 A class diagram.

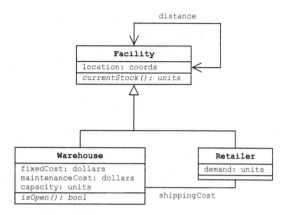

compartments. The first three compartments are used for the class name, attributes, and operations. Other compartments may be used in specific applications for other characteristics.

In Figure 4, we see a *specialization* relationship between Warehouse and Facility. A specialization indicates an *is-a* type of relationship: a Warehouse *is-a* Facility, so it incorporates all its properties. We can also see an *association* relationship between two Facilities, called **distance**. The two are differentiated graphically by the type of arrow. There is also an association between Warehouse and Retailer, called **shippingCost**. Notice that this association does not have an arrow associated with it, but is still valid. Arrows are optional in associations. They are elided here to illustrate a point, but are generally recommended to increase clarity.

The class diagram summarizes all the data used by the optimization problem (parameters), and all the information provided by it (decision variables). It is important for communicating requirements to those responsible for the rest of the IT infrastructure. Therefore, we reused as much functionality from the class diagram as possible. However, elements of a class in an optimization problem have important properties that distinguish them from their SE counterparts. The UML contains mechanisms we can use to describe these differences.

There are two major types of elements in mathematical programming: decisions and parameters. In stochastic programming, parameters may be deterministic or stochastic. Both decisions and parameters can be modeled as attributes of a class. Parameters that are not stochastic are only initialized once, when the class instance is created. The UML property {frozen} (in the UML, properties are expressed by their label in curly brackets) gives an attribute the behavior we desire. In the UML, unless specified otherwise, all attributes are {changeable}. This makes sense in general SE, but is undesirable in the MSPR, since typically only a few parameters are modeled as stochastic. The existing UML construct *note* can be used to indicate that all attributes are {frozen} by default.

Stochastic parameters do not perfectly fit into any concept currently in the UML. They are certainly {changeable}, but in a more specific way. So we create the new property {stochastic}, derived from {changeable}.

The UML has several mechanisms useful for representing decisions. Unfortunately, none are quite perfect. One can think of decisions as operations on a class (*e.g.*, we *open* a facility). Both are given actions as names; and both affect other characteristics of the class. In this view, opening or closing a facility is in fact an action taken on a facility. Unfortunately this view has difficulties. Unlike operations, MSPR decisions are not allowed to affect parameters of a class, although they affect the domains available to other decisions. In the OO framework, operations cannot change other operations (there are frameworks where this is allowed, like in functional programming). Thus, while operations and decisions share some characteristics, one can not be considered a subclass of the other.

A better approach is to define decisions as subclasses of attributes. We suggest defining a stereotype. Stereotyping is one of the extension mechanisms in the UML. The mechanism is used to create meta-classes with specific characteristics. This works very well for decision variables. In particular, the *tagged values* **upperBound** and **lowerBound** can be associated with the decision (in the UML, stereotypes are expressed by their label between guillemots) stereotype. The stereotype is used to define decision variables as special types of attributes.

In Figure 5, we can see all the classes needed to define the stochastic location-routing problem (SLRP) defined earlier. Figure 5 defines *roles* for some of the associations, indicated by a verb followed by a triangle ▶ or ◀ pointing from the subject to the object of the role. The role is an *adornment*, and has no direct translation to the MSPR framework. In particular, it is *not* holding the place of a decision variable. Diagram 5 implies that we are not concerned with which truck gets assigned to each route. If that decision were part of the model, an association class would need to be created and attached to the association between Truck and Route. This association class should then be reflected in the algebraic problem description. If it is not, then there is an inconsistency. Making these inconsistencies easy to spot is what we hope to achieve.

The *maximum* cardinality of each component is unambiguous in the class diagram. Given M_1 Warehouses and M_2 Retailers, a tool can deduce that there are $M_1 \times M_2$ ShippingCosts. Such a tool can also automate parts of the data acquisition

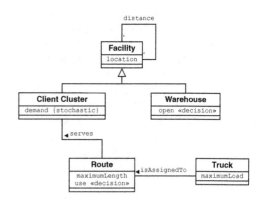

Fig. 5 Classes in the SLRP.

routines, as well as perform integrity checks. It is legal for a tool to allow certain additions to the syntax. With these additions, it is possible to generate equations automatically.

Decisions of arity > 1 present no difficulty. In particular, attributes with arrays can be used when convenient. Associations of arity > 2 are also easily handled within the UML. All that is needed is to draw the lines between classes in a manner that shows unambiguously that the associations involve tuples of classes as opposed to a set of classes taken two at a time. No normalization is required.

More important than generating equations automatically is having a graphical language that improves communication between different analysts. A professional with an IT background, who is likely to know where some of the desired information can be found, will appreciate having a description of the data in a familiar language. People interacting with the model solely at a decision maker level will also appreciate the information about the model contained in the diagram. For example, from the model in Figure 5 it is clear that direct shipments between the warehouse and individual Client Clusters are not available as a recourse action. This message can be conveyed precisely without the need for any mathematical notation or textual description. Another example is the relationship between **Truck** and **Route**. If the trucks all have the same **maximumLoad**, then the association **isAssignedTo** should not have a decision associated with it. However, if **maximumLoad** is different for each truck, and the smallest load is close to the typical demand for a cluster, then the **isAssignedTo** association could become a class containing a decision. Any person involved in the modeling process can spot this detail, and discuss its consequences, without the need for specialized training in OR.

5.2 Stochasticity Diagrams

The Stochasticity Diagram provides a concise view of the decision process. It documents that the right decisions are being considered at the right time, using the right information. It describes the point in time at which each piece of information becomes available with certainty; and the consequences of observing the information for the decision process. It is is a UML Statechart, with each state representing a decision process and each event representing the observation of some set of random variables.

Systems which model dynamic aspects of stochastic programming explicitly and associate single-stage LPs with each stage Fourer and Lopes (2008) are called filtration-oriented. The term comes from a type of stochastic process used to describe information release over time. The details of the definition of filtration are not relevant to this discussion, except that the filtration-oriented approach leads to a decomposition of the model that fits well with the OO paradigm. For more details on filtrations, see Neftci (2000). Figure 6 represents the filtration process for the SLRP.

Fig. 6 A simple state machine for a location-routing problem with 5 stages.

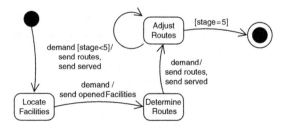

Every diagram has an *initial state* (the solid circle) and a *final state* (the other circle). In between, there are a number of other *states* (the round-edged boxes), each representing a set of decisions taken based on the same information. Each state has a *name*.

In between each pair of states there is an *event* (represented by an arc) that describes what new information causes the state transition. Each event may have a *name* and may take parameters. The parameters should be the random variables observed. An event may also have a *guard condition* (represented in between square brackets). When an event occurs, the transition only takes place if the guard condition is satisfied. A *signal* may also be sent when an event occurs, represented in the diagram by the **send** keyword followed by the name of the signal. The signal describes the decisions at period *t* that must be taken into account later. Conditional probabilities are not shown directly on the diagram. They are clearly important, but they are too much detail for this level of abstraction.

5.3 Element Diagrams

Element diagrams represent the same information as the algebraic model, but at a coarser level. Unlike activity graphs Schrage (2002) or diagrams from LPFORM Ma et al (1996) or gLPS Collaud and Pasquier-Boltuck (1994), element diagrams do not necessarily translate directly into algebraic expressions. Instead, they specify *which* elements are related, rather than specifically *how* they are related. The primary reason for not tying element diagrams directly to algebraic expressions is that element diagrams are used at modeling stages where the specific expressions that determine how elements are related may not be especially relevant. A problem owner or an IT person may be unaware of, uncomfortable with, or even unconcerned with the specific dynamics of the relationships between elements. However, he or she is likely to be interested in knowing that the expert has included the relationship in the model.

As an introduction, consider a problem without stochasticity. Figure 7, has an unadorned element diagram of the Traveling Salesperson Problem (TSP). While not useful for computation, Figure 7 contains a correct and complete representation of the major components of the model. There is an objective, to minimize (thus the triangle points down) the total distance; a decision (the diamond), the route to choose; and a constraint (the box), to visit all nodes. There are also *associations*

Fig. 7 An unadorned representation of the TSP.

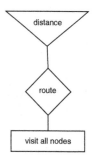

Fig. 8 An adorned representation of a typical formulation of the TSP

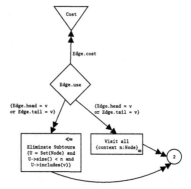

between the different elements in the diagram, represented by the lines connecting them. Each symbol is a specialization of the UML Class.

If adornments are used, the element diagram can express any linear program. In fact, when the element diagram is examined one set of constraints at a time, or one objective at a time, with every relationship expressed correctly, it represents an expression tree equivalent to one generated by a modeling language.

Figure 8 represents the following classical Dantzig-Fulkerson-Johnson TSP formulation in detail: Given a graph $G(V,E)$ with n nodes, let $\delta(U), U \subset V$ be the *cut* of node set U. Define a binary variable x_e, and a cost parameter c_e associated with each edge $e \in E$:

$$\min \quad \sum_{e \in E} c_e x_e$$

$$\sum_{e \in \delta(\{v\})} x_e = 2 \quad \forall v \in V$$

$$\sum_{\{e \in \delta(U)\}} x_e \geq 2 \quad \forall U \subset V, 2 \leq |U| \leq n-1$$

Figure 9 is the corresponding class diagram. Each constraint in Figure 8 has a symbol that identifies its type. Each constraint also includes an Object Constraint Language (OCL) expression in curly brackets. OCL expressions are used to specify multiplicity, and are not related to the constraints of an optimization problem.

Fig. 9 The Edge and Node
classes used in the TSP Element Diagram in Figure 8.

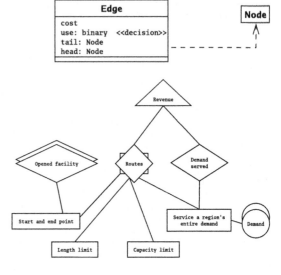

Fig. 10 The **determine route**
state in the SLRP.

OCL is a formal language defined as a subset of the UML to aid in clarification
of the semantics of models. In the UML, the enforcement of the OCL expressions
is left to the implementation UML (2003). A computer implementation is free to
replace the OCL with any other formal language, such as an AML.

Each association has a cardinality associated with it. The cardinality may be
elided, as in Figure 7. In most cases the association corresponds to a summation
or product. An OCL expression can be added to the association to specify which
instances of constraint and variable classes are related, as in Figure 8. An implementation may use these expressions to generate AML code.

Each association in Figure 8 has a double arrow (to avoid clashing with reserved
symbols in the UML) at one of its ends. The arrow indicates flow balance. An arrow
pointing toward the constraint is a credit, and an arrow pointing away from the
constraint is a debit. Each association may have a *name*. If so, then this name should
be a parameter related with each instance of the association. It is not the instance of
the parameter that is used for the name, but the class. For example, in Figure 8, c
is the mathematical object corresponding to the association *Edge.Cost* between the
decision and the objective, and not c_e.

Consider the SLRP. Figure 10 describes the **Determine Routes** state in Figure 6.
The double lines indicate stochasticity or externality. For example, the **facility.open**
decision was made before entering this state. It is represented as a decision, but it is
not mutable at this stage. It was received in this state as a signal sent by another state,
as indicated in Figure 6 by the **send openedFacilities** notation associated with the
two states involved. Similarly, the **routes** decision has an optional special marker on
it that indicates that this decision might influence decisions made in future stages.
The double lines on the **demand** parameter indicate that it is a random variable. All
double lines are adornments. The analyst should use judgment to determine when
to use them.

6 Illustrations from the literature

We now present a few classical examples taken from Ariyawansa and Felt (2001). For each example, we will provide a description and elided class, stochasticity and element diagrams.

6.1 Airlift Operations Schedule

The goal of this model Midler and Wollmer (1969) is to minimize the expected cost of airlift operations. Aircraft resources are allocated based on a forecast of the demands for specific routes. However, the actual demand is unknown. The recourse actions available are: allowing allocated flight time to go unused; switching aircraft from one route to another; and purchasing commercial flights.

6.1.1 The Class Diagram

The class diagram 11 describes **Flight** and **Plane**. Each plane has available hours. The most important parameters associated with each route are: **origin** and **destination**; **demand**, which is stochastic; **spot market cost**, which is the unit cost of purchasing commercial flights on that route; and **unused capacity cost**, the unit penalty for reserving Plane capacity and then leaving it unused. Each Route has two decisions associated with it: **spot purchase**, the amount of demand that will be covered by commercial flights; and **unused**, the amount of capacity reserved but left unused for this route.

The other classes are *association classes*. The **Assignment** and **Reassignment** have the same attributes, but are modeled as different classes. They both have **hours**, the time it takes for a given plane to fly a given route; **cost**, the unit cost of flying a given route with a given plane; and **capacity**, the number of units a given plane can carry when flying a given route. Because these parameters appear as members

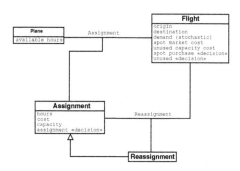

Fig. 11 Airlift operations class diagram

of Assignment instead of Plane, it is clear that in this model they depend on the specific combination of Plane and Route, as opposed to other plausible situations, where some parameters may depend only on Plane.

6.1.2 The Stochasticity Diagram

The stochasticity diagram 12 is simple. The first stage decision is to assign planes to routes; the second stage decision is to do any reassignments necessary.

6.1.3 The Element Diagrams

The first stage element diagram 13 prescribes that in this stage, assignments minimize cost, respecting the number of hours available for each flight. The second stage element diagram 14 is more sophisticated. There are two flows between **reassignment** and **Satisfy demand**. This indicates that reassignments may either increase or decrease the demand satisfied. The OCL constraint indicates which reassignments result in increases or decreases of satisfied demand. The expressions in the original paper involve each plane's carrying capacity, and ratios between flight-hours in different routes for each plane, but they are elided here.

6.2 Forest Planning

The goal of this model Gassmann (1989) is to maximize the revenue obtained from a forest area, by deciding which parts of the forest should be harvested at each point in time. The forest is segmented by the age of trees in a region, and each segment may

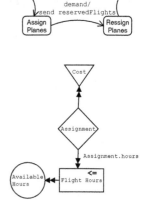

Fig. 12 Airlift operations stochasticity diagram

Fig. 13 Airlift first stage element diagram

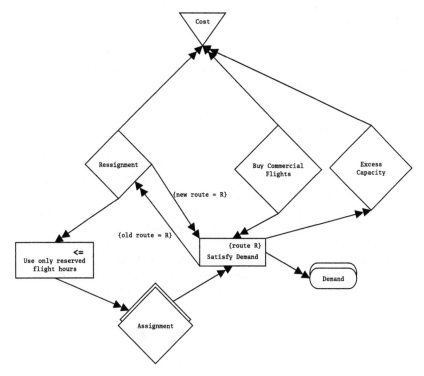

Fig. 14 Airlift second stage element diagram

Fig. 15 Forest planning class diagram.

be worth a different amount per unit area. Due to fire, disease, or other casualties, part of the trees that are not cut may be lost before they move into the next age group.

6.2.1 The Class Diagram

The class diagram 15 contains only one class and no associations. Even though an **age** method is present, it has no semantic meaning in optimization. It is present to illustrate that objects used within our language can be shared with other parties who may have different uses for them.

6.2.2 The Stochasticity Diagram

The stochasticity diagram 16 has a self-transition, which takes place every period. It is triggered by the random vector **casualties** and is processed so long as the stage is less than the total number of stages.

6.2.3 The Element Diagram

The element diagram 17 is associated with the **cut** state in Figure 16. Both cut and uncut forest have value. The amount of forest available in each category is determined by a **balance** constraint that considers the amount available in in the previous period, the amount cut in the previous period, and any casualties that may have occurred. The double arrow linking the **available** variable from the previous period to the balance constraint is hollow, in contrast to all the others. This is an optional adornment to indicate that this parameter is stochastic.

The amount of forest that can be cut now is limited by the available variable, as indicated by the **Availability** constraint. Lastly, the amount of timber the market

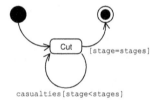

Fig. 16 Forest planning stochasticity diagram

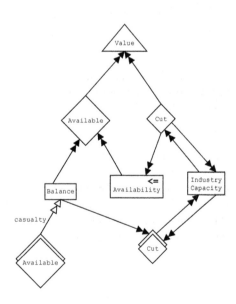

Fig. 17 Forest planning element diagram

is ready to accept is bounded above and below by the amount that was cut in the previous period. Thus, the **Industry capacity** constraint has arrows coming both in and out of both the current stage and previous stage **cut** variables. The Industry capacity constraint could be separated into a lower industry bound and an upper industry bound if desired.

6.3 Electrical Investment Planning

This model comes from Louveaux and Smeers (1998). The objective is to minimize total investment and maintenance costs for electricity generation. Several technologies are available, with different capacities, costs, availabilities, and lifetimes. Some of these characteristics are stochastic, and the goal is to balance all of them in determining an effective investment and operational schedule.

6.3.1 The Class Diagram

The class diagram 18 displays the major components of the model. Demand for electricity can be thought of as coming in different modes, which discretize the demand curve over a cycle. For a certain amount of time during a cycle (**duration** in the class diagram), an amount of power exceeding the previous mode (**power** in the class diagram) will be needed.

   The total demand (**demand** in the class diagram) for each **Demand Mode** can be produced by using several **Technologies**, each of which has: an **availability**, the proportion of time a plant using the production technology can be operated in a period; an **operating cost**, which is stochastic (it may depend, for example, on fuel costs); and a **planned capacity** already contracted for.

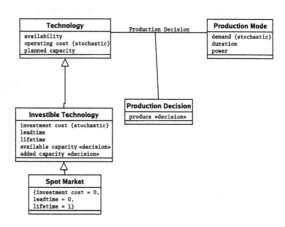

Fig. 18 Electricity investment class diagram.

In addition, it is possible to invest in certain technologies. In this case, one must take into account an **investment cost**, which is stochastic (it may depend, for example, on technological achievements), a **leadtime**, the delay between when the contract is signed and when the facility becomes operational; and also a **lifetime**, describing for how many periods the technology will be usable.

The decision maker may increase the **available capacity** of an **Investible Technology** (which is a subclass of technology), which when combined with the already contracted capacity, leadtime, and lifetime considerations, determines the **available capacity** at any point in time.

There is also a special type of Investible Technology called the **Spot Market**, in which typically the operating costs are very high. Spot Market purchases require no investment, have no leadtime, and only last for the current period.

6.3.2 The Stochasticity Diagram

The stochasticity diagram 19 illustrates that the relevant random variables to be observed are the demand and costs (both operating and investment). There is only one set of decisions, defined by the **Invest** state. The information exchanged between stages is the portfolio of current investments.

6.3.3 The Element Diagram

The element diagram 20 shows that there are two important constraints. **Satisfy demand** ensures that the amount produced or purchased in the spot market is sufficient to satisfy the demand for all modes. The **Capacity** constraint relates how capacity added in previous planning periods and capacity originally contracted affects the production capability at this stage.

The **added capacity** decision has a special marker to indicate that it will influence future decisions. **Demand**, **operating cost** and **investment cost** are marked stochastic, the first because of the ellipse with double lines, and the others because of the hollow double-arrows.

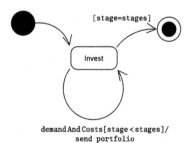

Fig. 19 Electricity investment
stochasticity diagram

Fig. 20 Electricity investment element diagram.

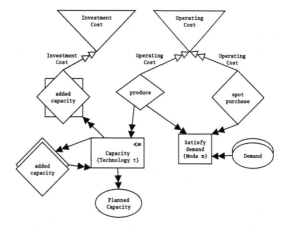

7 Conclusions and Further Work

Researchers have expressed concern with the increasing disconnect between academic models and those used in business environments Sodhi and Tang (2008). This disconnect, along with changes in the availability of timely information throughout the enterprise can sometimes hinder our ability to convey the value added by OR. This research addresses a small portion of this problem that fits within our expertise. We developed a graphical modeling language based on the UML to facilitate the communication of MSPR models between diverse stakeholders.

The extensive use of elision sets this work apart from previous OR research on modeling systems. While our language can describe linear programs in their entirety, it really is designed to produce an abstract summary of the model, which is a valuable modeling aid used extensively in fields involving information and decision making. Our language is most effective when communicating and documenting the general tradeoffs in a model and the information necessary to adequately analyze the situation underlying the model. The language should be used throughout the lifetime of a model. The development of the model should start with the creation of a set of diagrams, and those diagrams should be used to organize the mathematical expressions in the model. A computer system can guarantee consistency between different levels of abstraction. Future research along this direction should exploit new tools for collaboration available to the enterprise, like the Microsoft Surface.

We believe that the UML is sufficiently expressive, tractable, and extensible to be the basis for a graphical language like ours. The occasional compromises on expressiveness or simplicity we make are worth it when juxtaposed with the benefits of the UML (*i.e.* software support, familiarity, standardization). Other researchers may disagree, and design graphical languages which would perhaps be more clear by dropping the UML assumption. Even within the UML, there are different ways of describing stochastic optimization models. Perhaps a more elegant set of classes can be devised. Empirical research will help refine the design. Future research should also produce graphical languages for other types of OR problems, or show that this particular language can be generalized to cover other classes of problems well.

Ultimately, as with any language, practice will dictate which diagrams become common. The set of objects and diagrams proposed here, however, provide a formal starting point.

References

(2003) OMG Unified Modeling Language Specification. Object Management Group, version 1.5

Alonso-Ayuso A, Escudero LF, Garín A, M T Ortu n, Pérez G (2003) An approach for strategic supply chain planning under uncertainty based on stochastic 0-1 programming. J of Global Optimization 26(1):97–124, DOI http://dx.doi.org/10.1023/A:1023071216923

Ariyawansa KA, Felt AJ (2001) On a new collection of stochastic linear programming test problems. Tech. Rep. 4, Department of Mathematics, Washington State University, Pullman, WA 99164

Beraldi P, Conforti D, Violi A (2008) A two-stage stochastic programming model for electric energy producers. Comput Oper Res 35(10):3360–3370, DOI http://dx.doi.org/10.1016/j.cor.2007.03.008

Birge JR, Louveaux F (1997) Introduction to Stochastic Programming. Springer-Verlag

Bock C (2006) SysML and UML 2 Support for Activity Modeling. Systems Engineering 9(2):160–186

Brooke A, Kendrick D, Meeraus A (1988) GAMS A User's Guide. The Scientific Press

Cajori F (1993) History of Mathematical Notations. Dover Publications, Inc.

Checkland P (2000) Soft systems methodology: a thirty year retrospective. Systems Research and Behavioral Science

Choobineh J (1991) A diagramming technique for representation of linear programming models. Omega

Collaud G, Pasquier-Boltuck J (1994) glps: A graphical tool for the definition and manipulation of linear problems. European Journal of Operations Research

DeMarco T (1979) Structured analysis and system specification. Yourdon Press Upper Saddle River, NJ, USA

Felfernig A, Friedrich G, Jannach D, Zanker M (2002) Configuration knowledge representation using uml/ocl. LNCS

Fourer R, Lopes L (2008) StAMPL: A Filtration-Oriented Modeling Tool for Stochastic Programming, upcoming in INFORMS Journal on Computing

Fourer R, Gay DM, Kernighan BW (2002) AMPL A Modeling Language For Mathematical Programming, 2nd edn. Duxbury Press

Gassmann HI (1989) Optimzal harvest of a forest in the presence of uncertainty. Canadian Journal of Forest Research 19:1267–1274

Geoffrion AM (1987) An introduction to structured modeling. Management Science

Greenberg H (1993) A Computer-Assisted Analysis System for Mathematical Programming Models and Solutions: A User's Guide for ANALYZE. Kluwer Academic Publishers

Greenberg HJ (1996) A bibliography for the development of an intelligent mathematical programming system. ITORMS

Heikkinen VP (2003) Timber harvesting as a part of the portfolio management: A multiperiod stochastic optimisation approach. Manage Sci 49(1):131–142, DOI http://dx.doi.org/10.1287/mnsc.49.1.131.12752

Jackson M (1983) Systems Development. Prentice-Hall

Jones CV (1990) An introduction to graph-based modeling systems, part i: Overview. ORSA Jorunal on Computing

Jones CV (1991) An introduction to graph-based modeling systems, part ii: Graph-grammars and the implementation. ORSA Jorunal on Computing

Jones CV (1996a) Mimi/g: A graphical environment for mathematical programming and modeling. Interfaces

Jones CV (1996b) Visualization and Optimization. Operations Research/Computer Science Interface Series, Kluwer Academic Publishers

Jrjens J (2002) Umlsec: Extending uml for secure systems development. LNCS

Louveaux FV, Smeers Y (1998) Optimal investments for electricity generation: A stochastic model and a test-problem. In: Numerical Techniques for Stochastic Optimization, SpringerVerlag, chap 24, pp 445–453

Luján-Mora S, Trujillo J, Song IY (2002) Extending the uml for multidimensional modeling. LNCS

Ma P, F H Murphy, E A Stohr (1996) An Implementation of LPFORM. INFORMS Journal on Computing

Midler JL, Wollmer RD (1969) Stochastic programming models for scheduling airlift operations. Naval Research Logistics Quarterly 16:315–330

Neftci SN (2000) An Introduction to the MAthematics of Financial Derivatives. Academic Press

Powell SG (1997) The teachers' forum: From intelligent consumer to active modeler, two mba success stories. INTERFACES

Rosenhead J (1996) What's the problem? an introduction to problem structuring methods. Interfaces

Rubart J, Dawabi P (2002) Towards uml-g: A uml profile for modeling groupware. LNCS

Schrage L (2002) Optimization Modeling with Lingo, 4th edn. LINDO Systems Inc.

Sen S, Yu L, Genc T (2006) A stochastic programming approach to power portfolio optimization. Oper Res 54(1):55–72, DOI http://dx.doi.org/10.1287/opre.1050.0264

Sodhi MS, Tang CS (2008) The or/ms ecosystem: Strengths,weaknesses, opportunities and threats. Operations Research 56(2):267–277

Yu LY, Ji XD, Wang SY (2003) Stochastic programming models in financial optimization: A survey. AMO — Advanced Modeling and Optimization 5(1), URL citeseer.ist.psu.edu/yu03stochastic.html

AEON: Synthesizing Scheduling Algorithms from High-Level Models

Jean-Noël Monette, Yves Deville, and Pascal Van Hentenryck

Abstract This paper describes the AEON system whose aim is to synthesize scheduling algorithms from high-level models. AEON, which is entirely written in COMET, receives as input a high-level model for a scheduling application which is then analyzed to generate a dedicated scheduling algorithm exploiting the structure of the model. AEON provides a variety of synthesizers for generating complete or heuristic algorithms. Moreover, synthesizers are compositional, making it possible to generate complex hybrid algorithms naturally. Preliminary experimental results indicate that this approach may be competitive with state-of-the-art search algorithms.

Key words: Scheduling, Constraints, Modelling, Local Search, Job-Shop

1 Introduction

Scheduling problems are ubiquitous in industrial applications and have been the topic of significant research over several decades. Effective algorithms are now available for various classes of problems and general systems are available for modeling and solving complex problems. One of the difficulties with existing tools, however, is that modelers not only need to understand their application domain, but also need to be well-versed in the algorithmic and combinatorial aspects of solving the application at hand: Indeed, two applications which look essentially similar for a modeling standpoint may require fundamentally different approaches to obtain high-quality solutions.

Jean-Noël Monette, Yves Deville
INGI, UCLouvain, 1348 Louvain-la-Neuve, Belgium, e-mail: jean-noel.monette@uclouvain.be

Pascal Van Hentenryck
Brown University, Box 1910, Providence, RI 02912

J.W. Chinneck et al. (eds.), *Operations Research and Cyber-Infrastructure*, Operations Research/Computer Science Interfaces Series 47, DOI: 10.1007/978-0-387-88843-9_3,
© Springer Science+Business Media, LLC 2009

This work is a first step to address these limitations and to bridge the gap between high-level modeling and effective solving of scheduling applications. It presents the AEON[1] system which allows high-level scheduling models to be synthesized into effective algorithms by exploiting the model structure. Models in AEON are written with traditional high-level abstractions and their structure is analyzed to synthesize scheduling algorithms tailored to the applications at hand. Users state the models and only specify the synthesizer which then generates a scheduling algorithm for a specific resolution framework (e.g. greedy search, constraint programming, or local search). Synthesizers in AEON are compositional, which makes it possible to specify hybrid algorithms naturally.

The system has a number of benefits. From a user standpoint, AEON allows modelers to focus on describing their applications at a high level of abstraction, relieving them from delving into the algorithmic aspects. Moreover, since models reveal the structure of the applications, the AEON synthesizers are in a position to exploit the wealth of scheduling research in order to derive effective algorithms. Finally, because the model is independent of the solving technology, AEON makes it possible to apply various paradigms and to develop hybridizations whose potential had been demonstrated in a variety of practical applications. From an implementation standpoint, AEON also features several innovations. First, the model analysis is extensible and allows new classes of scheduling problems to be described using standard XML formats. Second, novel synthesizers can be added naturally and compositionally. Finally, several novel abstractions simplify the tasks of writing synthesizers. In particular, AEON provides the concepts of *model view*, which enables access to a general model and its solution through an interface specialized to the model at hand.

This paper extends and generalizes the research initiated in Van Hentenryck and Michel (2007) which demonstrated how to synthesize local-search algorithms from COMET models. The synthesizers proposed herein apply to the scheduling domain, consider various paradigms to solve scheduling applications (greedy algorithms, local search, and constraint programming), and are extensible and compositional. The models are similar in style to those used in ILOG Scheduler, OPL, and COMET, and earlier systems in constraint-based scheduling. ILOG Concert also provides a modeling layer that can be extracted by various solvers, but there is no attempt to synthesize search algorithms or their hybridizations. It is also useful to contrast the research to recent work in constraint programming concerning the design of default search procedures: See, for instance, Laborie and Godard (2007) which describes a Self-Adapting Large Neighborhood Search for scheduling applications, and Refalo (2004) for the use of impacts in directing the search. While their goal is to find a search procedure robust across a variety of models, our objective is to exploit the model structure to derive an effective search procedure for the model at hand and the chosen methodology. We view these approaches as orthogonal since robust search procedures must also be available for various classes of problems. However, revealing and exploiting the model structure is one of the main contributions of constraint programming and the search algorithm may significantly benefit from a structural synthesis.

---

[1] Aeon is another name for the Greek god of time Chronos. It means forever, eternity.

The rest of this paper presents an overview of the different parts of the system. Section 2 covers the use of the system and the available abstractions and solvers. In Section 3, the architecture is presented and some characteristics of the system are highlighted. Section 4 then shows how the system can be extended to deal with other families of problems or solvers. Section 5 presents and analyzes the experimental results.

2 Modelling and Solving Scheduling Problems

Figure 1 presents an AEON model for a Job-Shop Problem (JSP) and an associated synthesizer. The initialization of the input data in lines 1–6 is not shown. The model itself is given in lines 8–16. First, a schedule object is created. Then, the objects populating this schedule are created (lines 9–11), including activities, jobs, and machines. Next the constraints are stated: Machine requirements (lines 12–13) and precedences inside jobs (lines 14–15). Finally, the objective in line 16 minimizes the makespan.

The three last lines deal with the resolution of the model. Line 18 defines the synthesizer, which, in this case, synthesizes the hybridization of a greedy heuristic followed by a tabu search. It is easy to change the synthesizer: Simply replace `GreedyTabuSynthesizer` by `CPSynthesizer` to obtain a constraint-programming search. Line 19 applies the synthesizer to solve the model. This induces the analysis and classification of the model, the generation of the

```
1    range jobs = 1..nbjobs;
2    range machines = 0..nbmachines-1;
3    range tasks = 1..nbjobs*nbmachines;
4    int proc[tasks];
5    int mach[tasks];
6    int job[jobs,machines];
7
8    Schedule<Mod> s();
9    Job<Mod> J[i in jobs](s,IntToString(i));
10   Machine<Mod> M[i in machines](s,IntToString(i));
11   Activity<Mod> A[i in tasks](s,proc[i],IntToString(i));
12   forall(i in tasks)
13      A[i].requires(M[mach[i]]);
14   forall(i in jobs)
15      J[i].containsInSequence(all(j in machines)A[job[i,j]]);
16   s.minimizeObj(makespanOf(s));
17
18   GreedyTabuSynthesizer synth();
19   Solution<Mod> sol = synth.solve(s);
20   sol.printSolution();
```

Fig. 1 A Job-Shop Model and Its Synthesizer.

appropriate variables, constraints, and objectives for the solvers, and the execution of a search algorithm dedicated to the model. The synthesizer application produces a solution which can be queried and used in various ways. Line 19 simply prints the obtained solution.

As shown in Fig. 1, the modelling and solving parts are clearly separated. AEON features a rich set of abstractions to model a broad range of scheduling problems and constraints and objectives are stated using functions and methods. The remainder of this section reviews the set of abstractions that are available to model problems and to solve them.

The modelling classes end with "<Mod>" to denote that they are used for modelling[2]. Inside the system, other classes with names post-fixed with "<CP>" or "<LS>" are used for the actual search algorithms. For instance, the purpose of the class Activity<Mod> is completely different from the class Activity<CP>. Although they are associated with the same concept (an activity), the first modeling version provides methods to perform the analysis of the problem, while the CP version encapsulates variables to represent the starting and finishing dates of an activity and a constraint linking them. To simplify reading, the post-fix "<Mod>" is omitted in this section when it is clear that we refer to modelling classes.

Table 1 presents the modelling classes available in AEON at this stage. They are explained in the following. The central modelling class is Schedule (i.e. Schedule<Mod>). It is passed to all the other created objects and is responsible for the internal consistency of the model. To represent activities, there are two classes. Activity and MultiModeActivity represent single- and multi-mode activities respectively. At creation time, an activity receives as input a schedule, a processing time and a name. The processing time is either fixed or defined by lower and upper bounds. A MultiModeActivity is given the Schedule, the number of modes, and a name. The processing time of the modes are given separately for each mode. The methods available on activities (single- and multi-mode) allow to specify preemption, the membership to a Job, the resource requirements, and the precedences between activities. The requirements are mode-dependent but the remaining constraints are common to every modes. Precedence constraints can involve the start and the end of activities and jobs. They can also define delays. The aforementioned Job class represents groups of activities logically related. The activities are not necessarily ordered but they cannot be executed at the same time. Jobs share some features with activities: They can be grouped into other jobs and their ends and starts can be constrained with precedences. Lastly, activities and jobs can be defined as optional, meaning that their execution is not required.

Resources are represented by four classes, depending on the type of resource under consideration. The Machine class represents unary resources. Two activities that require the same machine cannot overlap in time. The Resource class represents renewable resources. At every moment, the sum of the requests of the activities being executed cannot exceed the capacity of the resource. On the contrary, the Reservoir class is used for non-renewable resources whose capacity

---

[2] In spite of a syntax similar to C++, such classes are not templated classes.

Table 1 Summary of the classes available for modelling.

Description	Classes
Schedule	`Schedule`
Activities	`Activity`
	`MultiModeActivity`
Jobs	`Job`
Resources	`Resource`
	`Machine`
	`Reservoir`
	`StateResource`
Objectives	`ScheduleObjective`
	`TaskObjective`
	`CompletionTime`
	`Lateness`
	`Tardiness`
	`Earliness`
	`UnitCost`
	`PiecewiseLinearFunction`
	`AbsenceCost`
	`AlternativeCost`
	`ModifObjective`
	`MultObjective`
	`ShiftObjective`
	`AgregObjective`
	`SumObjective`
	`MaxObjective`

is decreased after the execution of each activity. A minimum capacity can be defined for both the `Resource` and `Reservoir` classes. For these two classes and the `Machine` class, it is possible to define (periodic) breaks, i.e. time intervals of unavailability. The last kind of resource is the `StateResource` that represents a state of the world. The resource can only be in one state at a time. Two activities that require different states cannot overlap in time. For all kind of resources, it is possible to define sequence-dependent setup times and costs. The set of requirements of an activity (or of a mode of a multi-mode activity) has the form of a tree whose internal nodes are either conjunctions or disjunctions of simpler requests. External nodes are the basic requirements: a required machine, some required or provided amount of a resource, some consumed or produced amount of a reservoir, or a particular state of a state resource.

Objective functions are subclasses of `ScheduleObjective`. The subclasses are either simple or compound functions. Compound functions are obtained by summing or taking the maximum/minimum of other functions, or multiplying a function by a constant. Simple functions are the classical lateness, tardiness, earliness, and, more generally piecewise-defined linear functions based on the completion time of activities and jobs. The set of simple functions includes also cost functions associated with the modes of multi-mode activities, with the absence of optional activities or with the sequence-dependent setup of resources. The global objective function is passed to the `Schedule` object with a method that specifies if the function must be

Table 2 Summary of the classes available to solve.

Description	Classes
Synthesizers	`ScheduleSynthesizer`
	`CPSynthesizer`
	`TSSynthesizer`
	`SASynthesizer`
	`GreedySynthesizer`
	`SequenceSynthesizer`
	`ScheduleAnimator`
Solutions	`Solution`

minimized or maximized. The function `makespanOf` found in Fig. 1 is a shortcut for the makespan, or sum of the completion times, which is a common and important objective.

This set of abstractions makes it possible to model problems as various as classical shop problems (Job Shop, Open Shop, Flexible Shop, Flow Shop, Group Shop, Cumulative Shop, Just-In-Time Job Shop), variations of the Resource-Constrained Project Scheduling Problem (RCPSP, MRCPSP, RCPSP/max, MRCPSP/max) (Kolisch and Sprecher (1997)), the trolley problem (Van Hentenryck et al (1999)) and the NCOS and NCGS classes of MaScLib (Nuijten et al (2004)). This covers problems with different kind of objectives and different properties (disjunctive or cumulative, single- or multi-mode).

Although the modelling abstractions are able to represent a large set of problems, the set of problems that can be solved depends on the search that can be synthesized. Table 2 presents the available synthesis classes in AEON at this point. Currently, there are three underlying engines: Constraint Programming, Local Search (Tabu search and Simulated Annealing) and Greedy Search.[3] Their capabilities define the capabilities of the whole system. Based on these basis solvers, more complex solvers can also be synthesized. In particular, hybrid and animated solvers can be made out of other solvers. For instance, an animated solver wraps any underlying solver into a visual environment that shows the succession of (improving) solutions. Hybrid solvers can be as simple as a sequence of solvers, or can provide decomposition schemes parametrized by solvers for the various phases. Synthesizers also accept parameters, for instance to bound the allocated time. Line 16 of Fig. 1 shows how to create a synthesizer that is a sequence of two search algorithms. The first one greedily finds a feasible solution that will serve as initial solution to the second algorithm that is a Tabu Search.

3 Architecture

Figure 2 presents an overview of AEON centered around the resolution of a scheduling problem. Rounded boxes are the successive steps toward a solution. Only the first one, the modelling, involves the user. Subsequently, the model is analyzed and

---

[3] Future work will also consider MIP-based solvers for various classes of scheduling problems.

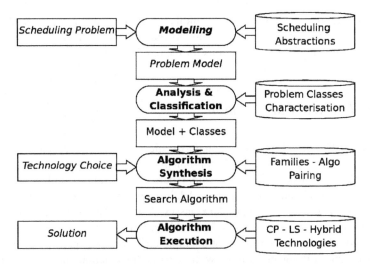

Fig. 2 Overview of AEON. Rounded boxes represent actions to solve the problem. Rectangles and Containers represent their inputs and outputs. The containers on the right are provided by the system, the rectangle on the left are inputs from, and output to, users and those between actions are transitional products. Italic text denotes user involvement.

categorized into some classes of problems. An algorithm is then synthesized and run, yielding a solution to the problem. The containers on the right hand side of Fig. 2 represent what is provided by the system to perform each step. The remainder of this section explains in more details how each step is performed. Section 4 describes how it is possible to enlarge those containers.

3.1 Modelling

Section 2 presented the modelling from a user point of view. Under the cover, when the model is executed, an internal representation of the problem is built. Most of the information is recorded in the modelling objects that were presented. For instance, the Activity class contains an attribute recording whether preemption is allowed or not. In addition, the Schedule object keeps a reference to all objects that were created. The information is recorded using graph structures: precedence relations into a digraph, objective functions and resource requests into rooted trees. The precedence constraints are labeled arcs of a graph whose nodes represent the start and end of activities, jobs and the schedule. In addition to the arcs explicitly added by the user, arcs are created to link the start of a job with the start of contained activities and the end of the job with the end of contained activities. There are also arcs to ensure that all activities and jobs are executed between the start and the end of the schedule. The trees representing objective functions and resource requests are necessary to represent combinations of simple functions or requirements. Such combinations are sums, products, and minimums/maximums in the case of objectives. They are conjunctions and disjunctions for the requirements.

3.2 Analysis and Classification

The goal of the second step is to categorize the model into one of the "known" classes. This classification is based on problem characteristics. Each class of problems is defined by a combination of pairs (characteristic,value). Table 3 presents a subset of the considered characteristics. Additionally, the last two columns specify the values for two well-known problem classes. A dash means that the value can be anything for this class of problems. This table presents a simplified version of the definition of classes. In fact, it is not a simple conjunction of pairs characteristic-value but rather a Boolean formula, with negation, disjunction and conjunction of simpler formulas. Atoms correspond to the pairs whose truth value is determined by the analysis of the model. If the value returned by the analysis is equal to the

Table 3 Partial Listing of Characteristics. The first column gives the characteristic, the second one defines the type of values. The third and fourth columns illustrate possible values for the Job-Shop (JSP) and RCPSP problems.

Characteristic	Type	JSP	RCPSP
Unit Processing Time	boolean	–	–
Fixed Processing Time	boolean	true	true
Preemption Allowed	enum	never	never
Common Release Dates	boolean	true	true
Common Deadlines	boolean	–	–
Deadlines Exist	boolean	false	false
Form of the Precedence Graph	enum	chains	DAG
Delay between Activities	boolean	false	false
No wait between Activities	boolean	false	false
Jobs inside Jobs	boolean	false	–
Number Of State Resources	integer	0	0
Maximum Capacity	integer	1	–
All Capacities are Equal	boolean	true	–
Reservoir Consumption	boolean	false	false
Reservoir Production	boolean	false	false
Setup Times	boolean	false	false
Disjunctive Requirements	boolean	false	false
All Activities in Jobs	boolean	true	false
Nb of Multi-Mode Activities	integer	0	0
Sum Of Requirements	integer	1	–
Objective Type	enum	minimize	minimize
Objective Form	enum	maximum	total
Objective Components	enum	completion time	lateness
Objective Scope	enum	all activities	one activity
All Due-Dates are equal	enum	–	–

expected one, the atomic formula receives the value true. A model belongs to a class of problem if the valuation of the formula defining this class is true.

Moreover, recurring sub-formulas are defined as higher-level characteristics or more general models from which other models may inherit. For instance, the JSP with Makespan is a special case of the JSP having the characteristic Makespan. The JSP is in turn a case of Disjunctive Problem. The hierarchy of categories forms a directed acyclic graph (DAG). This means that a problem categorized into some class is also member of all its ancestor classes. The output of the classification is thus a sequence of classes rather than a single class. This sequence represents a total order on the classes of the problem compatible with the DAG of classes. This means that, if a class inherits from another, it must appear before the ancestor in the sequence but the order of unrelated classes is arbitrarily fixed.

The analysis of characteristics in itself is achieved by a set of functions that gather information from the internal representation presented previously. Prior to the analysis, a normalization step is performed on the internal representation. In particular, the precedence graph is simplified to its transitive reduction in order to remove useless constraints. The trees for the requirements and the objective function are also simplified. For instance, a sum of sums is replaced by a single sum. Finally, useless objects (unused machines, empty jobs, for instance) are marked as such.

To be useful, the analysis must be robust with respect to modelling variations. AEON compiles models into a canonical form and the analysis is performed on the canonical form. For instance, the code of Fig. 3 shows an alternative model of a JSP. There are several differences (multi-mode activities, reservoirs, no jobs, explicit objective function) compared to the code in Fig. 1. However, AEON correctly categorizes it as a JSP, which is a highly desirable feature in practice. Indeed, it is the semantic of the model which is significant, not the syntax of how the meaning is described.

```
1   range machines;
2   range tasks;
3   int proc[tasks];
4   int mach[tasks];
5
6   Schedule<Mod> s();
7   Reservoir<Mod> M[i in machines](s,0,5,5,IntToString(i));
8   MultiModeActivity<Mod> A[i in tasks](s,1,IntToString(i));
9   forall(i in tasks) {
10      A[i].setProcTime(1,proc[i],proc[i]);
11      A[i].requires(1,M[mach[i]],3);
12  }
13  forall(i in tasks:i%nbmachines!=0)
14      A[i].precedes(A[i+1]);
15  s.minimizeObj(maxOf(all(i in tasks)completionTimeOf(A[i])));
16
17  GreedyTabuSynthesizer synth();
18  Solution<Mod> sol = synth.solve(s);
19  sol.printSolution();
```

Fig. 3 Alternative Model for the Job-Shop Problem

3.3 Algorithm Synthesis

The classes responsible for the synthesis are `ScheduleSynthesizer` and its subclasses (see Table 2). As reflected in Fig. 2, the input of the synthesis step is composed of three parts: the user model, its classification, and a choice made by the user for a particular solving technology. The chosen subclass of `ScheduleSynthesizer` defines the solving technology (for instance Constraint Programming for `CPSynthesizer`) and the `solve` method takes the model as an argument.

Based on the classification output, the synthesizer chooses the appropriate solving strategy. A strategy is a search algorithm specific to a class of problems that will be instantiated to a particular instance. Each synthesizer associates different strategies with the classes of problems. For instance, the `TSSynthesizer` class associates the Tabu Search of Dell'Amico and Trubian (1993) with the class Job-Shop Problem with Makespan. Each synthesizer might not define strategies for each class of problems but it is possible that it defines a strategy for a more general problems. As the output of the classification is a sequence of problem classes, the synthesizer will look for a strategy for the first class. If it does not exist, a strategy for the next class will be looked up. The sequence is visited while there is no matching strategy. In the worst case, the problem is recognized as a "general scheduling problem" for which there is a basic default search.

Once the strategy is chosen, it must be instantiated to the problem being solved. The synthesizer delegates this work to a subclass of the `Strategy` class. Roughly speaking, there is such a subclass for each existing pair of problem class and solving technology. Each `Strategy` subclass is responsible for setting up and running a search algorithm for the problem being solved. The difficulty is that although the class of the problem is known, it may be hard to find the suitable information to instantiate the search. To facilitate this step, AEON features a set of classes called views. The views are used to present the schedule and its components in a unified way, no matter how they were introduced. Different views correspond to different conceptions of the problem. The most general (`ScheduleView`) is a generic way to access the information, while specific views give direct access to the subset of useful information for some classes of problems. For instance, the `JobShopView` gives information for JSPs. It is meant to give the same interface no matter how the problem was modeled by the user (whether it was specified as in Fig. 1 or as in Fig. 3).

3.4 Algorithm Execution

The algorithm being actually run is different for each strategy. However they have in common that a solution is returned. Objects of the class `Solution` assign a value to each decision variable of the problem. This assignment is expressed in terms of the model objects. For instance, the method `getStartingTime` (`Activity<Mod> act`) returns the starting time of an activity. Beside the

```
1   Solution<Mod> solve(Schedule<Mod> sched){
2       JobShopView view(sched);
3       range Activities = view.getActivities();
4       range Jobs = view.getJobs();
5       range Machines = view.getMachines();
6       int[] duration =
7               all(i in Activities) view.getProcessingTime(i);
8       int[] machine = all(i in Activities) view.getMachine(i);
9       int[][] jobAct =
10              all(j in Jobs) view.getOrderedActivitiesOfJob(j);
11
12      JobshopAlgorithm  ls(LocalSolver(),Activities, Jobs,
13                          Machines, duration, machine, jobAct);
14      ls.solve();
15      SolutionView sol(view);
16      ls.saveSolution(sol);
17      return sol.getModelSolution();
18  }
```

Fig. 4 Solving a Job-Shop Problem

starting time, other decision variables of activities are the completion time, the set of resources effectively used, the mode (for multi-mode activities) and the presence or absence (for optional activities). The solution records also the value of the objective function under this assignment. The main benefit of solution objects is that the model stays independent. It can thus have several solutions that can be compared. Moreover, solutions serve to communicate between cooperating strategies. They can be used to perform an initial assignment, to provide an upper bound, or to guide heuristics.

Solutions are expressed in terms of the model but strategies deal with views. They need a `SolutionView` to express the solution in terms of the view. A `SolutionView` object is created from a view and the values for the decision variables are given in terms of this view. The underlying solution in terms of the model can then be retrieved from the solution view. Figure 4 shows the body of the `solve` method of the `DellAmico` class. It features the `JobShopView` and `SolutionView` classes. Line 2-10 shows the creation and the use of the view for Job-Shop problems. The actual search is delegated to another class named `JobshopAlgorithm` (lines 12-14). Line 15 creates the view for the solution from the view for the problem. This view is then fulfilled in line 16 and the actual solution is returned in line 17.

4 Adding Classes of Problems and Strategies

As the main concern of this work is to simplify the use of scheduling algorithms, it is also important to provide simple mechanisms to extend the system. In particular, the AEON architecture allows implementors to easily add classes of problems, synthesizers, and solving strategies. The extension of the modelling abstractions is not covered as it may need deeper modifications into the system. New classes of problems can be specified using XML files. Synthesizers and strategies are defined by extending existing classes.

4.1 Adding Classes of Problems

All classes of problems and high-level characteristics are defined in XML files. Each class is defined by its unique name and a structure of constraints that the problems of this class must respect. This structure is recursively made of the following elements:

- SimpleConstraint: The characteristic must have a given value.
- And: All constraints must be respected.
- Or: At least one constraint must be respected.
- Not: The constraint cannot be respected.
- IsA: The constraints of another given model must be respected.

The root element is called "Constraints" and corresponds to an "And". To add a new class, it is necessary to write an XML file that defines the constraints to satisfy. It is simple to reuse previous model thanks to *IsA* inheritance construct. For instance, Fig. 5 shows the file for the particular case of a JSP with two jobs that can be solved in polynomial time (Akers and Friedman (1955)). It is a conjunction of constraints, namely that it is a Job-Shop problem, that the objective function is the makespan, and that the number of jobs is two.

4.2 Adding Strategies

A new search strategy is created by extending class `Strategy`, which requires specifying two methods: `solve(Schedule<Mod> s)` and `solve(Schedule <Mod> sched, Solution<Mod> initSol)`. The first method implements the resolution of the problem from scratch and the second one solves

```
1  <?xml version="1.0" encoding="UTF-8"?>
2  <!DOCTYPE Model SYSTEM "models.dtd">
3  <Model ID="JobShopWithMakespanWithTwoJobs">
4    <Constraints>
5      <IsA Name="Makespan"/>
6      <IsA Name="JobShop"/>
7      <Constraint Name="nbJobs" Value="2"/>
8    </Constraints>
9  </Model>
```

Fig. 5 XML Definition of the Job-Shop with 2 jobs.

```
1  class MySynthesizer extends TSSynthesizer{
2    MySynthesizer():TSSynthesizer(){
3      registerStrategy("JobShopWithMakespanWithTwoJobs",
4                    new AkersAndFriedmanAlgorithm());
5    }
6  }
```

Fig. 6 Adding a new strategy to the TSSynthesizer

the problem, starting from an initial solution. This initial solution may be discarded, for instance in the case of a greedy solver. The body of these methods should use views. This is illustrated in Fig. 4, which shows the implementation of the first method. The implementation of the second one is similar. The only modification is the replacement of line 14 by the instruction `ls.solve(new SolutionView(view,initSol))` where a view of the initial solution is forwarded to the search algorithm.

A newly created strategy must then be linked to a class of problem by mean of a synthesizer. This pairing is done by the method `registerStrategy(string name, Strategy strategy)` defined in the `Synthesizer` class. This method associates a class (defined by its name) to a strategy. If another strategy was already associated with a synthesizer, the new one replaces the old one. This method is typically called inside the constructor of a new class of synthesizer. Figure 6 shows such a case, where a new synthesizer is defined as a subclass of `TSSynthesizer`. This means that a JSP with two jobs will be solved using the ad-hoc polynomial algorithm and all other problems will be solved with Tabu Search.

From this example, it is clear that the user choice for a particular search technology (in Fig. 2) can also be removed, allowing a completely black-box search. It suffices to create a default synthesizer with each class of problems, choosing the best possible strategy for each problem subclass. However, the "best" strategy is not necessarily unique even for a subclass: it may depend on the time constraints, the need to obtain lower and upper bounds, the desire for optimality, and the characteristics of the instances at hand. So providing the synthesizers increase the flexibility and effectiveness of the system.

4.3 Building New Strategies Compositionally

New strategies can also be built from simpler strategies. The architecture of AEON allows implementors to build composite searches by specialization or composition. The first possibility is to create a new strategy for a specialized class as shown in the previous subsection. At a more general level, a synthesizer can systematically create compound strategies from other synthesizers. Figure 7 presents the two possibilities for a simple compound: a Tabu Search followed by a CP search. Lines 1–14 illustrate a compound strategy for the JSP and lines 15-26 show the code of a synthesizer

```
1    class TS_CPJSP extends Strategy{
2      Strategy _s1;
3      Strategy _s2;
4      TS_CPJSP():Strategy(){
5        _s1 = new DellAmico();
6        _s2 = new CPJobShop();
7      }
8      Solution<Mod> solve(Schedule<Mod> s){
9        return _s2.solve(s,_s1.solve(s));
10     }
11     Solution<Mod> solve(Schedule<Mod> s,Solution<Mod> initSol){
12       return _s2.solve(s,_s1.solve(s, initSol));
13     }
14   }
15   class TS_CPSynthesizer extends ScheduleSynthesizer{
16     ScheduleSynthesizer _s1;
17     ScheduleSynthesizer _s2;
18     TS_CPSynthesizer():ScheduleSynthesizer(){
19       _s1 = new TSSynthesizer();
20       _s2 = new CPSynthesizer();
21     }
22     Solution<Mod> solve(Schedule<Mod> s){
23       string[] models = classify(s);
24       return _s2.solve(s,models,_s1.solve(s, models));
25     }
26   }
```

Fig. 7 Two implementations for a TS+CP strategy

chaining TS and CP. The methods `classify` and `solve` with several argument are defined in `ScheduleSynthesizer` and represent the different steps under the responsibility of the synthesizer: the classification and the resolution (with and without initial solution). It is interesting to see how the code of the compound synthesizer mimics the code of the compound strategy.

5 Experiments

The goal of this section is to show that the genericity of the system is compatible with effective and efficient solving of scheduling problems. To assess this, we chose to perform experiments on a few classical benchmark, the Job-Shop Problem with Makespan minimization (JSP), the Open-Shop Problem with Makespan minimization (OSP) and the Job-Shop Problem with total weighted tardiness minimization (JSTWT). For each benchmark, three synthesized search algorithms will be considered: A Local Search (LS), a Constraint Progamming approach (CP) and a compound where the Tabu Search gives an upper bound to the CP part (LS+CP). They will be compared with the COMET implementation (Van Hentenryck and Michel (2005)) of respectively the Tabu Search of Dell'Amico and Trubian (1993) for JSP,

Table 4 Mean Relative Error and running time (in seconds) for 4 algorithms. Ref. stands for the references algorithms, LS for Local Searches embedded in AEON, CP for Constraint Programming embedded in AEON and LS+CP for a compound of LS and CP. For CP and LS+CP, the number in parenthesis is the number of instances for which the search was complete and for which the running time is counted. For OSP, the column CP counts 2 values. The second one is a Large Neighborhood Search that can also be generated in AEON.

Problem	#Inst.	Average MRE				Average running time to best solution			
		Ref.	LS	CP/LNS	LS+CP	Ref.	LS	CP/LNS	LS+CP
JSP	78	2.08	2.09	54.40	2.03	2.6	3.1	4.4(30)	3.4(52)
OSP	80	1.68	1.70	1.58/0.01	0.85	24.1	25.0	8.0(49)/ <120	30.2(50)
JSPTW	22	4.28	3.87	97.88	4.14	24.4	24.3	-(0)	-(0)

the Tabu Search of Liaw (1999) for OSP and a Metropolis algorithm presented in Van Hentenryck and Michel (2004) for JSPTW.

The LS algorithms are counterparts of the original algorithms and have the same limits : 12,000 iterations for JSP and OSP and 600,000 iterations for JSPWT. The CP search is limited in time to $\max(300, 3*\#\text{activities})$ seconds, that is 25 minutes for the largest instances.

For local search algorithms, 20 runs for each instance were performed. The algorithms involving CP were only run once as they are much less variable. All runs were performed on a Intel Core 2 Duo, 1.66Ghz with 1 Gb of RAM.

Table 4 presents a summary of the results for classical benchmark instances. More detailed results are available online[4]. For each algorithm, the mean relative error (MRE) is given. The MRE is equal to $100*(UB-LB)/LB$ where UB is the value of the (average) makespan found by the algorithm and LB is the best lower bound known for the instance (taken from Zhang et al (2008, 2007); Van Hentenryck and Michel (2005); Laborie and Godard (2007)).

To show another hybrid approach, we also generated a Large Neighborhood Search (LNS) for the OSP. This search is particularly efficient and solved all but one of the 80 instances in less than 2 minutes, yielding a MRE of 0.01 as shown in column CP/LNS of Table 4.

This table shows that there is no significant difference between the search generated by AEON and a search that is written apart. Of course the CP approach is not always usable for larger instances but it is not restricted to AEON. On the contrary, the use of CP in conjunction with the Local Search permits to prove optimality of heuristically found solutions. In terms of running time, the CP approach is not competitive for large problems but the local search (LS) is competitive with the COMET implementation of the reference algorithms.

The cost of the use of AEON is illustrated on Fig. 8 where the total time used by the setup, analysis, classification and generation operations is reported in function of the number of activities in the problem. The plot exhibits a quadratic progression with a soft slope. For instances containing 500 activities, the classification time is less than 1.5 second.

---

[4] http://becool.info.ucl.ac.be/aeon

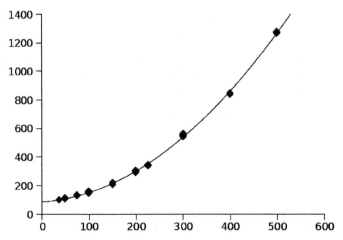

Fig. 8 Time (in milliseconds) to analyze a problem and generate the search in function of the number of activities.

6 Conclusion

This work presents AEON, a system to model and solve scheduling problems. Given a scheduling model specified in a high-level modeling language, AEON recognizes and classifies its structure, and synthesizes an appropriate search algorithm. The synthesized algorithm is specialized to a particular paradigm such as local search or constraint programming. The approach makes it possible to exploit structural information from the models to derive scheduling algorithms dedicated to classes of problems.

AEON has a number of fundamental features: First the model classification does not depend on the syntax or on the modeling choices. Models are transformed into a canonical form on which the analysis is performed, increasing the robustness of the modeling process. Second, AEON is an open and extensible system: New problem classes can be specified in standard XML format and new solving strategies can be added for all problem classes. Moreover, new synthesizers can be built from existing ones compositionally, building sequences of solvers or specializing decomposition algorithms (e.g., logical Benders decomposition) with different algorithms.

The experimental results demonstrated the feasibility of the approach. They show that the overhead of using AEON compared to dedicated algorithm is small and that the analysis cost is perfectly acceptable and grows quadratically with the problem size, taking about 1.5 seconds for 500 activities.

Our current work aims at defining a wide variety of scheduling algorithms for many problem classes. The inclusion of new algorithms, including large neighborhood search and parallel version of existing algorithms, is also under way and experimental results should be available soon. Long-term research will focus on two main directions. First, the automatic linearization of models will allow us to solve them using MIP technology or to obtain linear relaxations to provide lower bounds or guide the search. Second, robust default search should be built for various general classes of problems (e.g., disjunctive scheduling) when idiosyncratic constraints are present.

Acknowledgments

The authors want to thank the anonymous reviewers for their helpful comments. This research is partially supported by the Walloon Region, project Transmaze (516207) and by Interuniversity Attraction Poles Programme (Belgian State, Belgian Science Policy).

References

Akers S, Friedman J (1955) A non-numerical approach to production scheduling problems. Operations Research 3:429–442

Dell'Amico M, Trubian M (1993) Applying tabu search to the job-shop scheduling problem. Annals of Operations Research 41:231–252

Kolisch R, Sprecher A (1997) Psplib — a project scheduling problem library. European Journal of Operational Research 96:205–216, URL citeseer.ist.psu.edu/kolisch96psplib.html

Laborie P, Godard D (2007) Self-adapting large neighborhood search: Application to single-mode scheduling problems. In Proceedings MISTA-07, Paris

Liaw CF (1999) A tabu search algorithm for the open shop scheduling problem. Computers and Operations Research 26:109–126

Nuijten W, Bousonville T, Focacci F, Godard D, Le Pape C (2004) Towards an industrial manufacturing scheduling problem and test bed. PMS URL http://www2.ilog.com/masclib/

Refalo P (2004) Impact-based search strategies for constraint programming. In: CP 2004, Toronto (Canada), pp 557–571

Van Hentenryck P, Michel L (2004) Scheduling abstractions for local search. In: CP-AI-OR'04, Nice, pp 319–334

Van Hentenryck P, Michel L (2005) Constraint-Based Local Search. The MIT Press

Van Hentenryck P, Michel L (2007) Synthesis of constraint-based local search algorithms from high-level models. AAAI'07, Vancouver, British Columbia

Van Hentenryck P, Michel L, Laborie P, Nuijten W, Rogerie J (1999) Combinatorial optimization in OPL studio. In: Portuguese Conference on Artificial Intelligence, pp 1–15, URL citeseer.ist.psu.edu/article/vanhentenryck99combinatorial.html

Zhang CY, Li P, Rao Y, Guan Z (2007) A tabu search algorithm with a new neighborhood structure for the job shop scheduling problem. Computers & Operations Research 34:3229–3242

Zhang CY, Li P, Rao Y, Guan Z (2008) A very fast ts/sa algorithm for the job shop scheduling problem. Computers & Operations Research 35:282–294

Part 2
Optimization

Part 2.1
Integer Programming

A Branch-and-cut Algorithm for Integer Bilevel Linear Programs

S.T. DeNegre and T.K. Ralphs

Abstract We describe a rudimentary branch-and-cut algorithm for solving integer bilevel linear programs that extends existing techniques for standard integer linear programs to this very challenging computational setting. The algorithm improves on the branch-and-bound algorithm of Moore and Bard in that it uses cutting plane techniques to produce improved bounds, does not require specialized branching strategies, and can be implemented in a straightforward way using only linear solvers. An implementation built using software components available in the COIN-OR software repository is described and preliminary computational results presented.

Key words: Bilevel Programming, Integer Programming, Branch and Cut, Valid Inequality, Branch and Bound

1 Introduction

Standard mathematical programs consider decision problems in which there is a single decision-maker (DM) controlling all variables. Many real-world decision problems involve multiple, independent DMs, whose interests are not necessarily aligned. In this paper, we discuss solution methods for a class of models known as *integer bilevel linear programs* (IBLPs) that generalize standard integer linear programming (ILP) models by considering two sets of variables, each controlled by a separate DM.

S.T. DeNegre
Department of Industrial & Systems Engineering, Lehigh University, 200 W. Packer Avenue, Bethlehem, PA 18015, e-mail: sdenegre@lehigh.edu

T.K. Ralphs
Department of Industrial & Systems Engineering, Lehigh University, 200 W. Packer Avenue, Bethlehem, PA 18015, e-mail: ted@lehigh.edu

J.W. Chinneck et al. (eds.), *Operations Research and Cyber-Infrastructure*, Operations Research/Computer Science Interfaces Series 47, DOI: 10.1007/978-0-387-88843-9_4,
© Springer Science+Business Media, LLC 2009

The goal of the work described herein is to demonstrate that it is possible, in principle, to generalize the tremendously successful branch-and-cut framework commonly used to solve mixed integer linear programs to this very challenging computational setting. By developing techniques for IBLP that are analogous to those used in the ILP setting, we have been able to leverage the many advances that have occurred in solution technology for ILPs. Although our implementation is quite rudimentary and is intended only as a demonstration of concept, the algorithm improves on the branch-and-bound algorithm previously proposed by Moore and Bard (1990) in that it uses a basic cutting plane procedure to produce improved bounds, does not require specialized branching techniques, and can be implemented in a straightforward way using existing software.

Conceptually, the decisions in an IBLP are made in sequential order according to an implicit hierarchy. Top-level decisions are made first, after which the lower-level decisions are made under the mandates of those upper-level decisions. Formally, let $x \in \mathbb{R}^{n_1}$ represent a set of variables controlled by an *upper-level DM* or *leader* and let $y \in \mathbb{R}^{n_2}$ represent a set of variables controlled by a *lower-level DM* or *follower*. The canonical integer bilevel linear program is then given by

$$z_{IBLP} = \max \left\{ c^1 x + d^1 y \mid x \in \mathscr{P}_U \cap \mathbb{Z}^{n_1}, y \in \text{argmax}\{d^2 y \mid y \in \mathscr{P}_L(x) \cap \mathbb{Z}^{n_2}\} \right\},$$

where

$$\mathscr{P}_U = \left\{ x \in \mathbb{R}^{n_1} \mid A^1 x \le b^1, x \ge 0 \right\}$$

is the polyhedron defining the *upper-level feasible region*;

$$\mathscr{P}_L(x) = \left\{ y \in \mathbb{R}^{n_2} \mid G^2 y \le b^2 - A^2 x, y \ge 0 \right\}$$

is the polyhedron defining the *lower-level feasible region* with respect to a given $x \in \mathbb{R}^{m_1}$; $A^1 \in \mathbb{Q}^{m_1 \times n_1}$; $b^1 \in \mathbb{Q}^{m_1}$; $A^2 \in \mathbb{Q}^{m_2 \times n_1}$, $G^2 \in \mathbb{Q}^{m_2 \times n_2}$; and $b^2 \in \mathbb{Q}^{m_2}$. The defining characteristic of a bilevel program, in contrast with a standard mathematical program, is that the lower-level variables are required to consist of an optimal solution to an ILP whose right-hand side depends on the values chosen for the upper-level variables.

Bilevel models arise naturally in systems involving two opposing parties, such as in military and law enforcement applications. The essence of what makes these models difficult to analyze is the implicit adversarial relationship between the upper- and lower-level DMs stemming from the fact that improvements to the upper-level DM's objective usually come at the expense of a degradation in the lower-level DM's objective. In fact, without such an adversarial relationship, these systems become much easier to handle. In some cases, the adversarial relationship is explicit and direct, i.e., the upper-level DM's sole objective is to prevent the lower-level DM from achieving a known objective. Such systems, called *zero-sum*, arise in analyzing *interdiction problems* (see below).

Although bilevel linear programming (BLP) has received increased attention recently, the literature on IBLP remains scarce. Moore and Bard (1990) introduced a general framework for mixed integer bilevel linear programming (MIBLP), described associated computational challenges, and suggested a branch-and-bound algorithm. The vast majority of the remaining IBLP literature has been restricted to various special cases. Bard and Moore (1992) developed a specialized algorithm for binary bilevel programs. Dempe (2001) considered the case characterized by continuous upper-level variables and integer lower-level variables and used a cutting plane approach to approximate the lower-level feasible region. Wen and Yang (1990) considered the opposite case, where the lower-level problem is a linear program and the upper-level problem is an integer program. Linear programming duality was used to derive exact and heuristic solutions.

A closely related class of models mentioned above that has already proven its utility in practice is that of the *interdiction models*. Most research on these models has focused on the *network interdiction problem* (Wollmer, 1964; McMasters and Mustin, 1970; Ghare et al, 1971; Wood, 1993; Cormican et al, 1998; Israeli and Wood, 2002; Held and Woodruff, 2005; Janjarassuk and Linderoth, 2006; Royset and Wood, 2007; Lim and Smith, 2007; Morton et al, 2007), in which the lower-level DM represents an entity operating a network of some sort. The upper-level DM (or interdictor) attempts to reduce the network performance as much as possible via the removal (complete or otherwise) of portions (subsets of arcs or nodes) of the network. Here, we generalize the underlying concept behind these network interdiction models by allowing the lower-level problem to be completely general and introducing the "interdiction" of lower-level decision variables in order to obtain a class of models with a much wider range of application.

The remainder of the paper is composed as follows. In Section 2, we describe the mathematical models that we consider. In Section 3, we discuss the challenge of solving these models and the barriers to generalizing solution methods for single-level mathematical programming problems. In Section 4, we describe how to overcome these challenges and propose a branch-and-cut algorithm for IBLPs. Section 5 illustrates the algorithm via an example and provides some preliminary computational results. Finally, in Section 6, we provide conclusions and directions for future work.

2 Definitions and Notation

When discussing various relaxations, it will sometimes be convenient to refer to the matrices $A := [(A^1)^\top | (A^2)^\top]^\top$ and $G := [0 | (G^2)^\top]^\top$, and the vector $b := [(b^1)^\top | (b^2)^\top]^\top$. The region obtained by dropping the optimality requirement for the lower-level variables is then given by

$$\Omega^I = \{(x,y) \in \mathbb{Z}^{n_1} \times \mathbb{Z}^{n_2} \mid Ax + Gy \leq b, x, y \geq 0\}.$$

Removing the integrality requirements from Ω^I yields the polyhedral region

$$\Omega = \{(x,y) \in \mathbb{R}^{n_1} \times \mathbb{R}^{n_2} \mid Ax + Gy \leq b, x, y \geq 0\}.$$

For each upper-level solution $x \in \mathscr{P}_U \cap \mathbb{Z}^{n_1}$, we define the follower's *rational reaction set* to be

$$M^I(x) = \text{argmax}\{d^2y \mid y \in \mathscr{P}_L(x) \cap \mathbb{Z}^{n_2}\}.$$

If we set

$$\Omega^I_{\text{proj}} = \left\{ x \in \mathscr{P}_U \cap \mathbb{Z}^{n_1} \mid \exists y \text{ with } (x,y) \in \Omega^I \right\},$$

then any point (x,y) such that $x \in \Omega^I_{\text{proj}}$ and $y \in M^I(x)$ is called *bilevel feasible*. The IBLP problem can then be restated as that of determining

$$z_{IBLP} = \max_{(x,y) \in \mathscr{F}^I} c^1x + d^1y, \tag{IBLP}$$

where $\mathscr{F}^I = \left\{ (x,y) \mid x \in \Omega^I_{\text{proj}}, y \in M^I(x) \right\}$. We also define the continuous analog of $\mathscr{F}^I$ by

$$\mathscr{F} = \left\{ (x,y) \mid x \in \Omega_{\text{proj}}, y \in M(x) \right\},$$

where

$$\Omega_{\text{proj}} = \{ x \in \mathscr{P}_U \mid \exists y \text{ with } (x,y) \in \Omega \}$$

and

$$M(x) = \text{argmax}\{d^2y \mid y \in \mathscr{P}_L(x)\}.$$

Consistent with the existing literature (Bard, 1988; Bard and Moore, 1990; Moore and Bard, 1990; Bard and Moore, 1992), we assume that Ω^I is nonempty and bounded and that $\mathscr{P}_L(x) \cap \mathbb{Z}^{n_2} \neq \emptyset$ for all $x \in \mathscr{P}_U \cap \mathbb{Z}^{n_1}$. Further, we assume that if the lower-level DM's rational reaction set $M^I(x)$ is not a singleton, the upper-level DM is allowed to choose from among the alternatives one that is optimal with respect to the upper-level objective. This is the so-called *optimistic formulation* of the problem. The reader is referred to Loridan and Morgan (1996) for further insight on and discussion of alternative formulations.

3 Computational Challenges of IBLP

Because ILP is a special case of IBLP, it is clear that IBLP is also an $\mathscr{N}\mathscr{P}$-hard problem. In fact, in contrast to the ILP case, the question of IBLP feasibility is not even in $\mathscr{N}\mathscr{P}$, essentially because the question of whether a pair $(x,y) \in \mathbb{Z}^{n_1} \times \mathbb{Z}^{n_2}$ is feasible for a given IBLP is itself an ILP. Hansen et al (1992) show that even the continuous version of the problem (a BLP) is strongly $\mathscr{N}\mathscr{P}$-hard and Vicente et al (1994) adds that checking local optimality for BLPs is an $\mathscr{N}\mathscr{P}$-hard problem. All of this indicates that solving IBLPs in practice is likely to be extremely challenging.

A natural approach to developing algorithms for solving IBLPs is to consider generalizations of the techniques that are used for ILPs. It does not take long, however, to realize that our intuition does not easily carry over from the case of ILP to the case of IBLP. In a branch-and-bound algorithm for standard integer linear programming, integrality constraints are removed and the resulting linear program, which is easily seen to be a relaxation of the original ILP, is solved. The solution to this relaxed problem yields useful information about the original problem. In particular, we can make use of the following well-known rules to prune the branch and bound tree.

(R1) If the relaxed problem has no feasible solution, then neither does the original problem.
(R2) If the relaxed problem has a solution, then its value is a valid upper bound on the optimal value of the maximization original problem.
(R3) If the solution to the relaxed subproblem satisfies integrality restrictions, then it is optimal for the original problem.

Unfortunately, these rules cannot be extended in a straightforward way to IBLPs because dropping the integrality constraints from both upper and lower-level problems does not result in a relaxation, as the example in Figure 1 illustrates. In the figure, the polyhedron represents the set Ω, while the integer points in this polyhedron comprise the discrete set Ω^I. Within each of Ω and Ω^I, we have indicated points that satisfy the optimality constraint on the lower-level variables (i.e., the bilevel feasible solutions). From the figure, it is easy to see that $\mathscr{F} \subseteq \Omega$, $\mathscr{F}^I \subseteq \Omega^I$, and $\Omega^I \subseteq \Omega$. It is not the case, however, that $\mathscr{F}^I \subseteq \mathscr{F}$. Hence, the BLP obtained by dropping integrality constraints is not a relaxation of the IBLP.

In this example, optimizing over the continuous region $\mathscr{F}$ yields the integer solution $(8,1)$, with the upper-level objective value 18. However, the true solution to the IBLP is $(2,2)$, with objective value 22. From this, we observe that even when solutions to $\max_{(x,y)\in\mathscr{F}} c^1 x + d^1 y$ are in $\mathscr{F}^I$, they are not necessarily optimal. Thus, except in certain special cases, only Rule (R1) above remains valid if we simply remove integrality constraints from the IBLP to yield a BLP. Complicating matters further is the question of how to branch when faced with a solution that is integer but infeasible.

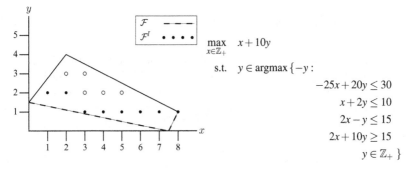

Fig. 1 The feasible region of IBLP (Moore and Bard, 1990).

4 Branch and Cut

As with many classes of mathematical programs, the most obvious route to achieving global optimality is the development of bounding procedures that can be used to drive a branch-and-bound algorithm. As we have just observed, however, the bounding, fathoming, and branching procedures employed in traditional LP-based branch-and-bound algorithms cannot be applied in a straightforward way. In this section, we describe how to overcome these challenges to develop a generalized branch-and-cut algorithm for IBLPs that follows the same basic paradigm used in ILP. This work improves on the branch-and-bound algorithm originally suggested by Moore and Bard (1990) in a number of significant ways that we point out below.

4.1 Bounding

Although removing the integrality restrictions on all variables does not result in a valid relaxation, removing the lower-level optimality constraint from the problem *does* yield the relaxation

$$\max_{(x,y)\in\Omega^I} c^1 x + d^1 y, \tag{1}$$

similar to one suggested by Moore and Bard (1990). Unfortunately, as we noted earlier, determining whether solutions to this relaxation are bilevel feasible is a difficult problem in itself.

In order to improve upon the bounds yielded by (1) and to avoid the potential difficulties associated with being forced to branch when faced with an infeasible integer solution, we consider here a branch-and-cut algorithm based on the iterative generation of linear inequalities valid for $\mathscr{F}^I$ and augmentation of the linear system describing Ω until an optimal member of $\mathscr{F}^I$ is exposed or we choose to branch. The procedures we suggest are analogous to those used in the case of ILP but also address the fact that integer solutions may not be feasible in this setting.

4.2 Generating Valid Inequalities

An inequality defined by (π_1, π_2, π_0) is called a *valid inequality* for $\mathscr{F}^I$ if $\pi_1 x + \pi_2 y \le \pi_0$ for all $(x,y) \in \mathscr{F}^I$. Unless $\mathrm{conv}(\mathscr{F}^I) = \Omega$, there exist inequalities that are valid for $\mathscr{F}^I$, but are violated by some members of Ω. In order to generate these inequalities, we must use information not contained in the linear description of Ω. For a point $(x,y) \in \mathbb{Z}^{n_1} \times \mathbb{Z}^{n_2}$ to be feasible for an IBLP, it must satisfy three conditions:

(C1) $(x,y) \in \Omega$,
(C2) $(x,y) \in \mathbb{Z}^{n_1} \times \mathbb{Z}^{n_2}$, and
(C3) $y \in M^I(x)$.

This is in contrast to standard ILPs, where we have only the first two conditions.

Because the first requirement is enforced by requiring membership in Ω, we must derive valid inequalities from the other two conditions. We start with the following straightforward, but useful observations.

Observation 1 *If the inequality (π_1, π_2, π_0) is valid for Ω^I, it is also valid for $\mathscr{F}^I$.*

Observation 2 *Let $(x, y) \in \Omega$ such that $y \notin M^I(x)$. If the inequality (π_1, π_2, π_0) is valid for $\Omega^I \setminus \{(x, y)\}$, it is also valid for $\mathscr{F}^I$.*

Observation 1 is derived from the relationship $\mathscr{F}^I \subseteq \Omega^I$ and allows us to separate fractional solutions to the LP resulting from removal of the lower-level optimality and integrality restrictions. Observation 2 states that we can separate points that are integer but not bilevel feasible. From these observations, we can derive two classes of valid inequalities to be used in a cutting plane procedure.

To initialize the cutting plane procedure, we must first solve the relaxation

$$\max_{(x,y) \in \Omega} c^1 x + d^1 y. \tag{LR}$$

If the solution $(\hat{x}, \hat{y})$ to (LR) does not satisfy condition (C2) above, we may apply standard cutting plane procedures used to separate points in $\Omega \setminus \Omega^I$ from $\Omega^I \supseteq \mathscr{F}^I$. For an overview of the various classes of valid inequalities used for separating fractional solutions from the convex hull of solutions to generic integer programs, see Cornuejols (2008). Any of the existing classes of valid inequalities are potential candidates for employment here, though the structure of each specific instance could be used to decide which classes are likely to be the most effective.

If $(\hat{x}, \hat{y})$ satisfies condition (C2), then we must check whether it satisfies condition (C3). This is done by solving the lower-level problem

$$\max_{y \in \mathscr{P}_L(x) \cap \mathbb{Z}^{n_2}} d^2 y \tag{2}$$

with the fixed upper-level solution $\hat{x}$. Let the solution to this IP be y^*. If $d^2 \hat{y} = d^2 y^*$, then $\hat{y}$ is also optimal for (2) and we conclude that $(\hat{x}, \hat{y})$ is bilevel feasible. Otherwise, we must again generate an inequality separating $(\hat{x}, \hat{y})$ from $\mathscr{F}^I$. In either case, however, $(\hat{x}, y^*)$ is bilevel feasible and provides a valid lower bound on the optimal solution value of the original IBLP.

Now suppose $d^2 \hat{y} < d^2 y^*$. In this case, $(\hat{x}, \hat{y})$ does not satisfy condition (C3) and is therefore not bilevel feasible. We may still use $(\hat{x}, y^*)$ to bound the original problem, but we would like to add an inequality to (LR) that is valid for $\mathscr{F}^I$ and violated by $(\hat{x}, \hat{y})$. The simple procedure encapsulated in the following proposition can be used to generate such an inequality.

Proposition 1. *Let $(\hat{x}, \hat{y}) \in \Omega^I$ be a basic feasible solution to (LR). Let J be the set of constraints that are binding at $(\hat{x}, \hat{y})$. Then*

$$\pi_1 x + \pi_2 y \leq \pi_0 - 1, \tag{3}$$

where $(\pi_1, \pi_2) = \sum_{j \in J}(a_j, g_j)$ and $\pi_0 = \sum_{j \in J} b_j$, is valid for $\mathscr{F}^I$.

Proof. The fact that $(\hat{x}, \hat{y})$ is a basic feasible implies that there exist $n = n_1 + n_2$ linearly independent constraints in the description of Ω that are binding at $(\hat{x}, \hat{y})$. Thus, the system $a'_j x + g'_j y = b_j, j \in J$ has a unique solution, namely $(\hat{x}, \hat{y})$. This, in turn, implies that $(\hat{x}, \hat{y})$ is the unique point of intersection between the hyperplane defined by the equation $\pi_1 x + \pi_2 y = \pi_0$ and the set Ω'. It follows that the inequality $\pi_1 x + \pi_2 y \leq \pi_0$ is valid for Ω'. Because the face of Ω induced by this inequality does not contain any other members of Ω' and there does not exist $(x, y) \in \mathbb{Z}^{n_1} \times \mathbb{Z}^{n_2}$ such that $\pi_1 x + \pi_2 y \in (\pi_0 - 1, \pi_0)$, this implies that the inequality $\pi_1 x + \pi_2 y \leq \pi_0 - 1$ is valid for $\Omega' \setminus \{(\hat{x}, \hat{y})\}$. Applying Observation 2 yields the result. $\square$

An example is shown in Figure 2 for the instance

$$\max_{x} \min_{y} \{y \mid -x + y \leq 2, -2x - y \leq -2, 3x - y \leq 3, y \leq 3, x, y \in \mathbb{Z}_+ \}.$$

In the figure, we can see the bilevel feasible region $\mathscr{F}^I = \{(0,2), (1,0), (2,3)\}$. Also shown in the figure is the bilevel feasible region $\mathscr{F}$ of the corresponding BLP. In this example, we start with the integer point $(1,3)$, an optimal solution to the LP

$$\max_{x,y} \{y \mid -x + y \leq 2, -2x - y \leq -2, 3x - y \leq 3, y \leq 3, x, y \in \mathbb{R}_+ \}.$$

It is easy to see that this point is not bilevel feasible, because the rational choice for the lower-level DM would be $y = 0$, when $x = 1$. Thus, we require a cut that separates $(1,3)$. Combining the constraints active at $(1,3)$ yields the half-space $\{(x,y) \in \mathbb{Z}^{n_1} \times \mathbb{Z}^{n_2} \mid -x + 2y \leq 5\}$ and applying the procedure described above, we obtain the new inequality

$$-x + 2y \leq 4,$$

which is valid for $\mathscr{F}^I$, but not satisfied by $(1,3)$. Note that after adding this cut, the optimal solution is obtained in the next iteration. Without the cutting plane procedure we have just described, we would be forced to branch after producing this solution in a branch-and-bound framework.

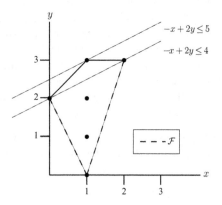

Fig. 2 An example of the bilevel feasibility cut.

The combination of this procedure, the bounding technique of Section 4.1, and the branching techniques given in Section 4.3 yields a branch-and-cut algorithm. However, it is clear that the procedure will fail on large-scale problems. In order to solve problems of interesting size, additional classes of valid inequalities derived from Condition (C3) are necessary. One such class that utilizes information from the value function of the lower-level ILP is described in DeNegre et al (2008).

4.3 Branching

As we have just described, an important advantage of our algorithm over its predecessor from Moore and Bard (1990), is the fact that we are not forced to branch after producing an infeasible integer solution and are therefore free to employ the well-developed branching strategies used in algorithms for traditional ILP, such as strong branching, pseudocost branching, or the recently introduced reliability branching (Achterberg et al, 2005). Of course, it is also possible to branch using disjunctions obtained from violations of Condition (C3). Although this is unnecessary for small problems, we believe such branching strategies may ultimately be necessary for larger problems. Specialized branching techniques for bilevel problems are discussed in DeNegre et al (2008).

4.4 A Branch-and-cut Algorithm

Putting together the procedures of the preceding three sections, we obtain a branch-and-cut algorithm that consists of solving the linear relaxation (LR), iteratively generating valid inequalities to improve the bound, and branching when necessary. In addition to the obvious advantage of producing potentially improved bounds, an advantage of this approach over the one proposed by Moore and Bard (1990) is that it relies only on the solution of standard ILPs and preserves all the usual rules of fathoming and branching. It therefore allows us to immediately leverage our vast knowledge of how to solve standard ILPs. The general framework of such an algorithm is described next.

Let

$$\max_{(x,y)\in\mathscr{F}_t} c^1 x + d^1 y. \qquad \text{(IBLP}^t)$$

be the IBLP defined at node t of the branch-and-cut tree. To process node t, we first solve the LP

$$z_{\text{LP}}^t = \max_{(x,y)\in\Omega_t} c^1 x + d^1 y. \qquad \text{(LP}^t)$$

and denote its solution by (x^t, y^t) (if it exists). If either the LP is infeasible or the optimal value of (LP^t) is less than the current lower bound L, we can fathom the current node. Otherwise we generate valid inequalities to separate the current solution from $\mathscr{F}^I$. If $(x^t, y^t) \in \Omega^I$, we check for bilevel feasibility. If the solution is feasible, we can stop. Otherwise, we add cuts of the form (3) to separate the current solution from $\Omega^I \setminus \{(x^t, y^t)\}$ if necessary and iterate. If a fractional solution is found, we either add cuts to separate the current solution from $\Omega^t \cap \mathbb{Z}^{n_1} \times \mathbb{Z}^{n_2}$ and iterate or else we branch. A general outline of the node processing subroutine is given in Algorithm 1.

Algorithm 1 Node Processing Loop

1: Solve (LP^t). If (LP^t) has an optimal solution, denote it (x^t, y^t). Then, depending on the outcome, do the following:

- If (LP^t) is infeasible, so is (IBLP^t) and the current node can be pruned.
- Else, if $z_{LP}^t \leq L$, the current node can be pruned.
- Else, go to Step 2.

2: Generate valid inequalities.

- If $(x^t, y^t) \in \Omega^I$, fix $x \leftarrow x^t$, and solve $z_{LL}^t = \max_{y \in \mathscr{P}_L(x^t) \cap \mathbb{Z}^{n_2}} d^2 y$. If $z_{LL}^t = d^2 y^t$ set $L \leftarrow c^1 x^t + d^1 y^t$ and prune the current node; else set

$$\Omega_{t+1} = \Omega_t \cap \left\{ (x, y) \in \mathbb{R}^{n_1} \times \mathbb{R}^{n_2} \mid \sum_{j \in J} (a_j x + g_j y) \leq \sum_{j \in J} b_j - 1 \right\},$$

where J is the set of active constraints in Ω_t at (x^t, y^t), set $t \leftarrow t + 1$, and go to Step 1.
- Else, either generate and add cuts valid for $\Omega^t \cap \mathbb{Z}^{n_1} \times \mathbb{Z}^{n_2}$ and go to Step 1 or BRANCH.

4.5 Specialized Methods for Binary IBLPs

The bilevel feasibility cut (3) ensures that bilevel infeasible solutions to (1) are not generated in future iterations. However, by design, it does not cut off any other integer points. This may result in the generation of a sequence of points $(x^*, y^1), (x^*, y^2), \ldots, (x^*, y^k)$ such that $y^i \notin M^I(x^*)$ for $i < k$. If $x \in \mathbb{B}^{n_1}$, information obtained from the lower-level problem can be used to avoid this problem. While checking bilevel feasibility, we obtain an optimal solution and associated objective value $z_L(x^*)$ for the lower-level problem (2). This leads to the implication $x = x^* \Rightarrow d^2 y \geq z_L(x^*)$. Let $I_0 := \{i \mid x_i^* = 0\}$ and $I_1 := \{i \mid x_i^* = 1\}$. Note that for $x \in \mathbb{B}^{n_1}$, we have that $\sum_{i \in I_0} x_i + \sum_{i \in I_1} (1 - x_i) = 0$ if and only if $x = x^*$. Otherwise, $\sum_{i \in I_0} x_i + \sum_{i \in I_1} (1 - x_i) \geq 1$. One way to model this implication is to introduce the constraint $\sum_{i \in I_0} x_i + \sum_{i \in I_1} (1 - x_i) + \delta \geq 1$, where $\delta \in \mathbb{B}$, which imposes the implication $x = x^* \Rightarrow \delta = 1$. Then, adding the constraint $d^2 y + m\delta \geq m + z_L(x^*)$, where $m = \min\{d^2 y - z_L(x^*) \mid (x, y) \in \Omega^I\}$, enforces $\delta = 1 \Rightarrow d^2 y \geq z_L(x^*)$, as desired. Exploring further such logical implications is an area of future research.

5 Computational Results

The branch-and-cut algorithm was implemented in C++, utilizing standard software components available from the Computational Infrastructure for Operations Research (COIN-OR) repository (Lougee-Heimer, 2003). The implementation uses the COIN-OR High Performance Parallel Search Framework (CHiPPS) to perform branch and bound, the MILP solver framework BLIS (part of CHiPPS), the COIN-OR LP Solver (CLP) for solving the LPs that arise in branch and cut, the SYMPHONY MILP solver for solving the lower-level ILPs, the Cut Generation Library (CGL) for generating cutting planes, and the Open Solver Interface (OSI) for interfacing with CHiPPS and SYMPHONY.

To our knowledge, the only other general IBLP algorithm proposed in the literature has been that of Moore and Bard (1990). We do not have the test set of Moore and Bard (1990) or an implementation of their algorithm available, so a comprehensive comparison to their algorithm is not feasible. In order to provide *some* basis for comparison, we did examine the branch-and-cut tree constructed by our algorithm on one of the examples from their original paper. The feasible region of the IBLP and our branch-and-cut tree are shown in Figure 3. In this simple case, our algorithm generated a total of seven nodes, and processed five, while the same example in the original paper required twelve nodes. Of course, this comparison is only a single instance, but examination of the two search trees does provide some evidence for our intuition that certain aspects of Moore and Bard's algorithm, such as the requirement to branch on integer variables, result in a less efficient search.

We also tested our algorithm on a set of interdiction problems, in which the lower-level problems were binary knapsack problems with a single constraint. The goal of the upper-level DM was to minimize the maximum profit achievable by the lower-level DM by fixing a subset of the variables in the lower-level problem to zero. A cost was associated with the fixing of each lower-level variable to zero and the upper-level problems contained a single constraint, representing the available interdiction budget. To create these instances, data files describing bicriteria

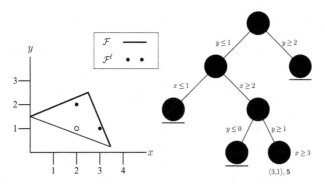

Fig. 3 Example 2 from Moore and Bard (1990) and the resulting branch-and-cut tree.

Table 1 Summary results from the knapsack interdiction.

	Maximum Infeasibility			Strong Branching		
$2n$	Avg Nodes	Avg Depth	Avg CPU (s)	Avg Nodes	Avg Depth	Avg CPU (s)
20	1801	16.45	3.17	1125	16.95	4.69
22	3538	18.25	6.63	1860	17.40	9.13
24	7034	20.20	13.27	3314	19.65	17.50
26	13867	22.00	27.54	6294	20.20	35.84
28	26155	23.85	60.08	11915	23.00	71.90
30	60626	26.65	124.84	23917	24.15	145.99
32	125840	26.75	249.19	45879	25.80	296.16
34	253965	29.65	516.65	–	–	–

knapsack problems were taken from the *Multiple Criteria Decision Making* library (Figueira, 2000). The first objective in each file was used to define a lower-level objective function, while the second objective provided a budget constraint. The available budget was then chosen to be $\lceil \sum_{i=1}^{n} a_i/2 \rceil$, where a_i is the cost of interdicting lower-level variable i. For a knapsack problem with n items, this construction yielded a problem with $2n$ variables and $n + 2$ constraints. All computational tests were performed on an Intel Xeon 2.4GHz processor with 4GB of memory. Summarized results of two sets of runs—one in which we used maximum infeasibility branching to select branching candidates and one in which we used strong branching, are shown in Table 1, where the results for each problem size reflect the average of 20 instances. Note that a dash indicates that no instances of the corresponding size were able to be solved due to memory requirements. These results look promising, but are preliminary at best. For these instances, strong branching reduced the size of the search tree significantly, but required more computation time. More fine-tuning of algorithm parameters is needed to determine the best branching strategy.

6 Conclusions

We have discussed the challenges associated with solving integer bilevel linear programming problems and described a branch-and-cut algorithm that can be seen as a generalization of the familiar algorithm used for solution of standard integer linear programs. The primary advantage of this approach is the ability to exploit the vast array of existing technology for solving ILPs techniques. The next step in the development of this approach is to include a wider range of the supplemental techniques that have proven critical in our ability to solve difficult integer linear programs in practice. These include such improvements as the development of preprocessing techniques, primal heuristics, additional classes of valid inequalities, branching rules based on disjunctions involving more than one variable, and more effective search strategies. In this paper, we have only suggested a starting point and much work remains to be done to make these methods practical for large-scale instances.

References

Achterberg T, Koch T, Martin A (2005) Branching rules revisited. Operations Research Letters 33(1):42–54

Bard J (1988) Convex two-level optimization. Mathematical Programming 40: 15–27

Bard J, Moore J (1990) A branch and bound algorithm for the bilevel programming problem. SIAM Journal on Scientific and Statistical Computing 11(2):281–292

Bard J, Moore J (1992) An algorithm for the discrete bilevel programming problem. Naval Research Logistics 39:419–435

Cormican K, Morton D, Wood R (1998) Stochastic network interdiction. Operations Research 46(2):184–197

Cornuejols G (2008) Valid inequalities for mixed integer linear programs. Mathematical Programming B 112:3–44

Dempe S (2001) Discrete bilevel optimization problems. Tech. Rep. D-04109, Institut fur Wirtschaftsinformatik, Universitat Leipzig, Leipzig, Germany

DeNegre S, Ralphs T, Guzelsoy M (2008) A new class of valid inequalities for mixed integer bilevel linear programs. Tech. rep., Lehigh University

Figueira J (2000) MCDM Numerical Instances Library. URL http://www.univ-valenciennes.fr/ROAD/MCDM/ListMOKP.html

Ghare P, Montgomery D, Turner W (1971) Optimal interdiction policy for a flow network. Naval Research Logistics Quarterly 18:27–45

Hansen P, Jaumard B, Savard G (1992) New branch-and-bound rules for linear bilevel programming. SIAM Journal on Scientific and Statistical Computing 13(5):1194–1217

Held H, Woodruff D (2005) Heuristics for multi-stage interdiction of stochastic networks. Journal of Heuristics 11(5-6):483–500

Israeli E, Wood R (2002) Shortest path network interdiction. Networks 40(2): 97–111

Janjarassuk U, Linderoth J (2006) Reformulation and sampling to solve a stochastic network interdiction problem. Tech. Rep. 06T-001, Lehigh University

Lim C, Smith J (2007) Algorithms for discrete and continuous multicommodity flow network interdiction problems. IIE Transactions 39(1):15–26

Loridan P, Morgan J (1996) Weak via strong stackelberg problem: New results. Journal of Global Optimization 8(3):263–287

Lougee-Heimer R (2003) The Common OPtimization INterface for Operations Research. IBM Journal of Research and Development 47(1):57–66

McMasters A, Mustin T (1970) Optimal interdiction of a supply network. Naval Research Logistics Quarterly 17:261–268

Moore J, Bard J (1990) The mixed integer linear bilevel programming problem. Operations Research 38(5):911–921

Morton D, Pan F, Saeger K (2007) Models for nuclear smuggling interdiction. IIE Transactions 39(1):3–14

Royset J, Wood R (2007) Solving the bi-objective maximum-flow network-interdiction problem. INFORMS Journal on Computing 19(2):175–184

Vicente L, Savard G, Judice J (1994) Descent approaches for quadratic bilevel programming. Journal of Optimization Theory and Applications 81:379–399

Wen U, Yang Y (1990) Algorithms for solving the mixed integer two-level linear programming problem. Computers & Operations Research 17(2):133–142

Wollmer R (1964) Removing arcs from a network. Operations Research 12(6): 934–940

Wood R (1993) Deterministic network interdiction. Mathematical and Computer Modelling 17(2):1–18

A Principled Approach to Mixed Integer/Linear Problem Formulation

J.N. Hooker

Abstract We view mixed integer/linear problem formulation as a process of identifying disjunctive and knapsack constraints in a problem and converting them to mixed integer form. We show through a series of examples that following this process can yield mixed integer models that automatically incorporate some of the modeling devices that have been discovered over the years for making the formulation tighter. In one case it substantially improves on the generally accepted model. We provide a theoretical basis for the process by generalizing Jeroslow's mixed integer representability theorem.

Key words: Mixed integer/linear programming, problem formulation, modeling, representability

1 Introduction

Mixed integer problem formulation is an art rather than a science, but it need not be unprincipled. A theorem of Jeroslow (1987), for example, provides guidance for writing formulations. It states that a problem can be given a mixed integer/linear formulation if and only if its feasible set is a union of finitely many polyhedra that satisfy a certain technical condition.

This suggests a disjunctive approach to mixed integer formulation. A union of polyhedra is represented by a disjunction of linear systems. So if we can understand a problem as presenting choices between discrete alternatives, we can perhaps write the choices as disjunctions of linear systems and convert each disjunction to a mixed integer formulation. In this way we obtain a mixed integer formulation for the entire problem.

Jeroslow's disjunctive formulations have the additional advantage that each disjunction receives a convex hull formulation, the tightest possible mixed

J.N. Hooker

Carnegie Mellon University, e-mail: john@hooker.tepper.cmu.edu

J.W. Chinneck et al. (eds.), *Operations Research and Cyber-Infrastructure*, Operations Research/Computer Science Interfaces Series 47, DOI: 10.1007/978-0-387-88843-9_5,
© Springer Science+Business Media, LLC 2009

integer/linear formulation. The continuous relaxation of the formulation describes the convex hull of the feasible set of the disjunction.

The disjunctive approach provides a useful device for creating mixed integer formulations for many problems, but in other cases it is impractical due to the large number of disjunctions required. Integer knapsack constraints are particularly troublesome, because the feasible set is a finite union of polyhedra only in the technical sense that each integer point is a polyhedron. Even this assumes that the feasible set is finite, and Jeroslow's theorem is in fact valid only when the integer variables in the mixed integer formulation are bounded. A purely disjunctive approach is therefore impractical and unnatural when the problem contains integer knapsack constraints, as many do.

We therefore propose that mixed integer/linear formulation combines two quite different kinds of ideas: disjunctions and integer knapsack constraints. We suggest that by identifying these two elements in a given problem, one can obtain practical mixed integer formulations in a reasonably principled way. Some of these formulations automatically incorporate nonobvious devices for tightening the formulation that are part of the folklore of modeling. In at least one case, the formulation is even better than the generally accepted one.

We ground this approach theoretically by extending Jeroslow's theorem in a straightforward way. We show that a problem has a mixed integer/linear formulation if and only if its feasible set is a union of finitely many *mixed integer polyhedra* satisfying a technical condition. A mixed integer polyhedron is, roughly speaking, a polyhedron in which some or all of the variables are required to be integer.

This is more general than Jeroslow's theorem because it allows for unbounded integer variables. It also incorporates integer knapsack constraints in a natural way, because disjunctions of linear systems become disjunctions of inequality systems that may contain integer knapsack inequalities. A problem consisting entirely of integer knapsack inequalities is a special case in which the formulation contains one disjunct. We also show that each disjunction receives a convex hull formulation, provided the individual disjuncts are convex hull formulations.

Williams (to appear) points out that a representable union of polyhedra can always be given a "big-M" formulation as well as a convex hull formulation. The big-M formulation is generally not as tight but contains fewer variables. Thus Jeroslow's representability theorem does not rely specifically on giving a convex hull formulation to disjunctions. We show that the same holds for general mixed integer representability. Any representable union of mixed integer polyhedra can be given a big-M mixed integer formulation as well as a convex hull formulation.

The paper has two main parts. The first deals with purely disjunctive formulations, while the second incorporates integer knapsack constraints. The first part begins with Jeroslow's result and illustrates it with a fixed charge problem. It also discusses the issue of when it is advantageous to combine several disjunctions into one long disjunction. Formulations are then derived for capacitated and uncapacitated facility location problems, using the disjunctive approach. The uncapacitated formulation avoids a typical beginner's mistake and thus shows how one may sidestep such pitfalls by following a principled method. Next, a lot sizing problem illustrates how logical constraints can assist problem formulation, although they can in principle be eliminated. Finally, we discuss big-M disjunctive formulations.

The second main part of the paper begins by generalizing Jeroslow's representability theorem, using both convex hull and big-M disjunctive formulations. We then formulate a modified facility location problem in which discrete variables account for the number of vehicles used to transport goods. This example shows how disjunctions of mixed integer systems, rather than linear systems, can occur in problem formulations. A package delivery problem then illustrates how a standard modeling trick falls automatically out of a principled approach. One can therefore obtain a tight model without knowing the "folklore" of modeling. It also illustrates how a principled approach leads one to include a redundant constraint that, according to conventional wisdom, can serve no purpose in the formulation. Nonetheless, this constraint makes the problem much easier to solve.

Some of the disjunctive formulations presented here appear in Hooker (2007). Several examples of mixed integer modeling in general can be found in Williams (1999).

2 Disjunctive Formulations

Disjunctive formulations are useful when one must make a choice from two or more alternatives. Problems typically present several such choices, and a disjunctive constraint can be written for each. If each constraint is a disjunction of linear systems, then it can be given a tight mixed/integer linear formulation, yielding a formulation for the problem as a whole.

We present in this section some examples in which a disjunctive analysis is the natural one. Further examples can be found in Hooker (2007). We begin with Jeroslow's result, which provides the theoretical basis for disjunctive formulation.

2.1 Bounded Mixed Integer Representability

Jeroslow (1987, 1989) defined a subset of $\mathbb{R}^n$ to be *bounded mixed integer representable* when it is the feasible set of a linear formulation with continuous and 0-1 variables. More precisely, $S \in \mathbb{R}^n$ is representable if there is a constraint set of the following form whose projection onto x is S:

$$Ax + Bu + Dy \geq b$$
$$x \in \mathbb{R}^n, \ u \in \mathbb{R}^m, \ y_k \in \{0,1\}, \ \text{all } k \tag{1}$$

The continuous variables u and discrete variables y can be viewed as auxiliary variables that help to define the feasible subset of $\mathbb{R}^n$.

The discrete variables are restricted to be 0-1 in this definition, but an equivalent definition can be obtained by replacing the 0-1 variables with general integer variables—provided the general integer variables are *bounded*. This is because a bounded integer variable y_k can be replaced by $\sum_{j=0}^{p} 2^j y_{kj}$, where each y_{kj} is 0-1, and a system of the form (1) results. Thus the term "bounded" in "bounded mixed integer representability" does not mean that the set to be represented is bounded. It means that the integer variables are bounded.

Jeroslow proved that $S \in \mathbb{R}^n$ is representable in this sense if and only if S is a union of finitely many polyhedra that have the same recession cone. The *recession cone* of a polyhedron P is the set of directions in which P is unbounded, or more precisely, the set of vectors $r \in \mathbb{R}^n$ such that, given any $u \in P$, $u + \beta r \in P$ for all $\beta \geq 0$.

The proof is based on the fact that representability in Jeroslow's sense is equivalent to representability by a disjunctive constraint of the form

$$\bigvee_{k \in K} \left(A^k x \geq b^k \right) \tag{2}$$

where K is finite. The disjunction (2) requires that x satisfy at least one of the linear systems $A^k x \geq b^k$. Each system $A^k x \geq b^k$ can be viewed as defining one of the polyhedra P_k that make up S, so that $S = \bigcup_{k \in K} P_k$.

Theorem 1 (Jeroslow). *A set $S \subset \mathbb{R}^n$ is bounded mixed integer representable if and only if S is the union of finitely many polyhedra having the same recession cone. In particular, S is bounded mixed integer representable if and only if S is the projection onto x of a mixed integer formulation with following form:*

$$x = \sum_{k \in K} x^k$$
$$A^k x^k \geq b^k y_k, \quad k \in K \tag{3}$$
$$\sum_{k \in K} y_k = 1, \quad y_k \in \{0, 1\}, \quad k \in K$$

The mixed integer formulation (3) represents the disjunctive problem (2). In particular, $y_k = 1$ when x satisfies the kth disjunct of (2). Note that x is disaggregated into a sum of continuous variables x^k, which play the role of auxiliary variables u in (1). Thus (3) has the form (1).

The mixed integer formulation (3) not only represents (2) but is a *convex hull formulation* of (2). That is, the continuous relaxation of (3) has a feasible set that, when projected onto x, is the convex hull of the feasible set of (2). The continuous relaxation of (3) is obtained by replacing $y_k \in \{0, 1\}$ with $y_k \geq 0$ for each k.

2.2 Example: Fixed-Charge Function

Bounded mixed integer representability is illustrated by the fixed-charge function, which occurs frequently in modeling. Suppose the cost x_2 of manufacturing quantity

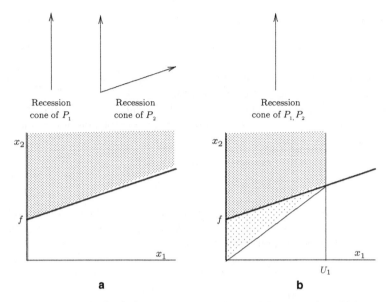

Fig. 1 (a) Feasible set of a fixed-charge problem, consisting of the union of polyhedra P_1 (heavy vertical line) and P_2 (shaded area). (b) Feasible set of the same problem with the bound $x_1 \leq U_1$, where P_2' is the darker shaded area. The convex hull of the feasible set is the entire shaded area.

x_1 of some product is to be minimized. The cost is zero when $x_1 = 0$ and is $f + cx_1$ otherwise, where f is the fixed cost and c the unit variable cost.

The problem can be viewed as minimizing x_2 subject to $(x_1, x_2) \in S$, where S is the set depicted in Figure 1(a). S is the union of two polyhedra P_1 and P_2, and the problem is to minimize x_2 subject to the disjunction

$$\begin{pmatrix} x_1 = 0 \\ x_2 \geq 0 \end{pmatrix} \vee \begin{pmatrix} x_2 \geq cx_1 + f \\ x_1 \geq 0 \end{pmatrix}$$

where the disjuncts correspond respectively to P_1 and P_2. In general there would be additional constraints in the problem, but we focus here on the fixed-charge formulation.

The recession cone of P_1 is P_1 itself, and the recession cone of P_2 is the set of all vectors (x_1, x_2) with $x_2 \geq cx_1 \geq 0$. Thus, by Theorem 1, S is not bounded mixed integer representable. Indeed, the formulation (3) becomes

$$\begin{aligned} x_1 &= x_1^1 + x_1^2 \quad x_1^1 \leq 0 \qquad -cx_1^2 + x_2^2 \geq fy_2 \quad y_1 + y_2 = 1 \\ x_2 &= x_2^1 + x_2^2 \quad x_1^1, x_2^1 \geq 0 \quad x_1^2 \geq 0 \qquad\qquad y_1, y_2 \in \{0, 1\} \end{aligned} \tag{4}$$

and does not correctly represent S, as can be seen by simplifying (4). Only one 0-1 variable appears, which can be renamed y. Also, we can set $x_1^2 = x_1$ (since $x_1^1 = 0$) and $x_2^1 = x_2 - x_2^2$, which yields

$$x_1 \geq 0, \ x_2 - x_2^2 \geq 0, \ x_2^2 - cx_1 \geq fy, \ y \in \{0, 1\}$$

Minimizing x_2 subject to this is equivalent to minimizing x_2 subject to

$$x_1 \geq 0, \quad x_2 - cx_1 \geq fy, \quad y \in \{0,1\}$$

The projection onto (x_1, x_2) is the union of the two polyhedra obtained by setting $y = 0$ and $y = 1$. The projection is therefore the set of all points satisfying $x_2 \geq cx_1$, $x_1 \geq 0$, which is clearly different from $P_1 \cup P_2$. The formulation is therefore incorrect.

However, if we place an upper bound U_1 on x_1, the problem is now to minimize x_2 subject to

$$\begin{pmatrix} x_1 = 0 \\ x_2 \geq 0 \end{pmatrix} \vee \begin{pmatrix} x_2 \geq cx_1 + f \\ 0 \leq x_1 \leq U_1 \end{pmatrix} \tag{5}$$

The recession cone of each of the resulting polyhedra P_1, P_2' (Figure 1b) is the same (namely, P_1), and the feasible set $S' = P_1 \cup P_2'$ is therefore bounded mixed integer representable. The convex hull formulation is

$$x_1^1 \leq 0 \qquad -cx_1^2 + x_2^2 \geq fy_2 \qquad x_1 = x_1^1 + x_1^2 \qquad y_1 + y_2 = 1$$
$$x_1^1, x_2^2 \geq 0 \qquad 0 \leq x_1^2 \leq U_1 y_2 \qquad x_2 = x_2^1 + x_2^2 \qquad y_1, y_2 \in \{0,1\}$$

Again the model simplifies:

$$x_1 \leq U_1 y, \quad x_2 \geq fy + cx_1, \quad x_1 \geq 0, \quad y \in \{0,1\} \tag{6}$$

Obviously, y encodes whether the quantity produced is zero or positive, in the former case $(y = 0)$ forcing $x_1 = 0$, and in the latter case incurring the fixed charge f. Big-M constraints like $x_1 \leq U_1 y$, which are very common in mixed integer models, can often be viewed as originating from upper bounds that are imposed to ensure that the polyhedra concerned have the same recession cone.

Big-Ms do not always have this origin, however. For example, a disjunctive constraint (2) can be given a *big-M disjunctive formulation*, which contains fewer continuous variables than a convex hull formulation but may not be as tight. This type of formulation is discussed further in Section 2.6.

2.3 Multiple Disjunctions

A mixed integer formulation may consist of multiple convex hull formulations, one for each disjunction. Such a formulation does not in general provide a convex hull relaxation for the problem as a whole. Consider, for example, the constraint set

$$\begin{pmatrix} x_1 = 0 \\ x_2 \in [0,1] \end{pmatrix} \vee \begin{pmatrix} x_2 = 0 \\ x_1 \in [0,1] \end{pmatrix} (a)$$

$$\begin{pmatrix} x_1 = 0 \\ x_2 \in [0,1] \end{pmatrix} \vee \begin{pmatrix} x_2 = 1 \\ x_1 \in [0,1] \end{pmatrix} (b) \tag{7}$$

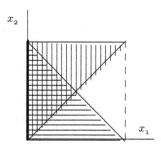

Fig. 2 Convex hull relaxation of (8a) (horizontal shading), convex hull relaxation of (8b) (vertical shading), continuous relaxation of (8) (heavy shading), and convex hull relaxation of (7) (heavy vertical line segment).

The convex hull formulations of the two disjunctions are

$$
\begin{array}{ll}
0 \leq x_1 \leq 1 - y_1, \ 0 \leq x_2 \leq y_1, \ y_1 \in \{0,1\} & (a) \\
0 \leq x_1 \leq 1 - y_2, \ 1 - y_2 \leq x_2 \leq 1, \ y_2 \in \{0,1\} & (b)
\end{array}
\tag{8}
$$

The feasible set of (8), projected onto x_1, x_2, is the heavy vertical line segment in Fig. 2, and its convex hull is the same line segment. The convex hulls described by continuous relaxations of (a) and (b) are

$$
\begin{array}{ll}
x_1 + x_2 \leq 1, \ x_1, x_2 \geq 0 & (a) \\
x_1 \leq x_2, \ x_1 \geq 0, \ x_2 \leq 1 & (b)
\end{array}
\tag{9}
$$

and also appear in the figure. The continuous relaxation of (8) corresponds to the intersection of these two convex hulls and is therefore weaker than a convex hull relaxation of (8).

A convex hull formulation can always be obtained for multiple disjunctions by taking the product of the disjunctions to obtain a single disjunction, which can then be given a convex hull formulation. That is, two disjunctions $A \vee B$ and $C \vee D$ can be written as a product $AC \vee AD \vee BC \vee BD$, where AC refers to the linear system consisting of both A and C. For example, the two disjunctions of (7) yield the product

$$
\begin{pmatrix} x_1 = 0 \\ x_2 \in [0,1] \end{pmatrix} \vee \begin{pmatrix} x_1 = 0 \\ x_2 = 1 \\ x_1, x_2 \in [0,1] \end{pmatrix} \vee \begin{pmatrix} x_1 = 0 \\ x_2 = 0 \\ x_1, x_2 \in [0,1] \end{pmatrix} \vee \begin{pmatrix} x_2 = 0 \\ x_2 = 1 \\ x_1 \in [0,1] \end{pmatrix}
\tag{10}
$$

The mixed integer formulation of (10) simplifies to $x_1 = 0, 0 \leq x_2 \leq 1$.

Although the convex hull formulation of the product simplifies in this example, formulating a product of disjunctions is not in general a practical option because the number of disjuncts grows exponentially. However, it may be useful to take a product of certain subsets of disjunctions. This can strengthen the relaxation, but only when the disjunctions have variables in common, due to the following lemma.

Lemma 1. *If two disjunctions D_1, D_2 of linear systems have no variables in common, then the convex hull formulations of D_1 and D_2, when taken together, already provide a convex hull formulation of $\{D_1, D_2\}$.*

Proof. Let F_i be the feasible set of D_i, for $i = 1, 2$. It suffices to show that $\text{conv}(F_1 \cap F_2) = \text{conv}(F_1) \cap \text{conv}(F_2)$, where $\text{conv}(F_i)$ is the convex hull of F_i. Obviously, $\text{conv}(F_1 \cap F_2) \subset \text{conv}(F_1) \cap \text{conv}(F_2)$. To show that $\text{conv}(F_1) \cap \text{conv}(F_2) \subset \text{conv}(F_1 \cap F_2)$, take any $\bar{x} \in \text{conv}(F_1) \cap \text{conv}(F_2)$, and let $\bar{x} = (\bar{u}, \bar{v})$, where u and v consist of the variables in D_1 and D_2, respectively. Since $\bar{x} \in \text{conv}(F_1)$,

$$(\bar{u}, \bar{v}) = \alpha(a^1, c^2) + (1 - \alpha)(b^1, d^2) \tag{11}$$

where $\alpha \in [0, 1]$ and $(a^1, c^2), (b^1, d^2) \in F_1$. Similarly,

$$(\bar{u}, \bar{v}) = \beta(c^1, a^2) + (1 - \beta)(d^1, b^2) \tag{12}$$

where $\beta \in [0, 1]$ and $(c^1, a^2), (d^1, b^2) \in F_2$. Using (11)–(12), it can be readily checked that $(\bar{u}, \bar{v})$ is a convex combination of four points:

$$\alpha\beta(a^1, a^2) + \alpha(1 - \beta)(a^1, b^2) + (1 - \alpha)\beta(b^1, a^2) + (1 - \alpha)(1 - \beta)(b^1, b^2) \tag{13}$$

where (11) is used to verify the first component $\bar{u}$ and (12) to verify the second component $\bar{v}$. But $(a^1, a^2) \in F_1 \cap F_2$ because $(a^1, c^2) \in F_1$, $(c^1, a^2) \in F_2$, and D_1 and D_2 have no variables in common. Similarly, the other three points belong to $F_1 \cap F_2$, and $\bar{x} \in \text{conv}(F_1 \cap F_2)$. $\square$

2.4 Example: Facility Location

A simple *capacitated facility location problem* illustrates how a disjunctive formulation can be developed in practice. There are m possible locations for facilities, and n customers who obtain products from the facilities. A facility installed at location i incurs fixed cost f_i and has capacity C_i. Each customer j has demand D_j, and the unit cost of shipping from facility i to customer j is c_{ij}. The problem is to decide which facilities to install, and how to supply the customers, so as to minimize total fixed and variable costs.

Each location i either receives a facility or not. If it does, the total shipments out of the location must be at most C_i, and a fixed cost is incurred. Otherwise nothing is shipped out of the location. Thus if x_{ij} is the quantity shipped from i to j, we have the disjunction

$$\begin{pmatrix} \sum_{j=1}^{n} x_{ij} \leq C_i \\ x_{ij} \geq 0, \text{ all } j \\ z_i = f_i \end{pmatrix} \vee \begin{pmatrix} x_{ij} = 0, \text{ all } j \\ z_i = 0 \end{pmatrix} \tag{14}$$

where z_i represents the fixed cost incurred at location i. In addition, each customer j must receive adequate supply:

$$\sum_{i=1}^{m} x_{ij} = D_j, \text{ all } j \qquad (15)$$

This can be viewed as a disjunction with one disjunct. The problem is to minimize

$$\sum_{i=1}^{m} \left(z_i + \sum_{j=1}^{n} c_{ij} x_{ij} \right) \qquad (16)$$

subject to (14) and (15).

Rather than writing a convex hull formulation for the product of the disjunctions (14) and the disjunction (15), which is a very complicated matter, we can formulate each disjunction individually. The convex hull formulation of (14) is

$$\sum_{j=1}^{n} x_{ij} \leq C_i y_i, \quad z_i = f_i y_i, \quad y_i \in \{0,1\}, \quad x_{ij} \geq 0, \text{ all } j \qquad (17)$$

and (15) is its own convex hull formulation. A mixed integer formulation can now be obtained by minimizing (16) subject to (15) and (17) for all i. This immediately simplifies to

$$\min \sum_{i=1}^{m} \left(f_i y_i + \sum_{j=1}^{n} c_{ij} x_{ij} \right) \quad (a)$$

$$\sum_{j=1}^{n} x_{ij} \leq C_i y_i, \text{ all } i \qquad (b) \qquad\qquad (18)$$

$$\sum_{i=1}^{m} x_{ij} = D_j, \text{ all } j \qquad (c)$$

$$y_i \in \{0,1\}, \quad x_{ij} \geq 0, \text{ all } i,j$$

This formulation is succinct enough, and its continuous relaxation tight enough, to be useful in practice.

A disjunctive approach to formulation can sometimes lead to tighter relaxations than one would obtain otherwise. A common beginner's mistake, for example, is to model the *uncapacitated facility location problem* as a special case of the capacitated problem. In the uncapacitated problem, there is no limit on the capacity of each facility, and x_{ij} represents the fraction of customer j's demand supplied by facility i, so that each $D_j = 1$. Although there is no capacity limit, one can observe that each facility will ship at most n units and therefore let $C_i = n$ in the formulation (18) for the capacitated problem. This is a valid formulation of the uncapacitated problem, but there is a much tighter one.

We start with a disjunctive conception of the problem. If facility i is installed, it supplies at most one unit to each customer and incurs cost f_i. If it is not installed, then it supplies nothing:

$$\begin{pmatrix} 0 \le x_{ij} \le 1, \text{ all } j \\ z_i = f_i \end{pmatrix} \vee \begin{pmatrix} x_{ij} = 0, \text{ all } j \\ z_i = 0 \end{pmatrix}$$

The convex hull formulation of this disjunction is

$$z_i = f_i y_i, \quad y_i \in \{0,1\}, \quad 0 \le x_{ij} \le y_i, \text{ all } j \tag{19}$$

This yields a tighter formulation than (18):

$$\min \sum_{i=1}^{m} \left(f_i y_i + \sum_{j=1}^{n} c_{ij} x_{ij} \right) \quad (a)$$

$$x_{ij} \le y_i, \text{ all } i, j \qquad (b)$$

$$\sum_{i=1}^{m} x_{ij} = 1, \text{ all } j \qquad (c)$$

$$y_i \in \{0,1\}, \quad x_{ij} \ge 0, \text{ all } i, j$$

$$\tag{20}$$

To see that it is tighter, note first that constraints in (18) and (20) are the same except for (b), and that (20b) implies (18b) because the latter is the sum of the constraints in the former. Furthermore, setting (for example) $y_i = 1/2$ for each i, $x_{ij} = 0$ for each i and $j \le n/2$, and $x_{ij} = 1$ for each i and $j > n/2$ (supposing n is even) satisfies the continuous relaxation of (18) but not that of (20).

This is an instance in which the more succinct relaxation is not the tighter one. The smaller formulation (18) with only $2m$ constraints (other than variable bounds) is not as tight as (20), which has $m(n+1)$ constraints.

2.5 Example: Lot Sizing with Setup Costs

A *lot sizing problem with set up costs* illustrates how logical relations among linear systems can be captured with logical constraints that involve the 0-1 variables. Logical constraints do not enhance the representability of mixed integer formulations, but they may be convenient in practice.

In the lot sizing problem, here is a demand D_t for a product in each period t. No more than C_t units of the product can be manufactured in period t, and any excess over demand is stocked to satisfy future demand. If there is no production in the previous period, then a setup cost of f_t is incurred. The unit production cost is p_t, and the unit holding cost per period is h_t. A starting stock level s_0 is given. The objective is to choose production levels in each period so as to minimize total cost over all periods.

Let x_t be the production level in period t and s_t the stock level at the end of the period. In each period t, there are three options to choose from: (1) start producing (with a setup cost), (2) continue producing (with no setup cost), and (3) produce nothing. If v_t is the setup cost incurred in period t, these correspond respectively to the three disjuncts

$$\begin{pmatrix} v_t \geq f_t \\ 0 \leq x_t \leq C_t \end{pmatrix} \vee \begin{pmatrix} v_t \geq 0 \\ 0 \leq x_t \leq C_t \end{pmatrix} \vee \begin{pmatrix} v_t \geq 0 \\ x_t = 0 \end{pmatrix} \tag{21}$$

There are logical connections between the choices in consecutive periods. If we schematically represent the disjunction (21) as

$$Y_t \vee Z_t \vee W_t \tag{22}$$

the logical connections can be written

$$\begin{aligned} Z_t &\Rightarrow (Y_{t-1} \vee Z_{t-1}) \\ Y_t &\Rightarrow (\neg Y_{t-1} \wedge \neg Z_{t-1}) \end{aligned} \tag{23}$$

where $\neg$ means "not" and $\wedge$ means "and." The inventory balance constraints are

$$s_{t-1} + x_t = D_t + s_t, \quad s_t \geq 0, \quad t = 1, \ldots, n \tag{24}$$

where s_t is the stock level in period t and s_0 is given. The problem is to minimize

$$\sum_{t=1}^{n} (p_t x_t + h_t s_t + v_t) \tag{25}$$

subject to (21) and (23) for all $t \geq 1$ and (24).

A convex hull formulation for (21) is

$$\begin{aligned} &v_t^1 \geq f_t y_t, \qquad v_t^2 \geq 0, \qquad v_t^3 \geq 0 \\ &0 \leq x_t^1 \leq C_t y_t, \quad 0 \leq x_t^2 \leq C_t z_t, \quad x_t^3 = 0 \\ &v_t = v_t^1 + v_t^2 + v_t^3, \, x_t = x_t^1 + x_t^2 + x_t^3 \\ &y_t + z_t + w_t = 1, \quad y_t, z_t, w_t \in \{0, 1\} \end{aligned} \tag{26}$$

Thus, $z_t = 1$ indicates a startup, $y_t = 1$ continued production, and $w_t = 1$ no production in period t. To simplify (26), we first eliminate w_t, so that $y_t + z_t \leq 1$. Since $x_t^3 = 0$, we can set $x_1 = x_t^1 + x_t^2$, which allows us to replace the two capacity constraints in (26) by $0 \leq x_t \leq C_t(y_t + z_t)$. Finally, v_t can replace v_t^1, because v_t is being minimized and v_t^2 and v_t^3 do not appear. The convex hull formulation (26) becomes

$$\begin{aligned} &v_t \geq f_t y_t, \quad 0 \leq x_t \leq C_t(y_t + z_t) \\ &y_t + z_t \leq 1, \quad y_t, z_t \in \{0, 1\} \end{aligned} \tag{27}$$

The logical constraints (23) can be formulated

$$z_t \leq y_{t-1} + z_{t-1}, \quad y_t \leq 1 - y_{t-1} - z_{t-1} \tag{28}$$

The second constraint is correct because we know $y_t + z_t \leq 1$. The entire problem can now be formulated as minimizing (25) subject to (24) and (27)–(28) for all $t \geq 1$.

The problem can also be formulated without logical constraints. We first write the logical constraints (23) as a set of disjunctions (i.e., in conjunctive normal form):

$$\neg Z_t \vee Y_{t-1} \vee Z_{t-1}$$
$$\neg Y_t \vee \neg Y_{t-1}$$
$$\neg Y_t \vee \neg Z_{t-1}$$

We now replace each negated term with the disjunction of the remaining terms in the disjunction (22) that contains it:

$$Y_t \vee W_t \vee Y_{t-1} \vee Z_{t-1}$$
$$Z_t \vee W_t \vee Z_{t-1} \vee W_{t-1} \tag{29}$$
$$Z_t \vee W_t \vee Y_{t-1} \vee W_{t-1}$$

We can now drop the logical constraints (28) and add convex hull formulations of the disjunctions in (29). This kind of maneuver can sometimes result in a tighter formulation, but it may not be worth the additional variables and constraints.

2.6 Big-M Disjunctive Formulations

A disjunction (2) of linear systems can be given a *big-M disjunctive formulation* as well as a convex hull formulation. The big-M formulation has fewer variables because the continuous variables are not disaggregated. It may be preferable in practice when there are a large number of disjuncts, even though its continuous relaxation can be significantly weaker than that of a convex hull formulation.

As noted earlier, Jeroslow's bounded representability theorem does not rely specifically on a convex hull formulation of disjunctions (Williams, to appear). Any finite union of polyhedra with the same recession cone can be given a big-M formulation as well as a convex hull formulation. We extend this result to general representability in Section 3.2.

A big-M disjunctive formulation for (2) has the form

$$A^k x \geq b^k - M^k(1 - y_k), \quad k \in K$$
$$\sum_{k \in K} y_k = 1, \quad y_k \in \{0,1\}, \quad k \in K \tag{30}$$

where M_k is set to a value sufficiently large that the kth disjunct is not constraining when $y_k = 0$. Thus the kth disjunct is enforced when $y_k = 1$, but through a different mechanism than in the convex hull formulation.

The formulation (30) is *sharp* when the M^ks are as small as possible. This is achieved by observing that if x does not belong to the polyhedron defined by the kth disjunct, then it must belong to at least one of the other polyhedra. Thus allows us to set

$$M^k = b^k - \min_{\ell \neq k} \left\{ \min_x \left\{ A^k x \mid A^\ell x \geq b^\ell \right\} \right\} \tag{31}$$

where the minima are taken componentwise; that is, $\min\{(\alpha_1, \alpha_2), (\beta_1, \beta_2)\} = (\min\{\alpha_1, \alpha_2\}, \min\{\beta_1, \beta_2\})$. Computation of the big-Ms in this manner requires solution of $(|K| - 1)\sum_{k \in K} m_k$ small linear programming problems of the form $\min_x \{A_i^k x \mid A^\ell x \geq b^\ell\}$, where m_k is the number of rows A_i^k of A^k, but the resulting formulation contains no disaggregated variables x^k. The linear programming problems must obviously be bounded, but this is assured by the condition that the polyhedra have the same recession cone.

If finite bounds $L \leq x \leq U$ are available for the variables $x = (x_1, \ldots, x_n)$, big-Ms can be calculated more rapidly using the formula

$$M^k = b^k - \sum_{j=1}^n \min\left\{0, A_j^k\right\} U_j - \sum_{j=1}^n \max\left\{0, A_j^k\right\} L_j$$

where A_j^k is column j of A^k. The resulting big-Ms, however, are in general larger than obtained by (31).

Sharp big-M formulations are sometimes convex hull formulations. This is true, for example, of the sharp big-M formulation for the fixed charge problem of Section 2.2. It simplifies to a formulation that is identical to the convex hull formulation (6). In other cases, however, a sharp big-M formulation can provide a relaxation much weaker than the convex hull. For example, the disjunction

$$\begin{pmatrix} -x_1 + x_2 \geq 1 \\ x_1, x_2 \in [0,2] \end{pmatrix} \vee \begin{pmatrix} 2x_1 - x_2 \geq 2 \\ x_1, x_2 \in [0,2] \end{pmatrix} \tag{32}$$

has the sharp big-M formulation

$$\begin{aligned}
-x_1 + 2x_2 &\geq -1 + 2y \\
2x_1 - x_2 &\geq 2 - 4y \\
x_1, x_2 &\in [0,2] \\
y_1 + y_2 &= 1, \quad y_1, y_2 \in \{0,1\}
\end{aligned} \tag{33}$$

The projection of the continuous relaxation onto (x_1, x_2) is described by $x_1 + x_2 \geq 0$, $x_1, x_2 \in [0,2]$ (Fig. 3). This is much weaker than the convex hull, which is described by $x_1 + x_1 \geq 1$, $x_1, x_2 \in [0,2]$. In fact, it adds nothing to the box constraints $x_1, x_2 \in [0,2]$ that are already part of both disjuncts.

Disjunctions of single linear inequalities (i.e., each $m_k = 1$) have special structure that allow one to eliminate the 0-1 variables y_k from a sharp big-M formulation and obtain a relatively simple formulation (Beaumont, 1990). This and other formulations are discussed in Hooker (2007).

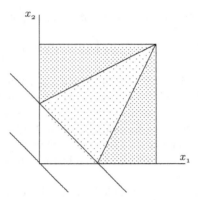

Fig. 3 Feasible set of disjunction (32) (dark shaded area), convex hull of the feasible set (entire shaded area), and feasible set of the continuous relaxation of the sharp big-M formulation (33) (entire box).

3 Knapsack Modeling

Mixed integer formulations frequently involve counting ideas that can be expressed as *knapsack inequalities*. For present purposes we can define a knapsack inequality to be any inequality of the form $ax \leq \alpha$, where some of the variables x_j may be required to take nonnegative integer values. Variable x_j can be interpreted as the quantity (integer or continuous) of item j that is chosen for some purpose (perhaps to be placed in a knapsack). The left-hand side of the inequality therefore counts the total quantity selected, perhaps weighting some items differently than others. The right-hand side places a bound on the total weight (perhaps the knapsack capacity).

Problems of this sort include set packing, set covering, and set partitioning problems. Capital budgeting problems provide textbook examples. Countless other problems use constraints of this form, containing both continuous and integer-valued variables.

Knapsack constraints capture a very different modeling idea that the disjunctive constraints discussed earlier. The bounded mixed integer representability theorem (Theorem 1) technically accounts for knapsack problems, provided the variables are bounded, but only by brute force. For example, a single knapsack constraint with bounded integer variables defines a feasible set consisting of integer lattice points. The points can be regarded as finitely many recession cones that have the same recession cone (namely, the origin).

However, Theorem 1 can be generalized to account for knapsack constraints in a more natural way. This also enhances representability, because the integer variables need not be bounded. We begin with this task and then illustrate how problem formulation based on this result can lead to tight formulations.

3.1 General Mixed Integer Representability

It is convenient at this point to assume that mixed integer formulations consist of rational data. This has no practical repercussions but allows us to generalize the idea of a recession cone more easily. We also regard a polyhedron as a set of the form $\{x \in \mathbb{R}^n \mid Ax \geq b\}$, where A, b consist of rational data.

We define a subset S of $\mathbb{R}^n \times \mathbb{Z}^p$ to be *mixed integer representable* if there is a constraint set of the following form whose projection onto x is S:

$$Ax + Bu + Dy \geq b$$
$$x \in \mathbb{R}^n \times \mathbb{Z}^p, \ u \in \mathbb{R}^m, \ y_k \in \{0, 1\}, \ \text{all } k \tag{34}$$

Let us say that a *mixed integer polyhedron* in $\mathbb{R}^{n+p}$ is the nonempty intersection of any polyhedron in $\mathbb{R}^{n+p}$ with $\mathbb{R}^n \times \mathbb{Z}^p$. We will show that a subset of $\mathbb{R}^n \times \mathbb{Z}^p$ is mixed integer representable if and only if it is the union of finitely many mixed integer polyhedra that have the same recession cone.

This requires that we define the recession cone of a mixed integer polyhedron. Let us say that rational vector d is a recession direction of mixed integer polyhedron $P \subset \mathbb{R}^n \times \mathbb{Z}^p$ if it is a recession direction of some polyhedron $Q \subset \mathbb{R}^{n+p}$ for which $P = Q \cap (\mathbb{R}^n \times \mathbb{Z}^p)$. Then the recession cone of P is the set of its recession directions. The definition is well formed because of the following lemma.

Lemma 2. *All polyhedra in $\mathbb{R}^{n+p}$ having the same nonempty intersection with $\mathbb{R}^n \times \mathbb{Z}^p$ have the same recession cone.*

Proof. Let $Q = \{x \in \mathbb{R}^{n+p} \mid Ax \geq b\}$ and $Q' = \{x \in \mathbb{R}^{n+p} \mid A'x \geq b'\}$ be polyhedra, and suppose that $Q \cap (\mathbb{R}^n \times \mathbb{Z}^p) = Q' \cap (\mathbb{R}^n \times \mathbb{Z}^p) = P$, where P is nonempty. It suffices to show that any recession direction d of Q is a recession direction of Q'. Take any $u \in P$. Since $u \in Q$, we have $u + \alpha d \in Q$ for any $\alpha \geq 0$. Furthermore, because d is rational, $u + \bar{\alpha} d \in Q \cap (\mathbb{R}^n \times \mathbb{Z}^p)$ for some sufficiently large $\bar{\alpha} > 0$. Now if d is not a recession direction of Q', then because $u \in Q'$, we have $u + \beta \bar{\alpha} d \notin Q'$ for some sufficiently large integer $\beta \geq 1$. Thus in particular $u + \beta \bar{\alpha} d \notin Q' \cap (\mathbb{R}^n \times \mathbb{Z}^p)$. But because β is integer, $u + \beta \bar{\alpha} d \in Q \cap (\mathbb{R}^n \times \mathbb{Z}^p)$. This violates the assumption that Q, Q' have the same intersection with $\mathbb{R}^n \times \mathbb{Z}^p$. $\square$

We can now state a necessary and sufficient condition for mixed integer representability. The proof is a straightforward extension of Jeroslow's proof (Jeroslow, 1987).

Theorem 2. *A nonempty set $S \subset \mathbb{R}^n \times \mathbb{Z}^p$ is mixed integer representable if and only if S is the union of finitely many mixed integer polyhedra in $\mathbb{R}^n \times \mathbb{Z}^p$ having the same recession cone. In particular, S is mixed integer representable if and only if S is the projection onto x of a mixed integer formulation of the following form:*

$$x = \sum_{k \in K} x^k$$

$$A^k x^k \geq b^k y_k, \quad k \in K$$

$$\sum_{k \in K} y_k = 1, \quad y_k \in \{0,1\}, \ k \in K \tag{35}$$

$$x \in \mathbb{R}^n \times \mathbb{Z}^p$$

Proof. Suppose first that S is the union of mixed integer polyhedra P_k, $k \in K$, that have the same recession cone. Each P_k has the form $\{x \mid A^k x^k \geq b^k\} \cap (\mathbb{R}^n \times \mathbb{Z}^p)$. It can be shown as follows that S is represented by (35), and is therefore representable, because (35) has the form (34). Suppose first that $x \in S$. Then x belongs to some P_{k^*}, which means that x is feasible in (35) when $y_{k^*} = 1$, $y_k = 0$ for $k \neq k^*$, $x^{k^*} = x$, and $x^k = 0$ for $k \neq k^*$. The constraint $A^k x^k \geq b^k y_k$ is satisfied by definition when $k = k^*$, and it is satisfied for other k's because $x^k = y_k = 0$.

Now suppose that x, y and x^k satisfy (35). Let $Q_k = \{x \mid A^k x \geq b^k\}$, so that $P_k = Q_k \cap (\mathbb{R}^n \times \mathbb{Z}^p)$. To show that $x \in S$, note that exactly one y_k, say y_{k^*}, is equal to 1. Then $A^{k^*} x^{k^*} \geq b^{k^*}$ is enforced, which means that $x^{k^*} \in Q_{k^*}$. For other k's, $A^k x^k \geq 0$. Thus, $A^k(\beta x^k) \geq 0$ for all $\beta \geq 0$, which implies that x^k is a recession direction for Q_k. Because by hypothesis all the P_ks have the same recession cone, all Q_ks have the same recession cone. Thus each x^k ($k \neq k^*$) is a recession direction for Q_{k^*}, which means that $x = x^{k^*} + \sum_{k \neq k^*} x^k$ belongs to Q_{k^*} and therefore to $\bigcup_{k \in K} Q_k$. But because $x \in \mathbb{R}^n \times \mathbb{Z}^p$, we have

$$x \in \left(\bigcup_{k \in K} Q_k\right) \cap (\mathbb{R}^n \times \mathbb{Z}^p) = \bigcup_{k \in K} (Q_k \cap (\mathbb{R}^n \times \mathbb{Z}^p)) = \bigcup_{k \in K} P_k$$

To prove the converse of the theorem, suppose that S is represented by (34). To show that S is a finite union of mixed integer polyhedra, let $P(\bar{y})$ be the set of all x that are feasible in (34) when $y = \bar{y} \in \{0,1\}^{|K|}$. Because S is nonempty, $P(\bar{y})$ is nonempty for at least one $\bar{y}$. Thus we let Y be the set of all $\bar{y}$ for which $P(\bar{y})$ is nonempty. So $P(\bar{y})$ is a mixed integer polyhedron for all $\bar{y} \in Y$, and $S = \bigcup_{\bar{y} \in Y} P(\bar{y})$. To show that the $P(\bar{y})$'s have the same recession cone, note that

$$P(\bar{y}) = \left\{ x \in \mathbb{R}^n \times \mathbb{Z}^p \ \middle| \ \begin{bmatrix} A & B & D \\ 0 & 0 & 1 \\ 0 & 0 & -1 \end{bmatrix} \begin{bmatrix} x \\ u \\ y \end{bmatrix} \geq \begin{bmatrix} b \\ \bar{y} \\ -\bar{y} \end{bmatrix} \text{ for some } u, y \right\}$$

But x' is a recession direction of $P(\bar{y})$ if and only if (x', u', y') is a recession direction of

$$\left\{ \begin{bmatrix} x \\ u \\ y \end{bmatrix} \in \mathbb{R}^n \times \mathbb{Z}^p \times \mathbb{R}^{m+|K|} \ \middle| \ \begin{bmatrix} A & B & D \\ 0 & 0 & 1 \\ 0 & 0 & -1 \end{bmatrix} \begin{bmatrix} x \\ u \\ y \end{bmatrix} \geq \begin{bmatrix} b \\ \bar{y} \\ -\bar{y} \end{bmatrix} \right\}$$

for some u', y'. The latter is true if and only if

$$\begin{bmatrix} A & B & D \\ 0 & 0 & 1 \\ 0 & 0 & -1 \end{bmatrix} \begin{bmatrix} x' \\ u' \\ y' \end{bmatrix} \geq \begin{bmatrix} 0 \\ 0 \\ 0 \end{bmatrix}$$

This means that the recession directions of $P(\bar{y})$ are the same for all $\bar{y} \in Y$, as desired.
□

The theorem says in part that any nonempty mixed integer representable subset of $\mathbb{R}^n \times \mathbb{Z}^p$ is the feasible set of some disjunction

$$\bigvee_{k \in K} \left(\begin{array}{c} A^k x \geq b^k \\ x \in \mathbb{R}^n \times \mathbb{Z}^p \end{array} \right) \tag{36}$$

This and the following lemma give us a technique for writing a convex hull formulation by conceiving the feasible set as a union of mixed integer polyhedra.

Lemma 3. *If each disjunct of (36) is a convex hull formulation, then (35) is a convex hull formulation of (36).*

Proof. It is clear that x satisfies (36) if any only if x satisfies (35) for some $(x^k, y_k \mid k \in K)$. It remains to show that, given any feasible solution $\bar{x}$, $(\bar{x}^k, \bar{y}_k \mid k \in K)$ of the continuous relaxation of (35), $\bar{x}$ belongs to the convex hull of the feasible set of (36). But $\bar{x}$ is the convex combination

$$\bar{x} = \sum_{k \in K^+} \bar{y}_k \frac{\bar{x}^k}{\bar{y}_k} \tag{37}$$

where $K^+ = \{k \in K \mid \bar{y}_k > 0\}$. Furthermore, each point $\bar{x}^k / \bar{y}_k$ satisfies $A^k(\bar{x}^k / \bar{y}_k) \geq b^k$ because $(\bar{x}^k, \bar{y}_k)$ satisfies $A^k \bar{x}^k \geq b^k \bar{y}_k$. Thus $\bar{x}^k / \bar{y}_k$ satisfies the continuous relaxation of the kth disjunct of (36) and so, by hypothesis, belongs to the convex hull of the feasible set of that disjunct. This and (37) imply that $\bar{x}$ belongs to the convex hull of the feasible set of (36). □

3.2 Big-M Mixed Integer Disjunctive Formulations

As noted earlier, any set that is bounded mixed integer representable can be represented by a big-M as well as a convex hull disjunctive formulation (Williams, to appear). This is likewise true of general mixed integer representable sets. Let us say that a *sharp big-M mixed integer disjunctive formulation* has the form

$$A^k x \geq b^k - M^k(1 - y_k), \quad k \in K$$
$$x \in \mathbb{R}^n \times \mathbb{Z}^p, \quad \sum_{k \in K} y_k = 1, \quad y_k \in \{0, 1\}, \quad k \in K \tag{38}$$

where

$$M^k = b^k - \min_{\ell \neq k} \left\{ \min_x \left\{ A^k x \mid A^\ell x \geq b^\ell, \, x \in \mathbb{R}^n \times \mathbb{Z}^p \right\} \right\} \qquad (39)$$

Theorem 3. *If set $S \subset \mathbb{R}^n \times \mathbb{Z}^p$ is the union of finitely many mixed integer polyhedra $P_k = Q_k \cap (\mathbb{R}^n \times \mathbb{Z}^p)$ (for $k \in K$) having the same recession cone, where $Q_k = \{x \mid A^k x \geq b^k\}$, then S is represented by the sharp big-M mixed integer disjunctive formulation (38).*

Proof. System (38) clearly represents S if every component of M^k as given by (39) is finite. We therefore suppose that some component i of some M^k is infinite, which implies that $\min \{A_i^k x \mid A^\ell x \geq b^\ell\}$ is unbounded for some $\ell \neq k$. Since P_ℓ is nonempty, this means there is a point $\bar{x} \in P_\ell$ and a rational direction d such that $A_i^k(\bar{x} + \alpha d)$ is unbounded in a negative direction as $\alpha \to \infty$, and such that $\bar{x} + \alpha d \in Q_\ell$ for all $\alpha \geq 0$. This means d is a recession direction of P_ℓ and therefore, by hypothesis, a recession direction of P_k. Thus by Lemma 2, d is a recession direction of Q_k. Since P_k is nonempty, there is an x' satisfying $A^k x' \geq b^k$, and for any such x' we have $A^k(x' + \alpha d) \geq b^k$ for all $\alpha \geq 0$. Thus $A^k(\bar{x} + \alpha d) \geq b^k + A^k(\bar{x} - x')$ for all $\alpha \geq 0$, which means that $A_i^k(\bar{x} + \alpha d)$ cannot be unbounded in a negative direction as $\alpha \to \infty$. $\square$

3.3 Example: Facility Location

An extension of the capacitated facility location problem considered earlier illustrates the usefulness of extending representability to disjunctions of mixed integer systems. Before, the cost of transporting quantity x_{ij} from facility location i to customer j was a continuous quantity $c_{ij} x_{ij}$. Now we suppose that goods transported on route (i, j) must be loaded into one or more vehicles, each with capacity K_{ij}, where each vehicle incurs a fixed cost c_{ij}. If w_{ij} is the number of vehicles used, then we have a disjunction of mixed integer systems for each location i:

$$\begin{pmatrix} \sum_{j=1}^n x_{ij} \leq C_i \\ 0 \leq x_{ij} \leq K_{ij} w_{ij}, \text{ all } j \\ z_i = f_i \\ w_{ij} \in \mathbb{Z}, \text{ all } j \end{pmatrix} \vee \begin{pmatrix} x_{ij} = 0, \text{ all } j \\ z_i = 0 \end{pmatrix} \qquad (40)$$

The mixed integer polyhedra defined by the two disjuncts have different recession cones. The cone for the first polyhedron is $\{(x_i, w_i) \mid x_i = 0, \, w_i \geq 0\}$ where $x_i = (x_{i1}, \ldots, x_{in})$ and $w_i = (w_{i1}, \ldots, w_{in})$, while the cone for the second is $\{(x_i, w_i) \mid x_i = 0\}$. However, if we add the innocuous constraint $w_i \geq 0$ to the second disjunct, the two disjuncts have the same recession cone and can therefore be given a convex hull formulation:

$$\sum_{j=1}^{n} x_{ij} \leq C_i y_i, \text{ all } i$$

$$0 \leq x_{ij} \leq K_{ij} w_{ij}, \text{ all } j \tag{41}$$

$$z_i = f_i y_i, \ y_i \in \{0,1\}, \ w_{ij} \in \mathbb{Z}, \text{ all } j$$

This yields a mixed integer formulation for the problem:

$$\min \sum_{i=1}^{m} \left(f_i y_i + \sum_{j=1}^{n} c_{ij} w_{ij} \right)$$

$$\sum_{j=1}^{n} x_{ij} \leq C_i y_i, \text{ all } i$$

$$0 \leq x_{ij} \leq K_{ij} w_{ij}, \text{ all } i, j \tag{42}$$

$$\sum_{i=1}^{m} x_{ij} = D_j, \text{ all } j$$

$$y_i \in \{0,1\}, \ w_{ij} \in \mathbb{Z}, \text{ all } i, j$$

Using a sharp big-M mixed integer formulation in place of the convex hull formulation (41) yields the same problem formulation (42).

3.4 Example: Package Delivery

A final example, adapted from Aardal (1998) and Trick (2005), illustrates how the approach presented here can result in a formulation that is superior to the standard formulation. A collection of packages are to be delivered by several trucks, and each package j has size a_j. Each available truck i has capacity Q_i and costs c_i to operate. The problem is to decide which trucks to use, and which packages to load on each truck, to deliver all the items at minimum cost.

We will formulate the problem by analyzing it as a combination of knapsack and disjunctive ideas. The decision problem consists of two levels: the choice of which trucks to use, followed by the choice of which packages to load on each truck. The trucks selected must provide sufficient capacity, which leads naturally to a 0-1 knapsack constraint:

$$\sum_{i=1}^{m} Q_i y_i \geq \sum_{j=1}^{n} a_j, \tag{43}$$

where each $y_i \in \{0,1\}$ and $y_i = 1$ when truck i is selected.

The secondary choice of which packages to load on truck i depends on whether that truck is selected. This suggests a disjunction of two alternatives. If the truck i is selected, then a cost c_i is incurred, and the items loaded must fit into the truck (a 0-1 knapsack constraint). If truck i is not selected, then no items can be loaded (another knapsack constraint). The disjunction is

$$
\begin{pmatrix} z_i \ge c_i \\ \sum_{j=1}^{n} a_j x_{ij} \le Q_i \\ x_{ij} \in \{0,1\}, \text{ all } j \end{pmatrix} \vee \begin{pmatrix} x_{ij} = 0, \text{ all } j \\ x_{ij} \in \{0,1\}, \text{ all } j \end{pmatrix} \tag{44}
$$

where z_i is the fixed cost incurred by truck i, and $x_{ij} = 1$ when package j is loaded into truck i. The feasible set is the union of two mixed integer polyhedra. They have the same recession cone if we add $z_i \ge 0$ to the second disjunct. If we suppose $y_i = 1$ when the first disjunct is enforced, the convex hull formulation of (44) is

$$
\begin{aligned}
& z_i \ge c_i y_i \\
& \sum_{j=1}^{n} a_j x_{ij} \le Q_i y_i \\
& y_i, x_{ij} \in \{0,1\}, \text{ all } j
\end{aligned} \tag{45}
$$

Finally, we make sure that each packaged must be shipped, which poses a set of knapsack constraints:

$$
\sum_{i=1}^{m} x_{ij} \ge 1, \ x_{ij} \in \{0,1\}, \text{ all } j \tag{46}
$$

Since (43) and (46) can be viewed as disjunctions having one disjunct, we have conceived the problem as consisting of disjunctions of mixed integer systems. If we minimize total fixed cost $\sum_i z_i$ subject to (43), (45), and (46), the resulting mixed integer model immediately simplifies to

$$
\begin{aligned}
& \min \sum_{i=1}^{m} c_i y_i && (a) \\
& \sum_{i=1}^{m} Q_i y_i \ge \sum_{j=1}^{n} a_j && (b) \\
& \sum_{j=1}^{n} a_j x_{ij} \le Q_i y_i, \text{ all } i && (c) \\
& \sum_{i=1}^{m} x_{ij} \ge 1, \ x_{ij} \in \{0,1\}, \text{ all } j && (d) \\
& y_i \in \{0,1\}, \ x_{ij} \in \{0,1\}, \text{ all } i, j
\end{aligned} \tag{47}
$$

This formulation differs in two ways from a formulation that one might initially write for this problem. First, one might omit the factor y_i from constraints (c), because these constraints ensure that each truck's load is within that truck's capacity. It is therefore natural to write simply the capacity Q_i on the right-hand side. However, a fairly well-known modeling device is to write $Q_i y_i$ instead, because this retains the validity of the formulation while making its continuous relaxation tighter. The approach recommended here allows one to derive the tighter formulation without knowing the device in advance.

Second, a standard formulation would not contain constraint (b), because due to (d) it is implied by the sum of constraints (c). According to conventional wisdom, there is no point is writing a constraint that is a nonnegative linear combination of other constraints. However, it is reported in Trick (2005) that the problem is far easier to solve with constraint (b) than without it, because the presence of (b) allows the solver to deduce lifted knapsack cuts, which create a much tighter continuous relaxation. Thus in this instance, a principled approach enables one to write a formulation that is superior to the standard one.

4 Conclusion

We have suggested how mixed integer problem formulation can be undertaken in a principled way. We by no means provide a method by which one can mechanically generate mixed integer formulations. Problem formulation remains an irreducibly creative act. Yet the framework presented here can give some guidance as to how to proceed.

Problems often pose choices between alternatives, and these can be represented as disjunctions of inequality systems. Counting ideas can be represented as integer knapsack constraints that appear among the inequality constraints. The disjunctions can be given convex hull or big-M formulations, resulting in a mixed integer formulation for the problem.

There may be a good deal of latitude as to how to view a problem as containing disjunctive and counting elements. Different interpretations of the problem can lead to different formulations. Even when the disjunctive constraints have been written, there is the issue as to whether some of them should be combined to obtain a tighter formulation.

Once the disjunctive constraints are finalized, the mixed integer formulation of each disjunct typically allows simplification. It may be possible to automate the simplification process, and this presents an interesting issue for future research.

Several additional research issues remain. (a) Are there sufficient conditions under which a big-M disjunctive formulation is a convex hull formation? (b) When is it advantageous to use a big-M rather than a convex hull disjunctive formulation? (c) Are there sufficient conditions under which a formulation containing logical constraints is a convex hull formulation? (d) When is it advantageous to replace logical constraints with convex hull disjunctive formulations?

In general, mixed integer problem formulation deserves more serious study that it has received. Jeroslow's work was a significant contribution, but much remains to be done. If the formulation process is better understood, it may be possible to develop more effective tools to assist practitioners in formulating problems. This in turn will allow more applications to benefit from the powerful solution technology that has been developed for mixed integer programming.

References

Aardal K (1998) Reformulation of capacitated facility location problems: How redundant information can help. Annals of Operations Research 82:289–309

Beaumont N (1990) An algorithm for disjunctive programs. European Journal of Operational Research 48:362–371

Hooker JN (2007) Integrated Methods for Optimization. Springer, New York

Jeroslow RG (1987) Representability in mixed integer programming, I: Characterization results. Discrete Applied Mathematics 17:223–243

Jeroslow RG (1989) Logic-Based Decision Support: Mixed Integer Model Formulation. Annals of Discrete Mathematics, North-Holland

Trick M (2005) Formulations and reformulations in integer programming. In: Barták R, Milano M (eds) Integration of AI and OR Techniques in Constraint Programming for Combinatorial Optimization Problems (CPAIOR 2005), Springer, Lecture Notes in Computer Science, vol 3524, pp 366–379

Williams HP (1999) Model Building in Mathematical Programming, 4th Ed. Wiley, New York

Williams HP (to appear) Logic and Integer Programming. Springer

Experiments with Branching using General Disjunctions

A. Mahajan and T.K. Ralphs

Abstract Branching is an important component of the branch-and-cut algorithm for solving mixed integer linear programs. Most solvers branch by imposing a disjunction of the form"$x_i \leq k \vee x_i \geq k+1$" for some integer k and some integer-constrained variable x_i. A generalization of this branching scheme is to branch by imposing a more general disjunction of the form "$\pi x \leq \pi_0 \vee \pi x \geq \pi_0 + 1$." In this paper, we discuss the formulation of two optimization models for selecting such a branching disjunction and then describe methods of solution using a standard MILP solver. We report on computational experiments carried out to study the effects of branching on such disjunctions.

Key words: branching, integer programming, general disjunctions

1 Introduction

In this paper, we consider the effect of using more general branching disjunctions in the well-known branch-and-cut algorithm for solving mixed integer linear programs (MILPs) than are typically considered by most solvers. Even though the method of selecting a branching disjunction is a crucial component of branch and cut, most solvers still only consider a very limited set of possible disjunctions when deciding how to branch. It is not clear whether the reason for this is (i) that it is not known how to generate more general branching disjunctions or (ii) the additional effort necessary to generate such disjunctions is not offset by gains in the overall

A. Mahajan
Department of Industrial and Systems Engineering, Lehigh University, Bethlehem, PA 18015, e-mail: asm4@lehigh.edu

T.K. Ralphs
Department of Industrial and Systems Engineering Lehigh University, Bethlehem, PA 18015, e-mail: ted@lehigh.edu

J.W. Chinneck et al. (eds.), *Operations Research and Cyber-Infrastructure*, Operations Research/Computer Science Interfaces Series 47, DOI: 10.1007/978-0-387-88843-9_6, © Springer Science+Business Media, LLC 2009

efficiency of the algorithm. In what follows, we address this question by formally stating the problem of selecting a "best" branching disjunction as an optimization problem, proposing a method to solve this optimization problem, and reporting on the effect of deploying this method of selection in a standard commercial solver. Our goal here is not to test the efficiency of our method for selecting disjunctions (it is demonstrably inefficient), but simply to answer the question of what gains could be realized in the overall efficiency of a branch-and-cut procedure (in terms of reducing the number of subproblems solved during the solution procedure) if "optimal" branching disjunctions could be determined.

1.1 Definitions

We consider the mixed integer linear program

$$\min cx$$
$$\text{s.t. } Ax \geq b \qquad\qquad\qquad (P)$$
$$x \in \mathbb{Z}^d \times \mathbb{R}^{n-d},$$

where $b \in \mathbb{Q}^m, c \in \mathbb{Q}^n$, and $A \in \mathbb{Q}^{m \times n}$ are the inputs and the variables with indices $1, 2, \ldots, d$ are required to take on integral values. If (P) does not have any feasible solution, then the optimal solution value is taken to be ∞. The linear programming (LP) relaxation of (P), obtained by dropping the integrality constraints, is the linear program

$$\min_{x \in \mathcal{P}} cx, \qquad\qquad\qquad (P^{LP})$$

where $\mathcal{P} = \{x \in \mathbb{R}^n \mid Ax \geq b\}$. Formally defining the problem of determining the "best" branching disjunction requires defining precisely what set of possible disjunctions we consider and by what criteria we evaluate them. To do this, we must first briefly describe the branch-and-bound procedure.

LP-based branch and bound is a recursive procedure for solving (P) in which a lower bound is first obtained by solving its LP relaxation (P^{LP}) (with the minimum taken to be ∞ if $\mathcal{P}$ is empty). If the bound obtained is at least as large as the value of the best feasible solution known (generated either by a separate heuristic procedure or as a by-product of solving the relaxation), then the current best solution is globally optimal and we are done. Otherwise, we determine a disjunction (usually binary) that is satisfied by all solutions to the original MILP, but not satisfied by the solution to the LP relaxation. Such a disjunction, referred henceforth to as a *valid branching disjunction*, is then used to partition the feasible region into subsets that define subproblems to which the algorithm can then be applied recursively until exhaustion. For a more complete description of the algorithm (and also of the branch-and-cut algorithm), see [Nemhauser and Wolsey, 1988, page 355]. Note that a *subproblem* refers to a restriction of the original problem resulting from the imposition of one or more branching disjunctions on the original instance. These subproblems should not be confused with the associated problem of selecting a branching disjunction, which is formulated below and then solved to determine an optimal branching disjunction.

Most solvers use branching disjunctions, called *variable disjunctions*, of the form "$x_i \leq k \vee x_i \geq k + 1$" for some integer k and some $i \leq d$, since these are always valid for (P). More generally, however, any $\pi \in \mathbb{Z}^d \times \{0\}^{n-d}$ and $\pi_0 \in \mathbb{Z}$ yields the disjunction "$\pi x \leq \pi_0 \vee \pi x \geq \pi_0 + 1$" (referred henceforth to as a *general disjunction* and denoted by the ordered pair (π, π_0)), which is also always valid for (P). Since the set of general disjunctions includes all variable disjunctions, considering this larger set should in principle be advantageous. It is this set of disjunctions we consider in what follows, though in the computational experiments, we were forced to further restrict the set in order to obtain results in a reasonable amount of time.

In its simplest form, the efficiency of the branch-and-bound procedure depends mainly on the number of subproblems generated. The goal of selecting the branching disjunctions is then to minimize the total number of subproblems to be solved. It is evident that the problem of selecting a branching disjunction that minimizes the total number of subproblems solved globally is extremely difficult—at least as hard as solving the original problem and likely much harder in practice. The approach taken by most solvers, and the one we shall take here, is to evaluate candidate branching disjunctions by assessing their effect using more myopic criteria. We defer discussion of the specific criteria employed in this study until Section 2 below.

1.2 Previous Work

Despite its importance as a component of the branch-and-bound procedure, relatively little effort has gone into improving methods by which branching disjunctions are determined. In practice, however, where branching is typically limited to variable disjunctions, some attention has been paid to selecting the "best" such disjunction. Linderoth and Savelsbergh [1999] performed extensive computational experiments to show that selecting a variable disjunction that will lead to maximum estimated increase in the lower bound of the subproblems is a good strategy. Such estimates are made primarily in one of two ways. *Strong branching* consists of making the estimates by partially solving each subproblem created by branching for each candidate variable disjunction. *Pseudo-cost branching* consists of estimating the change on the basis of the actual change that occurred when the candidate disjunction was previously imposed (in some other subproblem). Recently, Achterberg et al. [2005] showed empirically that using a hybrid approach, called *reliability branching*, yields better results in practice than either of above two approaches used alone.

The study of branching on general disjunctions is not new either and has been previously recognized as an important aspect of the theory of integer programming. In their survey, Aardal and Eisenbrand [2004] discussed the fact that when the dimension is fixed, polynomial time algorithms for solving integer programs can be obtained by branching on general disjunctions obtained by determining the so-called *thin directions* of the feasible region. These polynomial time algorithms are derived from the seminal work of Lenstra [H.W. Lenstra, 1983] and its extensions. It has also been shown, for instance by Krishnamoorthy and Pataki [2006], that certain specific problems can be solved "easily," if one branches on some particular general disjunction. On the other hand, few heuristics have been proposed that enhance computational performance of standard solvers by using general branching disjunctions. Fischetti and Lodi [2003] proposed a local branching heuristic that uses a general disjunction for branching such that one of the branches has a small feasible region but is more likely to contain feasible solutions with small objective function values. Owen and Mehrotra [2001] used a greedy heuristic to generate branching disjunctions with coefficients in $\{0, 1, -1\}$. Karamanov and Cornuéjols [2007] suggested branching using disjunctions that could be used for generating Mixed Integer Gomory cuts in the branch-and-cut algorithm. Some general branching disjunctions have also been shown to be useful for problems with specific structures like special ordered sets [Beale and Tomlin, 1970].

The remainder of the paper is organized as follows. In Section 2, we present two different criteria by which to select a branching disjunction and describe how to solve the problem of determining the optimal general disjunction with respect to these criteria. In Section 3, we analyze the results of computational experiments applying the methods from Section 2. In Section 4, we present our conclusions and indicate directions for future work in this area.

2 Selecting Branching Disjunctions

As previously described, selecting a branching disjunction based on its global effect is likely to be extremely difficult and we must therefore resort to more myopic (though still not theoretically efficient) selection procedures. The two criteria we use here to evaluate a branching disjunction are (i) lower bound improvement achieved after branching and (ii) width of $\mathcal{P}$ in the direction of the disjunction. The problem of finding an optimal general branching disjunction according to each of these criteria is formulated in the following two sections. It is known from the results of Sebő [1999] and our recent work [Mahajan and Ralphs, 2008] that the problem of optimizing over the set of general branching disjunctions with either of the above criteria is $\mathcal{NP}$-hard, even when the set of disjunctions is restricted in various ways.

2.1 Branching to Maximize Lower Bound

As previously mentioned, experiments by Linderoth and Savelsbergh [1999] and Achterberg et al. [2005] provided empirical evidence that selecting variable disjunctions on the basis of estimated increase in the lower bound after such a branching could result in a reduction in the number of subproblems solved. Therefore, we base our first criteria for choosing branching disjunctions on the same principle. The procedure is based on detecting infeasibility of the subproblems resulting from imposition of the branching disjunction, along with (possibly) an inequality requiring a certain target increase in the lower bound.

First, consider the integer program (P) and assume that $\mathcal{P}$ is not empty (otherwise, the problem is easy to solve). Let $(\hat{\pi}, \hat{\pi}_0) \in \mathbb{Z}^d \times \{0\}^{n-d} \times \mathbb{Z}$ be a disjunction that is used to branch after (P^{LP}) is solved. Then the LP relaxations associated with the two partitions created after branching are of the form

$$
\begin{array}{ccc}
\min cx & & \min cx \\
\text{subject to:} & \text{and} & \text{subject to:} \\
Ax \geq b & & Ax \geq b \\
\hat{\pi}x \leq \hat{\pi}_0 & & \hat{\pi}x \geq \hat{\pi}_0 + 1.
\end{array}
\tag{1}
$$

Now, consider the related linear programs

$$
\begin{array}{ccc}
z_L^* = \min \hat{\pi}x & & z_R^* = \min -\hat{\pi}x \\
\text{subject to:} & \text{and} & \text{subject to:} \\
Ax \geq b & & Ax \geq b.
\end{array}
\tag{2}
$$

The programs (1) are infeasible if and only if $z_L^* > \hat{\pi}_0$ and $z_R^* > -(\hat{\pi}_0 + 1)$. The dual of the programs (2) can be written as

$$
\begin{array}{ccc}
z_L^* = \max pb & & z_R^* = \max qb \\
\text{subject to:} & \text{and} & \text{subject to:} \\
pA = \hat{\pi} & & qA = -\hat{\pi} \\
p \geq 0 & & q \geq 0,
\end{array}
\tag{3}
$$

respectively. By imposing the requirement that $z_L^* > \hat{\pi}_0$ and $z_R^* > -(\hat{\pi}_0 + 1)$ and then combining the two dual formulations (3), one can conclude that the LPs (1) are both infeasible if and only if the system

$$
\begin{aligned}
pA - \pi &= 0 \\
qA + \pi &= 0 \\
pb - \pi_0 &\geq \delta \\
qb + \pi_0 &\geq \delta - 1 \\
p &\geq 0 \\
q &\geq 0 \\
(\pi, \pi_0) &\in \mathbb{Z}^{n+1},
\end{aligned}
\tag{4}
$$

has a solution for some $\delta > 0$ and with $\pi = \hat{\pi}, \pi_0 = \hat{\pi}_0$.

A sequence of MILPs of the form (4) can now be solved in order to find a branching disjunction whose imposition maximizes the resulting lower bound as follows.

Suppose it is desired to increase the lower bound resulting from imposition of the branching disjunction to some value exceeding a given target z_l. This is equivalent to requiring that both the following system of inequalities be infeasible.

$$
\begin{array}{lll}
Ax \geq b & & Ax \geq b \\
\hat{\pi}x \leq \hat{\pi}_0 & \text{and} & \hat{\pi}x \geq \hat{\pi}_0 + 1 \\
cx \leq z_l & & cx \leq z_l
\end{array}
\tag{5}
$$

Observe that dropping the branching constraints makes the systems (5) feasible, as long as $z_l > z_{LP}$. Using the approach described above, the problem of finding a suitable $(\hat{\pi}, \hat{\pi}_0)$ may now be written as that of finding a feasible solution to the system

$$
\begin{aligned}
pA - s_L c - \pi &= 0 \\
pb - s_L z_l - \pi_0 &\geq \delta \\
qA - s_R c + \pi &= 0 \\
qb - s_R z_l + \pi_0 &\geq \delta - 1 \\
p, s_L, q, s_R &\geq 0 \\
\pi \in \mathbb{Z}^n, \pi_0 &\in \mathbb{Z}.
\end{aligned}
\tag{6}
$$

The lower bound obtained after solving the LP relaxations (1) can be increased to at least z_l by imposing the branching disjunction $(\hat{\pi}, \hat{\pi}_0)$ if and only if $\pi = \hat{\pi}, \pi_0 = \hat{\pi}_0$ is a feasible solution to the system (6) for some $\delta > 0$. Note the similarity in the formulations (6) and (4). If there is a feasible solution to (6) with $s_L = s_R = 0$, then (4) is also feasible and consequently, imposition of the corresponding branching disjunction will make the LPs related to each member of partition infeasible.

If one treats z_l as a variable in formulation (6), then it becomes a nonlinear program because of the presence of bilinear terms $s_L z_l$ and $s_R z_l$. Hence, it is not straightforward to get the maximum value of z_l from this formulation. We overcome this difficulty by solving a sequence of parametric (feasibility) MILPs of the form (6) by treating z_l as a fixed parameter and choosing a suitable value for δ. By doing a binary search over a range of values for z_l and solving (6) in each iteration of the search, one can obtain the maximum value of the lower bound up to a desired level of accuracy. Additionally, if x^* is known to be a fractional optimal solution of the LP relaxation of the original problem (P), then the constraint $\pi_0 < \pi x^* < \pi_0 + 1$ may optionally be added to formulation (6).

2.2 Branching on Thin Directions

The second criterion by which we judge a branching disjunction (π, π_0) is by the width of $\mathcal{P}$ in the direction π, defined to be $\max_{x,y \in \mathcal{P}} \pi y - \pi x$. Intuitively, a branching disjunction with small associated width should be effective because it is likely that the volume of the union of the feasible regions of the subproblems resulting from imposition of such a disjunction will be significantly smaller than that of the polyhedron $\mathcal{P}$. For a polytope Q, the minimum width in the direction of any general branching disjunction is called the *integer width* and is defined to be

$$w(Q) = \min_{\pi} \max_{x,y \in \mathcal{P}} (\pi y - \pi x) \ s.t. \ \pi \in \mathbb{Z}^d \times \{0\}^{n-d}, \pi \neq \mathbf{0}.$$

Sebő [1999] showed that for a given polytope Q, the problem of determining whether $w(Q) \leq 1$ is $\mathcal{NP}$-complete, even when Q is a simplex. It is also known, from a result of Banaszczyk et al. [1999], that if Q is empty, then $w(Q) \leq Cn^{\frac{3}{2}}$, where C is a constant. Derpich and Vera [2006] tried to approximate the direction of the minimum integer width in order to assign priorities for branching on variables. They showed that the number of subproblems can be reduced when using this heuristic approach. Aardal and Eisenbrand [2004] discussed the fact that branching on thin directions leads to polynomial time algorithms for integer programs when the dimension is fixed. Hence, such branching directions seem empirically to be useful in reducing the number of subproblems to be examined during the solution procedure.

For a fixed $\hat{\pi}$, the dual of the LP

$$\max \hat{\pi}y - \hat{\pi}x$$
$$\text{subject to:}$$
$$Ax \geq b \qquad (7)$$
$$Ay \geq b,$$

can be written as

$$\min -qb - pb$$
$$\text{subject to:}$$
$$pA - \hat{\pi} = 0 \qquad (8)$$
$$qA + \hat{\pi} = 0$$
$$p,q \geq 0.$$

Thus, the problem of finding $w(\mathcal{P})$ can be equivalently expressed as the program

$$\min -qb - pb$$
$$\text{subject to:}$$
$$pA - \pi = 0$$
$$qA + \pi = 0 \qquad (9)$$
$$p,q \geq 0$$
$$\pi \in \mathbb{Z}^n \times \{0\}^{n-d}, \pi \neq \mathbf{0}.$$

Note that if there exists a feasible solution to formulation (4) described in the previous section, then $w(\mathcal{P}) < 1$. However, the converse is not true. Furthermore, if (P) does not have any continuous variables (i.e., if $d = n$) and if $\mathcal{P}$ is not full dimensional then $w(\mathcal{P}) = 0$. In such a case, one may end up obtaining the same solution from the formulation (9) for each subproblem. In order to overcome this difficulty, we modified the formulation to

$$
\begin{aligned}
&\min -qb - pb \\
&\text{subject to:} \\
&\quad pA - \pi = 0 \\
&\quad qA + \pi = 0 \\
&\quad \pi_0 + \delta \leq \pi x^* \leq \pi_0 + 1 - \delta \\
&\quad p, q \geq 0 \\
&\quad \pi \in \mathbb{Z}^n \times \{0\}^{n-d} \\
&\quad \pi_0 \in \mathbb{Z},
\end{aligned} \tag{10}
$$

where x^* is an optimal solution to the current LP relaxation and δ is a suitably small constant. The formulation (10) is only an approximation to finding the integer width of $\mathcal{P}$. However, it ensures that x^* violates the generated disjunction and also that $\pi \neq \mathbf{0}$.

3 Computational Experiments

In order to test the effect of selecting branching disjunctions using the formulations presented in the previous section, we performed a sequence of experiments using ILOG CPLEX 10.2 with the default selection method for branching disjunctions replaced by the ones previously described. Since our goal was only to discern the effectiveness of employing the disjunctions and not to test the efficiency of the method for determining them, our measure of effectiveness was reduction in total number of subproblems required to solve each instance. Thus, we are ignoring the time required to find the branching disjunctions, which was substantial in some cases.

Initial experiments were carried out on 91 instances selected from MIPLIB 3.0 [Bixby et al., 1998], MIPLIB 2003 [Achterberg et al., 2006], and the Mittelmann test set [Mittelmann, 2008]. The initial set was then reduced to 30 representative instances in order to complete experiments in reasonable time. Table 1 shows the size of these instances. The branching disjunctions were imposed using the callback functions provided with the CPLEX callable library. All experiments were run on 64-bit machines, each with 16GB RAM, 8 1.86GHz cores and 4MB cache. In all experiments, the best known objective function value was provided as upper bound to the solver to ensure that the solution procedure was not affected by the order in which subproblems were solved or other extraneous factors related to improvement in the upper bound.

Table 1 Number of constraints, variables, integer (including binary) variables and binary variables in the 30 instances used in experiments.

Instance	Cons	Vars	Ints	Bins	Instance	Cons	Vars	Ints	Bins
10teams	231	2025	1800	1800	mod008	6	319	319	319
aflow30a	479	842	421	421	neos6	1037	8768	8340	8340
bell3a	123	133	71	39	nug08	913	1632	1632	0
blend2	274	353	264	231	nw04	36	87482	87482	87482
egout	98	141	55	55	p0548	176	548	548	548
fiber	363	1298	1254	1254	pp08aCUTS	246	240	64	64
flugpl	18	18	11	0	qnet1	503	1541	1417	1288
gen	780	870	150	144	qnet1_o	456	1541	1417	1288
gesa2	1392	1224	408	240	ran10x26	297	520	260	260
gesa2_o	1248	1152	672	336	ran12x21	286	504	502	502
gt2	29	188	24	0	ran13x13	196	338	169	169
harp2	112	2993	2993	2993	rout	291	556	315	300
khb05250	101	1350	24	24	stein45	331	45	45	45
l152lav	97	1989	1989	1989	vpm1	234	378	168	168
lseu	28	89	89	89	vpm2	234	378	168	168

In the first experiment, a pure branch-and-bound procedure was used—other advanced techniques such as cutting planes, heuristics and probing were disabled. This allowed us to observe the effects of branching in isolation from the mitigating effects of applying these additional techniques. In the first experiment, a sequence of MILPs of the form (6) were solved to determine the disjunction yielding the maximum increase in lower bound. During initial testing, we concluded that optimizing over the entire set of general branching disjunctions was too time-consuming, as the MILPs (6) were sometimes extremely difficult to solve. We therefore imposed the following limitations for all tests.

1. π was restricted to the set $\{-M, -M+1, \ldots, M\}^n$. $M = 1$ was used in the first experiment and higher values were tried in other experiments.
2. Each π_i was replaced with two non negative variables substituting $\pi_i = \pi_i^+ - \pi_i^-$, $\pi_i^+, \pi_i^- \in [0, M]$. Such a transformation was used in order to make it easier for the solver to find heuristic solutions to the MILP formulation.
3. The constraint $\sum_{i=1}^n |\pi_i| \leq k$ was introduced to further restrict the search space. k was set to 2, 5, 10, 15 and 20 in different experiments.
4. A time limit of t seconds was imposed for solving any one MILP for selecting a branching disjunction. Additionally, a limit of $8t$ seconds was imposed on the time allowed to be spent in total on selecting any single branching disjunction. In the first experiment, t was set to 1000. Values of 50 and 100 were used in later experiments.
5. A total time limit of 20 hours was imposed for solving each instance. After 18 hours, only variable disjunctions were considered so that the problem could be solved to completion in the remaining two hours.

In case the search for a branching disjunction failed (because of time limits or because no solution was found), branching was carried out by considering variable disjunctions. Since it was not known how the selection rule of CPLEX works, the

LP relaxations of the subproblem resulting from the imposition of each candidate variable disjunction were solved explicitly in order to determine the optimal variable disjunction according to the criteria of maximum increase in lower bound. In cases where it was found that there was no variable disjunction whose imposition resulted in an increase in the lower bound, the default variable branching scheme of CPLEX was invoked. The number of subproblems solved when branching on general disjunctions was compared against that when branching only on variable disjunctions.

The number of subproblems generated during solution of each instance in the first experiment is shown in Table 2. N_k denotes the number of subproblems created when the search was restricted by addition of the constraint $\sum_{i=1}^{n} |\pi_i| \leq k$. Thus, N_1 denotes the number of subproblems when branching was done using only variable disjunctions (by selecting a variable disjunction after solving the resulting LP relaxations explicitly, as described above). The value r_k is defined to be $\frac{N_1}{N_k}$. Even though the experiments for Table 2 were carried out with 91 instances, only results for the 30 selected for further investigation are reported, since other instances showed similar results.

For all remaining experiments, the performance profiles of Dolan and Moré [2002] are used to display compactly, the results comparing number of subproblems solved in various experiments. A point (α, β) in such a plot indicates that a fraction β of all instances required less than α times the number of subproblems required in the experiment achieving the lowest total overall. Figure 1(a) shows a performance profile for the data in Table 2.

In the next two experiments, the time limit t imposed on the solution of each MILP was reduced to 100 seconds and 50 seconds, respectively. This was done to determine whether good branching disjunctions could still be found in a shorter amount of time. Figures 1(b) and 1(c) show the performance profile when t was fixed and k was varied.

The experiments described so far show that branching on disjunctions that maximize the subsequent lower bound increase does in fact lead to a significant reduction in the number of subproblems required to be solved. In general, the number of subproblems is also reduced when the set of disjunctions considered is larger (i.e., the number of non-zeros allowed in the vector π is increased).

Figures 2(a)-2(e) show the effect of time spent in selecting a branching disjunction when k is fixed. In general, when k is small, additional time spent selecting a disjunction pays a bigger dividend than when k is large. Figure 2(d) shows that when $k = 15$ the number of subproblems solved does not vary much as t is increased. When k is set to 20, the performance with $t = 50$ is nearly equivalent to that with $t = 1000$. One possible explanation is that for large values of k, if a feasible solution to the branching disjunction selection problem is not found quickly, then it is unlikely that a solution will be found even after substantial additional search time. Thus, even though branching on disjunctions that increase the lower bound appears promising, the problem of selecting disjunctions becomes increasingly difficult with the number of nonzero coefficients that are allowed in the description. This seems to be the case for the instance vpm1 in particular (see Table 2)—when k is changed

Table 2 Number of nodes (N_i) in branch and bound tree and the ratio $r_i = \frac{N_1}{N_i}$ for selected instances when $t = 1000$ seconds. The criterion for selecting the branching disjunction is to maximize the lower bound.

Instance	N_1	N_2	r_2	N_5	r_5	N_{10}	r_{10}	N_{15}	r_{15}	N_{20}	r_{20}
10teams	115	106	1.08	28	4.11	18	6.39	12	9.58	12	9.58
aflow30a	36634	19408	1.89	19485	1.88	20388	1.8	24112	1.52	20271	1.81
bell3a	16387	14377	1.14	8771	1.87	588	27.87	259	63.27	259	63.27
blend2	304	251	1.21	231	1.32	188	1.62	165	1.84	209	1.45
egout	2246	1044	2.15	554	4.05	572	3.93	676	3.32	558	4.03
fiber	18412	7676	2.4	7612	2.42	3039	6.06	3358	5.48	3324	5.54
flugpl	394	176	2.24	6	65.67	10	39.4	6	65.67	6	65.67
gen	100	100	1	100	1	100	1	100	1	100	1
gesa2	33526	24433	1.37	21664	1.55	21849	1.53	21849	1.53	21778	1.54
gesa2_o	98550	24777	3.98	24435	4.03	24661	4	24661	4	24661	4
gt2	340	10	34	10	34	12	28.33	10	34	12	28.33
harp2	432010	157377	2.75	174656	2.47	183306	2.36	174454	2.48	179130	2.41
khb05250	738	606	1.22	594	1.24	588	1.26	614	1.2	618	1.19
l152lav	60	40	1.5	32	1.88	28	2.14	34	1.76	30	2
lseu	4058	2365	1.72	226	17.96	78	52.03	58	69.97	58	69.97
mod008	2840	1678	1.69	296	9.59	102	27.84	68	41.76	52	54.62
neos6	5989	2131	2.81	2131	2.81	2131	2.81	2131	2.81	2131	2.81
nug08	14	6	2.33	4	3.5	6	2.33	6	2.33	5	2.8
nw04	30	24	1.25	16	1.88	12	2.5	12	2.5	12	2.5
p0548	1050	500	2.1	466	2.25	566	1.86	565	1.86	565	1.86
pp08aCUTS	1301300	486340	2.68	147271	8.84	166943	7.79	168905	7.7	231527	5.62
qnet1	42	30	1.4	24	1.75	20	2.1	22	1.91	18	2.33
qnet1_o	154	126	1.22	94	1.64	77	2	80	1.93	92	1.67
ran10x26	68449	34693	1.97	23309	2.94	24716	2.77	23704	2.89	21520	3.18
ran12x21	494558	280551	1.76	219967	2.25	208948	2.37	225980	2.19	212910	2.32
ran13x13	124716	87495	1.43	74699	1.67	57825	2.16	66008	1.89	58789	2.12
rout	219322	79399	2.76	65201	3.36	61806	3.55	61226	3.58	57673	3.8
stein45	31086	31177	1	21238	1.46	20594	1.51	20601	1.51	20601	1.51
vpm1	263111	40952	6.42	145	1814.56	32	8222.22	20	13155.55	5929	44.38
vpm2	273994	145152	1.89	77504	3.54	67014	4.09	69515	3.94	73687	3.72

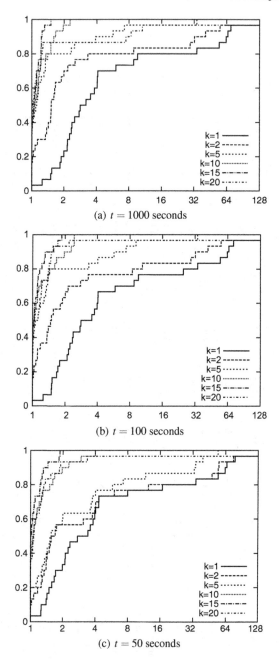

Fig. 1 Performance profile for number of subproblems when t is fixed and k is varied.

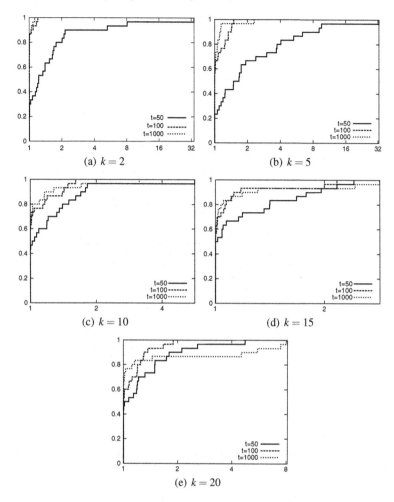

Fig. 2 Performance profile for number of subproblems when k is fixed and t (in seconds) is varied.

from 15 to 20, the number of subproblems goes up from 20 to 5929, presumably because the branching disjunction selection problem becomes so difficult that only a few effective disjunctions are found within the time limit.

In the next experiment, cutting planes were enabled to see how the branching disjunction selection method would perform in a branch-and-cut algorithm. In general, introduction of cutting plane generation should be expected to reduce the total number of subproblems. The default settings of CPLEX were used for cut generation, with the exception that MIR, Gomory, and flow (cover and path) cuts were disabled because the presence of these cuts caused numerical difficulties while solving some of the associated branching disjunction selection problems. Figure 3(a) shows the effect of adding cuts when $t = 100$ seconds and k has values 1, 2, and 5. It shows

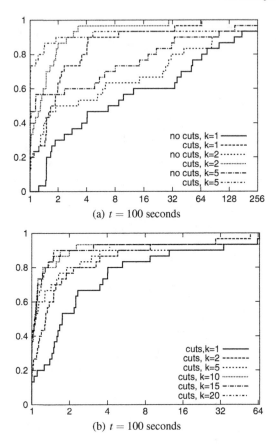

(a) $t = 100$ seconds

(b) $t = 100$ seconds

Fig. 3 Performance profile for number of subproblems when cuts are added to the original problem. t is fixed and k is varied.

that enabling cuts increases the performance of the solver significantly, even when branching on general disjunctions is used. Figure 3(b) shows how the performance varies when cuts are enabled and k is varied from 1 to 20. Figure 1(b) shows that, in the absence of cuts, around 80% of instances required at least half as many subproblems when branching on general disjunctions. When the cuts were enabled, this fraction dropped to 50%. So the effect of branching on general disjunctions is substantial even when the cuts are enabled, though it is not as dramatic.

To see the effect of increasing M, we performed one experiment with $M = 10$, $k = 15, t = 100$. Figure 4(a) shows a comparison of performance of this test against the others. The performance seems to be slightly worse than when $M = 1$. However, it could not be established whether this was due to larger coefficients in some of the disjunctions or because of the increased difficulty of the MILPs used to identify the disjunction. A similar experiment was carried with $M = 10, k = 15, t = 1000$ to see the effects for the case when more time was spent in finding disjunctions with

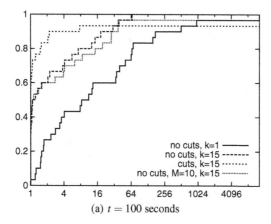

(a) $t = 100$ seconds

Fig. 4 Performance profile to compare the effect of branching for maximum lower bound when M is increased to 10.

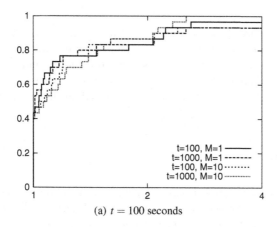

(a) $t = 100$ seconds

Fig. 5 Performance profile to compare the effects of changing t when M in increased.

$M > 1$. Figure (5(a)) shows that there are no considerable effects from spending more time or changing M. These experiments seem to suggest that k is probably a more important parameter than either t or M.

Finally, we experimented with selecting a branching disjunction along a "thin" direction by solving the formulation (10). Additional constraints, as described for the criteria of maximizing lower bound above, were also added. Figure 6(a) compares the number of subproblems solved when branching on "thin" directions with other experiments. The performance is seen to be comparable to that of branching on variable-disjunctions. One plausible reason why branching along thin directions did not perform as well as other criteria might be that most of the integer constrained variables in the test set were binary variables. For such problems, the integer width of the polytope associated with the LP relaxation of a subproblem is at most one.

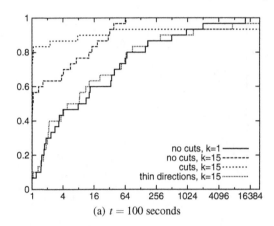

(a) $t = 100$ seconds

Fig. 6 Performance profile to compare the effect of branching on "thin" directions against other criteria.

Furthermore, there are typically a number of directions along which the width is one. So, for the case when the minimum width of the polytope is one, the formulation (8) selects any one of the many possible directions arbitrarily. One way to overcome this problem would be to resort to other criteria when the minimum width is found to be one. However, we have not yet pursued this line of research.

4 Conclusion

In this paper, we considered the use of general disjunctions of the form "$\pi x \leq \pi_0 \vee \pi x \geq \pi_0 + 1$" in branch and bound and branch and cut. We formulated the problem of selecting the optimal such disjunction using two different criteria and reported on the effect of using the associated optimization models to select branching disjunctions within the branch-and-bound framework of the commercial solver CPLEX. The naive approach to formulating and solving the branching disjunction selection problem described herein yielded mixed results. The optimization problems that arose turned out to be extremely difficult to solve using off-the-shelf software. Our experiments have given us many ideas as to how improve the efficiency of solving these problems and also how to develop fast heuristics for obtaining "good" disjunctions quickly. However, this is future work and was not the focus of this initial study.

With regard to the effectiveness of using more general disjunctions, our conclusion is that such an approach, if it can be made efficient, will undoubtedly yield improved solution times. We observed consistent substantial reductions in the number of subproblems required to be solved when using general disjunctions for branching. We therefore conclude that this is a fruitful line of future research, though much thought has to go into how to make solution of the formulations presented here efficient. Other interesting lines of research concern the development of additional criteria for selection of branching disjunctions and the study of the relationship between disjunctions used for generating valid inequalities and those used for branching. Both these topics have been addressed already to some extent, but certainly deserve further study.

5 Acknowledgement

The computational experiments were undertaken on a cluster provided by High Performance Computing at Lehigh University. CPLEX licences were made available by COR@L Labs at Lehigh University. The authors would also like to thank the reviewers for helpful comments and suggestions.

References

Aardal K, Eisenbrand F (2004) Integer programming, lattices and results in fixed dimenstion. Tech. rep., Probability, Networks and Algorithms

Achterberg T, Koch T, Martin A (2005) Branching rules revisited. Operation Research Letters 33:42–54

Achterberg T, Koch T, Martin A (2006) Miplib 2003. Operations Research Letters 34(4):1–12

Banaszczyk W, Litvak AE, Pajor A, Szarek SJ (1999) The flatness theorem for non-symmetric convex bodies via the local theory of banach spaces. Mathematics of Operations Research 24(3):728–750

Beale EML, Tomlin JA (1970) Special facilities in general mathematical programming system for non-convex problems using ordered sets of variables. In: Lawrence J (ed) Proceedings of the Fifth International Conference on Operations Research, pp 447–454

Bixby RE, Ceria S, McZeal CM, Savelsbergh MW (1998) An updated mixed integer programming library: Miplib 3. Tech. Rep. TR98-03, Rice University

Derpich I, Vera JR (2006) Improving the efficiency of branch and bound algorithm for integer programming based on "flatness" information. European Journal of Operational Research 174:92–101

Dolan ED, Moré JJ (2002) Benchmarking optimization software with performance profiles. Mathematical Programming 91:201–213

Fischetti M, Lodi A (2003) Local branching. Mathematical Programming 98:23–47, series B

HW Lenstra J (1983) Integer programming with a fixed number of variables. Mathematics of Operations Research 8:538–548

Karamanov M, Cornuéjols G (2007) Branching on general disjunctions, working Paper

Krishnamoorthy B, Pataki G (2006) Column basis reduction and decomposable knapsack problems. Submitted, available at http://www.optimization-online.org/ DB_HTML/2007/06/1701.html

Linderoth J, Savelsbergh M (1999) A computational study of search strategies for mixed integer programming. INFORMS Journal on Computing 11: 173–187

Mahajan A, Ralphs TK (2008) On the complexity of branching on general hyperplanes for integer programming. Working paper

Mittelmann H (2008) Mixed integer LP problems. Available at http://plato.la.asu. edu/ftp/milp/

Nemhauser GL, Wolsey LA (1988) Integer and Combinatorial Optimization. John Wiley & Sons, Inc.

Owen JH, Mehrotra S (2001) Experimental results on using general disjunctions in branch-and-bound for general-integer linear programs. Computational optimization and applications 20(2)

Sebő A (1999) An introduction to empty lattice simplices. In: Proceedings of the 7th International IPCO Conference on Integer Programming and Combinatorial Optimization, LNCS, pp 400–414

Part 2.2
Heuristics and Metaheuristics

A Weight Annealing Algorithm for Solving Two-dimensional Bin Packing Problems

Kok-Hua Loh[1], Bruce Golden[2], and Edward Wasil[3]

[1] School of Mechanical & Aerospace Engineering
Nanyang Technological University, Singapore 639798
khloh@ntu.edu.sg

[2] Robert H. Smith School of Business
Department of Decision and Information Technologies
University of Maryland, College Park, MD 20742
bgolden@rhsmith.umd.edu

[3] Kogod School of Business
American University, Washington, DC 20016
ewasil@american.edu

Summary. Weight annealing is a metaheuristic that has been recently proposed in the physics literature. We develop a weight annealing-based algorithm for solving four variants of the two-dimensional bin packing problem. We apply our algorithm to 500 benchmark instances and find that it quickly produces very high-quality solutions that are comparable to the best published results.

Key words: Two-dimensional bin packing; weight annealing; heuristics

1 Introduction

In the two-dimensional bin packing problem (denoted by 2BP), we have n rectangular items and each item has a specified width and height. We need to pack the items into a minimum number of identical bins that have width W and height H. The items have to be packed with their edges parallel to the edges of the bins and no two items can overlap.

Items may have a fixed orientation (O) or they may be rotated (R) through $90°$. There may be guillotine cutting (G) that produces items through a sequence of edge-to-edge cuts that are parallel to the edges of a bin or the cutting may be free (F). Lodi, Martello, and Vigo (1999b) proposed the following typology for two-dimensional bin packing problems: 2BP|O|G (items oriented, guillotine cutting required); 2BP|R|G (items rotated, guillotine cutting required); 2BP|O|F (items oriented, free cutting); 2BP|R|F (items rotated, free cutting). The authors mentioned

J.W. Chinneck et al. (eds.), *Operations Research and Cyber-Infrastructure*, Operations Research/Computer Science Interfaces Series 47, DOI: 10.1007/978-0-387-88843-9_7,
© Springer Science+Business Media, LLC 2009

industrial contexts of each problem including the application of 2BP|O|F to the placement of advertisements in newspapers.

Over the last eight years or so, several methods have been developed to solve each of the two-dimensional bin packing problems (all four variants are NP-hard). A good overview of methods for solving the 2BP developed through the late 1990s and early 2000s including descriptions of upper and lower bounds, exact algorithms, and metaheuristics is given by Lodi, Martello, and Vigo (2002).

Lodi, Martello, and Vigo (1999a) developed a tabu search algorithm for solving 2BP|O|G and applied their algorithm to problem instances taken from the literature including those proposed by Berkey and Wang (1987). The authors found that the solutions of tabu search were closer to known lower bounds than solutions produced by two well-known procedures (finite first-fit and finite best strip). Lodi, Martello, and Vigo (1999b) developed a unified tabu search framework (TS) for solving each of the four problems. They considered 10 classes of problems - six from Berkey and Wang (1987) and four from Martello and Vigo (1998) - and found that TS was effective in all cases. Faroe, Pisinger, and Zachariasen (2003) presented a heuristic based on guided local search (GLS) that solved both the three-dimensional and the two-dimensional bin packing problems. GLS produced solutions that were as good as those produced by TS on the 10 classes of two-dimensional problems. Monaci and Toth (2006) solved the 10 problem classes for the 2BP|O|F variant using a set covering heuristic (SCH). They compared SCH to the exact algorithm (EA) of Martello and Vigo (2001), the constructive algorithm (HBP) of Boschetti and Mingozzi (2003), TS, and GLS. The authors concluded that SCH is very competitive with the best procedures found in the literature.

In this paper, we propose an algorithm based on the concept of weight annealing (WA) to solve the four variants of 2BP. Weight annealing is a new metaheuristic that we have used to solve the one-dimensional bin packing problem (Loh, Golden, and Wasil (2008)). In Section 2, we briefly describe weight annealing. In Sections 3 and 4, we present our algorithms for solving problems with guillotine cuts (2BP|O|G and 2BP|R|G) and free cuts (2BP|O|F and 2BP|R|F), respectively. In Section 5, we conduct extensive computational experiments using 10 classes of problems, report results for all four variants, and compare our results to those found in the literature. In Section 6, we summarize our contributions.

What is noteworthy here is that we have taken a new metaheuristic (weight annealing) and, with moderate effort, applied it to two-dimensional bin packing problems, and obtained high-quality solutions that are comparable to the best results reported in the literature.

2 Weight Annealing

Ninio and Schneider (2005) proposed a weight annealing algorithm that allows a greedy heuristic to escape from a poor local optimum. Their algorithm assigns variable weights to different parts of the solution space and has four steps.

Step 1. Start with an initial configuration from a greedy heuristic solution using the original problem landscape.

Step 2. Determine a new set of weights based on the previous optimization run and insight into the problem.

Step 3. Perform a new run of the greedy heuristic using the new weights.

Step 4. Return to Step 2 until a stopping criterion is met.

Ninio and Schneider applied their weight annealing algorithm to five benchmark traveling salesman problems with 127 to 1,379 nodes and produced results that were comparable to the results of simulated annealing. The notion of changing the landscape to produce high-quality solutions to combinatorial optimization problems has been incorporated into several approaches including search space smoothing (Coy, Golden, Runger, and Wasil (1998)) and noising (Charon and Hudry (1993)).

3 Weight Annealing Algorithm for Problems with Guillotine Cuts

In this section, we describe the three phases of our weight annealing algorithm for solving 2BP|O|G and 2BP|R|G. We highlight key features of our algorithm including the initial solution, objective function, item swap (exchange) schemes, and weight assignments for solving 2BP|O|G. We describe the modifications to our algorithm that are needed to solve 2BP|R|G.

3.1 Phase 1

3.1.1 Initial Solution

We construct an initial solution using a hybrid first-fit procedure (HFF) from Chung, Garey, and Johnson (1982) that we have modified in the following way. We order the items by non-increasing height and select an item for packing with probability 0.5. In other words, we start with the first item on the ordered list and, based on a coin toss, we pack it into a bin if it is selected, or leave it on the ordered list if it is not selected. We continue down the ordered list until an item is selected for packing. We then go to the top of the ordered list and pack the second item in the same manner, and so on, until we reach the bottom of the list.

3.1.2 Objective Function for the Local Search

Using HFF, we pack items into horizontal levels where each level has width b_i and $b_i \leq W$ (bin width). To help minimize the total number of levels that are used, we swap (exchange) items between levels with an objective function that maximizes the sum of the squared level widths b_i, where $b_i = \sum_{j=1}^{m_i} t_{ij}$, m_i is the number of items in level i, and t_{ij} is the width of item j in level i. In the local search, we accept a swap between level i and level k if it results in an increase in $b_i^2 + b_k^2$. Our objective function is given by

$$maximize \; f = \sum_{i=1}^{p} b_i^2 \qquad (1)$$

where p is the number of levels. Our objective function is motivated by the one developed by Fleszar and Hindi (2002) for the one-dimensional bin packing problem.

We illustrate our objective function in Figure 1. We have two levels and we move item C from level 2 to level 1. This move results in the use of one less level, does not violate the bin width constraint of 10, and increases the objective function value from 68 to 100. We denote the swap of one item between levels as Swap (1,0). This type of swap was proposed by Fleszar and Hindi (2002) for moving one item between bins in a one-dimensional bin packing problem. We point out that Fleszar and Hindi also proposed Swap (1,1) which exchanges one item from a bin with one item from a different bin.

The objective function (1) is equivalent to minimizing the number of levels, but does not attempt to reduce the unused area in each level (this is a key weakness of HFF). We would like our objective function to minimize the number of levels used and also minimize the sum of the heights of the levels. We accomplish this with the following objective function

$$maximize \; f = \sum_{i=1}^{p} b_i^2 - \sum_{i=1}^{p} (Wh_i - A_i) \qquad (2)$$

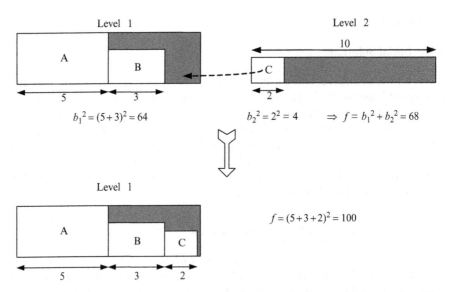

Fig. 1. Moving one item between two levels (called Swap (1,0)) uses one less level and increases the objective function value

where h_i is the height of level i and A_i is the sum of the areas of all items in bin i (that is, $A_i = \sum_{j=1}^{m_i} a_{ij}$ where m_i is the number of items in level i and a_{ij} is the area of item j in level i).

To summarize, in Phase 1 using the objective function (2), we try to pack all of the items into a minimum number of levels with minimum wasted space. Our local search procedure uses three types of swaps: Swap (1,0), Swap (1,1), and Swap (1, 2) (swap one item from a level with two items from a different level).

3.2 Phase 2

Using the solution produced in Phase 1, we apply a first-fit decreasing algorithm to generate an initial solution for the one-dimensional bin packing problem with items of size h_{ij}, where h_{ij} is the height of level j in bin i, and bins of height H. Let d_i be the stack height which is the sum of the heights of the levels in each bin. In order to minimize the total number of bins, we use swap schemes that exchange levels between all pairs of bins with an objective function that maximizes the sum of the squares of stack heights d_i, where $d_i = \sum_{j=1}^{m_i} h_{ij}$, and m_i is the number of levels in bin i. In the local search, we accept a swap between level i and level k if it results in an increase in $d_i^2 + d_k^2$. Our objective function is given by

$$maximize\ f = \sum_{i=1}^{q} d_i^2 \qquad (3)$$

where q is the number of bins. As in Phase 1, we use the three swap schemes (Swap(1,0), Swap(1,1), and Swap(1,2)) between all pairs of bins.

3.3 Phase 3

This phase can be regarded as post-optimization in which we try to fill unused space. We look at unused space within a level and the unused space at the top of a bin.

In order to fill the unused space within a level, we partition the level with a grid system that preserves the guillotine cutting constraint. In Figure 2, we show four ways of partitioning the unused space. In option 1, there are vertical partitions that originate from the top of each item. In option 2, there are horizontal partitions at the top right of each item. In option 3, both vertical and horizontal partitions are used. In option 4, there is a horizontal partition at the top of the level and vertical partitions beneath it. We select option 4 as it has partitions of varying dimensions to accommodate items of differing lengths and widths. We allow a feasible move to occupy a partition starting at its left edge or the remaining space to the right of an item already in that partition, but not the space above the item. In Figure 2, option 4, we show four items that have been moved in this way to fill unused space.

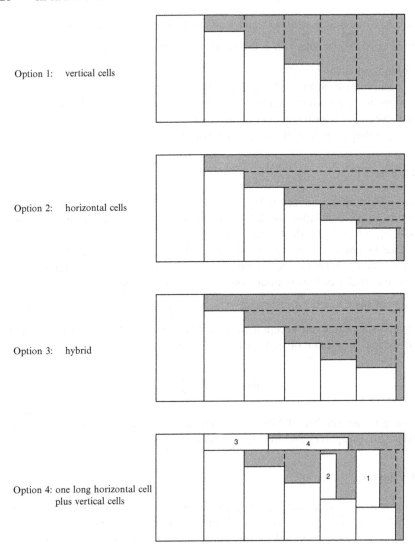

Option 1:   vertical cells

Option 2:   horizontal cells

Option 3:   hybrid

Option 4: one long horizontal cell
          plus vertical cells

Fig. 2. Four ways of partitioning unused space within a level

In the local search, our objective function is given by

$$maximize \ f = \sum_{i=1}^{q} A_i^2 \qquad (4)$$

where q is the number of bins and A_i is the sum of the areas of all items in bin i. For ease of implementation, we use only Swap (1,0) moves. Within each partition, only the remaining space to the right of an item can be filled up by additional items. In other words, the first item that we move to fill an empty space will have its left edge

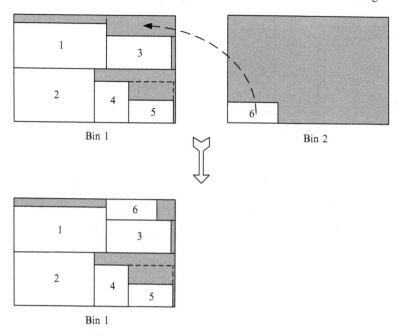

Fig. 3. Moving one item between bins to fill unused space

touching the left side of the partition. The next item will have its left edge touching the right edge of the first item and so on, as along as the sum of the item widths does not exceed the width of the partition.

We use the objective function in (4) and Swap (1,0) moves to fill the unused space at the top of a bin. We illustrate this type of move in Figure 3.

3.4 Weight Annealing

In our algorithm, we assign different weights to the bins and levels, and their items according to how well the bins and levels are packed. This distortion of item sizes allows for both uphill and downhill moves and is a key feature of our algorithm.

3.4.1 Weight Assignments

In Phase 1, for each level i, we assign weight w_i^T according to

$$w_i^T = (1 + Kr_i)^T \tag{5}$$

where W is the width of each bin, b_i is the width of level i, K is a constant, T is a temperature parameter, and the residual capacity of level i is $r_i = (W - b_i)/W$. The scaling parameter K controls the amount of size distortion for each item. K is typically set to a small value (e.g., 0.01). The size distortion for an item is proportional to the residual capacity of its level.

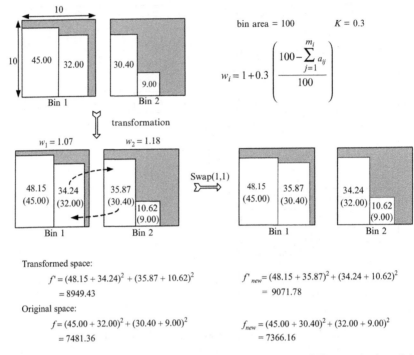

Fig. 4. A feasible uphill move in the transformed space is a downhill move in the original space

In Phase 2, for bin i, we compare the bin height H to the stack height d_i and assign weight w_i^T according to (5) where the residual capacity of bin i is $r_i = (H - d_i)/H$.

In Phase 3, for bin i, we compare A_i (the sum of the areas of all items in bin i) to the available bin area (HW) and assign weight w_i^T according to (5) where the residual capacity of bin i is $r_i = (HW - A_i)/(HW)$.

The use of weights increases the sizes of items in poorly packed bins and helps our algorithm to escape a poor local maximum through downhill moves. We illustrate this in Figure 4 where the bin area is 100, $K = 0.3$, and $T = 1$, and we make a Swap (1,1) move. We see that we have an uphill move in the transformed space (the objective function value increases) which is actually a downhill move in the original space (the objective function value decreases). We make a move as long as it is feasible in the original space. (We point out that, after the transformation, but before the swap, item sizes in bin 1 are 48.15 = 1.07 x 45 and 34.24 = 1.07 x 32.)

3.4.2 Weight Annealing Algorithm

In Table 1, we give our weight annealing algorithm for both variants of the two-dimensional bin packing problem with guillotine cuts (2BP|O|G, 2BP|R|G). We denote our algorithm by WA2BPG.

Table 1. Weight annealing algorithm for 2BP|O|G and 2BP|R|G

Step 0. Initialization.

 Parameters are K (scaling parameter), *nloop1, nloop2, nloop3, T* (temperature), and *Tred*.

 Set $K = 0.05$, *nloop1* = 20, *nloop2* = 100, *nloop3* = 50, $T = 1$, and *Tred* = 0.95.

 Inputs are height and width of each item, height and width of a bin, and lower bound (*LB*).

Step 1. Optimization runs.

 for $k = 1$: *nloop1* do

 Step 1.1 Perform Phase 1

  Construct an initial solution using modified hybrid first-fit procedure.

  set $T := 1$

  for $j = 1$: *nloop2* do

   Compute weight of level $i := w_i^T$ and weighted width of item j for all j.

   Do for all pairs of levels {

    Swap items between two levels.

    Allow item rotations for 2BP|R|G.

     Perform Swap (1,0).

     Perform Swap (1,1).

     Perform Swap (1,2).

   }

   $T := T \times Tred$

  end

 Step 1.2 Perform Phase 2

  set $T := 1$

  for $j = 1$: *nloop3* do

   Compute weight of bin $i := w_i^T$ and weighted height of level j for all j.

   Do for all pairs of bins {

    Swap levels between two bins.

     Perform Swap (1,0), exit j loop and k loop if *LB* is reached.

     Perform Swap (1,1), exit j loop and k loop if *LB* is reached.

     Perform Swap (1,2), exit j loop and k loop if *LB* is reached.

   }

   $T := T \times Tred$

  end

 Step 1.3 Perform Phase 3

  Determine the locations and sizes of the partitions.

  set $T := 1$

  for $j = 1$: nloop3 do

   Compute weight of bin i = wiT and weighted area of item j for all j.

   Do for all pairs of bins {

    Perform Swap (1,0), exit j loop and k loop if LB is reached.

    Allow item rotations for 2BP|R|G.

   }

  $T := T \times Tred$

  end

 end

Step 2. Outputs are the number of bins and the final distribution of items.

In Phase 1, WA2BPG starts with an initial solution that is generated by our modified hybrid first-fit procedure. Swapping operations with weight annealing are used to improve a solution. A temperature parameter (T) controls the amount by which a single weight can be varied. At the start, a high temperature $(T = 1)$ allows for higher frequencies of downhill moves. As the temperature is gradually cooled (the temperature is reduced via the parameter $Tred$ at the end of every iteration, that is, $T \times 0.95$), the amount of item distortion decreases and the problem space looks more like the original problem space. The lower bound is defined in Section 5.2.

We compute a weight for each level (according to $w_i^T = (1 + Kr_i)^T$) and then apply the weight to the width of each item in the level. The swapping process begins by comparing the items in the first level with the items in the second level, and so on, sequentially down to the last level in the initial solution and is repeated for every possible pair of levels.

For a current pair of levels (α, β), the swapping of items by Swap $(1,0)$ is carried out as follows. The algorithm evaluates whether the first item (item i) in level α can be moved to level β without violating the width constraint of level β in the original space. In other words, does level β have enough original residual capacity to accommodate the original width of item i? If the answer is yes (the move is feasible), the change in objective function value of the move in the transformed space is evaluated. If the change in objective function value is nonnegative, then item i is moved from level α to level β. After this move, the algorithm exits Swap $(1,0)$ and proceeds to Swap $(1,1)$. If the move of the first item is infeasible or the change in objective function value is negative, then the second item in level α is evaluated and so on, until a feasible move with a nonnegative change in objective function value is found or all items in level α have been considered and no feasible move with a nonnegative change has been found. The algorithm then performs Swap $(1,1)$ followed by Swap $(1,2)$. In each of the swapping schemes, we always make the first feasible swap that has a nonnegative change in the objective function value. We point out that the improvement step is carried out 100 times $(nloop2 = 100)$ starting with $T = 1$, followed by $T = 1 \times 0.95 = 0.95$, $T = 0.95 \times 0.95 = 0.9025$, etc.

In Phase 2, we solve a one dimensional bin packing problem treating each level as an item with size (height) h_{ij}. For bin i, we compute the stack height $d_i = \sum_{j=1}^{m_i} h_{ij}$, the residual capacity (r_i) based on the bin height H, and its weight w_i. We apply the same weight to all levels in the bin. We swap levels between bins. The improvement step is carried out 50 times $(nloop3 = 50)$ or until the lower bound is reached (we discuss the lower bounds in more detail in Section 5 on computational results).

In Phase 3, we try to move one item between bins to fill unused space. We start by determining the locations and sizes of unused space. For each bin i, we compute A_i (the sum of the areas of all items in bin i), the residual capacity r_i, and the weight w_i for each bin, and apply the same weight to all items in bin i. The improvement step is carried out 50 times $(nloop3 = 50)$ or until the lower bound is reached.

If we have not obtained the lower bound at the end of the first optimization run, we start another run with a new initial solution generated by our modified hybrid first-fit algorithm in Phase 1. We terminate the algorithm as soon as the lower bound is reached or after 20 runs (*nloop1* = 20).

3.4.3 Weight Annealing Algorithm for Problems with Non-oriented Items

We now describe the modifications to our algorithm that are needed to solve problems with items that can be rotated. WA2BPG solves the 2BP|R|G instances by allowing item rotations during Phase 1 and Phase 3.

During Phase 1, we allow for the rotation of an item through 90° to minimize the unused space within each level and each bin. In order to reduce computation time, we allow for only a feasible move to occupy a partition starting from its left edge or the remaining space to the right of an item already in the partition, but not the space above the item. We would like to rotate an item through 90° if this produces a tighter fit or results in a greater utilization of the unused space above an item that has its original orientation. We illustrate rotating two items in Figure 5. These rotations free a substantial amount of space to the right of the two items and this space can now be used by other items. In WA2BPG, during Phase 1, we allow an item rotation if it reduces a level's width (b_i), or if it results in a feasible swap with a nonnegative change in the objective function value.

During Phase 3 of WA2BPG for 2BP|O|G, an item from one bin will be moved into the unused space within a level or at the top of a bin if the move is feasible and improving. In Figure 6, item 6 is moved from bin 2 to bin 1 and now occupies two types of unused spaces – within a level and at the top of a bin.

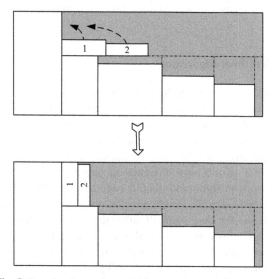

Fig. 5. Rotating items through 90 to produce a tighter packing

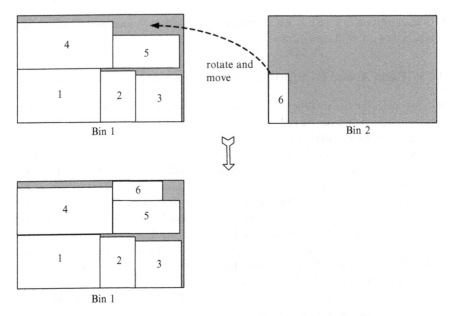

Fig. 6. Rotating an item through 90 and moving it to another bin

4 Weight Annealing Algorithm for Problems with Free Cuts

In this section, we describe our weight annealing algorithm for solving 2BP|O|F and 2BP|R|F.

4.1 Alternate Directions Algorithm

For problems with free cuts, Lodi, Martello, and Vigo (1999b) developed an alternate directions algorithm that exploited non-guillotine patterns by packing items in alternate directions. We adopt this feature for packing bins in our weight annealing algorithm. Specifically, we sort items by non-increasing height and then pack bands of items in alternate directions. We start by packing the first band from left to right at the bottom of a bin using a best-fit decreasing strategy. The first item in this band is placed in the lowest position with its left edge touching the left edge of the bin. The second item is placed in the lowest position with its left edge touching the right edge of the first item. We then pack all subsequent items in the same way as the second item until no items can be inserted into the band. In this way, we have produced the first left-to-right band. We now pack items in the opposite direction with the first right-to-left band above the first left-to-right band in the lowest position. We continue to pack items in alternate directions as long as the bin height constraint is not violated, or the stack height, which is defined as the top edge of the highest item amongst the stack of items in the bin, is less than the bin height. In Figure 7, we

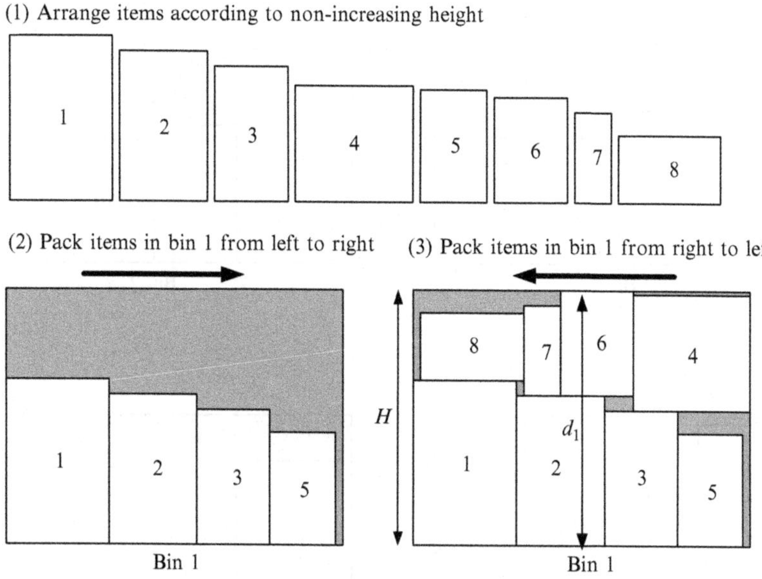

(1) Arrange items according to non-increasing height

(2) Pack items in bin 1 from left to right   (3) Pack items in bin 1 from right to left

Fig. 7. Packing items using the alternate directions algorithm

show how items are packed using the alternate-directions algorithm. We see that the stack height of items in bin 1 (this is the sum of the heights of item 2 and item 6) is $d_1 \leq H$.

4.2 Initial Solution

A feasible solution to 2BP|O|G is also a feasible solution to 2BP|O|F. We use the final solution to 2BP|O|G produced by WA2BPG as our initial solution.

4.3 Objective Function for the Local Search

In the local search, our objective function is given by

$$maximize \; f = \sum_{i=1}^{q} A_i^2 \tag{6}$$

where q is the number of bins and A_i is the sum of the areas of all items in bin i.

We select a pair of bins, swap items between bins (we can use Swap (1,0), Swap (1,1), and Swap (1,2)), and then repack each bin with the alternate directions algorithm. If a swap between bins is feasible and results in a nonnegative change in the objective function value, then we make the move. If not, we select another pair of bins for evaluation and continue for all pairs of bins. In Figure 8, we move one item from bin 1 to bin 2 with Swap (1,0), resulting in an increase in the objective

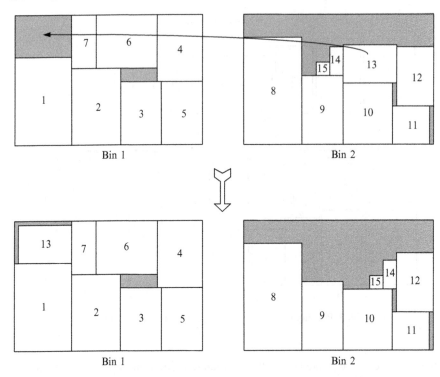

Fig. 8. Moving an item from bin 2 to bin 1 and then repacking bin 2

function value. We then repack bin 2 to increase the residual space for subsequent swaps. There is no need to repack bin 1 as item 13 is the last item to be moved in the alternative directions algorithm.

4.4 Weight Assignments

Clearly, for a solution to be feasible, we must have its stack height less than the bin height. For bin i, we compare the bin height H to the stack height d_i and assign weight w_i^T according to (5) where the residual capacity of bin i is $r_i = (H - d_i)/H$.

4.5 Post-optimization Processing

When packing items into a bin with the alternative directions algorithm, there can be dead spaces created in the bin. In Figure 9, we show an example of three dead spaces in bin 1. In a post-optimization process, we determine the coordinates and dimensions of these dead spaces and we try to fill them with a Swap (1,0) move. We use Swap (1,0) to move item 15 from bin 2 to the dead space in bin 1. We make this type of move in order to empty a less-filled bin ($A_2 < A_1$) which results in a larger objective function value.

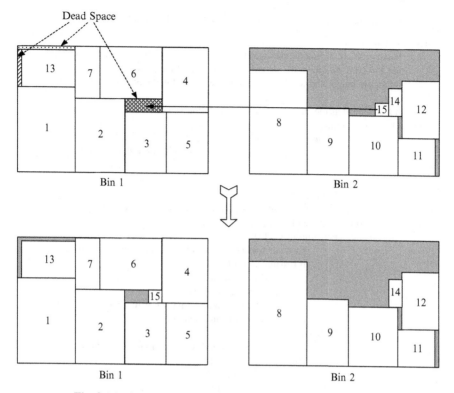

Fig. 9. Moving an item from bin 2 to bin 1 to occupy a dead space

4.6 Weight Annealing Algorithm

In Table 2, we give our weight annealing algorithm for both variants of the two-dimensional bin packing problem with free cuts (2BP|O|F, 2BP|R|F). We denote our algorithm by WA2BPF.

We point out that the solution generated by our algorithm to 2BP|O|F is a feasible solution to 2BP|R|F. To handle non-oriented items, we modify the post-optimization process to allow rotations of items through 90° to fill up dead spaces in a bin. In Figure 9, instead of moving item 15, we can now rotate item 14 and move it into the dead space between items 3 and 6. This produces a better packing and an increase in the objective function value.

5 Computational Results

5.1 Test Problems

In Table 3, we describe the six classes of randomly generated benchmark test problems from Berkey and Wang (1987). The height and width of an item are selected

Table 2. Weight Annealing Algorithm for 2BP|O|F and 2BP|R|F

Step 0. Initialization.

    Parameters are K (scaling parameter), *nloop1*, *nloop2*, T (temperature), and *Tred*.

    Set $K = 0.05$, *nloop1* = 20, *nloop2* = 50, $T = 1$, and *Tred* = 0.95.

    Inputs are height and width of each item, height and width of a bin, and lower bound (*LB*).

    Δf is defined as the change in objective function value.

Step 1. Optimization runs.

    for $k = 1$: *nloop1* **do**

        Construct an initial solution using the 2BP|O|G algorithm, exit k loop if *LB* is reached.

        Set $T := 1$

        for $j = 1$: *nloop2* **do**

        Compute weight of bin $i := w_i^T$ and weighted area of item j for all j.

        Do for all pairs of bins {

            Perform Swap (1,0).

                Evaluate feasibility and Δf of alternate directions packing.

                if feasible and $\Delta f \geq 0$

                    Swap the item.

                    Exit Swap (1,0) and

                    Exit k loop and j loop if *LB* is reached.

                else restore the original solution.

            Perform Swap (1,1).

                Evaluate feasibility and Δf of alternate directions packing,

                if feasible and $\Delta f \geq 0$

                    Swap the items.

                    Exit Swap (1,0) and

                    Exit k loop and j loop if *LB* is reached.

                else restore the original solution.

            Perform Swap (1,2).

                Evaluate feasibility and Δf of alternate directions packing.

                if feasible and $\Delta f \geq 0$

                    Swap the items.

                    Exit Swap (1,0) and

                    Exit k loop and j loop if *LB* is reached.

                else restore the original solution.

        }

        $T := T \times Tred$

        end

        Compute the sizes and coordinates of the dead spaces in all bins.

        Do for all pairs of bins. {

        Perform Swap (1,0).

            Evaluate feasibility and allow item rotations for 2BP|R|F.

            if feasible and $\Delta f \geq 0$

                Move the item.

                Exit k loop and j loop if *LB* is reached.

        }

    end

Step 2. Outputs are the number of bins and the final distribution of items.

Table 3. Six classes of problems from Berkey and Wang (1987)

Class	Item height, width	Bin height (H), width (W)
I	U[1, 10]	10
II	U[1, 10]	30
III	U[1, 35]	40
IV	U[1, 35]	100
V	U[1, 100]	100
VI	U[1, 100]	300

Table 4. Four classes of problems from Martello and Vigo (1998)

	Type Probabilities (%)			
Class	1	2	3	4
VII	70	10	10	10
VIII	10	70	10	10
IX	10	10	70	10
X	10	10	10	70

Type	Item width	Item height
1	U[2/3W, W]	U[1, 1/2H]
2	U[1, 1/2W]	U[2/3H, H]
3	U[1/2W, W]	U[1/2H, H]
4	U[1, 1/2W]	U[1, 1/2H]

$H = W = 100$

from a uniform distribution. The height and width of a bin are the same value (e.g., in Class I, a bin has $H = W = 10$). For each class, we set $n = 20, 40, 60, 80, 100$ and generate 10 instances; this produces 300 test instances.

In Table 4, we describe the four classes of randomly generated benchmark test problems from Martello and Vigo (1998). There are four types of items where the height and width of an item are selected from a uniform distribution with $H = W = 100$. Each class of problems is a mixture of the four item types (e.g., 70% of the items in Class VII are Type 1). For each class, we set $n = 20, 40, 60, 80, 100$ and generate 10 instances; this produces 200 test instances. Overall, we have a total of 500 test instances (the test problems of Berkey and Wang (1987) and Martello and Vigo (1998) are available at http://www.or.deis.unibo.it/research.html.)

5.2 Results for 2BP|O|F

We coded WA2BPF and WA2BPG in C/C++ and solved test problems on a 3 GHz Pentium 4 computer with 256 MB of RAM.

We start with 2BP|O|F since most of the published results pertain to this variant. However, it is not a straightforward task to compare results, given the way they have been reported in the literature.

Lodi, Martello, and Vigo (1999b) reported the *average ratios* for tabu search (TS solution value/ lower bound) for 10 problem instances computed on the 10 classes of problems, but did not provide the lower bounds they used. Furthermore, these ratios are different from the values reported in Lodi, Martello, and Vigo (1999a).

Faroe, Pisinger, and Zachariasen (2003) reported the *number of bins used* by GLS for the 10 classes, but no running times. They also gave the number of bins used by TS from Lodi, Martello, and Vigo (1999b) (although this paper reported only average ratios). Faroe, Pisinger, and Zachariasen also gave the lower bounds they say were reported in Lodi, Martello, and Vigo (1999a) (although this paper provided no such bounds).

Monaci and Toth (2006) thanked various researchers for providing "results, for each 2DBP instance, of their algorithms." Monaci and Toth (2006) reported the number of bins used by TS for the 10 problem classes. These results do not agree with the TS results given in Faroe, Pisinger, and Zachariasen (2003) (the TS results in Monaci and Toth are slightly better; perhaps they were updated through private communication with Lodi, Martello, and Vigo; however, the computation times for TS reported by Monaci and Toth are *exactly* the same as the times reported in Lodi, Martello, and Vigo (1999b)). Monaci and Toth (2006) provided lower bounds for each problem.

In Table 5, we show results from the literature for five algorithms and results for WA2BPF for the 10 classes of 2BP|O|F problems. In order to bring some consistency to our comparison of results, here are the bounds and algorithms given in Table 5.

LLMV	Lower bounds based on Lodi, Martello, and Vigo (1999a) that are given in Faroe, Pisinger, and Zachariasen (2003).
LB*	Lower bounds that are given in Monaci and Toth (2006).
TS	Tabu search results obtained by Lodi, Martello, and Vigo (1999b) that are given in Faroe, Pisinger, and Zachariasen (2003).
GLS	Guided local search results that are given in Faroe, Pisinger, and Zachariasen (2003).
EA	Exact algorithm results that are given in Monaci and Toth (2006). Monaci and Toth "ran the corresponding code [of Martello and Vigo (2001)] on [their] machine."
HBP(TL)	Constructive algorithm results that are given in Monaci and Toth (2006). This is Monaci and Toth's implementation of the the algorithm of Boschetti and Mingozzi (2003) with a time limit for computation.
SCH	Set covering heuristic results that are given in Monaci and Toth (2006).

In Table 5, for all 500 test instances, we see that SCH used 7,248 bins, closely followed by WA2BPF with 7,253 bins and HBP with 7,265 bins. GLS, EA, and TS needed more than 7,300 bins. The total number of bins used by SCH and WA2BPF are about 2.6% and 1.1% above the total number of bins for the lower bounds L_{LMV} and LB^*, respectively. Although the computers are different, WA2BPF and SCH are fast, taking 119.33 seconds and 148.46 seconds, respectively, to solve all 500 test

Table 5. Number of bins and running times for six algorithms that solve 10 classes of 2BP|O|F problems

Class	n	L_{LMV}	LB*	TS		GLS	EA	
				Bins	Time(s)	Bins	Bins	Time(s)
I	20	67	71	71	24.00	71	71	0.01
	40	128	134	136	36.11	134	134	4.62
	60	193	197	201	48.93	201	201	21.01
	80	269	274	282	48.17	275	275	15.01
	100	314	317	327	60.81	321	322	24.07
II	20	10	10	10	0.01	10	10	0.00
	40	19	19	21	0.01	19	20	3.00
	60	25	25	28	0.09	25	27	6.00
	80	31	31	33	12.00	32	34	9.00
	100	39	39	40	6.00	39	40	3.00
III	20	46	51	55	54.00	51	51	0.01
	40	88	92	98	54.02	95	95	12.01
	60	133	136	140	45.67	140	140	15.04
	80	184	187	199	54.31	193	195	24.01
	100	217	221	237	60.10	229	228	27.70
IV	20	10	10	10	0.01	10	10	0.00
	40	19	19	19	0.01	19	20	3.00
	60	23	23	26	0.14	25	27	12.00
	80	30	30	33	18.00	33	33	9.00
	100	37	37	38	6.00	39	40	9.00
V	20	60	65	67	36.02	65	65	0.01
	40	114	119	119	27.07	119	119	5.39
	60	172	179	182	56.77	181	180	15.19
	80	236	241	250	56.18	250	249	27.00
	100	273	279	295	60.34	288	286	27.01
VI	20	10	10	10	0.01	10	10	0.00
	40	15	15	21	0.03	18	19	12.00
	60	21	21	22	0.04	22	22	3.01
	80	30	30	30	0.01	30	30	0.01
	100	32	32	34	12.00	34	35	9.01
VII	20	53	55	55	12.02	55	55	0.06
	40	108	109	114	37.01	113	111	11.58
	60	155	156	163	36.44	161	162	18.00
	80	223	224	232	54.52	233	234	30.00
	100	268	269	276	47.43	276	276	21.00

(continued)

Table 5. (continued)

| | | | | TS | | GLS | EA | |
Class	n	L_{LMV}	LB*	Bins	Time(s)	Bins	Bins	Time(s)
VIII	20	55	58	58	18.04	58	58	0.00
	40	111	112	114	18.72	114	113	6.00
	60	159	159	162	20.99	163	164	15.00
	80	222	223	226	37.95	228	226	12.01
	100	273	274	284	52.66	282	281	21.00
IX	20	143	143	143	0.01	143	143	0.00
	40	274	278	277	24.05	278	278	0.01
	60	433	437	437	24.26	437	437	0.12
	80	569	577	575	54.31	577	577	3.51
	100	689	695	696	34.11	695	695	12.80
X	20	40	42	44	12.00	42	42	0.05
	40	71	74	75	25.18	74	74	2.28
	60	97	98	104	42.13	102	103	16.86
	80	123	123	130	47.30	130	132	28.29
	100	153	153	165	60.10	163	164	30.00
Total		7064	7173	7364	1436.09	7302	7313	524.69

| | | | | HBP(TL) | | SCH | | WA2BPF | |
Class	n	L_{LMV}	LB*	Bins	Time(s)	Bins	Time(s)	Bins	Time(s)
I	20	67	71	71	3.08	71	0.07	71	0.21
	40	128	134	134	9.68	134	3.93	134	0.06
	60	193	197	201	12.12	200	2.50	200	0.67
	80	269	274	275	3.08	275	2.50	275	3.07
	100	314	317	319	6.33	317	3.38	317	9.21
II	20	10	10	10	0.06	10	0.06	10	0.05
	40	19	19	19	0.46	19	0.31	20	0.04
	60	25	25	25	0.07	25	0.07	25	0.43
	80	31	31	31	0.48	31	0.07	31	13.89
	100	39	39	39	0.26	39	0.37	39	8.70
III	20	46	51	51	6.28	51	0.07	53	0.04
	40	88	92	94	6.48	94	1.10	94	2.15
	60	133	136	140	12.14	139	2.66	139	0.16
	80	184	187	190	9.93	190	6.09	189	3.16
	100	217	221	225	12.59	223	5.10	224	7.52
IV	20	10	10	10	0.07	10	0.06	10	0.05
	40	19	19	19	0.08	19	0.07	19	0.14
	60	23	23	25	6.13	25	1.86	25	0.05
	80	30	30	32	7.10	32	3.15	31	12.19
	100	37	37	38	4.04	38	2.32	38	0.36

(continued)

Table 5. (continued)

Class	n	L_{LMV}	LB*	HBP(TL)		SCH		WA2BPF	
				Bins	Time(s)	Bins	Time(s)	Bins	Time(s)
V	20	60	65	65	0.10	65	0.06	65	0.10
	40	114	119	119	9.31	119	1.21	119	0.17
	60	172	179	180	8.21	180	1.05	180	1.49
	80	236	241	248	18.80	247	8.82	247	2.66
	100	273	279	286	18.50	283	5.30	283	3.50
VI	20	10	10	10	0.07	10	0.07	10	0.04
	40	15	15	17	6.91	17	2.81	19	0.07
	60	21	21	21	0.16	21	0.35	22	0.05
	80	30	30	30	0.24	30	0.23	30	0.06
	100	32	32	34	6.39	34	2.75	33	21.00
VII	20	53	55	55	6.09	55	0.12	55	0.05
	40	108	109	112	10.25	111	1.41	111	2.12
	60	155	156	160	13.09	158	3.50	159	6.79
	80	223	224	232	24.24	232	15.71	232	0.27
	100	268	269	273	13.01	271	9.86	271	1.92
VIII	20	55	58	58	0.07	58	0.06	58	0.05
	40	111	112	113	3.47	113	0.49	113	0.21
	60	159	159	162	9.33	162	3.36	162	0.16
	80	222	223	225	6.36	224	3.90	224	0.33
	100	273	274	279	15.48	279	13.30	277	0.06
IX	20	143	143	143	0.06	143	0.06	143	0.19
	40	274	278	278	0.07	278	0.06	279	0.04
	60	433	437	437	0.08	437	0.07	438	0.12
	80	569	577	577	0.08	577	0.08	577	0.16
	100	689	695	695	0.11	695	0.11	695	0.23
X	20	40	42	42	4.78	42	0.12	43	0.29
	40	71	74	74	6.11	74	0.11	74	0.21
	60	97	98	102	16.13	101	4.20	102	0.16
	80	123	123	130	21.26	130	14.48	129	5.42
	100	153	153	160	26.63	160	19.07	159	9.26
Total		7064	7173	7265	345.85	7248	148.46	7253	119.33

TS	Silicon Graphics INDY R10000sc (195 MHz)
GLS	Digital 500au (500 MHz) with a 30 second time limit
EA, HBP(TL), SCH	Digital Alpha (533 MHz) with a 30 second time limit
WA2BPF	Pentium 4 (3 GHz)

instances. We point out that, in Class IX with $n = 40$, the TS solution of 277 reported by Faroe, Pisinger, and and Zachariasen (2003) is less than the lower bound of 278 given by Monaci and Toth (2006).

5.3 Results for 2BP|R|F

In Table 6, we show the results generated by WA2BPF on the 2BP|R|F problems (items can be rotated). WA2BPF used 7,222 bins and needed 66.66 seconds for all 500 test instances. Since the items can be rotated, 31 fewer bins were used when compared to the oriented solutions produced by WA2BPF that are given in Table 5.

Table 6. Number of bins and running times for WA2BPF on 10 classes of 2BP|R|F problems

Class	n	WA2BPF Bins	Time(s)	Class	n	WA2BPF Bins	Time(s)
I	20	71	0.21	VI	20	10	0.04
	40	134	0.06		40	19	0.07
	60	197	3.25		60	22	0.05
	80	274	0.25		80	30	0.06
	100	317	9.21		100	33	6.30
II	20	10	0.05	VII	20	55	0.05
	40	20	0.04		40	111	1.26
	60	25	0.11		60	156	4.31
	80	31	1.70		80	225	1.34
	100	39	1.50		100	269	1.87
III	20	52	0.04	VIII	20	58	0.05
	40	94	2.23		40	112	0.21
	60	138	0.16		60	159	0.17
	80	189	1.08		80	223	0.13
	100	224	3.12		100	274	0.57
IV	20	10	0.05	IX	20	143	0.10
	40	19	0.14		40	279	0.04
	60	25	0.05		60	438	0.12
	80	31	1.42		80	577	0.16
	100	38	0.36		100	695	0.23
V	20	65	0.10	X	20	43	0.29
	40	119	0.17		40	74	0.21
	60	180	0.66		60	101	5.96
	80	244	4.65		80	128	6.85
	100	283	2.17		100	159	3.44
				Total		7222	66.66

Lodi, Martello, and Vigo (1999b) published results produced by TS for the 10 classes of 2BP|R|F problems. They reported average ratio results. The lower bounds from an unpublished paper by Dell'Amico, Martello, and Vigo (1999) that were used by Lodi, Martello, and Vigo are not currently available, thereby making average ratio comparisons between WA2BPF and TS impossible.

5.4 Results for 2BP|O|G and 2BP|R|G

In Tables 7 and 8, we show the results generated by WA2BPG on the 2BP|O|G and 2BP|R|G problems. WA2BPG used 7,373 bins and needed 24.77 seconds to solve

Table 7. Number of bins and running times for WA2BPG on 10 classes of 2BP|O|G problems

Class	n	WA2BPG Bins	Time(s)	Class	n	WA2BPG Bins	Time(s)
I	20	72	0.12	VI	20	10	0.04
	40	137	0.06		40	19	0.07
	60	202	1.78		60	22	0.05
	80	277	0.72		80	30	0.06
	100	326	0.24		100	35	0.07
II	20	10	0.05	VII	20	56	0.07
	40	20	0.04		40	115	0.29
	60	26	0.41		60	164	0.22
	80	33	0.06		80	233	0.32
	100	40	0.07		100	275	0.27
III	20	54	0.04	VIII	20	60	0.06
	40	98	0.21		40	116	0.18
	60	143	0.94		60	163	0.60
	80	196	2.36		80	230	0.17
	100	230	2.28		100	283	0.17
IV	20	10	0.05	IX	20	143	0.19
	40	20	0.04		40	279	0.04
	60	26	0.06		60	438	0.12
	80	33	0.06		80	577	0.16
	100	39	0.19		100	695	0.23
V	20	67	0.04	X	20	44	0.15
	40	123	0.13		40	77	0.06
	60	185	0.35		60	105	0.12
	80	251	4.28		80	131	2.69
	100	291	3.45		100	164	0.34
				Total		7373	24.77

Table 8. Number of bins and running times for WA2BPG on 10 classes of 2BP|R|G problems

		WA2BPG				WA2BPG	
Class	n	Bins	Time(s)	Class	n	Bins	Time(s)
I	20	71	0.04	VI	20	10	0.04
	40	136	0.04		40	19	0.05
	60	201	3.47		60	22	0.05
	80	275	0.93		80	30	0.05
	100	323	0.37		100	34	1.96
II	20	10	0.04	VII	20	56	0.07
	40	20	0.24		40	110	0.83
	60	26	0.51		60	158	2.53
	80	32	0.88		80	227	1.21
	100	39	0.59		100	273	2.80
III	20	52	0.05	VIII	20	58	0.92
	40	95	0.24		40	113	0.07
	60	141	1.39		60	159	0.08
	80	193	0.81		80	223	1.97
	100	229	4.67		100	275	0.40
IV	20	10	0.05	IX	20	143	0.02
	40	19	0.80		40	278	0.05
	60	25	0.12		60	437	0.10
	80	33	0.06		80	577	0.15
	100	38	0.17		100	695	0.23
V	20	66	0.06	X	20	42	0.21
	40	120	0.48		40	74	0.08
	60	181	4.51		60	102	0.88
	80	248	3.35		80	130	0.33
	100	288	4.70		100	163	0.36
				Total		7279	44.01

the problems with oriented items, while it used 7,279 bins and needed 44.01 seconds to solve the problems with rotated items.

Lodi, Martello, and Vigo (1999b) published results produced by TS for the 10 classes of 2BP|O|G and 2BP|R|G problems. Again, comparisons based on average ratios cannot be made between WA2BPG and TS because the lower bounds used by Lodi, Martello, and Vigo were not published in their paper. Lodi, Martello, and Vigo (1998) published results produced by TS for 10 classes of 2BP|R|G problems. The ratios reported in the 1998 paper are different from the values reported in the 1999b paper. Lodi (2005) commented that the experiments in the two papers were run on different machines and probably with different parameter settings.

6 Conclusions

We developed an algorithm based on weight annealing that solved four variants of the two-dimensional bin packing problem. Overall, our algorithm produced high-quality results quickly. Specifically, with respect to oriented items and free cutting, our weight annealing algorithm generated results that were very comparable in terms of accuracy and computational speed to the best results found in the literature.

In summary, weight annealing is a straightforward, easy-to-implement meta-heuristic that produces very good results to bin packing problems. We expect to apply it to other combinatorial optimization problems in future work.

References

1. J. O. Berkey, P. Y. Wang. Two dimensional finite bin packing algorithms, *Journal of the Operational Research Society*, 38:423–429, 1987.
2. M. A. Boschetti, A. Mingozzi. Two-dimensional finite bin packing problems, *Part II: New upper and lower bounds*, 4OR, 2:135–147, 2003.
3. I. Charon, O. Hudry. The noising method: A new method for combinatorial optimization, *Operations Research Letters*, 14:133–137, 1993.
4. F. K. R. Chung, M. R. Garey, D. S. Johnson. On packing two-dimensional bins, *SIAM Journal on Algebraic and Discrete Methods*, 3:66–76, 1982.
5. S. Coy, B. Golden, G. Runger, E. Wasil. See the forest before the trees: Fine-tuned learning and its application to the traveling salesman problem, *IEEE Transactions on Systems, Man, and Cybernetics*, 28, 4:454–464, 1998.
6. M. Dell'Amico, S. Martello, D. Vigo, An exact algorithm for non-oriented two-dimensional bin packing problems, *in preparation*, 1999.
7. O. Faroe, D. Pisinger, M. Zachariasen, Guided local search for the three-dimensional bin-packing problem, *INFORMS Journal on Computing*, 15:267–283, 2003.
8. K. Fleszar, K. Hindi. New heuristics for one-dimensional bin-packing, *Computers & Operations Research*, 29:821–839, 2002.
9. A. Lodi. Private communication, 2005.
10. A. Lodi, S. Martello, D. Vigo. Neighborhood search algorithm for the guillotine non-oriented two-dimensional bin packing problem, in *Meta-Heuristics: Advances and Trends in Local Search Paradigms for Optimization, S. Voss. S. Martello, I. H. Osman, and C. Roucairol (eds.), Kluwer Academic Publishers, Boston, Massachusetts*, 22:125–139, 1998.
11. A. Lodi, S. Martello, D. Vigo. Approximation algorithms for the oriented two-dimensional bin packing problem, *European Journal of Operational Research*, 112:158–166, 1999a.
12. A. Lodi, S. Martello, D. Vigo. Heuristic and metaheuristic approaches for a class of two-dimensional bin packing problems, *INFORMS Journal on Computing*, 11:345–357, 1999b.
13. A. Lodi, S. Martello, D. Vigo. Recent advances on two-dimensional bin packing problems, *Discrete Applied Mathematics*, 123:379–396, 2002.
14. K-H. Loh, B. Golden, E. Wasil. Solving the One-dimensional Bin Packing Problem with a Weight Annealing Heuristic, *Computers & Operations Research*, 35(7):2283–2291, 2008.

15. S. Martello, D. Vigo. Exact solution of the two-dimensional finite bin packing problem, *Management Science*, 44:388–399, 1998.
16. S. Martello, D. Vigo. New computational results for the exact solution of the two-dimensional finite bin packing problem, *Technical report OR/01/06, Dipartimento di Elettronica, Informatica e Sistemistica, Universit di Bologna, Bologna, Italy*, 2001.
17. M. Monaci, P. Toth. A set-covering-based heuristic approach for bin-packing problems, *INFORMS Journal on Computing*, 18:71–85, 2006.
18. M. Ninio, J. J. Schneider. Weight annealing, *Physica A*, 349:649–666, 2005.

Solving the Maximum Cardinality Bin Packing Problem with a Weight Annealing-Based Algorithm

Kok-Hua Loh[1], Bruce Golden[2], and Edward Wasil[3]

[1] School of Mechanical & Aerospace Engineering
Nanyang Technological University
Singapore 639798
khloh@ntu.edu.sg

[2] Robert H. Smith School of Business
Department of Decision and Information Technologies
University of Maryland
College Park, MD 20742
bgolden@rhsmith.umd.edu

[3] Kogod School of Business
American University
Washington, DC 20016
ewasil@american.edu

Summary. In the maximum cardinality bin packing problem (MCBPP), we have n items with different sizes and m bins with the same capacity. We want to assign a maximum number of items to the fixed number of bins without violating the capacity constraint on each bin. We develop a heuristic algorithm for solving the MCBPP that is based on weight annealing. Weight annealing is a metaheuristic that has been recently proposed in the physics literature. We apply our algorithm to two data sets containing 4,500 randomly generated instances and show that it outperforms an enumeration algorithm and a branch-and-price algorithm.

Key words: Bin packing; weight annealing; heuristics; combinatorial optimization.

1 Introduction

In the maximum cardinality bin packing problem, we are given n items with sizes t_i, $i \in N = \{1, \ldots, n\}$, and m bins of identical capacity c. The objective is to assign a maximum number of items to the fixed number of bins without violating the capacity constraint. The problem formulation is given by

$$\text{maximize} \quad z = \sum_{i=1}^{n} \sum_{j=1}^{m} x_{ij} \tag{1}$$

J.W. Chinneck et al. (eds.), *Operations Research and Cyber-Infrastructure*, Operations Research/Computer Science Interfaces Series 47, DOI: 10.1007/978-0-387-88843-9_8,
© Springer Science+Business Media, LLC 2009

subject to

$$\sum_{i=1}^{n} t_i x_{ij} \leq c \qquad j \in \{1, \ldots, m\}$$

$$\sum_{j=1}^{m} x_{ij} \leq 1 \qquad i \in \{1, \ldots, n\}$$

$$x_{ij} = 0 \text{ or } 1 \qquad i \in \{1, \ldots, n\}, \ j \in \{1, \ldots, m\}$$

where $x_{ij} = 1$ if item i is assigned to bin j and $x_{ij} = 0$ otherwise.

The MCBPP is NP-hard (Labbé, Laporte, and Martello 2003). It has been applied in computing where we need to assign variable-length records to storage. The objective is to maximize the number of records stored in fast memory so as to ensure a minimum access time to the records given a fixed amount of storage space (Labbé, Laporte, and Martello 2003).

The MCBPP has been applied to the management of real-time multi-processors where the objective is to maximize the number of completed tasks with varying job durations before a given deadline (Coffman, Leung, and Ting 1978). It has been used to design processors for mainframe computers and the layout of electronic circuits (Ferreira, Martin, and Weismantel 1996).

A variety of bounds and heuristics have been developed for the MCBPP. Coffman, Leung, and Ting (1978) and Bruno and Downey (1985) provided probabilistic lower bounds. Kellerer (1999) considered this problem as a special case of the multiple knapsack problem where all items have the same profit and all knapsacks (or bins) have the same capacity and solved it with a polynomial approximation scheme for the multiple knapsack problem. Labbé, Laporte, and Martello (2003) developed several upper bounds and embedded them in an enumeration algorithm. Peeters and Degraeve (2006) solved the problem with a branch-and-price algorithm.

In this paper, we develop a heuristic algorithm for solving the MCBPP that is based on the concept of weight annealing. In Section 2, we describe weight annealing. In Section 3, we give the upper bounds and lower bounds that are used in our algorithm. In Section 4, we present our weight annealing algorithm. In Section 5, we apply our algorithm to 4,500 instances and compare our results to those produced by an enumeration algorithm and a branch-and-price algorithm. In Section 6, we summarize our contributions.

2 Weight Annealing

Ninio and Schneider (2005) proposed a weight annealing method that allowed a greedy heuristic to escape from a poor local optimum by changing the problem landscape and making use of the history of each optimization run. The authors changed the landscape by assigning weights to different parts of the solution space. Ninio and Schneider provided the following outline of their weight annealing algorithm.

Step 1. Start with an initial configuration from a greedy heuristic solution using the original problem landscape.

Step 2. Determine a new set of weights based on the previous optimization run and insight into the problem.

Step 3. Perform a new run of the greedy heuristic using the new weights.

Step 4. Return to Step 2 until a stopping criterion is met.

In their implementation, Ninio and Schneider required nonnegative values for all of the weights so their algorithm could look for good solutions. They used a cooling schedule with temperature T to change the values of the weights. When the value of T was large, there were significant changes to the weights. As T decreased, all weights approached a value of one. Ninio and Schneider applied their weight annealing to five benchmark traveling salesman problems with 127 to 1,379 nodes and generated results that were competitive with simulated annealing.

Weight annealing shares features with metaheuristics such as simulated annealing (e.g., a cooling schedule) and deterministic annealing (e.g., deteriorating moves) and similarities among these metaheuristics were presented by Ninio and Schneider (2005). In contrast to simulated annealing and deterministic annealing, weight annealing not only considers the value of the objective function, at each stage of an optimization run it also makes use of information on how well every part of the search space is being solved. By creating distortions in different parts of the search space (the size of the distortion is controlled by weight assignments based on insights gained from one iteration to the next), weight annealing seeks to expand and speed up the neighborhood search and focus computational efforts on the poorly solved regions of the search space.

3 Upper and Lower Bounds

3.1 Upper Bounds

Our algorithm uses upper bounds on the optimal value of the objective function (z^*) in (1) that were developed by Labbé, Laporte, and Martello (2003). The objective function value in (1) gives the maximum number of items that can be packed into the bins without violating bin capacities. Without loss of generality, we assume that the problem data are integers and $1 \leq t_1 \leq t_2 \leq \ldots \leq t_n \leq c$ (we refer to this as the ordered list throughout the rest of this paper).

The first upper bound for z^* developed by Labbé, Laporte, and Martello (2003) is given by

$$\bar{U}_0 = \max_{1 \leq k \leq n} \left\{ k \: : \: \sum_{i=1}^{k} t_i \leq mc \right\}. \tag{2}$$

Since the optimal solution is obtained by selecting the first z^* smallest items, all items with sizes t_i for which $i > \bar{U}_0$ can be disregarded.

Labbé, Laporte, and Martello (2003) derived the second upper bound $\bar{U}_1$ as follows. Let $Q(j)$ be the upper bound on the number of items that can be assigned to j bins. Then

$$Q(j) = \max\left\{ k \ : \ j \leq k \leq n, \sum_{i=1}^{k} t_i \leq jc \right\} \text{ for } j = 1,\ldots,m. \tag{3}$$

An upper bound on z^* is given by

$$U_1(j) = Q(j) + \lfloor Q(j)/j \rfloor (m - j) \tag{4}$$

since $\lfloor Q(j)/j \rfloor$ is an upper bound on the number of items that can be packed into each of the remaining $(m - j)$ bins. The upper bound is obtained by taking the minimum over all j, that is,

$$\bar{U}_1 = \min_{j=1,\ldots,m} U_1(j). \tag{5}$$

Note that $\bar{U}_1$ dominates $\bar{U}_0$.

The third upper bound $\bar{U}_2$ from Labbé, Laporte, and Martello (2003) is derived in the following way. Let i be the smallest item in an instance with m bins. Then $m\lfloor c/t_1 \rfloor$ is an upper bound on the number of items that can be assigned to m bins because $\lfloor c/t_1 \rfloor$ is an upper bound on the number of items that can be packed into one bin. A valid upper bound is given by

$$\bar{U}_2(i) = (i - 1) + m\lfloor c/t_1 \rfloor. \tag{6}$$

If i is not the smallest item, then an optimal solution will contain all items $j < i$, and by taking the minimum over all i, we obtain a valid upper bound

$$\bar{U}_2 = \min_{j=1,\ldots,n} U_2(i). \tag{7}$$

It follows that the best a priori upper bound is given by $U^* = \min\{\bar{U}_0, \bar{U}_1, \bar{U}_2\}$ (which is similar to what is given in Labbé, Laporte, and Martello (2003)). Since the optimal solution is obtained by selecting the first z^* smallest items, all items with sizes t_i for which $i > U^*$ can be disregarded. We point out that the time complexities for the computation of the bounds are given in the paper by Labbé, Laporte, and Martello (2003).

3.2 Lower Bounds

Our algorithm uses lower bounds developed by Martello and Toth (1990). Let I denote a one-dimensional bin packing problem instance. The lower bound L_2 on the optimal number of bins $z(I)$ can be computed in the following way.

Given any integer α, $0 \leq \alpha \leq c/2$, let

$$J_1 = \{j \in N \ : \ t_j > c - \alpha\},$$
$$J_2 = \{j \in N \ : \ c - \alpha \geq t_j > c/2\},$$
$$J_3 = \{j \in N \ : \ c/2 \geq t_j \geq \alpha\}, \qquad N = \{1,\ldots,n\},$$

then

$$L(\alpha) = |J_1| + |J_2| + max\left(0, \left\lceil \frac{\sum\limits_{j \in J_3} t_j - \left(|J_2|c - \sum\limits_{j \in J_2} t_j\right)}{c} \right\rceil\right) \tag{8}$$

is a lower bound on $z(I)$.

L_2 is calculated by taking the maximum over α, that is,

$$L_2 = max\{L(\alpha) : 0 \le \alpha \le c/2, \ \alpha \text{ integer}\} \tag{9}$$

In our algorithm, we use the Martello-Toth reduction procedure (denoted by MTRP and given in Martello and Toth 1990) to determine the lower bound L_3 which dominates L_2.

Let I be the original instance, z_1^r be the number of bins reduced after the first application of MTRP to I, and $I(z_1^r)$ be the corresponding residual instance. If $I(z_1^r)$ is relaxed by removing its smallest item, then we can obtain a lower bound by applying L_2 to $I(z_1^r)$ and this yields $L_1' = z_1^r + L_2(I(z_1^r)) \ge L_2(I)$. This process iterates until the residual instance is empty. For iteration k, we have a lower bound $L_k' = z_1^r + z_2^r + \ldots + z_k^r + L_2(I(z_k^r))$. Then

$$L_3 = max\{L_1', L_2', \ldots, L_{k_{max}}'\} \tag{10}$$

is a valid lower bound for I where k_{max} is the number of iterations needed to have the residual instance empty.

4 Weight Annealing Algorithm for the MCBPP

In this section, we present our weight annealing algorithm for the maximum cardinality bin packing problem which we denote by WAMC. Table 1 illustrates WAMC in pseudo code. We point out that a problem has been solved to optimality once we have found a feasible bin packing for the current instance defined by the theoretical upper bound U^* at Step 4 of our algorithm.

The number of items (n), the ordered list of item sizes, the bin capacity (c), and the number of bins (m) are inputs. For the ordered list, the data are integers and $1 \le t_1 \le t_2 \le \ldots \le t_n \le c$, where t_i is the size of item i.

4.1 Computing the Bounds

We begin by computing the three upper bounds and then setting $U^* = min\{\bar{U}_0, \bar{U}_1, \bar{U}_2\}$. Since the optimal solution of any instance is obtained by selecting the first z^* smallest items, we update the ordered list by removing any item i with size t_i for which $i > U^*$.

To improve the upper bound, we compute L_3 by applying MTRP. If L_3 is greater than m, it is not feasible to pack the items on the ordered list into m bins, so we can reduce U^* by 1. We update the ordered list by removing any item i with size t_i for which $i > U^*$. We iterate until $L_3 = m$.

Table 1. Weight annealing algorithm (WAMC) for the MCBPP

Step 0. Initialization

    Parameters are K (scaling parameter), $nloop1$, $nloop2$, T (temperature), and $Tred$.

    Set $K = 0.05$, $nloop1 = 20$, $nloop2 = 50$, $T = 1$, and $Tred = 0.95$.

    Inputs are number of items (n), the item size ordered list, bin capacity (c), and number of bins (m).

Step 1. Compute the upper bound $U^* = \{\bar{U}_0, \bar{U}_1, \bar{U}_2\}$.

Step 2. Set $n = U^*$.

    Remove item $i > U^*$ from the ordered list.

Step 3. Improve the upper bound.

    While $(L_3 > m)$ do\{

        $U^* = U^* - 1$.

        Remove item $i > U^*$ from the ordered list.

        Compute L_3.\}

Step 4. For $j = 1$ to $nloop1$

    Step 4.1 Construct initial solution with the ordered list with modified FFD algorithm.

    Step 4.2 Improve the current solution.

        Set $T = 1$.

        Compute residual capacity r_i of bin i.

        For $k = 1$ to $nloop2$

            Compute weights $w_i^T = (1 + Kr_i)^T$.

        Do for all pairs of bins\{

            Perform Swap (1,0)

                Evaluate feasibility and $\Delta f_{(1,0)}$.

                If $\Delta f_{(1,0)} \geq 0$

                    Move the item.

                    Exit Swap (1,0) and,

                    Exit j loop and k loop if m is reached.

              Exit Swap (1,0) if no feasible move with $\Delta f_{(1,0)} \geq 0$ is found.

            Perform Swap (1,1)

                Evaluate feasibility and $\Delta f_{(1,1)}$.

                If $\Delta f_{(1,1)} \geq 0$

                    Swap the items.

                    Exit Swap (1,1) and,

                    Exit j loop and k loop if m is reached.

              Exit Swap (1,1) if no feasible move with $\Delta f_{(1,1)} \geq 0$ is found.

            Perform Swap (1,2)

                Evaluate feasibility and $\Delta f_{(1,2)}$.

                If $\Delta f_{(1,2)} \geq 0$

                    Swap the items.

                    Exit Swap (1,2) and,

                    Exit j loop and k loop if m is reached.

              Exit Swap (1,2) if no feasible move with $\Delta f_{(1,2)} \geq 0$ is found.

            Perform Swap (2,2)

                Evaluate feasibility and $\Delta f_{(2,2)}$.

                If $\Delta f_{(2,2)} \geq 0$

                    Swap the items.

                    Exit Swap (2,2) and,

                    Exit j loop and k loop if m is reached.

              Exit Swap (2,2) if no feasible move with $\Delta f_{(2,2)} \geq 0$ is found.\}

      $T := T \times Tred$

      End of k loop

    End of j loop

Step 5. Outputs are the number of bins used and the final distribution of items.

4.2 Weight Annealing for the Bin Packing Problem

Next, we solve the one-dimensional bin packing problem with the current ordered list. We start with an initial solution generated by the first-fit decreasing procedure (FFD) that we have modified in the following way. We select an item for packing with probability 0.5. In other words, we start with the first item on the ordered list and, based on a coin toss, we pack it into a bin if it is selected, or leave it on the ordered list if it is not selected. We continue down the ordered list until an item is selected for packing. We then pack the second item in the same manner and so on, until we reach the bottom of the list. For each bin i in the FFD solution, we compute the bin load l_i which is the sum of sizes of items in bin i (that is, $l_i = \sum_{j=1}^{q_i} t_{ij}$, where t_{ij} is the size of item j in bin i and q_i is the number of items in bin i), and the residual capacity r_i which is given by $r_i = (c - l_i)/c$.

4.2.1 Objective Function

In conducting our neighborhood search, we use the objective function given by Fleszar and Hindi (2002):

$$\text{maximize } f = \sum_{i=1}^{p} (l_j)^2 \tag{11}$$

where p is the number of bins in the current solution. This objective function seeks to reduce the number of bins along with maximizing the sum of the squared bin loads.

4.2.2 Weight Assignment

A key feature of our procedure is the distortion of item sizes that allows for both up-hill and downhill moves. The changes in the apparent sizes of the items are achieved by assigning different weights to the bins and their items according to how well the bins are packed.

For each bin i, we assign weight w_i^T according to

$$w_i^T = (1 + Kr_i)^T \tag{12}$$

where K is a constant and T is a temperature parameter. We apply the weight to each item in the bin. The scaling parameter K controls the amount of size distortion for each item. T controls the amount by which a single weight can be varied. We start with a high temperature $(T = 1)$ and this allows more downhill moves. The temperature is reduced at the end of every iteration $(T \times 0.95)$, so that the amount of item distortion decreases and the problem space looks more like the original problem space.

At a given temperature T, the size distortion for an item is proportional to the residual capacity of its bin. At a local maximum, not-so-well packed bins will have large residual capacities. We try to escape from a poor local maximum with down-hill moves. To enable downhill moves, our weighting function increases the sizes of items in poorly packed bins.

Since the objective function tries to maximize the number of fully filled bins, the size transformation increases the chances of a swap between one of the enlarged items in this bin and a smaller item from another bin. Thus, we have an uphill move in the transformed space, which may be a downhill move in the original space. We make a swap as long as it is feasible in the original space.

4.2.3 Swap Schemes

We start the swapping process by comparing the items in the first bin with the items in the second bin, and so on, sequentially down to the last bin in the initial solution. Neighbors of a current solution can be obtained by swapping (exchanging) items between all possible pairs of bins. We use four different swapping schemes: Swap (1,0), Swap (1,1), Swap (1,2), and Swap (2,2). Fleszar and Hindi (2002) proposed the first two schemes.

In Swap (1,0), one item is moved from bin α to bin β. The change in the objective function value $(\Delta f_{(1,0)})$ that results from moving one item i with size $t_{\alpha i}$ from bin α to bin β is given by

$$\Delta f_{(1,0)} = (l_\alpha - t_{\alpha i})^2 + (l_\beta + t_{\alpha i})^2 - l_\alpha^2 - l_\beta^2. \tag{13}$$

In Swap (1,1), we swap item i from bin α with item j from bin β. The change in the objective function value that results from swapping item i with size $t_{\alpha i}$ from bin α with item j with size $t_{\beta j}$ from bin β is given by

$$\Delta f_{(1,1)} = (l_\alpha - t_{\alpha i} + t_{\beta j})^2 + (l_\beta - t_{\beta j} + t_{\alpha i})^2 - l_\alpha^2 - l_\beta^2. \tag{14}$$

In Swap (1,2), we swap item i from bin α with items j and k from bin β. The change in the objective function value that results from swapping item i with size $t_{\alpha i}$ from bin α with item j with size $t_{\beta j}$ and item k with size $t_{\beta k}$ from bin β is given by

$$\Delta f_{(1,2)} = (l_\alpha - t_{\alpha i} + t_{\beta j} + t_{\beta k})^2 + (l_\beta - t_{\beta j} - t_{\beta k} + t_{\alpha i})^2 - l_\alpha^2 - l_\beta^2. \tag{15}$$

In Swap (2,2), we swap item i and item j from bin α with item k and item l from bin β. The change in the objective function value that results from swapping item i with size $t_{\alpha i}$ and item j with size $t_{\alpha j}$ from bin α with item k with size $t_{\beta k}$ and item l with size $t_{\beta l}$ from bin β is given by

$$\Delta f_{(2,2)} = (l_\alpha - t_{\alpha i} - t_{\alpha j} + t_{\beta k} + t_{\beta l})^2 + (l_\beta - t_{\beta k} - t_{\beta l} + t_{\alpha i} + t_{\alpha j})^2 - l_a^2 - l_\beta^2. \tag{16}$$

For a current pair of bins (α, β), the swapping of items by Swap (1,0) is carried out as follows. The algorithm evaluates whether the first item (item i) in bin α can be moved to bin β without violating the capacity constraint of bin β in the original space. In other words, does bin β have enough original residual capacity to accommodate the original size of item i? If the answer is yes (the move is feasible), the change in objective function value of the move in the transformed space is evaluated. If $\Delta f_{(1,0)} \geq 0$, item i is moved from bin α to bin β. After this move, if bin α is empty and the total number of utilized bins reaches the specified number of bins (m), the algorithm stops and outputs the final results. If bin α is still partially filled, or the lower bound has not been reached, the algorithm exits Swap (1,0) and proceeds to Swap (1,1). If the move of the first item is infeasible or $\Delta f_{(1,0)} < 0$, the second item in bin α is evaluated and so on, until a feasible move with $\Delta f_{(1,0)} \geq 0$ is found or all items in bin α have been considered and no feasible move with $\Delta f_{(1,0)} \geq 0$ has been found. The algorithm then performs Swap (1,1), followed by Swap (1,2), and Swap (2,2). In each of the swapping schemes, we always take the first feasible move with a nonnegative change in objective function value that we find.

We point out that the improvement step (Step 4.2) is carried out 50 times $(nloop2 = 50)$ starting with $T = 1$, followed by $T = 1 \times 0.95 = 0.95$, $T = 0.95 \times 0.95 = 0.9025$, etc. At the end of Step 4, if the total number of utilized bins has not reached m, we repeat Step 4 with another initial solution. We exit the program as soon as the required number of bins reaches m or after 20 runs $(nloop1 = 20)$.

5 Computational Experiments

We now describe the test instances, present results generated by WAMC, and compare WAMC's results to those reported in the literature.

5.1 Test Instances

In this section, we describe how we generated two sets of test instances,

5.1.1 Test Set 1

We followed the procedure described by Labbé, Laporte, and Martello (2003) to randomly generate the first set of test instances. Labbé et al. specified the values of three parameters: number of bins $(m = 2, 3, 5, 10, 15, 20)$, capacity $(c = 100, 120, 150, 200, 300, 400, 500, 600, 700, 800)$, and range of item size $[t_{min}, 99]$ $(t_{min} = 1, 20, 50)$. For each of the 180 triples (m, c, t_{min}), we created 10 instances by generating item size t_i in an interval according to a discrete uniform distribution until the condition $\Sigma t_i > mc$ was met. This gave us a total of $180 \times 10 = 1,800$ instances which we denote by Test Set 1. We requested the 1,800 instances used by Labbé et al. (2003), but Martello (2006) replied that these instances were no longer available.

5.1.2 Test Set 2

Peeters and Degraeve (2006) extended the problems of Labbé et al. by multiplying the capacity c by a factor of 10 and enlarging the range of item size to $[t_{min}, 999]$. Rather than fixing the number of bins, Peeters and Degraeve fixed the expected number of generated items (denoted by $E(n')$). $E(n')$ is not an input for generating the instances; it is implicitly determined by the number of bins and capacity. Since the item sizes are uniformly distributed on the interval $[t_{min}, 999]$, the expected item size is $(t_{min} + 999)/2$ and $E(n') = 2cm/(t_{min} + 999)$. Given the number of expected items $\bar{n}$ as an input, the number of bins m must be $\bar{n}(t_{min} + 999)/2c$.

We randomly generated the second set of test instances with parameter values specified by Peeters and Degraeve: desired number of items ($\bar{n} = 100, 150, 200, 250, 300, 350, 400, 450, 500$), capacity ($c = 1000, 1200, 1500, 2000, 3000, 4000, 5000, 6000, 7000, 8000$), and range of item size $[t_{min}, 999]$ ($t_{min} = 1, 200, 500$). For each of the 270 triples ($\bar{n}, c, t_{min}$), we created 10 instances. This gave us a total of $270 \times 10 = 2,700$ instances which we denote by Test Set 2.

5.2 Computational Results

We coded WAMC in C and C++ and used a 3 GHz Pentium 4 computer with 256 MB of RAM. In the next two sections, we provide the results generated by WAMC on the two sets of test instances.

5.2.1 Results on Test Set 1

In Table 2, we show the average number of items (n) generated over 10 instances for each triple (m, c, t_{min}) in Test Set 1. In Table 3, we give the number of instances solved to optimality by WAMC. In Table 4, we give the average running time in seconds for WAMC.

Table 2. Average value of n over 10 instances for each triple (m, c, t_{min}) in Test Set 1

t_{min}	m	c									
		100	120	150	200	300	400	500	600	700	800
1	2	4	5	6	9	12	16	21	25	28	34
1	3	6	7	10	12	18	25	31	36	45	49
1	5	11	12	15	20	30	40	53	61	70	79
1	10	20	24	31	41	62	82	99	120	137	160
1	15	30	36	46	62	94	117	150	179	210	239
1	20	41	49	60	85	119	158	198	240	278	317
20	2	4	4	5	7	10	14	17	21	24	27
20	3	5	6	8	11	15	21	26	30	36	42
20	5	8	10	13	16	26	34	42	52	60	67
20	10	17	21	25	34	51	70	84	100	116	134
20	15	26	30	39	51	79	101	125	149	177	203
20	20	34	41	51	70	101	134	167	201	236	267
50	2	3	3	4	5	8	11	13	16	19	22
50	3	4	5	6	8	12	16	21	24	28	33
50	5	7	8	10	13	20	27	34	41	48	54
50	10	14	16	20	27	41	54	68	81	93	107
50	15	20	24	30	40	61	81	101	121	140	161
50	20	27	32	40	54	82	107	134	160	188	215

Table 3. Number of instances solved to optimality by WAMC in Test Set 1

t_{min}	m	c									
		100	120	150	200	300	400	500	600	700	800
1	2	10	10	10	10	10	10	10	10	10	10
1	3	10	10	10	10	10	10	10	10	10	10
1	5	10	10	10	10	10	10	10	10	10	10
1	10	10	10	10	10	10	10	10	10	10	10
1	15	10	10	10	10	10	10	10	10	10	10
1	20	9	10	10	10	10	10	10	10	10	10
20	2	10	10	10	10	10	10	10	10	10	10
20	3	10	10	10	10	10	10	10	10	10	10
20	5	10	10	10	10	10	10	10	10	10	10
20	10	9	10	9	10	10	10	10	10	10	10
20	15	10	10	9	10	10	10	10	10	10	10
20	20	9	10	10	10	10	10	10	10	10	10
50	2	10	10	10	10	10	10	10	10	10	10
50	3	10	10	10	10	10	10	10	10	10	10
50	5	10	10	10	9	10	10	10	10	10	10
50	10	10	10	10	9	10	10	10	10	10	10
50	15	10	10	10	10	10	10	10	10	10	10
50	20	10	10	10	10	10	10	10	10	10	10

Table 4. Average computation time (s) for WAMC over 10 instances for each triple (m, c, t_{min}) in Test Set 1

t_{min}	m	c									
		100	120	150	200	300	400	500	600	700	800
1	2	0.00	0.00	0.00	0.00	0.00	0.00	0.00	0.00	0.00	0.00
1	3	0.00	0.00	0.00	0.00	0.00	0.00	0.00	0.00	0.00	0.00
1	5	0.00	0.00	0.00	0.00	0.00	0.00	0.00	0.01	0.01	0.01
1	10	0.01	0.01	0.00	0.00	0.00	0.01	0.02	0.02	0.04	0.04
1	15	0.01	0.01	0.00	0.00	0.00	0.03	0.07	0.12	0.18	0.30
1	20	0.03	0.07	0.00	0.01	0.03	0.09	0.23	0.41	0.54	1.05
20	2	0.00	0.00	0.00	0.00	0.00	0.00	0.00	0.00	0.00	0.00
20	3	0.00	0.00	0.00	0.00	0.00	0.00	0.00	0.00	0.00	0.00
20	5	0.00	0.00	0.00	0.00	0.00	0.00	0.00	0.00	0.00	0.00
20	10	0.00	0.00	0.01	0.00	0.00	0.00	0.01	0.02	0.04	0.08
20	15	0.01	0.00	0.00	0.00	0.00	0.02	0.04	0.09	0.18	0.04
20	20	0.01	0.03	0.02	0.01	0.02	0.05	0.11	0.03	0.49	0.87
50	2	0.00	0.00	0.00	0.00	0.00	0.00	0.00	0.00	0.00	0.00
50	3	0.00	0.00	0.00	0.00	0.00	0.00	0.00	0.00	0.00	0.00
50	5	0.00	0.00	0.00	0.00	0.00	0.00	0.00	0.00	0.00	0.00
50	10	0.00	0.00	0.00	0.00	0.00	0.00	0.01	0.01	0.03	0.07
50	15	0.00	0.00	0.00	0.09	0.00	0.01	0.02	0.03	0.07	0.18
50	20	0.00	0.00	0.00	0.06	0.00	0.02	0.03	0.05	0.18	0.37

We see that WAMC found optimal solutions to 1,793 instances. On average, WAMC is very fast with most computation times less than 0.01 s and the longest average time about 1 s.

Labbé, Laporte, and Martello (2003) generated 1,800 instances and solved each instance using a four-step enumeration algorithm (which we denote by LLM) on a Digital VaxStation 3100 (a slow machine that is comparable to a PC486/33). We point out that our Test Set 1 and the 1,800 instances used by Labbé et al. are very similar (the average values of n that we give in Table 2 are nearly the same as those given by Labbé et al. (2003), but they are not exactly the same). In Table 5, we provide the number of instances solved to optimality by LLM. We see that LLM found optimal solutions to 1,759 instances. On average, LLM is fast with many computation times 0.01 s or less and the longest average time several hundred seconds or more.

Peeters and Degraeve (2006) followed the procedure of Labbé et al. (2003) and generated 1,800 instances. They solved each instance using a branch-and-price algorithm (denoted by BP) on a COMPAQ Armada 700M, 500 MHz Intel Pentium III computer with a time limit of 900 seconds. Peeters and Degraeve reported that BP solved 920 instances (". . . for those types of instances where the average CPU is significantly different from 0 . . .") to optimality. For these 920 instances, most of the computation times were less than 0.01 s. Although not listed in the paper explicitly, we believe that BP also solved the remaining 880 instances to optimality.

In summary, on three different sets of 1,800 instances generated using the specifications of Labbé et al. (2003), the number of optimal solutions found by BP, WAMC, and LLM were 1,800, 1,793, and 1,759, respectively.

Table 5. Number of instances solved to optimality by LLM reported in Labbé et al. (2003)

t_{min}	m	c									
		100	120	150	200	300	400	500	600	700	800
1	2	10	10	10	10	10	10	10	10	10	10
1	3	10	10	10	10	10	10	10	10	10	10
1	5	10	10	9	10	10	10	10	10	10	10
1	10	10	9	10	10	10	10	10	10	10	10
1	15	10	8	10	10	10	10	10	10	10	10
1	20	10	10	10	10	10	10	10	10	10	10
20	2	10	10	10	10	10	10	10	10	10	10
20	3	10	10	10	9	10	10	10	10	10	10
20	5	10	9	8	9	10	10	10	10	10	10
20	10	10	9	10	10	10	10	10	10	10	10
20	15	10	10	8	10	10	10	10	10	10	10
20	20	10	10	8	10	10	10	10	10	10	10
50	2	10	10	10	10	10	10	10	10	10	10
50	3	10	10	10	10	10	10	10	10	10	10
50	5	10	10	10	10	10	10	10	10	10	10
50	10	10	10	10	10	9	10	10	10	10	10
50	15	10	10	10	7	7	7	10	10	10	10
50	20	10	10	10	8	6	5	8	9	7	10

5.2.2 Results on Test Set 2

In Table 6, we show the average number of bins (n) over 10 instances for each triple $(\bar{n}, c, t_{min})$ in Test Set 2. In Table 7, we give the number of instances from Test Set 2 solved to optimality by WAMC. When the number of instances solved to optimality is less than 10 for WAMC, the maximum deviation from the optimal solution in terms of the number of items is shown in parentheses. In Table 7, we also provide the results generated by BP as reported in Peeters and Degraeve (2006). BP solved 2,700 instances that are similar to, but not exactly the same as, the instances in Test Set 2.

We see that WAMC found optimal solutions to 2,665 instances (there are a total of 2,700 instances). BP found optimal solutions to 2,519 instances.

WAMC performed better on instances with large bin capacities and BP performed better on instances with small bin capacities. WAMC solved all 1,080

Table 6. Average number of bins (m) over 10 instances for each triple $(\bar{n}, c, t_{min})$ in Test Set 2

$\bar{n}$	t_{min}	c									
		1000	1200	1500	2000	3000	4000	5000	6000	7000	8000
100	1	50	42	33	25	17	13	10	8	7	6
100	200	60	50	40	30	20	15	12	10	9	7
100	500	75	62	50	37	25	19	15	12	11	9
150	1	75	63	50	38	25	19	15	13	11	9
150	200	90	75	60	45	30	22	18	15	13	11
150	500	112	94	75	56	37	28	22	19	16	14
200	1	100	83	67	50	33	25	20	17	14	13
200	200	120	100	80	60	40	30	24	20	17	15
200	500	150	125	100	75	50	37	30	25	21	19
250	1	125	104	83	63	42	31	25	21	18	16
250	200	150	125	100	75	50	37	30	25	21	19
250	500	187	156	125	94	62	47	37	31	27	23
300	1	150	125	100	75	50	38	30	25	21	19
300	200	180	150	120	90	60	45	36	30	26	22
300	500	225	187	150	112	75	56	45	37	32	28
350	1	175	146	117	88	58	44	35	29	25	22
350	200	210	175	140	105	70	52	42	35	30	26
350	500	262	219	175	131	87	66	52	44	37	33
400	1	200	167	133	100	67	50	40	33	29	25
400	200	240	200	160	120	80	60	48	40	34	30
400	500	300	250	200	150	100	75	60	50	43	37
450	1	225	188	150	113	75	56	45	38	32	28
450	200	270	225	180	135	90	67	54	45	39	34
450	500	337	281	225	169	112	84	67	56	48	42
500	1	250	208	167	125	83	63	50	42	36	31
500	200	300	250	200	150	100	75	60	50	43	37
500	500	375	312	250	187	125	94	75	62	54	47

Table 7. Number of instances solved to optimality by WAMC in Test Set 2 and the number of instances solved to optimality by BP reported in Peeters and Degraeve (2006)

$\bar{n}$	t_{min}	\multicolumn{10}{c}{c}
		1000		1200		1500		2000		3000	
		BP	WAMC	BP	WAMC	BP	WAMC	BP	WAMC	BP	WAMC
100	1	10	10	10	10	10	10	10	10	10	10
	200	10	10	10	10	10	7(1)	10	10	10	10
	500	10	10	10	10	10	10	10	10	10	10
150	1	10	10	10	9(1)	10	10	10	10	10	10
	200	10	10	10	10	10	9(1)	10	10	10	10
	500	10	10	10	10	10	10	10	10	10	10
200	1	10	8(1)	10	8(1)	10	10	10	10	10	10
	200	10	10	10	10	10	10	10	10	10	10
	500	10	10	10	10	10	9(3)	10	10	10	10
250	1	10	9(1)	10	10	10	10	10	10	10	10
	200	10	10	10	9(1)	10	9(1)	10	10	10	10
	500	10	10	10	10	10	10	10	10	10	10
300	1	10	9(1)	10	8(1)	10	10	10	10	10	10
	200	10	10	10	10	10	8(1)	10	10	10	10
	500	10	10	10	10	10	10	10	10	10	10
350	1	10	9(1)	10	9(1)	10	10	10	10	10	10
	200	10	10	10	9(2)	10	10	10	10	10	10
	500	10	10	10	10	10	10	10	10	10	10
400	1	10	8(1)	10	10	10	10	10	10	10	10
	200	10	10	10	10	10	8(1)	10	10	10	10
	500	10	10	10	10	10	10	10	10	10	10
450	1	10	9(1)	10	8(1)	10	10	10	10	10	10
	200	10	10	10	9(2)	10	9(1)	10	10	9	10
	500	10	10	10	10	10	7(4)	10	10	10	10
500	1	10	9(1)	10	10	10	10	10	10	10	10
	200	10	10	10	10	10	9(1)	10	10	9	10
	500	10	10	10	10	10	10	10	10	10	10
	Total	270	261	270	259	270	255	270	270	268	270

( ) Maximum deviation from the optimal solution in terms of the number of items for WAMC.

Table 7. (continued)

$\bar{n}$	t_{min}	c									
		4000		5000		6000		7000		8000	
		BP	WAMC	BP	WAMC	BP	WAMC	BP	WAMC	BP	WAMC
100	1	10	10	10	10	10	10	10	10	10	10
	200	10	10	10	10	10	10	10	10	10	10
	500	10	10	10	10	10	10	10	10	10	10
150	1	10	10	10	10	10	10	10	10	10	10
	200	10	10	10	10	10	10	10	10	10	10
	500	10	10	10	10	10	10	10	10	10	10
200	1	10	10	10	10	10	10	10	10	10	10
	200	10	10	10	10	10	10	10	10	10	10
	500	10	10	10	10	10	10	10	10	10	10
250	1	10	10	10	10	10	10	10	10	10	10
	200	10	10	10	10	10	10	10	10	10	10
	500	10	10	10	10	10	10	10	10	10	10
300	1	10	10	10	10	10	10	10	10	10	10
	200	10	10	10	10	10	10	10	10	10	10
	500	10	10	1	10	3	10	3	10	10	10
350	1	10	10	10	10	10	10	10	10	10	10
	200	10	10	10	10	10	10	10	10	10	10
	500	10	10	0	10	0	10	0	10	9	10
400	1	10	10	10	10	10	10	10	10	10	10
	200	10	10	10	10	10	10	10	10	10	10
	500	10	10	0	10	0	10	0	10	0	10
450	1	10	10	10	10	10	10	10	10	10	10
	200	10	10	10	10	10	10	10	10	9	10
	500	10	10	0	10	0	10	0	10	0	10
500	1	10	10	10	10	10	10	10	10	10	10
	200	10	10	10	10	10	10	10	10	9	10
	500	7	10	0	10	0	10	0	10	0	10
	Total	267	270	221	270	223	270	223	270	237	270

instances with large bin capacities ($c = 5000, 6000, 7000, 8000$) to optimality, while BP solved 904 large-capacity instances to optimality. Over the 1,620 small-capacity bins ($c = 1000, 1200, 1500, 2000, 3000, 4000$), BP solved 1,615 instances to optimality, while WAMC solved 1,585 instances to optimality.

In Table 8, we show the average computation time in seconds for WAMC and BP for the instances solved to optimality. To illustrate, for the triple ($\bar{n} = 200$, $c = 1000$, $t_{min} = 1$), WAMC solved eight instances and averaged 0.1 s, while BP solved all 10 instances and averaged 0.5 s. We point out that for several triples (e.g., ($\bar{n} = 350$, $c = 5000$, $t_{min} = 500$)), BP did not solve any instance to optimality, so that no average computation time is provided in the table.

Over all 2,665 instances solved to optimality, WAMC had an average computation time of 0.20 s. Over all 2,519 instances solved to optimality, BP had an average

Table 8. Average computation time (s) for WAMC and BP on instances solved to optimality

$\bar{n}$	t_{min}	c									
		1000		1200		1500		2000		3000	
		BP	WAMC	BP	WAMC	BP	WAMC	BP	WAMC	BP	WAMC
100	1	0.1	0.2	0.1	0.9	0.3	0.3	0.0	0.0	0.0	0.0
	200	0.1	0.0	0.1	0.0	0.4	0.2(7)	0.1	0.0	0.0	0.0
	500	0.0	0.0	0.0	0.0	0.0	0.0	0.5	0.0	1.4	0.0
150	1	0.1	0.0	0.1	0.6(9)	2.3	0.1	0.0	0.1	0.0	0.1
	200	0.1	0.0	0.1	0.6	2.2	0.2(9)	1.7	0.1	0.0	0.1
	500	0.0	0.0	0.0	0.0	0.1	0.1	4.8	0.0	8.0	0.0
200	1	0.5	0.1(8)	3.0	0.6(8)	6.0	0.2	0.0	0.2	0.0	0.2
	200	0.2	0.0	0.3	0.3	6.1	8.9	3.3	0.2	0.0	0.2
	500	0.0	0.0	0.1	0.0	0.2	0.1(9)	6.1	0.0	24.3	0.1
250	1	1.7	0.1(9)	1.9	6.6	11.8	0.2	0.0	0.2	0.0	0.2
	200	0.3	0.0	0.8	0.1(9)	14.9	9.3(9)	15.5	0.3	0.0	0.2
	500	0.0	0.0	0.1	0.3	0.3	0.5	13.4	0.1	36.4	0.1
300	1	1.3	1.4(9)	7.2	3.4(8)	15.8	0.6	10.7	0.6	0.0	0.8
	200	0.5	0.0	0.6	0.9	27.4	5.0	43.8	0.6	39.8	0.5
	500	0.4	0.0	0.1	0.0	0.4	0.4	16.9	0.1	71.7	0.2
350	1	2.1	0.1(9)	29.3	5.4(9)	0.0	0.9	0.0	1.1	0.0	1.5
	200	0.6	0.1	1.4	0.1(9)	41.2	11.7	86.6	1.2	94.1	0.9
	500	0.0	0.0	0.1	0.1	0.6	0.8	27.7	0.1	117.9	0.3
400	1	3.3	0.1(8)	47.2	1.8	52.4	1.3	0.0	1.8	0.0	2.6
	200	0.8	0.1	1.6	0.0	68.7	6.3(8)	139.1	1.9	0.1	1.3
	500	0.0	0.0	0.2	0.1	0.8	2.5	39.5	0.2	165.0	0.4
450	1	8.2	5.2(9)	46.5	18.2(8)	128.6	1.8	35.2	2.3	0.0	3.3
	200	1.0	0.1	2.3	0.2(9)	88.8	4.2(9)	207.5	3.0	0.1(9)	1.7
	500	0.0	0.0	0.2	0.1	0.7	1.0(7)	50.7	0.3	237.4	0.6
500	1	13.2	0.2(9)	64.9	8.6	71.7	2.9	7.7	3.6	0.0	6.0
	200	1.6	0.1	1.7	0.1	127.6	5.2(9)	374.7	4.7	0.4(9)	2.3
	500	0.0	0.0	0.2	0.1	1.1	1.8	58.1	0.4	250.4	0.9

() When the number of instances solved to optimality is less than 10, the number solved to optimality is given in parentheses.

Table 8. (continued)

$\bar{n}$	t_{min}	4000 BP	4000 WAMC	5000 BP	5000 WAMC	6000 BP	6000 WAMC	7000 BP	7000 WAMC	8000 BP	8000 WAMC
100	1	0.0	0.0	0.0	0.0	0.0	0.0	0.0	0.0	0.0	0.0
	200	0.0	0.0	0.0	0.0	0.0	0.0	0.0	0.1	0.0	0.0
	500	0.6	0.0	1.5	0.0	0.6	0.0	0.0	0.0	0.0	0.1
150	1	0.0	0.1	0.0	0.1	0.0	0.1	0.0	0.8	0.0	0.1
	200	0.0	0.1	0.0	0.1	0.0	0.1	0.0	0.1	0.0	0.2
	500	13.9	0.1	10.9	0.1	10.3	0.1	0.3	0.1	0.7	0.2
200	1	0.0	0.3	0.0	0.3	0.0	0.3	0.0	0.3	0.0	0.2
	200	0.0	0.3	0.0	0.3	0.0	0.3	0.0	0.4	0.0	0.4
	500	47.8	0.1	41.2	0.1	23.9	0.1	0.8	0.2	9.7	0.3
250	1	0.0	0.2	0.0	9.2	0.0	0.1	0.0	0.1	0.0	0.1
	200	0.0	0.2	0.0	0.2	0.0	0.1	0.0	0.1	0.0	0.1
	500	98.8	0.1	268.6	0.2	204.0	0.1	50.4	0.1	6.3	0.1
300	1	0.0	1.2	0.0	1.2	0.0	1.1	0.0	1.1	0.0	1.3
	200	0.0	1.3	0.0	1.2	0.0	1.4	0.1	1.6	0.0	1.5
	500	239.6	0.4	326.6(1)	0.5	115.3(3)	0.6	16.7(3)	1.0	7.4	1.0
350	1	0.0	2.0	0.0	2.1	0.0	2.3	0.0	2.0	0.0	1.8
	200	0.0	2.2	0.0	2.2	0.0	2.3	0.0	2.0	0.0	2.8
	500	318.1	0.6	**(0)	0.7	**(0)	0.9	**(0)	1.1	99.6(9)	1.5
400	1	0.0	2.9	0.0	3.4	0.0	3.5	0.0	3.6	0.0	2.8
	200	0.0	3.2	0.0	3.3	0.0	4.6	0.0	4.4	0.0	3.6
	500	400.9	0.8	**(0)	1.0	**(0)	1.2	**(0)	1.6	**(0)	2.6
450	1	0.0	5.1	0.0	5.2	0.0	6.0	0.0	5.7	0.0	4.8
	200	0.1	5.0	0.1	4.8	0.0	5.8	0.0	6.8	0.0	6.3
	500	578.4	1.2	**(0)	1.3	**(0)	1.9	**(0)	2.7	**(0)	3.3
500	1	0.0	7.1	0.0	7.3	0.0	8.5	0.0	8.6	0.0	7.6
	200	0.1	6.8	0.2	7.4	0.0	8.2	0.0	9.9	0.0	8.9
	500	693.7	1.5	**(0)	2.0	**(0)	2.4	**(0)	3.1	**(0)	4.3

** BP did not solve any of the 10 instances to optimality.

computation time of 2.85 s. The Pentium III computer used by Peeters and Degraeve (2006) to run BP is much slower than the Pentium 4 computer that we used to run WAMC.

We point out that our weight annealing algorithm is a robust procedure that can be used to solve several variants of bin packing and knapsack problems such as the dual bin packing problem (see Loh (2006) for more details).

6 Conclusions

We developed a new algorithm (WAMC) to solve the maximum cardinality bin packing problem that is based on weight annealing. WAMC is easy to understand and easy to code.

WAMC produced high-quality solutions very quickly. Over 4,500 instances that we randomly generated, our algorithm solved 4,458 instances to optimality with an average computation time of a few tenths of a second. Clearly, WAMC is a promising approach that deserves further computational study.

References

1. J. Bruno, P. Downey. Probabilistic bounds for dual bin-packing, *Acta Informatica*, 22:333–345, 1985.
2. E. Coffman, J. Leung, D. Ting. Bin packing: Maximizing the number of pieces packed, *Acta Informatica*, 9:263–271, 1978.
3. C. Ferreira, A. Martin, R. Weismantel. Solving multiple knapsack problems by cutting planes, *SIAM Journal on Optimization*, 6:858–877, 1996.
4. K. Fleszar, K. Hindi. New heuristics for one-dimensional bin-packing, *Computers & Operations Research*, 29:821–839, 2002.
5. H. Kellerer. A polynomial time approximation scheme for the multiple knapsack problem, in *Randomization, Approximation, and Combinatorial Algorithms and Techniques* (D. Hochbaum, K. Jansen, J. Rolim, and A. Sinclair, editors), 51–62, Springer, Berlin, 1999.
6. M. Labbé, G. Laporte, S. Martello. Upper bounds and algorithms for the maximum cardinality bin packing problem, *European Journal of Operational Research*, 149: 490–498, 2003.
7. K-H. Loh. Weight annealing heuristics for solving bin packing and other combinatorial optimization problems: Concepts, algorithms, and computational results, Ph.D. dissertation, Robert H. Smith School of Business, University of Maryland, College Park, Maryland, 2006.
8. S. Martello, private communication, 2006.
9. S. Martello, P. Toth. Lower bounds and reduction procedures for the bin-packing problem, *Discrete Applied Mathematics*, 26:59–70, 1990.
10. M. Ninio, J. Schneider. Weight annealing, *Physica A*, 349:649–666, 2005.
11. M. Peeters, Z. Degraeve. Branch-and-price algorithms for the dual bin packing and maximum cardinality bin packing problem, *European Journal of Operational Research*, 170:416–439, 2006.

Part 2.3
Miscellaneous

Combinatorial Design of a Stochastic Markov Decision Process

Nedialko B. Dimitrov and David P. Morton

Abstract We consider a problem in which we seek to optimally design a Markov decision process (MDP). That is, subject to resource constraints we first design the action sets that will be available in each state when we later optimally control the process. The control policy is subject to additional constraints governing state-action pair frequencies, and we allow randomized policies. When the design decision is made, we are uncertain of some of the parameters governing the MDP, but we assume a distribution for these stochastic parameters is known. We focus on transient MDPs with a finite number of states and actions. We formulate, analyze and solve a two-stage stochastic integer program that yields an optimal design. A simple example threads its way through the paper to illustrate the development. The paper concludes with a larger application involving optimal design of malaria intervention strategies in Nigeria.

Key words: stochastic optimization, Markov decision process, action space design

1 Introduction

Markov decision processes (MDPs) have seen wide application to time-dynamic optimization under uncertainty; see, e.g., Puterman (2005). Much less attention has been paid to optimally designing an MDP, and that is the focus of this paper. We approach the problem of selecting the actions available when controlling the process via the MDP, using an integer program, and restrict attention to transient MDPs.

Nedialko B. Dimitrov
Graduate Program in Operations Research, The University of Texas at Austin, 1 University Station, C2200, Austin, TX, 78712, e-mail: ned@cs.utexas.edu

David P. Morton
Graduate Program in Operations Research, The University of Texas at Austin, 1 University Station, C2200, Austin, TX, 78712, e-mail: morton@mail.utexas.edu

J.W. Chinneck et al. (eds.), *Operations Research and Cyber-Infrastructure*, Operations Research/Computer Science Interfaces Series 47, DOI: 10.1007/978-0-387-88843-9_9,
© Springer Science+Business Media, LLC 2009

Mathematical programming has played a key role both in understanding and solving MDPs, almost from their inception (d'Epenoux, 1963; Manne, 1960). The survey Kallenberg (1994) provides an overview of linear programming approaches to solving MDPs. Linear programming formulations also play a central role in a recent class of approaches to approximate dynamic programming in which the value function in the linear program (LP) is replaced by an approximate (e.g., affine) value function that effectively reduces dimension (Adelman, 2007; de Farias and Roy, 2003, 2004; Schweitzer and Seidmann, 1985).

In a canonical MDP, the actions chosen to control the process in one state are not affected by the actions we choose in another state. However, we consider constrained MDPs, i.e., variants in which such constraints are present. These can be approached using Lagrange multipliers (Beutler and Ross, 1985) or via linear programming (Altman and Shwartz, 1991; Kallenberg, 1983). We consider constrained MDPs, primarily using a linear programming approach, but we turn to the Lagrangian approach when we consider a large-scale special case of a single-constraint MDP. Linear programming formulations can handle, in a natural way, constraints that involve the frequency with which we take particular actions in each state. These constraints concern the optimal control, or operation, of the process. On the other hand, the additional design stage we consider is on top of the MDP control, where we construct the actions that will be available in each state when operating the MDP. The design problem is combinatorial, as action-inclusion decisions are "yes-no" in nature. In addition, we consider resource constraints on these binary design variables. When selecting the MDP design, we may be uncertain with respect to some of the MDP's parameters, but these parameters are realized before we control the resulting system. We assume these uncertain parameters are governed by a known probability distribution, and so the resulting integer program used to design the system is a stochastic integer program.

The next section introduces our notation, formulates a basic MDP, and reviews how linear programming can be used to solve an MDP. The basic model is extended in simple ways in Section 3. Section 4 develops a stochastic integer program to optimally design an MDP. A simple example of growing complexity illustrates the ideas developed in these three sections. Section 5 considers a special structure that allows us to handle problem instances of larger scale, and applies that model to optimally design malaria intervention strategies in Nigeria.

2 A Basic Markov Decision Process

We begin by describing a discrete-time transient MDP or, more briefly, a system. At each time period $t \in \mathcal{T} = \{1, 2, \ldots\}$, we observe an individual in a state indexed by $s \in \mathcal{S}$, where $|\mathcal{S}|$ is finite, and we select an action $a \in A_s$, where $|A_s|$ is also finite. We collect a one-step reward $r_{s,a}$, and the individual probabilistically transitions to state $s' \in \mathcal{S}$ via $p(s' \mid s, a)$. The initial position of the individual is governed by the probability mass function w_s, $s \in \mathcal{S}$, and we let $w = (w_s)_{s \in \mathcal{S}}$ be the associated

$|\mathcal{S}|$-vector. Note that the set of available actions, A_s, the one-step reward, $r_{s,a}$, and the one-step transition probabilities, $p(s' \mid s, a)$, do not depend on the time index t. Our goal is to maximize the total expected reward, i.e., *value*, we collect by specifying a policy $\pi = (\delta^1, \delta^2, \ldots)$, where $\delta^t \in \times_{s \in \mathcal{S}} A_s$ gives our decision rule in time period t and $\delta_s^t \in A_s$ denotes the action taken in period t if the individual is in state s. Let P_δ denote the $|\mathcal{S}| \times |\mathcal{S}|$ transition matrix with $[P_\delta]_{s,s'} = p(s' \mid s, \delta_s)$, and let $P_\pi^t = P_{\delta^1} P_{\delta^2} \cdots P_{\delta^t}$. We denote by $r_\delta = (r_{s,\delta_s})_{s \in \mathcal{S}}$ the $|\mathcal{S}|$-vector of one-step rewards under decision rule δ. The problem of maximizing the system's value can then be formulated as:

$$\max_{\pi = (\delta^1, \delta^2, \ldots)} w^\top \sum_{t=0}^{\infty} P_\pi^t r_{\delta^{t+1}}. \tag{1}$$

We say that a policy π is transient if $\sum_{t=0}^{\infty} P_\pi^t$ is finite, and we call our system transient if this series is finite for every policy π. A policy, π, is said to be stationary if $\pi = (\delta, \delta, \ldots)$ for some δ, i.e., the action taken in period t depends on the individual's state but not t. It is well known that a system is transient if and only if every stationary policy is transient; and, for transient systems, the maximum (optimal) value in model (1) can be achieved by a stationary policy (Blackwell, 1962; Derman, 1962; Veinott, Jr., 1969).

Let V_s denote the optimal value, given that the individual begins in state $s \in \mathcal{S}$, i.e., the optimal value of model (1) if we were to take $w = e_s$, where e_s is the unit vector with a 1 in the s-th component. The optimality principle, i.e., Bellman's recursion, states

$$V_s = \max_{a \in A_s} \left[r_{s,a} + \sum_{s' \in \mathcal{S}} p(s' \mid s, a) V_{s'} \right]. \tag{Bellman}$$

Here, the optimal value in state s is equal to the one-step reward from that state plus the expected optimal value after transitioning, maximized over all actions in state s. Assuming we have solved the Bellman recursion for all V_s, $s \in \mathcal{S}$, we can use the distribution governing the individual's initial position to form our optimal expected total reward, $w^\top V = \sum_{s \in \mathcal{S}} w_s V_s$, where $V = (V_s)_{s \in \mathcal{S}}$.

Following work that began with d'Epenoux (1963) and Manne (1960), we can rewrite (Bellman) as a system of inequalities, coupled with *minimizing* $\sum_{s \in \mathcal{S}} w_s V_s$, which has the effect of pushing each value V_s onto the largest of its inequalities over $a \in A_s$. This allows us to solve the Bellman recursions via the following LP:

$$\min_V \quad \sum_{s \in \mathcal{S}} w_s V_s$$
$$\text{s.t.} \quad V_s - \sum_{s' \in \mathcal{S}} p(s' \mid s, a) V_{s'} \geq r_{s,a}, \quad s \in \mathcal{S}, a \in A_s. \tag{BellmanLP}$$

Provided $w_s > 0$, $s \in \mathcal{S}$, the optimal decision variables in this LP solve the Bellman recursion, and for any given initial distribution $w_s \geq 0$, $s \in \mathcal{S}$, the optimal value of this LP is our optimal expected total reward.

The dual of (BellmanLP) will also prove useful. With $x_{s,a}, s \in \mathscr{S}, a \in A_s$, denoting dual variables associated with the inequality constraints of (BellmanLP), and x representing the associated vector, we have the dual LP:

$$\max_{x} \quad \sum_{s \in \mathscr{S}} \sum_{a \in A_s} r_{s,a} x_{s,a}$$

$$\text{s.t.} \quad \sum_{a \in A_s} x_{s,a} - \sum_{s' \in \mathscr{S}} \sum_{a \in A_{s'}} p(s \mid s', a) x_{s',a} = w_s, \quad s \in \mathscr{S}$$

$$x_{s,a} \geq 0, \qquad\qquad\qquad\qquad\qquad s \in \mathscr{S}, a \in A_s.$$

(BellmanLPD)

The decision variables, $x_{s,a}$, represent the expected number of times, over the individual's transient lifetime, that he is in state s and we perform action a. The equality constraint is a type of flow-balance constraint, stipulating that the expected number of times the individual is in a state must equal the expected number of times he enters that state, including inflow from the mass function, w_s, specifying the individual's initial position. Any basic feasible solution to (BellmanLPD) has the property that for each $s \in \mathscr{S}$, we have $x_{s,a} > 0$ for at most one $a \in A_s$. This provides a linear-programming proof that we can solve model (1) using a stationary and non-randomized policy (Wagner, 1960). (We return to this issue in the context of constrained MDPs below.) So, having found an optimal basic solution to (BellmanLPD) we can extract an optimal stationary policy by the following rule: In state $s \in \mathscr{S}$ if $\sum_{a \in A_s} x_{s,a} > 0$ then select the single action $a \in A_s$ with $x_{s,a} > 0$, and otherwise select any action $a \in A_s$. Said another way, we can take the (single) basic variable for each $s \in \mathscr{S}$ as an indicator specifying the action to take in that state.

The linear programming approach to solving an MDP is often less efficient than using special-purpose algorithms such as policy iteration (Howard, 1960; Puterman, 2005). That said, it provides several advantages: First, the linear programming approach most easily handles certain types of constrained MDPs, i.e., MDPs with constraints that restrict the class of policies that can be employed. Second, the linear programming approach also handles, in a natural way, the addition of a "design stage" on top of the MDP. As we have already seen, viewing an MDP as an LP can provide structural insight. Finally, when using an LP to solve the MDP we can make use of open-source and commercially-available software. We return to these issues below but first discuss an example. Throughout the paper, variants of this example illustrate the models we consider.

Example 1. Suppose an individual moves randomly on the grid network depicted in Figure 1. The top-left cell (northwest corner) and the bottom-right cell (southeast corner) are special. We seek to guide the individual to the northwest corner, but he vanishes from the grid if he first reaches the southeast corner. The set of grid cells, i.e., nodes in the individual's spatial network, form $\mathscr{S}$. There are five actions, A_s, available in each cell: do nothing, close a one-way door blocking the north exit, the south exit, the east exit, or the west exit. If we do nothing, the individual has a $\frac{1}{4}$ probability of transitioning to the adjacent cell to the north, south, east, or west in the next time period. If we close a one-way door blocking one of the cell's exits, the individual has a $\frac{1}{3}$ probability of exiting to each of the remaining three neighboring cells. The doors are one-way since they block movement out of, but not into, the cell. The special cells are different: If the individual reaches the northwest corner, or the southeast corner he departs the grid in the next time step, regardless of the action we

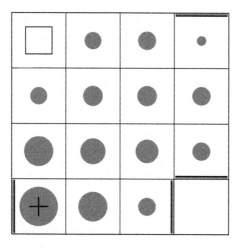

Fig. 1: An optimal solution to the MDP from Example 1. The individual starts at the dark plus sign in the southwest corner. We wish to maximize the probability the individual reaches the northwest corner, before reaching the southeast corner. The grid is a taurus, so going north from the top row leads to the bottom row, and going west from the left column leads to the right column, etc. The one-way doors we close are indicated, with their darker sides facing the cell from which they block movement. The relative sizes of the circles indicate the expected number of times the individual is in each cell. In this example, we simply block transit to the southeast corner and wait for the individual to eventually be absorbed in the northwest corner. The expected number of steps until the individual exits the system is 13.25.

take. In the former case we receive a unit reward. The one-step reward for the latter case, along with that of all other cells, is 0. As a result, the goal is to maximize the probability the individual reaches the northwest corner prior to reaching the southeast corner and vanishing. Equivalently, the goal can viewed as "protecting" the southeast corner, i.e., as minimizing the probability the individual is allowed to transit into that cell.

This stylized example is motivated by applications in nuclear smuggler interdiction. In a full fledged application, the cells of the grid are nodes in an arbitrary network, with each node representing a physical location and an edge between nodes representing a path the smuggler could take between locations. The individual moving probabilistically through the network models a nuclear smuggler's movements through the locations. The MDP optimizers, the defense force, have certain actions available, such as placing nuclear detectors, that limit the smuggler's transition probability from one place to another. Then, the goal of the optimization is to place nuclear detectors in such a way so as to protect the major cities of the defense force.

We assume that the individual begins in the southwest corner, i.e., the associated w_s is 1. The grid is a taurus, i.e., it wraps around on the east-west and north-south "borders" in the figure. Figure 1 shows an optimal policy, which seals off the southeast corner. Even though we have the option to close a door in each cell, we only do so in the four cells required to block transit to that corner. The relative sizes of the circles in the figure indicate $\sum_{a \in A_s} x_{s,a}$, i.e., the expected number of times the individual is in that cell. □

Note that the system of Example 1 is transient. That is, for every stationary policy, the individual eventually reaches either the northwest or southeast corner and then exits the system with probability one. Note that it is impossible to "box in" the individual, and while we can seal off transition to the northwest corner or the southeast corner, it is impossible to do both. Even in modifications of the problem formulation in which we fail to formally satisfy the transient condition, any policy that obtains positive reward results in the individual exiting the system with probability one. (For related notions of so-called proper and improper policies, see Bertsekas and Tsitsiklis, 1991 and Eaton and Zadeh, 1962.)

Example 2. Here, we modify the model of Example 1 by reducing each of the positive transition probabilities with the multiplicative factor $(1-\lambda)$, for $0 < \lambda < 1$. Thus the individual vanishes from a (standard) cell with probability λ, and this creates "time pressure" for us to guide the individual to the northwest corner. Our goal, as before, is to maximize the probability the individual reaches the northwest cell before he vanishes. The solution to this example is displayed in Figure 2. Here, we close many more doors to guide the individual towards the northwest corner as quickly as possible. □

In the next section, we show how the multiplicative factor in Example 2 can instead be interpreted as a discount factor. The next section also formulates a constrained MDP that induces "time pressure" as in Example 2, albeit for a different reason.

3 Simple Modeling Extensions

We label the modeling extensions we consider in this section as being simple for two reasons. First, from a computational perspective they do not significantly alter the difficulty of the associated MDP that we seek to solve. Second, the model extensions

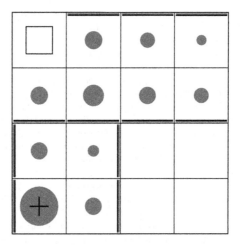

Fig. 2: An optimal solution to the MDP from Example 2. Refer to Figure 1 for a description of the graph notation. There is a small probability that the individual disappears from the grid at each step. This adds time pressure and so we are more aggressive in closing doors to guide the individual to the northwest corner more quickly. Compare this with the results of Figure 1. (Note this solution also solves the model of Example 1.) The expected number of steps until leaving the system is 8.00, and the probability the individual reaches the northwest corner can be made arbitrarily close to 1 as λ shrinks to zero.

we consider here are (now) "simple" in the sense that they are well-understood, having been explored in the literature. Our motive for presenting them here is that they will prove useful in understanding the scope of MDPs that we can optimally design using the ideas of the subsequent section.

3.1 Random Replication and Branching MDPs

In some settings, we need to model richer population dynamics than that described in Section 2, where a *single* individual moves from state to state and eventually exits the system. As an example, we consider an extension that allows for random replication. Specifically, given that an individual is in state s and we take action a, that individual has probability $\beta_{s,a}$ of replicating, i.e., of producing another individual who then evolves in expectation in a manner identical to that of his progenitor. (Except for the act of replicating, individuals in the system do not interact.) We can capture this by altering the standard Bellman recursion to account for such replication as follows:

$$V_s = \max_{a \in A_s} \left[r_{s,a} + \sum_{s' \in \mathscr{S}} p(s' \mid s,a)V_{s'} + \beta_{s,a} \sum_{s' \in \mathscr{S}} p(s' \mid s,a)V_{s'} \right]. \qquad \text{(R-Bellman)}$$

The (R-Bellman) recursion captures the fact that with probability $\beta_{s,a}$ the individual creates a replicate who then garners the same expected reward as his progenitor for the remainder of the process.

Here, the potential replication happens after we collect the one-step reward for performing action a, but we could instead have replication occur before collecting the reward. The replication need not be created in the same state, either. For example, if we would like to replicate from an individual in state s and create the copy in state s' with probability $\beta_{s,a}$, we can simply add $\beta_{s,a}V_{s'}$ to the expression for V_s.

The (R-Bellman) recursion directly translates into an LP in the same way as the original Bellman recursion. Specifically, we replace the constraint of (BellmanLP) with

$$V_s - \sum_{s' \in \mathscr{S}} p(s' \mid s,a)(1 + \beta_{s,a})V_{s'} \geq r_{s,a}, \quad s \in \mathscr{S}, a \in A_s.$$

Note that the resulting model with replication is exactly of the form of our original model with $p(s' \mid s,a)$ replaced by $p(s' \mid s,a)(1 + \beta_{s,a})$.

Our development here can be generalized so that an individual can generate multiple offspring in one step. In Section 2, we defined $p(s' \mid s,a)$ as the probability that the individual transits to state s' given that he is in s and we take action a. We can replace this with the following dynamics: An individual in state s and subjected to action a generates a finite, nonnegative, number of individuals in the next time period. And, $p(s' \mid s,a)$, called the transition rate, is the expected number of individuals that transit to state s'. Further, the system can begin with more than a single individual. Instead a finite number of individuals can appear in the system, and w_s is redefined as being the expected number of individuals that are initially in state s. Such MDPs are known as *branching* MDPs. The notions of a transient policy and transient system are unchanged in that they hinge on convergence of $\sum_{t=0}^{\infty} P_\pi^t$. Similarly, stationary policies achieve maximum system value. Such policies can be achieved by solving (BellmanLPD) and employing the rules outlined in Section 2. Branching MDPs have a long history in dynamic programming, going back to the original work of Bellman (1957).

3.2 Nontransient Stochastic Processes

For the special case we considered in Section 2, in which the population consists of (at most) one individual, and $\sum_{s' \in \mathscr{S}} p(s' \mid s, a) \leq 1$ for each $s \in \mathscr{S}, a \in A_s$, the system is termed substochastic. A system is termed stochastic if instead $\sum_{s' \in \mathscr{S}} p(s' \mid s, a) = 1$ for each $s \in \mathscr{S}, a \in A_s$. In the latter case, the population always consists of exactly one individual, and hence, the system is not transient in the sense described above. An ergodic Markov chain is an example of such a process. (In Examples 1 and 2, this would correspond to an individual who wanders the grid forever.) In this setting, alternative measures of total system reward must be introduced to ensure the system's value is finite. Perhaps the simplest approach here is to introduce a discount factor $0 < \rho < 1$ and modify model (1) so that we maximize the expected present value of reward:

$$\max_{\pi = (\delta^1, \delta^2, \dots)} w^\top \sum_{t=0}^{\infty} \rho^t P_\pi^t r_{\delta^{t+1}}. \tag{2}$$

A system was previously (under $\rho = 1$) termed transient provided $\sum_{t=0}^{\infty} P_\pi^t$ converged for every policy π, and we can see here that if we require the same property of $\sum_{t=0}^{\infty} \rho^t P_\pi^t$, the development of Section 2 again carries over. Viewed another way, we can think of replacing a stochastic transition matrix P_δ by the substochastic matrix ρP_δ, which has the effect of putting us in the transient setting.

From a modeling perspective, we usually think of ρ as discounting future rewards due to the decreased value of receiving income in future time periods. However, mathematically we see that ρ can also be viewed as "discounting" the transition probabilities. We used this idea in Example 2, increasing the probability the individual vanishes from the grid at each step by using a discount factor of $\rho = 1 - \lambda$. We now see this is equivalent to discounting the unit reward we obtain when the individual reaches the northwest corner. Under either interpretation, we have created time pressure to guide the individual to the northwest corner more quickly.

3.3 Constrained MDPs

Our original MDP, i.e., model (1), does not constrain the policy $\pi = (\delta^1, \delta^2, \dots)$ beyond requiring the action taken in each state in each time period, δ_s^t, come from the set A_s. This can be extended to a setting where limited resources are allocated in order to take actions, and hence, actions taken in one state and in one time period constrain those available in other states and time periods. That is, we restrict the class of available policies by requiring $\pi \in \Pi$ for some constraint set Π, which requires, e.g., that we obey a budget constraint.

Before developing this in more detail, we turn to the notion of randomized policies, relaxing our notion of a decision rule from the beginning of Section 2. Let $\delta_{s,a}^t = \mathbb{P}(\delta_s^t = a)$, $a \in A_s$. That is, given that we are in state s in period t, $\delta_{s,a}^t$ is the probability we choose action $a \in A_s$. We say this relaxes the space of feasible policies because as stated, model (1) requires that we deterministically choose one action in each time period in each state, i.e., it requires that the policy be nonrandomized. Now, for a fixed state s, we allow $\delta_{s,a}^t$ to be positive for more than one $a \in A_s$. All we require is that for all time periods t and states s, we have $\sum_{a \in A_s} \delta_{s,a}^t = 1$, stipulating that we have a randomized choice of action in each state s.

Even when we allow for randomized policies, model (1) can be solved by a nonrandomized stationary policy, i.e., one in which for each $s \in \mathscr{S}$, all but one of the probabilities $\delta_{s,a}^t$, $a \in A_s$, takes value zero, and these are the same for all time periods t. We pointed to this fact in Section 2, following the dual LP (BellmanLPD), where we indicated that an optimal basic solution to the dual LP has at most one $x_{s,a}$ positive for each A_s. In the solutions of Examples 1 and 2 using nonrandomized stationary policies means that in each cell we either do nothing or close one of the four exits, with probability one.

We extend our earlier notation and let P_{δ^t} denote the $|\mathscr{S}| \times |\mathscr{S}|$ transition matrix with $[P_{\delta^t}]_{s,s'} = \sum_{a \in A_s} \delta_{s,a}^t p(s' \mid s,a)$. We similarly extend the reward vector r_{δ^t} to denote the expected reward under a randomized decision rule. In introducing a budget constraint, we let $c_{s,a}$ be the cost of performing action a in state s and let c_{δ^t} be the $|\mathscr{S}|$-vector of expected one-step costs under randomized decision rule $\delta^t = (\delta_{s,a}^t)_{s \in \mathscr{S}, a \in A_s}$. With b denoting the available budget, and under this set of extended notation and allowing randomized policies, we formulate the following budget-constrained MDP:

$$
\max_{\pi = (\delta^1, \delta^2, \ldots)} w^\top \sum_{t=0}^{\infty} P_\pi^t r_{\delta^{t+1}}
$$

$$
\text{s.t.} \quad w^\top \sum_{t=0}^{\infty} P_\pi^t c_{\delta^{t+1}} \le b.
$$

(3)

We cannot solve (3) by simply solving the recursion (Bellman), which optimizes over $a \in A_s$, separately for each s, because this ignores the fact that the policy is now constrained by

$$
\pi \in \Pi = \left\{ \pi = (\delta^1, \delta^2, \ldots) \ge 0 : w^\top \sum_{t=0}^{\infty} P_\pi^t c_{\delta^{t+1}} \le b, \sum_{a \in A_s} \delta_{s,a}^t = 1, \forall t, s \right\}.
$$

It is important to recognize that the additional budget constraint is with respect to the *expected* cost we incur over the individual's transient lifetime.

As an alternative to the budget constraint in (3), we can scale the budget b by the expected lifetime of the individual, i.e., we formulate:

$$\max_{\pi=(\delta^1,\delta^2,\ldots)} \quad w^\top \sum_{t=0}^{\infty} P_\pi^t r_{\delta^{t+1}}$$
$$\text{s.t.} \quad w^\top \sum_{t=0}^{\infty} P_\pi^t c_{\delta^{t+1}} \le b w^\top \sum_{t=0}^{\infty} P_\pi^t e, \tag{4}$$

where $e = (1,1,\ldots,1)^\top$. The constraint in (4) captures the situation in which b is earned in each time period of the individual's transient lifetime, and that, in expectation, the costs incurred by carrying out actions a must be covered by these earnings.

By augmenting the dual LP (BellmanLPD) with one of the following budget constraints, we can solve the respective models (3) and (4):

$$\sum_{s\in\mathscr{S}} \sum_{a\in A_s} c_{s,a} x_{s,a} \le b \tag{5a}$$

$$\sum_{s\in\mathscr{S}} \sum_{a\in A_s} c_{s,a} x_{s,a} \le b \sum_{s\in\mathscr{S}} \sum_{a\in A_s} x_{s,a}. \tag{5b}$$

Optimal solutions to models (3) and (4) can be achieved by randomized stationary policies. Suppose we have solved the augmented dual LP (BellmanLPD) and obtained solution $x = (x_{s,a})$. Then, we can extract such an optimal policy as follows. If $\sum_{a\in A_s} x_{s,a} > 0$ then we take action $a \in A_s$ in state s according to:

$$\delta_{s,a} = \mathbb{P}(\delta_s = a) = \frac{x_{s,a}}{\sum_{a\in A_s} x_{s,a}}, \tag{6}$$

and the action we take is arbitrary if $\sum_{a\in A_s} x_{s,a} = 0$. Restated, if the individual is expected to visit state s then we take action a with the probability specified in (6) and, of course, if the individual does not visit state s then the action we take is irrelevant. Here, if we have an optimal basic solution and only one budget constraint, then there will be at most one state $s \in \mathscr{S}$ that has $\delta_{s,a} > 0$ for multiple actions, and this probability will be positive for (at most) two actions. More generally, if we append m resource constraints then the policy will be randomized in at most m states. (See, e.g., the discussion in Feinberg and Shwartz, 1995 and Ross, 1989.) Intuitively, randomized policies arise because any stationary policy typically either under- or over-utilizes the budget, but randomization enables full consumption of the budget.

Example 3. We consider an instance of the budget-constrained model (3), similar to that in Example 1, albeit with a modified grid and initial position for the individual, as indicated in Figure 3. As in Example 1, the individual is equally likely to transit to any of the four neighboring cells if we choose the "do nothing" action in that state. If we close a one-way door, the individual cannot transit to the corresponding neighbor cell, and is equally likely to move to each of the remaining three neighboring cells in the next time period. As before, the goal is to maximize the probability the individual reaches the northwest cell before reaching the southeast cell and vanishing. Closing a one-way door costs $c_{s,a} = 0.2$, except for the doors that directly block transit to the southeast corner. Those four one-way doors are considerably more expensive to close, with $c_{s,a} = 2$. The "do

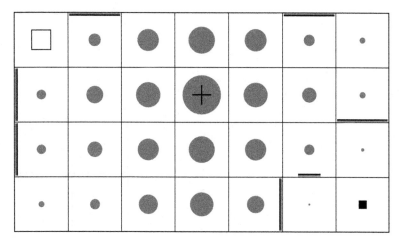

Fig. 3: The figure shows an instance of the budget-constrained model (3) and its solution. The cost of closing a door blocking transit to the southeast corner is very high. Thus, unlike in Figure 1, an optimal policy cannot simply block-off transit to that cell. The relative sizes of the black square in the southeast corner and the white square in the northwest corner, indicate the relative probabilities of the individual first reaching those cells. The solution consumes all of the available budget by randomizing the policy used in a cell near the southeast corner. There, a door is closed blocking transit to the south with probability 0.44 and otherwise we choose the "do nothing" action with probability 0.56. The total expected time for the individual in the system is 31.49 time periods.

nothing" action has zero cost, and the available budget is b = 1. We solve this model instance using the dual LP (BellmanLPD), augmented with budget constraint (5a), and the solution is displayed in Figure 3. Due to the budget constraint, it is no longer possible to simply block-off transit to the southeast corner, and the relative sizes of the squares in the northwest and southeast corners indicate the probabilities of the individual first reaching these respective cells (0.72 and 0.28). The solution is randomized in only one cell, near the southeast corner, where we close a one-way door blocking transit to the south with probability 0.44. We incur a cost each time the individual is blocked by a door, and we must stay within budget b. This induces a time pressure for the individual to vanish, and of course the objective is to maximize the probability he does so via the northwest corner. □

Example 4. We now modify Example 3 only in that we consider the budget constraint of model (4) instead of that of model (3). So, we solve the instance using the dual LP (BellmanLPD), augmented with budget constraint (5b). Figure 4 displays the solution. □

Examples 3 and 4 maximize the probability the individual reaches the northwest corner (or, equivalently minimizes the probability he reaches the southeast corner) subject to a budget constraint. In Example 3, for instance, we could exchange the role of the constraint and the objective, and instead formulate:

$$\min_{\pi=(\delta^1,\delta^2,\dots)} \quad w^\top \sum_{t=0}^{\infty} P_\pi^t c_{\delta^{t+1}}$$

$$\text{s.t.} \quad w^\top \sum_{t=0}^{\infty} P_\pi^t r_{\delta^{t+1}} \geq \alpha. \tag{7}$$

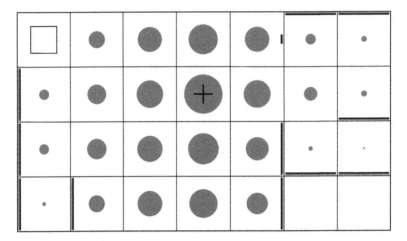

Fig. 4: The figure shows an instance of the budget-constrained model (4) and its solution. The model instance is identical to that in Figure 3 except that now the available budget scales with the expected time the individual spends in the system before vanishing. The optimal policy shown in the figure leads to an expected time in the system of 46.05 periods. Compare this with the expected time in Figure 3. The longer expected time in the system effectively increases the budget, and thus we are able to completely block-off transit to the southeast corner. In this solution, we have a randomized policy in a cell blocking transit to the east near the northeast corner.

In (7), we require the policy achieve a prespecified probability, α, that the individual reaches the northwest corner prior to vanishing, and we seek a policy that does so at minimum expected cost. This model contains what is known in stochastic programming as a chance-constraint (Prékopa, 1995), and in our current setting can be solved, e.g., using the appropriate variant of the dual LP (BellmanLPD).

4 Optimally Designing an MDP

So far, our discussion has centered on selecting a policy that optimally *controls* a system. The system dynamics are such that we observe the system's state and then take an action, possibly subject to budget constraints, which restrict the control policies we can choose. We now consider a one-time system "design" decision in which we seek to (optimally) form the set of actions that we will have available when we later solve the "operations" problem of optimally controlling the system via the MDP model. The design problem is a combinatorial optimization problem that constructs the sets A_s, $s \in \mathscr{S}$, subject to resource constraints, where the objective function is the optimal value of the MDP we design. We begin with an integer programming formulation of this problem, and discuss solution methods. Then, we show that this formulation can also capture the situation where we face a budget-constrained MDP, but restrict attention to the class of stationary nonrandomized policies. Finally, we consider the problem of optimally designing an MDP, when the parameters governing the MDP are random. These parameters are known only through a probability distribution at the time when we design the MDP, but are realized prior to selecting the MDP's control policy.

4.1 An Integer Programming Formulation

With $A = (A_s)_{s \in \mathscr{S}}$ and with $\mathscr{A}$ denoting the set of all feasible action-set choices, we can extend the budget-constrained MDP (3) to include a design stage as follows:

$$
\begin{aligned}
\max_{A \in \mathscr{A}} \max_{\pi = (\delta^1, \delta^2, \ldots)} \quad & w^\top \sum_{t=0}^\infty P_\pi^t r_{\delta^{t+1}} \\
\text{s.t.} \quad & w^\top \sum_{t=0}^\infty P_\pi^t c_{\delta^{t+1}} \leq b \\
& \sum_{a \in A_s} \delta_{s,a}^t = 1, t \in \mathscr{T}, s \in \mathscr{S} \\
& \delta_{s,a}^t \geq 0, t \in \mathscr{T}, s \in \mathscr{S}, a \in A_s \\
& \delta_{s,a}^t = 0, t \in \mathscr{T}, s \in \mathscr{S}, a \notin A_s.
\end{aligned}
\tag{8}
$$

In the final three constraints of (8) we have made explicit the dependence of the MDP control policy on the design decision $A = (A_s)_{s \in \mathscr{S}}$.

We seek to reformulate (8), for a class of action-set restrictions $\mathscr{A}$, in a computationally tractable manner, and we do so using a mixed-integer program (MIP). We redefine A_s to index all *candidate* actions in state $s \in \mathscr{S}$. A binary variable $z_{s,a}$ is used to indicate whether ($z_{s,a} = 1$) or not ($z_{s,a} = 0$) we will have access to action a in state s when controlling the system in the MDP. The following formulation represents model (8) when the set of action sets we can form are subject to multiple knapsack-style constraints defined by resource levels b^i, $i \in I$, and action-design costs, $c_{s,a}^i$, $s \in \mathscr{S}, a \in A_s, i \in I$:

$$
\max_z \quad h(z) \tag{9a}
$$

$$
\text{s.t.} \quad \sum_{s \in \mathscr{S}} \sum_{a \in A_s} c_{s,a}^i z_{s,a} \leq b^i, i \in I \tag{9b}
$$

$$
z_{s,a} \in \{0,1\}, s \in \mathscr{S}, a \in A_s, \tag{9c}
$$

where

$$
h(z) = \max_x \quad \sum_{s \in \mathscr{S}} \sum_{a \in A_s} r_{s,a} x_{s,a} \tag{10a}
$$

$$
\text{s.t.} \quad \sum_{a \in A_s} x_{s,a} - \sum_{s' \in \mathscr{S}} \sum_{a \in A_{s'}} p(s \mid s', a) x_{s',a} = w_s, s \in \mathscr{S} \tag{10b}
$$

$$
\sum_{s \in \mathscr{S}} \sum_{a \in A_s} c_{s,a} x_{s,a} \leq b \tag{10c}
$$

$$x_{s,a} \geq 0, s \in \mathscr{S}, a \in A_s \tag{10d}$$

$$x_{s,a} \leq M_{s,a} z_{s,a}, s \in \mathscr{S}, a \in A_s, \tag{10e}$$

and where the $M_{s,a}$, $s \in \mathscr{S}, a \in A_s$, are sufficiently large. The objective function of (9a), given as the optimal value in (10), is an MDP parameterized by the design decisions z. Binary constraints (9c) are yes-no restrictions on including action a for state s, and constraints (9b) require the designed action sets to satisfy our resource constraints. The MDP given by (10a)-(10d) captures the budget-constrained MDP (3), as discussed in Section 3.3. Constraints (10e) disallow use of action a in state s when $z_{s,a} = 0$, and when $z_{s,a} = 1$, $M_{s,a}$ being sufficiently large means that these constraints are vacuous. One way to find such values of $M_{s,a}$ is to solve auxiliary MDPs with $z_{s,a} = 1$ for all s and a that maximize $\sum_{a \in A_s} x_{s,a}$ for each s or maximize $x_{s,a}$ for each s and a. (Of course, tighter values of $M_{s,a}$ can be found.) We can solve model (9) by forming a single optimization model in which we simultaneously optimize over z and x, i.e.,

$$\max_{z,x} \sum_{s \in \mathscr{S}} \sum_{a \in A_s} r_{s,a} x_{s,a}$$

s.t. (9b)-(9c) and (10b)-(10e).

With Z denoting the constraint set defined by (9b)-(9c), note that $h(z)$ is concave over the convex hull of Z, at least when we view h as an extended real-valued function that takes value $h(z) = -\infty$ if the LP (10) is infeasible for a specific $z \in Z$. This permits solving (9) by Benders' decomposition (Benders, 1962; Van Slyke and Wets, 1969), in which we iteratively solve a master program to select the value of z and solve the MDP (10) for that z, building up in the master program a combination of optimality cuts that form an outer-linearization of $h(z)$ and feasibility cuts that eliminate choices of $z \in Z$ that lead to an infeasible MDP. Such an approach has the advantage that we need not solve the MDP (10) by linear programming but can instead use more computationally efficient methods such as policy iteration applied to the budget-constrained MDP.

It is worth noting that the design problem presented in this section can be solved using standard MDP techniques by increasing the state space of the MDP by a multiplicative factor exponential in the length of the decision variable z. To do this, we could introduce an initial virtual state where the available actions are all possible settings of the decision variable z. A particular setting of z then forces MDP to transition with probability 1 to a set of states specific to that setting of z, where only the actions allowed in z are available. Our formulation, in essence, removes this exponential blowup in the state space.

4.2 A Nonrandomized Stationary Policy

Consider the variant of the budget-constrained MDP (3) in which we require $\pi = (\delta, \delta, \ldots)$, i.e., a stationary policy. So, we consider the following model:

$$\max_{\pi=(\delta,\delta,\ldots)} \quad w^\top \sum_{t=0}^{\infty} P_\pi^t \, r_{\delta^{t+1}}$$

$$\text{s.t.} \quad w^\top \sum_{t=0}^{\infty} P_\pi^t \, c_{\delta^{t+1}} \leq b \tag{11}$$

$$\delta \in \times_{s\in\mathscr{S}} A_s,$$

and we disallow randomized policies, as indicated by the final constraint in (11). Even though this model does not involve design, per se, we can solve it with a specialization of the integer programming model developed in the previous section. Specifically, we can use:

$$\max_{z,x} \quad \sum_{s\in\mathscr{S}} \sum_{a\in A_s} r_{s,a} x_{s,a}$$

$$\text{s.t.} \quad \sum_{a\in A_s} z_{s,a} = 1, s \in \mathscr{S}$$

$$\text{(9c) and (10b)-(10e)},$$

where we have specialized constraints (9b) to $\sum_{a\in A_s} z_{s,a} = 1, s \in \mathscr{S}$. This requires us to select exactly one of the actions in each state, i.e., we require a nonrandomized strategy. For such a binary solution z, there are only $|\mathscr{S}|$ variables $x_{s,a}$ that can be nonzero by the forcing constraints (10e), and the values of these variables, $x = x(z)$, are fully specified by the $|\mathscr{S}| \times |\mathscr{S}|$ system of equations (10b). Constraint (10c) forbids selection of nonrandomized strategies via z that lead to an $x(z)$, which violates the resource constraint.

4.3 Designing an MDP under Stochastic Parameters

The parameters of the budget-constrained MDP (3) are $p(s \mid s',a)$, $r_{s,a}$, w_s, $c_{s,a}$, for $s \in \mathscr{S}, a \in A_s$ and b. Here, we model the situation in which these parameters are known only through a probability distribution at the time we must select the action-set design decisions $z = (z_{s,a})$. We denote by ξ the vector of all the random MDP parameters, and we also include in ξ one additional random parameter, $I_{s,a}$, $s \in \mathscr{S}, a \in A_s$. Parameter $I_{s,a}$ is an indicator random variable. If we include action a in state s as part of our design decision, and $I_{s,a}$ takes value one then we will have access to that action when selecting our control policy for the system. However, when $I_{s,a}$ takes value zero we will not have access to that action, even if it has been selected via $z_{s,a} = 1$. This models exogenous factors disallowing a particular action.

With these constructs we formulate the following two-stage stochastic integer program in which the MDP models our recourse:

$$\max_{z} \quad \mathbb{E}_\xi \, h(z,\xi)$$

$$\text{s.t. (9b)-(9c)}, \tag{12}$$

where

$$h(z, \xi) = \max_x \sum_{s \in \mathscr{S}} \sum_{a \in A_s} r_{s,a} x_{s,a} \qquad (13a)$$

$$\text{s.t. } (10b)\text{-}(10d) \qquad (13b)$$

$$x_{s,a} \leq I_{s,a} M_{s,a} z_{s,a}, s \in \mathscr{S}, a \in A_s. \qquad (13c)$$

We emphasize the timing of decisions and realizations of uncertainty in model (12). When we select z, the random vector $\xi = (p(s \mid s', a), r_{s,a}, w_s, c_{s,a}, b, I_{s,a})$ is known only through its probability distribution. Then, we realize $\xi = \xi(\omega)$ for some sample point $\omega \in \Omega$, and knowing this we select the optimal control policy for the corresponding MDP. This control policy depends on the realization of the MDP's parameters and of course, the system design z.

Example 5. Consider the following example of model (12), built on a variant of Example 3, in which only the individual's initial position, $w = (w_s)$, is stochastic. In order to close a one-way door when controlling the individual's movement in the MDP (using $x_{s,a}$), we must have installed that door in the design stage (using $z_{s,a}$). In the design stage, we have a knapsack constraint on the $z_{s,a}$. In particular, we are cardinality constrained and can install 6 doors. After the design stage, there are three equally-likely scenarios, with the individual beginning in one of the cells indicated by the plus signs in Figure 5. While solving the MDP for a particular scenario, the budget constraint for closing installed doors is identical to that in Example 3. The solution is shown in Figure 5. An

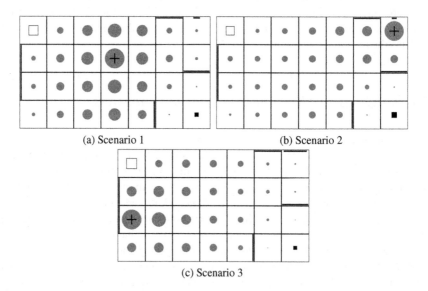

(a) Scenario 1   (b) Scenario 2

(c) Scenario 3

Fig. 5: An optimal solution to the three-scenario design problem from Example 5. In the design stage we are allowed to install 6 doors. After the design stage, there are three equally-likely scenarios, with the individual starting in one of the three cells indicated by crosses in the figure. Each scenario has a budget constraint on closing doors that is identical to the constraint in Example 3. In the optimal solution, we install a door in the northeast corner that is only used with probability 0.25, 0.18, and 0.87 in the first, second, and third scenarios, respectively. The individual is guided to the northwest corner with probability 0.692 (over all scenarios).

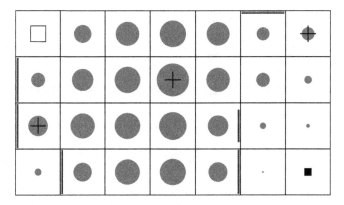

Fig. 6: An optimal solution to the one-scenario design problem from Example 5. In the design stage we are allowed to install 6 doors. After the design stage, there is one scenario, with the individual starting uniformly randomly in one of the three cells indicated by crosses in the figure. The scenario has a budget constraint on closing doors that is identical to that in Example 3. In the optimal solution, we install a door in the southeast that is only used with probability 0.74. The individual is guided to the northwest corner with probability 0.696. As expected, this is greater than the probability of exiting from the northwest corner in the three-scenario case presented in Figure 5.

interesting feature of the optimal solution is the door installed in the northeast corner. The door is used with probability 0.25, 0.18, and 0.87 in the randomized control policies in the first, second, and third scenarios, respectively. The individual exists at the northwest cell with probability 0.692 over all scenarios.

It also interesting that this example, with three equally likely scenarios, is different, and has a different optimal solution, than the case where there is one scenario with the individual starting with probability $1/3$ in each of the three respective cells. Consider model (12). If ξ is simply $w = (w_s)$, as in this example, then $h(z,\xi)$ is concave in ξ. Thus, we have $\mathbb{E}_\xi h(z,\xi) \leq h(z,\mathbb{E}\,\xi)$. The three-scenario case is a maximization over z of the left-hand side of the inequality. The one-scenario case is a maximization over z of the right-hand side of the inequality. Thus, based on the inequality, we know that the objective function value of the one-scenario case should be at least as large as the objective function value in the three-scenario case. In our instances, in the one-scenario case, the individual arrives at the northwest cell with probability 0.696. The solution of the one-scenario case is shown in Figure 6. □

5 A Special Case with Application

Consider the special case of the MDP where the actions do not affect the transition probabilities. In other words, $p(s' \mid s,a) = p(s' \mid s,a')$ for all a and a' in A_s, and we will denote this transition probability by simply $p(s' \mid s)$. The rewards and costs, on the other hand, can still depend on the actions.

Consider the equalities in (BellmanLPD),

$$\sum_{a\in A_s} x_{s,a} - \sum_{s'\in\mathscr{S}} \sum_{a\in A_{s'}} p(s\mid s',a)x_{s',a} = w_s, \quad s\in\mathscr{S}.$$

In our special case, defining $e_s = \sum_{a\in A_s} x_{s,a}$, we can rewrite the equalities as

$$\sum_{a\in A_s} x_{s,a} - \sum_{s'\in\mathscr{S}} p(s\mid s') \sum_{a\in A_{s'}} x_{s',a} = w_s, \quad s\in\mathscr{S}$$

$$e_s - \sum_{s'\in\mathscr{S}} p(s\mid s')e_{s'} = w_s, \quad s\in\mathscr{S},$$

which gives us a linear system in the $|\mathscr{S}|$-vector e.

Solving the linear system for e, we can then reformulate (BellmanLPD) as

$$\max_{y} \quad \sum_{s\in\mathscr{S}} \sum_{a\in A_s} r_{s,a}e_s y_{s,a}$$

$$\text{s.t.} \quad \sum_{a\in A_s} y_{s,a} = 1, \quad s\in\mathscr{S} \qquad \text{(SpecBellmanLPD)}$$

$$y_{s,a} \geq 0, \quad s\in\mathscr{S}, a\in A_s,$$

where $y_{s,a}$ can be interpreted as the probability we perform action a given that the individual is in state s. In other words, this reformulation solves directly for the randomized policy $\delta_{s,a}$, instead of using extraction rule (6). The budget constraints for this special-case MDP can be reformulated in a similar way. For example, to capture the specialized budget constraint (5a) we add

$$\sum_{s\in\mathscr{S}} \sum_{a\in A_s} c_{s,a}e_s y_{s,a} \leq b. \qquad (14)$$

We can follow the steps described in Section 4 to perform optimal design in the special case. When performing MDP design as in (12), the special case reformulation only affects the recourse function $h(z,\xi)$. When using decision variables $y_{s,a}$ to reformulate the linear program (13) which defines $h(z,\xi)$, we may take $M_{s,a} = 1$. Again, there will be computational advantages to finding tighter values of $M_{s,a}$ but because the $y_{s,a}$ variables denote probabilities, the unit bound suffices. The special case reformulation gives us several additional advantages in evaluating the recourse function, and we now discuss these in turn.

5.1 Nonlinear Dependencies

The first advantage of (SpecBellmanLPD) over (BellmanLPD) is that we can easily capture nonlinear dependencies between the rewards, or costs, and the expected number of times the individual is in a state. In (BellmanLPD), the decision variables are $x_{s,a}$, representing the expected number of times we perform action a in state s.

The objective function of (BellmanLPD) depends linearly on the expected number of visits to a particular state. For example, if we lose a dollar when the state is visited once, we lose twelve dollars when the state is visited twelve times.

On the other hand, in (SpecBellmanLPD), the decision variables are the $y_{s,a}$ and the $r_{s,a}e_s$ are constants. The term $r_{s,a}e_s$ captures the linear dependence explained in the previous paragraph. However, in (SpecBellmanLPD), we need not stick to this linear dependence. For example, after computing the e_s, the expected number of visits to state s, we can compute an arbitrary function of s, a, and e_s to substitute for the expression $r_{s,a}e_s$. In this way, we are able to capture nonlinear dependencies between the number of times a state is visited and the reward. For example, we can now express (negative) rewards such as losing as many dollars as the square root of the expected number of times we visit a state. A similar argument applies to the costs in (14). Though we can capture some nonlinear dependencies, in (SpecBellmanLPD) there is still a linear relationship between the rewards and the probability we select an action in a state, $y_{s,a}$.

5.2 Greedy Algorithm Through Lagrangian Relaxation

A second advantage of (SpecBellmanLPD) is that we do not need to solve it as a linear program, but can instead solve it with a fast greedy algorithm. Imagine solving (SpecBellmanLPD), i.e., without the inclusion of a budget constraint such as the one in (14). For each state s, we can simply select the action $a \in A_s$ with the greatest reward, i.e., set $y_{s,a} = 1$ and $y_{s,a'} = 0$ for all other $a' \in A_s$.

When we add a budget constraint such as (14) to (SpecBellmanLPD), the problem does not immediately decompose as nicely. Of course, we can choose to solve the budget-constrained problem as a linear program, but there can be computational advantages in large-scale instances to decomposing the problem by coupling a Lagrangian relaxation with a line-search as follows. A Lagrangian relaxation of (SpecBellmanLPD) under budget constraint (14) is:

$$\max_{y} \quad \sum_{s \in \mathcal{S}} \sum_{a \in A_s} (r_{s,a}e_s - \lambda c_{s,a}e_s)y_{s,a}$$

$$\text{s.t.} \quad \sum_{a \in A_s} y_{s,a} = 1, \qquad s \in \mathcal{S}$$

$$y_{s,a} \geq 0, \qquad s \in \mathcal{S}, a \in A_s,$$
$$\text{(RelaxSpecBellmanLPD)}$$

where λ is the Lagrange multiplier for the budget constraint.

To solve the budget-constrained version of model (SpecBellmanLPD) via model (RelaxSpecBellmanLPD), we must search for the appropriate value of λ. In the usual setting, a value of λ that is too small leads to a solution that exceeds the budget, and if λ is too large we under-utilize the budget. A simple bisection search allows us to find the "right" value of λ. Of course, the advantage of this approach over directly solving the budget-constrained (SpecBellmanLPD) is that, like model

(SpecBellmanLPD), model (RelaxSpecBellmanLPD) separates by state for each value of λ, i.e., it can be solved by the greedy algorithm described above. For more on constrained MDPs, see the discussion in the survey of Kallenberg (1994), and for more on the use of Lagrangian relaxation to deal with an MDP with a single budget constraint, like we consider here, see, e.g., Beutler and Ross (1985).

5.3 An Application

As an example, we apply our special-case model to finding optimal malaria intervention strategies in Nigeria. We divide Nigeria using a one arc-minute grid, creating $269,228$ spatial cells, which form the states of the MDP. The "individual" that moves among these states is malaria, or vectors (mosquitoes) carrying the disease. We consider minimizing three objective functions: the deaths caused by malaria, the economic impact of malaria, and a mixture of these two objectives. A more detailed description of this application, albeit without the "design decisions" z (see below), is contained in Dimitrov et al (2008).

In each cell, we have 18 available strategies. Each strategy has an associated cost, and an associated effectiveness in reducing the negative reward in the objective function. Table 1 provides a summary of the purchasing costs and effects of some basic intervention strategies considered in the model. Data on the cost and effectiveness of each strategy were gathered from the malaria literature. Since it is reasonable to assume that the listed strategies do not affect the transition probabilities of the disease vectors across the landscape, we are in the special MDP case described earlier in this section.

In solving the malaria application, we optimally select a set of distribution centers in Nigeria using the ideas in Section 4. In addition to purchasing costs, the costs of the intervention strategies used in the MDP take into account a model of distribution costs. The distribution costs of intervention strategies to a cell, depend linearly on

Table 1: Purchase costs and benefits of intervention strategies can be gathered from the malaria literature (Guyatt et al, 2002; Kayentao et al, 2004; Kiszewski et al, 2007; van Eijk et al, 2004). ACT stands for artemisinin-based combination therapy. IPT stands for intermittent preventative treatment. IRS stands for indoor residual spraying. LLIN stands for long lasting insecticide-treated nets. RDT stands for rapid diagnostic tests. These are the basic strategies included in the model. The model includes 18 strategies total. Some strategies not listed in the table are ACT targeted to children under 5 years old and combinations of strategies such as IPT and LLIN at the same time.

Strategy	Purchase Cost (US $/person)	Benefit
ACT	0.67	Reduce Number Infected by 50%
IPT	0.18	Reduce Pregnant Mortality Rate by 65%
IRS	1.08	Reduce Number Infected by 75%
LLIN	1.17	Reduce Number Infected by 63%
RDT	0.70	Decrease Intervention Costs by 25%

the distance of that cell to the nearest distribution center. The optimization model is allowed to select three of Nigeria's five most populated cities as distribution centers.

Following the description of the special MDP case in this section, to construct the malaria model we need an initial distribution of the disease vectors, $w = (w_s)$, and the transition probabilities for the malaria vector, $p(s \mid s')$. Then, we can solve the linear system that specifies the vector e, and hence construct the reformulated model (SpecBellmanLPD), with a budget constraint.

All of the calculations described in the previous paragraph are solely used to calculate the rewards of the reformulated program. In our malaria model, the rewards of the reformulated program depend only on the number of individuals infected by malaria.

One way to calculate the rewards in the reformulated program is to first estimate the initial distribution of disease vectors w by using a regression from a number of ecological and environmental factors. Then, we could use suitability data for disease vectors to obtain transition probabilities (Moffett et al, 2007). Finally, we could empirical data to estimate the number of infected individuals in a cell, given the number of disease vectors and the population of the cell.

However, a more direct way of achieving the same goals is to estimate the entomological inoculation rate (EIR), defined as the average number of infectious bites per person per year using a linear regression from the ecological and environmental factors, factors such as "Mean Diurnal Temperature Range" and "Precipitation During Driest Quarter." We can then use the EIR values to determine the percentage of infected individuals within each cell. The relationship between EIR and the percentage of infected individuals is nonlinear (Beier et al, 1999). Once we have the percentage of infected individuals and the population of each cell, we go on to calculate the number of deaths and the lost productivity in each cell. We use this second, more direct approach in our calculations.

The results of the multivariate linear regression used to determine the distribution of EIR values across Nigeria are provided in Figure 7. EIR values were found to be highest in the coastal areas, while low values were observed in the northeast. This variation appears to result from both the small mean diurnal temperature range in the coastal regions and from the large amount of rainfall that these regions encounter throughout the year. Malaria vector abundance is greatest in areas that have consistently high temperatures and consistent precipitation. The EIR values are thus compatible with our understanding of the ecological factors that are important to malaria transmission.

So, design variables z (see Section 4) select the location of distribution centers, and once those locations are selected we solve a budget-constrained version of the special-case model (SpecBellmanLPD). And, in the results we now report, we do so for a range of budget values b in constraint (14). In general, for different values of b, we expect that different subsets of the distribution centers could be selected. However, in our computational instances this did not turn out to be the case. That is, over a range of different budgets and objective functions, the optimal distribution center locations did not change, and were consistently the three locations in the coastal areas. Figure 8 graphically displays the possible distribution center

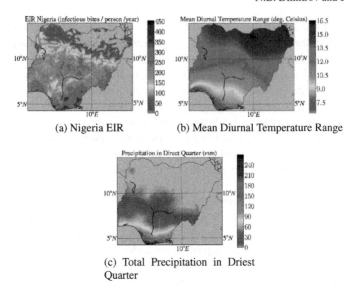

(a) Nigeria EIR   (b) Mean Diurnal Temperature Range

(c) Total Precipitation in Driest
Quarter

Fig. 7: Results of the multivariate linear regression. Figure 7a depicts the variation in EIR values across Nigeria, as measured in terms of the number of infective bites per person per year. The regression indicated that the EIR values were largely a function of temperature and precipitation. To help indicate this dependence, Figure 7b depicts the mean diurnal temperature range across Nigeria, while Figure 7c depicts the total precipitation of the driest quarter of the year, as measured in mm of rainfall.

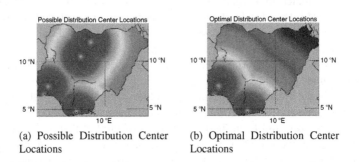

(a) Possible Distribution Center   (b) Optimal Distribution Center
Locations   Locations

Fig. 8: Results of optimal distribution center selection. Figure 8a displays the locations of Nigeria's five most populated cities: Lagos, Kano, Ibadan, Kaduna, and Port Harcourt. The optimization is allowed to select three of these to be distribution centers. The distribution costs of intervention strategies depend linearly with the distance to the nearest distribution center. Figure 8b displays the locations selected by the optimization. Even though the optimization is run separately for different budgets and objective functions, Lagos, Ibadan, and Port Harcourt are consistently selected as distribution centers. Retrospectively, this selection is intuitive as the distribution centers are targeted towards the coastal areas, where malaria is most prevalent. (see Figure 7)

locations—Lagos, Kano, Ibadan, Kaduna, and Port Harcourt—as well as the optimal locations—Lagos, Ibadan, and Port Harcourt. Retrospectively, the clustering of distribution centers around the coastal areas is intuitive as those areas have the greatest malaria prevalence, as pictured in Figure 7a.

The optimal intervention strategies for three different objectives are provided in Figure 9. The map in Figure 9a depicts the optimal strategy for limiting malaria

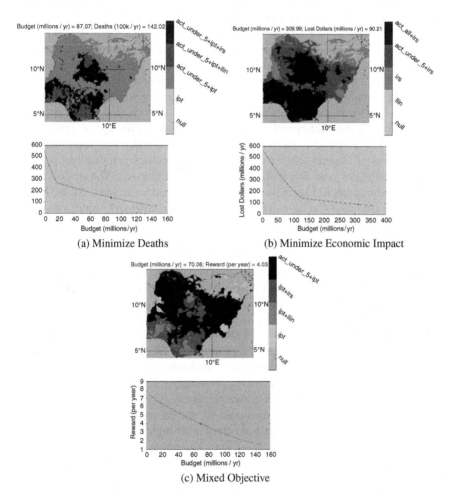

(a) Minimize Deaths

(b) Minimize Economic Impact

(c) Mixed Objective

Fig. 9: Optimal intervention strategies. Figure 9a depicts both the optimal strategy for limiting malaria mortality at a selected budget, and the effects of adopting the optimal strategy for each of a range of budgets. Figure 9b depicts the same information, but for the minimization of economic loss due to malaria. Figure 9c depicts the results when limiting a mixture of economic loss and mortality. With each of the objectives, at small budgets, strategies were initially targeted to areas of high population density. This reflects the high cost effectiveness of implementing strategies in urban areas. An interesting result of the analysis is the kinks visible in graphs of Figures 9a and 9b. These kinks represent a decrease in the cost effectiveness of the remaining available strategies as the budget is increased.

mortality at a selected budget. The different colors in the map represent different actions, with the occurrence of a particular color in a particular area representing the performance of the associated action in that area as part of the overall intervention strategy. The map thus indicates that at a budget of 87.64 million dollars per year, the optimal intervention strategy involves the distribution of IPT to pregnant women and ACT to children under the age of five across most of the country. In highly populated areas, these actions are supplemented with IRS and LLIN. The graph in Figure 9a depicts the effects on mortality of adopting the optimal intervention strategies associated with a range of budgets. The x-axis indicates the budget, in millions of dollars per year, while the y-axis indicates the number of deaths from malaria, in hundreds of thousands per year. The red dot indicates the budget and corresponding number of deaths for the map shown in Figure 9a.

Malaria mortality is assumed to be limited to pregnant women and young children. That is why, in increasing the budget, the first strategy to be implemented is IPT, followed by the distribution of ACT to children under the age of five. Providing both IPT to pregnant women and ACT to children under five years old, in all relevant areas of Nigeria, costs roughly 17 million dollars per year and prevents 290,000 deaths per year, at a cost of 60 dollars per life saved. The abrupt change of slope in the graph in Figure 9a is located at this budget amount. As the budget is increased beyond 17 million dollars per year, more expensive strategies such as LLIN and IRS become optimal. These strategies are first implemented in the major population centers, as can be seen in Figure 9a.

Figure 9b shows the results when the goal is instead to reduce the economic impact of malaria. The format of the figure is identical to that of Figure 9a, however the effects of adopting the different intervention strategies are presented in terms of lost economic productivity, rather than malaria mortality.

At small budget amounts, the economic consequences of malaria infection are reduced through the distribution of LLINs to highly populated areas. As the budget is increased, these areas are supplemented with IRS. As the budget is further increased, IRS is distributed throughout the majority of the country. Covering the majority of the country with IRS costs approximately 131 million dollars per year and prevents 422 million dollars in economic damages. The abrupt change in slope in Figure 9b is located at this budget amount. As the budget is further increased, ACT is distributed to all individuals in areas with high population densities, and elsewhere to children under the age of five. The change in slope seen in Figure 9b reflects the lower efficiency of this strategy, as compared to that of distributing LLINs and IRS.

Figure 9c depicts an optimal strategy for a selected budget when considering both economic damage and mortality. Any aggregation of these two measures requires the implicit assignment of a dollar value to human life, which will always be controversial. So as not to endorse any particular such value, Figure 9c simply represents the effects of assigning an arbitrary economic cost to mortality. For this reason, the graph in Figure 9c is presented in terms of a unitless quantity referred to as "Reward." This graph indicates that as the budget increases, the optimal strategies exhibit the combined characteristics of the optimal strategies for limiting economic loss and mortality individually. At the lowest budget, the majority of the country is provided with IPT. As the budget increases, ACT is provided to children under the age of five. However, before the entire country has been provided with with IPT and ACT, LLINs are distributed to the major population centers, with IRS provided to the outlying areas. As the budget is further increased, IRS and ACT are provided across the country. The model is able to produce results for the assignment of any value to the loss of human life.

For these calculations, we used the special case algorithm described in Section 5.2. Specifically, when solving the MDP for a particular design, i.e. selection of distribution centers, and a particular budget, we performed a search for the correct value of the Lagrange multiplier. To compute an optimal design for each budget requires approximately 1.5 minutes on a modern laptop, while each iteration of the underlying greedy algorithm requires 0.3 seconds.

Acknowledgements

We thank Alexander Moffett and Sahotra Sarkar from the University of Texas Section for Integrative Biology for their help in constructing the malaria application. This research was supported by the National Science Foundation under Grants CBET-0736231 and CMMI-0653916.

References

Adelman D (2007) Dynamic bid-prices in revenue management. Operations Research 55:647–661

Altman E, Shwartz A (1991) Sensitivity of constrained Markov decision problems. Annals of Operations Research 32:1–22

Beier JC, Killeen GF, Githure JI (1999) Entomological inoculation rates and plasmodium falciparum malaria prevalence in Africa. American Journal of Tropical Medicine and Hygiene 61:109–113

Bellman RE (1957) Dynamic Programming. Princeton University Press

Benders JF (1962) Partitioning procedures for solving mixed-variables programming problems. Numerische Mathematik 4:238–252

Bertsekas DP, Tsitsiklis JN (1991) An analysis of stochastic shortest path problems. Mathematics of Operations Research 16:580–595

Beutler FJ, Ross KW (1985) Optimal policies for controlled Markov chains with a constraint. Journal of Mathematical Analysis and Application 112:236–252

Blackwell D (1962) Discrete dynamic programming. Annals of Mathematical Statistics 33:719–726

Derman C (1962) On sequential decisions and Markov chains. Management Science 9:16–24

Dimitrov N, Moffett A, Morton DP, Sarkar S (2008) Markov decision processes for optimal malaria control, working paper, Graduate Program in Operations Research, The University of Texas at Austin

Eaton JH, Zadeh LA (1962) Optimal pursuit strategies in discrete state probabilistic systems. Transactions of the ASME, Series D, Journal of Basic Engineering 84:23–29

van Eijk AM, Ayisi JG, ter Kuile FO, Otieno JA, Misore AO, et al (2004) Effectiveness of intermittent preventive treatment with sulphadoxine-pyrimethamine for control of malaria in pregnancy in western Kenya: a hospital based study. Tropical Medicine and International Health 9:351–360

d'Epenoux F (1963) A probabilistic production and inventory problem. Management Science 10:98–108, english translation of an article published in *Revue Francaise de Recherche Opérationnelle* 14, 1960.

de Farias DP, Roy BV (2003) The linear programming approach to approximate dynamic programming. Operations Research 51:850–856

de Farias DP, Roy BV (2004) On constraint sampling for the linear programming approach to approximate dynamic programming. Mathematics of Operations Research 29:462–478

Feinberg EA, Shwartz A (1995) Constrained markov decision models with weighted discounted rewards. Mathematics of Operations Research 20:302–320

Guyatt HL, Corlett SK, Robinson TP, Ochola SA, Snow RW (2002) Malaria prevention in highland Kenya: indoor residual house-spraying vs. insecticide-treated bednets. Tropical Medicine and International Health 7:298–303

Howard RA (1960) Dynamic Programming and Markov Processes. MIT Press, Cambridge, MA

Kallenberg LCM (1983) Linear programming and finite Markovian control problems. Tech. Rep. 148, Mathematical Centre Tracts, Amsterdam

Kallenberg LCM (1994) Survey of linear programming for standard and nonstandard Markovian control problems. part i: Theory. Mathematical Methods of Operations Research 40:1–42

Kayentao K, Kodio M, Newman RD, Maiga H, Doumtabe D, et al (2004) Comparison of intermittent preventive treatment with chemoprophylaxis for the prevention of malaria during pregnancy in Mali. The Journal of Infectious Diseases 191:109–116

Kiszewski A, Johns B, Schapira A, Delacollette C, Crowell V, et al (2007) Estimated global resources needed to attain international malaria control goals. Bulletin of the World Health Organization 85:623–630

Manne AS (1960) Linear programming and sequential decisions. Management Science 6:259–267

Moffett A, Shackelford N, Sarkar S (2007) Malaria in Africa: Vector species niche models and relative risk maps. PLoS ONE 2:e824

Prékopa A (1995) Stochastic Programming. Kluwer Academic Publishers, Dordrecht

Puterman ML (2005) Markov Decision Processes: Discrete Dynamic Programming. John Wiley & Sons, Inc., Hoboken, New Jersey

Ross KW (1989) Randomized and past dependent policies for markov decision processes with finite action set. Operations Research 37:474–477

Schweitzer P, Seidmann A (1985) Generalized polynomial approximations in Markovian decision processes. Journal of Mathematical Analysis and Applications 110:568–582

Van Slyke RM, Wets R (1969) L-shaped linear programs with applications to optimal control and stochastic programming. SIAM Journal on Applied Mathematics 17:638–663

Veinott, Jr AF (1969) Discrete dynamic programming with sensitive discount optimality criteria. The Annals of Mathematical Statistics 40:1635–1660

Wagner HM (1960) On the optimality of pure strategies. Management Science 6:268–269

A Primal-Dual Slack Approach to Warmstarting Interior-Point Methods for Linear Programming

Alexander Engau, Miguel F. Anjos, and Anthony Vannelli

Abstract Despite the many advantages of interior-point algorithms over active-set methods for linear programming, one of their practical limitations is the remaining challenge to efficiently solve several related problems by an effective warmstarting strategy. Similar to earlier approaches that modify the initial problem by shifting the boundary of its feasible region, the contribution of this paper is a new but relatively simpler scheme which uses a single set of new slacks to relax the nonnegativity constraints of the original primal-dual variables. Preliminary computational results indicate that this simplified approach yields similar improvements over cold starts as achieved by previous methods.

Keywords: interior-point methods – linear programming – warmstarting

1 Introduction

In this paper, we study linear programs (LPs) in standard primal form

$$\min c^T x \tag{1a}$$
$$\text{s.t. } Ax = b \tag{1b}$$
$$x \geq 0 \tag{1c}$$

Alexander Engau, Postdoctoral Fellow
University of Waterloo, Waterloo, ON N2L 3G1, Canada, e-mail: aengau@alumni.clemson.edu

Miguel F. Anjos, Associate Professor
University of Waterloo, Waterloo, ON N2L 3G1, Canada, e-mail: anjos@stanfordalumni.org

Anthony Vannelli, Professor and Dean
University of Guelph, Guelph, ON N1G 2W1, Canada, e-mail: vannelli@uoguelph.ca

J.W. Chinneck et al. (eds.), *Operations Research and Cyber-Infrastructure*, Operations Research/Computer Science Interfaces Series 47, DOI: 10.1007/978-0-387-88843-9_10, © Springer Science+Business Media, LLC 2009

where the constraint matrix $A \in \mathbb{R}^{m \times n}$, the right-hand-side vector $b \in \mathbb{R}^m$, and the cost coefficient $c \in \mathbb{R}^n$ denote the problem data, and $x \in \mathbb{R}^n$ is the decision variable. The dual problem of (1) with dual variable $y \in \mathbb{R}^m$ and nonnegative slack $s \in \mathbb{R}^n$ is

$$\max b^T y \tag{2a}$$

$$\text{s.t. } A^T y + s = c \tag{2b}$$

$$s \geq 0 \tag{2c}$$

Since the seminal work by Karmarkar (1984), interior-point methods (IPMs) have become the algorithms of choice to efficiently solve LPs as well as convex (conic) optimization problems (Roos et al 2006). In contrast to active-set methods that move along the boundary of the feasible region, most prominently including Dantzig's simplex method, IPMs typically generate a sequence of intermediate interior points along the trajectory of analytic centers (the so-called "central path"), which converges to an optimal solution of the LP as the algorithm reduces the associated centrality measure to zero. IPMs are well-developed in theory and already widely used in many practical applications, however, an aspect that is still under active investigation is the development of effective warmstarting strategies.

By warmstarting we mean the use of information obtained from solving an initial LP instance, particularly its optimal solution, to accelerate or otherwise facilitate the re-optimization of one or more closely related problems with only minor changes from the original problem structure by adding or removing some variables and/or constraints, or some numerical changes due to (small) perturbations of the original problem data. The former situation typically occurs when solving LPs as subproblems for (mixed-)integer linear programs within the context of branch-and-bound, branch-and-cut, cutting-plane or other sequential decomposition schemes, and several papers have already considered this case (Mitchell and Todd 1992, Mitchell and Borchers 1996, Gondzio 1998, Gondzio and Vial 1999, Mitchell 2000, Elhedhli and Goffin 2004, among others). For the latter, data changes in right-hand side or cost vectors naturally arise in Benders or Dantzig-Wolfe decomposition, respectively, as well as in many engineering or financial contexts that, for example, deal with frequent variation of product specifications or market prices. Fewer papers have addressed this case (Freund 1991a,b, Yildirim and Wright 2002, Gondzio and Grothey 2003, Benson and Shanno 2007) that we also discuss in this paper.

It is widely recognized that the major challenge in warmstarting an IPM lies in the fact that optimal or nearly-optimal solutions that lie on or close to the boundary of the nonnegative feasible region are typically not sufficiently interior to be suited as initial iterate for an interior-point algorithm. In particular, because all nonbasic variables will assume very small values after converging to a nearly-optimal solution, starting an IPM from such a point often causes numerical instabilities or other difficulties that enable only very little progress, if at all. Therefore, and in contrast with active-set methods for which the optimal solution of the original LP instance is typically a very good starting point for a closely related problem, IPMs usually perform better when (re-)started from well-centered points in close proximity to the central path although possibly still quite far from an optimal solution, compared to points that are much closer but badly centered.

Based on these observations, the predominant solution strategy among the aforementioned papers was the storage of intermediate iterates of the original problem, which allows to retreat along its central path until a "good" warmstarting point is found, good in the sense that it is also sufficiently close to the new central path of the modified problem. First proposed by Mitchell and Todd (1992) and further studied by Mitchell and Borchers (1996), related approaches are analyzed more recently by Yildirim and Wright (2002) and Gondzio and Grothey (2003) who also give explicit bounds on the permissible problem perturbation so that the resulting infeasibilities at a previous iterate can be absorbed by one full Newton step to continue a feasible path-following IPM. In support of these approaches, some computational experiments have been reported and have shown encouraging preliminary results (Gondzio and Grothey 2003, John and Yildirim 2008).

In the present paper, we study an alternative scheme that, instead of maintaining a solution pool of previous iterates, modifies the new problem to allow a warm start from an (exact or approximate) optimal solution of the initial problem. In this case, to overcome the persistent problem of vanishing primal variables and dual slacks, we employ an idea similar to Freund's infeasible-start shifted-barrier methods (Freund 1991a,b, 1996) and Benson and Shanno's exact primal-dual penalty method approach (Benson and Shanno 2007) that modify the original problem by shifting the boundary of the nonnegative feasible region to temporarily allow these variables to become negative. Unlike these methods, however, we do not actually change the problem by introducing new shift or penalty parameters, but we merely choose the new but equivalent problem formulation that explicitly introduces the corresponding slack variables for all nonnegative constraints. As a major benefit of this approach, therefore, we are able to remove the difficulty to properly choose and possibly update any additional problem parameters, while achieving a similar warm start performance as obtained by the previous methods.

2 Preliminaries

In preparation of the discussion of our new warmstarting scheme, we first review the basic primal-dual path-following interior-point algorithm and several related warmstarting approaches that have been proposed in the existing literature. Throughout this paper, we adopt the standard notation typically used in this context and denote by $X \in \mathbb{R}^{n \times n}$ and $S \in \mathbb{R}^{n \times n}$ the diagonal matrices of the vectors $x \in \mathbb{R}^n$ and $s \in \mathbb{R}^n$, respectively. Moreover, for any vector norm $\|.\|$ and any matrix $A \in \mathbb{R}^{m \times n}$, we let

$$\|A\| := \max\{\|Ax\| : \|x\| = 1, x \in \mathbb{R}^n\} \tag{3}$$

be the associated subordinate matrix norm so that, in particular, $\|Ax\| \leq \|A\| \cdot \|x\|$ if $\|.\|$ denotes one of the most-commonly used ℓ_1, ℓ_2, or ℓ_∞-norms.

2.1 Interior-Point Methods and Algorithms

While a variety of IPMs have been proposed over the last thirty years, including different variants of the affine-scaling, target-following, or potential-reduction methods (Roos et al 2006), probably the most often used are the so-called primal-dual path-following methods (Wright 1997) that stem from the logarithmic barrier formulation

$$\min c^T x - \mu \sum_{i=1}^{n} \log(x_i) \text{ s.t. } Ax = b \tag{4}$$

of problem (1). These methods perform a sequence of Newton iterations applied to the first-order (Karush-Kuhn-Tucker) optimality conditions

$$Ax = b \tag{5a}$$

$$A^T y + s = c \tag{5b}$$

$$XSe = \mu e \tag{5c}$$

where (5a) and (5b) ensure primal and dual feasibility, respectively, and (5c) describes complementary slackness for the decreasing barrier parameter or centrality measure μ. It is well known that for every $\mu > 0$, this system has a unique solution, and the set of these solutions forms the so-called central path which converges to an optimal solution of LP for μ tending to zero. Moreover, it is easy to see that for a primal-dual feasible solution (x, y, s) and $\mu = x^T s / n$, the quantity $n\mu$ measures the duality gap $c^T x - b^T y$ between the objective values of the original primal-dual pair.

To solve the resulting Newton system associated with the KKT conditions (5)

$$\begin{bmatrix} A & 0 & 0 \\ 0 & A^T & I \\ S & 0 & X \end{bmatrix} \begin{bmatrix} \Delta x \\ \Delta y \\ \Delta s \end{bmatrix} = \begin{bmatrix} r_b \\ r_c \\ \mu e - XSe \end{bmatrix} \tag{6}$$

where the residuals $r_b = b - Ax$ and $r_c = c - A^T y - s$ may be zero or nonzero, most algorithms either solve the equivalent symmetric indefinite system

$$\begin{bmatrix} 0 & A \\ A^T & -D^{-2} \end{bmatrix} \begin{bmatrix} \Delta y \\ \Delta x \end{bmatrix} = \begin{bmatrix} r_b \\ r_c - \mu X^{-1} e + s \end{bmatrix} \tag{7}$$

where $D = X^{1/2} S^{-1/2}$, or compute the Cholesky factorization of the symmetric positive definite system $AD^2 A^T$ that arises in the so-called normal equations

$$AD^2 A^T \Delta y = r_b + AD^2 (r_c - \mu X^{-1} e + s). \tag{8}$$

The missing terms in (7) and (8) can then be found by the simple back substitution

$$\Delta s = r_c - A^T \Delta y \tag{9a}$$

$$\Delta x = \mu S^{-1} e - x - D^2 \Delta s. \tag{9b}$$

Once the Newton direction $(\Delta x, \Delta y, \Delta s)$ at a current iterate has been computed, a corresponding step is taken which guarantees that the new iterate is still interior and, depending on the particular IPM used, belongs to some pre-specified neighborhood of the central path. Then the barrier parameter is updated, and this procedure is repeated until all termination criteria for residuals and solution accuracies are satisfied. This basic IPM is outlined with some more details as Algorithm 1.

Algorithm 1: Primal-Dual Path-Following IPM

Input: initial point $z^0 = (x^0, y^0, s^0)$, scalar $\sigma \in [0,1]$, tolerances $\varepsilon_b > 0, \varepsilon_c > 0, \varepsilon_d > 0$;

Initialization: set $k = 0$ and compute $r_b^k = b - Ax^k$, $r_c^k = c - A^T y^k - s^k$, $\mu^k = \sigma {x^k}^T s^k / n$;

while $\max \left\{ \frac{\|r_b^k\|}{\varepsilon_b}, \frac{\|r_c^k\|}{\varepsilon_c}, \frac{(x^k)^T s^k}{\varepsilon_d} \right\} > 1$ **do**

    solve the Newton system (6) for $(\Delta x^k, \Delta y^k, \Delta s^k)$;

    set $\alpha^k < \min \left\{ 1, \frac{x_i^k}{|\Delta x_i^k|}, \frac{s_i^k}{|\Delta s_i^k|} : \Delta x_i < 0, \Delta s_i < 0, i = 1, \ldots, n \right\}$;

    set $(x^{k+1}, y^{k+1}, s^{k+1}) = (x^k, y^k, s^k) + \alpha^k (\Delta x^k, \Delta y^k, \Delta s^k)$;

    set $k = k + 1$ and update r_b^k, r_c^k, and μ^k;

end

The initial point $z^0 = (x^0, y^0, s^0)$ in Algorithm 1 must satisfy that $(x^0, s^0) > 0$ but can otherwise be chosen either primal-dual feasible ($r_b^0 = 0$ and $r_c^0 = 0$) or infeasible (at least one of r_b^0 and r_c^0 is nonzero). Correspondingly, we also call Algorithm 1 a feasible or infeasible IPM, and in either case it is easy to show that

$$r^{k+1} = (1 - \alpha^k) r^k = \prod_{j=0}^{k} (1 - \alpha^j) r^0 \qquad (10)$$

for both r_b and r_c, so that a feasible IPM preserves feasibility of its starting point, whereas an infeasible IPM (IIPM) can always establish feasibility by taking a full Newton step with $\alpha^k = 1$ (but at the risk of possibly leaving the interior). While the early development of IPMs was primarily focused on feasible approaches that still enjoy slightly better complexity bounds in theory, in practice IIPMs typically outperform their feasible counterparts and are nowadays widely considered to be the more powerful algorithms for LP.

2.2 Warmstarting Interior-Point Algorithms

Similar to the notation adopted in Yildirim and Wright (2002), we now denote the problem data of an LP instance by the triplet $d = (A, b, c)$ and assume that $d = d^\circ + \Delta d$, where $d^\circ = (A^\circ, b^\circ, c^\circ)$ is the initial LP with a known optimal solution $z^\circ = (x^\circ, y^\circ, s^\circ)$, and $\Delta d = (\Delta A, \Delta b, \Delta c)$ is a (small) problem perturbation of d°.

Since z° is optimal for the initial data instance d°, it also satisfies its KKT conditions (5) and, in particular, is primal-dual feasible. However, for the new instance d, this previous solution typically becomes infeasible because

$$r_b = b - Ax^\circ = (b^\circ + \Delta b) - (A^\circ + \Delta A)x^\circ = \Delta b - \Delta A x^\circ \tag{11a}$$

$$r_c = c - A^T y^\circ - s = (c^\circ + \Delta c) - (A^\circ + \Delta A)^T y^\circ - s = \Delta c - \Delta A^T y^\circ \tag{11b}$$

are nonzero, in general. Hence, to re-establish feasibility we may either move from z° to some other close but feasible point or take a first full Newton step which, from (10), will re-establish feasibility also for all following iterates. These approaches have recently been investigated by Yildirim and Wright 2002 (with computational results reported in John and Yildirim 2008) who proposed the (weighted) least-squares adjustments (LSA)

$$\min_{\Delta x} \|\Sigma \Delta x\| \text{ s.t. } A(x^\circ + \Delta x) = b, x^\circ + \Delta x \geq 0 \tag{12a}$$

$$\min_{\Delta y, \Delta s} \|\Lambda \Delta s\| \text{ s.t. } A^T(y^\circ + \Delta y) + (s^\circ + \Delta s) = c, s^\circ + \Delta s \geq 0 \tag{12b}$$

where Σ and Λ can be chosen as identities (P(lain)LSA), the inverses X^{-1} and S^{-1} (W(eighted)LSA), or $X^{-1}S$ and $S^{-1}X$ (J(ointly)WLSA). A benefit of this approach is that the solution to (12) can be given explicitly but with the drawback that the new point $(x, y, s) = (x^\circ + \Delta x, y^\circ + \Delta y, s^\circ + \Delta s)$ may not be well-centered, in general.

An alternative to the above LSA adjustment is the pure Newton adjustment

$$A\Delta x = r_b \tag{13a}$$

$$A^T \Delta y + \Delta s = r_c \tag{13b}$$

$$X^\circ \Delta s + S^\circ \Delta x = 0 \tag{13c}$$

whose solution, however, is slightly more difficult and also requires a Cholesky factorization of $AD^2 A^T$ if reduced to its equivalent normal equations. Related to the above approaches, Gondzio and Grothey (2003) also provide theoretical bounds on the permissible problem perturbation so that all resulting infeasibilities can be absorbed by one full Newton step from a previous iterate to continue a feasible path-following IPM while staying within some predescribed neighborhood of the central path. In a more recent paper (Gondzio and Grothey 2008), the same authors propose an alternative warmstarting strategy that uses sensitivity analysis to identify those starting point components that cause blocking of the current Newton step, with the aim of constructing a modified search direction in which larger steps are possible.

In this paper, we choose a different approach that, instead of keeping track of previous iterates to retreat along the central path, re-establish feasibility, and continue a feasible IPM, makes explicit use of the resulting infeasibilities to define a new (infeasible) starting point as initial iterate for an IIPM. Since these algorithms have been proven to be theoretically competitive and shown to outperform their feasible counterparts in practice, it seems reasonable to initially ignore that the starting point is infeasible and achieve its feasibility in the course of the algorithm. Nevertheless, we still cannot directly restart from an (approximate or exact) optimal solution for which the duality gap is typically very close to zero so that several variables will have almost completely vanished and only very small steps can be taken to maintain their interiority. To remedy this situation, the most common approach is to temporarily allow x and s to become negative by shifting the boundary of their feasible nonnegative region, which was first proposed in the shifted-barrier methods by Freund (1991a,b, 1996, also Polyak 1992), later extended for column-generation problems by Mitchell (1994), and recently used by Benson and Shanno (2007) in their primal-dual penalty method.

In the first paper, Freund (1991a) introduces the new potential function

$$F(x,\beta) = q\log(c^T x - \beta) - \sum_{i=1}^{n} \log(x_i + h_i(c^T x - \beta)) \tag{14}$$

where $q = n + \sqrt{n}$, $h > 0$ is a given and fixed positive shift vector, and β is a known lower bound on the optimal objective function value. For this function, he proposes a new potential-reduction algorithm that, under relatively mild assumptions, achieves a constant decrease of duality gap and primal-dual infeasibilities in $O(nL)$ steps, or, under some more restrictive assumptions, in $O(\sqrt{n}L)$ steps (as usual, here L denotes the bit length of the problem input data).

In a related second paper and primarily studied from a theoretical point of view, Freund (1991b) proposes to solve a sequence of shifted-barrier problems

$$\min c^T x - \varepsilon \sum_{i=1}^{n} \log(x_i + \varepsilon h_i) \tag{15a}$$

$$\text{s.t. } Ax = b \tag{15b}$$

$$x + \varepsilon h > 0 \tag{15c}$$

where $h > 0$ is again a positive shift vector, for a sequence of values $\varepsilon > 0$ that converges to zero. For this case, he shows that for suitable h and initial $\varepsilon = \varepsilon^0$, the number of iterations required to achieve $\varepsilon \leq \varepsilon^*$ is bounded by $\lceil 6\sqrt{n}\ln(\varepsilon^0/\varepsilon^*) \rceil$. Since the proper choices of both h and ε^0 depend on a priori knowledge of an approximate center of the dual feasible region, however, these results are mostly theoretical and the approach, in general, not fully satisfactory for practical implementation.

Related to the modified barriers by Polyak (1992), the third method examined by Freund (1996) works with the so-called infeasible-start shifted-barrier problem

$$\min (c + \varepsilon(A^T y^\circ + s^\circ - c))^T x - \mu\varepsilon \sum_{i=1}^{n} \log(x_i) \tag{16a}$$

$$\text{s.t. } Ax = b + \varepsilon(Ax^\circ - b) \tag{16b}$$

$$x > 0 \tag{16c}$$

and achieves an iteration complexity of $O(nL)$ for a suitably chosen starting point. Moreover, for those starting points that are feasible, the proposed algorithm further reduces the iteration count to at most $O(\sqrt{n}L)$, thereby matching today's best known complexity bound for any feasible IPM.

In the specific context of warmstarting IPMs, a related approach to Freund's shifted-barrier methods is the exact primal-dual penalty method recently proposed by Benson and Shanno (2007) which introduces a set of auxiliary variables ξ and ψ that relax the nonnegativity constraints on x and s and are penalized in the primal and dual objective function, respectively.

$$\min c^T x + d^T \xi \qquad\qquad \max b^T y - u^T \psi \qquad\qquad (17a)$$

$$\text{s.t. } Ax = b \qquad\qquad\qquad \text{s.t. } A^T y + s = c \qquad\qquad (17b)$$

$$0 \leq x + \xi \leq u \qquad\qquad\qquad -\psi \leq s \leq d \qquad\qquad (17c)$$

$$\xi \geq 0 \qquad\qquad\qquad\qquad \psi \geq 0 \qquad\qquad (17d)$$

This formulation is exact because, for sufficiently large penalty parameters d and u, the optimal values for ξ and ψ will be zero and the upper bound inequalities $x + \xi \leq u$ and $s + \psi \leq d$ hold with a positive slack (the method itself is based on an IPM and, thus, not exact, in general). Benson and Shanno highlight that the Newton system associated with (17) can be reduced to a form similar to (6) for the original LP, so that the computational effort per iteration is not substantially different than that of solving the original problem. Hence, whereas the initialization of the new variables ξ and ψ can be accomplished relatively easily, the only potential drawback of this method remains the proper initial choice and necessity of possible later updates of the penalty parameters, which are of a high importance for the overall performance of this approach. In particular, while too small choices do not yield an optimal solution for the original LP and require repeated updates after spending unnecessary time on any initially formulated penalty problem, Benson and Shanno also report that too large values cause numerical errors and negatively affect the stability of both algorithm and its final solution. In spite of these difficulties, the general approach seems to work well as demonstrated on a subset of the Netlib LP test problems and a group of mixed-integer linear programs using the (I)IPM implemented in their software package LOQO (Vanderbei 1999). Most recently, Gondzio and Grothey (2008) further build on these results and also combine this method with their unblocking technique based on sensitivity analysis.

3 New Warmstarting Scheme

We recall from our discussion so far that there are mainly two challenges in solving a perturbed problem instance $d = d^\circ + \Delta d$ from a warmstarting point $z^\circ = (x^\circ, y^\circ, s^\circ)$, that is optimal for the initial problem d° or possibly the last iterate of an IPM with (sufficiently) small duality gap $n\mu^\circ = x^{\circ T} s^\circ \gtrsim 0$. The first problem, that z° is typically primal-dual infeasible for d, is not of our major concern and relatively easily dealt with by using an infeasible IPM. The second hurdle, that several of the components of x° and s° are very close or equal to zero, is more critical but can be handled by shifting the boundary of the nonnegative feasible region to (at least temporarily) allow x and s to also take negative values and, thus, enable longer Newton steps and more rapid progress during the initial iterations of the interior-point algorithm.

Following on these two ideas and adopting the notation used by Benson and Shanno for the formulation of their primal-dual penalty approach (17), in this paper we choose the similar but simpler scheme which only uses a new set of slacks to relax the nonnegativity constraints of the original primal-dual variables.

$$\min c^T x \qquad\qquad \max b^T y \qquad\qquad (18a)$$

$$\text{s.t. } Ax = b \qquad\qquad \text{s.t. } A^T y + s = c \qquad\qquad (18b)$$

$$x - \xi = 0 \qquad\qquad s - \psi = 0 \qquad\qquad (18c)$$

$$\xi \geq 0 \qquad\qquad \psi \geq 0. \qquad\qquad (18d)$$

Note that this formulation is also exact and, in fact, equivalent to the original primal-dual pair but does not depend on any additional parameters. Furthermore, because x and s are now unrestricted, there is no problem to initialize $(x^0, y^0, s^0) = (x^\circ, y^\circ, s^\circ)$ even if x° and s° contain elements that are zero as long as the initial slacks ξ^0 and ψ^0 are chosen sufficiently interior.

Before we analyze this formulation with respect to the standard worst-case iteration bound for IIPMs and address the initialization of the new slack variables in detail, we first derive its corresponding Newton system to show that the required computations per iteration remain essentially unchanged compared to the original LP. Similar to (5), the (KKT) optimality conditions of (18) for a centrality measure μ are given by

$$Ax = b \qquad\qquad (19a)$$

$$A^T y + s = c \qquad\qquad (19b)$$

$$x - \xi = 0 \qquad\qquad (19c)$$

$$s - \psi = 0 \qquad\qquad (19d)$$

$$\Xi \Psi e = \mu e \qquad\qquad (19e)$$

with corresponding Newton system

$$\begin{bmatrix} A & 0 & 0 & 0 & 0 \\ 0 & A^T & I & 0 & 0 \\ I & 0 & 0 & -I & 0 \\ 0 & 0 & I & 0 & -I \\ 0 & 0 & 0 & \Psi & \Xi \end{bmatrix} \begin{bmatrix} \Delta x \\ \Delta y \\ \Delta s \\ \Delta \xi \\ \Delta \psi \end{bmatrix} = \begin{bmatrix} r_b \\ r_c \\ r_x \\ r_s \\ \mu e - \Xi \Psi e \end{bmatrix} \qquad (20)$$

where $r_b = b - Ax$ and $r_c = c - A^T y - s$ as before, and $r_x = \xi - x$ and $r_s = \psi - s$. Using that $\Delta \xi = \Delta x - r_x$ and $\Delta \psi = \Delta s - r_s$, we can further simplify (20) yielding

$$\begin{bmatrix} A & 0 & 0 \\ 0 & A^T & I \\ \Psi & 0 & \Xi \end{bmatrix} \begin{bmatrix} \Delta x \\ \Delta y \\ \Delta s \end{bmatrix} = \begin{bmatrix} r_b \\ r_c \\ \mu e - \Xi \Psi e + \Xi R_s e + \Psi R_x e \end{bmatrix} \tag{21}$$

which has the exact same structure as (6) and, in particular, can be further reduced to the augmented (symmetric indefinite) system

$$\begin{bmatrix} 0 & A \\ A^T & -D^{-2} \end{bmatrix} \begin{bmatrix} \Delta y \\ \Delta x \end{bmatrix} = \begin{bmatrix} r_b \\ r_c + \mu \Xi^{-1} e - \psi + r_s + \Xi^{-1} \Psi r_x \end{bmatrix} \tag{22}$$

where now $D = \Xi^{1/2} \Psi^{-1/2}$ but otherwise identical to (7). Finally, and similar to (9), after solving this system or the corresponding normal equations for Δx and Δy, we can find Δs, $\Delta \xi$, and $\Delta \psi$ by the three simple back substitutions

$$\Delta s = r_c - A^T \Delta y \tag{23a}$$

$$\Delta \xi = \Delta x - r_x \tag{23b}$$

$$\Delta \psi = \Delta s - r_s. \tag{23c}$$

Hence, the computations required to solve the Newton systems for the reformulated problem (18) are essentially the same as for the original problem, so that the addition of slacks should not increase the solution effort for the individual iterations.

3.1 Analysis of the new warmstarting scheme

Despite many advances in the development of IIPMs, the best worst-case iteration bound, up to a constant factor C, remains the one first established by Mizuno (1994)

$$Cn \log \left(\max \left\{ \frac{\|r_b^0\|}{\varepsilon_b}, \frac{\|r_c^0\|}{\varepsilon_c}, \frac{\zeta^2 n}{\varepsilon_d} \right\} \right) \tag{24}$$

where $\zeta \geq \|(x^*, s^*)\|_\infty$ for some optimal solution $z^* = (x^*, y^*, s^*)$ or, theoretically, $\zeta = 2^L$ for a problem instance with integer data of bit length L (Roos et al 2006). A similar complexity analysis to that by Mizuno (1994)[1] shows that for our reformulated problem (18), the argument of the logarithmic term in (24) takes the form

$$\max \left\{ \frac{\|r_b^0\|}{\varepsilon_b}, \frac{\|r_c^0\|}{\varepsilon_c}, \frac{\|r_x^0\|}{\varepsilon_x}, \frac{\|r_s^0\|}{\varepsilon_s}, \frac{\zeta^2 n}{\varepsilon_d} \right\} \tag{25}$$

where r_b^0, r_c^0, r_x^0, and r_s^0 denote the initial residuals of the four equality constraints in (19), ε_b, ε_c, ε_x, ε_s, and ε_d are the individual error tolerances for feasibility and

---

[1] The full details of this analysis are included in a forthcoming working paper.

duality, respectively (in the following, we shall assume a uniform tolerance ε), and $\zeta \geq \|(\xi^*, \psi^*)\|_\infty = \|(x^*, s^*)\|_\infty$ remains the same as before.

To compare the iteration bound in (24) for a traditional IIPM cold start from $(x^0, y^0, s^0) = (\zeta e, 0, \zeta e)$ with the bound in (25) for a warm start of the reformulated problem (18) from $(x^0, y^0, s^0, \xi^0, \psi^0) = (x^\circ, y^\circ, s^\circ, \zeta e, \zeta e)$, we first note that both approaches start from an initial duality gap of $n\mu = (\zeta e)^T(\zeta e) = \zeta^2 n$ and, thus, result in identical worst-case iteration bounds especially if $\zeta^2 n$ dominates the other residual norm. For $\|r_x\|$ and $\|r_s\|$, this turns out to be always the case.

Proposition 1. *Let $\zeta \geq \|(x^\circ, s^\circ, 1)\|_\infty$, where (x°, s°) are optimal for the initial LP instance d°, and let $r_x^0 = \xi^0 - x^0$ and $r_s^0 = \psi^0 - s^0$ be the residuals of the initial point $(x^0, y^0, s^0, \xi^0, \psi^0) = (x^\circ, y^\circ, s^\circ, \zeta e, \zeta e)$ for (18). Then $\max\left\{\|r_x^0\|, \|r_s^0\|\right\} \leq \zeta^2 n$.*

Proof. Because $(\xi^0, \psi^0) = (\zeta e, \zeta e) \geq (x^\circ, s^\circ) \geq 0$, it follows immediately that $r_x^0 = \zeta e - x^\circ \geq 0$ and $r_s^0 = \zeta e - s^\circ \geq 0$ and thus

$$\|r_x^0\| = \|\zeta e - x^\circ\| \leq \|\zeta e\| = \zeta \|e\| \leq \zeta^2 n \tag{26a}$$

$$\|r_s^0\| = \|\zeta e - s^\circ\| \leq \|\zeta e\| = \zeta \|e\| \leq \zeta^2 n \tag{26b}$$

to give the result. $\square$

Hence, as long as we initialize the new slacks ξ^0 and ψ^0 to values at least as large as the previous optimal solutions x° and s°, the new residuals r_x^0 and r_s^0 do not increase the worst-case iteration bound of the standard IIPM. Clearly, because our objective is to relax (especially the small) elements of x° and s°, this condition will be satisfied for our initialization scheme described in Section 3.2.

Next, we investigate the residuals r_b and r_c for the primal and dual infeasibilities and establish a bound on the maximal problem perturbation so that their residual norms for the warm-start bound in (25) do not exceed their corresponding cold-start residual norms in (24). We quantify the problem perturbation Δd and the new data $d = d^\circ + \Delta d$ in terms of the initial data d° using scalars $\alpha, \alpha', \beta, \gamma \geq 0$ so that

$$\|\Delta A\| \leq \alpha \|A^\circ\| \quad \Rightarrow \quad (1-\alpha)\|A^\circ\| \leq \|A\| \leq (1+\alpha)\|A^\circ\| \tag{27a}$$

$$\|\Delta A^T\| \leq \alpha' \|A^{\circ T}\| \quad \Rightarrow \quad (1-\alpha')\|A^{\circ T}\| \leq \|A^T\| \leq (1+\alpha')\|A^{\circ T}\| \tag{27b}$$

$$\|\Delta b\| \leq \beta \|b^\circ\| \quad \Rightarrow \quad (1-\beta)\|b^\circ\| \leq \|b\| \leq (1+\beta)\|b^\circ\| \tag{27c}$$

$$\|\Delta c\| \leq \gamma \|c^\circ\| \quad \Rightarrow \quad (1-\gamma)\|c^\circ\| \leq \|c\| \leq (1+\gamma)\|c^\circ\| \tag{27d}$$

Proposition 2. *Let $\delta_b = \max\{2\alpha, 2\beta\}$ and $\delta_c = \max\{2\gamma, \alpha'\}$. If*

$$(\delta_b, \delta_c) \leq \left(\frac{\|b^\circ - \zeta A^\circ e\|}{\|b^\circ\| + \zeta \|A^\circ\| \|e\|}, \frac{\|c^\circ - \zeta e\|}{\|c^\circ\| + \|A^{\circ T}\| \|y^\circ\|} \right) \tag{28}$$

then the respective residual norms $\|r_b^0\|$ and $\|r_c^0\|$ in (25) for a warm start of (18) are not larger than their corresponding cold-start residuals in (24).

Proof. We first derive lower bounds on the residual norms $\|r_b^0\|$ and $\|r_c^0\|$ for the new problem instance d when (cold)started from $(x^0, y^0, s^0) = (\zeta e, 0, \zeta e)$.

$$\|r_b^0\|_{cold} = \|b - Ax^0\| = \|(b^\circ + \Delta b) - \zeta(A^\circ + \Delta A)e\| \tag{29a}$$

$$\geq \|b^\circ - \zeta A^\circ e\| - (\|\Delta b\| + \zeta\|\Delta A\|\|e\|) \tag{29b}$$

$$\geq \|b^\circ - \zeta A^\circ e\| - (\beta\|b^\circ\| + \alpha\zeta\|A^\circ\|\|e\|) \tag{29c}$$

$$\|r_c^0\|_{cold} = \|c - A^T y^0 - s^0\| = \|(c^\circ + \Delta c) - 0 - \zeta e\| \tag{29d}$$

$$\geq \|c^\circ - \zeta e\| - \|\Delta c\| \geq \|c^\circ - \zeta e\| - \gamma\|c^\circ\| \tag{29e}$$

Similarly, we obtain the following two upper bounds when (warm)starting the reformulated problem (18) from $(x^0, y^0, s^0, \xi^0, \psi^0) = (x^\circ, y^\circ, s^\circ, \zeta e, \zeta e)$

$$\|r_b^0\|_{warm} = \|\Delta b - \Delta A x^\circ\| \tag{30a}$$

$$\leq \|\Delta b\| + \zeta\|\Delta A\|\|e\| \leq \beta\|b^\circ\| + \alpha\zeta\|A^\circ\|\|e\| \tag{30b}$$

$$\|r_c^0\|_{warm} = \|\Delta c - \Delta A^T y^\circ\| \tag{30c}$$

$$\leq \|\Delta c\| + \|\Delta A^T\|\|y^\circ\| \leq \gamma\|c^\circ\| + \alpha'\|A^{\circ T}\|\|y^\circ\| \tag{30d}$$

where (30a) and (30c) follow as in (11). Finally, combining the two bounds from (29) and (30) with the initial assumptions on δ_b and δ_c in (28) gives

$$\|r_b^0\|_{cold} - \|r_b^0\|_{warm} \geq \|b^\circ - \zeta A^\circ e\| - 2(\beta\|b^\circ\| + \alpha\zeta\|A^\circ\|\|e\|) \tag{31a}$$

$$\geq \|b^\circ - \zeta A^\circ e\| - \delta_b(\|b^\circ\| + \zeta\|A^\circ\|\|e\|) \geq 0 \tag{31b}$$

$$\|r_c^0\|_{cold} - \|r_c^0\|_{warm} \geq \|c^\circ - \zeta e\| - (2\gamma\|c^\circ\| + \alpha'\|A^{\circ T}\|\|y^\circ\|) \tag{31c}$$

$$\geq \|c^\circ - \zeta e\| - \delta_c(\|c^\circ\| + \|A^{\circ T}\|\|y^\circ\|) \geq 0 \tag{31d}$$

to conclude the proof.   □

Furthermore, if the inequalities in (28) hold strictly, then the warm-start residuals are strictly smaller than their corresponding cold-start residuals, thus leading to an improvement of the theoretical worst-case iteration bound if the larger of the two (cold-start) residual norms also dominates the initial duality gap $\zeta^2 n$.

Corollary 1. *Let* $\delta = \max\{\alpha, \beta, \gamma\}$. *Then* $\zeta^2 n \leq \max\{\|r_b^0\|, \|r_c^0\|\}$ *in particular if*

$$\delta \leq \max\left\{\frac{\|b^\circ - \zeta A^\circ e\| - \zeta^2 n}{\|b^\circ\| + \zeta\|A^\circ\|\|e\|}, \frac{\|c^\circ - \zeta e\| - \zeta^2 n}{\|c^\circ\|}\right\} \tag{32}$$

Proof. Similar to the proof of Proposition 2, this result follows directly by combining the bounds from (29) with (32). In particular, if the maximum in (32) is achieved by either the first or second argument, then either the first or the second of the two following inequalities

$$\|r_b^0\| - \zeta^2 n \ge \|b^\circ - \zeta A^\circ e\| - (\beta \|b^\circ\| + \alpha \zeta \|A^\circ\| \|e\|) - \zeta^2 n \tag{33a}$$

$$\ge \|b^\circ - \zeta A^\circ e\| - \delta(\|b^\circ\| + \zeta \|A^\circ\| \|e\|) - \zeta^2 n \ge 0 \tag{33b}$$

$$\|r_c^0\| - \zeta^2 n \ge \|c^\circ - \zeta e\| - \gamma \|c^\circ\| - \zeta^2 n \tag{33c}$$

$$\ge \|c^\circ - \zeta e\| - \delta \|c^\circ\| - \zeta^2 n \ge 0 \tag{33d}$$

will be satisfied, and the result follows. □

In general, however, whereas the upper bounds given by (28) in Proposition 2 are usually positive and, thus, always satisfied for a positive but sufficiently small problem perturbation, the bounds given by (32) in Corollary 1 may also become negative so that the initial duality gap $\zeta^2 n$ may exceed both cold- and warm-start residual even for $\Delta d = 0$ and $d = d^\circ$.

Our last remark pertains to the final duality gap $n\mu$ upon termination of the (I)IPM outlined in Algorithm 1. Throughout the above discussion, we implicitly assumed a uniform value ε for each of the tolerances ε_b, ε_c, ε_x, ε_s and ε_d, but the modification of the above results for varying values is only notationally tedious and otherwise straightforward. Nevertheless, we shall point out that for the two approaches compared above, the duality tolerance ε_d actually applies to two different products, namely $x^T s$ in standard form and $\xi^T \psi$ in the reformulated problem (18). As the next result shows, in general, this requires to use a slightly smaller tolerance for $\xi^T \psi$ in order to actually guarantee that $n\mu = x^T s \le \varepsilon_d$.

Proposition 3. *Let* $(x^*, y^*, s^*, \xi^*, \psi^*)$ *be the final iterate when solving problem* (18) *with tolerances* ε_b, ε_c, ε_x, ε_s, *and* ε_d. *If* $\psi^{*T} \xi^* \le \varepsilon_d - \varepsilon_x \varepsilon_s$, *or if* $\psi^{*T} \xi^* \le \varepsilon_d$ *and* $(s^*, x^*) \ge 0$, *then* $x^{*T} s^* \le \varepsilon_d$.

Proof. Based on the termination criterion in Algorithm 1, we first note that the final residuals $r_x^* = \xi^* - x^*$ and $r_s^* = \psi^* - s^*$ satisfy that $\|r_x^*\| \le \varepsilon_x$ and $\|r_s^*\| \le \varepsilon_s$, respectively. Furthermore, because $\xi^0 \ge x^\circ$ and $\psi^0 \ge s^\circ$ for the initial iterates, it follows that $r_x^0 = \xi^0 - x^\circ \ge 0$ and $r_s^0 = \psi^0 - s^\circ \ge 0$ so that (10) implies that

$$\xi^k - x^k = r_x^k = \prod_{j=0}^{k-1}(1 - \alpha^j)r_x^0 \ge 0 \tag{34}$$

and similarly, $r_s^k = \psi^k - s^k \ge 0$ for all $k \ge 0$. Hence, the first part now follows from

$$x^{*T} s^* = (\xi^* - r_x^*)^T (\psi^* - r_s^*) \le \xi^{*T} \psi^* + r_x^{*T} r_s^* \tag{35a}$$

$$\le (\varepsilon_d - \varepsilon_x \varepsilon_s) + \|r_x^*\| \|r_s^*\| \le \varepsilon_d \tag{35b}$$

where (35a) is clear because $\xi^* \ge 0$ and $\psi^* \ge 0$. In particular, if also $x^* \ge 0$ and $s^* \ge 0$, then (34) implies that $\xi^* \ge x^* \ge 0$ and $\psi^* \ge s^* \ge 0$ and, thus, $x^{*T} s^* \le \xi^{*T} \psi^*$ which also gives the second part and concludes the proof. □

In principle, this result indicates two potential drawbacks of our approach when used in practice, namely the necessity to choose a smaller termination tolerance for the final duality gap as well as the possibility of remaining negative components in the final iterate x^* and s^* upon termination of the IIPM. From a numerical point of view, however, the difference $\varepsilon_x \varepsilon_s$ is typically very small and can be ignored for all practical purposes. Furthermore, negative values $x_i^* < 0 \leq \xi_i^*$ or $s_i^* < 0 \leq \psi_i^*$ are usually negligible as well because they are necessarily of very small magnitude

$$|x_i^*| \leq \xi_i^* - x_i^* = r_{xi}^* \leq \|r_x^*\| \leq \varepsilon_x \tag{36}$$

and similarly, $|s_i^*| \leq \varepsilon_s$. Hence, negative entries of x or s usually indicate a true value of zero for sufficiently small termination tolerances ε_x and ε_s.

3.2 Initialization of the slack variables

Our above analysis has shown that for solving a standard primal-dual LP instance $d = d^\circ + \Delta d$ by an IIPM, we always maintain (or improve) the (theoretical) complexity in both individual iterations and overall iteration count also for the reformulated problem (18) with $(x^0, y^0, s^0) = (x^\circ, y^\circ, s^\circ)$ and additional primal-dual slacks ξ and ψ. Moreover, by preserving the optimal values for the initial instance d°, we found that for sufficiently small perturbations Δd, the residual norms $\|r_b^0\|$ and $\|r_c^0\|$ are smaller than for a cold start, so that we expect to start from a point closer to an optimal solution and, thus, converge in a fewer number of iterations, in general.

For the initialization of ξ and ψ, so far we have assumed that $(\xi^0, \psi^0) = (\zeta e, \zeta e)$ where $\zeta \geq \|(\xi^*, \psi^*)\|_\infty = \|(x^*, s^*)\|_\infty$ and (x^*, s^*) belong to some optimal solution. In practice, however, it is clear that we do not know such a solution a priori and, therefore, need to choose initial values for ξ and ψ by some other means. First, based on our objective to relax (especially the small) elements of x° and s°, and to not simply carry over the numerical difficulties from small entries in x° and s° to ξ and ψ, respectively, we will always choose $(\xi^0, \psi^0) \geq (x^\circ, s^\circ)$ which also ensures that the new starting point will not be significantly smaller in magnitude than $\|(x^*, s^*)\|_\infty$, provided the problem perturbation Δd is small enough for (x^*, y^*, s^*) to not deviate too much from the optimal solution $(x^\circ, y^\circ, s^\circ)$ for the initial problem.

Second, because we know from (10) that every iteration reduces all residuals by the same factor $1 - \alpha^k$, we also propose to start from initial residuals $r_x^0 = \xi^0 - x^\circ$ and $r_s^0 = \psi^0 - s^\circ$ that are similar in size to r_b^0 and r_c^0 as measured by the maximal residual $\rho = \|(r_b, r_c, 1)\|_\infty$. Furthermore, and in agreement with several other authors (Gondzio 1998, Yildirim and Wright 2002, Gondzio and Grothey 2003) who justify the choice of an initial point that is also well-centered, similar to the weighting matrices for the JWLSA in (12) we let

$$r_x^0 = (X^\circ)^{1/2}(S^\circ)^{-1/2}\rho e \tag{37a}$$

$$r_s^0 = (X^\circ)^{-1/2}(S^\circ)^{1/2}\rho e \tag{37b}$$

so that the associated initial slacks ξ^0 and ψ^0 achieve uniform complementarity

$$\Xi^0 \Psi^0 e = (X^\circ + R_x^0)(S^\circ + R_s^0)e = \mu e + 2\sqrt{\mu}\rho e + \rho^2 e = (\sqrt{\mu} + \rho)^2 e. \quad (38)$$

The obvious drawback of this approach, however, is that it does not grant a warm start from an exact optimal solution (x°, s°), for which some components are equal to zero so that the inverses of X° and S° in (37) are not defined everywhere, in general. In addition, even for an approximate solution with a nonzero but small centrality measure $\mu = x^{\circ T} s^\circ \gtrsim 0$, some variables will be of very small value and, thus, yield a very large starting point that may unnecessarily slow down the convergence of the algorithm. To avoid these problems, we first note that if (x°, s°) is well-centered with $x_i s_i = \mu \gtrsim 0$ and x_i small, then s_i is necessarily much larger (or vice versa) and, therefore, may not need to be relaxed at all. Hence, if we already knew which variables are or are about to become basic, then we would not be concerned about these variables reducing to zero and could directly warmstart from their previous optimal values without the need for additional slacks.

The identification of basic and nonbasic variables in an IPM framework is addressed in several recent papers (Facchinei et al 2000, Oberlin and Wright 2006, among others) and an older survey by El-Bakry et al (1994) that describes a variety of different indicator functions including the primal variables and dual slacks themselves, the ratios of primal variables and dual slacks, and the ratio of subsequent iterates (the so-called Tapia indicator). In spite of the known difficulties with especially the two former approaches, note that the primal-dual indicator defined by

$$\frac{x_i^\circ}{s_i^\circ} < \tau \quad \Rightarrow \quad x_i^\circ \to 0 \text{ and } s_i^\circ > 0 \quad (39a)$$

$$\frac{s_i^\circ}{x_i^\circ} < \tau \quad \Rightarrow \quad s_i^\circ \to 0 \text{ and } x_i^\circ > 0 \quad (39b)$$

for some indicator threshold $\tau \in [0, 1]$ corresponds precisely to the (squared) ratios in (37) and, therefore, is particularly well-suited for our particular purpose.

For the primal-dual indicator in (39), it is easy to see that $\tau \leq 1$ ensures that at most one of the two inequalities can be satisfied, so that either x_i or s_i is predicted to become zero but never both. Furthermore, and in addition to the discussion in El-Bakry et al (1994), we observe that if (x°, s°) is a perfectly-centered solution so that $x_i^\circ s_i^\circ = \mu$ for all i, then the primal-dual indicator is in fact equivalent to using the variables as indicators themselves, because

$$\frac{x_i^\circ}{s_i^\circ} < \tau \quad \Leftrightarrow \quad x_i^\circ < \sqrt{\mu\tau} < \sqrt{\mu/\tau} < s_i^\circ \quad (40a)$$

$$\frac{s_i^\circ}{x_i^\circ} < \tau \quad \Leftrightarrow \quad s_i^\circ < \sqrt{\mu\tau} < \sqrt{\mu/\tau} < x_i^\circ \quad (40b)$$

so that we refrain from slacking x_i° (or s_i°), or equivalently, set $\xi_i^0 = x_i^\circ$ (or $\psi_i^0 = s_i^\circ$) only if it exceeds the value $\sqrt{\mu/\tau}$. More precisely, in extension of (37) and to preserve validity of the uniform complementarity products in (38), we now let

$$(r_{xi}^0, r_{si}^0) = \begin{cases} ((2\sqrt{\mu}\rho + \rho^2)/s_i^\circ, 0) & \text{if } x_i^\circ < \sqrt{\mu\tau} < \sqrt{\mu/\tau} < s_i^\circ \\ (0, (2\sqrt{\mu}\rho + \rho^2)/x_i^\circ) & \text{if } s_i^\circ < \sqrt{\mu\tau} < \sqrt{\mu/\tau} < x_i^\circ \\ (\sqrt{x_i^\circ/s_i^\circ}\rho, \sqrt{s_i^\circ/x_i^\circ}\rho) & \text{if } \sqrt{\mu\tau} \leq (x_i^\circ, s_i^\circ) \leq \sqrt{\mu/\tau} \end{cases} \quad (41)$$

Finally, for the specific choice of the indicator threshold, is is apparent from (40) and our above discussion that larger values for τ may lead to smaller starting points but, at the same time, relax fewer variables at the risk of preserving the numerical difficulties from initial values that are too close to zero. On the other hand, by choosing τ small, we obtain a larger starting point but may avoid those problems (provided the starting point is not too large to cause problems itself). In particular, El-Bakry et al (1994) mention conservative strategies that choose primal-dual indicator thresholds similar in magnitude to the final centrality measure, $\tau = \mu$, thus leading to an upper bound of 1 in (41) below which all variables will be relaxed. While this choice was proposed for the early identification of zero variables during an IPM, it is important to note that in our context we already know the final iterate so that this choice is too conservative in general. In particular, we have found that the best warmstarting results can be achieved for very aggressive choices with threshold values across the complete range up to $\tau = 1$. For the exact details, we refer to the next section reporting our computational results.

4 Computational Results

We tested the above warmstarting scheme on selected LP problems from the Netlib test suite following the framework described by Benson and Shanno (2007). In particular, we picked only those problems for which $m + n \leq 1000$, and we further eliminated all those instances for which perturbations resulted in an infeasible or unbounded problem. Although our current method treats the particular case of LPs only, we have used the (freely available) semidefinite-quadratic-linear solver SDPT3 (Toh et al 1999) to enable the direct extension also to more general conic optimization problems in the future. In any way, because our objective here is to evaluate the performance of our new warmstarting scheme rather than to conduct a comprehensive comparison with other proposed methods, and because we only compare the iteration count ratio between a warm and cold start and otherwise treat the specific solver as a black box, the particular choice of solver should not be of major relevance for the results presented in this paper. However, our approach relies to some degree on effectively handling free variables in an interior-point framework, so that it was also convenient to use the recent modification of the SDPT3 code by Anjos and Burer (2007) that avoids their otherwise common representation as the difference of two nonnegative blocks. Finally, because SDPT3 is based on the software package MATLAB[©], we used the Netlib problems in .mat-format that are available from the COAP[2] collection of LP test problems.

---

[2] http://www.math.ufl.edu/~hager/coap/testcases.html

For each case, we first solved the original problem with initial data d° to obtain an optimal solution $(x^\circ, y^\circ, s^\circ)$. The subsequent perturbation $\Delta d = (\Delta A, \Delta b, \Delta c)$ was defined following the scheme in Benson and Shanno (2007), which is repeated here for the specific case of the cost perturbation Δc. Namely, for each entry Δc_i, we first generated a uniformly distributed random number $\eta \in [-1, 1]$ and perturbed the initial cost c_i° only if $\eta < \min\{0.1, 20/n\}$, so that at most 10% or 20 entries were changed on average. To determine the magnitude of the perturbation, we then generated a second random number $\varepsilon \in [-1, 1]$ and set

$$\Delta c_i = \begin{cases} \varepsilon\delta & \text{if } c_i^\circ = 0 \\ \varepsilon\delta c_i^\circ & \text{otherwise} \end{cases} \tag{42}$$

where the parameter δ was set to different values to observe the effects of different perturbation levels similar to (27). The right-hand side vector b° was perturbed analogously, and the only difference for the constraint matrix perturbation ΔA was that we preserved any existing sparsity structure of A° also for $A = A^\circ + \Delta A$.

Using the default settings in SDPT3, we then solved the perturbed problem in standard form by a cold start, and the reformulated problem (18) from the initial point $(x^0, y^0, s^0) = (x^\circ, y^\circ, s^\circ)$ and with $(\xi^0, \psi^0) = (x^\circ + r_x^0, s^\circ + r_s^0))$ defined according to (41) to obtain the new optimal solutions (x^*, y^*, s^*) and $(x^*, y^*, s^*, \xi^*, \psi^*) \approx (x^*, y^*, s^*, x^*, s^*)$, respectively. From the iteration counts for cold and warm start, we computed the Warm-to-Cold-start-iteration-Ratio (WCR = number of warm-start iterations / number of cold-start iterations) for both individual and simultaneous perturbation of A, b, and c, and for three different perturbation levels $\delta \in \{0.001, 0.01, 0.1\}$. In addition, for each instance we recorded the total number of entries of A, b, and c that had been perturbed (Pert), the solution differences

$$\frac{\|x^\circ - x^*\|}{1.0 + \|x^\circ\|} \qquad \frac{\|y^\circ - y^*\|}{1.0 + \|y^\circ\|} \qquad \frac{\|s^\circ - s^*\|}{1.0 + \|s^\circ\|} \tag{43}$$

and a quantity B↔N that "guesses" the number of changes to the active sets for the optimal solutions x° and x^* by using the primal-dual indicator in (39) with threshold $\tau = 10^{-5}$. While the detailed results for all individual problems are available online[3], Tables 1, 2, and 3 summarize these results for each combination of perturbation type Δ and perturbation level δ, where the (#) entries indicate how many problems remained both feasible and bounded for that particular combination.

The results in Table 1 are obtained from the original initialization scheme in (37) without indicator, whereas Tables 2 and 3 follow the scheme given in (41) and use the primal-dual indicator with threshold values of $\tau = \mu^\circ = (x^\circ)^T s^\circ / n$ (approximately 10^{-8} by using the default duality tolerance in SDPT3) and $\tau = 1$, respectively. As mentioned previously in the text, and despite several systematic differences between the results across the three tables, we first observe that the performance of our warm-starting scheme does not change dramatically from either using or abandoning an indicator, although the indicator clearly improves its performance and, in particular,

---

[3] http://mfa.research.uwaterloo.ca/EngauAnjosVannelli_2008a/warmstart.html

Table 1 Perturbations and WCR Statistics Without Indicator ($\tau = 0$)

(Feasible) Perturbations				WCR Statistics					Solution Differences			
Δ	δ	Pert	(#)	avg	stdv	min	med	max	$\|x^* - x^\circ\|$	$\|y^* - y^\circ\|$	$\|s^* - s^\circ\|$	B↔N
b	0.001	10.6	16	0.34	0.16	0.11	0.36	0.66	1.9e-003	1.2e-002	1.5e-002	1.45
b	0.01	11.3	17	0.41	0.21	0.15	0.42	0.86	4.6e-003	2.6e-002	4.3e-002	4.64
b	0.1	11.6	18	0.60	0.35	0.15	0.56	1.32	7.3e-003	4.3e-002	4.7e-002	3.04
c	0.001	15.9	18	0.42	0.16	0.15	0.43	0.76	2.7e-003	2.9e-001	3.4e-002	2.20
c	0.01	15.9	17	0.58	0.21	0.22	0.56	1.08	6.5e-003	2.2e-001	6.9e-002	2.04
c	0.1	15.4	14	1.08	0.79	0.34	0.90	3.43	7.5e-003	7.1e-001	2.8e-001	0.61
A	0.001	19.5	20	0.48	0.27	0.14	0.49	1.40	1.9e-002	1.0e-001	1.5e+001	1.65
A	0.01	19.0	18	0.54	0.27	0.20	0.49	1.33	3.6e-003	1.3e-001	3.0e+001	2.00
A	0.1	19.2	16	0.97	0.45	0.43	0.81	1.98	1.0e-002	2.8e+001	5.6e+002	2.14
Abc	0.001	44.6	16	0.43	0.17	0.18	0.46	0.73	6.3e-003	1.2e+000	1.9e+000	3.01
Abc	0.01	41.4	13	0.61	0.19	0.39	0.62	1.00	1.5e-002	2.8e-001	2.8e-001	2.74
Abc	0.1	39.3	11	1.27	0.47	0.61	1.36	1.95	1.4e-002	4.1e-001	4.2e-001	1.53

Table 2 Perturbations and WCR Statistics With Primal-Dual Indicator Threshold $\tau = \mu$

(Feasible) Perturbations				WCR Statistics					Solution Differences			
Δ	δ	Pert	(#)	avg	stdv	min	med	max	$\|x^* - x^\circ\|$	$\|y^* - y^\circ\|$	$\|s^* - s^\circ\|$	B↔N
b	0.001	11.6	18	0.30	0.15	0.11	0.27	0.63	1.4e-003	2.3e-002	3.8e-002	1.82
b	0.01	10.9	16	0.40	0.20	0.12	0.36	0.99	2.6e-003	3.5e-002	3.7e-002	1.12
b	0.1	11.6	18	0.54	0.40	0.15	0.51	1.94	3.6e-003	2.2e-001	1.9e-001	1.88
c	0.001	16.2	22	0.39	0.14	0.16	0.40	0.68	3.2e-002	2.4e-001	2.6e-002	0.79
c	0.01	16.2	21	0.52	0.24	0.18	0.48	1.22	1.8e-002	3.3e-001	6.3e-002	0.82
c	0.1	15.9	19	1.17	0.73	0.24	0.92	3.30	8.7e-001	1.1e+000	8.5e-001	1.65
A	0.001	19.4	22	0.41	0.19	0.16	0.39	0.86	1.5e-002	1.5e-001	5.1e+000	0.80
A	0.01	19.5	21	0.56	0.31	0.19	0.45	1.44	1.1e-002	1.3e-001	6.6e+000	0.33
A	0.1	19.3	21	0.83	0.44	0.29	0.63	1.92	8.2e-002	2.5e-001	2.7e+000	0.69
Abc	0.001	45.8	18	0.44	0.16	0.20	0.43	0.73	4.7e-003	4.1e-002	4.0e-002	2.06
Abc	0.01	45.8	17	0.61	0.27	0.28	0.51	1.32	3.1e-003	7.2e-002	7.4e-002	1.04
Abc	0.1	44.4	17	1.21	0.57	0.43	1.31	2.29	8.5e-003	2.4e-001	2.4e-001	1.87

Table 3 Perturbations and WCR Statistics With Primal-Dual Indicator Threshold $\tau = 1$

(Feasible) Perturbations				WCR Statistics					Solution Differences			
Δ	δ	Pert	(#)	avg	stdv	min	med	max	$\|x^* - x^\circ\|$	$\|y^* - y^\circ\|$	$\|s^* - s^\circ\|$	B↔N
b	0.001	11.3	18	0.26	0.14	0.10	0.19	0.60	3.5e-004	1.5e-003	6.4e-003	3.18
b	0.01	11.0	17	0.32	0.15	0.13	0.27	0.64	3.7e-004	2.2e-001	1.7e-001	3.33
b	0.1	11.8	18	0.38	0.17	0.15	0.40	0.78	6.2e-004	8.0e-002	8.2e-002	3.94
c	0.001	16.0	22	0.35	0.15	0.10	0.37	0.63	1.2e-002	1.9e-001	1.1e-002	0.77
c	0.01	16.4	22	0.42	0.17	0.18	0.40	0.82	1.3e-002	2.7e-001	9.9e-002	2.29
c	0.1	16.6	18	0.64	0.21	0.25	0.62	1.20	2.1e-001	5.4e-001	3.3e-001	1.19
A	0.001	19.4	23	0.36	0.17	0.14	0.38	0.79	8.6e-002	1.2e-001	2.6e-001	0.84
A	0.01	19.5	23	0.43	0.16	0.16	0.44	0.92	1.4e-001	1.9e-001	3.1e-001	1.03
A	0.1	19.4	22	0.60	0.19	0.28	0.60	1.08	1.0e-002	7.4e-001	2.3e+000	1.79
Abc	0.001	45.2	18	0.38	0.14	0.17	0.42	0.65	1.4e-003	2.5e-002	2.8e-002	0.76
Abc	0.01	44.5	17	0.52	0.19	0.23	0.52	0.94	5.8e-003	1.6e-001	1.6e-001	1.96
Abc	0.1	43.7	16	0.84	0.31	0.45	0.73	1.52	5.5e-003	6.3e-001	6.3e-001	2.67

increases the number of problems (#) that are successfully solved. Second, by comparing Tables 2 and 3, we also find that the more conservative threshold of $\tau = \mu$ is clearly outperformed by the more aggressive choice of $\tau = 1$, which also dominated the other intermediate values from 10^{-8} to 10^{-1} which we tested but whose results, for sake of space and lack of much additional insight, are not included in this paper.

For each individual set of results, our warmstarting schemes appears most favorable towards changes in the right-hand side b, although this may be caused by the chosen perturbation scheme (42) resulting in fewer perturbations and, in effect, smaller solution differences for changes in the typically smaller-sized vectors b compared to changes in either A or c. In particular, we also find that the WCRs for the individual perturbations increase only relatively minor when changing A, b, and c simultaneously, for which results have not been reported by Benson and Shanno (2007) and Gondzio and Grothey (2008) and in spite of the significant increase in the total number of perturbations (Pert). It is also noteworthy that the indicated number of changes to the active set does not seem to have a major impact, provided the indicator reliably identified the optimal basis for the corresponding solutions.

In any case, it is to be expected that a warm start works better for smaller perturbation levels δ, which can be seen best from the associated performance profiles in Figures 1, 2, and 3. These plots give on the abscissa the percentage of problems that did not exceed a certain WCR, that is given on the ordinate and varied between

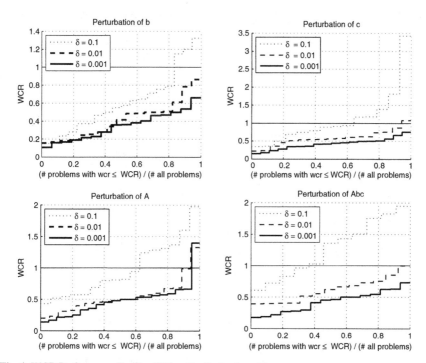

Fig. 1 WCR Performance Profiles Without Indicator ($\tau = 0$)

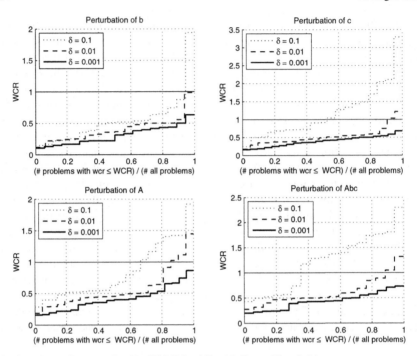

Fig. 2 WCR Performance Profiles With Primal-Dual Indicator Threshold $\tau = \mu$

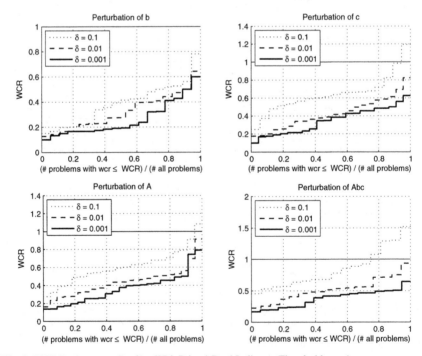

Fig. 3 WCR Performance Profiles With Primal-Dual Indicator Threshold $\tau = 1$

its minimum and maximum values that are given together with mean, median, and standard deviation as WCR statistics in Tables 1, 2, and 3. These plots indicate that our new warmstarting scheme is able to reduce the number of iterations on the vast majority of problems and, for the particular choice of $\tau = 1$ in Figure 3, for all problems with small and medium perturbations $\delta \in \{0.001, 0.01\}$. Although the claim of an ultimate percentage seems rather meaningless in view of the variation within the data, averaging between all twelve combinations for $\tau = 1$ suggests an overall reduction in the number of iterations of over 50%, which confirms the good results found by previous authors for the warmstarting of interior-point algorithms.

Finally, some remarks regarding the testing framework are in order. As pointed out also by other papers (Benson and Shanno 2007, Gondzio and Grothey 2008), a wealth of successful heuristics has by now been proposed for warmstarting an IPM, but no attempt has so far been made to rigorously compare these different strategies in a unified environment. One issue is the current lack of a meaningful suite of reoptimization test problems. Although we use the same (randomized) perturbation scheme as the two aforecited papers, the resulting problems are still (possibly quite) different, thus leading to questionable conclusions if one directly compares the numbers reported in different papers. To achieve a meaningful comparison, all approaches should be applied to the exact same problems and ideally use the same computing architecture and solver. This, however, creates its own issues as Benson and Shanno (2007, using LOQO) and we (using SDPT3) rely on efficient handling of free variables, unlike Gondzio and Grothey (2008) who make use of their parallel code OOPS. We propose the resolution of these issues as important future work.

5 Conclusions

In this paper, we have presented a new scheme for warmstarting interior-point methods for linear programming and provided both theoretical and computational evidence for its good performance. In spite of the still predominant perception that IPMs cannot be efficiently warmstarted in general, this paper confirms the results reported by previous authors that warmstarting IPMs is possible and may lead to reductions in the number of iterations of roughly 50% on average.

This paper builds on several ideas from the existing IPM literature, which most prominently include the various approaches that permit negative primal variables and dual slacks by moving the boundary of the nonnegative feasible region using shifted barriers or penalized auxiliary variables. In contrast to these methods, however, our approach is novel in that it does not actually modify the original problem but merely chooses a new but equivalent formulation which explicitly introduces new sets of slacks to remove the nonnegativity constraints from the original primal-dual variables. Intentionally starting from an initial point that is primal-dual infeasible, which is different from other warmstarting approaches reviewed in this paper, allows us to keep all original variables at their previous optimal values while only adjusting the new slacks to be sufficiently interior and reaching common feasibility in the course of the subsequent iterations of an infeasible IPM.

As one possible enhancement of our approach, we also address the use of indicator functions to detect variables that are still far from zero and do not require further relaxation by an additional slack variable. Although this introduces the challenge to properly set the associated indicator threshold, the computational results indicate that the good performance of our method can be preserved for a wide variety of choices although best for thresholds well above the final duality gap. In particular, this highlights another benefit of our approach: its non-dependency on parameters that require extensive "fine-tuning" to make the method work in practice.

To further advance the warmstarting approach presented in this paper, we are currently investigating the possibility of replacing the current primal-dual indicator with more sophisticated ones like the Tapia indicator. Because this requires keeping track of the previous iterates, which at the moment we do not, another possible extension is to then combine our new warmstarting scheme with the strategy to maintain a pool of previous iterates from which a new warmstarting point can be chosen or suitably adjusted. An interesting third direction is the more general modification of the presented scheme, that so far only handles numerical changes in the problem data, to also accommodate changes in the problem structure in the context of decomposition and LP and SDP relaxations for integer or mixed-integer linear programs. Finally, whereas by now several warmstarting approaches are proposed for linear and general nonlinear programming, more specific results for the important class of semidefinite programs are still outstanding but of high relevance due to frequent advantages of SDP over LP relaxations, especially for many combinatorial optimization problems.

Acknowledgements We thank the three anonymous referees and the ICS09 program committee for their valuable comments and suggestions on an earlier version of this manuscript.

References

Anjos MF, Burer S (2007) On handling free variables in interior-point methods for conic linear optimization. SIAM J Optim 18(4):1310–1325

Benson HY, Shanno DF (2007) An exact primal-dual penalty method approach to warmstarting interior-point methods for linear programming. Comput Optim Appl 38(3):371–399

El-Bakry AS, Tapia RA, Zhang Y (1994) A study of indicators for identifying zero variables in interior-point methods. SIAM Rev 36(1):45–72

Elhedhli S, Goffin JL (2004) The integration of an interior-point cutting plane method within a branch-and-price algorithm. Math Program 100(2, Ser. A):267–294

Facchinei F, Fischer A, Kanzow C (2000) On the identification of zero variables in an interior-point framework. SIAM J Optim 10(4):1058–1078

Freund RM (1991a) A potential-function reduction algorithm for solving a linear program directly from an infeasible "warm start". Math Programming 52(3, Ser. B):441–466

Freund RM (1991b) Theoretical efficiency of a shifted-barrier-function algorithm for linear programming. Linear Algebra Appl 152:19–41

Freund RM (1996) An infeasible-start algorithm for linear programming whose complexity depends on the distance from the starting point to the optimal solution. Ann Oper Res 62:29–57

Gondzio J (1998) Warm start of the primal-dual method applied in the cutting-plane scheme. Math Programming 83(1, Ser. A):125–143

Gondzio J, Grothey A (2003) Reoptimization with the primal-dual interior point method. SIAM J Optim 13(3):842–864

Gondzio J, Grothey A (2008) A new unblocking technique to warmstart interior point methods based on sensitivity analysis. SIAM J Optim 19(3):1184–1210

Gondzio J, Vial JP (1999) Warm start and ε-subgradients in a cutting plane scheme for block-angular linear programs. Comput Optim Appl 14(1):17–36

John E, Yildirim EA (2008) Implementation of warm-start strategies in interior-point methods for linear programming in fixed dimension. Comput Optim Appl 41(2):151–183

Karmarkar N (1984) A new polynomial-time algorithm for linear programming. Combinatorica 4(4):373–395

Mitchell JE (1994) An interior point column generation method for linear programming using shifted barriers. SIAM J Optim 4(2):423–440

Mitchell JE (2000) Computational experience with an interior point cutting plane algorithm. SIAM J Optim 10(4):1212–1227

Mitchell JE, Borchers B (1996) Solving real-world linear ordering problems using a primal-dual interior point cutting plane method. Ann Oper Res 62:253–276

Mitchell JE, Todd MJ (1992) Solving combinatorial optimization problems using Karmarkar's algorithm. Math Programming 56(3, Ser. A):245–284

Mizuno S (1994) Polynomiality of infeasible-interior-point algorithms for linear programming. Math Programming 67(1, Ser. A):109–119

Oberlin C, Wright SJ (2006) Active set identification in nonlinear programming. SIAM J Optim 17(2):577–605

Polyak R (1992) Modified barrier functions (theory and methods). Math Programming 54(2, Ser. A):177–222

Roos C, Terlaky T, Vial JP (2006) Interior point methods for linear optimization. Springer, New York

Toh KC, Todd MJ, Tütüncü RH (1999) SDPT3 – a MATLAB software package for semidefinite programming, version 1.3. Optim Methods Softw 11/12(1-4):545–581

Vanderbei RJ (1999) LOQO: an interior point code for quadratic programming. Optim Methods Softw 11/12(1-4):451–484

Wright SJ (1997) Primal-dual interior-point methods. Society for Industrial and Applied Mathematics (SIAM), Philadelphia, PA

Yildirim EA, Wright SJ (2002) Warm-start strategies in interior-point methods for linear programming. SIAM J Optim 12(3):782–810

Linear Dynamic Programming and the Training of Sequence Estimators

Christopher Raphael* and Eric Nichols[†]

Abstract We consider the problem of finding an optimal path through a trellis graph when the arc costs are linear functions of an unknown parameter vector. In this context we develop an algorithm, Linear Dynamic Programming (LDP), that simultaneously computes the optimal path for all values of the parameter. We show how the LDP algorithm can be used for supervised learning of the arc costs for a dynamic-programming-based sequence estimator by minimizing empirical risk. We present an application to musical harmonic analysis in which we optimize the performance of our estimator by seeking the parameter value generating the sequence best agreeing with hand-labeled data.

Key words: dynamic programming, optimal sequence, partially observable Markov decision processes

1 Introduction

Dynamic programming (DP) is a well-established technique for finding the optimal path through a trellis graph in which the score of the path is represented as a sum of arc scores traversed along the path. The history of DP goes back at least to (Bellman 1957), though perhaps much further. In this work we introduce an extension of the DP algorithm, we call linear dynamic programming (LDP). LDP also addresses a situation in which we seek the best scoring path through a trellis. However, in the

Christopher Raphael
School of Informatics, Indiana Univ., e-mail: craphael@indiana.edu

Eric Nichols
School of Informatics, Indiana Univ., e-mail: epnichols@gmail.com

* The author acknowledges the support of NSF grant IIS-0812244.

† The author acknowledges the support of NSF grant IIS-0738384.

J.W. Chinneck et al. (eds.), *Operations Research and Cyber-Infrastructure*, Operations Research/Computer Science Interfaces Series 47, DOI: 10.1007/978-0-387-88843-9_11, © Springer Science+Business Media, LLC 2009

LDP case the arc scores are known linear functions of an unknown parameter. In this context, LDP finds the optimal path *simultaneously* for *all* values of the parameter. LDP mirrors regular DP by recursively constructing the score of the best possible path to each intermediate trellis node. The score of this path, as a function of the parameter, is shown to be the maximum of a finite collection of linear functions. This form can be carried through the DP iteration exactly. While meaningful complexity analysis remains open, we demonstrate the feasibility of this approach in the domain of musical harmonic analysis.

While we find the LDP formulation interesting in its own right, we developed the approach with a specific aim: LDP serves as an alternative to maximum likelihood parameter estimation methods in sequence estimation problems using hidden Markov models (HMMs). One vexing aspect of the HMM training algorithms, for both labeled and unlabeled data, is the focus on data likelihood, rather than a criterion of more direct interest, such as recognition performance. LDP can be used to directly optimize recognition performance on a training set. This direct approach is embraced by a host of other machine learning algorithms, though we extend the approach to sequence estimators.

The algorithm we use to perform the LDP iteration is a close cousin to *value iteration* in partially observable Markov decision processes (POMDPs) (Kaelbling et. al. 1998), (Murphy 2000), (Cassandra et. al. 1997), (Sondik 1971), (White 1991), though our problem formulation seems to have little in common with POMDPs. We expect that the wealth of knowledge concerning POMDP solvers has much to contribute to our LDP approach, though, at present, we have not yet exploited this connection. This work demonstrates that the algorithmic approaches of POMDPs find application in a more general setting.

We demonstrate our training approach with an application to musical harmonic analysis. In this domain we associate a harmonic label, such as chord and key, to each measure or beat of the music, while seeking the optimal harmonic labeling of the music using DP. Our notion of optimality considers both agreement between our harmonic sequence and the observable data, as well as prior knowledge concerning harmonic sequences. We parameterize our DP trellis graph so that each arc score is a linear function of an unknown parameter that weights the contributions of several relevant features. We choose the parameter by finding the value that gives optimal performance on a labeled training set, as well as presenting the performance on separate test data.

2 Linear Dynamic Programming

2.1 Traditional Dynamic Programming

Suppose we have a trellis graph with finite set of nodes, S, as depicted in Figure 1. By "trellis", we mean that every node, $s \in S$, has an associated level, $l(s) \in \{1, \ldots, N\}$,

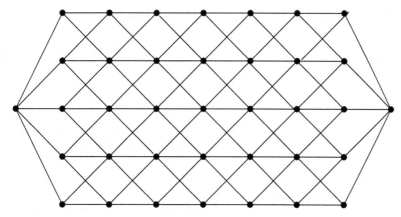

Fig. 1 A dynamic programming trellis structure.

while the arcs of the graph, $A \subset S \times S$, only connect nodes at adjacent levels:

$$A \subseteq \{(s,t) : l(t) = l(s) + 1\}$$

More general definitions are possible. A path through the trellis is a sequence $(s_1, \ldots, s_n)$ such that $l(s_1) = 1$ and $(s_m, s_{m+1}) \in A$ for $m = 1, \ldots, n-1$. We will call a path $(s_1, \ldots, s_n)$ a complete path if $n = N$. We define the score of a path as $c(s_1, \ldots, s_n) = \sum_{m=1}^{n-1} c(s_m, s_{m+1})$, where $c(s,t)$ is some fixed score for each arc $(s,t) \in A$.

Dynamic programming (DP) seeks a complete path $s_1^*, \ldots, s_N^*$ having *maximal* score. We denote the optimal score to a node s_n at level n as

$$c^*(s_n) = \max_{s_1, \ldots, s_{n-1}} c(s_1, \ldots, s_{n-1}, s_n)$$

where the maximum is over all paths ending in s_n. The well known Viterbi algorithm (Viterbi 1967), with roots going at least as far back as (Bellman 1957), defines $c^*(s) = 0$ for states with $l(s) = 1$ and computes the function, c^*, recursively as

$$c^*(t) = \max_{s \in \mathrm{Pred}(t)} c^*(s) + c(s,t) \tag{1}$$

$$a(t) = \arg \max_{s \in \mathrm{Pred}(t)} c^*(s) + c(s,t)$$

for $n = 2, \ldots, N$, where $\mathrm{Pred}(t) = \{s \in S : (s,t) \in A\}$. We choose arbitrarily from the optimal predecessor when the arg max is not unique. An optimal path $s_1^*, s_2^*, \ldots, s_n^*$ to any state, s_n^*, at level n is then recovered by defining $s_m^* = a(s_{m+1}^*)$ for $m = n - 1, \ldots, 1$. A globally optimal complete path can be found by tracing back an optimally scoring state at level N,

$$s_N^* = \arg \max_{s:l(s)=N} c^*(s)$$

2.2 An Extension to Simultaneous Computation

Now suppose that the arc scores, $\{c(s,t)\}$, are no longer fixed, but rather depend on some parameter, $\theta \in \Re^D$, through:

$$c_\theta(s,t) = \theta^T \beta(s,t) + \beta_0(s,t)$$

where $\beta(s,t) \in \Re^D$ and $\beta_0(s,t) \in \Re$ are known. For instance, the trellis of Figure 1 may have M categories of arcs, each having a common, yet unknown arc score. In this case θ would represent the M-dimensional vector of arc scores while $\beta(s,t)$ would be the vector that is 1 only in the component corresponding to the category of (s,t) and 0 for other components, and $\beta_0(s,t) = 0$. We now consider computing the optimal path through the DP recursion of Eqn. 1, *simultaneously* for *all* values of the parameter θ.

The key observation is the following. Note that the score of any particular path $s_1, \ldots, s_n$, viewed as a function of θ, given by

$$c_\theta(s_1, \ldots, s_n) = \sum_{m=1}^{n-1} \theta^T \beta(s_m, s_{m+1}) + \beta_0(s_m, s_{m+1})$$

is clearly affine in θ. Thus the score of the *optimal* path to s_n, also viewed as a function of θ, is a maximum of affine functions

$$c_\theta^*(s_n) = \max_{s_1, \ldots, s_{n-1}} c_\theta(s_1, \ldots, s_n) \tag{2}$$

where the maximum is taken over all paths $s_1, \ldots, s_{n-1}$ ending in s_n. The number of paths in the maximization of Eqn. 2 grows exponentially in n, so such a representation will not be useful from an algorithmic perspective. However, many paths may be suboptimal for *all* values of θ; for such paths all descendant paths will also be suboptimal for all θ and can be eliminated from consideration.

To this end, define the *surviving* paths to be

$$B(s_n) = \bigcup_{\theta \in \Re^D} \{(s_1, \ldots, s_n) : c_\theta(s_1, \ldots, s_n) = c_\theta^*(s_n)\}$$

These are the paths ending in s_n that are optimal for at least one value of θ. Then we have

$$c_\theta^*(s_n) = \max_{(s_1, \ldots, s_n) \in B(s_n)} c_\theta(s_1, \ldots, s_n) \tag{3}$$

since the discarded paths contribute nothing to the maximum of Eqn. 2. The paths in $B(s_n)$ are those that *could* be prefixes of an optimal complete path for some θ.

The function of θ, $c_\theta^*(s_n)$, is rather interesting geometrically. First of all, as a maximum of affine functions, $c_\theta^*(s_n)$ must be convex. For each path $(s_1, \ldots, s_n)$, define the associated region of optimality to be

$$R(s_1, \ldots, s_n) = \{\theta : c_\theta^*(s_n) = c_\theta(s_1, \ldots, s_n)\}$$

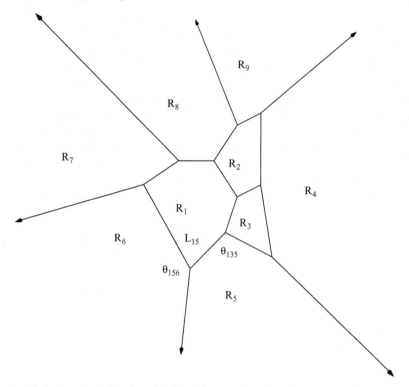

Fig. 2 $c_\theta^*(s_n)$ viewed as a function of θ. The $R(s_1, \ldots, s_n)$ regions for various paths are the simplices labeled as R_k in the figure.

Thus $R(s_1, \ldots, s_n)$ is non-empty if and only if $(s_1, \ldots, s_n) \in B(s_n)$. Each nonempty region, $R(s_1, \ldots, s_n)$, can be shown to be a simplex, and on such regions $c_\theta^*(s_n)$ is, by definition, affine in θ. Figure 2 depicts a possible configuration of the regions, $R(s_1, \ldots, s_n)$, for a two-dimensional parameter space, $\theta = (\theta_1, \theta_2)$. On each region R_k of the figure, $c_\theta^*(s_n)$ is affine in θ. The affine functions associated with two neighboring regions are equal along the segment that separates the regions.

The essential computation of our linear dynamic programming (LDP) algorithm is to compute the sets $\{B(s)\}_{l(s)=n+1}$ recursively from the sets $\{B(s)\}_{l(s)=n}$, as follows. Since, for any fixed θ, an optimal path at level $n+1$ must be an extension of some optimal path at level n, we know that

$$B(t) \subseteq \tilde{B}(t) \stackrel{\text{def}}{=} \bigcup_{(s,t) \in A} B(s) \circ t$$

where by $B(s) \circ t$ we mean extending the paths in $B(s)$ by t. We will obtain $B(t)$ from $\tilde{B}(t)$ by removing any superfluous paths, $(s_1, \ldots, s_n, t)$ whose score, $c_\theta(s_1, \ldots, s_n, t)$ is suboptimal for all θ. That is, $B(t)$ is the *smallest* subset of $\tilde{B}(t)$ having

$$\max_{\pi \in B(t)} c_\theta(\pi) = \max_{\pi \in \tilde{B}(t)} c_\theta(\pi) \tag{4}$$

This "filter" computation, which allows us to compute $B(t)$ from $\tilde{B}(t)$, is the subject of a good deal of research in the POMDP community (Kaelbling et. al. 1998), (Murphy 2000), (Cassandra et. al. 1997), (Sondik 1971) (White 1991), as it forms the computational workhorse for value iteration techniques. There are many techniques for performing filtering, though the search for computationally attractive approaches is a source of ongoing research in POMDPs. We will not not discuss filtering techniques here in any detail. However, a popular approach due to (White 1991) iteratively constructs $B(t)$ by comparing each new affine function of $\tilde{B}(t)$ with a set of current "survivors" already shown to be somewhere optimal. By solving a linear program, the new function can be shown either to not be in $B(t)$, or the algorithm identifies a new member of $\tilde{B}(t)$ that must be in $B(t)$.

The LDP algorithm constructs a search tree of possible paths. In the tree, a path at depth n corresponds to a path through the first n levels of the trellis. Such a tree is depicted in Fig. 3 for a trellis having only two states per level, labeled 0 and 1, thus two children for each nonterminal node. Each surviving path $s_1,\ldots,s_n$ in the

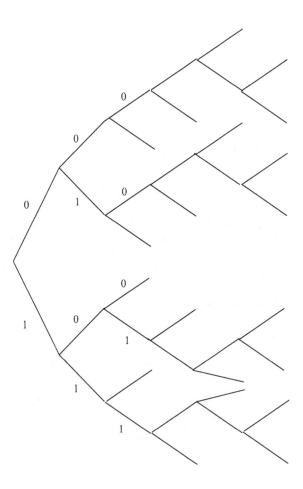

Fig. 3 The search tree of potentially optimal paths generated by the LDP algorithm for a trellis graph having only two states, 0 and 1, for each level. A terminal node in the graph indicates a path $s_1,\ldots,s_n$ for which $R(s_1,\ldots,s_n)$ is empty. Such a path requires no exploration of its children in the graph.

search tree has an associated set, $R(s_1, \ldots, s_n)$, of parameter values, θ, for which the path is optimal (with respect to other paths ending in s_n). Thus, unlike in the regular DP computation, we may have many surviving paths ending in state s_n — each optimal for a different range of parameter values. The task of the filter operation is to determine which sets, $R(s_1, \ldots, s_n)$, are empty since these paths need not be considered further in the search tree. Along a particular path $s_1, s_2, \ldots$, we have

$$R(s_1) \supseteq R(s_1, s_2) \supseteq R(s_1, s_2, s_3) \ldots$$

This follows since, by the basic reasoning of DP, if $(s_1, \ldots, s_n)$ is an optimal path for some fixed θ, then so is $(s_1, \ldots, s_{n-1})$. That is, if $\theta \in R(s_1, \ldots, s_n)$ then $\theta \in R(s_1, \ldots, s_{n-1})$

The LDP algorithm constructs this search tree level by level, generating children for each tree node at level n whose corresponding path, $(s_1, \ldots, s_n)$, has non-empty $R(s_1, \ldots, s_n)$. If computationally necessary, perhaps additional nodes (paths) are pruned. The paths that reach the final trellis node are the paths that are optimal for some value of θ.

3 Linear Dynamic Programming for Training in Sequence Estimation

The hidden Markov model (HMM) has proved to be a powerful and flexible approach for analyzing data sequences, with successes in many application domains including speech recognition (Rabiner 1989), gesture recognition (Starner and Pentland 1995), handwriting recognition (Hu et. al. 1996), various applications in Bioinformatics, e.g. (Karplus et. al. 1998), musical score following (Raphael 1999), and many others. In the HMM, recognition is often accomplished using dynamic programming (DP) to find the mostly likely sequence of hidden states given the observed data. This corresponds to finding the best scoring path through the state space trellis. One of the most attractive aspects of the HMM is automatic training procedures for estimating model parameters. However, a possible weakness of these training methods is their focus on a criterion not directly related to recognition performance. That is, HMM training algorithms such as the Baum-Welch algorithm, for unlabeled data, and straightforward empirical probability, for labeled data, optimize the *data likelihood* rather than a quantity, such as *recognition error rate*, that explicitly measures the quality of labellings produced by the recognition algorithm. In this section we show how LDP can serve as a reasonable alternative to maximum likelihood techniques for parameter estimation in sequence estimation problems.

Suppose we observe a sequence of N data observations and wish to estimate a corresponding sequence of labels that explain the data. A time-honored approach builds an $|S| \times N$ trellis graph where S is our collection of possible labels or states. Labeling of the data can be accomplished by assigning arc scores in a reasonable manner and computing the trellis path giving the best score through DP. Of course, the resulting sequence strongly depends on the choice of arc scores. At a minimum the arc scores should encourage a reasonable "vertical" correspondence between the labels and associated data observations. For instance, some data observations are likely to occur under some states, so arcs leading to these states should receive high scores. In addition, the arc scores can be chosen to prefer *a priori* desirable label sequences over less plausible ones, perhaps even enforcing certain "horizontal" constraints on the label sequence.

Now we introduce a way of *learning* the arc scores automatically. Suppose that our arc scores are each known linear functions of an unknown parameter, θ. We will choose θ as the value whose associated DP state sequence most closely matches a ground truth sequence. This value of θ can be found with LDP. Thus we address a problem of *supervised* learning. We emphasize that we are *not* trying to optimize the DP score over θ — this problem is unbounded if θ is unrestricted. Rather, we seek θ giving the best agreement between its associated DP state sequence and the ground truth. Thus, our approach *directly* optimizes a criterion we care about, such as the number of recognition errors we commit. Our optimality criterion, however, can be anything we choose — thus we may optimize a loss function incorporating a more nuanced assessment of the "badness" of different errors than does the 0-1 loss function. We will present such a loss function in the next section. In contrast, traditional HMM training techniques optimize the data likelihood, which is not of direct relevance to recognition performance.

Our approach does not address the issue of *generalization error* (Bishop 2006) in any meaningful sense, since we simply optimize the unregularized performance on a training set. Thus we hope that the training set is large enough that we do not over-fit during this process.

The approach of optimizing performance on a training set is certainly an old and well-established one in the machine learning community. What is novel here is our LDP method for optimizing training performance over a family of *sequence* estimators. We know of no other work that seeks to directly optimize the performance of a sequence estimator on a training set.

4 Application to Harmonic Analysis

The problem of *functional harmonic analysis* seeks to partition a piece of music into labeled sections, the labels giving the local *harmonic state*. The label usually consists of a key, e.g. C Major or G minor, and a chord symbol such as I, ii, iii, IV, V, vi, vii for the triads built on the scale degrees indicated by the roman numerals. For instance, the label (A major, IV) corresponds to the triad built on the fourth scale degree, (D,F♯,A), in the key of A major. Since harmony represents a significant part of what listeners respond to in music, its analysis is fundamental to a host of musical applications including expressive rendering, improvisational accompaniment systems, and may also constitute a one-dimensional reduction of music suitable for some search and retrieval applications. Past efforts in this area include (Pardo and Birmingham 2002), (Raphael and Stoddard 2003) (Temperley 2001), While the problem holds promise for a wide range of musical applications, the evaluation of such work remains difficult, primarily due to the scarcity of ground truth data as well as a suitable evaluation metric (not all errors are equally bad).

Our recognition approach uses DP to find the best scoring path through the lattice composed by an $S \times N$ array of states, where N is the number of measures or beats in the piece and S is the number of possible harmonic labels we consider. Our score function consists of two components: a data score and a path score. The data score encourages close agreement between each measure label and the pitches of that measure. The path score rewards paths that are more musically plausible, independent of the data. Our recognized sequence is then computed as the lattice path that minimizes the sum of these scores. We focus here on the problem of *learning* the data and path scores in a way that optimizes the path quality using a hand-labeled training set.

More explicitly, our score function, $C_\theta(s_1 \ldots, s_N)$, is composed as

$$C_\theta(s_1^N) = D_\theta(s_1, \ldots, s_N) + P_\theta(s_1, \ldots, s_N) \tag{5}$$

where the path, $(s_1, \ldots, s_N)$ is a sequence of labels, one for each measure. The data score, $D_\theta(s_1, \ldots, s_N) = \sum_{n=1}^N d_\theta(s_n, x_n)$, is represented as

$$d_\theta(s_n, x_n) = \sum_{i=1}^3 \sum_{j=1}^4 \theta_{ij}^d \delta_{ij}(s_n, x_n) \tag{6}$$

where x_n is the collection of pitches in the nth measure and the counts, $\delta_{ij}(s_n, x_n)$, are as follows. Each harmonic label, s_n, divides the possible chromatic pitches into four categories: those that are

1. the root of the chord
2. in the chord but not the root
3. in the scale but not the chord
4. outside the scale

Similarly, the pitches in a measure are divided into those that begin

1. on the downbeat of the measure
2. on a beat but not the downbeat
3. elsewhere in the measure

In Eqn. 6, $\delta_{ij}(s_n, x_n)$ counts the notes in the nth measure that are in position category i and of chromatic type j. To avoid degeneracies in which families of parameter assignments correspond to essentially identical choices, we further assume $\sum_j \theta_{ij}^d = 0$, thus reducing the effective length of the parameter θ^d.

The path score $P_\theta(s_1^N) = \sum_{n=1}^{N-1} p_\theta(s_n, s_{n+1})$ is the sum of modulation and progression components:

$$p_\theta(s_n, s_{n+1}) = \theta^m M(s_n, s_{n+1}) + \sum_{i=1}^{3} \theta_i^h H_i(s_n, s_{n+1})$$

where $M(s_n, s_{n+1})$ is an indicator function for key change. If $M(s_n, s_{n+1}) = 1$, the $\{H_i\}$ terms act as indicators for various classes of harmonic motion such as progressive (up a fifth) and regressive (down a fifth). As above, we assume $\sum_i \theta_i^h = 0$. In total, considering the linear constraints, In all, our parameter θ has dimension 12. Intuitively, the various terms in our objective function, C_θ, may be relevant for describing the quality of a particular path. Since we can only optimize a univariate quantity we choose as our optimality criterion a linear combination of these terms. θ gives the weights used in forming the linear combination C_θ.

The LDP algorithm terminates with a collection of paths that are each optimal on a particular region of θ values. We perform training by selecting a value for θ whose associated path is the best of the surviving paths, according to some measure of goodness.

This measure of goodness is *entirely distinct* from the score function described above, and can be chosen arbitrarily. In the case of harmonic analysis, we believe some errors are worse than others and should be penalized accordingly. For instance, the difference between the ii chord and the IV chord may be subtle and subjective in some cases. We address this issue by assigning a penalty for recognizing the true chord (from hand-labeled ground truth) with a possibly different chord as the number of pitch classes in the symmetric difference between the two chords. Thus there is no cost for getting a chord correct and cost of 2 for confusing chords ii and IV, since each has one pitch class not contained in the other. Similarly, our cost for the key attribute is formed by counting the number of pitch classes in the symmetric difference of the two scales. These two attributes are weighted equally and summed over the entire analysis sequence to form our goodness function for comparing paths.

Rather than trying to optimize *simultaneously* over our 12-dimensional parameter space, instead we have successively optimized over the various one-dimensional components of θ, using a simple one-dimensional implementation of the LDP algorithm. This technique is clearly inferior to simultaneous optimization over θ. While it is, in principle, possible to perform simultaneous optimization, this area remains to focus of ongoing work on our part. For our present purposes, we focus here on the essential idea of using LDP for training a sequence recognizer. However, the simultaneous optimization problem remains a source of ongoing research for us, with potential to draw on the relevant POMDP literature. The one-dimensional filtering problem is quite simple since, given a collection of one-dimensional linear functions, we only need discover which are maximal over some interval. It is straightforward to solve this one-dimensional problem in a computationally efficient manner, though we omit the details here.

Our first experiments involved performing the LDP algorithm with no pruning. In this case we observed a steady increase in the number of surviving paths at each stage of the trellis, though far less than the exponentially growing number of paths present if no filtering is performed. Figure 4 shows how the number of surviving paths grows as a function of trellis level over several one-dimensional iterations of our algorithm. This demonstrates that the overwhelming majority of paths are pruned, but also suggests difficulties with the scalability of the basic algorithm. We expect that some pruning, with the possibility of losing potentially optimal paths, will be necessary in more ambitious problems.

In the remaining experiments we used techniques analogous to beam search (Yu and Fern 2007) to decrease the number of paths that are propagated through the algorithm. In this case, as we progress through the trellis, we narrow the considered range of each particular component, θ_k, according to our path quality metric, to focus on what *seems* to be the right region in parameter space. In effect, we "tunnel in" on the best region in the one-dimensional parameter space under consideration. Figure 5 shows our symmetric difference "goodness" measure for the

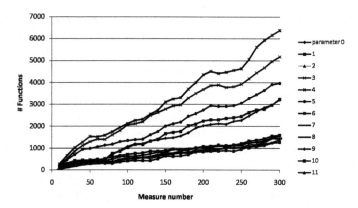

Fig. 4 Number of linear functions for each iteration of the algorithm.

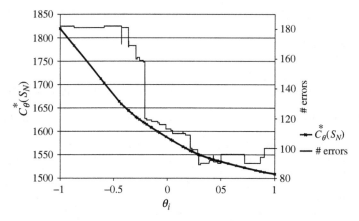

Fig. 5 After performing LDP on a particular component of θ, the resulting optimal cost and our symmetric difference penalty function, both as functions of θ_k. Training is accomplished by optimizing the latter criterion over the possible paths indexed by θ_k.

surviving paths after a typical iteration of the algorithm for this beam search version. Unlike the $c_\theta^*(s_n)$ function, which is convex in θ, our "goodness" measure can have arbitrary dependence on θ.

Using this procedure, we trained our algorithm on the *Grande Valse Brilliante* of Chopin using hand-labeled ground truth. In this experiment we limited the set of possible harmonic labels to the 27 (key,chord) pairs encountered in the piece. Note that, due to the nature of our data and path scores in Eqn. 5, parameter values trained from a restricted set of harmonic labels can still be applied to recognition problems using a different set of labels. Using this LDP implementation we were able to improve our path quality measure from 2203 to 173, starting with a random initial configuration for θ. The resulting configuration after our optimization terminates corresponded to a total summed symmetric difference (SSD) of 73 between the recognized chord pitch classes and the ground truth chord pitch classes, as well as an SSD of 100 between the two scale sequences. This corresponds to 0.24 chord errors and 0.33 scale errors per measure.

We then applied this learned parameter to the Chopin *Petit Chien* (the "Minute Waltz") using a collection of 14 labels. This resulted in an SSD of 186 chord pitch class errors and 40 scale pitch class errors, corresponding to 1.33 chord errors and 0.29 scale errors per measure. Finally, we tried retraining the algorithm with a larger collection of 80 labels and used the learned θ with the test data and a larger collection of 132 chord labels. This experiment resulted in a better chord error rate of 1.06 but much worse scale error rate of 1.2, suggesting that the selected best path often "borrowed" chords from other keys. The lack of any significant quantity of ground truth data, or agreement on the collection of possible labels, makes comparisons with other approaches difficult.

The analysis is available for download as a midi file at http://www.music.informatics.indiana.edu/papers/informs08/ that demonstrates the resulting analysis by superimposing the the recognized triads over the piano music while printing out the chord labels as they are played.

References

1. Bellman R., "Dynamic Programming", Princeton University Press, Princeton, New Jersey, 1957.
2. Bishop, C., "Pattern Recognition and Machine Learning", Springer, New York, New York 2006.
3. Cassandra A., Littman M., Zhang N., "Incremental Pruning: A Simple, Fast, Exact Method for Partially Observable Markov Decision Processes", *Proc. Thirteenth Annual Conf. on Uncertainty in Artif. Intel. (UAI–97)* 1997.
4. Hu J., Brown M. K., and Turin W., "HMM based on-line handwriting recognition", 18, pp. 1039-1045, 1996.
5. Karplus K., Barrett C., and Hughey R., "Hidden Markov models for detecting remote protein homologies", *Bioinformatics*, 14-10, 846-856, 1998.
6. Kaelbling L, Littman M., and Cassandra A., "Planning and Acting in Partially Observable Stochastic Domains", *Artificial Intelligence* 101, 1-2, pp. 99-134, 1998.

7. Murphy K., "A survey of POMDP solution techniques", *Technical Report, U. C. Berkeley*, 2000.
8. Pardo B. and Birmingham W. P., "Algorithms for Chordal Analysis", *Computer Music Journal*, 26-2, 27-49, 2002.
9. Rabiner L., "A Tutorial on Hidden Markov Models and Selected Applications in Speech Recognition", *Proceedings of the IEEE*, 77-2, pp. 257-285, 1989.
10. Raphael C., "Automatic Segmentation of Acoustic Musical Signals Using Hidden Markov Models", *IEEE Transactions on Pattern Analysis and Machine Intelligence*, 21-4, 360-370, 1999.
11. Raphael C., Stoddard J., "Harmonic analysis with probabilistic graphical models", *Proceedings of the International Symposium on Music Informatics Retrieval (ISMIR)* 2003.
12. Sondik E. J., "The optimal control of partially observable Markov processes", *Ph.D. Thesis* Stanford Univ., 1971.
13. Starner T. and Pentland A., "Real-Time American Sign Language Recognition From Video Using Hidden Markov Models", *SCV95, 5B Systems and Applications*, 1995.
14. Temperley D., "The cognition of basic musical structures", *MIT Press* Cambridge, MA, 2001.
15. Viterbi A., "Error bounds for convolutional codes and an asymptotically optimum decoding algorithm", *IEEE Transactions on Information Theory*, 13-2, pp. 260-269, 1967.
16. White C. C., "Partially observed Markov decision processes: A survey", *Annals of Operations Research* 32, 1991.
17. Xu, Y. and Fern, A. "On Learning Linear Ranking Functions for Beam Search", *Proceedings of 24th Int. Conf. on Machine Learning*, 1047–1054, 2007.

Part 3
Applications

Part 3.1
Cyberinfrastructure

Approximate Algorithms for Maximizing the Capacity of the Reverse Link in Multiple–Class CDMA Systems

Arash Abadpour and Attahiru Sule Alfa

Abstract Code Division Multiple Access (CDMA) has proved to be an efficient and stable means of communication between a group of users which share the same physical medium. With the rising demands for high–bandwidth multimedia services on mobile stations, it has become necessary to devise methods for more rigorous management of capacity in these systems. While a major method for regulating capacity in CDMA systems is through power control, the mathematical complexity of the related model inhibits useful generalizations. In this paper, a linear and a quadratic approximation for the aggregate capacity of the reverse link in a CDMA system are proposed. It is shown that the error induced by the approximations is reasonably low and that rewriting the optimization problem based on these approximations makes the implementation of the system in a multiple–class scenario feasible. This issue has been outside the scope of the available methods which work on producing an exact solution to a single–class problem.

Key words: Quality of Service, CDMA, Optimization, Capacity, Multiple Classes of Service

1 Introduction

In Code Division Multiple Access (CDMA), several independent users access a common communication medium by modulating their symbols with preassigned spreading sequences. The success of this strategy depends on the proper handling

Arash Abadpour
Deptartment of Electrical and Computer Engineering, University of Manitoba
e-mail: abadpour@ee.umanitoba.ca

Attahiru Sule Alfa
Deptartment of Electrical and Computer Engineering, University of Manitoba
e-mail: alfa@ee.umanitoba.ca

J.W. Chinneck et al. (eds.), *Operations Research and Cyber-Infrastructure*, Operations
Research/Computer Science Interfaces Series 47, DOI: 10.1007/978-0-387-88843-9_12,
© Springer Science+Business Media, LLC 2009

of the multiple access interference (MIA). The MIA could be either suppressed through the implementation of advanced signal processing methods such as multi-user detection and receiver beam–forming, or it could be managed through efficient power control (Hanly and Tse (1999)) and signature selection. In this paper, we look at the management of capacity in a single–cell system through power control, where certain conditions have to be met in order to guarantee an efficient and stable communication (see a survey in Zhang et al (2005)).

The basic approach to the power management problem is to define a set of constraints and then to find the solution which is binding for all of them. An example of this approach is to find the set of transmission powers which provide a given (often identical) signal to interference ratio (SIR) for all the stations in a cell (Hanly (1995)). For example, in Ishikawa and Umeda (1997), the researchers work on capacity design and analysis of the call admission control using a fixed–SIR approach (also see Viterbi et al (1994); Shin et al (1999)). A comprehensive and generalized treatment of this topic can be found in Yates (1995). The fixed–SIR approach is carried out through open–loop power control by individual stations as guided by power messages transmitted by the base station (Smith and Gervelis (1996)).

With the introduction of multimedia services to wireless CDMA communications, the goal is no more to provide fixed capacity to all of the users (Ulukus and Greenstein (2000)), but to maximize the aggregate capacity given a set of constraints (Hanly and Tse (1999)). In fact, the addition of other types of services to the conventional voice–only communication channels has urged the need for more control over the rates at which different stations transmit (Frodigh et al (2001)). This control is necessary in order to maximize system performance measures including the aggregate capacity (Gilhousen et al (1991)). The implementation of capacity maximization in multimedia–enabled networks is in contrast with voice–only systems in which the sole purpose of the power control mechanism is to eliminate the near–far effect through providing every station with a fixed SIR (Gilhousen et al (1991)). For the coverage of the early works on achieving multiple rates (Ottosson and Svensson (1995)) through maintaining fixed chip–rate and different transmission powers refer to Baier et al (1994); Chih-Lin and Sabnani (1995).

The maximization of the capacity, in this paper, is attempted at the reverse link (uplink), because this link is often the limiting link in CDMA communication systems (Bender et al (2000); Parkvall et al (2001)). For the coverage of the early works on the capacity of the reverse link, accompanied by results gathered from field tests refer to Padovani (1994); Evans and Everitt (1999). Among different channels on the reverse link, this paper concentrates on the traffic channels, due to the more demanding conditions they need to satisfy in establishing stable communications (Yang (1998b)). The work presented here is different from power control strategies used in the forward link (Kim et al (2003)), mainly due to the stringent requirements of the reverse link (Verdu (1989)). It is worth to mention that this present work analyzes the system at chip–level, as opposed to some others which also include the different transmission rates of the individual stations (Sung and Wong (2001)).

To reach a practically sound framework, it is important to consider a set of practical constraints to be satisfied in the system. While the minimal set of constraints considered by different researchers always includes a minimum Quality of Service (QoS) bound (Hosein (2004)), it is observed that this constraint, in the absence of others, can effectively cause very unfair systems (Oh et al (2003); Jafar and Goldsmith (2003)). This issue could be dealt with by incorporating fairness constraints into the problem. This, however, would increase the complexity of the solver. Moreover, adding more constraints into the problem makes the analysis of the problem, and development of a solver algorithm, harder.

The existence of different services in modern wireless systems has led to the need to define different classes of service (Lee et al (2005)). This, for example, means potentially different guaranteed minimum QoS levels for different users. Moreover, different users may have different significances to the service provider, for example because of their premium rates. The fact that the constraints are met at different points for different stations makes the application of many of the methods developed previously impossible, unless changes are made to them to fulfill the new demand. This is essentially because a majority of the previous algorithm were designed for the case in which all the stations reside in the same class (Hosein (2003); Oh and Soong (2006)).

In this paper, we look at the problem of maximizing the aggregate capacity of the reverse link in a CDMA network. Hence, the aggregate capacity is defined as the weighted summation of the capacities of the mobile stations. Also, we consider the case in which there are separate minimum SIR constraints for different stations. The problem analyzed here also includes a maximum aggregate received power constraint and separate limits on the transmit powers of each station. Furthermore, each station has its own maximum bandwidth constraint. We will show how this problem can be approximately solved using linear or quadratic programming.

The rest of this paper is organized as follows. Section 2 contains the proposed method, Section 3 presents some experimental results and, finally, Section 4 concludes the paper.

2 Proposed Method

This section contains the analysis of the reverse–link capacity maximization in a multiple–class system. Here, we assume that during the time it takes for the solver to produce a solution the system is in a steady state. This model is based on the assumption that the system is analyzed in time slots of T_s, where $T_s \gg \frac{1}{W}$ (W is the bandwidth), and that the coherence time of the most rapidly varying channel is greater than T_s. Therefore, in each time slot, path–loss propagation coefficients can be assumed to be constant (Oh et al (2003)). It is also worth to mention that the typical time interval during which the shadowing factor is nearly constant for a mobile station is a second or more (Torrieri (2004)). Hence, for solvers which take significantly less than a second to produce a solution shadowing can be ignored as well.

The rest of this section is organized as follows. First, in Section 2.1, the system model is presented. Then, a set of substitute variables are defined in Section 2.2, from which, in Section 2.3, two approximations for the objective function are derived. These approximations are used to generate the canonical representations depicted in Section 2.4. Then, after the issue of the addition of other constraints into the problem is addressed in Section 2.5, Section 2.6 presents the proposed algorithms as well as a complexity analysis.

2.1 System Model

Assume that there are M mobile stations with reverse link gains of $g_1, \cdots, g_M$, which satisfy $g_1 > \cdots > g_M$. Denote the transmit power of the i-th mobile station as p_i and the maximum transmission power of the i-th station as p_i^{max},

$$0 \le p_i \le p_i^{max}, \forall i. \tag{1}$$

With a background noise of I, the SIR for the signal coming from the i-th station, as perceived by the base station, is calculated as,

$$\gamma_i = \frac{p_i g_i}{I + \sum_{j=1, j \neq i}^{M} p_j g_j}. \tag{2}$$

Here, we assume that Shannon's formula can be used to approximately relate SIR to the bandwidth, thereby writing $C_i = B \log_2 (1 + \gamma_i)$. The adoption of the maximum bound given by Shannon's theorem is based on previously–developed models (see Kandukuri and Boyd (2000); Hanly and Tse (1999); Huawei (2005) for example). Moreover, we omit the constant B for notational convenience and therefore analyze relative capacities. Using these notations, in this section, we consider the problem defined as maximizing,

$$C = \sum_{i=1}^{M} \alpha_i C_i, \tag{3}$$

subject to,

$$\begin{cases} \gamma_i \ge \gamma_i^{min}, \forall i, \\ C_i \le C_i^{max}, \forall i, \\ \sum_{i=1}^{M} p_i g_i \le P^{max}, \\ 0 \le p_i \le p_i^{max}, \forall i. \end{cases} \tag{4}$$

Here, the constants γ_i^{min}, C_i^{max}, and p_i^{max} are the minimum SIR, the maximum capacity, and the maximum transmission power of the i-th station, respectively and α_i is the significance of station i ($\alpha_i > 0$). In other words, the values of the α_is demonstrate the "interest" of the system in each particular station. Accordingly, these values can indicate priority, for example for providing more urgency to calls made by emergency vehicles, or be based on the premium rate each station has signed on to pay for the service. Through grouping the stations into classes of identical values for these parameters, this model will be applicable to a multiple–class scenario.

Setting $\alpha_i = 1$, $\gamma_i^{min} = \gamma$, $C_i^{max} = \eta$, and $p_i^{max} = p_{max}$ this problem will reduce to the single–class problem titled as the NSC in Abadpour et al (2007b). In Abadpour et al (2007b) an algorithm is proposed which solves the NSC in an M–station cell in $O(M^3)$ flops.

The goal of the rest of this section is to solve the more generalized problem of maximizing (3) subject to (4), in which different stations not only have different significances, denoted by different values of α_i, but also have their own individual constraints. In these circumstances, the mathematical method introduced in Abadpour et al (2006) and used for tackling the NSC (Abadpour et al (2007b)) and its single–class generalizations (Abadpour et al (2007a)) will not work, because the constraints are now specific to the stations and therefore the methodology used previously will fail.

2.2 Substitute Variables

Here, we propose a new set of substitute variables and then rewrite the optimization problem, using approximations, as a linear or a quadratic programming problem.

Define the new set of variables,

$$\varphi_i = \frac{\gamma_i}{1 + \gamma_i} = \frac{p_i g_i}{\sum_{j=1}^{M} p_j g_j + I}, \forall i. \tag{5}$$

Note that,

$$C_i = -\log_2 (1 - \varphi_i). \tag{6}$$

Derivation shows that,

$$p_i g_i = I \frac{\varphi_i}{1 - \sum_{j=1}^{M} \varphi_j}. \tag{7}$$

Thus, if $\sum_{i=1}^{M} \varphi_i < 1$, a set of positive φ_is will produce a set of positive p_is.

Using (5), the conditions given in (4) can be rewritten as linear constraints for φ_is as,

$$\begin{cases} \varphi_i^{min} \leq \varphi_i \leq \varphi_i^{max}, \forall i, \\ \sum_{i=1}^{M} \varphi_i \leq \frac{X^{max}}{X^{max} + 1}, \\ l_i \sum_{j=1}^{M} \varphi_j + \varphi_i \leq l_i, \forall i. \end{cases} \tag{8}$$

Here,

$$
\begin{cases}
\varphi_i^{min} = \dfrac{\gamma_i^{min}}{\gamma_i^{min}+1}, \\
\varphi_i^{max} = 1 - 2^{-C_i^{max}}, \\
X^{max} = \dfrac{p^{max}}{I}, \\
l_i = \dfrac{p_i^{max} g_i}{I}.
\end{cases}
\tag{9}
$$

Note that the second condition in (8) results in $\sum_{i=1}^{M} \varphi_i \leq 1$, satisfying the condition needed for (7) to produce positive p_is. Define the $M \times 1$ vectors φ, φ^{min} and φ^{max} as the sequence of all values of φ_i, φ_i^{min} and φ_i^{max}, respectively. Furthermore, we define,

$$
\mathbf{A} = \begin{bmatrix} \mathbf{1}_{1 \times M} \\ \mathbf{1}_{M \times M} + diag\left[\dfrac{1}{l_1}, \cdots, \dfrac{1}{l_M}\right] \end{bmatrix},
\tag{10}
$$

$$
\mathbf{b} = \begin{bmatrix} \dfrac{X^{max}}{X^{max}+1} \\ \mathbf{1}_{M \times 1} \end{bmatrix}.
\tag{11}
$$

Now, (8) can be written as,

$$
\begin{cases}
\varphi^{min} \leq \varphi \leq \varphi^{max}, \\
\mathbf{A}\varphi \leq \mathbf{b}.
\end{cases}
\tag{12}
$$

While we will use (12) as the set of constraints for the optimization problem, to be given later in the paper, this set of inequalities can also be used for identifying the feasible region for φ. This issue is not discussed in this paper.

2.3 Approximation of the Objective Function

The formulation of the objective function, in its present form, as a function of the φ_is, includes fractional and logarithmic terms and is hard to work with. Thus. we devise two methods, a linear and a quadratic one, to approximate C as a first–degree or a second–degree function of the φ_is. With the linear representation of the constraints, given in (12), this would make the application of standard linear and quadratic programming methods to the problem analyzed here possible.

For small γ_i, We have,

$$
C_i = \log_2(1+\gamma_i) \simeq \frac{1}{ln2}\gamma_i \simeq \frac{1}{ln2}\varphi_i.
\tag{13}
$$

The approximation used here can be written as,

$$ln(1+x) \simeq \frac{x}{1+x}, x \in [\gamma, 2^\eta - 1], \tag{14}$$

and yields a linear approximation of C_i in terms of φ_i. Another approximation is given below,

$$C_i \simeq \frac{1}{ln2} \gamma_i = \frac{1}{ln2} \frac{\varphi_i}{1 - \varphi_i} \simeq \frac{1}{ln2} \varphi_i (1 + \varphi_i). \tag{15}$$

This is a second order approximation of C_i in terms of φ_i and uses the following approximation,

$$ln(1+x) \simeq \frac{x}{1+x} \left(1 + \frac{x}{1+x}\right), x \in [\gamma, 2^\eta - 1]. \tag{16}$$

The appropriateness of the two approximations demonstrated in (14) and (16) is investigated in Figure 1. Here, the nominal values of $\gamma = -30dB$ and $\eta = 0.3$ are used, demonstrated using the shaded area. Based on Figure 1–b, both approximations induce less than 10% error. Note that as p_i increases, and thus so do γ_i and φ_i, the error induced by either approximation goes up. However, the second order approximation is always more accurate than the linear approximation (see Figure 1–a). It is also important to emphasize that while the linear approximation is conservative, i.e. it produces smaller values than the exact formulation, the second order formulation approximates the capacity by a laregr value. Therefore, the second order approximation overestimates the aggregate capacity which it attempts to maximize.

2.4 Canonical Representation

Defining the $M \times 1$ vector α, as the sequence of all α_is, we use the linear approximation, given in (13), to rewrite the objective function as,

$$C \simeq \frac{1}{ln2} \sum_{i=1}^M \alpha_i \varphi_i = \mathbf{f}^T \varphi. \tag{17}$$

Here,

$$\mathbf{f} = \frac{1}{ln2} \alpha. \tag{18}$$

Similarly, the quadratic approximation, given in (15), results in,

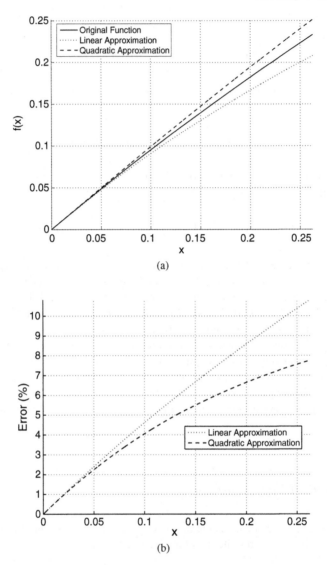

(a)

(b)

Fig. 1 Investigating the properness of the approximations given in (14) and (16). The shaded areas show the working interval. Note that, as shown in (14) and (16), here we approximate $ln(1+x)$ in terms of $\frac{x}{1+x}$. Thus, the fact that the quadratic approximation exhibits a line in the $(x, f(x))$ plane should not mislead the reader. (a) The exact values compared with the two different approximations. (b) Relative error induced by the two approximations.

$$C \simeq \frac{1}{ln2} \sum_{i=1}^{M} \alpha_i \left(\varphi_i + \varphi_i^2 \right) = \frac{1}{2} \varphi^T \mathbf{H} \varphi + \mathbf{f}^T \varphi, \qquad (19)$$

where,

$$\mathbf{H} = \frac{2}{ln2} diag\left[\alpha_1, \cdots, \alpha_M\right]. \tag{20}$$

The maximization of either (17) or (19) has to be carried out subject to the constraints shown in (8) and using linear or quadratic programming, respectively. We call these two algorithms the M^1SC and the M^2SC, respectively. These algorithms will be presented in detail in Section 2.6.

2.5 Addition of Other Constraints

The approximations proposed here are also helpful when a new constraint is to be added to the problem. The reader is referred to the case of adding a new constraint to the NSC, addressed in Abadpour et al (2007a), which led to the definition of the N^+SC. There, to tackle the unfairness of the solution to the NSC, a capacity–share constraint was added to the problem, as,

$$\tilde{C}_i = \frac{C_i}{C} \leq \frac{1}{\mu}\frac{1}{M}, 0 < \mu < 1. \tag{21}$$

Adding this constraint to the NSC almost quadrupled the code complexity of the solver (Abadpour et al (2007a)). Here, we demonstrate the straightforward approach which yields the addition of the new constraint to the approximate problems.

Using (3) Equation (21) can be written as,

$$\sum_{j=1}^{M} \alpha_j \varphi_j \geq M\mu\varphi_i, \forall i. \tag{22}$$

This translates into,

$$(M\mu\mathbf{I}_{M \times M} - \alpha\mathbf{1}_{1 \times M})\varphi \leq \mathbf{0}_{M \times 1}. \tag{23}$$

We argue that the addition of any constraint which can be written as a linear function of the φ_is could be performed similarly.

2.6 Proposed Algorithms

Using the formulation developed in Section 2.4, the two algorithms of the M^1SC and the M^2SC can be written as the three steps of,

1. Generating $\mathbf{A}, \mathbf{b}, \mathbf{f}$ and $\mathbf{H}$,

2. Solving either φ=linprog($\mathbf{f},\mathbf{A},\mathbf{b},\varphi^{min},\varphi^{max}$), for the case of the M^1SC, or φ=quadprog($\mathbf{H},\mathbf{f},\mathbf{A},\mathbf{b},\ \varphi^{min},\varphi^{max}$), for the case of the M^2SC, and, finally,
3. Calculating C_is using (6), p_is using (7), and C using (3).

Note that, as the matrix $\mathbf{H}$, defined in (20), is positive–definite, the computational complexity of the M^2SC is polynomial (Kozlov et al (1979)). The linear programming–based approach, namely the M^1SC, will take up polynomial time as well (Gill et al (1982)).

3 Experimental Results

The proposed algorithms are implemented in MATLAB 7.0 and executed on a Pentium IV 3.00GHZ personal computer with 1GB of RAM running Windows xp.

Here, the work is carried out in a circular cell of radius $R = 2.5Km$. For the station i at the distance d_i from the base station, only the path–loss is considered, and is modeled as given in Rappaport and Milstein (1992), as follows,

$$g_i = Cd_i^n. \qquad (24)$$

For a comprehensive review of the subject refer to Rappaport (2002). Here, C and n are constants equal to 7.75×10^{-3} and -3.66, respectively, when d_i is in meters. Equivalently, with d_i in kilometers, C will equal 1.2283×10^{-13} (see Yang (1998a); Oh and Wasserman (1999); Goodman and Mandayam (2000)). To produce a sequence $\mathbf{g}$ of length M, a set of $3M$ points are placed in the $[-R,R] \times [-R,R]$ square, based on a two dimensional uniform distribution. Then, from those in the circle with radius R centered at the origin, M points are picked.

The base parameters used in this study are $\gamma = -30dB$, $I = -113dBm$, $P_{max} = -113dBm$, $p_{max} = 23dBm$, and $\eta = 0.3$. These values are partly based on the data given in Goodman and Mandayam (2000); Goodman (1997); Yang (1998a). Note that, here, the values of I and P_{max} comply with the notion of limiting the blocking probability, as defined in Viterbi and Viterbi (1993). The conversion from dB to watts is performed according to $xdB \equiv 10^{\frac{1}{20}x}$. Also, $xdBm \equiv 10^{\frac{1}{10}x}mw$.

In order to evaluate the performance of the proposed methods, in comparison to each other as well to the exact method, namely the NSC, first, a cell containing 15 stations, as shown in Figure 2–(a), is considered.

In order to be able to apply the NSC and the proposed algorithms on the same problem, we set $\alpha_i = 1$, $\gamma_i^{min} = \gamma$, $C_i^{max} = \eta$, and $p_i^{max} = p_{max}$, for all the stations. This setting reduces the general problem to what the NSC is capable of calculating the solution to, thus providing a platform for comparing the M^1SC and the M^2SC with the NSC.

It takes $8.6ms$ for the NSC to produce a solution to the given problem. Using the first–order approximation, the M^1SC solves the same problem in $26.6ms$ and the M^2SC, which is based on a second–order approximation, takes $23.4ms$ to finish. Therefore, utilization of the second–order approximation results in more than 10%

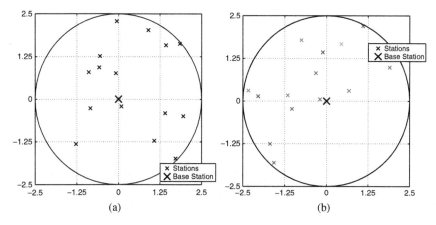

Fig. 2 Sample problems defined in 15–station cells. (a) All α_is are one. (b) None unity α_is visualized using different shades of gray.

decline in the computational complexity of the solver. Similar observation is made for problems with different sizes and locaitons of stations. It is worth to mention that the application of the approximations almost triples the computational complexity. This is mainly due to the fact that the exact algorithms go through a list of candidate points (Abadpour et al (2007b)), whereas the approximate algorithms use numerical search at their core. Nevertheless, the approximations enable us to solve the problem in a multiple–class framework, a scenario which is out of the scope of the exact algorithm.

Comparison of the aggregate capacity values generated by the three problems, we observe values of $C = 0.735$, $C = 0.734$, and $C = 0.735$, produced by the NSC, the M^1SC, and the M^2SC, respectively (values are relative). The more accurate result of the M^2SC is notable. Numerically, the M^1SC has caused 0.16% error in the aggregate capacity whereas the M^2SC is accurate up to four decimal places.

Comparing the M^1SC with the exact algorithm, the mean deviation in the values of p_i is 11.50%. The minimum and the maximum deviation of the same variable is 0.08% and 52.08%, respectively. Similar figures are observed for values of C_i (mean of 11.70%, minimum of 0.085% and maximum of 53.00%). Analyzing the solution generated by the M^2SC, however, the deviation in p_is and C_is is zero per cent up to four decimal places.

In the next experiment, the performance of the two algorithms, the M^1SC and the M^2SC, in a truly multiple–class system are compared. In order to do so, a sample problem is generated, as shown in Figure 2–(b). Here, darkness of each station demonstrates its corresponding value of α_i (the darker a stations is, the higher the corresponding value of α_i is). Using the M^1SC, it takes about $29.7ms$ to solve this problem, whereas the M^2SC demands $28.1ms$ to find the solution to the same problem (about 5% less). Furthermore, there is 1.09% difference between the aggregate capacity values calculated by the two algorithms.

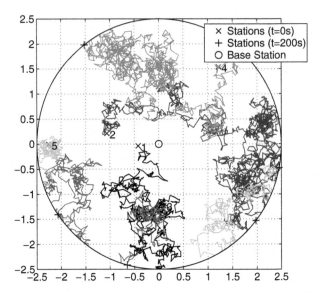

Fig. 3 Pattern of movement of the stations used in the dynamic analysis of the M^2SC.

Based on the results stated in the above, another experiment is carried out in order to analyze the behavior of the M^2SC in a simulation which spans a given period of time. In this experiment, the movements of $M = 5$ stations in a cell are simulated and the corresponding problems are solved. Here, the movements are modeled using a discrete random walk with the speed at each moment chosen based on a uniform random variable between zero and $5Km/h$ (Jabbari and Fuhrmann (1997)). Here, we assume that no station leaves the cell or enters it. In this setting, the system is analyzed in a time span of $T = 200s$, during which the resulting problem is solved every $dt = 100ms$. Figure 3 shows the random walk of the stations during the experiment. The solutions produced for all the corresponding problems are aggregated in Figure 4. Here, each row represents one station. The graphs on the left present the transmission powers of the stations in this time span while the graphs to the right show the regarding capacities. Figure 5 shows the aggregate capacity of the system during the experiment and, finally, Figure 6 presents the capacity shares of the stations during this experiment.

4 Conclusions

The problem of maximizing the aggregate capacity of the uplink in a single–cell CDMA system was analyzed in this paper. As an extension to the available methods, the case of multiple–class systems was analyzed. As opposed to the previous studies which assume identical constraints for all the mobile stations, it was argued that in practical systems, customers constitute different classes and therefore

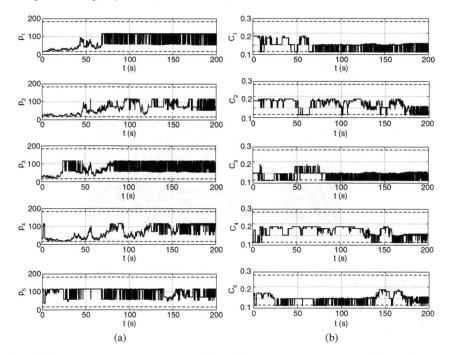

Fig. 4 Transmission powers and the capacities of different stations over the time in the dynamic experiment. (a) Transmission powers. (b) Capacities.

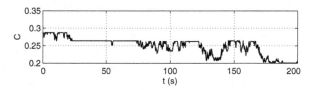

Fig. 5 Aggregate capacity during the experiment.

should be treated accordingly. It was shown that, through using approximations, the problem can be solved using linear or quadratic programming. While utilizing a second–degree approximation yields a more accurate outcome, it overestimates the capacities and therefore may result in spurious results, due to the fact that the aim of the problem is the maximization of the aggregate capacity. First–order approximation, on the other hand, is conservative but induces more error. Nevertheless, both algorithms are well inside a 5%–error margin. The proposed algorithms, however, are computationally more expensive due to the utilization of numerical optimization in them. The paper also contains analysis of the problem in a time span, during which the stations perform a random walk inside a cell.

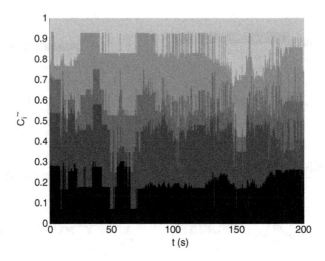

Fig. 6 Capacity shares of the stations during the experiment. Each shade of gray represents one station.

References

Abadpour A, Alfa AS, Soong AC (2006) Closed form solution for QoS–constrained information–theoretic sum capacity of reverse link CDMA systems. In: Proceedings of the second ACM Q2SWinet 2006, Torremolinos, Malaga, Spain, pp 123–128

Abadpour A, Alfa AS, Soong AC (2007a) Capacity–share controlled information–theoretic sum capacity of reverse link single–cell CDMA systems. In: 2007 IEEE 65th Vehicular Technology Conference, (VTC2007 Spring), Dublin, Ireland

Abadpour A, Alfa AS, Soong AC (2007b) A more realistic approach to information–theoretic sum capacity of reverse link CDMA systems in a single cell. In: Proceedings of the IEEE International Conference on Communications (ICC 2007), Glasgow, Scotland

Baier A, Fiebig UC, Granzow W, Koch W, Teder P, Thielecke J (1994) Design study for a CDMA–based third-generation mobile radio system. IEEE Journal on Selected Areas in Communications 12:733–743

Bender P, Black P, Grob M, Padovani R, Sindhushayana N, Viterbi A (2000) CDMA/HDR: A bandwidth–efficient high–speed wireless data service for nomadic users. IEEE Communications Magazine 38 (7):70–77

Chih-Lin I, Sabnani KK (1995) Variable spreading gain CDMA with adaptive control for integrated traffic in wireless networks. In: Proceedings of IEEE VTC, pp 794–798

Evans JS, Everitt D (1999) On the teletraffic capacity of CDMA cellular networks. IEEE Transactions on Vehicular Technology 48 (1):153–165

Frodigh M, Parkvall S, Roobol C, Johansson P, Larsson P (2001) Future–generation wireless networks. IEEE Personal Communications 8 (5):10–17

Gilhousen K, Jacobs I, Padovani R, Viterbi A, Jr LW, III CW (1991) On the capacity of a cellular cdma system. IEEE Transactions on Vehicular Technology 40 (2):303–312

Gill PE, Murray W, Wright MH (1982) Practical Optimization. Academic Press

Goodman D, Mandayam N (2000) Power control for wireless data. IEEE Personal Communications Magazine 7:48–54

Goodman DJ (1997) Wireless Personal Communications Systems. Addison–Wesley Wireless Communications Series, Readings, Massachusetts

Hanly SV (1995) An algorithm of combined cell–site selection and power control to maximize cellular spread spectrum capacity. IEEE Journals on Selected Areas in Communications 13 (7):1332–1340

Hanly SV, Tse D (1999) Power control and capacity of spread–spectrum wireless networks. Automatica 35 (12):1987–2012

Hosein P (2003) Optimal proportionally fair rate allocation for CDMA reverse links. In: Proceedings of the Sixth International Symposium on Wireless Personal Multimedia Communications, Yokosuka, Japan

Hosein P (2004) Optimality conditions for throughput maximization on the reverse link for a CDMA network. In: Proceedings of the IEEE Eighth International Symposium on Spread Spectrum Techniques and Applications, pp 764–768

Huawei (2005) Soft frequency reuse scheme for UTRAN LTE. 3GPP TSG RAN WG1 Meeting #41, R1–050507

Ishikawa Y, Umeda N (1997) Capacity design and performance of call admission control in cellular CDMA systems. IEEE Journal on Selected Areas in Communications 15 (8):1627–1635

Jabbari B, Fuhrmann WF (1997) Teletraffic modeling and analysis of flexible hierarchical cellular networks with speed-sensitive handoff strategy. IEEE Journal on Selected Areas in Telecommunications 15 (8):1539–1548

Jafar SA, Goldsmith A (2003) Adaptive multirate CDMA for uplink throughput maximization. IEEE Transactions on Wireless Communications 2:218–228

Kandukuri S, Boyd S (2000) Simultaneous rate and power control in multirate multimedia CDMA systems. In: IEEE Sixth International Symposium on Spread Spectrum Techniques and Applications, NJIT, NJ, pp 570–574

Kim DI, Hossain E, Bhargava VK (2003) Downlink joint rate and power allocation in cellular multirate WCDMA systems. IEEE Transactions on Wireless Communications 2 (1):69–80

Kozlov MK, Tarasov SP, Khachiyan LG (1979) Polynomial solvability of convex quadratic programming. Doklady Akademiia Nauk SSSR (translated in Soviet Mathematics Doklady, 20) 248:1108–111

Lee JW, Mazumdar RR, Shroff NB (2005) Downlink power allocation for multi–class wireless systems. IEEE/ACM Transactions on Networking 13 (4):854–867

Oh SJ, Soong ACK (2006) QoS–constrained information–theoretic sum capacity of reverse link CDMA systems. IEEE Transactions on Wireless Communications 5 (1):3–7

Oh SJ, Wasserman K (1999) Adaptive resource allocation in power constrained CDMA mobile networks. In: IEEE Wireless Communications and Networking Conference, pp 510–514

Oh SJ, Zhang D, Wasserman KM (2003) Optimal resource allocation in multi–service CDMA networks. IEEE Transactions on Wireless Communications 2:811–821

Ottosson T, Svensson A (1995) multirate schemes in DS/CDMA systems. In: Proceedings of IEEE VTC, pp 1006–1010

Padovani R (1994) Reverse link performance of IS–95 based cellular syste,s. IEEE Personal Communications Third Quarter:28–34

Parkvall S, Dahlman E, Frenger P, Beming P, Persson M (2001) The evolution of WCDMA toward higher speed downlink packet data access. In: Proceedings of IEEE VTC'01–Spring, Vol. 3, pp 2287–2291

Rappaport T, Milstein L (1992) Effects of radio propagation path loss on DS–CDMA cellular frequency reuse efficiency for the reverse channel. IEEE Transactions on Vehicular Technology 41 (3):231–242

Rappaport TS (2002) Wireless communications: principles and practice. Prentice Hall, Upper Saddle River, N.J.

Shin SM, Cho CH, Sung DK (1999) Interference-based channel assignment for DS–CDMA cellular systems. IEEE Transactions on Vehicular Technology 48 (1):233–239

Smith C, Gervelis C (1996) Cellular System Design & Optimization. McGraw–Hill Series on Telecommunications

Sung CW, Wong WS (2001) Power control and rate management for wireless multimedia CDMA systems. IEEE Transactions on Communications 49 (7):1215–1226

Torrieri D (2004) Principles of Spread-Spectrum Communication Systems. Springer

Ulukus S, Greenstein L (2000) Throughput maximization in CDMA uplinks using adaptive spreading and power control. In: IEEE Sixth International Symposium on Spread Spectrum Techniques and Applications, pp 565–569

Verdu S (1989) The capacity region of the symbol–asynchronous gaussian multiple–access channel. IEEE Transactions on Information Theory 35 (4):733–751

Viterbi A, Viterbi A (1993) Erlang capacity of a power controlled CDMA system. IEEE Journal on Selected Areas in Communications 11 (6):892–900

Viterbi AJ, Viterbi AM, Gilhousen KS, Zehavi E (1994) Soft handoff extends CDMA cell coverage and increases reverse link capacity. IEEE Journal on Selected Areas in Communications 12 (8):1281–1288

Yang SC (1998a) CDMA RF System Design. Artech House Publishing, Boston

Yang SC (1998b) CDMA RF System Engineering. Artech House Publishers, Boston, London

Yates RD (1995) A framework for uplink power control in cellular radio systems. IEEE Journal on Selected Areas in Communications 13 (7):1341–1347

Zhang J, Wang C, Li B (2005) Resource management in DS–CDMA cellular networks. In: Pan Y, Xiao Y (eds) Design and Analysis of Wireless Networks, Nova Science Publishers, Inc., Hauppauge, NY, pp 99–111

Mathematical Formulations and Metaheuristics Comparison for the Push-Tree Problem

Marco Caserta, Andreas Fink, Andrea Raiconi, Silvia Schwarze, and Stefan Voß

Abstract The Push-Tree Problem is a recently addressed optimization problem, with the aim to minimize the total amount of traffic generated on information broadcasting networks by a compromise between the use of "push" and "pull" mechanisms. That is, the push-tree problem can be seen as a mixture of building multicast trees with respect to nodes receiving pieces of information while further nodes may obtain information from the closest node within the tree by means of shortest paths. In this sense we are accounting for tradeoffs of push and pull mechanisms in information distribution. The objective of this paper is to extend the literature on the problem by presenting four mathematical formulations and by defining and applying some metaheuristics for its resolution.

Key words: Push-Tree Problem, Multicast Tree, Metaheuristics, Reactive Tabu Search, Simulated Annealing

Marco Caserta
Institute of Information Systems (IWI), University of Hamburg, Von-Melle-Park 5, 20146 Hamburg, Germany e-mail: marco.caserta@uni-hamburg.de

Andreas Fink
Faculty of Economics and Social Sciences, Helmut-Schmidt-University, Holstenhofweg 85, 22043 Hamburg, Germany e-mail: andreas.fink@hsu-hamburg.de

Andrea Raiconi
Department of Statistics, Probability and Applied Statistics, University of Rome "La Sapienza", P.le A. Moro 5, 00185 Roma, Italy e-mail: andrea.raiconi@uniroma1.it

Silvia Schwarze
Institute of Information Systems (IWI), University of Hamburg, Von-Melle-Park 5, 20146 Hamburg, Germany e-mail: schwarze@econ.uni-hamburg.de

Stefan Voß (corresponding author)
Institute of Information Systems (IWI), University of Hamburg, Von-Melle-Park 5, 20146 Hamburg, Germany e-mail: stefan.voss@uni-hamburg.de

J.W. Chinneck et al. (eds.), *Operations Research and Cyber-Infrastructure*, Operations Research/Computer Science Interfaces Series 47, DOI: 10.1007/978-0-387-88843-9_13,

1 Introduction

Many real-word information distribution systems may be modeled as a weighted graph where some information stored in a specified node (the information source) must be broadcasted to a subset of the other nodes. Usually in a realistic scenario this information will not be static but will evolve over time, which necessitates as primary issue finding the most appropriate way to transmit the information to the interested nodes (called request nodes) whenever their local copy becomes outdated.

Let us suppose that the functionality of the whole network relies strictly on the dynamic transmission of the information from the source, and therefore each request node needs to be quickly informed of every update. An obvious solution would then be transmitting all these updates on a minimum cost multicast tree involving the source and the request nodes. It is clear that under these assumptions our problem reduces to the well-known Steiner tree problem. Though being $\mathcal{N}\mathcal{P}$-hard, the problem has been extensively studied with respect to approximation algorithms as well as metaheuristics and exact approaches (see Voß (2006) for a recent survey). The broadcasting operation performed by the source in this scenario is known as *push* mechanism.

On the contrary, it could also be the case that although the source keeps updating the information with a certain rate, the request nodes of our network can rely for a long period of time on previous copies and need to be informed about all the occurred changes with much lower rates (an example of this scenario could be the information caching at the basis of the Internet Domain Name System). In that case a considerable amount of the traffic generated by the push operations described above would be wasted; a much more reasonable solution would consist in an explicit information request performed by each node whenever it needs it. Assuming that each node chooses the cheapest possible path to communicate with the source, the optimal solution in this case becomes a Shortest Path Tree, that is widely known as a polynomially solvable problem (see, e.g., Papadimitriou and Steiglitz (1982)). Each operation request of this type is known as *pull*.

If we now consider a heterogeneous network, which shares characteristics of both scenarios discussed above in different regions, it becomes clear that a combination of push and pull operations could be the most convenient choice. That is, the source could use the push mechanism to keep a selection of nodes updated; at this point, each of these nodes is capable to handle pull operations coming from any request node not directly updated. We give a visual representation of this situation in Figure 1.

The optimal set of connections needed by the source to update the selected set of nodes defines a subtree of the graph which is called push-tree; since determining the optimal paths from any request node excluded from the push-tree to any node belonging to it is an easy task, the entire problem is characterized by the choice of such tree, and that is why the name of the overall optimization problem refers just to it.

Figure 1 shows the connection between the push-tree and some related problems. In fact, the information replication performed on the push tree nodes is similar to

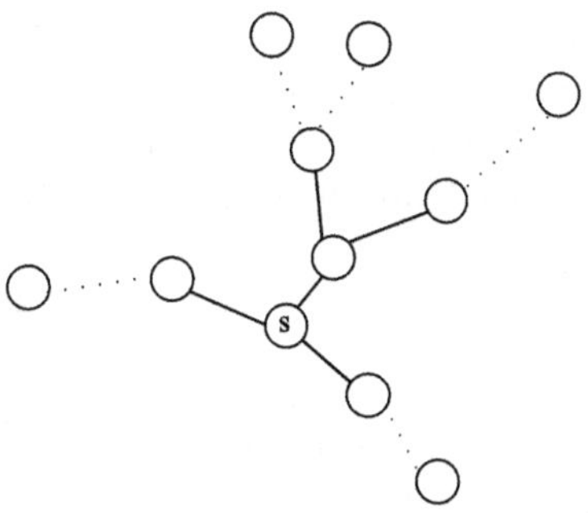

Fig. 1 Push-tree example:
each node in the push-tree
(consisting of the solid edges)
is kept updated, so each
other node that needs the
information can choose the
nearest amongst them to
perform its request.

the problem of placing replicas (mirroring) of some resource in order to meet the request of the clients and minimizing the replication cost addressed, e.g., in Tang and Xu (2004). Moreover, as shown in the figure, each path between the source and a request node can be considered as divided in two parts, with the push mechanism operating on the first and the pull mechanism on the second part, and this relates to some other works based on multilevel network design, such as, e.g., Mirchandani (1996). However, while these works are more related to a fixed cost assigned to the choices made, the push-tree refers to the variable cost associated to the levels of traffic generated by the use of the two mechanisms.

The push-tree problem has been introduced in Havet and Wennink (2001, 2004). In these works they formalize the problem and, as we will see in the next section, they prove it to be polynomially solvable in a special case and present an approximation algorithm for the general undirected case. Moreover, they present some robustness results for their algorithm in the case of changes in the request nodes set or in the update and request rates. These results are further extended in Havet (2002). In Facundo et al. (2007) the authors have performed some computational results on the heuristic algorithm in Havet and Wennink (2004). To the best of our knowledge neither mathematical programming formulations nor any advanced metaheuristics have been proposed for the push-tree problem so far. In this paper we strive to overcome this situation.

The remaining sections of the paper are organized as follows. Section 2 presents a more formal description of the problem and summarizes some already known results. Section 3 presents our mathematical formulations. Section 4 describes our metaheuristic approaches. Computational results are reported in Section 5 and conclusions are considered in Section 6.

2 Problem Formulation and Known Results

Let $G = (V, E)$ be an undirected graph. For each edge $(i, j) \in E$, let $l_{ij} \geq 0$ be its length (or weight). Moreover, given a subgraph H of G, let l_H be the length of all its edges. Let $s \in V$ be the source node and $R \subseteq V \setminus \{s\}$ be the set of request nodes. Let

$\mu \geq 0$ be the update rate of the source (i.e., the number of times that the information in s changes per time unit) and r_v be the request rate for each node $v \in R$. We look for the subgraph PT of G and the paths P_v from each $v \in R$ to some node in PT such that the following function is minimized:

$$\mu l_{PT} + \sum_{v \in R} r_v l_{P_v} \tag{1}$$

Obviously l_{P_v} will be 0 if v itself belongs to PT. Moreover, PT will be surely a tree, since a cycle would imply an additional cost while connecting the same set of nodes. The values for μ and r_v determine the size of the push tree: if μ is sufficiently small ($\mu < r_v \quad \forall v \in R$) the push-tree would include every request node (i.e., would be the optimal Steiner tree for $R \cup \{s\}$ as the set of basic or required nodes). On the other hand, if $\mu > \sum_{v \in R} r_v$, the push-tree would be composed of just node s (and the optimal solution would be given by the shortest path tree from every request node to s).

Now let us consider the case in which the input graph G is a tree. The exact linear algorithm presented in Havet and Wennink (2004) is based on the following observation: removing a single edge e from G would disconnect it into two components, and e is part of the path to the source for each request node in the component not containing s. Let $\Lambda(e)$ be the sum of all the request rates of the request nodes in the component without the source; if e is not in the push-tree, its contribution to the objective function is $\Lambda(e)l_e$, otherwise it will obviously be μl_e. Therefore, the optimal push-tree will be composed of all the edges e such that $\mu < \Lambda(e)$. Figure 2 summarizes the procedure; note that the edge lengths are not necessary to find the optimal solution (but they are obviously required to determine its actual value).

The exact algorithm for the tree case suggests a two-step class of heuristics for the general case: determine a tree of the graph (called *routing tree*) and execute the exact algorithm for this tree. What differentiates these approaches is the routing tree construction method.

Fig. 2 Optimal push-tree in a tree: request nodes are represented by squares, with their request rate reported inside. $\Lambda(e)$ is reported for each edge. The considered value for μ is 4. The push-tree is composed of the thick edges.

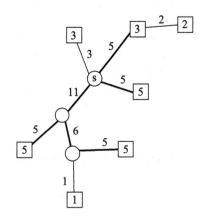

Two natural possibilities are to consider a minimum spanning tree or a shortest path tree routed at the source, which can be easily computed. However, in Havet and Wennink (2004) it was proven that both of these approaches can be arbitrarily bad, i.e., there is at least a push-tree instance such that the ratio between the solution produced with any of these approaches and the actual optimal solution grows to infinity. We could then consider the Steiner tree problem on $R \cup \{s\}$. The problem is $\mathcal{NP}$-hard itself. However, it is proven in Havet and Wennink (2004) that assuming a given heuristic approximating the Steiner tree problem with ratio ρ, then

$$\frac{w(T)}{w^*} \leq \rho \frac{\mu}{r_m} \tag{2}$$

where $w(T)$ is the objective function value if the Steiner tree heuristic is used for the first step of the two-step push-tree heuristic, w^* is the optimal objective function value and r_m is the smallest nonzero request rate on the network. In particular, well-known heuristics approximating the Steiner tree problem with ratio $2 - 2/|R|$, like the Prim-based cheapest insertion heuristic (Takahashi and Matsuyama, 1980), also approximate this problem with a ratio less than $2(\mu/r_m)$.

In the following, unless differently specified, wherever we refer to the routing tree heuristic we are considering a routing tree built with the Prim-based Steiner tree heuristic. However, as it is clear from (2) even an optimal solution for the Steiner tree problem would not necessarily result in an optimal solution for the push-tree problem. We present an example of that in Figure 3, which shows the optimal Steiner tree on a well-known instance for Steiner tree problems, the incidence graph i160–003 of the SteinLib library (Koch et al., 2001). Let us consider node 1 as the source node, all the other terminal nodes (2–7) as request nodes, an update rate μ of 5 and a request rate equal to 2 for all the request nodes. The push-tree built on this tree is composed of the edge $(1, 156)$. However, this achieves an objective function value of 6012, as can be easily computed. If we use instead the shortest path tree routed at the source, the constructed push-tree only consists of the source node, and the value of the objective function is 6008 (in fact, this is the optimal objective function value for this instance).

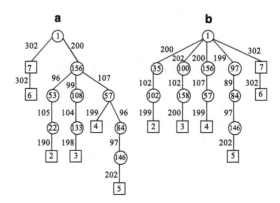

Fig. 3 (a) Optimal Steiner tree, with a total edge weight of 2297. The evaluating function of the related push-tree problem is 6012. (b) Shortest Path tree, with a total edge weight of 2702. The evaluating function of the related push-tree problem is 6008.

3 Mathematical Models for the Push-Tree Problem

In order to compare the results of our heuristics with the exact solutions, we present four different mathematical formulations.

Let $G = (V, E)$ be the input graph. In both formulations we consider a directed version of the graph, containing both arcs (i, j) and (j, i) for each edge (i, j) of the original undirected graph both having the same weights associated to them. We will refer to the following input parameters:

- $n > 0$: cardinality of V;
- $s \in V$: source node;
- $\mu \geq 0$: update rate of the source;
- $R \subseteq V \setminus \{s\}$: set of request nodes;
- $r_i \geq 0 \quad \forall i \in R$: request rate for each request node;
- $BS(i) \subseteq E \quad \forall i \in V$: set of arcs from other nodes to i;
- $FS(i) \subseteq E \quad \forall i \in V$: set of arcs from i to other nodes;
- $l_{ij} \geq 0 \quad \forall (i, j) \in E$: length of the arc (i, j);
- $A_{ij} \geq 0 \quad \forall i \in R, j \in V$: length of the shortest path between i and j in G (trivially $A_{ii} = 0 \quad \forall i \in R$);
- $S_i > 0 \quad \forall i \in V \setminus \{s\}$: minimum number of hops between s and i in G.

Moreover, we define the following binary variables:

$$x_i = \begin{cases} 1 & \text{if node } i \text{ belongs to the push-tree,} \\ 0 & \text{otherwise.} \end{cases} \quad \forall i \in V \quad (3)$$

$$z_{ij} = \begin{cases} 1 & \text{if the arc } (i, j) \text{ belongs to the push-tree,} \\ 0 & \text{otherwise.} \end{cases} \quad \forall (i, j) \in E \quad (4)$$

$$a_{ij} = \begin{cases} 1 & \text{if } j \text{ is the node of the push-tree} \\ & \text{with the shortest path from } i, \\ 0 & \text{otherwise.} \end{cases} \quad \forall i \in R, j \in V \quad (5)$$

Trivially, a_{ii} must be set to 1 if $i \in R$ belongs to the push-tree.

3.1 Single-commodity Flow Formulation

The first formulation that we describe is a single-commodity flow formulation as it can be found for various tree-like problems. In this formulation we will consider an additional set of integer variables y_{ij} defined on each arc $(i, j) \in E$, representing the amount of flow passing through arc (i, j).

$$\min \mu \left(\sum_{(i,j) \in E} l_{ij} \cdot z_{ij} \right) + \sum_{i \in R} r_i \left(\sum_{j \in V} A_{ij} \cdot a_{ij} \right) \quad (6)$$

subject to

$$x_s = 1 \tag{7}$$

$$x_i = \sum_{(j,i)\in BS(i)} z_{ji} \quad \forall i \in V \setminus \{s\} \tag{8}$$

$$\sum_{j\in V} a_{ij} = 1 \quad \forall i \in R \tag{9}$$

$$x_j \geq a_{ij} \quad \forall i \in R, j \in V \tag{10}$$

$$\sum_{(s,j)\in FS(s)} y_{sj} = \sum_{i\in V\setminus\{s\}} x_i \tag{11}$$

$$\sum_{(j,i)\in BS(i)} y_{ji} - \sum_{(i,k)\in FS(i)} y_{ik} = x_i \quad \forall i \in V \setminus \{s\} \tag{12}$$

$$y_{ij} \leq (n-1)z_{ij} \quad \forall (i,j) \in E \tag{13}$$

$$y_{ij} \geq z_{ij} \quad \forall (i,j) \in E \tag{14}$$

$$x_i \in \{0,1\} \quad \forall i \in V \tag{15}$$

$$a_{ij} \in \{0,1\} \quad \forall i \in R, j \in V \tag{16}$$

$$y_{ij} \in \{0,1,\ldots\} \quad \forall (i,j) \in E \tag{17}$$

$$z_{ij} \in \{0,1\} \quad \forall (i,j) \in E \tag{18}$$

The objective function (6) minimizes the total amount of traffic on the network. Constraint (7) imposes the source node as part of the solution. Constraints (8) define each other node as part of the push-tree if and only if it is reached by some arc belonging to it. Constraints (9) impose that each request node is associated to exactly one node of the graph, while constraints (10) ensure that such nodes belong to the push-tree. Constraints (11)-(14) impose the flow balancing constraints: the source produces exactly one unit of flow for each other node in the solution, each of them retains one unit, and there can be flow only on arcs belonging to the push-tree. This guarantees the construction of a connected acyclic solution.

While this seems to be a natural formulation there may be ways to enhance it. For instance, variables x_i may be replaced based on constraints (8) and, e.g., the following constraints added:

$$\sum_{(i,j)\in FS(i)} z_{ij} \leq (n-1) \sum_{(k,i)\in BS(i)} z_{ki} \quad \forall i \in V \setminus \{s\} \tag{19}$$

These constraints impose that if a node different from the source has some arcs leaving it in the solution, then it must have been reached by some other node. Moreover, the maximum amount of flow that can reach a given node is bounded by its distance in terms of hops from the source: let us suppose that a given node i belongs to the push-tree and is connected to the source by exactly S_i hops. Since no more than $n-1$ units of flow are produced by the source and each node along the path from s to i will retain one of them, no more than $n-S_i$ units of flow can reach node i. That is, the right hand side of 13 may be strengthened as follows:

$$y_{ij} \leq (n - S_i) z_{ij} \qquad \forall (i, j) \in E \tag{20}$$

An immediate option coming to mind is to modify the formulation in defining a multi-commodity flow formulation. In such a formulation we would consider a different binary flow variable y_{ij}^k, for each node $k \in V \setminus \{s\}$ and each $(i, j) \in E$, whose value is 1 if a unit of flow directed to node k uses (i, j) to reach its destination. Related flow balancing constraints should have the following meaning: the source produces exactly one unit of flow for each other node in the solution, each of them retains one unit directed to itself and forwards all the others, and there can be flow only on arcs belonging to the push-tree. Moreover, the maximum amount of flow units that can reach a given node is bounded by its distance in terms of hops from the source like in the proposed modification of the single-commodity model.

3.2 Miller-Tucker-Zemlin Formulation

The second formulation implements the Miller-Tucker-Zemlin subtour elimination constraints (Miller et al., 1960). In this formulation we consider a set of integer variables u_i defined on each node $i \in V$ such that if arc (i, j) is part of the push-tree then $u_i < u_j$.

$$\min \mu \left(\sum_{(i,j) \in E} l_{ij} \cdot z_{ij} \right) + \sum_{i \in R} r_i \left(\sum_{j \in V} A_{ij} \cdot a_{ij} \right) \tag{21}$$

subject to

$$x_s = 1 \tag{22}$$

$$x_i = \sum_{(j,i) \in BS(i)} z_{ji} \qquad \forall i \in V \setminus \{s\} \tag{23}$$

$$\sum_{j \in V} a_{ij} = 1 \qquad \forall i \in R \tag{24}$$

$$x_j \geq a_{ij} \qquad \forall i \in R, j \in V \tag{25}$$

$$\sum_{(i,j) \in FS(i)} z_{ij} \leq (n - 1) \sum_{(k,i) \in BS(i)} z_{ki} \qquad \forall i \in V \setminus \{s\} \tag{26}$$

$$u_s = 0 \tag{27}$$

$$u_i \leq (n - 1) x_i \qquad \forall i \in V \setminus \{s\} \tag{28}$$

$$u_i \geq x_i \qquad \forall i \in V \setminus \{s\} \tag{29}$$

$$u_i + 1 \leq u_j + (n - 1)(1 - z_{ij}) \qquad \forall (i, j) \in E \tag{30}$$

$$x_i \in \{0, 1\} \qquad \forall i \in V \tag{31}$$

$$a_{ij} \in \{0, 1\} \qquad \forall i \in R, j \in V \tag{32}$$

$$u_i \in \{0, 1, \ldots\} \qquad \forall i \in V \tag{33}$$

$$z_{ij} \in \{0, 1\} \qquad \forall (i, j) \in E \tag{34}$$

The objective function (21) and constraints (22)-(25) are assumed to have the same meaning as in the previous model. Constraints (26) impose that if a node different from the source has some arcs outgoing from it in the solution, then it must have been reached by some other node. Constraints (27)-(30) avoid the creation of cycles in the solution by setting the source's sequencing variable to 0 and by imposing the sequencing variable of a given node j to be greater than the one of a node i if (i, j) belongs to the solution, and together with constraints (26) guarantee a connected acyclic solution.

This formulation may be modified, too, e.g., in the same way as the single-commodity flow formulation by substituting variables x_i as well as by some lifting of constraints (30), e.g., in the following way:

$$nz_{ij} + u_i - u_j + (n-2)z_{ji} \leq n-1 \qquad \forall (i,j) \in E \qquad (35)$$

4 Metaheuristics

It seems of interest to verify whether existing metaheuristics can be adapted to it in order to produce good quality solutions. The metaheuristics implemented to achieve this objective are simulated annealing and reactive tabu search. Both techniques have been used in conjunction with four different methods to produce solutions and neighborhoods. Before describing our metaheuristics, we will present these methods as well as the solution representation used.

4.1 Routing Tree-based Neighborhoods

These two neighborhood generation schemes are basically an extension of the routing tree heuristic: iteratively, new routing trees are built and their related push-trees are found and evaluated as previously described. Feasible solutions for these approaches can be obtained with a first execution of the basic routing tree heuristic.

Steiner Routing Tree Neighborhoods:

Each new solution is obtained by applying a Steiner tree heuristic on a given set of required nodes. This tree is then used as routing tree. The neighborhood of the current solution is composed of all the routing trees obtained by selecting as set of required nodes the same of our current solution, except for one added or one dropped, and avoiding to drop any node from the set of request nodes R or the source node s (that must obviously be in each routing tree).

MS Routing Tree Neighborhoods:

Each new solution is obtained by computing a minimum spanning (MS) tree on a given set of nodes. This tree is then used as routing tree. The neighborhood of the current solution is composed of all the routing trees obtained by selecting as set of nodes the same of our current solution, except for one added or one dropped, and avoiding to drop any node from the set of request nodes R or the source node s (that must obviously be in each routing tree). This type of neighborhoods could lead to infeasible solutions (i.e., the set of selected nodes could be disconnected, like in the example in Figure 4). Infeasible solutions are taken into account by means of appropriate penalties in their evaluation, i.e., we add a large penalty for each selected node disconnected from the push-tree.

4.2 Push-Tree-based Neighborhoods

Instead of building routing trees, these two methods are focused on the direct construction of new push-trees. Each new push-tree is evaluated using equation (1). The shortest paths between each request node and every other node can be computed in advance using the Floyd-Warshall algorithm (see, e.g., Papadimitriou and Steiglitz (1982)). The push-tree of the starting solution can be obtained either with a routing tree heuristic or considering just the source node s (i.e., considering the shortest path tree as first solution). Note that for the latter case the worst case error ratio reported in Havet and Wennink (2004) has not been proven.

Fig. 4 Simple example leading to infeasibility for MS Routing Tree Neighborhoods. The set of required nodes considered is composed of the nodes that have to be included in the routing tree for a given neighbor of the current solution. A Steiner Routing Tree could be easily found by considering the edges connecting node 3 to node 4 and node 5 and by using node 2 to connect node s and node 3. However, an MS Routing Tree using just the set of required nodes can not be found, since node s is not directly connected to any of the other nodes of the set.

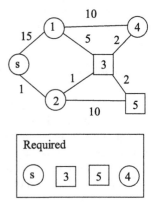

Steiner Push-Tree Neighborhoods:

Each new solution is obtained by applying a Steiner tree heuristic on a given set of required nodes. This tree is then used as push-tree. The neighborhood of the current solution is composed of all the push-trees obtained by selecting as set of required nodes the same of our current solution, except for one added or one dropped, and avoiding to drop the source node s (that must obviously be in each push-tree).

MS Push-Tree Neighborhoods:

Each new solution is obtained by computing a MS tree on a given set of nodes. This tree is then used as push-tree. The neighborhood of the current solution is composed of all the push-trees obtained by selecting as set of nodes the same of our current solution, except for one added or one dropped, and avoiding to drop the source node s (that must obviously be in each push-tree). If the solution appears to be disconnected, then only the component containing s is considered as push-tree.

4.3 Solution Representation

The solutions for all of these approaches can be represented with a bit vector defined on the nodes of the given graph. In the Steiner neighborhoods the activated bits represent the required nodes, while the bits set to 0 represent the possible Steiner nodes for the heuristic. In the MS neighborhoods the activated bits represent the nodes that we want to cover, while the bits set to 0 represent nodes that must be excluded from the tree. Each move from the current solution to any of its neighbors corresponds to a bit switch on any of these nodes, except for the nodes that must always be activated, i.e., the nodes in $R \cup \{s\}$ for the Routing Tree neighborhoods, and s for the Push-Tree neighborhoods.

We are now ready to introduce our metaheuristics.

4.4 Simulated Annealing

Simulated Annealing (SA) extends basic local search. The concept of SA may be described as follows: Starting from an initial solution, successively a candidate move is randomly selected; this move is accepted if it leads to a solution with a better objective function value than the current solution, otherwise the move is accepted with a probability depending on the deterioration Δ of the objective function value. The acceptance probability is computed according to the Boltzmann function as $e^{-\Delta/T}$, using a temperature T as control parameter. Various authors describe robust realizations of this general SA concept.

Following Johnson et al. (1989), the value of T is initially high, which allows many worse moves to be accepted, and is gradually reduced through multiplication by a parameter *coolingFactor* according to a geometric cooling schedule. Given a parameter *sizeFactor*, *sizeFactor* · n_{size} candidate moves are tested (n_{size} denotes the neighborhood size) before the temperature is reduced. The starting temperature is determined as follows: Given a parameter *initialAcceptanceFraction* and based on an abbreviated trial run, the starting temperature is set so that the fraction of accepted moves is approximately *initialAcceptanceFraction*. A further parameter, *frozenAcceptanceFraction* is used to decide whether the annealing process is frozen and should be terminated. Every time a temperature is completed with less than *frozenAcceptanceFraction* of the candidate moves accepted, a counter is increased by one, while this counter is re-set to 0 each time a new best solution has been obtained. The whole procedure is terminated when this counter reaches a parameter *frozenLimit*. For our implementation we follow the parameter setting of Johnson et al. (1989), which was reported to be robust for different problems. Namely, we use $\alpha = 0.95$, *initialAcceptanceFraction* $= 0.4$, *frozenAcceptanceFraction* $= 0.02$, *sizeFactor* $= 16$ and *frozenLimit* $= 5$.

4.5 Reactive Tabu Search

Like simulated annealing, tabu search extends the concepts of local search to overcome local optimality. This is done by using information about the search history to guide future choices. Based on some sort of memory certain moves may be forbidden, we say they are set tabu (and appropriate move attributes such as a certain index indicating a specific node are put into a list, called tabu list). The search may imply acceptance of deteriorating moves when no improving moves exist or all improving moves of the current neighborhood are set tabu. At each iteration a best admissible neighbor may be selected. A neighbor, respectively a corresponding move, is called admissible, if it is not tabu. See Glover and Laguna (1997) for a survey on tabu search.

Reactive Tabu Search (RTS) aims at the automatic adaptation of the tabu list length (Battiti, 1996): if the tabu memory indicates that the search is revisiting formerly traversed solutions, then the tabu list size is increased. A possible specification can be described as follows: Starting with a tabu list length ls of 1 it is increased to $\min\{\max\{ls+2, ls \times 1.2\}, b_u\}$ every time a solution has been repeated, taking into account an appropriate upper bound b_u (to guarantee at least one admissible move). If there has been no repetition for some iterations, we decrease it to $\max\{\min\{ls-2, ls/1.2\}, 1\}$. To accomplish the detection of a repetition of a solution, one may apply a trajectory based memory using hash codes.

For RTS, it is appropriate to include means for diversifying moves whenever the tabu memory indicates that we are trapped in a certain region of the search space. As a trigger mechanism one may use, e.g., the combination of at least three solutions each having been traversed three times. A very simple escape strategy is to perform randomly a number of moves (depending on the average of the number of iterations between solution repetitions).

We consider a given time limit as termination criterion.

5 Computational Results

Previous works on the push-tree problem with numerical results (Facundo et al., 2007) do not specify in detail how data is generated. Since the problem has strong connections with the Steiner tree problem, we decided to test our methods on already studied instances for this problem, that had to be obviously adapted to fit our new parameters.

We consider two different datasets. The first one is made of 18 instances and is Dataset B of the OR-Library (Beasley, 1990). These instances are randomly generated connected graphs, with a weight between 1 and 10 for each edge. These instances were generated according to the following parameters: $n = 50, 75, 100$ number of nodes, $n_r = \frac{1}{6}n, \frac{1}{4}n, \frac{1}{3}n, \frac{1}{2}n$ number of basic nodes which need to be connected (in our case it will be the number of request nodes plus the source), and a number of edges e specified to achieve an average node degree of 2.5 and 4.

The second group of instances is one of the so-called *incidence* datasets. The parameters for these instances are $n = 160$, $n_r = \log n, \sqrt{n}, 2\sqrt{n}$ and $\frac{n}{4}$, while the values chosen for graph densities are $m = \frac{3n}{2}, n \ln n, \frac{n(n-1)}{2}, 2n$ and $\frac{n(n-1)}{10}$, for a total of 100 different instances. All the considered datasets can be found on SteinLib[1].

To adapt the instances to our particular problem, we assumed the basic node with smallest index to be the source. Moreover, our choice of parameters for update and request rates was to set μ to 5 and r_i to 2 for each $i \in R$.

All computations for the metaheuristics have been made on a workstation with 1 GB RAM and a 2.8 GHz Intel Xeon processor. The metaheuristic framework HOTFRAME (Fink and Voß, 2002) has been used for the implementations. Optimal solutions refer to the application of CPLEX 10 with OPL Studio on a workstation with 2 GB RAM and a 3.2 GHz Intel Xeon processor. Times are measured in seconds.

In the tables we refer to the mathematical models and metaheuristics as follows:

SC: Single-Commodity Flow Formulation
MTZ: Miller-Tucker-Zemlin Formulation
SASR: Simulated Annealing with Steiner Routing Tree Neighborhoods
RTSR: Reactive Tabu Search with Steiner Routing Tree Neighborhoods
SAMR: Simulated Annealing with MS Routing Tree Neighborhoods
RTMR: Reactive Tabu Search with MS Routing Tree Neighborhoods
SASPs: Simulated Annealing with Steiner Push-Tree Neighborhoods, source s used as first push-tree

---

[1] *See Koch et al. (2001) as well as http://elib.zib.de/steinlib/steinlib.php .*

RTSPs: Reactive Tabu Search with Steiner Push-Tree Neighborhoods, source s used as first push-tree
SAMPs: Simulated Annealing with MS Push-Tree Neighborhoods, source s used as first push-tree
RTMPs: Reactive Tabu Search with MS Push-Tree Tree Neighborhoods, source s used as first push-tree
SASPh: Simulated Annealing with Steiner Push-Tree Neighborhoods, first push-tree obtained with the routing tree heuristic
RTSPh: Reactive Tabu Search with Steiner Push-Tree Neighborhoods, first push-tree obtained with the routing tree heuristic
SAMPh: Simulated Annealing with MS Push-Tree Neighborhoods, first push-tree obtained with the routing tree heuristic
RTMPh: Reactive Tabu Search with MS Push-Tree Tree Neighborhoods, first push-tree obtained with the routing tree heuristic

5.1 Mathematical Models

The comparison between the two proposed models has been made on the first ten instances of the B dataset. It takes into account two factors: the total computational time and the quality of the linear programming relaxation returned. As can be seen in Table 1, the Miller-Tucker-Zemlin formulation returned slightly better relaxations on average, and resulted to be more efficient than the Single-Commodity flow formulation in terms of computational time. For each instance, the optimal solution value is given in the *opt* column.

The proposed models might be expected as "weakest models" for the push-tree problem. For many tree-like problems one might even assume that the single commodity formulation behaves better than the MTZ-formulation. Surprisingly, here

Table 1 Mathematical models comparison

n	n_r	e	opt	SC relax	SC time	MTZ relax	MTZ time	SCmod relax	SCmod time
50	9	63	217	113.19	0.922	125.03	0.969	126.87	0.75
50	13	63	290	116.65	2.735	114.47	4.719	117.84	2.75
50	25	63	440	280	5.328	280.59	6.234	291.69	4
50	9	100	172	89.5	19.078	85.74	1.688	90.87	8
50	13	100	159	102.11	5.297	100.95	0.672	103.88	4
50	25	100	385	224.5	>10000	218.06	56.921	227.15	>10000
75	13	94	344	179.1	4.797	180.11	4.438	185.71	5.25
75	19	94	337	176.25	11.375	176.64	29.578	185.13	6
75	38	94	681	428.37	39.015	458.51	5	442.49	25.75
75	13	150	243	145.97	113.922	144.78	3.172	147.9	68.17
	average		326.8	185.564		188.488		191.953	

this seems not to be the case. Therefore, the results regarding these two formulations are interesting in themselves. Modifying the single-commodity flow formulation along the lines described at the end of Section 3.1 (columns SCmod in Table 1) allowed us to slightly improve the results of the relaxation. Overall, however, these formulations do not seem to provide good bounds as can be seen from the large gaps between the relaxations and the optimal solutions.

We also explored the multi-commodity formulation following the above mentioned natural definition of flow variables, but the results were not as good as expected (providing much higher computation times and similar linear relaxations compared to the single commodity and MTZ formulations).

5.2 Metaheuristic Comparisons on the B Dataset

On this dataset, we tried both our heuristics with all the possible combinations of neighborhoods and starting solutions presented above. Results as well as computational times are reported in Tables 2–4. Regarding tabu search, for which a time limit had to be given, such a limit was fixed to three times the computational time of the related simulated annealing time on that instance. This was done since the metaheuristics on this dataset are generally quite fast, so we wanted to investigate whether additional time could help to improve the results when the optimum is not reached. Nevertheless, as Table 4 shows, the best result for these heuristics was found generally much earlier than this limit. In Table 2 column *heu* reports the value obtained by the routing tree heuristic on each instance, while column *opt* reports the optimal solution found by means of our mathematical models.

We applied Friedman's test (Hollander and Wolfe, 1999) on the results obtained, in terms of solution value, total execution time and best solution time, in order to obtain some statistical rankings between the different algorithms. Rankings are shown in Figures 5-7. In particular, as we can see, the heuristics with Push-Tree neighborhoods are the clear winners regarding solution quality, since the four Routing Tree heuristics perform significantly worse (they reject the null hypothesis that the performances are not statistically different). In particular, the heuristics with Steiner Push-Tree neighborhoods are the best ranked (as we can see from Table 2, SASPs, RTSPs and RTSPh found the optimal solution in all instances except one, and SASPh in all of them except two). Regarding total solution time, the tabu search approaches are obviously ranked worse than the respective simulated annealing ones, since we gave higher time limits. Among the SA approaches, the best ranked are the ones with MS Push-Tree neighborhoods (SAMPs and SAMPh), while the ones with Steiner Push-Tree neighborhoods (SASPs and SASPh) are the only ones rejecting the null hypothesis. Finally, regarding best solution times, the SA with Steiner Push-Tree neighborhood heuristics (SASPs and SASPh) are the only ones performing significantly worse, while the heuristics with Steiner Routing Tree neighborhoods (SASR and RTSR) are the overall best ranked.

Table 2 Solution Comparisons for the B dataset

n	n_r	e	heu	SASR	RTSR	SAMR	RTMR	SASPs	RTSPs	SAMPs	RTMPs	SASPh	RTSPh	SAMPh	RTMPh	opt
50	9	63	217	217	217	217	217	217	217	217	217	217	217	217	217	**217**
50	13	63	309	299	299	299	299	290	290	299	302	290	290	299	299	**290**
50	25	63	441	441	441	441	441	440	440	454	454	440	440	440	440	**440**
50	9	100	185	172	172	172	172	172	172	172	172	172	172	172	172	**172**
50	13	100	162	160	160	160	160	159	159	159	159	159	159	160	160	**159**
50	25	100	421	397	397	397	397	385	385	385	388	385	385	388	394	**385**
75	13	94	360	344	344	349	344	344	344	344	344	344	344	344	344	**344**
75	19	94	371	344	344	344	344	337	337	337	337	337	337	370	370	**337**
75	38	94	682	682	682	682	682	681	681	681	681	681	681	681	681	**681**
75	13	150	267	245	245	245	245	243	243	243	271	243	243	243	243	**243**
75	19	150	312	302	302	302	302	302	302	320	302	312	302	312	312	**302**
75	38	150	538	534	534	533	533	518	518	518	518	518	518	518	518	**518**
100	17	125	546	540	542	540	540	525	525	525	525	525	525	525	525	**525**
100	25	125	751	721	721	721	721	715	715	715	732	715	715	715	715	**715**
100	50	125	1029	1024	1024	1024	1024	1007	1007	1007	1010	1007	1007	1014	1014	**1007**
100	17	200	419	363	363	363	363	363	363	363	363	363	363	363	372	**363**
100	25	200	378	362	365	364	367	364	364	364	398	364	364	370	370	**362**
100	50	200	682	674	674	670	670	666	666	673	668	666	666	673	668	**666**
average			448.33	434.5	434.78	434.61	434.5	429.33	429.33	432	435.61	429.89	429.33	433.56	434.11	**429.22**

Table 3 Total Time Comparisons for the B dataset

n	n_r	e	SASR	RTSR	SAMR	RTMR	SASPs	RTSPs	SAMPs	RTMPs	SASPh	RTSPh	SAMPh	RTMPh
50	9	63	0.91	2.73	5.79	17.37	6.21	18.63	0.41	1.23	6.06	18.18	0.27	0.81
50	13	63	10.67	32.01	3.01	9.03	5.77	17.31	0.44	1.32	5.27	15.81	0.28	0.84
50	25	63	1.07	3.21	0.67	2.01	6.12	18.36	0.43	1.29	6.09	18.27	3.05	9.15
50	9	100	1.30	3.90	0.74	2.22	5.78	17.34	0.46	1.38	5.33	15.99	0.36	1.08
50	13	100	1.14	3.42	0.8	2.40	5.81	17.43	0.51	1.53	6.05	18.15	0.32	0.96
50	25	100	1.28	3.84	0.85	2.55	7.04	21.12	3.51	10.53	7.22	21.66	3.04	9.12
75	13	94	2.56	7.68	1.72	5.16	17.87	53.61	0.9	2.70	13.11	39.33	0.8	2.40
75	19	94	2.83	8.49	1.86	5.58	15.18	45.54	0.96	2.88	14.08	42.24	0.84	2.52
75	38	94	2.74	8.22	1.71	5.13	18.2	54.60	1.06	3.18	17.26	51.78	9.47	28.41
75	13	150	2.77	8.31	1.96	5.88	20.03	60.09	0.92	2.76	17.76	53.28	0.92	2.76
75	19	150	27.91	83.73	1.93	5.79	18.28	54.84	1.11	3.33	6.38	19.14	4.72	14.16
75	38	150	3.32	9.96	2.14	6.42	23.5	70.50	1.32	3.96	16.97	50.91	8.09	24.27
100	17	125	6.37	19.11	103.4	310.20	35.16	105.48	2.21	6.63	36.45	109.35	2.04	6.12
100	25	125	5.20	15.60	41.48	124.44	34.11	102.33	1.74	5.22	36.93	110.79	1.64	4.92
100	50	125	5.99	17.97	4.38	13.14	39.72	119.16	2.35	7.05	36.66	109.98	1.81	5.43
100	17	200	6.34	19.02	26.19	78.57	38.19	114.57	3.7	11.10	34.09	102.27	3.05	9.15
100	25	200	5.57	16.71	4.47	13.41	31.78	95.34	3.5	10.50	25.44	76.32	1.9	5.70
100	50	200	55.54	166.62	4.12	12.36	32.7	98.10	12.04	36.12	31.76	95.28	19.11	57.33
average			7.97	23.92	11.51	34.54	20.08	60.24	2.09	6.26	17.94	53.82	3.43	10.29

Table 4 Best Solution Time Comparisons for the B dataset

n	n_r	e	SASR	RTSR	SAMR	RTMR	SASPs	RTSPs	SAMPs	RTMPs	SASPh	RTSPh	SAMPh	RTMPh
50	9	63	0.01	0.01	0.01	0.01	2.42	0.01	0.01	0.01	0.01	0.01	0.01	0.01
50	13	63	0.01	0.01	0.1	0.17	2.72	0.01	0.13	0.02	0.01	0.02	0.01	0.01
50	25	63	0.01	0.01	0.01	0.01	0.7	0.02	0.04	0.04	0.01	0.01	0.01	0.01
50	9	100	0.34	0.01	0.11	0.68	0.01	0.02	0.02	0.02	0.02	0.02	0.02	0.01
50	13	100	0.01	0.01	0.01	0.01	2.08	0.26	0.02	0.02	1.89	0.67	0.01	0.01
50	25	100	0.18	0.54	0.15	0.06	2.84	0.04	0.58	0.05	2.98	0.08	0.9	4.91
75	13	94	0.01	0.02	0.02	0.02	0.03	0.03	0.07	0.04	0.06	0.08	0.04	0.04
75	19	94	0.01	0.01	0.26	1.44	6.67	0.03	0.1	0.08	5.35	0.1	0.02	0.02
75	38	94	0.01	0.01	0.01	0.01	7.6	0.09	0.08	0.14	6.3	0.13	4.46	1.17
75	13	150	0.01	0.02	0.02	0.03	8.44	0.05	0.06	0.06	0.06	0.06	0.03	0.04
75	19	150	0.02	0.01	0.28	0.78	8.89	0.13	0.39	0.08	0.01	0.16	0.01	0.01
75	38	150	0.02	0.02	0.03	0.04	13.13	0.21	0.46	3.92	0.14	0.09	3.51	4.42
100	17	125	2.45	1.82	60.89	21.64	0.09	0.06	1.02	0.09	0.17	0.12	0.94	0.08
100	25	125	0.02	0.04	2.39	0.4	18.56	0.55	0.1	0.17	0.06	0.06	0.05	0.05
100	50	125	0.8	12.7	0.65	0.09	23.61	1.84	0.12	0.28	17.41	0.28	0.06	0.07
100	17	200	0.07	0.72	0.79	49.16	15.23	0.09	2.26	3	15.9	0.83	1.7	0.14
100	25	200	0.65	3.57	1.45	11.14	17.37	0.09	1.95	0.25	9.71	0.68	0.05	0.07
100	50	200	0.8	0.09	0.62	0.09	18.82	1.8	4.26	15.88	19.4	5.84	11.12	9.24
average			0.3	1.09	3.77	4.77	8.29	0.3	0.65	1.34	4.42	0.51	1.28	1.13

5.3 Metaheuristic Comparisons on the i160 Dataset

On this dataset both metaheuristics were tried, too, with all the possible combinations of neighborhoods and starting solutions. Results as well as computational

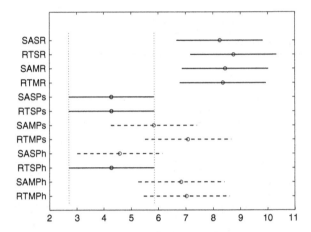

Fig. 5 Solution quality statistical ranks comparison for the B dataset

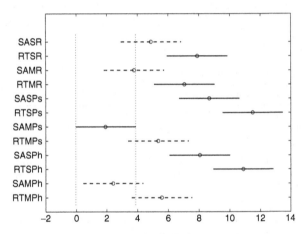

Fig. 6 Total time statistical ranks comparison for the B dataset

times are reported in Tables 5–10.[2] The time limit for the tabu search was fixed to 2000 seconds per instance; however, as can be seen in Tables 9/10, also on these instances the best results were generally found much earlier than the limit. The column *heu* in Table 5 (and its continuation in Table 6) reports the value obtained by the routing tree heuristic on each instance. Since we were not able to find the optimal solutions on instances of this size, the column *LB* in Table 5 (and Table 6) reports the lower bounds obtained by the linear programming relaxation of our slightly modified single-commodity flow model (SCmod). As can be seen, the solutions obtained by our heuristics are much closer to this lower bound than to the original routing tree heuristic.

---

[2] Note that tables are split for better readability. Average values in Tables 6, 8, and 10 are calculated over the results of two continued tables, respectively.

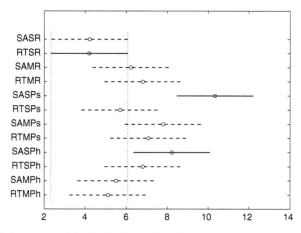

Fig. 7 Best solution time statistical ranks comparison for the B dataset

The statistical rankings obtained by Friedman's test are shown in Figures 8-10. As for the previous dataset, the heuristics with Steiner Push-Tree neighborhoods (SASPs, RTSPs, SASPh and RTSPh) perform better than the others, and between them, the tabu search approaches have better rankings than the SA ones. All the other heuristics perform significantly worse, therefore there is not the clear distinction between push-tree neighborhoods and routing tree neighborhoods that could be seen in Figure 5. Another interesting remark is that for every type of heuristic taken into account the RTS approach is ranked better than the respective SA. Regarding total solution time, the tabu search approaches are obviously the worse ones and equally ranked, since we set the 2000 seconds time limit. Among the simulated annealing approaches, the ones based on MS Push-Tree neighborhoods (SAMPs and SAMPh) confirm to be the top ranked, as for dataset B, while all the others reject the null hypothesis.

Finally considering best solution times, the Reactive Tabu Search with MS Push-Tree neighborhood and source node as starting solution (RTMPs) is the top ranked, while all the others perform significantly worse.

6 Conclusions

In this paper we addressed an optimization problem for information distribution systems, namely the Push-Tree Problem. From an algorithmic point of view the previous research provided an exact algorithm for tree networks and an approximation algorithm for the general case. In this paper we have shown that metaheuristic approaches can be adapted to improve the solutions provided by this algorithm. Our approaches have been tested on two classes of instances, differing in both dimensions and structure of the networks. Further research is focused on extending

Table 5 Solution Comparisons for the i160 dataset

n	n_r	e	heu	SASR	RTSR	SAMR	RTMR	SASPs	RTSPs	SAMPs	RTMPs	SASPh	RTSPh	SAMPh	RTMPh	LB
160	7	240	7081	6207	6173	6173	6729	6173	6173	6173	6173	6173	6173	6545	6545	4965.11
160	7	240	6039	5817	5817	5817	5817	5641	5641	5641	5641	5641	5641	5641	5641	4701.43
160	7	240	6192	6012	6012	6012	6192	6008	6008	6008	6008	6008	6008	6008	6008	5085.68
160	7	240	7510	6596	6596	6596	7310	6596	6596	6596	6596	6596	6596	6596	6696	4765.10
160	7	240	8017	6300	6388	6414	6678	6294	6294	6388	6388	6294	6294	6388	6388	4757.04
160	7	812	5187	4784	4486	5187	4674	4481	4481	4736	4481	4481	4481	4481	4486	3472.08
160	7	812	4806	4770	4612	4806	4806	4612	4612	4870	4672	4612	4612	4612	4612	3614.65
160	7	812	4825	4301	4301	4301	4301	4301	4301	4301	4301	4301	4301	4301	4301	3530.19
160	7	812	5492	4920	4842	4763	4763	4763	4763	4845	4763	4763	4763	4763	4763	3775.17
160	7	812	5132	4709	4518	4864	4587	4518	4518	4549	4518	4518	4518	4549	4518	3714.82
160	7	12720	6457	3360	3259	3360	3259	3259	3259	3259	3259	3259	3259	3259	3259	2755.04
160	7	12720	6794	3400	3303	3400	3303	3303	3303	3303	3303	3303	3303	3303	3303	2724.94
160	7	12720	4979	3309	3306	3309	3306	3306	3306	3306	3306	3306	3306	3306	3306	2742.04
160	7	12720	5596	3375	3325	3375	3325	3338	3325	3338	3325	3338	3325	3338	3325	2766.74
160	7	12720	5861	3333	3305	3333	3305	3305	3305	3305	3305	3305	3305	3305	3305	2787.40
160	7	320	6796	6210	6199	6199	6199	6024	6024	6029	6029	6024	6024	6029	6309	4389.61
160	7	320	7123	6100	6204	6334	6257	6100	6100	6100	6100	6100	6100	6100	6100	4518.82
160	7	320	5833	5150	5150	5150	5370	5150	5150	5150	5150	5150	5150	5150	5150	4397.10
160	7	320	6882	5684	5684	5684	5684	5684	5684	5684	5684	5684	5684	5684	5746	4283.24
160	7	320	6246	6063	5762	5747	5762	5747	5747	5940	5762	5747	5747	5762	5762	4385.45
160	7	2544	4828	4213	3863	4228	4117	3861	3861	4277	3861	3861	3861	4277	3861	3145.73
160	7	2544	4973	3847	3836	4325	3895	3836	3836	4164	3847	3847	3836	3911	3847	3109.47
160	7	2544	5939	4041	3736	3896	3728	3728	3728	4209	3728	3728	3728	3728	3919	3197.34
160	7	2544	3913	3874	3874	3895	3895	3847	3847	4132	3876	3847	3847	3874	3874	3254.97
160	7	2544	4020	3991	3991	4020	4020	3944	3944	4231	3944	3944	3944	4020	4020	3200.47
160	12	240	10295	9985	9933	9933	10269	9923	9923	9923	9923	9923	9923	9923	9923	8259.67
160	12	240	10775	9843	9660	9660	9843	9660	9660	9660	9660	9660	9660	9843	10166	7665.07
160	12	240	10413	10139	10139	10139	10139	10114	10114	10114	10114	10114	10114	10139	10139	7903.57
160	12	240	13122	10751	10737	10737	11353	10565	10565	10565	10565	10565	10565	10565	10565	7748.62
160	12	240	10951	8753	8753	8753	8753	8753	8753	9270	8753	8753	8753	9916	9270	7383.34
160	12	812	12398	7415	7415	8119	7771	7413	7413	7613	7462	7413	7413	7413	7501	6341.07
160	12	812	8205	7611	7611	7638	7638	7299	7299	7611	7603	7299	7299	7299	7299	6350.28
160	12	812	8784	7169	7494	8478	8117	7167	7167	7977	7631	7167	7167	7752	7752	6216.91
160	12	812	8645	7894	7722	7843	7857	7590	7590	7949	7590	7590	7590	7843	7843	6403.51
160	12	812	8038	7644	7201	7652	7652	7091	7091	7797	7091	7091	7091	7620	7620	6255.66
160	12	12720	11391	5378	5305	5378	5305	5305	5305	5305	5305	5305	5305	5305	5305	4742.39
160	12	12720	11362	5441	5274	5441	5274	5274	5274	5274	5274	5274	5274	5274	5274	4735.96
160	12	12720	11953	5377	5283	5377	5283	5283	5283	5283	5283	5283	5283	5283	5283	4754.73
160	12	12720	10296	5367	5292	5367	5292	5305	5292	5305	5292	5294	5292	5294	5292	4735.02
160	12	12720	11989	5308	5278	5308	5278	5308	5278	5308	5278	5278	5278	5278	5278	4732.11
160	12	320	10518	9008	9026	8835	8835	8835	8835	9310	8864	8835	8835	10185	9006	7169.11
160	12	320	10567	8708	8708	9195	8708	8708	8708	9805	8708	8708	8708	8708	8708	7248.38
160	12	320	11194	9412	9563	9652	9652	9091	9091	9353	9091	9091	9091	9353	9353	7662.42
160	12	320	10915	9085	9057	9095	9653	9057	9057	9057	9057	9057	9057	9113	9095	7494.08
160	12	320	11317	9487	9487	9487	9622	9487	9487	9487	9487	9487	9487	9830	9894	7710.66
160	12	2544	11571	6407	6149	6682	6389	6149	6149	6535	6371	6149	6149	6578	6371	5354.99
160	12	2544	12791	6308	6308	6537	6444	6270	6270	6403	6315	6302	6270	6348	6676	5399.55
160	12	2544	7310	6663	6411	6674	6546	6251	6251	6407	6407	6251	6251	6461	6461	5464.68
160	12	2544	6481	6481	6391	6481	6481	6367	6367	6390	6401	6367	6390	6391	6391	5584.31
160	12	2544	8762	6668	6511	6848	6589	6338	6338	6628	6465	6338	6338	6511	6511	5502.42
160	24	240	21120	18629	18822	18954	18954	18629	18629	19085	19085	18629	18629	18993	19672	15283.94
160	24	240	21584	18934	18934	18934	19247	18885	18885	19111	18885	18885	18885	19009	19009	15458.18
160	24	240	22301	20117	20048	20470	20076	19848	19848	20514	19880	19848	19848	20221	19848	16762.23
160	24	240	22018	19018	19018	19688	19018	18745	18745	19703	18745	18745	18745	18898	20150	15489.51
160	24	240	19325	19028	19028	19028	19307	18994	18994	19059	19042	18994	18994	19048	19006	16349.08
160	24	812	17389	14100	13993	14050	14049	13738	13738	14409	14378	13738	13738	14194	13946	12288.97
160	24	812	16502	14172	13686	14423	14243	13455	13455	13643	13846	13455	13455	13969	13969	12385.53
160	24	812	24168	14056	13852	15191	13951	13592	13629	14036	13648	13592	13592	14217	13830	12454.21
160	24	812	18843	14834	14458	15193	14322	13711	13711	14487	13711	13711	13711	13825	14431	12735.66
160	24	812	24717	14009	14244	14122	13672	13525	13525	13934	13915	13525	13525	14647	13542	12265.51
160	24	12720	24078	10086	10034	10086	10034	10034	10034	10034	10034	10034	10034	10034	10034	9498.48
160	24	12720	23185	10067	9949	10067	9949	9949	9949	9949	9949	10036	9949	10036	9949	9465.31
160	24	12720	24104	10180	10036	10180	10036	10053	10036	10053	10036	10053	10036	10053	10036	9487.60
160	24	12720	21822	10095	10036	10095	10036	10036	10036	10036	10036	10036	10036	10036	10036	9467.15
160	24	12720	24283	10058	10056	10058	10056	10058	10056	10058	10056	10058	10056	10058	10056	9484.78
160	24	320	25509	18060	18405	18865	18177	17311	17311	18185	17311	17311	17311	17676	17311	14694.45
160	24	320	23778	17633	17347	18420	18318	17252	17252	18245	17252	17252	17252	19625	19625	14888.51
160	24	320	19576	16605	16071	17788	17694	15995	15995	16371	16371	15995	15995	17703	17703	14617.12
160	24	320	17479	16537	16537	17025	17025	16529	16529	16591	16529	16529	16529	16529	16529	15447.32
160	24	320	21749	18113	18052	18305	19013	17852	17852	18085	17857	17852	17852	18220	18220	15068.52
160	24	2544	23422	12434	11993	12013	11722	11614	11614	11921	11767	11614	11614	12754	11614	10646.95
160	24	2544	22767	12314	12048	12898	11884	11908	11796	12369	12030	11858	11796	12707	11906	10765.84
160	24	2544	24592	12212	11922	11998	11809	11641	11641	11703	11661	11566	11566	13000	11661	10581.05
160	24	2544	22979	12137	12061	12286	11915	11619	11619	12504	11828	11619	11783	12087	11984	10644.20
160	24	2544	21859	12224	11833	12097	12103	11772	11772	12757	12051	11772	11772	12637	12451	10663.21

Table 6 Solution Comparisons for the i160 dataset – Continued

n	n_r	e	heu	SASR	RTSR	SAMR	RTMR	SASPs	RTSPs	SAMPs	RTMPs	SASPh	RTSPh	SAMPh	RTMPh	LB
160	40	240	40019	33860	33860	33995	33995	33426	33426	33611	33598	33426	33426	33598	33598	28094.31
160	40	240	37326	32254	32254	32254	32446	31752	31752	32316	32035	31752	31752	31752	32235	26568.41
160	40	240	41231	32273	32308	32305	33197	31614	31614	31796	31682	31614	31614	32066	31682	27068.78
160	40	240	35379	31781	31642	31781	32617	31219	31219	31330	32072	31219	31219	32447	32447	25767.01
160	40	240	37381	31971	31983	32643	32871	31181	31181	31905	31664	31181	31181	31829	31198	26517.60
160	40	812	35639	22013	22013	22178	22085	21695	21695	22082	21803	21744	21711	23166	22982	20417.50
160	40	812	40862	22044	21826	22191	21826	21596	21588	21656	21963	21588	21588	22586	22151	19998.66
160	40	812	38899	22427	22576	22344	22188	21616	21616	22026	22162	21785	21616	22443	22368	20197.08
160	40	812	37523	21728	21257	21451	21441	21001	21181	22305	21493	21181	21001	22012	21559	19732.45
160	40	812	43418	21831	21767	21804	21827	21479	21458	22461	21816	21479	21458	22464	21605	20067.56
160	40	12720	41639	16389	16389	16389	16389	16389	16389	16389	16389	16389	16389	16389	16389	15834.48
160	40	12720	39639	16360	16360	16360	16360	16360	16360	16360	16360	16360	16360	16360	16360	15827.79
160	40	12720	41970	16372	16372	16372	16372	16372	16372	16372	16372	16372	16372	16372	16372	15792.49
160	40	12720	39128	16406	16406	16406	16406	16413	16406	16413	16406	16406	16406	16406	16406	15850.16
160	40	12720	40762	16336	16336	16336	16336	16336	16336	16336	16336	16336	16336	16336	16336	15805.85
160	40	320	30583	26672	26344	28003	28003	26274	26274	26274	26274	26274	26274	27259	27273	23497.31
160	40	320	34665	28094	28094	28766	29684	27605	27605	28310	28209	27605	27605	28568	28600	25310.66
160	40	320	32954	27749	27749	28795	29513	27183	27183	27183	27263	27183	27183	27183	27183	24188.96
160	40	320	34835	27519	27519	27799	27934	26600	26600	26803	26600	26600	26600	27372	26600	24360.06
160	40	320	31247	27708	27683	27739	27945	26811	26811	27054	27271	26811	26811	27170	27506	24586.61
160	40	2544	42423	18660	18660	18675	18906	18755	18444	19407	18923	18444	18444	19042	18965	17379.88
160	40	2544	41694	19110	18877	18877	18885	18661	18669	19265	19065	18661	18644	19372	18951	17376.74
160	40	2544	39714	18334	18435	18566	18308	18308	18308	18635	18569	18334	18308	19644	18473	17143.93
160	40	2544	43417	19069	18412	18504	18375	18499	18375	19382	18375	18486	18375	19250	18829	17302.06
160	40	2544	42227	18754	18649	18935	18649	18748	18506	18911	18731	18605	18504	19358	18764	17279.24
average			19202.9	12640.3	12555	12782		12751.9	12390.6	12383.9	12662.9	12493.4	12389.7	12382.7	12737.8	12633.7	10917.17

Table 7 Total Time Comparisons for the i160 dataset

n	n_r	e	SASR	RTSR	SAMR	RTMR	SASPs	RTSPs	SAMPs	RTMPs	SASPh	RTSPh	SAMPh	RTMPh
160	7	240	15.22	2000	214.51	2000	69.39	2000	4.72	2000	68.62	2000	4.67	2000
160	7	240	14.92	2000	205.74	2000	69.63	2000	5.39	2000	68.81	2000	4.64	2000
160	7	240	133.28	2000	200.39	2000	65.35	2000	4.07	2000	66.88	2000	5.24	2000
160	7	240	15.56	2000	261.41	2000	68.14	2000	4.75	2000	66.97	2000	5.15	2000
160	7	240	167.2	2000	212.04	2000	68.99	2000	4.07	2000	68.63	2000	5.02	2000
160	7	812	161.25	2000	11.45	2000	88.34	2000	7.76	2000	85.52	2000	9.23	2000
160	7	812	201.16	2000	11.44	2000	87.44	2000	7.89	2000	90.1	2000	8.14	2000
160	7	812	277.69	2000	15.18	2000	90.61	2000	7.91	2000	80.04	2000	8.42	2000
160	7	812	152.59	2000	28.29	2000	91.45	2000	7.91	2000	93.87	2000	8.41	2000
160	7	812	388.75	2000	21.28	2000	89.74	2000	6.85	2000	86.89	2000	8.29	2000
160	7	12720	1590.7	2000	1477.11	2000	975.73	2000	1025.84	2000	1045.92	2000	1017.57	2000
160	7	12720	1690.17	2000	1707.29	2000	963.61	2000	992.3	2000	1000.35	2000	936.98	2000
160	7	12720	1235.26	2000	1201.37	2000	1014.13	2000	989.44	2000	977.86	2000	1027.99	2000
160	7	12720	1421.34	2000	1388.61	2000	1016.05	2000	1054.21	2000	992.7	2000	933.11	2000
160	7	12720	849.69	2000	800.58	2000	1044.74	2000	1048.66	2000	924.74	2000	941.11	2000
160	7	320	14.87	2000	249.31	2000	71.76	2000	5.75	2000	76.26	2000	5.6	2000
160	7	320	15.08	2000	281.67	2000	73.23	2000	5.22	2000	71.99	2000	5.73	2000
160	7	320	14.46	2000	280.7	2000	71.28	2000	4.47	2000	66.25	2000	5.49	2000
160	7	320	15.14	2000	225.57	2000	84.31	2000	5.21	2000	69.52	2000	5.49	2000
160	7	320	165.9	2000	263.64	2000	80.31	2000	5.82	2000	73.62	2000	6.4	2000
160	7	2544	163.4	2000	24.46	2000	167.53	2000	19.12	2000	175	2000	18.49	2000
160	7	2544	464.29	2000	24.27	2000	171.64	2000	20.45	2000	173.18	2000	20.38	2000
160	7	2544	458.07	2000	27.98	2000	165.37	2000	20.29	2000	158.78	2000	20.21	2000
160	7	2544	319.01	2000	24.84	2000	169.48	2000	20.25	2000	188.89	2000	17.19	2000
160	7	2544	313.38	2000	21.56	2000	167.04	2000	15.86	2000	181.49	2000	17.48	2000

Table 8 Total Time Comparisons for the i160 dataset – Continued

n	n_r	e	SASR	RTSR	SAMR	RTMR	SASPs	RTSPs	SAMPs	RTMPs	SASPh	RTSPh	SAMPh	RTMPh
160	12	240	258.2	2000	279.85	2000	86.12	2000	5.44	2000	86.52	2000	5.57	2000
160	12	240	15.08	2000	243.78	2000	99.91	2000	5.37	2000	100.07	2000	5.41	2000
160	12	240	15.57	2000	246.36	2000	85.03	2000	5.61	2000	89.66	2000	5.62	2000
160	12	240	14.45	2000	177.28	2000	72.83	2000	4.99	2000	66.37	2000	5.32	2000
160	12	240	14.9	2000	282.9	2000	75.69	2000	6.12	2000	66.57	2000	5.35	2000
160	12	812	87.27	2000	13.18	2000	98.41	2000	9.22	2000	91.36	2000	8.53	2000
160	12	812	202.19	2000	17.54	2000	98.42	2000	10.08	2000	94.06	2000	8.34	2000
160	12	812	223.93	2000	13.61	2000	91.28	2000	9.49	2000	87.85	2000	11.94	2000
160	12	812	247.59	2000	20.63	2000	104.17	2000	7.92	2000	87.49	2000	8.72	2000
160	12	812	301.95	2000	13.14	2000	95.76	2000	9.36	2000	81.86	2000	7.71	2000
160	12	12720	1629.56	2000	1653.05	2000	901.54	2000	954.08	2000	926.41	2000	1022.11	2000
160	12	12720	2738.4	2000	2718.67	2000	971.65	2000	962.61	2000	1001.16	2000	994.78	2000
160	12	12720	1961.43	2000	1945.66	2000	907.95	2000	928.71	2000	972.63	2000	896.94	2000
160	12	12720	1918.07	2000	1923.71	2000	990.24	2000	992.96	2000	936.94	2000	1041.39	2000
160	12	12720	2084.33	2000	2097.89	2000	1136.96	2000	1066.48	2000	966.12	2000	963.42	2000
160	12	320	15.47	2000	87.36	2000	85.48	2000	6.59	2000	83.18	2000	5.77	2000
160	12	320	108.79	2000	80.82	2000	87.08	2000	5.5	2000	78	2000	5.78	2000
160	12	320	120.78	2000	19.3	2000	74.88	2000	6.11	2000	73.02	2000	6.38	2000
160	12	320	18.56	2000	229.66	2000	80.02	2000	12.73	2000	84.85	2000	5.9	2000
160	12	320	225.81	2000	14.45	2000	83.89	2000	9.57	2000	82.55	2000	6.42	2000
160	12	2544	282.71	2000	24.47	2000	201.74	2000	19.97	2000	167.95	2000	20.82	2000
160	12	2544	539.43	2000	372.67	2000	162.54	2000	19.95	2000	161.95	2000	19.57	2000
160	12	2544	277.19	2000	25.09	2000	174.46	2000	20.01	2000	160.05	2000	45.83	2000
160	12	2544	340.94	2000	21	2000	169.66	2000	19.62	2000	165.51	2000	18.03	2000
160	12	2544	279.79	2000	32.8	2000	169.32	2000	21.29	2000	177.65	2000	21	2000
160	24	240	194.62	2000	13	2000	104.98	2000	5.8	2000	95.84	2000	6.08	2000
160	24	240	16.13	2000	11.36	2000	113.38	2000	7.47	2000	103.61	2000	6.34	2000
160	24	240	21.2	2000	11.26	2000	98.55	2000	5.92	2000	95.1	2000	5.34	2000
160	24	240	214.99	2000	78.64	2000	91.54	2000	11.75	2000	81.07	2000	11.22	2000
160	24	240	147.6	2000	172.19	2000	96.69	2000	5.86	2000	92.7	2000	5.58	2000
160	24	812	306.53	2000	20.95	2000	134.38	2000	10.21	2000	117.13	2000	9.15	2000
160	24	812	297.91	2000	13.23	2000	94.8	2000	11	2000	87.22	2000	9.06	2000
160	24	812	389.51	2000	15.18	2000	106.22	2000	13.96	2000	93.19	2000	16.06	2000
160	24	812	257.55	2000	12.97	2000	108.14	2000	8.6	2000	87.44	2000	10.14	2000
160	24	812	290.63	2000	13.46	2000	89.28	2000	11.37	2000	83.69	2000	8.81	2000
160	24	12720	2652.08	2000	2683.6	2000	1113.87	2000	1062.54	2000	979.5	2000	1015.33	2000
160	24	12720	1429.13	2000	1426.65	2000	926.16	2000	1018.53	2000	904.59	2000	877.69	2000
160	24	12720	1471.06	2000	1556.71	2000	982.68	2000	1056.08	2000	1089.34	2000	950.28	2000
160	24	12720	1237.66	2000	1265.64	2000	947.09	2000	1072.29	2000	986.51	2000	984.99	2000
160	24	12720	1802.63	2000	1797.3	2000	944.38	2000	958.06	2000	995.03	2000	881.13	2000
160	24	320	204.12	2000	17.82	2000	92.63	2000	7.24	2000	101.03	2000	8	2000
160	24	320	27.36	2000	14.67	2000	106.2	2000	6.41	2000	104.11	2000	8.38	2000
160	24	320	15.05	2000	11.12	2000	87.48	2000	5.71	2000	84.55	2000	6.15	2000
160	24	320	110.71	2000	11.12	2000	81.27	2000	7.23	2000	79.73	2000	6.81	2000
160	24	320	231.43	2000	14.65	2000	119.99	2000	5.9	2000	80.75	2000	7.44	2000
160	24	2544	306.65	2000	314.58	2000	174	2000	20.71	2000	176.63	2000	60.1	2000
160	24	2544	417.3	2000	359.95	2000	186.83	2000	63.58	2000	188.95	2000	47.58	2000
160	24	2544	376.71	2000	263.04	2000	182.51	2000	49.56	2000	167.25	2000	29.02	2000
160	24	2544	494.87	2000	345.8	2000	186.3	2000	20.36	2000	165.88	2000	66.11	2000
160	24	2544	527.52	2000	375.47	2000	182.2	2000	63	2000	169.01	2000	37.36	2000
160	40	240	133.14	2000	15.23	2000	99.21	2000	7.11	2000	90.91	2000	9.97	2000
160	40	240	293.95	2000	166.41	2000	96.47	2000	6.92	2000	92.35	2000	12.96	2000
160	40	240	141.29	2000	11.61	2000	113.82	2000	7.96	2000	107.2	2000	9.5	2000
160	40	240	22.1	2000	11.91	2000	133.85	2000	6.27	2000	131.31	2000	5.71	2000
160	40	240	243.54	2000	14.97	2000	104.28	2000	7.02	2000	98.39	2000	6.62	2000
160	40	812	347.04	2000	159.94	2000	112.84	2000	9.23	2000	123.69	2000	19.56	2000
160	40	812	401.47	2000	154.96	2000	103.46	2000	11.8	2000	113.69	2000	12.6	2000
160	40	812	306.99	2000	202.31	2000	102.59	2000	13.28	2000	99.68	2000	11.98	2000
160	40	812	330.1	2000	142.23	2000	119.79	2000	8.88	2000	119.03	2000	14.73	2000
160	40	812	314.21	2000	169.55	2000	108.8	2000	37.69	2000	113.89	2000	10.48	2000
160	40	12720	811.02	2000	820.17	2000	991.35	2000	953.91	2000	1012.44	2000	1013.44	2000
160	40	12720	777.45	2000	760.26	2000	853.42	2000	892.28	2000	910.55	2000	911.59	2000
160	40	12720	732.19	2000	763.2	2000	959.04	2000	1086.24	2000	1023.58	2000	942.29	2000
160	40	12720	760.61	2000	756.98	2000	796.52	2000	831.28	2000	859.02	2000	831.89	2000
160	40	12720	749.32	2000	726.67	2000	890.91	2000	951.14	2000	914.2	2000	914.08	2000
160	40	320	358.73	2000	12.21	2000	101.63	2000	7.49	2000	102.25	2000	6.1	2000
160	40	320	158.25	2000	12.06	2000	162.06	2000	6.79	2000	159.3	2000	8.82	2000
160	40	320	232.95	2000	15.2	2000	108.47	2000	11.5	2000	111.11	2000	8.73	2000
160	40	320	397.84	2000	11.86	2000	110.14	2000	8.26	2000	105.93	2000	7.19	2000
160	40	320	190.79	2000	135.56	2000	117.77	2000	10.9	2000	116.04	2000	7.2	2000
160	40	2544	264.6	2000	244.81	2000	186.09	2000	31.11	2000	162.88	2000	48.75	2000
160	40	2544	254.08	2000	209.82	2000	177.62	2000	20.11	2000	173.54	2000	59.59	2000
160	40	2544	286.9	2000	221.22	2000	175.25	2000	97.38	2000	179.25	2000	66.09	2000
160	40	2544	384.86	2000	213.91	2000	188.43	2000	34.11	2000	188.31	2000	67.83	2000
160	40	2544	286.37	2000	211.54	2000	203.06	2000	51.07	2000	180.05	2000	76.72	2000
	average		468.02	2000	387.21	2000	285.99	2000	210.33	2000	283.41	2000	203.52	2000

Table 9 Best Solution Time Comparisons for the i160 dataset

n	n_r	e	SASR	RTSR	SAMR	RTMR	SASPs	RTSPs	SAMPs	RTMPs	SASPh	RTSPh	SAMPh	RTMPh
160	7	240	0.15	0.97	119.4	38.83	56.58	0.15	0.18	0.1	54.05	0.46	0.01	0.01
160	7	240	2.79	1.86	79.06	1.72	51.71	0.17	0.18	0.13	0.01	0.01	0.01	0.01
160	7	240	0.04	0.12	74.4	0.01	0.01	0.01	0.01	0.01	0.3	0.28	0.24	0.23
160	7	240	2.84	109.68	51.3	17.95	50.88	0.16	1.54	0.16	46.88	0.86	0.28	760.39
160	7	240	8.01	0.19	164.79	1.05	0.1	0.16	0.01	0.01	0.22	0.38	0.15	0.21
160	7	812	0.11	0.28	0.01	51.4	0.58	0.21	1.52	0.23	64.98	1.28	0.58	0.54
160	7	812	0.24	49.37	0.01	0.01	63.41	0.23	0.11	0.14	0.36	0.52	0.3	0.46
160	7	812	128.74	0.59	4.44	1.13	71.18	0.24	0.08	0.14	0.64	0.43	0.7	0.38
160	7	812	0.12	0.17	17.78	11.41	76.22	0.25	0.06	0.14	0.85	0.53	0.28	0.36
160	7	812	0.09	1.48	11.33	457.36	67.12	0.22	0.14	0.14	0.6	0.7	0.36	0.47
160	7	12720	0.12	1.46	0.3	1.66	844.99	1.54	883.11	1.49	907.49	4.54	880	4.64
160	7	12720	0.11	1.43	0.3	1.66	735.6	1.59	748.54	1.49	778.86	8.59	727.19	8.56
160	7	12720	1.46	1.46	1.65	1.77	812.14	1.55	798.54	1.63	861.53	3.37	902.58	3.04
160	7	12720	22.85	1.41	24.28	1.63	835.82	1.53	852.56	1.52	881.28	3.66	824.32	3.28
160	7	12720	0.97	1.4	1.02	1.65	933.59	1.53	927.65	1.53	715.14	4.63	719.17	4.4
160	7	320	1.51	0.99	120.05	138.29	54.64	0.2	0.06	0.11	52.27	1.43	1.49	46.75
160	7	320	0.09	1.72	203.67	1.05	0.14	0.17	0.08	0.15	0.54	0.66	0.3	0.36
160	7	320	0.09	0.14	134.32	112.66	0.1	0.18	0.05	0.11	51.62	0.62	0.25	0.35
160	7	320	1.42	0.14	115.89	1807.39	61.47	0.17	1.06	0.11	0.41	0.54	1.61	133.21
160	7	320	35.14	2.52	182.89	102.38	54.44	0.2	0.16	0.15	53.35	16.03	0.28	0.34
160	7	2544	139.83	1.22	3.65	0.82	132.6	0.35	0.07	0.24	138.5	10.29	0.31	0.72
160	7	2544	0.12	0.28	0.36	2.19	0.18	0.41	3.29	0.47	172.98	2.04	3.83	0.92
160	7	2544	0.63	0.27	0.27	0.63	149.83	0.34	20.09	0.27	136.62	1.02	0.51	0.73
160	7	2544	0.14	0.28	0.6	0.64	148.65	2.12	0.1	0.27	175.75	1.42	0.42	0.52
160	7	2544	0.44	2.35	0.01	0.01	139.76	0.37	0.12	0.26	143.98	56.03	0.01	0.01
160	12	240	217.13	0.22	170.18	0.19	0.12	0.17	1.76	0.22	0.35	0.27	0.3	0.24
160	12	240	0.06	1841.64	120.65	0.19	47.8	0.22	0.5	0.46	49.19	1.12	1.59	0.24
160	12	240	0.08	0.13	0.18	0.19	0.29	0.15	0.22	0.22	49.64	2.07	0.22	0.24
160	12	240	0.12	166.5	164.8	0.18	60.56	0.15	0.11	0.15	0.42	0.52	0.2	0.34
160	12	240	1.38	0.13	140.6	367.18	54.07	0.23	0.37	0.29	45.23	0.77	0.22	29.13
160	12	812	49.41	375.31	3.58	1673.22	0.17	0.22	0.28	0.24	65.14	4.18	0.44	1.72
160	12	812	0.06	0.17	6.73	120.4	83.16	0.35	0.11	0.22	0.7	0.81	0.45	0.54
160	12	812	180.82	0.48	0.23	0.68	69.69	0.31	3.54	0.24	64.36	1.18	0.3	0.46
160	12	812	0.07	2.61	9.89	81.6	73.42	0.24	0.12	0.23	61.46	1.27	0.28	0.39
160	12	812	179.11	4.09	0.32	0.4	79.38	0.24	2.73	0.14	69.61	0.73	0.01	0.01
160	12	12720	0.12	1.48	0.3	1.53	794.22	1.61	850.12	1.5	815.01	30.93	904.95	30.95
160	12	12720	0.11	1.47	0.3	1.62	824.3	1.55	807.03	1.53	805.99	11.33	796.18	11.16
160	12	12720	0.12	1.46	0.3	1.56	710.58	1.54	729.31	1.51	759.88	8.46	700.1	9.42
160	12	12720	21.82	1.39	22.52	1.53	888.91	1.53	885.07	1.58	719.26	19.77	787.38	20.29
160	12	12720	21.87	1.44	24.35	1.65	841.39	1.54	776.29	1.56	692.3	8.8	693.66	10
160	12	320	0.52	0.22	79.14	4.02	0.12	0.19	0.16	0.18	44.94	1.27	0.32	241.1
160	12	320	55.04	3.68	27.01	24.56	60.43	0.19	0.16	0.23	0.52	0.66	0.44	1.35
160	12	320	0.11	240.3	9.82	0.97	54.67	0.24	0.28	0.3	55.46	0.97	0.45	0.8
160	12	320	0.1	30.8	110.82	120.42	57.97	0.31	8.92	0.3	53.19	1.16	0.44	0.6
160	12	320	0.31	0.3	5.84	168.92	48.78	0.34	5.88	0.37	53.78	0.75	0.29	0.39
160	12	2544	263.03	4.05	0.56	0.8	186.62	0.34	0.24	0.45	1.02	1.78	1.03	1.51
160	12	2544	539.24	0.27	192.97	0.98	146.52	30.09	0.18	0.46	113.57	32.2	0.57	2.14
160	12	2544	1.13	0.67	0.27	51.78	0.18	0.58	0.08	0.48	123.82	10.67	0.38	0.54
160	12	2544	0.01	0.47	0.01	0.01	154.21	7.38	1.18	0.46	135.42	32.45	0.84	0.5
160	12	2544	129.8	77.09	0.64	0.8	169.1	4.72	0.09	0.46	161.63	63.61	0.59	1.15
160	24	240	83.29	0.23	4.06	19.87	0.5	0.97	0.35	0.46	54.45	1.54	2.18	8.5
160	24	240	2.26	1.36	3.02	178.45	77.81	7.7	3.88	0.91	59.08	3.55	2.38	1.17
160	24	240	0.18	76.18	1.76	50.52	56.23	0.41	0.37	0.65	43.48	1.52	0.31	1.02
160	24	240	44.79	4.97	0.53	106.27	47.97	0.59	8.03	0.93	46.2	2.8	7.07	0.4
160	24	240	79.2	588.53	86.39	171.57	62.56	12.74	0.34	0.34	60.79	10.03	0.25	0.37
160	24	812	101.29	0.9	11.34	71.18	87.11	6.83	0.63	29.34	74.94	4.89	0.52	1.05
160	24	812	273.32	136.32	0.35	1288.64	76.94	1.98	0.46	0.5	68.24	4.95	1.75	0.36
160	24	812	274.39	711.05	4.23	1723.08	93.81	0.53	0.41	0.52	60.57	2.03	9.13	13.28
160	24	812	218.45	1088.02	3.59	223.22	84.85	0.69	0.21	0.5	69.66	3.89	0.82	1.01
160	24	812	0.11	1786.11	3.76	310.84	79.88	4.04	0.33	0.41	64.13	3.1	0.57	82.73
160	24	12720	21.62	1.23	21.35	1.48	878.25	1.63	827.53	1.49	766.59	28.8	794.37	27.66
160	24	12720	23.94	1.24	23.11	1.5	807.57	1.56	896.15	1.49	787.61	12.58	761.23	12.71
160	24	12720	1369.37	1.28	1436.37	1.38	818	1.61	870.46	1.6	896.12	14.22	785.62	15.83
160	24	12720	20.84	1.3	21.86	1.48	776.76	1.48	880.16	1.6	633.9	43.69	618.65	41.91
160	24	12720	22.58	1.22	21.79	1.43	827.79	1.59	835.45	1.56	866.88	980.09	760.4	949.55
160	24	320	13.23	167.43	9.22	486.52	62.87	97.95	0.14	0.59	51.41	1.84	3.74	4.61
160	24	320	15.05	663.23	5.34	81.77	58.98	0.4	0.29	0.56	52.69	3.15	4.14	0.73
160	24	320	0.11	79.02	1.81	0.51	51.23	0.87	0.26	0.49	54.17	1.45	0.56	0.26
160	24	320	91.46	1.2	1.84	338.16	62.93	1.39	0.54	0.37	0.29	0.4	0.23	0.35
160	24	320	130.47	1302.02	6.29	17.05	73.06	54.02	1.17	0.54	50.65	40.05	0.3	0.66
160	24	2544	280.22	6.7	243.83	58.64	133.4	0.56	20.5	0.85	138.53	8.05	0.78	2.42
160	24	2544	0.1	0.25	232.74	24.01	156.73	6.08	1.62	1.28	173.51	20.01	0.67	2.68
160	24	2544	262.54	9.37	239.91	0.92	0.71	26.45	0.55	0.66	126.93	3.78	1.35	2.79
160	24	2544	307.9	0.26	193.88	1.08	168.76	50.37	0.19	0.91	121.26	57.49	1.46	2.73
160	24	2544	276.14	2.83	231.68	305.77	140.92	4.31	0.29	0.9	125.09	2.6	0.97	4.96

Table 10 Best Solution Time Comparisons for the i160 dataset – Continued

n	n_r	e	SASR	RTSR	SAMR	RTMR	SASPs	RTSPs	SAMPs	RTMPs	SASPh	RTSPh	SAMPh	RTMPh
160	40	240	3.42	7.31	6.32	1.12	54.2	210.78	0.32	1.14	53.6	12.13	5.8	12.12
160	40	240	112.89	400.64	51.92	40.66	53.41	38.07	0.36	0.92	50.85	0.95	8.12	0.72
160	40	240	73.42	433.69	2.17	98.86	56.71	21.99	0.29	0.66	49.37	19.97	5.47	9.39
160	40	240	3.12	6.5	2.18	16.94	55.18	7.28	0.42	1.25	56.97	7.88	0.2	0.45
160	40	240	80.88	1147.9	5.36	69.88	65.31	3.32	0.22	0.65	55.97	1.37	0.59	1
160	40	812	164.37	261.83	68.05	1276.11	81.15	10.19	0.48	0.84	81.91	597.9	12.92	11.06
160	40	812	401.36	38.87	36.28	995.58	81.08	2.29	0.41	0.78	57.87	3.9	0.52	10.76
160	40	812	161.3	1541.58	73.89	1.51	82.68	2.6	0.53	1.02	68.48	2.95	0.81	5.29
160	40	812	148.81	1561.94	8.9	1099.36	70.42	47.35	0.18	0.87	77.18	46.28	7.55	5.78
160	40	812	172.3	196.84	41.22	1741.68	65.21	3.29	0.96	0.74	74.2	5.53	3.54	124.97
160	40	12720	588.43	1.01	593.39	1.2	835.51	1.69	806	1.53	706.87	23.54	681.82	24.3
160	40	12720	558.73	1.16	543.53	1.26	674.77	1.6	712.97	1.53	550.16	119.65	539.25	116.19
160	40	12720	578.75	1.07	608.71	1.2	671.52	1.67	768.77	1.6	634.48	29.44	572.39	29.62
160	40	12720	598.66	1.12	605.61	1.34	560.44	1.59	571.26	1.52	576.7	23.75	564.48	21.75
160	40	12720	658.2	1.07	641.59	1.18	587.98	1.63	632.23	1.52	687.81	26.34	689.64	24.22
160	40	320	180.27	347.72	2.05	154.36	62.48	9.19	3.25	0.81	65.47	5.81	1.72	0.58
160	40	320	54.65	868.25	3.01	208.22	59.14	1.51	2.3	0.83	59.48	7.16	4.07	17.07
160	40	320	97.93	68.3	5.01	262	57.32	1.21	7.2	0.71	60.26	1.28	0.41	1.75
160	40	320	383.36	264.6	2.39	100.54	61.76	1.32	0.5	0.67	56.92	1.83	2.59	32.61
160	40	320	107.97	1481.51	40.93	325.42	56.1	2.43	0.21	0.61	59.46	4.11	0.37	1.2
160	40	2544	192.56	172.6	136.13	30.54	166.83	21.48	1.24	1.07	145.71	18.4	1.27	5.2
160	40	2544	218.7	204.5	143.51	39.52	143.5	125.65	0.76	1.05	131.8	94.9	1.26	428.36
160	40	2544	249.53	31.97	152.91	145.96	141.61	2.85	0.41	1.08	165.84	6.06	1.28	136.13
160	40	2544	296.23	2.66	142.67	0.97	146.9	47.03	0.32	1.08	173.33	34.34	1.07	6.02
160	40	2544	257.51	0.39	154.61	40.4	185.91	6.2	1.18	1.03	133.07	65.36	1.1	5.18
	average		124.27	186.15	92.86	175.95	215.11	9.29	161.77	0.99	204.62	27.75	148.24	35.47

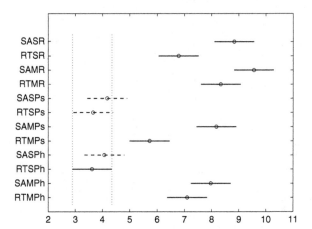

Fig. 8 Solution quality statistical ranks comparison for the i160 dataset

both the set of considered test instances, the parameters regarding update and request rates (so far, we restricted to a very limited but realistic set of values) and the number of implemented metaheuristics. Moreover, further improvements for the mathematical programming formulations are worth being investigated.

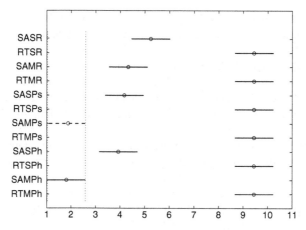

Fig. 9 Total time statistical ranks comparison for the i160 dataset

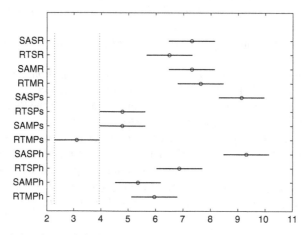

Fig. 10 Best solution time statistical ranks comparison for the i160 dataset

References

R. Battiti. Reactive search: Toward self-tuning heuristics. In V.J. Rayward-Smith, I.H. Osman, C.R. Reeves, and G.D. Smith, editors, *Modern Heuristic Search Methods*, pages 61–83. Wiley, Chichester, 1996.

J.E. Beasley. OR-Library: Distributing test problems by electronic mail. *Journal of the Operational Research Society*, 41:1069–1072, 1990.

K.V. Martínez Facundo, J.A. Saucedo Martínez, J. Á. Segura Ramiro, M. A. Urbano Vázquez, and R. Z. Ríos Mercado. El problema del árbol de empuje en sistemas de telecomunicaciones. *Ingenierías*, 10 (36), 2007.

A. Fink and S. Voß. HOTFRAME: A heuristic optimization framework. In S. Voß and D. Woodruff, editors, *Optimization Software Class Libraries*, pages 81–154. Kluwer, Boston, 2002.

F. Glover and M. Laguna. *Tabu Search*. Kluwer, Boston, 1997.

F. Havet. Robustness of a routing tree for a push tree problem. Technical Report 4464, INRIA, 2002.

F. Havet and M. Wennink. The push tree problem. In *SPAA 01: 13th ACM Symposium on Parallel Algorithms and Architectures*, pages 318–319, 2001.

F. Havet and M. Wennink. The push tree problem. *Networks*, 44:281–291, 2004.

M. Hollander and D.A. Wolfe. *Nonparametric Statistical Methods, 2nd Edition*. John Wiley & Sons, 1999.

D. S. Johnson, C. R. Aragon, L. A. McGeoch, and C. Schevon. Optimization by simulated annealing: An experimental evaluation; part I, graph partitioning. *Operations Research*, 37:865–892, 1989.

T. Koch, A. Martin, and S. Voß. SteinLib: An updated library on Steiner tree problems in graphs. In D.-Z. Du and X. Cheng, editors, *Steiner Trees in Industries*, pages 285–325. Kluwer, Boston, 2001.

C.E. Miller, A.W. Tucker, and R.A. Zemlin. Integer programming formulation of traveling salesman problems. *Journal of the Association of Computing Machinery*, 7:326–329, 1960.

P. Mirchandani. The multi-tier tree problem. *INFORMS Journal on Computing*, 8: 202–218, 1996.

C. H. Papadimitriou and K. Steiglitz. *Combinatorial Optimization: Algorithms and Complexity*. Prentice-Hall, Englewood Cliffs, New Jersey, 1982.

H. Takahashi and A. Matsuyama. An approximate solution for the Steiner problem in graphs. *Math. Japonica*, 24:573–577, 1980.

X. Tang and J. Xu. On replica placement for QoS-Aware content distribution. In *Proceedings of the 23rd Annual Joint Conference of the IEEE Computer and Communications Societies (INFOCOM)*, volume 2, pages 806–815, 2004.

S. Voß. Steiner tree problems in telecommunications. In M. Resende and P.M. Pardalos, editors, *Handbook of Optimization in Telecommunications*, pages 459–492. Springer, New York, 2006.

Two-Edge Disjoint Survivable Network Design Problem with Relays

Abdullah Konak, Sadan Kulturel-Konak, and Alice E. Smith

Abstract In this paper, we study the network design problem with relays considering network survivability. This problem arises in telecommunications and logistic systems. The design problem involves selecting two edge-disjoint paths between source and destination node pairs and determining the location of the relays in the network to minimize the network cost. A constraint is imposed on the distance that a signal or commodity can travel in the network without being processed by a relay. An efficient and effective meta-heuristic approach is proposed to solve large sized problems and compared with construction heuristics and an exact approach run for up to 24 hours using CPLEX.

Keywords: Network Design, Survivability, Relays, Genetic Algorithm

1 Introduction

The network design problem with relays (NDPR) is first introduced by Cabral et al. (2007) in the context of a telecommunication network design problem. In this paper, we study the two-edge connected network design problem with relays

Abdullah Konak
Information Sciences and Technology, Penn State Berks
Tulpehocken Rd. PO Box 7009, Reading, PA19610 USA
konak@psu.edu

Sadan Kulturel-Konak
Management Information Systems, Penn State Berks
Tulpehocken Rd. PO Box 7009, Reading, PA19610 USA
sadan@psu.edu

Alice E. Smith
Department of Industrial & Systems Engineering, Auburn University
3301 Shelby Center, Auburn, AL 36849 USA
smithae@auburn.edu

J.W. Chinneck et al. (eds.), *Operations Research and Cyber-Infrastructure*, Operations
Research/Computer Science Interfaces Series 47, DOI: 10.1007/978-0-387-88843-9_14,
© Springer Science+Business Media, LLC 2009

(2ECON-NDPR), which is an extension of the NDPR by considering survivability in the network design. A survivable network has the ability to restore network services after catastrophic edge or node failures. Network survivability is an important concern in telecommunication network design as network topologies are becoming sparse because of high capacity fiber-optic links which can transmit large amount of data. Traditionally, the survivability of a network against component failures is achieved by imposing redundant paths between nodes. For many real-life network applications, a level of redundancy to protect against a single edge or node failure is sufficient since component failures are so rare that the probability of observing another failure during a repair is almost zero (Monma and Shallcross 1989; Magnanti et al. 1995). Therefore, network design researchers mainly focus on two-edge and two-node connectivity problems, which assure network connectivity against a single component failure. In this paper, we consider two-edge connectivity (2ECON) in the context of NDPR. However, our approach can be extended to two-node connectivity (2NCON) as well.

The 2ECON-NDPR is briefly defined as follows. An undirected network $G = (V, E)$ with node set $V = \{1, 2, \ldots, N\}$ and edge set $E = \{(i, j) : i, j \in V, i < j\}$ is given. Each edge (i, j) is associated with a cost of $c_{i,j}^e$ and a distance of $d_{i,j}$. $|K|$ commodities, representing point-to-point traffics, are simultaneously routed on the network; each commodity k has a single source node $s(k)$ and a single destination node $t(k)$. For each commodity k, two edge-disjoint paths from node $s(k)$ to node $t(k)$ are to be determined. The first path $(p_1(k))$ is dedicated as the primary path for the routing of commodity k, and the second path $(p_2(k))$ is reserved as a backup path in case path $p_1(k)$ fails. In other words, the connectivity between nodes $s(k)$ and $t(k)$ for each commodity k is expected to be one edge fault tolerant similar to the two-edge connected network design problem (Monma and Shallcross 1989). In the 2ECON-NDPR, however, an upper bound λ is imposed on the distance that commodity k can travel on a path from node $s(k)$ to node $t(k)$ without visiting a special node, which is called a relay. A relay may correspond to different facilities on real life networks. For example, in digital telecommunication networks, the signal can be transmitted only for a limited distance without losing its fidelity due to attenuation and other factors, and therefore, it has to be regenerated at certain intervals during its transmission. In this case, a relay corresponds to a telecommunication facility in which the signal is regenerated into its original form. Different from the classic multi-commodity network design problem, in the 2ECON-NDPR some nodes of the network have to be dedicated as relays in which the signal is regenerated. A fixed cost, c_i^v, is occurred when a relay is located at node i. The objective function of the 2ECON-NDPR is to minimize the network design cost while making sure that each commodity k can be routed from node $s(k)$ to node $t(k)$ through two edge-disjoint paths on each of which the distances between node $s(k)$ and the first relay, between any consecutive relays, and between node $t(k)$ and the last relay are less than the upper bound λ. A network flow based formulation of the 2ECON-NDPR on a directed network, $G = (V, E)$, where edge set E includes both edges (i, j) and (j, i) is given as follows:

Decision Variables:

$x_{i,j}$ binary edge decision variable such that $x_{i,j} = 1$ if edge (i,j) is included in the solution , 0 otherwise.

y_i binary relay decision variable such that $y_i = 1$ if a relay is located at node i, 0 otherwise.

$f_{i,j}^k$ binary flow decision variable such that $f_{i,j}^k = 1$ if edge (i,j) is used by commodity k, 0 otherwise.

$u_{k,i}^p$ total distance traveled on a path p by commodity k before node i without visiting a relay.

$v_{k,i}^p$ total distance traveled on a path p by commodity k after node i without visiting a relay.

Formulation 2ECON-NDPR:

$$\text{Min } z = \sum_{i \in V} c_i^v y_i + \sum_{(i,j) \in E, i < j} c_{i,j}^e x_{i,j} \tag{1}$$

$$\sum_{(i,j) \in E} f_{i,j}^k - \sum_{(j,i) \in E} f_{j,i}^k = \begin{cases} 2 & i = s(k) \\ -2 & i = t(k) \\ 0 & otherwise \end{cases} \quad k \in K, i \in V \tag{2}$$

$$u_{k,i}^p \geq v_{k,j}^p + d_{j,i} - (1 - f_{j,i}^k)2\lambda \quad k \in K, i \in V, p \in \{1,2\}, (j,i) \in E \tag{3}$$

$$u_{k,i}^p \leq \lambda \quad k \in K, i \in V, p \in \{1,2\} \tag{4}$$

$$v_{k,i}^p \geq u_{k,i}^p - \lambda y_i \quad k \in K, i \in V, p \in \{1,2\} \tag{5}$$

$$f_{i,j}^k + f_{j,i}^k \leq x_{i,j} \quad k \in K, (i,j) \in E, i < j \tag{6}$$

$$y_i, x_{i,j}, f_{i,j}^k \in \{0,1\}$$

$$u_{k,i}^p, v_{k,i}^p \geq 0$$

In the above formulation, Constraint (2) is a set of standard node flow balance constraints to make sure that two unit flows are sent from source node $s(k)$ to destination node $t(k)$. Constraint (3) is used to calculate the total distance traveled by commodity k to node i without visiting a relay on path p. Note that Constraint (3) is valid due to Constraint (6) which limits the flow of the same commodity on each edge to one unit. Constraint (3) becomes $u_{k,i}^p \geq v_{k,j}^p + d_{j,i}$ if commodity k is routed through edge (i,j). If node j is not a relay, then $v_{k,j}^p \geq u_{k,j}^p$ due to Constraint (5), and using this inequality, Constraint (3) can be rewritten as follows:

$$u_{k,i}^p \geq u_{k,j}^p + d_{j,i} \tag{7}$$

On path p, inequality (7) is used to calculate the total distance traveled by commodity k from a relay node to node i without visiting any relay node. This distance is represented by decision variable $u_{k,i}^p$ in the formulation. Constraint (4) is the relay constraint that makes sure that the total distance traveled by commodity k on path p

without visiting a relay node is less than λ at each node. Constraint (5) resets the total distance of path p at a relay node. Note that if node j is a relay, both $v_{k,j}^p$ and $u_{k,j}^p$ can be zero in Constraint (5). Therefore, inequality (7) and Constraint (3) are reduced to $u_{k,i}^p \geq d_{j,i}$ at node i after visiting relay node j. Constraint (6) makes sure that edge (i, j) cannot be used for routing if it is not included in the solution, as well as edge (i, j) cannot be used by each commodity k more than once by restricting flows to one unit. Constraints (2) and (6) make sure that there exist 2-edge disjoint paths between every source and destination pair in the network.

Cabral et al. (2007) formulate a path based integer programming model of NDPR and propose a column generation approach which can also be applied in the case of the 2ECON-NDPR. Unfortunately, the column generation approach cannot be practically used to prove the optimality of a solution in the case of large problem instances since all feasible paths and relay locations combinations have to be generated as a priori. Therefore, they recommend using a subset of all feasible paths and relays combinations. Although this approach does not guarantee optimality, superior solutions can be found in reasonable CPU time. In addition, they proposed four different construction heuristics in which a solution is constructed by taking into consideration one commodity at a time. In this paper, we modify three of their construction heuristics to solve the 2ECON-NDPR, which are used as benchmarks to test the performance of our approach. More recently, Kulturel-Konak and Konak (2008) study the NDPR and propose a hybrid local search-genetic algorithm (GA) where a specialized crossover operator based on random paths between source and destination nodes are utilized, and local search procedures are used to investigate new solutions. These local search procedures are not directly applicable to the 2ECON-NDPR. In this paper, we modify this hybrid GA's specialized crossover operator for the 2ECON-NDPR, and the new crossover operator is coupled with customized mutation strategies and a simple heuristic to determine location of relays. Therefore, there is no need for computationally expensive local search procedures.

The NDPR is closely related to a set of well-known network design problems such as the Steiner tree problem, the hop-constrained network design problem, the constrained shortest path problem, and the facility location problem. In the hop constrained network design problem, hop constraints impose an upper bound on the number of edges between some source and some destination nodes due to reliability (LeBlanc and Reddoch 1990) or performance concerns (Balakrishnan and Altinkemer 1992). Several papers (Choplin 2001; Randall et al. 2002; Kwangil and Shayman 2005) address optical network design problems considering restricted transmission range due to optical impairments, which is one of the main motivations in the NDPR.

Similar to the Steiner tree problem, all nodes are not required to be connected in the 2ECON-NDPR. Voss (1999) considers the hop-constrained Steiner tree problem and proposes a solution approach based on tabu search and mathematical programming. Gouveia and Magnanti (2003) consider the diameter-constrained minimum spanning and Steiner tree problems where an upper-bound is imposed on the number of edges between any node pairs. Gouveia (1996) proposes two different mathematical models for the hop-constrained minimum spanning tree problem as well as

Lagrangean relaxation and heuristic approaches to solve the problem. Subsequently, Gouveia and Requejo (2001) develop an improved Lagrangean relaxation approach to the problem. In addition, due to relay decision variables, the 2ECON-NDPR is closely related to the facility location problem (Hakimi 1964).

The objective of this paper is to develop a meta-heuristic approach, namely a genetic algorithm, for the 2ECON-NDPR to solve large problem instances effectively and efficiently. To our best knowledge, 2ECON-NDPR has not previously been studied.

2 A Genetic Algorithm Approach to 2ECON-NDPR

In this section, we describe a genetic algorithm to find good solutions to the 2ECON-NDPR. The parameters and notation used in the GA are given as follows:

z a solution

$z.x_{i,j}$ edge decision variable of solution z such that $z.x_{i,j} = 1$ if edge (i, j) is selected in solution z, 0 otherwise.

$z.y_i$ relay decision variable of solution z such that $z.y_i = 1$ if a relay is located at node i, 0 otherwise.

$z.p_i(k)$ the ith path of commodity k of solution z.

$E(z)$ edge set of solution $z, E(z) \subset E$

$V(z)$ node set of solution $z, V(z) \subset V$

μ population size

t_{max} maximum number of generations (stopping criteria)

P population

OP offspring population

$P[i]$ the ith member in the population

U uniform random number between 0 and 1

2.1 Encoding, Fitness, and Solution Evaluation

By definition, a feasible solution to the 2ECON-NDPR does not have to be a fully connected network. A solution is feasible if at least two edge-disjoint paths exist between source node $s(k)$ and destination node $t(k)$ of each commodity k such that on both paths, the distances between node $s(k)$ and the first relay, between any consecutive relays, and between the last relay and node $t(k)$ and are less than the upper bound λ. This observation is used in the encoding of the GA to represent solutions. Basically, a solution z includes the primary and secondary edge-disjoint paths for each commodity and the relay decision variables, i.e., a solution is represented as $z = \{p_1(1), \ldots, p_1(k); p_2(1), \ldots, p_2(k); y_1, \ldots, y_N\}$. The crossover and mutation operators of the GA generate the edge-disjoint paths $\{p_1(1), \ldots, p_1(k); p_2(1), \ldots, p_2(k)\}$ of an offspring using the edges inherited from two randomly selected parents; and therefore, they ensure two edge-disjoint paths between the source and destination nodes of each commodity. For a given path, relay decision variables $\{y_1, \ldots, y_N\}$ are determined using a simple heuristic during the crossover. This heuristic also ensures feasibility of the paths with respect to the relay constraint. Since the procedures of the GA always generate feasible solutions, the population is ranked according to the cost.

2.2 Specialized Crossover Operator

In a GA, the function of the crossover operator is to create new solutions by recombining the edges of existing solutions. The representation of solutions in the GA is permutation based. When used with the permutation based encodings, traditional GA crossover operators such as single-point or uniform crossover may generate highly infeasible solution structures which have to be repaired by using special repair algorithms. There are a number of crossover operators specially designed for permutation encodings (see (Fogel et al. 1999) for a survey), which can be used to recombine the corresponding paths of parents to create offspring. For example, the corresponding paths of two solutions a and b can be recombined (i.e., crossover $a.p_1(k)$ with $b.p_1(k)$ and $a.p_2(k)$ with $b.p_2(k)$ for each commodity k). There are a few drawbacks associated with such a crossover operator. Firstly, $a.p_1(k)$ and $b.p_1(k)$ may not share any common nodes, which will make the crossover impossible in this case. Secondly, $a.p_1(k)$ and $b.p_2(k)$ or $a.p_2(k)$ and $b.p_1(k)$ may have many overlapping edges. In this case, the crossover of $a.p_1(k)$ with $b.p_1(k)$ must be coordinated with the crossover of $a.p_2(k)$ with $b.p_2(k)$ since the paths of the offspring must be disjoint. Thirdly, the paths of the commodities tend to overlap as the routes of different commodities may share many edges in the 2ECON-NDPR (i.e., $a.p_1(k)$ may share many edges with $a.p_1(j)$ and $a.p_2(j)$ where $k \neq j$). If such dependences between the paths are not considered, an offspring may end up having a much higher number of edges than its parents. Therefore, these dependences between the paths should be considered in order to design an effective crossover for the 2ECON-NDPR.

Because of the reasons briefly discussed above, a specialized crossover is developed based on the Suurballe-Tarjan algorithm (Suurballe and Tarjan 1984). The Suurballe-Tarjan algorithm finds the shortest pair of edge-disjoint paths between a source and a destination node in polynomial time. The crossover operator of the GA is a random construction heuristic in which an offspring solution is constructed from the union of two parent solutions by considering one commodity at a time in a random order of commodities. In Figure 1, a step-by-step example of the crossover and mutation is demonstrated for a problem with two commodities. In the figure, relay nodes are identified by solid circles. The first step in the crossover is randomly selecting two parent solutions, say a and b. After selecting parents, they are combined as illustrated in Figure 1-step (ii), and each edge $(i, j) \in E$ of the combined solution is assigned to a temporary cost $tc_{i,j}$ as follows:

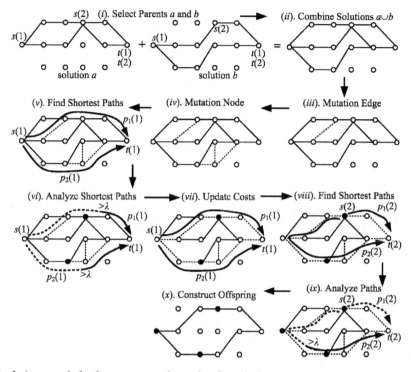

Fig. 1 An example for the crossover and mutation. Dotted edges represent low cost edges.

$$tc_{i,j} = \begin{cases} U \times (c_{i,j}^e + c_i^v + c_j^v) & (i,j) \in E(a) \cup E(b), \\ \infty & \text{otherwise.} \end{cases} \qquad (8)$$

Mutation is applied on the combined solution by adding new edges and/or a node. The details of the mutation operators are discussed in the following section. In Figure 1, steps (*iii*) and (*iv*) provide example for edge and node mutations, respectfully. Newly added edges to the combined solution during mutation are assigned random costs (U), which are significantly smaller cost than the ones given in equation (8), so that these new edges are encouraged to be used in the offspring. In Figure 1, such low cost edges are identified by dotted edges.

After mutation, for each commodity k in a random order, two edge-disjoint shortest paths, $p_1(k)$ and $p_2(k)$, from node $s(k)$ to node $t(k)$ are found using the Suurballe-Tarjan algorithm (Suurballe and Tarjan 1984). In Figure 1, step (v) demonstrates the edge-disjoint shortest paths $p_1(1)$ and $p_2(1)$ from node $s(1)$ to node $t(1)$. Note that in this example, commodity 1 is randomly selected as the first commodity to be routed.

After determining paths $p_1(k)$ and $p_2(k)$ of commodity k, the locations of the relays on paths $p_1(k)$ and $p_2(k)$ are determined using a simple heuristic. To do so, starting from node $s(k)$ or $t(k)$ (randomly and uniformly selected), each edge $(i,j) \in p_1(k)$ is sequentially examined whether a relay should be located at node

i or not. After examining edge (i, j), a relay is located at node i if and only if the total distance between node j and the previous relay on path $p_1(k)$ is more than λ. The same procedure is repeated for $p_2(k)$ to determine the locations of relays on this path. For example in step (vi), the total distance exceeds λ after traversing the fourth edge on path $p_1(1)$ and the third edge on path $p_2(1)$. Therefore, two relays are allocated on the fourth node of $p_1(1)$ and the third node of $p_2(1)$ for the feasibility of these paths.

Finally, $tc_{i,j}$ is set to zero for all edges $(i, j) \in p_1(k) \cup p_2(k)$ in order to encourage the paths of the unassigned commodities to use already assigned edges. This is illustrated in step (vii) where edges of $p_1(1)$ and $p_2(1)$ are dotted, indicating low costs. The example continues with commodity 2. In step $(viii)$, two edge-disjoint paths from node $s(2)$ to node $t(2)$ are found. In step (ix), these paths are analyzed to locate any necessary relay stations. The resulting offspring is shown in step (x). The pseudo code of the crossover operator is presented in the next section.

2.3 Mutation

The purpose of mutation in a GA is to introduce new solution structures (genes) to existing solutions so that local minima can be avoided. In traditional GA mutation, the structure of a solution is randomly changed. A mutation operator of the GA for the 2ECON-NDPR should perturb the edge-disjoint paths by introducing new edges and nodes, which do not exist in parent solutions, while maintaining the edge disjoint paths. The mutation operators of this GA add randomly selected edges or nodes to the parent solutions selected for the crossover. To increase the probability of using these newly added edges and nodes, their costs are set to very small random numbers with respect to existing ones. Then, the crossover operator is applied. By adding new edges and nodes to the parent solutions before applying crossover, the offspring is assured to have two edge-disjoint paths for each commodity. The GA has the following two mutation operators:

Mutation-Edge: Randomly select an edge (i, j) such that $(i, j) \notin \{E(a) \cup E(b)\}, i \in \{V(a) \cup V(b)\}$, and $j \in \{V(a) \cup V(b)\}$ and set $tc_{i,j} := U$. The objective of this mutation is to encourage an offspring to include an edge which does not exist in its parents.

Mutation-Node: Randomly select a node i such that $i \notin \{V(a) \cup V(b)\}$ and there exist at least two edges $(i, j) \in E$ where $j \in \{V(a) \cup V(b)\}$, and then set $tc_{i,j} := U$ for all edges (i, j) where $j \in \{V(a) \cup V(b)\}$. The objective of this mutation is to route commodities through a new node which does not exist in the parents.

The procedure of the mutation and crossover is given below. As mentioned earlier, the mutation operators are applied to the randomly selected parents before applying the crossover. These two mutation operators are sequentially applied independently with the probability of ρ (mutation rate) as given in the procedure below. By setting the cost of new edges introduced by the mutation operators to a random number (U), which is much smaller than the cost of the existing edge on the parents, these new edges are encouraged to be used in the offspring instead of the existing edges of the parents. Mutating the parents before crossover provides significant computational efficiency compared to mutating the offspring by eliminating the need for checking the existence of two edge-disjoint paths between each source and destination pair.

Procedure Crossover_Mutation()

Randomly select two solutions a and b from P to create offspring z.
for each edge $(i, j) \in E$ **do** {
    if edge $(i, j) \in E(a) \cup E(b)$ **then** set $tc_{i,j} := U \times (c_{i,j}^e + c_i^v + c_j^v)$
                else set $tc_{i,j} := \infty$}
if $(U < \rho)$ **then** apply *Mutation-Edge*
if $(U < \rho\,)$ **then** apply *Mutation-Node*
for each $k \in K$ in a random sequence **do** {
    find edge disjoint shortest paths $p_1(k)$ and $p_2(k)$ using random costs
    for $q := 1, ..., 2$ **do** {
        set $Q := 0$
        for each edge $(i, j) \in p_q(k)$ **do** {
            set $z.x_{i,j} := 1$
            $Q = Q + d_{i,j}$
            if $Q > \lambda$ **then** { set $z.y_i := 1$ and $Q := d_{i,j}$ }
            set $tc_{i,j} := 0$
        }
    }
Return offspring z

2.4 Overall Algorithm

The important features of the GA are follows:

- The GA is a generational GA where entire population is replaced by offspring generated by the Crossover_Mutation() operator. The GA retains only the best feasible solution found so far in the population between iterations. All other solutions in the next generation are newly generated offspring.
- In the selection procedure, the offspring population is sorted according to the cost. The best μ offspring are selected for the next generation.
- Duplicate solutions are discouraged in the population. If the population has a multiple copies of a solution, only one of them is actually ranked, and the others are placed at the bottom of the population list, and they are not compared with the others. Since comparison of solutions is performed during the ranking procedure, minimum additional computational effort is needed to discover identical solutions in the population. With this approach, the population is discouraged to converge to a single solution, which can be the case in GA. In our initial experiments, we found better results by avoiding identical solutions in the population.

The pseudo code of the GA is given in the following.

Procedure GA

> Randomly generate μ solutions
> **for** $t := 1,\ldots,t_{max}$ **do** {
> //Crossover
> set $i := 0$;
> **do** {
> > $OP[i] := $ Crossover_Mutation();
> > Evaluate $OP[i]$;
> > Update best feasible solution of necessary
> > set $i := i + 1$;
> } **while** $(i < 2\mu$)
> Rank OP by penalizing duplicate solutions.
> **for** $j := 1,\ldots,\mu$ **do** set $P[j] := OP[j]$;
}

3 Construction Heuristics

This section presents three construction heuristics based on the ones proposed by Cabral et al. (2007) for the NDPR. As mentioned earlier, in their study, a solution is constructed by considering one commodity at the time using a path based integer programming formulation to solve the NDPR with a single commodity. We used the same approach to construct solutions using the formulation 2ECON-NDPR. The formulation 2ECON-NDPR is a difficult integer programming model to be optimally solved. However, it can be optimally solved in a reasonable time if only a single commodity is considered at a time, which enables us to develop construction heuristics for the 2ECON-NDPR in the similar fashion to those defined in (Cabral et al. 2007) and use the resulting solutions as benchmarks.

Let 2ECON-NDPR(k) represent the formulation of the 2ECON-NDPR with a single commodity k. The formulation 2ECON-NDPR(k) can be used in the three construction heuristics as follows:

Increasing Order Construction Heuristic (IOCH): In this heuristic, the optimal two edge-disjoint paths and relay locations are found for each commodity k by solving the 2ECON-NDPR(k). Let k^* represent the commodity with the minimum cost solution 2ECON-NDPR(k) among all commodities. The paths and relay nodes of the 2ECON-NDPR(k^*) solution are included in the solution, and their associated costs are set to zero. Then, the 2ECON-NDPR(k) is solved again for the remaining commodities using the updated costs, and the paths and relays of the minimum cost solution are added to the solution, and their associated costs are set to zero. The procedure continues in a similar fashion until all commodities are considered. The procedure of IOCH is given below:

Procedure IOCH

Set $z.x_{i,j} := 0$ for each $(i, j) \in E$ and $z.y_i := 0$ for each $i \in V$
while $K \neq \emptyset$ {
    Solve the 2ECON-NDPR(k) for each $k \in K$
    Let k^* be the commodity with the minimum 2ECON-NDPR(k) solution
    Let $(\mathbf{x}^*, \mathbf{y}^*)$ be decision variables of the 2ECON-NDPR(k^*)
    for each $(i, j) \in E$ **do** {
        if $x_{i,j}^* = 1$ **then** set $z.x_{i,j} := 1$ and $c_{i,j}^e := 0$
    }
    for each $i \in V$ **do** {
        if $y_i^* = 1$ **then** $z.y_i := 1$ and $c_i^v := 0$
        $K := K \quad \backslash k^*$
}
Return solution z

Decreasing Order Construction Heuristic (DOCH): This heuristic is the opposite of the IOCH such that the solution is constructed starting from the maximum cost 2ECON-NDPR(k) solution to the minimum cost one. The procedure of the DOCH is be the same as procedure IOCH with a single difference: k^* represents the commodity with the maximum cost 2ECON-NDPR(k) solution among all available commodities.

Random Order Construction Heuristic (ROCH): In this heuristic, a solution is constructed one commodity at a time in a similar fashion to IOCH and DOCH, but in a random order of the commodities. In each iteration a commodity k is selected randomly among available commodities, and the 2ECON-NDPR(k) is solved.

4 Experimental Results & Discussions

In the experimental study, two different problem groups, 80 and 160 nodes are used. For each problem group, the x and y coordinates and cost of each node i are randomly generated from integer numbers between 0 and 100. The cost and distance of each edge (i, j) are defined as the Euclidian distance between nodes i and j. Two different values of λ, 30 and 35, are tested. Edges longer than λ are not considered in the problems. Therefore, the number of edges (M) for each problem depends on λ. For example, the 160 node problem with $\lambda = 35$ has 3,624 edges and the ones with $\lambda = 30$ has 2,773 edges. In addition, three different levels of $K, 5, 10$ and 15, are considered. The source and the destination nodes of commodities for each problem are randomly selected but forced to be far apart from each other so that the problems are not trivial to solve. In Table 1, the problems are named using their parameters (e.g., the problem with 160 nodes, 10 commodities and $\lambda = 35$ is named as 160-10-35).

Table 1 Results of the Test Problems

Problem $(N-K-\lambda)$	M	GA Best	GA Avg.	GA % Coef. Var	Avg. CPU Sec*	IP Model (% Opt. Gap)	IOCH	DOCH	ROCH
80-5-30	641	616.2	623.5	0.39	285	662.8 (32%)	758.9	773.0	746.7
80-5-35	853	527.7	527.8	0.02	309	593.7 (29%)	701.8	722.0	718.4
80-10-30	641	708.3	715.2	0.50	363	757.5 (35%)	1,025.5	1070.3	973.7
80-10-35	853	628.3	647.7	0.81	369	662.7 (31%)	1,004.9	1,018.8	922.8
80-15-30	641	880.5	914.3	2.16	432	934.8 (42%)	1,265.0	1,281.2	1,151.2
80-15-35	853	805.8	853.5	2.59	391	879.2 (41%)	1,236.7	1,169.7	1,126.0
160-5-30	2,773	420.6	453.7	5.17	348	545.1 (38%)	598.5	654.5	590.1
160-5-35	3,624	421.0	443.8	3.67	366	496.8 (33%)	568.8	625.5	599.6
160-10-30	2,773	590.9	617.6	2.96	494	769.5 (46%)	879.8	1,018.9	932.2
160-10-35	3,624	560.9	596.3	3.40	509	651.0 (36%)	913.6	926.0	861.7
160-15-30	2,773	705.5	745.0	4.60	642	876.4(45%)	1,128.4	1,159.3	1,077.7
160-15-35	3,624	696.9	739.9	3.41	688	835.8 (43%)	1,155.4	1126.8	1,075.2

*The computational experiments were performed on a PC with 2.66GHZ Intel Dual-Core CPU and 4GB memory.

Table 1 presents the results found by the GA, the construction heuristics, and the integer programming. To gauge GA's results, formulation 2ECON-NDPR was solved using CPLEX V9.0 with a time limit of 24 CPU hours. Unfortunately, none of the problems could be solved to optimality within the time limit. Therefore, the best feasible solutions found and their percent optimality gaps at the termination are reported in Table 1. In the construction heuristics, each sub-problem 2ECON-NDPR(k) was solved using CPLEX V9.0 with a time limit of 1,800 CPU seconds. If the optimal solution of 2ECON-NDPR(k) could not be obtained within this time limit, the best feasible solution was used in the construction heuristics.

The GA was run for 30 random replications with parameters $\mu = 50$, $\rho = 0.1$, and $t_{\max} = 1000$. The best feasible solution, the average, and the percent coefficient of variation of random 30 runs are provided in the table. In each case, the GA was able to find a significantly better solution than the best solution found by integer programming. As it can be seen in the table, the GA outperforms the construction heuristics in all problems. The GA and the construction heuristics are similar in the way solutions are created one commodity at a time. In the construction heuristics, the solution for a single commodity is optimal for that commodity and they are therefore myopic. In the GA, on the other hand, the solution for a single commodity is randomly generated using random costs in the crossover and mutation. Therefore, the GA may consider a broader range of solutions than the greedy construction heuristics.

The GA is highly robust over random replications. The percent coefficient of variation is less than 5% for all cases. As seen in the CPU times, the GA scales well. Computationally, the most expensive operation of the GA is the Suurballe-Tarjan algorithm to find the shortest pairs of edge-disjoint paths, which can be done in $O(M \log_{1+M/N} N)$ (Suurballe and Tarjan 1984). Since the Suurballe-Tarjan algorithm runs for each commodity, CPU time depends on the number of the commodities routed in the network. However, we observed that after finding the shortest

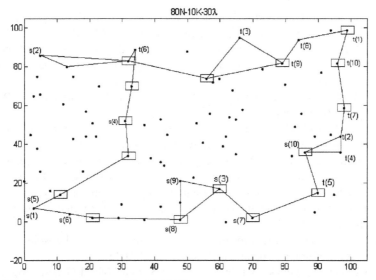

Fig. 2 The best GA solution found for 80-10-30.

paths for the first few commodities, the shortest paths for the remaining ones are determined much faster since they tend to overlap with the already added paths. Therefore, the CPU times did not linearly increase with the number of commodities as it might be expected. Overall, the GA is capable of solving large size problems in reasonably short times. Figure 2 illustrates the best solution found for problem 80-10-30 by the GA.

5 Conclusions and Future Research

In this paper, a GA with specialized crossover and mutation operators was developed to solve the survivable network design problem with relays for the first time. Our initial experiments demonstrate that the GA is very promising in both computational efficiency and in optimization performance. The proposed crossover approach can be extended to other survivable network design problems such as node-disjoint network design problem as a further research.

References

Balakrishnan, A, Altinkemer, K (1992) Using a hop-constrained model to generate alternative communication network design. ORSA Journal on Computing 4: 192-205

Cabral, EA, Erkut, E, Laporte, G, et al. (2007) The network design problem with relays. European Journal of Operational Research 180: 834-844

Choplin, S (2001). Virtual path layout in ATM path with given hop count. Proceedings of the First International Conference on Networking-Part 2, Colmar, France, Springer-Verlag.

Fogel, DB, Bäck, T, Michalewicz, Z (1999) Evolutionary Computation 1. IOP Publishing Ltd, Bristol, UK

Gouveia, L (1996) Multicommodity flow models for spanning trees with hop constraints. European Journal of Operational Research 95: 178-190

Gouveia, L, Magnanti, TL (2003) Network flow models for designing diameter-constrained minimum spanning and Steiner trees. Networks 41: 159-173

Gouveia, L, Requejo, C (2001) A new Lagrangean relaxation approach for the hop-constrained minimum spanning tree problem. European Journal of Operational Research 132: 539-552

Hakimi, SL (1964) Optimum locations of switching centers and absolute centers and medians of graph. Operations Research 12: 450-459

Kulturel-Konak, S, Konak, A (2008) A Local Search Hybrid Genetic Algorithm Approach to the Network Design Problem with Relay Stations. in S. Raghavan, B. L. Golden and E. Wasil (ed) Telecommunications Modeling, Policy, and Technology. Springer, New York

Kwangil, L, Shayman, MA (2005) Optical network design with optical constraints in IP/WDM networks. IEICE Transactions on Communications E88-B: 1898-1905

LeBlanc, L, Reddoch, R (1990). Reliable link topology/capacity design and routing in backbone telecommunication networks. First ORSA Telecommunications SIG Conference.

Magnanti, TL, Mirchandani, P, Vachani, R (1995) Modeling and solving the two-facility capacitated network loading problem. Operations Research 43: 142-157

Monma, CL, Shallcross, DF (1989) Methods for designing communications networks with certain two-connected survivability constraints. Operations Research 37: 531-541

Randall, M, McMahon, G, Sugden, S (2002) A simulated annealing approach to communication network design. Journal of Combinatorial Optimization 6: 55-65

Suurballe, JW, Tarjan, RE (1984) A quick method for finding shortest pairs of disjoint paths. Networks 14: 325-336

Voss, S (1999) The Steiner tree problem with hop constraints. Annals of Operations Research 86: 321-345

Part 3.2
Routing

Generating Random Test Networks for Shortest Path Algorithms

Dennis J. Adams-Smith and Douglas R. Shier

Abstract One of the pillars in the empirical testing of algorithms is the generation of representative and suitably informative test problems. We investigate the particular case of generating random test networks for shortest path problems and discuss several methods proposed for generating such networks. Both analytic and simulation results reveal several pitfalls to avoid in the generation of test networks. We also identify two particular generation methods having desirable characteristics.

Key words: network generator, random test problems, shortest paths

1 Introduction

Networks are pervasive in our technological society, where transportation, logistics, telecommunication, and computer networks play an increasingly important role. A variety of exact and heuristic algorithms are regularly used to route goods, messages, and tasks. Typically there are competing algorithms available for solving network optimization problems, so that both theoretical and empirical analyses are used to identify bottleneck operations and to assess the relative efficiencies of network algorithms. Ideally, one would like to delineate portions of the parameter space (e.g., number of nodes, number of edges) over which certain algorithms are preferred.

To aid in the empirical evaluation of algorithms, both standard benchmark problems and randomly generated problems are used. Benchmark problems are typically real-world problems possessing characteristics of networks encountered

Dennis J. Adams-Smith
Department of Mathematical Sciences, Clemson University, Clemson SC 29634-0975, e-mail: dadamss@clemson.edu

Douglas R. Shier
Department of Mathematical Sciences, Clemson University, Clemson SC 29634-0975, e-mail: shierd@clemson.edu

J.W. Chinneck et al. (eds.), *Operations Research and Cyber-Infrastructure*, Operations Research/Computer Science Interfaces Series 47, DOI: 10.1007/978-0-387-88843-9_15,
© Springer Science+Business Media, LLC 2009

in transportation and communication applications. It is common to supplement the testing of algorithms on real-world problems by also generating random test problems. Such random generation has a number of advantages: the experimenter can vary the network parameters (and thus systematically explore the parameter space), the generated problems can be analyzed by statistical means (Coffin, Saltzman, 2000), and an unlimited set of synthetic problems can be readily reproduced by other investigators.

In this paper, we focus on the generation of random test networks for shortest path algorithms, which are important not only for efficient solution of routing and scheduling problems, but also for problems that arise in cartography, data compression, and DNA sequencing (Ahuja et al., 1993). The remainder of this section provides relevant terminology. In Section 2 we survey a number of generation methods that have been deployed in the testing of shortest path algorithms. Exact results for an illustrative small example are provided in Section 3, and more extensive computational results from our simulation experiments are discussed in Section 4. Conclusions and areas for further research are presented in Section 5.

A (directed) network $G = (N, E)$ consists of a set N of n nodes and a set E of m directed edges. The cost of edge (i, j) is denoted c_{ij}. The number of incoming edges to a node is its *indegree* and the number of outgoing edges is its *outdegree*. The *density* δ of network G is defined as $\delta = \frac{m}{n}$; it represents the average indegree, as well as the average outdegree, of a node in G.

A root node r is also specified. Network G is *root-connected* if there is a (directed) path from the root node r to every other node in the network. The *single-source shortest path problem* involves finding a minimum cost directed path from the source node r to every other node in the network. A solution to this problem is given by a *shortest path tree*: that is, a tree rooted at r whose (unique) r-j path is a shortest path from node r to node j. Notice that in a root-connected network, every node is accessible from the source r and so a shortest path tree spans the entire node set N. We argue that root-connectivity is a highly desirable property for randomly generated test networks. In this way, each generated network will require a shortest path algorithm to work to its fullest: finite shortest path distances will need to be found for *every* node in N, not just some (uncontrolled) subset of N. This requirement has the added benefit of reducing variability in solution times when R replications of an experiment are conducted with a fixed network size, but a randomly generated topology and cost structure.

2 Approaches for Generating Random Networks

The goal of generating random networks for use in shortest path algorithm testing is to (randomly) generate a certain number R of networks $G = (N, E)$ of fixed size $n = |N|$, $m = |E|$ that are root-connected. We investigate seven generation approaches. The first method generates a truly random root-connected network, which becomes our "gold standard" against which other approaches will be measured.

The remaining methods generate a random sparse structure and then randomly add the remaining edges; the random structure takes the form of a spanning tree, a Hamiltonian cycle, or a structure based on indegrees. Once such a "random" topology has been fully constructed, edge costs c_{ij} can be generated according to various cost models (e.g., uniform or normal). For the most part, we will focus on the network topology, and not the costs. In particular, we will emphasize the trade-offs between "true randomness" (uniformity) and computational effort in the various generation methods.

2.1 $G_{n,m}$ with Root-Connectivity

Using the $G_{n,m}$ random graph model (Bollobás, 1985), we randomly generate m distinct directed edges joining the n nodes. (The method for doing this is straightforward, but to ensure distinct edges it is advantageous to employ a hash function (Aho et al., 1974).) In this procedure each selection of m edges will be as equally likely as any other selection of m edges. This method has been used in various computational studies of shortest path algorithms (Dial et al., 1979; Glover et al., 1985). By contrast, we insist here that the generated network G should be root-connected. Computationally, it is advantageous to first check the indegree of every node in the generated network G. If every node has indegree at least one, then we conduct a breadth-first search from the root r to check that every node is reachable from r. If either check fails, the network is discarded and a new candidate network is generated. Since the $G_{n,m}$ method produces networks uniformly among all (n, m) networks, it will produce root-connected networks uniformly among all such networks and is henceforth denoted the *Uniform* method. We repeat this process until we have generated R root-connected test networks of fixed size (n, m).

Unfortunately, this technique is computationally demanding, especially when network densities are low. Erdős and Rényi (1959) specify a threshold density of $\delta > 0.5 \ln n$ random edges before it is reasonable to expect (weak) connectivity — and this is connectivity in the *undirected* sense, not root-connectivity. Thus, we may need to generate and subsequently reject large numbers of networks before finding acceptable ones. As one example, it was necessary to generate 2,122,478 random networks with 100 nodes and 250 edges ($\delta = 2.5$) in order to produce 200 that were root-connected.

2.2 Rooted Spanning Tree Structures

Because of the large overhead of generating networks only to discard most of them for lack of root-connectivity, several methods have been proposed that ensure root-connectivity by first growing a spanning tree on the n nodes; the remaining $m - (n - 1)$ edges are then randomly added. Several methods have been developed for evolving such a spanning tree T, rooted at node r.

2.2.1 Prim's Algorithm

Initially, we set $T = \{r\}$. A natural method to grow a rooted spanning tree is to successively pick a random node $i \in T$ and connect it to a randomly selected node $j \notin T$. Conceptually this can be viewed as an implementation of Prim's MST algorithm (Ahuja et al., 1993) on the complete directed graph with uniform edge weights. Previous computational studies have employed this method (Gilsinn, Witzgall, 1973; Hulme, Wisniewski, 1978; Van Horn et al., 2003). However, this method might create trees with a demonstrable bias, since the longer a node is in the current tree T the more often it will be selected as the origin node i; hence it will have a higher (out) degree than nodes i added later in the process. Consequently, the rooted tree T generated by Prim is unlikely to be uniformly drawn from the set of all spanning trees rooted at r. In particular, the outdegree in T of the root node r should be on average higher than occurs under uniform generation. After adding the additional $m - (n - 1)$ random edges, the root should then continue to have too large an outdegree in the generated network G. These predictions are supported by both analytic and simulation results; see Sections 3 and 4.

2.2.2 Kruskal's Algorithm

Analogous to using Prim's algorithm to create a spanning tree rooted at r, we can similarly adapt Kruskal's MST algorithm (Ahuja et al., 1993). Conceptually, we create a complete undirected network on n nodes and assign random edge weights. Then we apply Kruskal's algorithm to find a (minimum) spanning tree in this weighted complete network. Whereas at each iteration of Prim's algorithm, nodes are added to the current tree T, Kruskal's algorithm adds edges to the current forest at each iteration. This is classically accomplished by sorting the edges according to their (random) weights and then examining the edges in order of nondecreasing weight. Equivalently, we can simply examine the edges in a fixed, random order. If the edge connects two nodes in different subtrees, we retain it and merge the associated subtrees. In this way, subtrees will grow and merge until a spanning tree T is created. We then perform a breadth-first search from the root r and direct all edges outward to obtain a rooted spanning tree. Again the additional $m - (n - 1)$ edges are randomly added to T. As the computational results in Section 4 indicate, this method is a (surprisingly) less biased approach than Prim's method.

2.2.3 Broder's Random Walk

Broder (1989) describes a random walk algorithm for producing a spanning tree in an arbitrary connected, undirected graph H. This method produces spanning trees *uniformly* over all the spanning trees of H. Conceptually, we can apply this method to the complete graph on n nodes to create a random rooted spanning tree T. Namely, we initialize $T = \{r\}$ and begin the random walk at node r. At each step, we continue the random walk (by selecting a random neighbor of the current node $i \in T$) until we encounter a node $j \notin T$; at this point we add to the current tree T the directed edge (i, j). The random walk then continues from node j. We stop once all nodes are in T. Early in the process, edges are more likely to lead to a node outside the current tree, while later on we are more likely to continue walking among the nodes of T in search of a new node $j \notin T$ to add. By using a random walk among the nodes, Broder's method reduces the bias introduced by Prim's algorithm, in which nodes that have been in the tree longer have higher outdegree. This method has been used in a recent computational study of label-correcting shortest path algorithms (Bardossy, Shier, 2006).

2.2.4 Wilson's Random Walk

Wilson (1996) proposes creating a rooted spanning tree by a random walk of a directed graph H. This method is guaranteed to produce rooted spanning trees uniformly from all r-rooted spanning trees of H. Here, we initialize $T = \{r\}$ and begin the random walk at a random node $j \notin T$. We continue a random walk from j tracing out a path P until we encounter a node $i \in T$. At this point all edges of P are added to T. By keeping a successor function on the nodes of P, we can ensure that this path is a *simple* path: i.e., it contains no embedded directed cycles. For example, suppose the current path is $P = [i_1, i_2, i_3, i_4]$ with $\mathrm{succ}(i_1) = i_2$, $\mathrm{succ}(i_2) = i_3$, and $\mathrm{succ}(i_3) = i_4$. If the next random step takes us back to node i_2 and then continues on to node i_5, we would update $\mathrm{succ}(i_4) = i_2$ and $\mathrm{succ}(i_2) = i_5$. Following the updated successors then traces out the simple path $P = [i_1, i_2, i_5]$, in effect "cancelling" out the directed cycle traversed in the random walk. By continuing this process, the edges of a spanning tree directed into the root node r will be grown. Once every node is in T, we can reverse all edges to obtain a rooted spanning tree directed away from the root r. Notice that Wilson's walk, which conducts a random walk *outside* the current tree, adds an entire path P to the tree; however, extraneous cycles may be traversed before adding new valid edges to the current T.

2.3 Hamiltonian Cycle Generator

Rather than adding $n - 1$ edges to form a rooted spanning tree, one can create a random Hamiltonian cycle, involving the addition of n edges. This is easily done by creating a random permutation $\pi_1, \pi_2, \ldots, \pi_n$ of $\{1, 2, \ldots, n\}$ and then adding the edges $(\pi_1, \pi_2), \ldots, (\pi_{n-1}, \pi_n), (\pi_n, \pi_1)$. Then the remaining $m - n$ additional edges are randomly added to the network. Several computational studies (Goldberg, 2001; Klingman et al., 1974; Mondou et al., 1991; Skriver, Andersen, 2000) have used this type of generation technique. A possible drawback to this approach is that the graph density must be high enough to expect a naturally occurring directed Hamiltonian cycle. For *undirected* random graphs G, there is a threshold function on the density for the likely appearance of a Hamiltonian cycle: namely, we need $\delta > 0.5 \ln n$ to expect the occurrence of a Hamiltonian cycle in G. Consequently, this generation method might be creating a structure that will distort the resulting distribution of sparse test networks.

2.4 One-In Generator

To avoid the possible pitfalls in creating a fixed structure before adding random edges, while still reducing the computational overhead associated with the Uniform method in Section 2.1, we propose a "one-in" method. This method starts by creating an edge directed into every node (except the root r) from a random predecessor. We then add the remaining $m - (n - 1)$ random edges and check the resulting graph for root-connectivity via a breadth-first search. If the check fails, the network is discarded and a new candidate is generated. By ensuring that no node is isolated (except possibly the root), this approach saves much of the computational overhead associated with the Uniform method. For example, whereas the Uniform method in Section 2.1 required generating 2,122,478 random networks with 100 nodes and 250 edges in order to find 200 that were root-connected, the One-In method generated only 228 random networks to find 200 that were root-connected.

3 Analytic Results

We begin by presenting exact analytic results for the various generation methods, obtained by examining a small, but revealing, example with $n = 4$ nodes, $m = 8$ edges and root node $r = 1$. Of the 12 possible directed edges between 4 nodes, we select only 8, so there are $\binom{12}{8} = 495$ possible graphs of this type. Of these, only 456 are root-connected. The remaining 39 are simply those graphs whose $12 - 8 = 4$ nonselected edges contain a cutset $(X, \bar{X})$ with $1 \in X$. Specifically, if $X = \{1\}$, $X = \{1,2,3\}$, $X = \{1,2,4\}$, or $X = \{1,3,4\}$ we can remove the three edges of the cutset $(X, \bar{X})$ plus any of 9 other choices for the fourth edge. If $X = \{1,2\}$, $X = \{1,3\}$, or $X = \{1,4\}$, we remove all four edges of $(X, \bar{X})$. Altogether, there are a total of $4 \times 9 + 3 \times 1 = 39$ possible graphs (on 4 nodes and 8 edges) that are not root-connected.

Since the Uniform method generates each of the 456 root-connected graphs with equal probability, we can exactly calculate certain theoretical measures associated with this generation technique. In particular, we compute the mean root degree (the outdegree of node r), the mean number of nodes $D_2(G)$ at distance 2 from r in G, and the rooted diameter of G (the maximum distance from r to any of the other nodes of G). This yields the entries in the first row of Table 1. Results for the other generation techniques appear in the remaining rows.

Table 1 Exact results for graphs with 4 nodes, 8 edges

Method	Mean Root Degree	Mean $D_2(G)$	Mean Diameter
Uniform	2.059	0.862	1.803
Prim	2.481	0.511	1.471
Kruskal	2.333	0.649	1.590
Random Spanning Tree	2.333	0.649	1.591
Hamiltonian Cycle	2.000	0.929	1.857
One-In	2.111	0.790	1.701

Table 2 Frequency distribution of the 16 spanning trees using the Prim and Kruskal methods

	T_1	T_2	T_3	T_4	T_5	T_6	T_7	T_8
Root Degree	1	2	1	2	2	1	1	1
Prim Frequency	1	3	1	3	3	1	2	1
Kruskal Frequency	11	11	11	11	11	11	12	11

	T_9	T_{10}	T_{11}	T_{12}	T_{13}	T_{14}	T_{15}	T_{16}
Root Degree	1	1	1	2	2	3	1	2
Prim Frequency	1	2	1	3	3	6	2	3
Kruskal Frequency	11	12	11	11	11	12	12	11

First we note that the mean root degree for the Uniform method is slightly larger than the graph density $\delta = \frac{m}{n} = 2$; this occurs because we are averaging over the 456 root-connected graphs $G_1, G_2, ..., G_{456}$ rather than the 495 random graphs. Next we examine the generation methods based on first producing a rooted spanning tree and then generating additional random edges. As seen in Table 1, the Prim method produces highly biased graphs, with an average root degree much larger than that for the Uniform method. This bias can be explained as follows. In this example there are $n^{n-2} = 4^2 = 16$ rooted spanning trees $T_1, T_2, ..., T_{16}$; these spanning trees are shown explicitly in (Adams-Smith, Shier, 2008). Rather than generating these T_i uniformly, Prim's method generates them according to the frequency distribution shown in Table 2. This table also lists the root degree of each spanning tree T_i. Notice that T_{14}, which has the largest root degree, occurs with by far the largest Prim frequency, verifying our suspicion that the Prim method favors spanning trees with large root degrees. By contrast, if these T_i are uniformly generated, then the mean root degree of the spanning tree would be 1.5; using the Prim frequencies, however, produces the larger mean root degree of 1.833. Table 2 also shows the frequency of occurrence of the 16 rooted spanning trees obtained using Kruskal's method. Interestingly enough, in this case the spanning trees are generated approximately uniformly and the mean root degree turns out to be 1.5 (the same as if generated uniformly).

The generation methods of Broder and Wilson do uniformly generate the spanning trees T_i and then randomly add the remaining edges. After creating such a spanning tree, here containing 3 edges, there are $\binom{9}{5} = 126$ ways to pick 5 additional

Table 3 Frequency distribution of the 456 root-connected graphs among 2016 generated graphs

Number of Appearances	Number of Graphs	Number of Appearances	Number of Graphs
1	39	7	24
2	48	8	21
3	114	9	27
4	60	10	0
5	54	11	0
6	63	12	6

distinct edges from the 9 remaining, giving $16 \cdot 126 = 2016$ ways to generate a root-connected $(4,8)$-graph. However, the 456 root-connected graphs G_i do *not* appear with equal probability among these 2016 generated $(4,8)$-graphs; see Table 3.

In summary, Table 1 shows that the Prim method produces the largest bias in terms of generated graphs, according to any of the three metrics used. On the other hand, both the Hamiltonian Cycle and One-In methods are the closest to the Uniform method, which guarantees uniform generation of the root-connected graphs. While the Kruskal method does not ensure uniform generation of the initial spanning tree T, it gives results virtually the same as those of Broder and Wilson (which do ensure uniform generation of T). The spanning tree methods of Kruskal, Broder and Wilson show intermediate bias, situated between the Hamiltonian Cycle/One-In and Prim methods. The lesson here is that uniformly generating a spanning tree and then adding random edges does not produce graphs that are sufficiently representative for our purposes.

4 Computational Results

The analytic results in Section 3 show that clear differences appear in the various generation techniques for the small sample network studied. In this section, we study randomly generated larger networks having n nodes and m edges, with R replications for each fixed n and m. Specifically, we investigate $n = 100, 200, 400$ and a range of densities: $\delta = 2.5, 3, 3.5, 4, 4.5, 5, 6$ for $n = 100$; $\delta = 3, 3.25, 4, 5, 7.5, 10, 12.5, 15, 17.5, 20, 22.5, 25$ for $n = 200$; and $\delta = 5, 6.25, 7.5, 10, 12.5, 15$ for $n = 400$. To ensure consistency, all generation algorithms were coded in MATLAB and computational results were obtained using MATLAB 7.2.0.283 (R2006a), executed on a Sun V440 with 16GB RAM, 4x1.6GHz CPU, running Solaris 10. Some representative results are presented in Table 4 for $n = 200$ and $m = 800$ (i.e., $\delta = 4$), and in Table 5 for $n = 400$ and $m = 4000$ (i.e., $\delta = 10$). All results are averaged over $R = 200$ repetitions. Since the rooted diameter turned out to be a less discriminating measure, we have only listed standard deviations for the first two measures.

Tables 4 and 5 order the generation methods approximately by their similarity to the Uniform method. Note that in each table, the mean root degree ranks the

Table 4 Computational results for networks with $n = 200$, $m = 800$, $R = 200$

Method	Root Degree		$D_2(G)$		Diameter
	Mean	Std Dev	Mean	Std Dev	Mean
Uniform	4.195	1.946	15.955	8.001	6.465
One-In	3.995	1.888	15.300	7.855	6.335
Hamiltonian Cycle	3.860	1.601	14.490	6.458	6.350
Wilson	4.950	1.951	19.595	7.979	6.020
Kruskal	4.980	2.093	19.810	8.279	5.955
Broder	5.025	2.092	20.040	8.339	5.925
Prim	8.890	2.710	40.900	10.803	5.175

Table 5 Computational results for networks with $n = 400$, $m = 4000$, $R = 200$

Method	Root Degree		$D_2(G)$		Diameter
	Mean	Std Dev	Mean	Std Dev	Mean
Uniform	9.890	3.021	85.280	23.119	4.030
Hamiltonian Cycle	9.900	2.756	86.060	22.834	4.015
One-In	10.145	3.128	88.125	25.022	4.040
Wilson	10.810	3.160	92.260	24.261	4.020
Broder	10.910	3.177	93.610	25.281	4.025
Kruskal	11.345	3.257	96.760	24.586	4.015
Prim	15.145	3.570	131.585	25.188	3.975

generation methods in exactly the same order as the mean $D_2(G)$ value; this is to be expected since a larger number of nodes adjacent to the root tends to produce a larger number of nodes at distance 2 from the root. Given the generally high correlation between these two metrics (root degree and $D_2(G)$), we focus on the root degree in comparing the various generation techniques. These tables show that the One-In and Hamiltonian Cycle methods produce networks with characteristics most similar to the desired Uniform method. Broder, Wilson, and Kruskal produce networks with a demonstrable bias (specifically, a much higher mean root degree). The Prim method produces extremely atypical networks; for example, Table 4 shows that the mean root degree is over twice as large as that for the Uniform method.

We carried out a standard two-sample t-test (with unequal variances) to compare the mean root degrees of networks generated by the different methods, for the data in Tables 4 and 5. This analysis showed that there were no statistically significant differences between the One-In and Hamiltonian Cycle methods (at the $\alpha = .05$ significance level), nor were there significant differences between these methods and the Uniform method. Also, there were no statistically significant differences in comparing the Broder, Wilson, and Kruskal methods. On the other hand, we found that the Broder, Wilson, and Kruskal methods had significantly larger means than that for the Uniform method (at the $\alpha = .001$ significance level). The mean root degree for Prim was at least 11 standard deviations greater than the means for Broder, Wilson, and Kruskal.

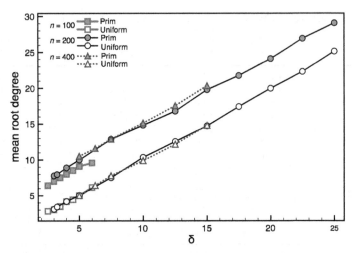

Fig. 1 Prim versus Uniform as a function of δ

These conclusions hold for other network sizes. Namely, the generation techniques cluster into the groups {Uniform, One-In, Hamiltonian Cycle}, {Broder,
Wilson, Kruskal}, and {Prim}, with the groups ranked by their proximity to the
"gold standard" Uniform method. More extensive tabulations are available (Adams-
Smith, Shier, 2008) for the entire range of network sizes (n, m) studied.

Figure 1 compares the mean root degree, as a function of the density δ, for the
Prim method and the Uniform method. It is clear that the substantial bias for Prim
persists at all network sizes (n, m) studied. Examination of Figure 1 suggests that
this bias increases with the number of nodes n. In fact, using a result from the theory
of recursive trees (Smythe, Mahmoud, 1995), we can show that the average root
degree of Prim-generated networks grows as $\delta + O(\ln n)$, establishing that the bias
of the Prim method indeed increases with the number of nodes n. Figure 2 compares
the One-In and Hamiltonian Cycle methods to Uniform for networks with 200 nodes
and varying densities; for comparsion, one of the random spanning tree methods
(Wilson) is also displayed. We can see that One-In and Hamiltonian Cycle track
fairly closely the Uniform method. Figure 3 verifies this conclusion for $n = 100$ and
$n = 400$ as well.

5 Conclusions

Both analytic and simulation results have demonstrated that the characteristics of
"random" test networks generated by alternative techniques can vary substantially,
especially when measured relative to our gold standard Uniform method. Since the
Uniform method can be computationally demanding for the generation of large test
networks (too many networks are rejected as not being root-connected), we have

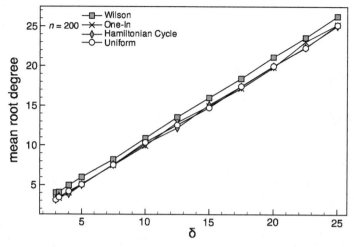

Fig. 2 One-In, Hamiltonian Cycle, and Wilson versus Uniform as a function of δ: $n = 200$

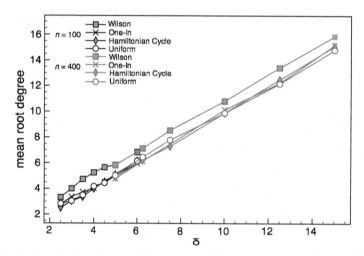

Fig. 3 One-In, Hamiltonian Cycle, and Wilson versus Uniform as a function of δ: $n = 100, n = 400$

studied here six other generation approaches. While the Prim method is often used, and is computationally viable, it displays clear bias in the various metrics presented here. To a large extent this bias results from the nonuniform generation of the initial spanning tree T. The Broder and Wilson methods do ensure uniform generation of the spanning tree T, yet they still produce nonuniform test networks, though with not such a pronounced bias as the Prim-generated networks. The Kruskal method, another MST-based approach, is surprisingly less biased than the Prim method; however its implementation involves ranking all $O(n^2)$ edges of the complete undirected graph and is computationally less efficient. The two best methods identified are the Hamiltonian Cycle and One-In methods. Both of these methods are easy to

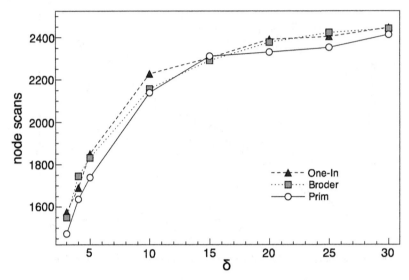

Fig. 4 Number of node scans for FIFO as a function of δ using One-In, Broder, and Prim

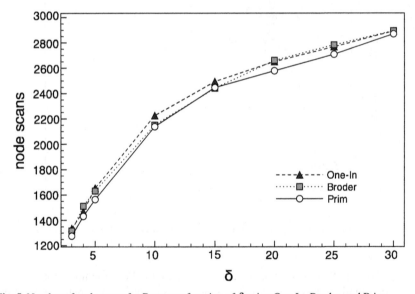

Fig. 5 Number of node scans for Pape as a function of δ using One-In, Broder, and Prim

implement and are computationally feasible. The Hamiltonian Cycle method is generally applicable except when the network is very sparse, in which case the underlying graph would not be expected to contain a Hamiltonian cycle. The One-In method is applicable in all cases, though it does require checking for root-connectivity after a potential network has been generated. This does not however appear to impose a large computational burden.

A natural next step is to investigate the extent to which these different network characteristics can affect the conclusions of empirical studies conducted on network algorithms. As a first step in that direction, we have studied two standard shortest path algorithms (FIFO and Pape) and have counted the number of *node scans* (Bardossy, Shier, 2006) to find a shortest path tree rooted at node $r = 1$ in randomly generated networks with $n = 1000$ nodes. Results for selected generation methods are shown for the two algorithms in Figures 4 and 5, averaged over $R = 100$ replications at each network density δ. We can see that Prim tends to create easier problems (fewer node scans) over a wide range of densities δ for both FIFO and Pape, whereas One-In tends to create more demanding problems. By comparison, the Broder method creates problems of intermediate complexity; specifically it tends to create easier problems at lower densities but harder ones at higher densities.

Acknowledgements The authors are appreciative of the thoughtful suggestions provided by Neil Calkin in developing the One-In generation approach.

References

Adams-Smith DJ, Shier DR (2008) Random generation of shortest path test networks. http://www.math.clemson.edu/˜shierd/Shier/

Aho AV, Hopcroft JE, Ullman JD (1974) The design and analysis of computer algorithms. Addison-Wesley, Reading, MA

Ahuja RK, Magnanti TL, Orlin JB (1993) Network flows: Theory, algorithms, and applications. Prentice Hall, Englewood Cliffs, NJ

Bardossy MG, Shier DR (2006) Label-correcting shortest path algorithms revisited. In: F. Alt et al. (eds.) Perspectives in Operations Research, pp. 179–197. Springer, New York

Bollobás B (1985) Random graphs. Academic Press, London

Broder A (1989) Generating random spanning trees. 30th Annual Symposium on the Foundations of Computer Science, pp. 442–447. IEEE Computer Society, Piscataway, NJ

Coffin M, Saltzman MJ (2000) Statistical analysis of computational tests of algorithms and heuristics. INFORMS J Comput 12: 24–44

Dial R, Glover F, Karney D, Klingman D (1979) A computational analysis of alternative algorithms and techniques for finding shortest path trees. Networks 9: 215–248

Erdős P, Rényi A (1959) On random graphs I. Publ Math-Debrecen 6: 290–297

Gilsinn J, Witzgall C (1973) A performance comparison of labeling algorithms for calculating shortest path trees. NBS Technical Note 772, U.S. Department of Commerce

Glover F, Klingman D, Phillips N, Schneider R (1985) New polynomial shortest path algorithms and their computational attributes. Manage Sci 31: 1106–1128

Goldberg AV (2001) Shortest path algorithms: Engineering aspects. In: Algorithms and Computation, Lecture Notes in Computer Science 2223, pp. 502–513. Springer, Berlin

Hulme B, Wisniewski J (1978) A comparison of shortest path algorithms applied to sparse graphs. Sandia Technical Note 78-1411, Sandia Laboratories

Klingman D, Napier A, Stutz J (1974) NETGEN: A program for generating large scale capacitated assignment, transportation, and minimum cost flow network problems. Manage Sci 20: 814–821

Mondou JF, Crainic T, Nguyen S (1991) Shortest path algorithms: A computational study with the C programming language. Comput Oper Res 18: 767–786

Skriver AJV, Andersen KA (2000) A label correcting approach for solving bicriterion shortest-path problems. Comput Oper Res 27: 507–524

Smythe RT, Mahmoud HM (1995) A survey of recursive trees. Theor Probab Math Stat 51: 1–27

Van Horn M, Richter A, Lopez D (2003) A random graph generator. 36th Annual Midwest Instruction and Computing Symposium. Duluth, MN. http://www.micsymposium.org/mics_2003/VanHorn.PDF

Wilson D (1996) Generating random spanning trees more quickly than the cover time. Proceedings of the Twenty-Eighth Annual ACM Symposium on the Theory of Computing, pp. 296–303. ACM, New York

A Branch-and-Price Algorithm for Combined Location and Routing Problems Under Capacity Restrictions

Z. Akca, R.T. Berger, and T.K. Ralphs

Abstract We investigate the problem of simultaneously determining the location of facilities and the design of vehicle routes to serve customer demands under vehicle and facility capacity restrictions. We present a set-partitioning-based formulation of the problem and study the relationship between this formulation and the graph-based formulations that have been used in previous studies of this problem. We describe a branch-and-price algorithm based on the set-partitioning formulation and discuss computational experience with both exact and heuristic variants of this algorithm.

Key words: branch-and-price, facility location, vehicle routing, column generation

1 Introduction

The design of a distribution system begins with the questions of where to locate the facilities and how to allocate customers to the selected facilities. These questions can be answered using location-allocation models, which are based on the assumption that customers are served individually on out-and-back routes. However, when customers have demands that are less-than-truckload and thus can receive service from routes making multiple stops, the assumption of individual routes will not accurately capture the transportation cost. Therefore, the integration of location-allocation and routing decisions may yield more accurate and cost-effective solutions.

Z. Akca
Department of Industrial and Systems Engineering, Lehigh University, Bethlehem, PA 18015, e-mail: zea2@lehigh.edu

R.T. Berger
18 Whittemore Street, Concord, MA 01742, e-mail: rosemary.berger@verizon.net

T.K. Ralphs
Department of Industrial and Systems Engineering, Lehigh University, Bethlehem, PA 18015, e-mail: ted@lehigh.edu, http://coral.ie.lehigh.edu/~ted

J.W. Chinneck et al. (eds.), *Operations Research and Cyber-Infrastructure*, Operations Research/Computer Science Interfaces Series 47, DOI: 10.1007/978-0-387-88843-9_16, © Springer Science+Business Media, LLC 2009

In this paper, we investigate the so-called *location and routing problem* (LRP). Given a set of candidate facility locations and a set of customer locations, the objective of the LRP is to determine the number and location of facilities and construct a set of vehicle routes from facilities to customers in such a way as to minimize total system cost. The system cost may include both the fixed and operating costs of both facilities and vehicles. In this study, we consider an LRP with capacity constraints on both the facilities and the vehicles.

Vehicle routing models in general have been the subject of a wide range of academic papers, but the number of these devoted to combined location and routing models is much smaller. Laporte (1988) surveyed the work on deterministic LRPs and described different formulations of the problem, solution methods used, and the computational results published up to 1988. Min et al (1998) classified both deterministic and stochastic models in the LRP literature with respect to problem characteristics and solution methods.

Solution approaches for the LRP can be divided broadly into heuristics and exact methods, with much of the literature devoted to heuristic approaches. Most heuristic algorithms divide the problem into subproblems and handle these subproblems sequentially or iteratively. Examples of heuristics developed for the LRP can be found in Perl and Daskin (1985), Hansen et al (1994) and Barreto et al (2007).

Many fewer papers have been devoted to the study of exact algorithms for the LRP and most of these have been based on the so-called two-index vehicle flow formulation. Laporte and Nobert (1981) solved a single depot model with a constraint relaxation method and a branch-and-bound algorithm. They reported solving problems with 50 customer locations. Laporte et al (1983) solved a multi-depot model using a constraint relaxation method and Gomory cutting planes to satisfy integrality. They were able to solve problems with at most 40 customer sites. Laporte et al (1986) applied a branch-and-cut algorithm to a multi-depot LRP model with vehicle capacity constraints. They used subtour elimination constraints and chain barring constraints that guarantee that each route starts and ends at the same facility. They reported computational results for problems with 20 customer locations and 8 depots. Finally, Belenguer et al (2006) provided a two-index formulation of the LRP with capacitated facilities and capacitated vehicles and presented a set of valid inequalities for the problem. They developed two branch-and-cut algorithms based on different formulations of the problem. They reported that they could solve instances with up to 32 customers to optimality in less than 70 CPU seconds and could provide good lower bounds for the rest of the instances, which had up to 134 customers.

Berger (1997) developed a set-partitioning-based model for a special case of the LRP with route length constraints and uncapacitated vehicles and facilities. Berger et al (2007) extended that work to develop an exact branch-and-price algorithm in which they solved the pricing problem as an elementary shortest path problem with one resource constraint. They reported computational results for problems with 100 customers and various distance constraints. Akca et al (2008) developed an exact solution algorithm using branch-and-price methodology for the integrated location routing and scheduling problem (LRSP), which is a generalization of the LRP. In the LRSP, the assumption that each vehicle covers exactly one route is removed and the decision of assigning routes to vehicles subject to the scheduling constraints is considered in conjunction with the location and routing decisions. They considered instances with capacitated facilities and time- and capacity-limited vehicles. They provided solutions for instances with up to 40 customers.

In this study, we utilize a variant of the model presented by Akca et al (2008) to solve the LRP under capacity restrictions and modify their exact algorithm for the LRSP to solve the LRP. We develop a number of variants and heuristic extensions of the basic algorithm and report on our computational experience solving both randomly generated instances and instances from the literature. The remainder of the paper is organized as follows. Section 2 presents a formal description of the problem, provides two formulations, and investigates the relationship between the formulations. Section 3 describes details of the heuristic and the exact algorithms for the set-partitioning formulation. Section 4 provides some computational results evaluating the performance of the algorithms. Section 5 concludes the paper.

2 Problem Definition and Formulations

The objective of the LRP is to select a subset of facilities and construct an associated set of vehicle routes serving customers at minimum total cost, where the cost includes the fixed and operating costs of both facilities and vehicles. The constraints of the problem are as follows: (i) each customer must be serviced by exactly one vehicle, (ii) each vehicle must be assigned to exactly one facility at which it must start and end its route, (iii) the total demand of the customers assigned to a route must not exceed the vehicle capacity, and (iv) the total demand of the customers assigned to a facility must not exceed the capacity of the facility. In the literature, most of the exact methods developed for the described LRP or its special cases are based on the two-index vehicle flow formulation of the problem. To the best of our knowledge, an exact solution algorithm based on a set-partitioning formulation has not been applied to the case of the LRP with capacity constraints. The theoretical relationship between the two-index formulation and the set-partitioning formulation can be understood by considering a closely related three-index formulation that we present below. We show that applying Dantzig-Wolfe decomposition to the three-index formulation yields the set-partitioning formulation. This is turn shows that the bounds yielded by the LP relaxation of the set-partitioning model must be at least as tight as those of the three-index formulation.

2.1 Vehicle Flow Formulation

We let I denote the set of customers, J denote the set of candidate facilities, and $V = I \cup J$. To bypass the decision of assigning vehicles to facilities, we assume that each facility has its own set of vehicles and that a vehicle located at facility j can only visit customer locations and the facility j during its trip. Let H_j be the set of vehicles located at facility j, $\forall j \in J$ and H be the set of all vehicles, $H = \bigcup_{j \in J} H_j$. We define the following parameters and decision variables:

Parameters:

$$D_i = \text{demand of customer } i, \, \forall i \in I,$$
$$C_j^F = \text{capacity of facility } j, \, \forall j \in J,$$
$$C^V = \text{capacity of a vehicle,}$$
$$F_j = \text{fixed cost of opening facility } j, \, \forall j \in J,$$
$$O_{ik} = \text{operating cost of traveling arc } (i,k) \, \forall i,k \in V.$$

Decision Variables:

$$x_{ikh} = \begin{cases} 1 \text{ if vehicle } h \text{ travels directly from location } i \text{ to location } k, \, \forall i \in V, k \in V, \\ \quad h \in H \\ 0 \text{ otherwise,} \end{cases}$$

$$y_{ih} = \begin{cases} 1 \text{ if vehicle } h \text{ visits customer } i, \, \forall i \in I, h \in H \\ 0 \text{ otherwise,} \end{cases}$$

$$t_j = \begin{cases} 1 \text{ if facility } j \text{ is selected to be open, } \forall j \in J \\ 0 \text{ otherwise.} \end{cases}$$

A vehicle flow formulation of the LRP is as follows:

(VF-LRP) Minimize $\displaystyle\sum_{j \in J} F_j t_j + \sum_{h \in H} \sum_{i \in V} \sum_{k \in V} O_{ik} x_{ikh}$ \hfill (1)

s.t. $\displaystyle\sum_{h \in H} \sum_{k \in V} x_{ikh} = 1 \qquad \forall i \in I,$ \hfill (2)

$\displaystyle\sum_{k \in V} x_{ikh} - \sum_{k \in V} x_{kih} = 0 \qquad \forall i \in V, h \in H,$ \hfill (3)

$\displaystyle\sum_{k \in V} x_{kih} - y_{ih} = 0 \qquad \forall i \in I, h \in H,$ \hfill (4)

$\displaystyle y_{ih} - \sum_{k \in S} \sum_{l \in V \setminus S} x_{klh} \leq 0 \qquad \forall S \subseteq I, i \in S, h \in H,$ \hfill (5)

$\displaystyle\sum_{i \in I} D_i y_{ih} - C^V \leq 0 \qquad \forall h \in H,$ \hfill (6)

$\displaystyle\sum_{h \in H_j} \sum_{i \in I} D_i y_{ih} - C_j^F t_j \leq 0 \qquad \forall j \in J,$ \hfill (7)

$x_{ikh} \in \{0,1\} \, \forall i,k \in V, h \in H,$ \hfill (8)

$y_{ih} \in \{0,1\} \, \forall i \in I, h \in H,$ \hfill (9)

$t_j \in \{0,1\} \, \forall j \in J.$ \hfill (10)

In (VF-LRP), the objective function (1) seeks to minimize the total cost, which includes the fixed cost of the selected facilities and the operating cost of the vehicles. Vehicle fixed costs can easily be incorporated into the model by increasing the cost of traveling from the facility to each customer location by a fixed amount. Constraints (2) specify that exactly one vehicle must service customer i. Constraints (3) require that each vehicle should enter and leave a location the same number of times. Constraints (4) determine the assignment of customers to vehicles. Constraints (5) eliminate subtours, i.e. routes that do not include a facility. Constraints (6) are vehicle capacity constraints. Constraints (7) ensure that the capacity of a facility is not exceeded by demand flows to customer locations. For notational convenience, we assume that variables associated with travel between different facilities or travel between a customer and a facility using a truck not associated with that facility are fixed to zero. Constraints (8), (9), and (10) are the set of binary restrictions on the variables.

2.2 Set-Partitioning Formulation

Here we utilize a modified version of the set-partitioning formulation for the LRSP presented by Akca et al (2008). We define the set P to be a set indexing all vehicle routes feasible with respect to vehicle capacity and originating from and returning to the same facility. We let $P_j \subseteq P$ index routes associated with vehicles assigned to facility j for $j \in J$. In addition to the parameters and sets defined for (VF-LRP), we use the following parameters and decision variables:
Parameters:

$$O_p = \text{operating cost of route } p \in P,$$

$$a_{ip} = \begin{cases} 1 & \text{if customer } i \in I \text{ is assigned to route } p \in P, \text{ and} \\ 0 & \text{otherwise.} \end{cases}$$

Decision Variables:

$$z_p = \begin{cases} 1 & \text{if route } p \in P \text{ is selected, and} \\ 0 & \text{otherwise,} \end{cases}$$

$$t_j = \begin{cases} 1 & \text{if facility } j \in J \text{ is selected to be open, and} \\ 0 & \text{otherwise,} \end{cases}$$

The formulation is as follows:

$$\textbf{(SPP) Minimize} \quad \sum_{j \in J} F_j t_j + \sum_{p \in P} O_p z_p \tag{11}$$

$$\text{subject to} \quad \sum_{p \in P} a_{ip} z_p = 1 \quad \forall i \in I, \tag{12}$$

$$\sum_{p \in P_j} \sum_{i \in I} D_i a_{ip} z_p - C_j^F t_j \leq 0 \quad \forall j \in J, \tag{13}$$

$$z_p \in \{0,1\} \ \forall p \in P, \tag{14}$$

$$t_j \in \{0,1\} \ \forall j \in J. \tag{15}$$

The objective function (11) seeks to minimize the total cost, which includes the fixed cost of the selected facilities and the operating cost of the vehicles. Constraints (12) guarantee that each customer location is served by exactly one route. Constraints (13) ensure that the total demand of the selected routes for a facility does not exceed the facility capacity. Constraints (14) and (15) are standard binary restrictions on the variables.

2.3 Comparing the Formulations

Observe that the three-index formulation (VF-LRP) exhibits a high degree of symmetry under the assumption that the vehicle fleet assigned to each facility is homogeneous. This is due to the fact that the assignment of routes to a specific vehicle is essentially arbitrary, i.e., the cost of a given solution to (VF-LRP) is invariant under permutation of the indices assigned to specific vehicles. This symmetry can be dealt with either (i) by using a two-index formulation, which requires the addition of an exponential number of valid inequalities to the formulation or (ii) by applying Dantzig-Wolfe decomposition (DWD). Laporte et al (1986) and Belenguer et al (2006) have each developed branch-and-cut algorithms using the former approach. Here, we explore the latter approach.

As is standard in DWD, we decompose the constraints of (VF-LRP) into two subsystems. The *master problem* is defined by constraints (2) and (7), while the *subproblem* is defined by constraints (3), (4), (5), (6), (8), (9), and (10). All constraints of the subproblem are indexed by the set J and it is therefore immediate that the subproblem decomposes by facility. The objective of each of the resulting single-facility subproblems is to generate least-cost routes for all vehicles assigned to the facility, though without the constraint that customers appear on exactly one route. For each candidate facility $j \in J$, the set of integer solutions of the decomposed subproblem can be represented by the set of vectors

$$\{(x,y,t) \in \mathbb{Z}^{(|V| \times |V| \times |H_j|) \times (|V| \times |H_j|) \times \{0,1\}} \mid (x,y,t) \text{ satisfies } (3)_j, (4)_j, (5)_j,$$
$$(6)_j, (8)_j, (9)_j, (10)_j\},$$

which is described only by those constraints associated with facility j and specifies values only for those variables associated with vehicles assigned to facility j. Hence, the index j for the constraints represents the set of constraints associated with facility j. Let E be a set indexing the members of all of the above sets, with E_j the indices for vectors associated with facility j only, so that $E = \cup_{j \in J} E_j$. For a facility j and an index $q \in E_j$, the corresponding member (x^q, y^q, t^q) of the above set is then a vector with the following interpretation: for each pair $(i,k) \in |V| \times |V|$ and $h \in H_j$, the parameter $x_{ikh}^q = 1$ if vehicle h travels on arc (i,k) in solution q and is 0 otherwise; for each $i \in I$ and $h \in H_j$, $y_{ih}^q = 1$ if customer i is visited by vehicle h in solution q and is 0 otherwise; and $t^q = 1$ if facility j is open in solution q. Note that the variable t indicating whether the facility is open does not appear in any of the linear constraints of the subproblem and can hence be set to either 0 or 1 without affecting feasibility.

Because the subproblem decomposes as described above, solutions to the original problem can be seen as vectors obtained by "recomposing" convex combinations of the members of E_j for each $j \in J$. In other words, any solution (x, y, t) to the LP relaxation of the original problem can be written as:

$$x_{ikh} = \sum_{q \in E} x_{ikh}^q \theta_q \quad \forall i, k \in V, h \in H, \tag{16}$$

$$y_{ih} = \sum_{q \in E} y_{ih}^q \theta_q \quad \forall i \in I, h \in H, \tag{17}$$

$$t_j = \sum_{q \in E_j} t^q \theta_q \quad \forall j \in J, \tag{18}$$

$$\sum_{q \in E_j} \theta_q = 1 \qquad \forall j \in J, \tag{19}$$

$$\theta_q \geq 0 \qquad \forall q \in E. \tag{20}$$

Using (16) - (20), we can then formulate the LP relaxation of the master problem as:

(MDW) Minimize $\displaystyle\sum_{q \in E} \tilde{C}_q \theta_q$

$$\text{s.t.} \qquad \sum_{q \in E} b_{iq} \theta_q = 1 \ \forall i \in I, \tag{21}$$

$$\sum_{q \in E_j} \sum_{i \in I} b_{iq} D_i \theta_q - C_j^F \sum_{q \in E_j} \theta_q t^q \leq 0 \ \forall j \in J, \tag{22}$$

$$\sum_{q \in E_j} \theta_q = 1 \ \forall j \in J, \tag{23}$$

$$\theta_q \geq 0 \ \forall q \in E, \tag{24}$$

where

$$b_{iq} = \sum_{h \in H} \sum_{k \in I} x_{ikh}^q = \sum_{h \in H} y_{ih}^q, \quad \forall i \in I, q \in E,$$

$$\tilde{C}_q = F_q t^q + \sum_{i \in V} \sum_{k \in V} \sum_{h \in H} O_{ik} x_{ikh}^q, \quad \forall q \in E,$$

where $F_q = F_j$ when $q \in E_j$ for $j \in J$. Here, b_{iq} can be interpreted as the number of times customer i is visited in solution q, and $\tilde{C}_q$ is the cost of solution q (including facility fixed cost) for all $q \in E$.

The similar forms of (SPP) and (MDW) should now be evident, but to rigorously show their equivalence, we need to dissect the relationship between set E_j and P_j for a given facility $j \in J$. A member of set E_j consists of a collection of routes assigned to vehicles located at facility j. A member of set P_j, on the other hand, is a single route that can be assigned to any vehicle at facility j. Therefore, a member of E_j can be constructed by associating at most $|H_j|$ members of set P_j and some number of empty routes (zero vectors representing vehicles that are not used) to the vehicles assigned to facility j.

Now, by utilizing the integrality requirements from the original problem and carefully eliminating the indices of symmetric solutions from E, we get a much smaller set that we will show is in one-to-one correspondence with collections of members of P_j of cardinality at most $|H_j|$. We proceed as follows:

1. First, as the vehicles associated with a given facility j are identical, a set of routes from P_j can be assigned to vehicles in any arbitrary order and each route can also visit the customers in either clockwise or counterclockwise order. Hence, we obtain different members of E_j that are all equivalent from the standpoint of both feasibility and cost. To eliminate superfluous equivalent members of E_j, we divide the members of set E_j into equivalence classes, where two members of E_j are considered equivalent if the set of customers assigned to the facility and the partition of that set of customers defined by the routes are identical. It is clear that any two members of E_j that are equivalent by this definition will have exactly the same impact on both cost and feasibility. We then form equivalence classes from which all but one member may safely be eliminated from E_j.

2. Let $\hat{\theta}$ represent a solution to (MDW) for which the corresponding solution in the original space obtained by applying equations (16)-(18) is feasible for the original problem (VF-LRP). From (16) and (8), along with the fact that x_{ikh}^q is binary for $q \in E$, we get that $x_{ikh}^q = 1$ whenever $\hat{\theta}_q > 0$ in the solution to (MDW). In other words, all members q of E_j with $\hat{\theta}_q > 0$ must correspond to routes visiting exactly the same customers in exactly the same order. Hence, we must in fact have $\hat{\theta}_q = 1$ for exactly one $q \in E_j$ for each $j \in J$ and so $\theta_q \in \{0,1\}$ for all $q \in E$.

3. It then follows easily that index q can be removed from E_j if there exist vehicles $h_1, h_2 \in H_j$ such that $x_{ikh_1}^q = x_{ikh_2}^q \ \forall i, k \in V$, where $x_{ikh_1}^q > 0$ for some $i, k \in I$ (i.e., this is not an empty route). In this case, vehicles h_1 and h_2 define exactly the same set of routes, which means that $b_{iq} > 1$ for some $i \in I$. Because of constraint (21), such a solution must have $\hat{\theta}_q = 0$.

4. Finally, from (18) and (22), we can conclude that if $\hat{\theta}_q = 1$ and we have $x_{ikh}^q > 0$ for some $i, k \in V$ and $h \in H$, then t^q must be 1. Hence, we can eliminate any solutions for which $t^q = 0$ that does not correspond to a zero solution (i.e., closed facility). All of this allows us to rewrite (22) in the form

$$\sum_{q \in E_j} \sum_{i \in I} b_{iq} D_i \theta_q - C_j^F \sum_{q \in E_j} \theta_q \leq 0 \ \forall j \in J. \tag{25}$$

If we restrict set E_j according to the rules described above and call the restricted set $\bar{E}_j$ for each $j \in J$, then we can finally conclude the following.

Proposition 1. *There is a one-to-one correspondence between subsets of P_j with cardinality less than $|H_j|$ and members of $\bar{E}_j$.*

The proof follows easily from the definition of sets P_j and $\bar{E}_j$ and the restriction rules. By replacing set E_j with $\bar{E}_j$ for all $j \in J$ in (MDW), as well as replacing (22) with (25) and adding the constraint $\theta_q \in \{0,1\}$ for all $q \in E$, we obtain a new (equivalent) formulation (MDW'). Then, we finally have the equivalence of (SPP) and (MDW) as follows

Proposition 2. *There is a one-to-one correspondence between solutions to (SPP) and solutions to (MDW') such that corresponding solutions also have the same objective function value. Thus, (SPP), (MDW'), and (MDW) are all equivalent.*

3 Solution Algorithm

3.1 Branch-and-Price

Having shown that (SPP) is equivalent to a DWD of (VF-LRP), we now discuss an exact solution algorithm based on a branch-and-price implementation utilizing the formulation (SPP). First, we strengthen the original formulation by adding the following additional valid constraints:

$$\sum_{p \in P_j} a_{ip} z_p - t_j \leq 0 \qquad \forall i \in I, \forall j \in J, \tag{26}$$

$$\sum_{j \in J} t_j \geq N^F, \tag{27}$$

$$\sum_{p \in P_j} z_p = v_j \qquad \forall j \in J, \tag{28}$$

$$\sum_{j \in J} v_j \geq \left\lceil \frac{\sum_{i \in I} D_i}{C^V} \right\rceil \tag{29}$$

$$v_j \geq t_j \qquad \forall j \in J, \tag{30}$$

$$v_j \in \mathbb{Z}^+ \qquad \forall j \in J, \tag{31}$$

where v_j represents the number of vehicles used at facility j, $\forall j \in J$ and N^F is a lower bound on the number of facilities that must be opened in any integer solution, calculated as follows:

$$N^F = \operatorname{argmin}_{\{l=1,\ldots,|J|\}} \left(\sum_{t=1}^{l} C^F_{j_t} \geq \sum_{i \in I} D_i \right) \quad \text{s.t. } C^F_{j_1} \geq C^F_{j_2} \geq \ldots \geq C^F_{j_n}.$$

Constraints (26) force a facility to be open if any customer is assigned to it. Constraint (27) sets a lower bound on the total number of facilities required in any integer feasible solution. Constraints (26) (from Berger et al (2007) and Akca et al (2008)) and constraint (27) (from Akca et al (2008)) are shown computationally to improve the LP relaxation of the model. Constraints (28) are only added to facilitate branching on the integrality of the number of vehicles at each facility in the branch-and-price algorithm. Constraint (29) sets a lower bound for the total number of vehicles in the solution. Finally, constraints (30) force the number of vehicles used at a facility to be at least 1 if the facility is open. We refer to formulation (11)–(15) and (26)–(31) as (SP-LRP) in the rest of the paper.

The formulation (SP-LRP) contains a variable for each possible vehicle route originating from each facility. Hence, the number of routes will be too large to enumerate even for small instances. To solve the LP relaxation of models that contain exponentially many columns, column generation algorithms can be used. By solving a sequence of linear programs and dynamically generating columns eligible to enter the basis, such an algorithm implicitly considers all columns but generates only those that may improve the objective function. In order to generate integer solutions, a branch-and-bound approach is used in combination with the column generation and the overall approach is referred to as branch-and-price. Desrochers et al (1992), Vance et al (1994), Berger et al (2007), and Akca et al (2008) provide examples of branch-and-price algorithms from the literature.

Here, we modify the branch-and-price algorithm used in Akca et al (2008) to solve the LRSP. Therefore, some parts of the algorithm are described only briefly. For details, we refer the reader to Akca et al (2008). To initialize the algorithm, we construct a *restricted master problem* (RMP), that is, an LP relaxation of (SP-LRP) that contains all facility variables (t_j for $j \in J$) and vehicle variables (v_j for $j \in J$), but only a subset of the vehicle route variables (z_p for $p \in P$). The branch-and-price algorithm consists of two main components: an algorithm for solving the *pricing problem* or *column generation subproblem*, which is used to construct new columns in each iteration, and *branching rules*, which specify how to partition the feasible region into subsets to which the algorithm is then applied recursively until exhaustion.

At each iteration of the solution process for the LP relaxation of (SP-LRP), the objective of the column generation subproblem is to find a feasible vehicle route originating from each facility $j \in J$ with minimum reduced cost with respect to the current dual solution of the RMP. The reduced cost of a given route $p \in P$ is

$$\hat{C}_p = O_p - \sum_{i \in N} a_{ip}\pi_i + \sum_{i \in N} a_{ip}D_i\mu_j + \sum_{i \in N} a_{ip}\sigma_{ji} - v_j, \tag{32}$$

where π, μ, σ and v are the dual variables associated with constraints (12), (13), (26), and (28), respectively, from the RMP. Hence, the column generation subproblem for facility $j \in J$ can be formulated as follows:

$$\text{Minimize} \quad \sum_{i \in M} (\sum_{k \in I} (O_{ik} - \pi_k + D_k\mu_j + \sigma_{jk})x_{ik} + O_{ij}x_{ij}) - v_j \tag{33}$$

$$\text{s.t.} \qquad\qquad y_j = 1, \tag{34}$$

$$\sum_{k \in M} x_{ik} = \sum_{k \in M} x_{ki} = y_i \qquad \forall i \in I, \tag{35}$$

$$y_i - \sum_{k \in S} \sum_{l \in V \setminus S} x_{kl} \leq 0 \qquad \forall S \subseteq I, i \in S, \tag{36}$$

$$\sum_{i \in I} D_i y_i - C^V \leq 0, \tag{37}$$

$$x_{ik} \in \{0,1\} \; \forall i,k \in M, \tag{38}$$

$$y_i \in \{0,1\} \; \forall i \in M, \tag{39}$$

where $M = I \cup \{j\}$, $x_{ik} = 1$ if link (i,k) is used in solutions, and $y_i = 1$ if customer i is assigned to the route.

The column generation subproblem above can be seen as an instance of the well-known *elementary shortest path problem with resource constraints* (ESPPRC), which is well-studied and arises as a subproblem in many different routing applications. To cast the above subproblem as an ESPPRC, we consider a network with $|I| + 2$ nodes, one node for each customer, one for the facility j as a source node and a copy of the facility j as a sink node. We assign each customer node a demand equal to its demand in the original problem and let the cost of each arc (i,l) in the network equal the coefficient of x_{il} in (33). A shortest path from source to sink visiting a customer at most once (called *elementary*) and satisfying the constraint that the total demand of customers included in the path does not exceed the vehicle capacity then corresponds to a vehicle route. The total cost of the path plus the fixed cost $-v_j$ is the reduced cost of the associated column.

To solve the ESPPRC, we use Feillet et al (2004)'s label setting algorithm with a single resource (the vehicle capacity). In the algorithm, each path from source to sink that is not dominated by another with respect to vehicle capacity, cost, and the set of nodes that can still be visited is explored. More details on the variants of this approach that were used in the computational experiments are given in Section 3.2 below.

When the pricing problem cannot identify any more columns with negative reduced cost, then the current solution to the LP relaxation of the master problem is optimal. If this optimal LP solution is not integral, then we are forced to branch. Devising good branching rules is an important step in developing a branch-and-price algorithm. Since the LP relaxations of the new nodes generated after branching are also solved using column generation, the branching constraints must be incorporated into the pricing problem and the columns to be generated must satisfy branching constraints for the node. Therefore, the specific branching rules employed may affect the structure of the pricing problem, causing it to become more difficult to solve. Here, we implement the same four branching rules we used for our work on the LRSP: branching on fractional variables t and v, forcing/forbidding the assignment of a specific customer to a specific facility, and forcing/forbidding flow on a single arc (originally used in Desrochers and Soumis (1989)). All branching rules can easily be incorporated into the pricing problem without changing the structure. Details on the effect of these rules on the pricing problem and the implementation of them can be found in Akca et al (2008).

3.2 Solving the Column Generation Subproblem

The ESPPRC is an NP-hard optimization problem, but small instances may generally be solved effectively in practice using dynamic programming-based labeling algorithms. In general, the number of labels that must be generated and evaluated in the label setting algorithm increases as either the number of customers or the vehicle capacity increases. To enhance efficiency, we therefore augment the basic scheme with some heuristic versions of the algorithm, since it is not necessary to find the column with the most negative reduced cost in every iteration. We refer to the exact pricing algorithm (that is guaranteed to produce a column with the smallest reduced cost) as ESPPRC. The following are heuristic versions of the exact algorithm and are not guaranteed to produce a column with negative reduced cost when one exists.

ESPPRC-LL(n). The ESPPRC algorithm keeps all non-dominated labels at each node. Depending on the size of the instance, the number of labels kept can become very large. In this heuristic version proposed by Dumitrescu (2002), we set a limit n on the number of unprocessed labels stored at each node. At each iteration, labels are sorted based on reduced cost and among the unprocessed labels, the n with smallest reduced cost are kept and the rest are permanently deleted. Therefore, the ESPPRC-LL(n) algorithm tends to terminate much more quickly than the ESPPRC for small values of n.

ESPPRC-CS(n). The ESPPRC algorithm is efficient for instances with small numbers of customers. In addition, the total number of customers in a route is restricted by the vehicle capacity. To be able to take advantage of this, we choose a subset of customers C_S with size n based on the cost of arcs in the network (coefficients of link variables in (33)). Since the objective of the pricing problem is to find a route with smallest reduced cost, we determine the n customers in the subset by constructing a minimum spanning tree over the customer locations. We stop the spanning tree algorithm when we have n customers in the tree. The first customer in the subset (and the tree) is chosen based on the cost of the links from source to customers. Then to find valid vehicle routes, we run ESPPRC that include only customers in C_S.

2-Cyc-SPPRC-PE(n). The shortest path problem with resource constraints (SPPRC) is a relaxation of the ESPPRC in which the path may visit some customers more than once. The SPPRC is solvable in pseudo-polynomial time, but use of this further relaxation of the column generation subproblem results in reduced bounds. Eliminating solutions containing cycles of length two strengthens this relaxation of the pricing problem and improves the bound (for details of the algorithm, see Irnich and Desaulniers (2005)). We refer to this pricing algorithm as 2-Cyc-SPPRC. In addition, we can also generate paths that are elementary with respect to a given subset of customers. We call the resulting algorithm 2-Cyc-SPPRC-PE(n), where n is the size of the customer set to be considered. At each iteration of the pricing problem, for each facility, the algorithm consists of the following steps:

1. Solve the 2-Cyc-SPPRC.
2. Consider the column with minimum cost and choose at most m customers that are visited more than once. Let C_{E1} be the set of these customers. If the set is empty, stop (the path is already elementary).
3. Solve 2-Cyc-SPPRC-PE(m) with set C_{E1} from step 2.
4. Pick at most m customers that are visited more than once. Let C_{E2} be the set of these customers. Let $C_{E3} = C_{E1} \cup C_{E2}$ and $m_3 = |C_{E3}|$. If the set is empty, let $C_{E3} = C_{E1}$ and stop.
5. Solve 2-Cyc-SPPRC-PE(m_3) with set C_{E3}.

In our experiments, we generally had the same set of customers C_{E3} in every step of the column generation. Thus, we decided to determine set C_{E3} for each facility at the first iteration of column generation at each node, and we use the same set for the rest of the iterations at the node.

For computational testing, we implemented four variants of the branch-and-price algorithm based on the above pricing schemes.

- *Heuristic Branch-and-Price* (HBP): The purpose of this algorithm is to provide a good upper bound. At each node of the tree, we use ESPPRC-CS(n) and ESPPRC-LL(m) with small values of n and m (n is chosen to be 12 to 15 depending on the average demand and the vehicle capacity, while m is chosen to be 5 or 10). In addition, we also used combinations of ESPPRC-CS(n) and ESPPRC-LL(m) for larger values of n. In the algorithm, we use an iteration limit for the number of pricing problems solved at any node of the tree. If the number of iterations exceeds the limit, we branch.
- *Elementary Exact Branch-and-Price* (EEBP): The purpose of this algorithm is to prove the optimality of the solution or provide an integrality gap. At each node of the tree, we use ESPPRC-CS(n), ESPPRC-LL(m) and ESPPRC.
- *2 Step Elementary Exact Branch-and-Price* (EEBP-2S): In this variant, HBP is run first to generate initial columns and an upper bound. Then, EEBP is initiated with the columns and the upper bound obtained from HBP.
- *Non-elementary Exact Branch-and-Price (NEBP)*: This is similar to elementary exact branch-and-price algorithm except that the pricing problem solved is 2-Cyc-SPPRC-PE(n).

4 Computational Results

In this section, we discuss the performance of our branch-and-price algorithm for the LRP on two sets of instances. The first set contains the LRP instances used in Barreto et al (2007) that are available from Barreto (2003). We used these instances to test the performance of our HBP and NEBP algorithms. The second set of instances were random instances we generated to test the performance of our EEBP and EEBP-2S algorithms. We evaluate the effect of facility capacity constraints and other parameters using this set of instances. For all of our experiments, we used a Linux-based workstation with a 1.8 GHz processor and 2GB RAM.

4.1 Instances From the Literature

To the best of our knowledge, there are no benchmark instances available specifically for the LRP. Barreto et al (2007) used the instances in the literature available for other types of problems to construct a set of LRP instances. They report lower bounds found by applying a branch-and-cut algorithm to the two-index formulation

Table 1 Performance of Heuristic Branch-and-Price

Instance	LB[1]	Barreto et al (2007)		Heuristic Branch-and-Price		
		UB[2]	Gap	UB	Gap	CPU(s)
Gaskell67-21x5	424.9*	435.9	2.59	424.9	0	1.2
Gaskell67-22x5	585.1*	591.5	1.09	585.1	0	41.5
Gaskell67-29x5	512.1*	512.1	0	512.1	0	67.7
Gaskell67-32x5	556.5	571.7	2.73	562.3	1.04	10801.8
Gaskell67-32x5-2	504.3*	511.4	1.41	505.8	0.3	85.6
Gaskell67-36x5	460.4*	470.7	2.24	460.4	0	1077.6
C69-50x5	549.4	582.7	6.06	565.6	2.95	239.4
C69-75x10	744.7	886.3	19.01	852.1	14.42	10802.3
C69-100x10	788.6	889.4	12.78	929.5	17.86	10836.6
Perl83-12x2	204*	204	0	204.0	0	0.2
Perl83-55x15	1074.8	1136.2	5.71	1121.8	4.37	10800.0
Perl83-85x7	1568.1	1656.9	5.66	1668.2	6.38	10813.8
Min92-27x5	3062*	3062	0	3062.0	0	4.2
Min92-134x8	–	6238	–	6421.6	–	10850.9
Dsk95-88x8	356.4	384.9	8	390.6	9.58	10808.9

[1] Reported by Barreto (2004), found using branch-and-cut
[2] Reported by Barreto et al (2007), found using a heuristic
* Branch-and-cut used in Barreto (2004) proves the optimality

of the problem (Barreto, 2004) and upper bounds found by applying a sequential heuristic based on clustering techniques (Barreto et al, 2007). They listed 19 instances, three of which have more than 150 customers, too large for our approach to work efficiently. We removed these three instances plus one more with 117 customers and fractional demand, since we assume integer demands. The labels of the instances denote the source of the instance and the number of customers and facilities in the instances (for more details about the references, see Barreto (2003)).

We first ran HBP with a time limit of 3 CPU hours, focusing on producing quality upper bounds. Table 1 presents the instances we tested and compares the results with the upper bounds reported in Barreto et al (2007). Since neither our HBP nor Barreto et al (2007) can provide a valid lower bound for the problem, we used the best lower bounds as found in Barreto (2004) (second column in Table 1) to measure the quality of our upper bound. The "Gap" in Table 1 is the percent gap between the upper bound and the LB listed in the second column. HBP is capable of finding better upper bounds (usually optimal) for the instances of small and medium size. In these cases, the computation time is also very short. However, for larger instances, the upper bounds reported by Barreto et al (2007) are generally better. In addition, their heuristic algorithm is very efficient—they report that in most of the instances, it provides the result in less than one second.

Next, we used the EEBP-2S algorithm to test the ability to produce lower bounds and prove optimality. With this algorithm, we could not solve all of the instances within the total time limit of 5 CPU hours (3 CPU hours for HBP and 2 CPU hours

Table 2 Performance of 2 Step Elementary Exact Branch-and-Price

Instance	LB	OPT/BestIP	Gap	CPU(s)	Total CPU(s)
Gaskell67-21x5[1]	424.9	424.9	0	3.0	3.0
Gaskell67-22x5	585.1	585.1	0	2999.9	3041.4
Gaskell67-32x5	544.1	562.3	3.24%	8453.1	19254.9
Perl83-12x2[1]	204.0	204.0	0	0.2	0.2
Min92-27x5	3062.0	3062.0	0	833.6	837.8

[1] EEBP algorithm is used

Table 3 Performance of Non-elementary Exact Branch-and-Price

Instance	LB	OPT/BestIP	Gap	CPU(s)
Gaskell67-29x5	441.2	512.1	13.85%	14411.5
Gaskell67-32x5-2	494.4	505.8	2.26%	5654.8
Gaskell67-36x5	455.5	460.4	1.05%	100.1
C69-50x5	526.2	565.6	6.96%	2634.1
C69-75x10	693.5	852.1	18.62%	8785.8
Perl83-55x15	852.3	1121.8	24.02%	319.5
Perl83-85x7	1272.4	1668.2	23.73%	1379.6

for EEBP). The lower bounds found by our algorithm, along with the best integer solution found, optimality gap, and computation time are reported in Table 2. Note that because Gaskell67-21x5 and Perl83-12x2 are very easy to solve, we used the EEBP algorithm instead of the EEBP-2S algorithm in these cases.

Finally, for instances that we could not provide lower bounds by using the EEBP or the EEBP-2S algorithm, we used the NEBP algorithm with a time limit of 5 CPU hours or evaluated node limit of 50 nodes. The results are reported in Table 3. For the instances C69-100x10, Min92-134x8 and Dsk95-88x8, we could not solve even the root node within the time limit.

In general, the lower bounds found by using branch-and-cut (Barreto, 2004) are better than our lower bounds. However, in some cases, their computation times are much larger than our time limits. The HBP algorithm can provide good upper bounds, but for the medium and large size problems, we need to improve our lower bounding, perhaps by adding dynamic cut generation to our algorithm in order to close the optimality gap.

4.2 Random Instances

On random instances, Laporte et al (1986) provided computational results for an exact method (branch-and-cut algorithm) for the capacitated LRP. Belenguer et al (2006) also developed a branch-and-cut algorithm for the capacitated LRP, but neither the details of the instances nor the computational results are publicly available. Therefore, we evaluated our algorithm by generating random instances as in Laporte et al (1986), where they generated instances with 10, 15 and 20 customers and 4 to 8 facilities. In addition to these, we generated instances with 30 and 40 customers and 5 facilities to test the performance of the algorithm on larger instances. The coordinates of the customers and the facilities and the demand of each customer were generated using a Uniform distribution on [0,100]. We then calculated the Euclidean distance between each pair of customers and between customers and facilities and rounded the calculated distance to two decimal places. Demand for each customer was rounded to the nearest integer. Vehicle capacity C^V was calculated as

$$C^V = (1 - \alpha)max_{i \in I}\{D_i\} + \alpha \sum_{i \in I} D_i, \qquad (40)$$

where α was a parameter and the values were chosen in set $\{0, 0.25, 0.5, 0.75, 1\}$.

4.2.1 Small and Medium Random Instances

Laporte et al (1986) solved location and routing problems with capacitated vehicles, but they did not have a facility capacity. Instead, they had a lower and upper bound for the total number of facilities that could be open in a solution. In this experiment, in order to provide a better comparison of our algorithm with that of Laporte et al (1986), we removed constraint (13) from the SP-LRP. We set N^F, the minimum number of open facilities in (27), to 1, and we added constraint $\sum_{j \in J} t_j \leq M^F$, where M^F be the maximum number of facilities that can be open in any solution. Facility and vehicle fixed costs were set to be zero. As in Laporte et al (1986), three groups of instances with different numbers of customers and facilities were available. For each group, five different vehicle capacities were calculated by changing α. Some details about the instances are listed in Table 4.

Tables 5, 6 and 7 present the results achieved with our branch-and-price algorithm. Instances listed in these tables are labeled with the number of customers, facilities and with letters $\{a,b,c,d,e\}$ based on the α value used. For example, the instance $r10x4$-a-1 has 10 customers, 4 facilities and $\alpha = 0$. The integer from 1 to 3 after the letters represents the id of the instances within the same group. The tables present the name of each instance, the LP solution value at the root node, the optimal solution value, the number of evaluated nodes, and the CPU time in seconds. In these instances, we first ran the EEBP algorithm for 5 minutes and if the algorithm did not terminate within 5 minutes, we switched to the EEBP-2S algorithm. Table 5

Table 4 Details for the instances

# of Customers	# of Facilities	N^F	M^F	# of instances	α
10	4	1	3	3	$\{0, 0.25, 0.5, 0.75, 1\}$
15	6	1	4	3	$\{0, 0.25, 0.5, 0.75, 1\}$
20	8	1	5	3	$\{0, 0.25, 0.5, 0.75, 1\}$

Table 5 Performance of Elementary Exact Branch-and-Price for 10 customer instances

Instance	LP	OPT.	# of Nodes	CPU(s)
r10x4-a-1	472.11	472.11	1	0.00
r10x4-a-2	421.44	421.44	1	0.00
r10x4-a-3	548.28	548.28	1	0.02
r10x4-b-1	313.01	313.18	3	0.04
r10x4-b-2	297.57	305.27	19	0.08
r10x4-b-3	352.66	354.92	3	0.03
r10x4-c-1	257.25	257.25	1	0.06
r10x4-c-2	259.76	259.76	1	0.04
r10x4-c-3	296.82	296.82	1	0.05
r10x4-d-1	243.42	257.25	21	0.52
r10x4-d-2	250.04	250.04	1	0.04
r10x4-d-3	296.82	296.82	1	0.04
r10x4-e-1	226.46	226.46	1	0.32
r10x4-e-2	225.82	225.82	1	0.17
r10x4-e-3	272.85	272.85	1	0.31

Table 6 Performance of Elementary Exact Branch-and-Price for 15 customer instances

Instance	LP	OPT.	# of Nodes	CPU(s)
r15x6-a-1	435.2	435.2	1	0.01
r15x6-a-2	663.32	663.32	1	0.01
r15x6-a-3	411.45	411.45	1	0.01
r15x6-b-1	313.46	313.46	1	0.31
r15x6-b-2	414.65	414.65	1	0.21
r15x6-b-3	285.01	285.01	1	0.12
r15x6-c-1	313.46	313.46	1	3.1
r15x6-c-2	392.75	392.75	1	1.98
r15x6-c-3	279.82	279.82	1	5.37
r15x6-d-1	313.36	313.46	3	4.92
r15x6-d-2	378.76	378.76	1	9.41
r15x6-d-3	279.82	279.82	1	14.13
r15x6-e-1	305.86	312.18	5	9.82
r15x6-e-2[+]	374.86	374.86	1	16.62[+]
r15x6-e-3	274.22	274.22	1	300.01

[+] The EEBP-2S algorithm was used, total time is reported.

presents the results for instances with 10 customers, Table 6 presents instances with 15 customers, and Table 7 presents instances with 20 customers. We marked the instances with a "+" sign if the EEBP-2S algorithm was used. For problems with at least 20 customers, we needed to use the EEBP-2S algorithm. The branch-and-price algorithm was very successful in finding the optimal solution quickly. In general, our computation times were much smaller than those reported by Laporte et al (1986),

Table 7 Performance of Elementary Exact Branch-and-Price for 20 customer instances

Instance	LP	OPT.	# of Nodes	CPU(s)
r20x8-a-1	639.77	653.11	57	0.41
r20x8-a-2	542.23	551.58	25	0.98
r20x8-a-3	760.42	760.42	1	0.05
r20x8-b-1	415.3	417.13	7	8.35
r20x8-b-2	383.19	383.19	1	6.32
r20x8-b-3	439.18	447.72	121	37.32
r20x8-c-1[+]	398.34	398.34	1	26.25[+]
r20x8-c-2[+]	363.86	363.86	1	110.87[+]
r20x8-c-3[+]	402.85	402.85	1	28.74[+]
r20x8-d-1[+]	392.26	392.26	1	10.04[+]
r20x8-d-2[+]	359.49	359.49	1	200.29[+]
r20x8-d-3[+]	402.85	402.85	1	124.24[+]
r20x8-e-1[+]	392.28	392.28	1	12.39[+]
r20x8-e-2[+]	355.39	355.39	1	82.77[+]
r20x8-e-3[+]	402.46	402.46	1	103.27[+]

[+] The EEBP-2S algorithm is used, total time is reported.

but it is difficult to make a fair comparison, given advances in computing technology. In most of the instances, the LP solution found by our algorithm at the root node was the optimal.

The instances become more difficult when the vehicle capacity increases (α increases) because the number of labels generated in the pricing problem depends directly on the vehicle capacity. Laporte et al (1986) observed the reverse effect with regard to their branch-and-cut algorithm. The number of cuts generated increases and the problem gets more difficult when the vehicle capacity is small. This is most likely due to the fact that the problem structure becomes more like that of the traveling salesman problem (TSP) as the capacity is increased and the TSP is much easier to solve by branch and cut than as a capacitated routing problem.

To strictly differentiate the instances from those with a single depot, we experimented with changing the value of parameter N^F, the minimum number of open facilities, to 2 and ran the r15x6 and r20x8 b and c instances. There were no significant changes in the computational times or the number of evaluated nodes. We then added facility capacities to the same set of problems and ran our algorithm again. Table 8 presents the computational results, as well as the facility capacity values used for the facilities. The capacity value was chosen in order to require at least two open facilities. The computational results do not show any significant difference from those of the uncapacitated instances. For larger instances, we expect that the LP solution times will tend to increase if the master problem has facility capacity constraints. Adding a facility capacity to a two-index vehicle flow formulation requires an additional set of constraints (Belenguer et al, 2006), the size of which can be large. In a branch-and-cut algorithm, it may require additional time to generate this set of constraints.

Table 8 Instances with Capacitated Facilities

Instance	Fac. Cap	LP	OPT.	# of Nodes	Total Time
cr15x6-c-1	600	299.07	299.07	1	1.15
cr15x6-c-2	600	392.75	392.75	1	2.53
cr15x6-c-3	600	279.82	279.82	1	1.86
cr15x6-d-1	700	299.07	299.07	1	0.57
cr15x6-d-2	700	378.76	378.76	1	6.42
cr15x6-d-3	700	279.82	279.82	1	11.01
cr20x8-c-1	750	398.34	398.34	1	40.46
cr20x8-c-2	750	363.86	363.86	1	88.12
cr20x8-c-3	750	402.85	402.85	1	15.25
cr20x8-d-1	900	392.29	392.29	1	29.1
cr20x8-d-2	750	359.49	359.49	1	257.94
cr20x8-d-3	900	402.85	402.85	1	31.3

Laporte et al (1986) report that adding facility fixed costs to the problem makes the problem easier. We added facility fixed costs to r15x6 and r20x8 b and c instances. The performance of the branch-and-price algorithm was not affected in instances with 15 customers. However, for some of the 20 customer instances, the computational times exceeded 2 CPU hours (for the results, see Akca (2008)).

4.2.2 Large Random Instances

In this section, we present the results of applying our algorithm to larger capacitated random instances. We generated 6 instances with 30 customers and 6 instances with 40 customers. Each instance had 5 facilities with capacity constraints. The facilities had a fixed cost of 100. The characteristics of each instance are listed in Table 9. The first column includes the name of each instance, labeled based on the number of customers and facilities and the vehicle capacity. For instances in group "a" the vehicle capacity value (listed in the fourth column) was chosen to be 7 times the average demand and for group "b", the vehicle capacity value was 5.5 times the average demand. Facility capacity (listed in the second column) was chosen based on total demand such that at least two facilities (the minimum number of facilities is listed in the third column) should be open in an integer solution.

We used the EEBP-2S algorithm in which the HBP and EEBP algorithms were both used with a time limit of 3 CPU hours. Table 10 presents the results of both steps. The algorithm was very successful in finding optimal or near-optimal solutions for these larger instances. Some details, such as the number of open facilities, the number of vehicles used at each open facility, the average number of customers in each route (vehicle), and the number of customers in the longest route, are presented in Table 9.

Table 9 Characteristics of the Instances and the Optimal Solutions

Instance				OPT/BestIP Solution Info			
Name	Fac. Cap.	N^F	L^V	# of Fac.	# of Vec.	Avg. # of Cust/route	# of Cust. longest route
cr30x5a-1	1000	2	350	2	3,2	6	8
cr30x5a-2	1000	2	350	2	3,2	6	7
cr30x5a-3	1000	2	350	2	3,3	5	7
cr30x5b-1	1000	2	275	2	3,2	6	8
cr30x5b-2	1000	2	275	2	4,3	4.29	7
cr30x5b-3	1000	2	275	2	3,4	4.29	6
cr40x5a-1	1750	2	340	2	3,3	6.67	8
cr40x5a-2	1750	2	390	2	3,4	5.71	8
cr40x5a-3	1750	2	370	2	3,3	6.67	7
cr40x5b-1	1750	2	275	2	3,5	5	7
cr40x5b-2	1750	2	275	2	3,5	5	7
cr40x5b-3	1750	2	325	2	5,3	5	7

Table 10 Performance of the EEBP-2S for Instances up to 40 Customers with Capacitated Facilities and Facility Fixed Cost

Instance	HBP		EEBP					Total
	IP	CPU(s)	LP	IP	Gap	# of N.	CPU(s)	CPU (s)
cr30x5a-1	819.53	43.5	810.29	819.5	0	33	993.3	1036.8
cr30x5a-2	823.49	7202.3	790.49	823.49	2.55	500	10806.5	18008.8
cr30x5a-3	702.29	44.2	687.72	702.19	0	51	917.9	962.1
cr30x5b-1	880.02	164.3	865.47	880.01	0	251	6420.6	6585
cr30x5b-2	825.32	8.3	815.95	825.3	0	7	33.2	41.5
cr30x5b-3	884.62	13.4	881.33	884.55	0	19	41.7	55.1
cr40x5a-1	928.11	631.8	911.39	928.11	1.49	11	10882.8	11514.6
cr40x5a-2	888.37	378.4	871.66	888.37	0.93	13	11052.9	11431.3
cr40x5a-3	947.24	173	939.54	947.24	0.18	28	10862	11035
cr40x5b-1	1052.07	257.3	1043.62	1052	0	627	8084.6	8342
cr40x5b-2	981.52	60.1	976.88	981.27	0	47	862.5	922.7
cr40x5b-3	964.32	62.6	959.05	964.23	0	45	963	1025.6

5 Conclusion

We have presented a set-partitioning-based formulation for the capacitated location and routing problem, which to our knowledge is the first of its kind for this class of problem. We have demonstrated that it can be obtained by applying Dantzig-Wolfe decomposition to the graph-based formulation employed in most previously reported research. We have described a branch-and-price algorithm and reported on our experience using it to solve both problems from the literature and randomly generated instances. Our experiments indicate that the algorithm is very effective at producing quality solutions and can handle larger instances than previously suggested approaches, which have been primarily based on two-index formulations. The approach, however, does not seem as effective at producing quality lower bounds. This is likely due to the absence of dynamic cut generation. The next step in this research will be to incorporate the generation of known classes of valid inequalities into our algorithm. This should produce an algorithm exhibiting the advantages of both the branch-and-price and branch-and-cut approaches.

References

Akca Z (2008) Location Routing and Scheduling Problems: Models and algorithms. Working paper, COR@L Lab, Lehigh University

Akca Z, Berger RT, Ralphs TK (2008) Modeling and Solving Location Routing and Scheduling Problems. Working paper, COR@L Lab, Lehigh University

Barreto S (2003) LRP instances. URL http://sweet.ua.pt/iscfl43

Barreto S (2004) Analysis and Modelling of Location-Routing Problems (in portuguese). Phd thesis, University of Aveiro, Aveiro, Portugal

Barreto S, Ferreira C, Paixao J, Santos BS (2007) Using Clustering Analysis in a Capacitated Location-Routing Problem. European Journal of Operational Research 127(3):968–977

Belenguer JM, Benavent E, Prins C, Prodhon C, Wolfler-Calvo R (2006) A Branch and Cut method for the Capacitated Location-Routing Problem. Service Systems and Service Management, 2006 International Conference on 2:1541–1546

Berger RT (1997) Location-Routing Models for Distribution System Design. PhD thesis, Department of Industrial Engineering and Management Sciences, Northwestern University

Berger RT, Coullard CR, Daskin M (2007) Location-Routing Problems with Distance Constraints. Transportation Science 41:29–43

Desrochers M, Soumis F (1989) A Column Generation Approach to the Urban Transit Crew Scheduling Problem. Transportation Science 23(1):1–13

Desrochers M, Desrosiers J, Solomon MM (1992) A New Optimization Algorithm for the Vehicle Routing Problem with Time Windows. Operations Research 40(2):342–354

Dumitrescu I (2002) Constrained Path and Cycle Problems. PhD thesis, Department of Mathematics and Statistics, University of Melbourne

Feillet D, Dejax P, Gendreau M, Gueguen C (2004) An Exact Algorithm for the Elementary Shortest Path Problem with Resource Constraints: Application to Some Vehicle Routing Problems. Networks 44(3):216–229

Hansen PH, Hegedahl B, Hjortkjaer S, Obel B (1994) A Heuristic Solution to the Warehouse Location-Routing Problem. European Journal of Operational Research 76:111–127

Irnich S, Desaulniers G (2005) Column Generation, Springer, chap Shortest Path Problems with Resource Constraints, pp 33–65. GERAD 25th Anniversary Series

Laporte G (1988) Location Routing Problems. In: Golden B, Assad A (eds) Vehicle Routing: Methods and Studies, North-Holland, Amsterdam, pp 293–318

Laporte G, Nobert Y (1981) An Exact Algorithm for Minimizing Routing and Operating Cost in Depot Location. European Journal of Operational Research 6: 224–226

Laporte G, Nobert Y, Pelletier Y (1983) Hamiltonian Location Problems. European Journal of Operational Research 12:82–89

Laporte G, Nobert Y, Arpin D (1986) An Exact Algorithm for Solving a Capacitated Location-Routing Problem. Annals of Operations Research 6:293–310

Min H, Jayaraman V, Srivastava R (1998) Combined Location-Routing Problems: A Synthesis and Future Research Directions. European Journal of Operational Research 108(1):1–15

Perl J, Daskin MS (1985) A Warehouse Location-Routing Model. Transportation Research 19(B):381–396

Vance PH, Barnhart C, Johnson E, Nemhauser GL (1994) Solving Binary Cutting Stock Problems by Column Generation and Branch and Bound. Computational Optimization and Applications 3:111–130

Using Oriented Random Search to Provide a Set of Alternative Solutions to the Capacitated Vehicle Routing Problem

Angel A. Juan, Javier Faulin, Rubén Ruiz, Barry Barrios, Miquel Gilibert, and Xavier Vilajosana

Abstract In this paper we present SR-GCWS, a simulation-based algorithm for the Capacitated Vehicle Routing Problem (CVRP). Given a CVRP instance, the SR-GCWS algorithm incorporates a randomness criterion to the classical Clarke and Wright Savings (CWS) heuristic and starts an iterative process in order to obtain a set of alternative solutions, each of which outperforms the CWS algorithm. Thus, a random but oriented local search of the space of solutions is performed, and a list of "good alternative solutions" is obtained. We can then consider several properties per solution other than aprioristic costs, such as visual attractiveness, number of trucks employed, load balance among routes, environmental costs, etc. This allows the decision-maker to consider multiple solution characteristics other than just those defined by the aprioristic objective function. Therefore, our methodology provides more flexibility during the routing selection process, which may help to improve the quality of service offered to clients. Several tests have been performed to discuss the effectiveness of this approach.

Key words: Capacitated Vehicle Routing Problem, heuristics, Monte Carlo simulation

Angel A. Juan, Miquel Gilibert and Xavier Vilajosana
Dep. of Computer Science and Telecommunication, Open University of Catalonia,
Rambla Poblenou, 156, 08018 Barcelona, Spain
{ajuanp, mgilibert, xvilajosana}@uoc.edu

Javier Faulin and Barry Barrios
Dep. of Statistics and Operations Research, Public University of Navarre,
Campus Arrosadia, 31006 Pamplona, Spain
javier.faulin@unavarra.es, bcubeb3@mit.edu

Rubén Ruiz
Dep. of Statistics, Applied OR and Quality, Valencia University of Technology,
Camino de Vera, s/n, 46022 Valencia, Spain
rruiz@eio.upv.es

J.W. Chinneck et al. (eds.), *Operations Research and Cyber-Infrastructure*, Operations
Research/Computer Science Interfaces Series 47, DOI: 10.1007/978-0-387-88843-9_17,
© Springer Science+Business Media, LLC 2009

1 Introduction

In the Capacitated Vehicle Routing Problem (CVRP), a fleet of vehicles supplies customers using resources available from a depot or central node. Each vehicle has the same capacity (homogeneous fleet) and each customer has a certain demand that must be satisfied. Additionally, there is a cost matrix that measures the costs associated with moving a vehicle from one node to another. These costs usually represent distances, traveling times, number of vehicles employed or a combination of these factors. More formally, we assume a set Ω of $n+1$ nodes, each of them representing a vehicle destination (depot node) or a delivery point (demanding node). The nodes are numbered from 0 to n, node 0 being the depot and the remaining n nodes the delivery points. A demand $q_i > 0$ of some commodity has been assigned to each non-depot node i ($1 \leq i \leq n$). On the other hand, $E = \{(i,j)/i,j \in \Omega \; ; \; i < j\}$ represents the set of the $n \cdot (n+1)/2$ existing edges connecting the $n+1$ nodes. Each of these links has an associated aprioristic cost, $c_{ij} > 0$, which represents the cost of sending a vehicle from node i to node j. These c_{ij} are assumed to be symmetric ($c_{ij} = c_{ji}$, $0 \leq i,j \leq n$), and they are frequently expressed in terms of the Euclidean distance, d_{ij}, between the two nodes. The delivery process is to be carried out by a fleet of NV vehicles ($NV \geq 1$) with equal capacity, $C \gg \max\{q_i/1 \leq i \leq n\}$. Some additional constraints associated to the CVRP are the following (Laporte et al. 2000):

1. Each non-depot node is supplied by a single vehicle
2. All vehicles begin and end their routes at the depot (node 0)
3. A vehicle cannot stop twice at the same non-depot node
4. No vehicle can be loaded exceeding its maximum capacity

Different approaches to the CVRP have been explored during the last decades (Toth and Vigo 2002, Golden et al. 2008). These approaches range from the use of pure optimization methods, such as linear programming, for solving small-size problems with relatively simple constraints to the use of heuristics and meta-heuristics that provide near-optimal solutions for medium and large-size problems with more complex constraints. Most of these methods focus on minimizing an aprioristic cost function subject to a set of well-defined constraints. However, real-life problems tend to be complex enough so that not all possible costs, e.g., environmental costs, work risks, etc., constraints and desirable solution properties, e.g., time or geographical restrictions, balanced work load among routes, solution attractiveness, etc., can be considered a priori during the mathematical modeling phase (Poot et al. 2002, Kant et al. 2008). For that reason, there is a need for more flexible methods that provide a large set of alternative near-optimal solutions with different properties, so that decision-makers can choose among different alternative solutions according to their concrete necessities and preferences. Furthermore, in a recent critical review by (Laporte 2007), the author clearly states "When reporting results, most researchers concentrate on solution quality and computing time. While these two measures are undoubtedly important, they do not tell the whole story. Other qualities such as simplicity of implementation and flexibility are also important (...) It is also important to design algorithms that can easily handle the numerous side constraints that arise in practice". Consequently, the main purpose of this paper is to present SR-GCWS, a hybrid algorithm that combines the classical Clarke & Wright Savings (CWS) heuristic with Monte Carlo Simulation (MCS) to generate a set of alternative solutions for a given CVRP instance. Each solution in this set outperforms the CWS heuristic, but it also has its own characteristics and therefore constitutes an alternative possibility for the decision-maker where several side constraints can be considered.

The rest of the paper is structured as follows: Section 2 reviews some relevant CVRP literature, including the use of MCS in VRP; Section 3 introduces the main ideas behind our approach; Section 4 explains in detail the methodology we used to introduce randomness in the classical CWS algorithm; Section 5 discusses some advantages of our approach over other existing approaches; Section 6 explains how this algorithm has been implemented by means of the object-oriented programming paradigm; Section 7 discusses some experimental results; finally, Section 8 concludes this paper and highlights its main contributions.

2 Review of Related Work

Exact methods have achieved decent levels of performance, like the sophisticated method by (Baldacci et al. 2008) where exact solutions to problems up to 100 customers are solvable. However, the success rate is variable, as noted by (Laporte 2007). The computational times are extreme in some cases and adding new real constraints is a challenge in such specialized exact methodologies.

The Clarke and Wright's Savings (CWS) algorithm (Clarke and Wright 1964) is probably the most cited method to solve the CVRP. This method uses the concept of savings associated to each edge. At each step, the edge with the most savings is selected if and only if the two corresponding routes can feasibly be merged and if the selected edge comprises of nodes that are not interior to its respective route (a node is interior to a route if it is not adjacent to the depot). The CWS algorithm usually provides "good solutions", especially for small and medium-size problems, but it also presents difficulties in some cases (Gaskell 1967). Another important approach to the CVRP is the Sweep method (Gillett and Miller 1974). There are several variants of the CWS. For instance, (Mole and Jameson 1976) generalized the definition of the savings function, introducing two parameters for controlling the savings behavior. Similarly, (Holmes and Parker 1976) developed a procedure based upon the CWS algorithm, using the same savings function but introducing a solution perturbation scheme in order to avoid poor quality routes. (Beasley 1981) adapted the CWS method to the optimization of inter-customer travel times. Correspondingly, (Dror and Trudeau 1986) developed a version of the CWS method for the Stochastic VRP. Two years later, (Paessens 1988) depicted the main characteristics of the CWS method and its performance in generic VRP. Recently, the CWS heuristic has been finely tuned by means of genetic algorithms experimentation by (Battarra et al. 2009).

The methodology we present in this paper combines the CWS algorithm with the use of Monte Carlo simulation (MCS), which can be defined as a set of techniques that make use of random number generation to solve certain stochastic or deterministic problems (Law 2007). MCS has proved to be extremely useful for obtaining numerical solutions to complex problems which cannot be efficiently solved by using analytical approaches. (Buxey 1979) was probably the first author in combining MCS along with the CWS algorithm to develop an algorithm for the CVRP. His method was redesigned by (Faulin and Juan 2008), who introduced an entropy function to guide the random selection of nodes. MCS has also been used by (Fernández de Córdoba et al. 2000) to solve the CVRP.

Other related heuristics that have been proposed to solve the VRP are the GRASP procedures (Feo and Resende 1995). Likewise, the use of meta-heuristics in VRP became popular during the nineties. Additionally, and as of late, new powerful hybrid metaheuristics are being proposed. Some of the most important papers on the use of heuristics and meta-heuristics in that moment were (Gendreau et al. 1994), which introduced the Tabu Route algorithm, and (Laporte et al. 2000), which includes a thorough discussion of classical and modern heuristics. Some years later, (Tarantilis and Kiranoudis 2002) presented the Boneroute for routing and fleet management, and (Toth and Vigo 2003) the Granular Tabu Search as a new method to solve the CVRP.

Moreover, other important references about meta-heuristics that can be applied to CVRP are (Alba and Dorronsoro 2004, Berger and Barkaoui 2003), who introduced some genetic algorithms in routing, and (Prins 2004), who developed a new evolutionary algorithm for the VRP. Additional high performing notorious genetic search methods are those proposed by (Mester and Bräysy 2005, Mester and Bräysy 2007). Advanced crossover operators are put forward by (Nagata 2007).

Large sized problems are solved efficiently by means of variable neighborhood search methods by (Kytöjoki et al. 2007). Also (Pisinger and Ropke 2007) proposed the use of general local search methods working over adaptive large neighborhoods.

Obviously, due to space limitations, a complete review of the vast VRP literature is not given here. For more detailed reviews, the reader is referred to (Cordeau et al. 2004, Laporte 2007, Gendreau et al. 2008).

3 Our Approach to the CVRP

As we have explained before, our goal here is to develop a methodology that provides the decision-maker with a set of alternative near-optimal or "good" solutions for a given CVRP instance. We are not especially interested in obtaining the best solution from an aprioristic point of view –that is, the solution that minimizes the aprioristic costs as expressed in the objective function. As we have already pointed, in practical real situations there are important cost factors, constraints and desirable solution properties that usually can not be modeled or accounted for a priori. Once generated, this list of alternative "good" solutions can be stored in a solutions database so that the decision-maker can perform retrieval queries according to different criteria or preferences regarding the desirable properties of an ideal "real-life" solution.

In order to generate this set of "good" solutions, we will make use of Monte Carlo Simulation –and, in particular, of a random selection criterion–, to randomize the CWS algorithm and perform an oriented random search in the space of feasible solutions. To be more specific, given a CVRP instance, we generalize the CWS algorithm in two ways:

- First, we introduce a random behavior in the solution-construction process of the CWS algorithm: each time a new edge must be selected from the list of available edges, we apply a selection criterion which assigns exponentially diminishing probabilities to each eligible edge based on the edge's savings value and on a user-defined parameter β, where $0 < \beta < 1$. Roughly speaking, this parameter can be interpreted as the probability of selecting the edge with the highest savings value at each step of the solution-construction process (a more detailed explanation about this selection criterion is given in Section 4).
- Second, we perform a number of iterations, $nIter \geq 1$, of the randomized CWS algorithm. In this iterative process, different values of the β parameter are explored in what constitutes a simultaneous random search and parameter fine-tuning process.

To be more precise, our approach is based on a series of simple steps (Fig. 1):

1. Given a CVRP instance, construct the corresponding data model and use the classical CWS algorithm to solve it.
2. Choose a value for the parameter β for adding random behavior to the algorithm (a fine-tuning analysis might be necessary at this stage).

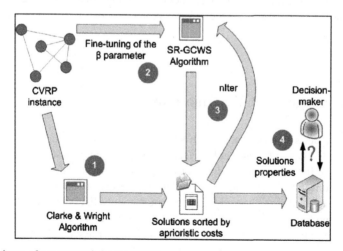

Fig. 1 Scheme of our approach for the CVRP

3. Start an iterative process to generate solutions using the SR-GCWS algorithm with the user-defined values for parameters β and *nIter* (notice that an alternative stopping criterion, such as the maximum computation time allowed or the desired number of "good" solutions, could also be used instead of this second parameter).

4. At each iteration, save the resulting solution in a database only if it outperforms the one provided by the CWS algorithm (i.e., we will consider that a solution is a "good" one only if it outperforms the CWS solution from an aprioristic costs perspective). The resulting database should allow sending filtering queries regarding different solution properties.

Since the parameter β is restricted to the interval $(0, 1)$ we expect that this parameter will be easy to fine-tune in most practical situations. In different tests that we have developed, using a default value between $\beta = 0.2$ and $\beta = 0.3$ has shown to provide good results without requiring any fine-tuning process. As an alternative to the use of these default values, a fine-tuning process could be performed by just running a set of short-run simulations (covering just some hundreds or thousands of iterations) with different values of this parameter. The parameter value that provides the best solution in the short-run simulations can be then selected to run a long-run simulation (covering some thousands or even millions of iterations). Nevertheless, a lot of computation time could be required in order to perform a large number of iterations, especially in the case of large CVRP instances with hundreds of nodes. In these cases, Parallel and Grid Computing techniques (PGC) could be employed to accelerate significantly the generation of "good" solutions (Mohcine et al. 2007).

Due to its nature, we call the resulting algorithm the Generalized CWS of the SimuRoute project (SR-GWCS) or, more formally SR-GWCS(β,*nIter*). Using this notation, it is easy to verify that SR-GWCS($0.\hat{9}$,1) is just the classical CWS heuristic.

The next section discusses in more detail the random process that the SR-GWCS algorithm employs to select edges from the savings list at each step of a given iteration.

4 Randomizing the CWS Algorithm

As we have described before, at each step of an iteration of the SR-GCWS algorithm, an edge has to be randomly selected from the savings list. This savings list is simply the list of available edges sorted by their corresponding savings values. Our algorithm introduces randomness in this process by assigning a probability of (approximately) β to the first edge in the sorted savings list –the one with the most savings–, and by assigning probabilities to the rest of the nodes according to an exponential diminishing pattern, so that edges with higher associated savings receive higher probabilities of being selected (Fig. 2).

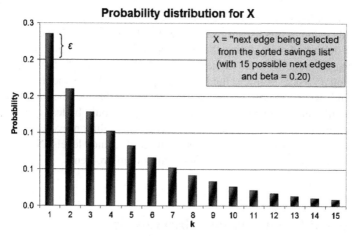

Fig. 2 Assignment of probabilities to edges

To do this probability assignment process we use the fact that:

$$\sum_{k=1}^{+\infty} \beta \cdot (1 - \beta)^{k-1} = 1, \forall \beta \in (0,1) \tag{1}$$

Therefore, considering the random variable X = "next edge being selected from the sorted savings list" and assuming that, at a particular step, the savings list contains l eligible edges ($l \geq 1$) sorted from higher savings (edge 1) to lower savings (edge l), we can define the following probability distribution:

$$P(X = k) = \begin{cases} \beta + \varepsilon \text{ if } k = 1 \\ \beta \cdot (1 - \beta)^{k-1} \text{ if } 1 < k \leq l \end{cases} \tag{2}$$

Where:

$$\varepsilon = \sum_{k=l+1}^{+\infty} \beta \cdot (1 - \beta)^{k-1} = 1 - \sum_{k=1}^{l} \beta \cdot (1 - \beta)^{k-1} \tag{3}$$

Our methodology also allows introducing some interesting "risky/conservative" strategies for the routing selection. In effect, notice that high values of β are conservative in the sense that, each time a new edge has to be selected to define a new merging operation between two routes, they promote the selection of those edges with the highest savings values. On the contrary, low values of this parameter help to promote the selection of edges other than the ones with the highest savings values, which contributes to explore a wider region of the space of solutions. In fact, this "risky/conservative" strategy is also intrinsically built in the random selection process for any given value of β: notice from equation (2) that, at each step, the probability of selecting the edge with the highest savings value is given by the sum of two terms. The second term, ε, is approximately zero at the beginning of any iteration, when the number of edges in the savings list is large, but it continuously increases its value as this list shrinks after each edge selection. The collateral effect is the one described next: during the first steps of a given iteration the probability of selecting the edge with the highest savings will be relatively low –especially if we are using a "risky" or low value for β, say $\beta = 0.2$–, but as the iteration evolves this probability experiments a continuous increase. At the end, the logic behind this strategy is that initial steps in a solution-construction could be less conservative in order to explore more alternative routes but, as the solution evolves, these steps become more conservative in order to keep high efficiency levels. Notice that this approach also contributes to avoid the local minimum problem.

5 Additional Comments and Observations

As it has been described before, our approach makes use of an iterative process to generate a set of random solutions which outperform the classical CWS algorithm. Each of these solutions is a set of roundtrip routes that, altogether, satisfy all nodes demand by visiting and serving them. Furthermore, each of these solutions will have their own unique characteristics regarding properties such as total aprioristic cost, number of routes or vehicles, visual attractiveness, load balancing, environmental costs, etc., thus providing more alternatives to the decision-maker, who can choose the ideal solution according to a set of preferences or non-aprioristic constraints or additional costs.

The SR-GCWS algorithm has many desirable characteristics. First of all, it is a simple method which requires little instantiation. With little effort, similar algorithms based on the same key basic idea could be easily developed for other routing problems and, in general, for other combinatorial optimization problems. Second, SR-GCWS returns not only one solution or set of routes for the CVRP problem, like most existing algorithms, but rather a relatively large set of solutions. Such behavior is highly desirable, as it allows for multiple criteria decision making as the set of solutions can be ranked according to different objectives. Notice that this is somewhat different to Genetic Algorithms (GAs). While GAs maintains a population of solutions as SR-GCWS does, the size of this population is usually limited to 100 or even less, which is less than what our SR-GCWS algorithm can provide. Moreover, some of the most efficient heuristics and metaheuristics are not used in practice because of the difficulties they present when dealing with real-life problems and restrictions (Kant et al. 2008). On the contrary, simulation-based heuristics, like the one presented here, tend to be more flexible and, therefore, they seem more appropriate to deal with real restrictions and dynamic work conditions.

6 Software Implementation

We have used an object-oriented approach to implement the described methodology as a computer program. In order to do this, we have employed the Java programming language. The implementation process is not a trivial task, since there are some details which deserve special attention, in particular: (i) the use of a good random number generator, (ii) a correct design of the different classes, so that convenient cohesion and coupling levels will be reached, and (iii) the code levels of accuracy and effectiveness –as an example of this, to perform mathematical operations the use of the package `java.lang.StrictMath` is usually preferred over the use of the more classical package `java.lang.Math`.

Regarding the generation of random numbers and variates, we have employed the SSJ library (L'Ecuyer 2002). In particular, we have used the subclass GenF2W32, which implements a generator with a period value equal to $2^{800}-1$.

Furthermore, we needed a software implementation of the classical CWS heuristic in order to be able to test the efficiency of our approach against the CWS approach. Since we did not find any available implementation for the CWS algorithm –either on the Internet or in any book or journal–, we have developed our own object-oriented implementation of this algorithm. As a matter of fact, there are several variants of the CWS heuristic, so we decided to base our implementation in the one described in the following webpage from the Massachusetts Institute of Technology: <web.mit.edu/urban_or_book/www/book/chapter6/6.4.12.htm>

7 Experimental Results

In order to test the efficiency of our approach, we started by using some CVRP instances referenced in (Toth and Vigo 2002). We also used other CVRP instances from the TSPLIB, a library of instances freely available from the University of Heidelberg at:
<www.iwr.uniheidelberg.de/groups/comopt/software/TSPLIB95/>.

At first, we were somewhat concerned with the results of our CWS implementation, since they did not seem to perfectly match the expected results. After discussing this matter with Professor Vigo, we understood that the expected CWS results should be considered with caution, since some of them were obtained by using CWS implementations that were not making use of real numbers, but only integer numbers. Moreover, sometimes these integers were obtained by rounding, while other times they were obtained by direct truncation. These details may have a significant impact over the CWS results, even for the same instance. Because of this, we decided to construct and use our own CVRP instances, which always use real numbers of high precision (all numbers and calculations in our code use the `double` Java type).

7.1 Case 1: a small size CVRP

As a first CVRP instance to test our algorithm, we generated a random set of 20 nodes (nodes 1 to 20) uniformly distributed inside the square defined by the corner points $(-100, -100)$, $(-100, 100)$, $(100, 100)$ and $(100, -100)$. The depot (node 0, with no demand), was placed at the square center. The demand for each node was randomly generated (with an average demand of 83 and a maximum individual demand of 144). Finally, a value of 345 was assigned as the vehicle total capacity. Fig. 3 shows the scatterplot for this instance together with the solution provided by the classical CWS heuristic. Each point represents a node, and the corresponding number represents its identification number. In this example, the traveling cost from one node to other was calculated as the Euclidean distance between the two nodes. Thus, the CWS heuristic provided a solution with a total cost of 1,221.81.

Similarly, we solved this instance by employing our SR-GCWS algorithm: using a standard PC (Intel Centrino Duo CPU, 1.6 GHz and 2 GB RAM). It took less than seven seconds to perform 10,000 iterations (i.e., to generate 10,000 random solutions); after those iterations SR-GCWS provided 138 alternative solutions with a lower cost than the CWS heuristic, with a minimal cost solution of 1,173.47, which is represented in Fig. 4. Notice that this solution significantly differs from the one provided by the CWS algorithm in at least two aspects other than the total cost, i.e.: it employs only 5 routes while the CWS employed 6 routes, and its routes do not overlap, which increases the visual attractiveness of the proposed solution.

Therefore, it seems reasonable to conclude that in small-size scenarios, SR-GCWS can easily offer a considerable number of alternative solutions that outperform the solution provided by the CWS heuristic.

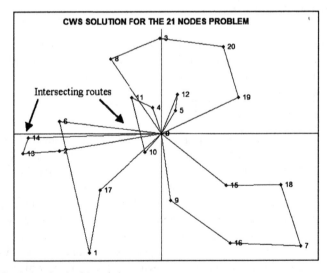

Fig. 3 CWS solution for the 21-node instance

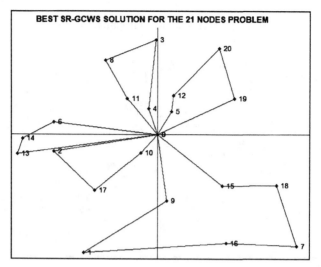

Fig. 4 SR-GCWS solution for the 21-node instance

7.2 Case 2: a medium size CVRP

As a second CVRP instance, we generated a random set of 50 nodes (nodes 1 to 50) uniformly distributed inside the square defined by the points $(-1000, -1000)$, $(-1000, 1000)$, $(1000, 1000)$ and $(1000, -1000)$. As before, the depot was node 0 and it had zero demand. Demands for nodes other than the depot were randomly generated, with an average demand of 162 and a maximum individual demand of 290. Finally, a value of 1,266 was assigned as the vehicle total capacity. Again, we solved this instance by using the CWS heuristic (Fig. 5) and by using the SR-GCWS algorithm (Fig. 6).

The solution given by the CWS heuristic has a cost of 17,356.33. After 10,000 iterations, processed in approximately two minutes of computing time, the SR-GCWS algorithm provided 136 different solutions with a lower cost than the CWS one. The best of these solutions has a total cost of 17,146.51. Moreover, while the CWS solution has unbalanced routes with a 3,873.41 cost route, routes in the GCWS solution are more balanced, with a maximum cost of 3,229.73.

Again, it seems reasonable to conclude that also for medium-size scenarios, SR-GCWS can easily offer a considerable number of alternative solutions that outperform the CWS heuristic.

7.3 Other cases: two large size CVRPs

To test how our algorithm performs in large size scenarios with an important number of nodes, we also generated two random CVRP instances containing 126 and

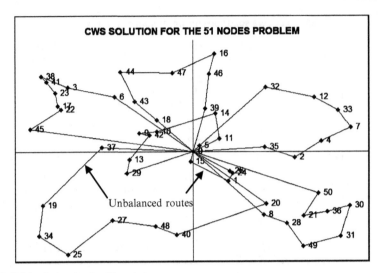

Fig. 5 CWS solution for the 51-node instance

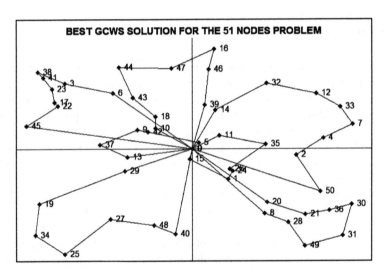

Fig. 6 SR-GCWS solution for the 51-node instance

251 nodes respectively. A value of 1,850 was randomly assigned to be the vehicle capacity for the 126 nodes scenario. In the case of the 251 nodes scenario, a value of 1,150 was randomly assigned as the corresponding vehicle capacity. As before, we solved each of these scenarios both by using the CWS algorithm and by using the SR-GCWS algorithm.

For the 126 nodes scenario, the CWS algorithm provided a solution with a total cost of 22,641.17. In this case, the SR-GCWS algorithm employed about six

Table 1 Summary of results for the different cases

Case (Number of nodes)	CWS Solution	Best SR-GCWS Solution	Number of SR-GCWS solutions improving CWS	Time (s)
Case 1 (21)	1,221.81	1,173.47	138	7
Case 2 (51)	17,356.33	17,146.51	136	126
Case 3 (126)	22,641.17	22,012.60	146	401
Case 4 (251)	31,632.49	30,779.79	18	625

and a half minutes to perform 1,000 iterations. From these iterations, a total of 146 solutions outperforming the CWS solution were obtained. The best of these solutions has a total cost of 22,012.60.

In the case of the 251 nodes scenario, the CWS algorithm provided a solution with a total cost of 31,632.49. This time, the SR-GCWS algorithm employed about ten minutes to perform 100 iterations. At the end of this process, a total of 18 solutions outperforming the CWS were obtained, with a minimum cost of 30,779.79. Notice that both in these large size scenarios, the respective numbers of iterations to run were reduced to avoid larger computation times. As discussed before, in these large size scenarios the use of Parallel and Grid Computing could significantly improve the results in most practical situations without having to wait for longer computation times.

Table 1 shows a summary of our results for the previously discussed tests.

8 Conclusions

We have presented here the SR-GCWS algorithm, which combines Monte Carlo simulation and the Clark and Wright heuristic to provide a set of alternative solutions for the Capacitated Vehicle Routing Problem. The SR-GCWS algorithm has proven to be effective in scenarios of different sizes, ranging from instances with a reduced number of nodes to instances with a considerable number of nodes.

One major advantage of simulation-based algorithms is the fact that they provide not only a good solution to the decision maker, but a set of alternative good solutions than can be ranked according to different criteria. Another major advantage of our approach is the flexibility of simulation-based algorithms, which allows them to deal with realistic situations defined by complex restrictions and dynamic working conditions. In our opinion, simulation techniques offer a new way to explore some traditional combinatorial problems, such as the CVRP and many others of similar characteristics.

9 Acknowledgements

This work has been partially financed by the United States Department of Transportation under grant DTOS59-06-00035 and by the Spanish Ministry of Education and Science under grant TRA2006-10639.

References

Alba, E. and B. Dorronsoro. 2004. Solving the Vehicle Routing Problem by using Cellular Genetic Algorithms. In Jens Gottlieb and Günter R. Raidl, editors, Evolutionary Computation in Combinatorial Optimization – EvoCOP 2004, LNCS 3004, 11–20, Coimbra, Portugal, 5–7 April, 2004. Springer-Verlag

Baldacci, R., Christofides, N. and Mingozzi, A. 2008. An exact algorithm for the vehicle routing problem based on the set partitioning formulation with additional cuts. Mathematical Programming, 115(2): 351–385

Battarra, M., Golden, B. and Vigo, D. 2009. Tuning a parametric Clarke-Wright heuristic via a genetic algorithm. In press at Journal of the Operational Research Society. doi: 10.1057/palgrave.jors.2602488

Beasley, J. 1981. Adapting the Savings Algorithm for Varying Inter-Customer Travel Times. Omega, 9, 658–659

Berger, J. and M. Barkaoui. 2003. A Hybrid Genetic Algorithm for the Capacitated Vehicle Routing Problem. In E. Cantó-Paz, editor. Proceedings of the International Genetic and Evolutionary Computation Conference – GECCO03, LNCS 2723, 646–656, Illinois. Chicago, USA. Springer-Verlag

Buxey, G.M. 1979. The Vehicle Scheduling Problem and Monte Carlo Simulation. Journal of Operational Research Society, 30, 563–573

Clarke, G. and J. Wright. 1964. Scheduling of Vehicles from a central Depot to a Number of Delivering Points. Operations Research, 12, 568–581

Cordeau, J.F., Gendreau, M., Hertz, A., Laporte, G., and J.S. Sormany. 2004. New Heuristics for the Vehicle Routing Problem. In A. Langevin and D. Riopel, editors, Logistics Systems: Design and Optimization. Kluwer Academic Publishers

Dror, M. and P. Trudeau, P. 1986. Stochastic Vehicle Routing with Modified Savings Algorithm. European Journal of Operational Research, 23, 228–235

Faulin, J. and A. Juan. 2008. The ALGACEA-1 Method for the Capacitated Vehicle Routing Problem. International Transactions in Operational Research, 15, 1–23

Feo, T.A. and M.G.C. Resende. 1995. Greedy Randomized Adaptive Search Procedures. Journal of Global Optimization, 6, 109–133

Fernández de Córdoba, P., García Raffi, L.M., Mayado, A. and J.M. Sanchis. 2000. A Real Delivery Problem Dealt with Monte Carlo Techniques. TOP, 8, 57–71

Gaskell, T.J. 1967. Bases for the Vehicle Fleet Scheduling. Operational Research Quarterly, 18, 281–295

Gendreau, M., Hertz, A. and G. Laporte. 1994. A Tabu Search Heuristic for the Vehicle Routing Problem. Management Science, 40, 1276–1290

Gendreau, M., Potvin, J.-Y., Bräysy, O., Hasle, G. and Løkketangen, A. 2008. Metaheuristics for the vehicle routing problem and its extensions: A categorized bibliography. In Bruce, G., Raghavan, S. and Wasil, E., editors, The Vehicle Routing Problem: Latest Advanced and New Challenges. Springer, Dordrecht

Gillet, B.E. and L.R. Miller. 1974. A Heuristic Algorithm for the Vehicle Dispatch Problem. Operations Research, 22, 340–349

Golden, B., Raghavan, S. and E. Edward Wasil (eds.). 2008. The Vehicle Routing Problem: Latest Advances and New Challenges. Springer

Holmes, R.A. and R.G. Parker. 1976. A Vehicle Scheduling Procedure Based Upon Savings and a Solution Perturbation Scheme. Operational Research Quarterly, 27, 83–92

Kant, G., Jacks, M. and C. Aantjes. 2008. Coca-Cola Enterprises Optimizes Vehicle Routes for Efficient Product Delivery. Interfaces, 38: 40–50

Kytöjoki, J., Nuortio, T., Bräysy, O. and Gendreau, M. 2007. An efficient variable neighborhood search heuristic for very large scale vehicle routing problems. Computers and Operations Research, 34: 2743–2757

Laporte, G. 2007. What you should know about the Vehicle Routing Problem. Naval Research Logistics, 54: 811–819

Laporte, G., Gendreau, M., Potvin, J.Y. and F. Semet. 2000. Classical and Modern Heuristics for the Vehicle Routing Problem. International Transactions in Operational Research, 7, 285–300

Law, A. 2007. Simulation Modeling & Analysis. McGraw-Hill

L'Ecuyer, P. 2002. SSJ: A Framework for Stochastic Simulation in Java. In Proceedings of the 2002 Winter Simulation Conference, pp. 234–242

Mester, D. and Bräysy, O. 2005. Active guided evolution strategies for the large scale vehicle routing problems with time windows. Computers and Operations Research, 32: 1165–1179

Mester, D. and Bräysy, O. 2007. Active-guided evolution strategies for the large-scale capacitated vehicle routing problems. Computers and Operations Research, 34: 2964–2975

Mole, R.H. and S.R. Jameson. 1976. A Sequential Route-building Algorithm Employing a Generalised Savings Criterion. Operational Research Quarterly, Vol. 27, 503–511

Mohcine, J., Contassot-Vivier, S. and Couturier, R. (2007). Parallel Iterative Algorithms: From Sequential to Grid Computing. Chapman & Hall/CRC.

Nagata, Y. 2007. Edge aseembly crossover for the capacitated vehicle routing problem. In Cotta, C. and van Hemert, J., editors, Lecture Notes in Computer Science, vol 4446. Springer-Verlag, Berlin Heidelberg

Paessens, H. 1988. The Savings Algorithm for the Vehicle Routing Problem. European Journal of Operational Research, 34, 336–344

Pisinger, D. and Ropke, S. 2007. A general heuristic for vehicle routing problems. Computers and Operations Research, 34: 2403–2435

Poot, A., Kant, G. and A Wagelmans. 2002. A savings based method for real-life vehicle routing problems. Journal of the Operational Research Society, 53, 57–68

Prins, C. 2004. A Simple and Effective Evolutionary Algorithm for the Vehicle Routing Problem. Computers and Operations Research, 31, 1985–2002

Tarantilis, C.D. and C.T. Kiranoudis. 2002. Boneroute: an Adaptive Memory-Based Method for Effective Fleet Management. Annals of Operations Research, 115, 227–241

Toth, P. and D. Vigo. 2002. The Vehicle Routing Problem. SIAM Monographs on Discrete Mathematics and Applications. SIAM

Toth, P. and D. Vigo. 2003. The Granular Tabu Search and its Application to the Vehicle Routing Problem. INFORMS Journal on Computing, 15, 333–346

Optimizing Paths in the Presence of Spherical Impediments

Meike Verhoeven and David L. Woodruff

Abstract This paper provides formulations, solution methods and computational results for continuous shortest path problems in the presence of spherical impediments in 3D space. We extend line-of-site methods developed for 2D obstacles to create starting solutions for a non-linear solver in the 3D world and demonstrate that the addition of intersection points and surface arcs provides a significant boost. We compare our sophisticed method with a simple grid search. An important conclusion is that a grid performs reasonably well and in fact is preferred when the penalties for traversing the impediments are low. When better solutions in the presence of high penalty impediments are needed, we provide a method based on a network of intersection and tangency points which is used to construct a starting point for a non-linear solver.

Key words: Optimal Path, Sensors, Impediments.

1 Introduction

Some RFID antennae, underwater sea mines, security systems and some simple types of air defense systems impede objects within a range that is useful to model as spherical. There are many situations where one might want to be able to find the shortest path between two points when travel within the range of an impediment adds a penalty to the distance (or speed). It can also be an important sub-problem to the problem of selecting impediments for interdiction, selecting impediments to probe, or the problem of designing a robust sensor network. We use words such as

Meike Verhoeven
Mathematics Institute, Universität Duisburg-Essen, Campus Duisburg, D-47048 Duisburg
Germany
e-mail: meike.verhoeven@gmx.de

David L. Woodruff
Graduate School of Management, UC Davis, Davis CA, 95616 USA
e-mail: dlwoodruff@ucdavis.edu

J.W. Chinneck et al. (eds.), *Operations Research and Cyber-Infrastructure*, Operations
Research/Computer Science Interfaces Series 47, DOI: 10.1007/978-0-387-88843-9_18,
© Springer Science+Business Media, LLC 2009

impediments and *penalty* for locutional convenience even though in some applications we might be interested in solving a sub-problem for which the master problem considers things such as sensors that do not impeded, but are still modeled as adding a penalty to the distance.

We concern ourselves with situations where the sensors or impediments are reasonably modeled as having a clear spherical range. Travel outside the range of the impediments is without penalty or reward and travel inside the range of an impediment is penalized (or rewarded) in proportion to the distance traveled within the range. This results in a penalty function with gradients that are discontinuous when they are not constant, which preclude the effective use of many classic methods of solving path problems using the calculus of variations [5] and the methods used in planning paths for unmanned air vehicles [9] or aircraft in the presence of radar or senors with a penalty that is continuous [11].

There has been significant work reported in the literature on two dimensional problems where the impediments are obstacles, which is an extreme form of impediment. In particular, very good methods have been proposed for finding optimal paths when there are polygonal obstacles [6]. Earlier work on this problem (e.g., [8]) used *visibility graphs* [10], which were extended by Fishkind et al [7] to the problem of circular obstacles. The basic idea, which we extend in §3, is to build a graph that connects points that include those that must be visited in a shortest path and then find the shortest path through the graph. Extension to three dimensions and the ability to traverse the impediments adds complications that we address in this paper.

The next section describes problem formulations. The problem is ultimately discontinuous and non-convex, but local optima can be found by a commercial solver so in §3 we discuss algorithms for finding good starting solutions. Implementations of the algorithms, problem instances for testing and computational results are described in §4. The paper closes with conclusions and directions for further research.

2 Formulations

A general formulation seeks the best path through a connected, closed set of points $A \subset \Re^D$ from $a \in A$ to $b \in A$ where the presence of impediments affects the evaluation of the quality of the path. We will represent the path as a continuous function $p : [0,1] \to A$. For each point in A a function $f : A \to \Re^+$ allows us to measure the distance plus the penalty. The problem, then, is to

$$\min_p \int_0^1 f(p(t))dt$$

subject to:

$$p(0) = a$$
$$p(1) = b$$
$$p \in C([0,1], A).$$

However $C([0,1], \mathcal{A})$ is the space of continuous functions, which renders this formulation uncomputable except in special cases. Consequently, we consider approximations to the general problem.

Rather than allowing a fully general penalty function such as $f(\cdot)$, we exploit a finite list of impediments $\mathcal{S} \subset \mathcal{A}$ where each member $s \in \mathcal{S}$ has a penalty $c_s \in (-1, \infty)$ and an associated indicator function $\delta_s(\cdot)$ such that $\delta_s(x)$ takes the value one if point x is in the *range* of impediment s. This allows us to split the penalty function and to write our problem formulation as:

$$\min_p \int_0^1 \left(p(t) + \sum_{s \in \mathcal{S}} c_s \delta_s(p(t)) \right) dt \quad \text{(P)}$$

subject to:

$$p(0) = a$$
$$p(1) = b$$
$$p \in C([0,1], \mathcal{A}).$$

If $c_s < 0$ then impediment s is a navigation aid and otherwise it is an impediment of some sort, such as an impediment whose range is to be avoided. Having c_s bounded below by -1 is an artifact of standardizing to a unit penalty for portions of the path not in the range of an impediment. To simplify the generation of test instances and coding of algorithms, we make use of a cube as the region $\mathcal{A}$.

A straightforward solution method is to discretize the space and approximate the integration with a sum. If we create a finite set of points $\mathcal{G} \subset \mathcal{A}$, then for $i, j \in \mathcal{G}$ the path is given by variables p_{ij} which are one if the arc from i to j is in the path and zero otherwise. The version of problem (P) on a grid $\mathcal{G}$ is called (G) and is written as a shortest path problem:

$$\min_p \sum_{i,j \in \mathcal{G}} \left[D_{ij} p_{ij} \left(1 + \sum_{s \in \mathcal{S}} c_s \beta(s, i, j) \right) \right] \quad \text{(G)}$$

subject to:

$$\sum_{i \in \mathcal{G}} I_{ai} p_{ai} = 1$$
$$\sum_{i \in \mathcal{G}} I_{ib} p_{ib} = 1$$
$$\sum_{i \in \mathcal{G}} I_{ik} p_{ik} - \sum_{j \in \mathcal{G}} I_{kj} p_{kj} = 0, \quad k \in \mathcal{G} \setminus \{a, b\}$$

where the elements of incidence matrix, I_{ij}, have the value one if i and j are neighbors and zero otherwise; i.e., it indicates the presence of an arc between grid points i and j. The elements of the distance matrix, D_{ij} give the distances between neighboring points i and j. For the moment, we leave unspecified the definition of the neighborhood, but we have in mind a rectangular grid with the neighbors of i being those points immediately adjacent on the grid coordinates and the diagonals. This formulation assumes that a and b are both in the set $\mathcal{G}$. We have replaced $\delta_s(i)$ with $\beta(s, i, j)$, which gives the portion of the line segment between i and j that is in the range of impediment s. If the problem is to be solved using a general purpose solver, then these values must be pre-computed; however, if a shortest path algorithm is used, they can be computed as needed. The main point is that it is a shortest path problem so once the data is made available it can be computed rapidly for large instances. Unfortunately, for three dimensional problems the instances become *very* large even for modest resolution.

Smaller problem instances can be achieved using a piecewise linear formulation that exploits the fact that the impediment regions are spherical. Each impediment, s has a range with radius r_s. In this formulation, rather than creating a fixed grid *a priori*, we allow the points that define the path to be placed optimally. The path is represented by a vector of breakpoints, p, of length M. Each element $p_i \in \mathcal{A}$ gives the location of the ith point in the path. The trick is to treat the impediment range indicator function as a variable rather than as data: $\tilde{\delta}_s(i)$ is one if the line from p_i to p_{i+1} passes through the range of impediment s and zero otherwise. The formulation makes use of the vector norm, given by $\| \cdot \|$ to establish a length for $\tilde{\delta}$ and determine the path cost. Hence, the formulation has a non-linear objective function and a non-convex feasible region:

$$\min_{p,\tilde{\delta}} \sum_{i=1}^{M-1} \left(\|p_i - p_{i+1}\| \left(1 + \sum_{s \in \mathcal{S}} c_s \tilde{\delta}_s(i) \right) \right) \quad \text{(L)}$$

subject to:

$$p_1 = a$$
$$p_M = b$$
$$p_i \in \mathcal{A}, \quad i = 1, \ldots, M$$
$$\tilde{\delta}_s(i) \in \{0,1\} \quad s \in \mathcal{S}, i = 1, \ldots, M$$
$$\min_{\lambda}\{\|(\lambda p_i + (1-\lambda)p_{i+1}) - s\| : \lambda \in [0,1]\} \geq r_s(1 - \tilde{\delta}_s(i)),$$
$$s \in \mathcal{S}, i = 1, \ldots, M-1$$

With spherical impediments the minimum for the left hand side of the final constraint is given by

$$\|p_i - s\| \qquad , \text{if} \ -\frac{(p_i - p_{i+1})\cdot(p_{i+1} - s)}{\|p_i - p_{i+1}\|^2} < 0$$

$$\|p_{i+1} - s| \qquad , \text{if} \ -\frac{(p_{i+1} - s)\cdot(p_i - p_{i+1})}{\|p_i - p_{i+1}\|^2} > 1$$

$$\frac{\|(p_i - p_{i+1}) \times (p_{i+1} - s)\|}{\|(p_i - p_{i+1})\|} \qquad , \text{otherwise}$$

where $\times$ stand for the cross product and $\cdot$ for the dot product. The minimal distance between the line that goes through p_i and p_{i+1} and the center of s is $\frac{\|(p_i - p_{i+1}) \times (p_{i+1} - s)\|}{\|(p_i - p_{i+1})\|}$. If this point of minimal distance lies between p_i and p_{i+1} this equals the minimum distance between the connecting line and s. Otherwise the minimal distance of the connecting line is the distance to the closer endpoint of the two.

Remark 1 *The problem (L) is identical to the original problem (P), but with restricting the path to all piecewise linear paths with M supporting points instead of $C([0,1], \mathcal{A})$. Since this is a subset (L) gives an upper bound for (P).*

For M → ∞ the set of feasible path converges to the original set and therefore also the value of the objective function.

Since this problem has a non-linear objective function and a non-convex feasible region good starting points are needed to make sure to find a good solution. In the next section we will discuss some methods to find starting solutions.

3 Starting Solutions for Problem (L)

The basic idea for finding a good starting solution is to create a network and find the shortest path through it. The nodes in this network should represent the character of the problem. We generate nodes using tangency and intersection points as we now describe. Formulas that we use to compute the exact locations of these points are given in the Appendix.

3.1 Tangency Points

The shortest path between two points whose direct connection is interdicted by an impediment that should not be entered, is the straight connection on a line that is tangential to the impediment, the shortest path on the surface of the sphere (in the three dimensional case this is a part of a great circle) to another point of the sphere connecting to the ending point of another line tangential to the impediment and then to follow this line. So tangential points are essential points on shortest path when avoiding the impediments and therefore we include them among the nodes of the network. This is basically the idea behind visibility graphs (see, e.g., [7]) reported in the literature for 2D problems. In the two dimensional case for every impediment s and every point $p \in \mathcal{A}$ (outside the impediment) there exist exactly two points on the surface of s so that the connecting line to p is tangential to s. In the following we will refer to the set of these points as the **tangency points**. They are often exploited by algorithms for two dimensional problems.

For the three dimensional case the corresponding points for a point p and a sphere s generally form a complete great circle of s. That is why we choose the **tangency points** for this case to be the points on the great circle of tangency between s and the starting point (and the end point) that are closest from the line connecting between starting point and endpoint.

3.2 Intersection Points and Surface Arcs

Intersection points and surface arcs have not been exploited in the literature to date, but we found them to be helpful for our problems. In order to generate good starting solutions for problems where the impediment ranges are to be avoided we begin with the observation given as Remark 2.

Remark 2 *For every shortest path that avoids all impediments, there are corresponding paths that follow the edges of $\mathcal{A}$ and/or the edges of the impediment ranges that can be reached from the shortest path without crossing an impediment.*

When trying to find a path on the surfaces of the spheres or the boundary of $\mathcal{A}$, the points of interest are those where the impediment ranges intersect with each other or the boundary of $\mathcal{A}$. So these points should be added as nodes in the network.

For D=2, if the impediment ranges that are circles in general position, then for every pair of impediments there are either no points of intersection or exactly two. If $\mathcal{A}$ is a rectangle then there are either zero or two points of intersection with each circle. So this gives at most $2\sum_{k=1}^{|\mathcal{S}|}(|\mathcal{S}|-k)$ nodes for the intersections.

For D=3 the points of intersection form a complete circle. Since later on it is hard to allocate the nodes in the network when only having the three dimensional coordinates, we establish a plane for each sphere. A stereographic projection of the intersection circles on to these planes results in ellipses and helps reduce the network creation to be essentially the same as the two-dimensional case. To discuss the ellipses and the resulting network, it is useful to refer to the sphere for which a plane is defined as the *primary* sphere for that plane. The *secondary* spheres for a particular plane are those spheres that intersect with the primary sphere. Therefore, each secondary sphere results in an ellipse on the plane for the primary sphere. Since we are using a stereographic projection, only those secondary spheres whose circles of intersection with the primary sphere intersect each other will result in intersections of the ellipses on the planes. Such intersections are assigned nodes as in the two dimensional setting. Other ellipses that are isolated on the plane must be assigned nodes at arbitrary points on the ellipses; we use points of tangency with a line parallel to the x-axis. This results in two nodes per isolated ellipse.

3.3 Generating Arcs

Once the set of nodes, N, is constructed the corresponding arcs must be added to the network. For our network there are two classes of arcs:

- **Straight connections** For every pair $n_i, n_j \in N$ of distinct nodes an arc is added to the network that stands for the straight line connection. Therefore the length of this arc is set to the euclidean distance between n_i and n_j plus the fraction of penalty for every impediment this line goes through.
- **Surface connections** For every pair $n_i, n_j \in N$ of distinct nodes that lies on the surface of the same impediment s an arc that follows the surface is added to the network. The length of the arc is the length of the path on the surface plus potential penalty cost for impediments in $S \setminus \{s\}$ where this paths goes through.

For both cases the arcs are only added to the network if they lie completely in $\mathcal{A}$; if they both lie in the region, then the lower cost arc is added. Since for every pair

$n_i, n_j \in N$ of distinct nodes only the cheaper arc of the two is added, the number of arcs in the network is at most

$$\sum_{k=1}^{|N|} (|N| - k) = 2|N|(|N| - 1).$$

4 Computational Results

In this section we describe test instances, algorithm implementations and results of our computational experiments. We are particularly interested in being able to apply these methods to solve sub-problems where the locations of the impediments vary, either because they are design variables or because their locations are uncertain. Hence, we are interested in the average performance of the algorithms both in terms of quality and time.

4.1 Instances

To simplify the parameterization of instances and to facilitate comparison, we use a square region for $\mathcal{A}$ with sides of unit length. For every instance we use a fixed number of spheres with radius and penalty that are selected randomly from a given interval. For most experiments, the starting point and ending point are placed in opposite corners of the region.

Figure 1 shows an examples of a problem instance with 10 small spheres. This example was chosen because it is relatively easy to see most of the spheres. For many problem instances, particularly those with larger spheres, it is difficult to visualize. This is one of the reasons that optimization software is needed to find good paths.

4.2 Implementations

All implementations were done in Xpress-Mosel and run on a 2.8 GHz dual core processor under Linux.

4.2.1 Algorithm G

This algorithm solves problem (G) where the space is discretized with a regular rectangular grid with k points per unit in each dimension. There are a number of reasonable possibilities for placing arcs that we explored experimentally. We let G(k,c) denote the algorithm where arcs are only parallel to the coordinate axes meaning

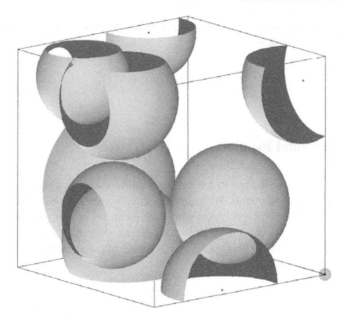

Fig. 1 An example of a problem instance.

that the nodes that only differ in one coordinate by $\frac{1}{k-1}$ are connected by an arc. For G(k,d) we also add the arcs that are diagonal in two dimensions meaning that they are connecting nodes that differ in two coordinates by $\frac{1}{k-1}$. For the three dimensional case we also establish the algorithm G(k,dd) that additionally includes the three dimensional diagonal that means that nodes that differ in all three coordinates by $\frac{1}{k-1}$ are added. It is clear that more arcs will require greater time, but result in a better solution. This tradeoff is explored in §4.6.

In order to give some sense of what these solutions look like, Figure 2 shows the solution generated by G(20,dd) to the problem shown in Figure 1.

4.3 Algorithms SU, TA, SUTA, and SUSITA

Algorithms SU and TA implement the surface and tangency points methods of creating nodes for the shortest path network as described in §3.2 and §3.1, respectively. Algorithm SUTA creates nodes for points of tangency and well as surface intersection. Algorithm SUSITA is the same, except that each point of tangency is connected only with the two closest points of tangency not on the same sphere. This results in a dramatic reduction in the number of arcs and therefore in the computational effort with only moderate impact on solution quality.

Figure 3 shows the results of algorithm SU added to the solution from G(20,dd) as shown in Figure 2. The difference between the two algorithms is clearly shown. Algorithm SU goes from sphere to sphere hugging the surfaces. As we will see, this can produce better results than the grid when the spheres imply a large penalty.

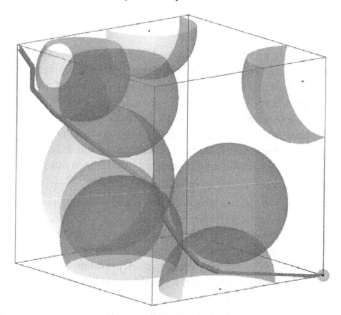

Fig. 2 Solution generated by G(20,dd) to the problem shown in Figure 1.

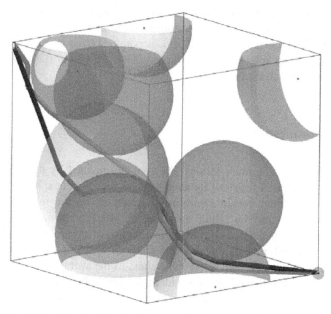

Fig. 3 Results of algorithm Su displayed along with the solution from G(20,dd) as shown in Figure 2.

4.3.1 Algorithm L

This algorithm solves problem (L) using the Xpress SLP package [3]. As noted
in §2, one of the constraints of the problem contains a minimization that can be
divided into three cases and replaced by a non-linear term. In order to implement this
efficiently, we can add the first two cases to the problem since these constraints do
not preclude a feasible solution in any case (if the endpoint of a line is in a sphere you
have to pay the penalty). The third constraint, which says that the minimum distance
between the line and the center must be smaller than the radius or the penalty must
be paid, is only allowed to be binding if the point of minimum distance lies between
the endpoints. So this constraint must be binding iff $0 \leq \frac{\|(p_i - p_{i+1}) \times (p_{i+1} - s)\|}{\|(p_i - p_{i+1})\|} \leq 1$.
Hence, two additional integer variable for every arc are needed, which makes $2|S|M$
extra variables for the complete implementation.

Our main interest is in studying the different ways to generate starting solutions,
so we fix the parameters of Xpress SLP using out-of-the-box values. As a practical
matter, the SLP package works best on our problem instances when the variables
are bounded. Consequently, we bound the variables and then iteratively re-solve the
problem. Based on experimentation, we found that a good way to do this was to
bound the variables to move in each dimension by 0.02 times the distance from a
to b and to re-solve five times starting from the previous solution. The algorithm's
running time is somewhat sensitive to the number of support points M. For the sake
of consistent comparisons between starting solution methods, we set M to 15 for
all runs summarized here. The algorithm L is parameterized by the algorithm that
generates its starting solution. For example L(SU) is problem (L) with a starting
point generated by paths on surfaces.

4.4 Main Results

Table 1 summarizes the main results. The runs are divided by the magnitude of
the randomly generated penalties for each of the 7 impediment spheres. The "Low
Penalty" instances had penalties uniformly generated on the interval (0,1), the
"Medium" on (2,3), and the "High" penalties on (10,20). For each penalty class,
nine instances were generated with impediment radii randomly generated between
0.3 and 0.8. Five different starting solution methods were applied to each instance
as shown in the table. Each cell of the table contains the average deviation from the
best solution found, followed by the standard deviation, then the average total time
in seconds, followed by the standard deviation.

The most striking result is that using only points of tangency to create the graph
works very poorly, as shown in the row labeled L(TA). The other important point is
that for low penalties, a grid is the most effective way to find a starting solution for
problem (L). For higher penalties, a more sophisticated starting point is needed. As
we will see in §4.6, adding resolution to the grid is computationally very expensive.
Hence, the algorithms that create a graph using lines of intersection and tangency

Table 1 Results for instances with seven spheres with random size and penalty. Each cell of the table contains the average deviation from the best solution found, followed by the standard deviation, then the average total time in seconds, followed by the standard deviation. The "Low Penalty" instances had penalties uniformly generated on the interval (0,1), the "Medium" on (2,3), and the "High" penalties on (10,20). For each penalty class, nine instances were generated with impediment radii randomly generated between 0.3 and 0.8.

Algorithm	Low Penalty				Medium Penalty				High Penalty			
	Gap	σ_{gap}	CPU	σ_{cpu}	Gap	σ_{gap}	CPU	σ_{cpu}	Gap	σ_{gap}	CPU	σ_{cpu}
L(G(20,dd))	0.2%	0.3%	166	53	6.0%	10.3%	129	40	15.2%	17.7%	100	40
L(TA)	12.3%	9.6%	64	14	58.1%	45.5%	64	20	180.6%	170.6%	50	20
L(SU)	3.6%	2.9%	124	52	8.9%	8.6%	98	43	13.4%	20.3%	51	43
L(SUTA)	1.9%	3.1%	399	119	5.9%	7.1%	376	114	11.6%	18.5%	256	114
L(SUSITA)	3.5%	3.0%	120	54	8.9%	8.6%	99	43	13.4%	20.3%	51	43

are preferred for instances with high penalties. The high values for the standard deviation of the solution gap, particularly for high penalties, are due to the fact that among the algorithms SU, SUTA, and SUSITA each found the best solution for some instances.

For high penalty instances, SU and SUSITA did not differ in their average performance because most of the arcs chosen for inclusion in the graph by SUSITA were on the surface of the spheres. Algorithm SUTA provides slightly better results at the expense of increased time. This is because some of the distant tangential connections are sometimes better than the near connections, which are all that SUSITA considers.

4.5 Experiments with More Spheres

To see the effect of adding more spheres, consider Table 2. The results are based nine random instances: three each with 15, 20 and 25 spheres. The penalties were medium, i.e., uniformly random on (2,3) and the radii were sampled from (0.2,0.4). There is a significant increase in time for the more sophisticated methods, but the only increase for the grid is due to the execution the non-linear solver for problem (L). Hence, for problems with large numbers of impediments, a grid may be preferred.

4.6 Experiments Concerning Grid Structure

To explore the tradeoffs between grid structure, solution time and solution quality, we solve nine instances each with seven randomly placed spheres with sizes drawn randomly from (0.4,0.8) and penalties drawn from (2,3). To avoid giving an advantage to any of the algorithms we place the start and end point randomly on two opposite sides.

Table 2 Larger number of Spheres. The results from nine random instances: three each with 15, 20 and 25 spheres. The penalties were medium, i.e., uniformly random on (2,3) and the radii were sampled from (0.2,0.4). As in Figure 1, for each algorithm we show the average and standard deviations of the gap to the best solution and the average and standard deviation of the number of CPU seconds.

	Avg. Gap	St. Dev.	Avg. CPU	St. Dev.
Grid20dd	6.6%	13.6%	171	95
L(Su)	7.9%	15.2%	466	531
L(SuSiTa)	7.9%	15.2%	466	526
L(Ta)	46.9%	32.0%	45	27

Table 3 Grid experiments with 9 instances, each with 7 randomly placed spheres and starting and ending points placed randomly on two opposite sides. As in Figure 1, for each algorithm we show the average and standard deviations of the gap to the best solution and the average and standard deviation of the number of CPU seconds.

	Avg. Gap	St. Dev.	Avg. CPU	St. Dev.
L(G(10,c))	17.8%	6.7%	1	0
L(G(20,c))	11.8%	6.3%	9	4
L(G(30,c))	9.2%	5.7%	62	48
L(G(40,c))	7.1%	6.1%	485	512
L(G(10,d))	10.1%	3.8%	2	1
L(G(20,d))	4.2%	2.1%	32	13
L(G(30,d))	2.5%	1.8%	262	148
L(G(35,d))	1.1%	1.9%	775	559
L(G(10,dd))	7.0%	4.7%	3	1
L(G(20,dd))	2.8%	2.5%	55	21
L(G(30,dd))	1.1%	1.6%	502	259

Each instance is solved with the three different definitions of neighborhood with the number of grid points k adjusted so as to keep the run times in close proximity. The results are shown in Table 3. As one would expect, increasing the grid resolution improves solution quality at the expense of solution time. We selected G(20,dd) because the time required was comparable to the other methods and because parameters with slightly better performance required significantly more time.

5 Conclusions and Directions for Further Research

We have provided formulations, algorithms and computational results for continuous shortest path problems in the presence of spherical impediments in 3D space. We have extended line-of-site methods developed for 2D obstacles to create starting solutions for a non-linear solver and demonstrated that the addition of intersection points and surface arcs provides a significant boost. An important conclusion is that a simple grid performs reasonably well and in fact is preferred when the penalties for traversing the impediments are low. This is an important result, because a grid is simple to program and not sensitive to the shapes of the impediments. For many practical applications, a grid can be used to construct an adequate starting point for further refinement by a non-linear solver or for direct use. When better solutions are needed, a network of intersection and tangency points can be constructed and used to find a shortest path that works well as a starting point.

The work could be extended to add a trip length constraint, where the Euclidean travel distance irrespective of impediments is limited. This sort of formulation is important in many applications, for example those involving aircraft [2]. Carlyle, Johannes and Wood [1] have developed a shortest path algorithm that is very effective even though this constraint adds considerable complication. Hence, starting points for (L) are computationally possible using either a grid or the surface and tangency points.

The model could also be extended to consider the case where instead of impediments, there are aides with spherical range. The formulation for problem (L) requires no changes for this case, but the starting points should be selected by constructing a grid that includes the centers of the spheres and perhaps other key points.

Given the 3D benchmark instances, it would also be useful to construct fast heuristics for situations where solutions are needed quickly. Any such work would be greatly aided by improved visualization methods. These things remain as future research.

The problem of finding the shortest path between two points when travel within the range of an impediment adds a penalty can be an important sub-problem to the problem of selecting impediments for interdiction, selecting impediments to probe, and design of robust impediment network. It is also an interesting problem in its own right for which we have provided algorithms, benchmark instances and insights into when simply using a grid is preferred and when more sophisticated algorithms are needed.

Acknowledgment

This work was sponsored in part by the Air Force Office of Sponsored Research under grant F49620-01-0327. The graphics software used in the figures was developed by Jaya Sreevalsan-Nair.

References

1. Carlyle, W. M., J.O. Royset, and R.K. Wood, "Lagrangian Relaxation and Enumeration for Solving Constrained Shortest-Path Problems," *Networks*, to appear, 2008.
2. Carlyle, W. M., J.O. Royset, and R.K. Wood, "Routing Military Aircraft With A Constrained Shotest-path Algorithm," Technical Report, Operations Research Department Naval Postgraduate School Monterey, California, USA, 2007

3. Dash Optimization, *Xpress-SLP, version 2006a*, Blisworth House, Church Lane, Blisworth, Northants NN7 3BX, UK, 2006.
4. Eberly, D., "Intersection of Ellipses," http://www.geometrictools.com/Documentation/IntersectionOfEllipses.pdf, 2000.
5. Gelfand, I.M. and S.V. Fomin, *Calculus of Variations*, Prentice-Hall, Englewood Cliffs, NJ, 1963.
6. Hershberger, J. and S. Suri, "An Optimal Algorithm for Euclidean Shortest Paths on a Plane," *SIAM Journal on Computing*, 28, 1999, 2215–2256.
7. Fishkind, D.E., C.E. Priebe, K. Giles, L.N. Smith and V. Aksakalli, "Disambiguation Protocols Based on Risk Simulation," *IEEE Transactions on Systems, Man, and Cybernetics, Part A*, 137, (2007) 814–823.
8. Kapoor, S., S.N. Maheshwari and J.S.B. Mitchell, "An Efficient Algorithm for Euclidean Shortest Paths Among Polygonal Obstacles in the Plane," *Discrete Computational Geometry*, 18, 1997, 377–383.
9. Kim, J. and J.P. Hespanha, "Discrete Approximations to Continuous Shortest-Path: Applications to Minimum-Risk Path Planning for Groups of UAVs," *Proceedings of the 42nd IEEE Conference on Decision and Control*, 2003, 1734–1740.
10. Rao N.S.V., "Robot Navigation in Unknown Generalized Polygon Terrains Using Vision Sensors," *IEEE Transactions on Systems, Man, and Cybernetics*, 20, 1995, 947–962.
11. Zabarankin, M., Uryasev, S., and R. Murphey. "Aircraft Routing under the Risk of Detection", *Naval Research Logistics*, 53 (2006), 728–747.

Appendix - Projection and Intersection Formulas

The points of intersection of two spheres form a circle but since it is difficult to work with the surface arcs in three dimensions, we project the circles of intersection via stereographic projection on to planes, where they form ellipses. Therefore it suffices to just evaluate a few points of each intersection in three dimensions to compute the coefficients of the corresponding ellipse.

We are given intersecting spheres with center (a,b,c) and radius R and with center(d,e,f) and radius r. To find the points of intersection we move the coordinate system so that the center of the first sphere lies in the origin. Then the center of the second sphere has the coordinates (d-a,e-b,f-c). We assume without loss of generality that $d - a <> 0$ and turn our coordinate system so that both of the other coordinates of the center of the second sphere are zero. For that we use the rotation matrices

$$A = \begin{pmatrix} 1 & 0 & 0 \\ 0 & \cos(\alpha) & -\sin(\alpha) \\ 0 & \sin(\alpha) & \cos(\alpha) \end{pmatrix} \text{ and } B = \begin{pmatrix} \cos(\beta) & 0 & \sin(\beta) \\ 0 & 1 & 0 \\ -\sin(\beta) & 0 & \cos(\beta) \end{pmatrix} \text{ so } (d-a,e-b,f-c)AB =$$

$$\begin{pmatrix} (d-a)\cos(\beta) + (e-b)\sin(\alpha)\sin(\beta) - (f-c)\cos(\alpha)\sin(\beta) \\ (e-b)\cos(\alpha) + (f-c)\sin(\alpha) \\ (d-a)\sin(\beta) - (e-b)\sin(\alpha)\cos(\beta) + (f-c)\cos(\alpha)\cos(\beta)) \end{pmatrix}^T \equiv g$$

We choose α and β so that the transformed center of the second sphere, g, has the desired properties. With $\alpha = \arctan(-\frac{e-b}{f-c})$ for $f - c <> 0$ and $\alpha = \frac{\pi}{2}$ otherwise it follows that $g_2=0$. With $\beta = \arctan(-\frac{\sqrt{(e-b)^2+(f-c)^2}}{d-a})$ for $f-c <> 0$ and $\beta = \arctan(\frac{e-b}{d-a})$ otherwise, it also follows that $g_3=0$.

Using these values of α and β, $g_1 = \sqrt{(d-a)^2+(e-b)^2+(f-c)^2}$, which is the distance between the spheres.

In this coordinate system the spheres have the formulas

$$x^2+y^2+z^2 = R^2$$
$$(x-g_1)^2+y^2+z^2 = r^2$$

So the points of intersection of the spheres form a circle with $x = \frac{R^2-r^2+g_1^2}{2g_1}$ and radius $\tilde{r} = \frac{\sqrt{4g_1^2R^2-(R^2-r^2+g_1^2)^2}}{2g_1}$.

If we turn this circle back to the original coordinate system we get

$$(x,\cos(\theta)\tilde{r},\sin(\theta)\tilde{r})B^{-1}A^{-1}$$

$$= \begin{pmatrix} x\cos(\beta)+\sin(\theta)\tilde{r}\sin(\beta) \\ \cos(\theta)\tilde{r}\cos(\alpha)+x\sin(\beta)\sin(\alpha)-\sin(\theta)\tilde{r}\cos(\beta)\sin(\alpha) \\ \cos(\theta)\tilde{r}\sin(\alpha)-x\sin(\beta)\cos(\alpha)+\sin(\theta)\tilde{r}\cos(\beta)\cos(\alpha) \end{pmatrix}^T$$

for $\theta \in [0, 2\pi]$.

To get the ellipse of intersection in the two dimensional stereographic projection, we select 5 arbitrary points on the intersection circle and perform the projection for the first sphere (i.e., the first sphere is the primary sphere for this projection):

$$(u,v,w) \longmapsto \left(\frac{2Ru}{2R-w}, \frac{2Rv}{2R-w} \right)$$

for points (u,v,w) on the sphere with origin in $(0,0,R)$ and radius R.

We get 5 points lying on the two-dimensional Ellipse $x^2+axy+by^2+cx+dy+e = 0$ so that we can get the coefficients of the ellipse by solving this system of 5 linear equations.

Once we have the ellipses in two dimension, we can easily construct arcs and find the points of intersection of three spheres, so we can construct the network as described in §3.2.

Part 3.3
Miscellaneous

Tailoring Classifier Hyperplanes to General Metrics

John W. Chinneck

Abstract Finding a hyperplane that separates two classes of data points with the minimum number of misclassifications is directly related to the following problem in linear programming: given an infeasible set of linear constraints, find the smallest number of constraints to remove such that the remaining constraints constitute a feasible set (the Maximum Feasible Subsystem problem). This relationship underlies an effective heuristic method for finding separating hyperplanes in classification problems [Chinneck 2001]. This paper shows how to tailor the maximum feasible subsystem hyperplane placement heuristic so that it can provide good values for metrics other than total accuracy. The concepts are demonstrated using accuracy-related metrics such as precision and recall, balancing the population accuracies, and balancing the accuracies on each side of the hyperplane, but the principles also apply to other metrics such as the Gini index, entropy, etc. Customizations such as these may prove useful in developing better decision trees.

Key words: classification, separating hyperplanes, infeasibility analysis

1 Introduction

Linear programming (LP) is frequently used to determine the best way to place a separating hyperplane in classification problems (e.g. Glover [1990], Bennett and Mangasarian [1992], Xiao [1993], and Bennett and Bredensteiner [1997]). One LP-based approach recognizes that the problem of placing a separating hyperplane so that the number of misclassified points is minimized is easily transformed into an equivalent problem of analyzing infeasible LPs known variously as the Maximum Satisfiability Problem, the Maximum Feasible Subsystem Problem, the Minimum Unsatisfied Linear Relation Problem, or the Minimum Cardinality IIS Set Covering

John W. Chinneck

Systems and Computer Engineering, Carleton University, Ottawa, Ontario K1S 5B6, Canada

J.W. Chinneck et al. (eds.), *Operations Research and Cyber-Infrastructure*, Operations Research/Computer Science Interfaces Series 47, DOI: 10.1007/978-0-387-88843-9_19, © Springer Science+Business Media, LLC 2009

Problem [Amaldi 1994, Parker 1995, Chinneck 2001]. The different versions of the infeasible LP analysis problem concentrate on finding the maximum cardinality subset of linear constraints that can be satisfied simultaneously, or on the related dual problem of finding the minimum cardinality subset of constraints to remove such that the remaining constraints comprise a feasible set. We will refer to these problems collectively as the Maximum Feasible Subsystem problem (MAX FS). See Chinneck [2001] and references for some history of approaches to solving this problem.

For a binary classification problem consisting of data points belonging to either type 0 or type 1, the classification problem is converted to a linear program as follows [Chinneck 2001]:

Given: a training set of I data points ($i = 1 \dots I$) in J dimensions ($j = 1 \dots J$), in which the value of attribute j for point i is denoted by d_{ij}, and the class of each point is known (either Type 0 or Type 1).
Define a set of linear constraints as follows (one constraint for each data point):

- for each point of Type 0 : $\Sigma_j d_{ij} w_j \leq w_0 - \in$
- for each point of Type 1 : $\Sigma_j d_{ij} w_j \geq w_0 + \in$

$$(1)$$

where $\in$ is a small positive constant (often set at 1). Note that the variables are the unrestricted w_j, where $j = 0 \dots J$, while the d_{ij} are known constants.

If the data are completely classifiable by a single hyperplane, then any feasible solution to the LP resulting from the conversion will yield a set of values for the w_j that defines the separating hyperplane $\Sigma_j w_j x_{ij} = w_0$, and there is no need for further analysis. In the usual case in which the data points cannot be completely classified by a single hyperplane, then the LP resulting from the conversion is infeasible. Finding a solution to the MAX FS problem in this infeasible LP solves the classification problem of identifying the smallest set of data points to remove such that all of the remaining points are completely classified by a single hyperplane. The actual hyperplane is easily found once the data set has been modified by removal of those points: any feasible solution to the resulting LP suffices, though some choices may be better than others. The points removed will in general be incorrectly classified by the resulting hyperplane, so any solution to the MAX FS problem determines a hyperplane that misclassifies the smallest number of points.

MAX FS is known to be NP-hard [Sankaran 1993; Chakravarti 1994; Amaldi and Kann 1995]. However, there are very good heuristic algorithms for its solution [Chinneck 1996, 2001]; these are reviewed below. An important aspect of these heuristics is that they remove constraints (or points in the classification problem) one by one en route to finding a large (frequently maximum) cardinality feasible subsystem of constraints, and hence a large cardinality set of completely classifiable data points. In the classification context, this means that there is an opportunity to tailor the operation of the algorithms for specific purposes, such as:

- maintaining the relative population accuracies of type 0 and type 1 points (i.e. *specificity* and *sensitivity*) within a narrow band,

- balancing the specificity and sensitivity as closely as possible,
- balancing the zone accuracies (i.e. *precisions*) on both sides of the classifier hyperplane,
- favouring the precision on one side of the classifier hyperplane,
- adjusting for misclassification costs,
- working towards better values of hyperplane selection criteria such as the Gini index,
- taking remedial steps when the classifier returns a degenerate hyperplane that puts all points on one side.

Some of these special variants can address the difficulties that arise when there is a dominant type that comprises most of the data points. In such a case, most hyperplane placement methods tend to simply classify all or nearly all of the data points as being of the dominant type, which gives high overall accuracy due to the prevalence of points of the dominant type. The problem of dominant populations becomes even more severe as the analysis moves to the lower reaches of a developing decision tree. Some of the variants can also address issues such as the need to reduce false-positive or false-negative predictions.

In general, the relative size of the two populations affects hyperplane placement and accuracy assessment (see Flach [2003] for a detailed analysis), and this effect needs to be explicitly considered by new methods that e.g. try to balance the accuracy of each population, or that try to balance the accuracy on either side of the hyperplane.

The variants of the original algorithm will be especially useful in developing decision trees. Decision trees result when the hyperplane placement method is applied repeatedly: first to the overall data set, then to the data on the nominal type 0 side of the initial hyperplane, then to the data on the nominal type 1 side of the initial hyperplane, etc. No further hyperplanes are created when certain stopping conditions are met, e.g. the population of one side of a hyperplane is almost entirely of one type, or is too small (see Rokach and Maimon [2008] for background on decision trees)

Many decision tree construction methods use a greedy approach that chooses the hyperplane (or *rule*) that maximizes the overall accuracy at the current node, but this can be counter-productive. For example, it may be better to separate out a small but highly accurate zone early in the tree, even though the associated hyperplane has a much lower overall accuracy than competing hyperplanes at this node. As Fürnkranz and Flach [2003] point out, the value of the decision rule at a node in the tree lies not in its ability to discriminate between positive and negative examples, but in its potential for being refined into a high-quality rule. There are numerous ways to estimate the worth of a particular separating hyperplane at a node (e.g. Gini index, entropy, etc.; see Fürnkranz and Flach [2003]), so there is obvious value in algorithm variants that tend to return hyperplanes that give better measures on these scores.

Section 2 describes the ways in which the algorithm for solving the MAX FS problem can be tailored. Section 3 presents specific variants that control various accuracy-related metrics, illustrating the differing effects via a two-dimensional data set. Section 4 discusses the characteristics of these particular variants, and Section 5 presents ideas on how these may be used to construct better decision trees.

1.1 Measuring Accuracy

The algorithm variants in this paper concentrate on various types of accuracy metrics, hence clear definitions are needed. All definitions are combinations of these basic elements:

- Initial populations:

  - Pop_0: initial population of type 0 points
  - Pop_1: initial population of type 1 points
  - Pop_T: initial population total ($pop_T = pop_0 + pop_1$)

- Final, or post-classification populations:

  - Pop_{00}: population of type 0 points classified as type 0 (*true negatives*)
  - Pop_{11}: population of type 1 points classified as type 1 (*true positives*)
  - Pop_{01}: population of type 0 points classified as type 1 (*false positives*)
  - Pop_{10}: population of type 1 points classified as type 0 (*false negatives*).

Note that the total population of points classified as type 0 (i.e. the *type 0 zone population*) is $pop_{00} + pop_{10}$ and the total population of points classified as type 1 (i.e. the *type 1 zone population*) is $pop_{11} + pop_{01}$.

Using these elements, we define three types of accuracy:

Overall Accuracy or *Total Population Accuracy*: $A_T = (pop_{00} + pop_{11})/pop_T$

Population Accuracy, the accuracy for each individual type:

- $A_{p0} = pop_{00}/pop_0$
- $A_{p1} = pop_{11}/pop_1$

A_{p1} is also variously known as the *true positive rate, sensitivity* and *recall*. A_{p0} is also variously known as the *true negative rate*, and *specificity*.

Zone Accuracy, the accuracy for the nominal zones created by a single hyperplane:

- $A_{z0} = pop_{00}/(pop_{00} + pop_{10})$
- $A_{z1} = pop_{11}/(pop_{11} + pop_{01})$

A_{z1} is also variously known as *precision, confidence* and *positive prediction accuracy*. A_{z0} is also known as *negative prediction accuracy*.

Consider the simple hyperplane example shown in Fig. 1. The zone to the upper left is nominally type 0 (white dots) and the zone to the lower right is nominally type 1 (black dots). The population counts are as follows: $pop_0 = 14$, $pop_1 = 14$, $pop_T = 28$, $pop_{00} = 11$, $pop_{11} = 10$, $pop_{10} = 4$, $pop_{01} = 3$. The corresponding accuracies are $A_T = (11 + 10)/28 = 0.75$, $A_{p0} = 11/14 = 0.786$, $A_{p1} = 10/14 = 0.714$, $A_{z0} = 11/(11 + 4) = 0.733$, $A_{z1} = 10/(10 + 3) = 0.769$. Note that the accuracies are all different.

Note that the various accuracy definitions are not the only metrics for choosing the best hyperplane from among a selection of candidate hyperplanes at a node in a developing decision tree. Other metrics such as the Gini index and entropy,

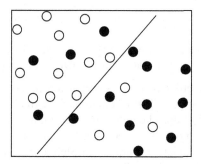

Fig. 1 Separating hyperplane.

among others, can also be used. We will concentrate on the accuracy measures listed above in this paper, but the other metrics can be handled in the same algorithmic framework.

1.2 Placing Classifier Surfaces via the Maximum Feasible Subsystem Heuristic

The basic algorithm for solving the MAX FS problem is briefly reviewed below; consult the original articles [Chinneck 1996, 2001] for details.

The initial infeasible LP (1) is first converted to an elastic form by adding appropriate nonnegative elastic variables [Brown and Graves 1975], analogous to artificial variables in an ordinary phase 1 LP formulation. In the classification application we deal only with row inequalities, which are converted to elastic form as shown in Eqn. 2. A nonnegative elastic variables e_i is added to each row with the appropriate sign.

nonelastic row	elastic row
$\Sigma_j d_{ij} w_j \leq w_0 - \in$	$\Sigma_j d_{ij} w_j - e_i \leq w_0 - \in$
$\Sigma_j d_{ij} w_j \geq w_0 + \in$	$\Sigma_j d_{ij} w_j + e_i \geq w_0 + \in$

$$(2)$$

The associated elastic objective minimizes the sum of the elastic variables. This amounts to determining the minimum sum of the constraint violations in the initial un-elasticized model, and is called the *sum of the infeasibilities* (SINF). If SINF equals zero, then the initial un-elasticized model is feasible. Each nonzero elastic variable indicates a violated constraint in the initial un-elasticized model; this *number of infeasibilities* (NINF) is another measure of the infeasibility of the initial un-elasticized model.

Algorithm 1 presents a simplified version of the basic heuristic algorithm for solving the MAX FS problem. Refinements which improve the efficiency of the algorithm are omitted for clarity. The main ideas in Algorithm 1 are:

- constraints are removed one at a time until those remaining constitute a feasible set,
- at each iteration, a subset of the constraints are candidates for removal,
- the candidate constraint that most reduces SINF is removed permanently.

For the classification problem, the input set of constraints is derived from the data points by the conversion described in Equation 2, normally with $\in = 1.0$, though any positive constant will do. The output of Algorithm 1 is a subset of constraints corresponding to a subset of the data points that constitutes a linearly separable set. Similarly the list of candidate constraints in Step 4 corresponds to a list of data points in the classification problem. The algorithm tailoring described in this paper mainly deals with adjusting this list of candidate data points, usually by completely removing one type of point from the list.

There are several different ways to construct the initial list of candidate constraints in Step 4, using different figures of merit. The most accurate method lists all of the constraints to which the elastic objective function is sensitive [Chinneck 1996]. While quite accurate, this method is slower due to the number of LPs that must be solved (however each LP is similar to the last, so advanced starts are very effective). A faster variant [Chinneck 2001] uses a short list of candidates based on the degree of sensitivity of the elastic objective function to the constraint, and is nearly as accurate. We use the original version throughout this paper.

INPUT: an infeasible set of linear constraints.

1. Elasticize the constraints by adding appropriate elastic variables.
2. Solve the elastic LP.
3. If SINF= 0 then exit.
4. Construct the list of candidate constraints for removal, in decreasing order of figure of merit.
5. For each candidate constraint:

    5.1. Temporarily remove the candidate constraint.
    5.2. Solve the reduced elastic LP and note the new value of SINF.
    5.3. Reinstate the candidate constraint.

6. Permanently remove the candidate constraint whose temporary removal gave the smallest value of SINF.
7. Go to Step 2.

OUTPUT: maximum cardinality feasible subset of constraints.
Alg. 1: Finding a maximum cardinality feasible subset of constraints.

After Alg. 1 has rendered the data set completely classifiable by a single hyperplane, several different methods are available for placing the final hyperplane. Some examples:

a) Use the final hyperplane determined by the feasible solution found in Step 2 of Algorithm 1 just before exiting in Step 3.

b) Maximize the total slack of the constraints associated with the retained points. Each retained point tries to push the separating hyperplane as far away from itself as it can. This tends to push the plane towards the zone associated with the minority type.

c) Averaging. First place a hyperplane as close as possible to the type 1 zone by minimizing the total slack of the constraints associated with the remaining type 1 points. Now perform a similar operation for the type 0 zone. Finally, average the coefficients in the two hyperplanes.

d) Minimize the total slack of the constraints associated with the removed (misclassified) points, while correctly classifying the retained points.

Another good option is to place the final hyperplane using a support vector machine [Cristianini and Shawe-Taylor, 2000], but this has not been tested. The experiments reported later use method (d) for the final hyperplane placement.

2 Customizing Hyperplane Placement

There are 3 ways to tailor the operation of Alg. 1 so that good values of specific metrics can be achieved. These are (i) adjusting the list of candidate constraints in Step 4, (ii) assigning weights to the elastic variables in Eqn. 1, and (iii) using a different figure of merit in Steps 5.2 and 6. These are discussed in detail below. Since adjusting the list of candidates has the greatest impact on the accuracy measures, we rely on that method of customization in the examples below.

2.1 Adjusting the List of Candidates

The most important factor in guiding the hyperplane placement is the adjustment of the list of candidate points for removal (i.e. Step 4 of Alg. 1).

Each solution of an elastic LP in Step 2 of Alg. 1 yields a new temporary hyperplane which does not completely separate the two data types (complete separation happens only for the reduced final dataset output by Alg. 1). However each temporary hyperplane provides a basis for identifying candidate data points for removal. In the LP problem, candidate constraints are either (i) violated constraints, or (ii) constraints that are tight. In the classification problem, these correspond to (i) points misclassified by the temporary hyperplane, and (ii) points that are at a distance of exactly $\in$ from the temporary hyperplane. In this second case, the point is in some sense holding the temporary hyperplane in place.

In the majority of cases, especially early in the process, the points removed belong mainly to category (i), i.e. are misclassified by the current temporary hyperplane. Consider the effect of removing a misclassified type 0 point from the dataset. The next hyperplane no longer attempts to correctly classify this point, and so can move away from it, possibly correctly classifying a few more type 1 points as it does so. In general, the type 1 zone will become larger, and the type 0 zone will become smaller. However, in giving up several type 1 points, the final type 0 zone accuracy will generally increase, while the final type 0 population accuracy will generally decrease. There is an inherent conflict between increasing the population accuracy and increasing the zone accuracy for a given point type.

Population accuracy of a given type is increased simply by claiming more and more of the points as being of that type, i.e. by removing only points of the other type. For example, we can achieve a type 0 population accuracy of 100% simply by claiming all points as being of type 0. This obviously has a negative impact on the population accuracy of type 1, and also on the zone accuracy of type 0.

An avenue for influencing the zone or population accuracy is choosing which type of point is eligible for removal at the next iteration of Alg. 1. This is done by pruning the list of candidate constraints in Step 4 of Alg. 1 of all constraints associated with one or the other type. Which point type is pruned from the list at each iteration is chosen based on the goal of the particular customization. In rare cases the list of candidates is emptied by this technique, in which case the original list is reinstated and used.

Note that pruning of the list of candidates can be guided by any evaluation metric, not just one of the accuracy measures as in the examples presented later. The Gini index, entropy, or any other metric could be used.

2.2 Adjusting the Weights on the Elastic Variables

A second way to adjust the hyperplane placement is to differentially weight the elastic variables described in Eqn. 1. In Alg. 1, the elastic variables associated with both types of data points are weighted equally; however it is straightforward to assign different weights to the two types, perhaps reflecting the relative costs of misclassification errors, or the relative sizes of the constituent populations. Minimization of SINF is then replaced by minimizing the weighted sum of the elastic variables. This causes the LP solution to misclassify fewer of the more highly weighted points. As before, the set of points is completely linearly classifiable when the weighted sum of the elastic variables is zero. This will produce a different list of candidates at each iteration as compared to the unweighted version, typically increasing the list of low-weight candidates and reducing the list of high-weight candidates.

2.3 Selecting the Figure of Merit

Constraints (points) on the list of candidates may influence the positioning of the temporary hyperplane when removed; those not on the list cannot. However exactly where the temporary hyperplane will move after the candidate is removed is not known beforehand, hence the necessity of checking the effect before deciding which candidate to remove permanently. In the original algorithm, SINF is the figure of merit for deciding which candidate to drop permanently. As shown empirically, this works well when the goal is minimizing the total number of violated constraints (or misclassified points).

In principle, any other figure of merit can be used in place of SINF reduction in Steps 5.2 and 6 of Alg. 1 to choose which candidate to drop permanently. For example, we could evaluate the new value of the Gini index after dropping each candidate, choosing to permanently drop the candidate that produces the best value of the Gini index.

2.4 Interactions

Note that the three methods of tailoring interact. Weighting the elastic variables tends to produce hyperplanes that reduce the number of costly misclassifications in favour of more of the cheaper misclassifications, as opposed to minimizing the total number of misclassifications as in the unweighted version. Of course, the hyperplane so produced determines the list of candidates, and pruning the list in various ways has direct effects on the accuracy-related metrics as well as indirect effects on other metrics. At the same time, the selection of the figure of merit may work in a complementary fashion, such as reducing the Gini index. How best to adjust all three customizations simultaneously is the subject of ongoing research.

3 Customizations for Controlling Accuracy

The goal of Alg. 1 is to maximize the overall accuracy of the separating hyperplane. To demonstrate how Alg. 1 can be tailored to pursue diverse metrics, five new variations for different kinds of accuracy metrics are presented in the following sections. These methods have objectives such as maximizing the zone accuracy of one type, balancing the zone accuracies of the two types, balancing the relative populations, etc.

Recall that the general effect of removing a type 1 point (i.e. pruning type 0 points from the list of candidates) has these effects:

- Final population accuracy: type 0 improves, type 1 worsens.
- Final zone accuracy: type 0 worsens, type 1 improves.
- Final zone populations: zone 0 increases, zone 1 decreases.

This happens because the hyperplane moves farther back into the type 1 zone since it no longer has to accommodate the type 1 point that has been eliminated. Removing a type 0 point has the analogous opposite effect.

Some definitions are necessary:

- Kept points:

  - Pop_{k0}: population of type 0 points kept.
  - Pop_{k1}: population of type 1 points kept
  - Pop_{kT}: total population of points kept.
  - Pop_{k00}: population of type 0 points kept and correctly classified by current hyperplane
  - Pop_{k10}: population of type 1 points kept and incorrectly classified by current hyperplane

- Removed points:

  - Pop_{r0}: population of type 0 points removed.
  - Pop_{r1}: population of type 1 points removed

Finally, some of the algorithms make use of a *threshold* control parameter, which takes a value between 0 and 1.

The effects of the various algorithms are demonstrated using a two-dimensional data set derived from the *pima* dataset [Blake and Merz 1998] by keeping only the plasma glucose (horizontal axis) and body mass index (vertical axis) features, and eliminating all data points having missing values. The resulting *pima2d* data set consists of 752 instances (488 of type 0, 264 of type 1). Fig. 2 shows the hyperplane placed by Alg. 1, which seeks maximum overall accuracy. The populations and accuracies associated with Fig. 2 are summarized in Table 1.

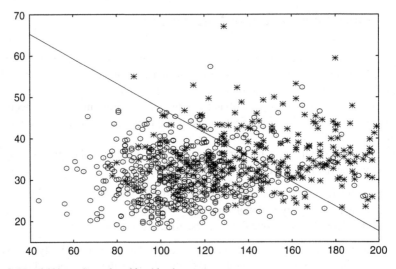

Fig. 2 Pima2d hyperplane placed by Alg. 1.

Table 1 Pima2d confusion matrix for Alg. 1.

		Actual type				Overall	
		0	**1**	pop_z	A_z %		
Nominal type	**0**	442	125	567	77.95	**Wrong**	171
	1	46	139	185	75.14	**Correct**	581
	pop_i	488	264			**Total**	752
	A_p %	90.57	52.65			A_T %	77.26

INPUT: rand-ordered list of candidate constraints and associated points, *MinPopFrac0, MinPopFrac1*.

1. If $pop_{k0}/pop_{kT} < MinPopFrac0$ then eliminate type 0 points from candidate list.
2. If $pop_{k1}/pop_{kT} < MinPopFrac1$ then eliminate type 1 points from candidate list.

Alg. 2: Pruning the candidate list to control the population fractions.

The overall accuracy is moderate at 77.26%, but note that the population accuracy for type 0 is quite high (90.57%) because 567 points are nominally type 0 even though there are only 488 actual type 0 points.

3.1 Controlling the Population Fractions

This algorithm tries to prevent the elimination of a smaller population by a larger one by working to keep the population fractions within a specified range. The algorithm stops eliminating points of one type if their removal forces one of the population fractions outside pre-set bounds. The bounds are defined by a threshold parameter, in this case a small maximum deviation fraction, *MaxDevFrac*. The fraction of the total remaining points associated with the smaller population is maintained in the range $\pm MaxDevFrac \times$ (original population fraction).

For example, consider a data set having 60 type 0 points and 40 type 1 points and *MaxDevFrac* = 0.25. The smaller type 1 population fraction is maintained in the range $0.4 \pm 0.25(0.4)$, i.e. between 0.3 and 0.5 of the total population of points remaining. As a consequence, the type 0 population fraction is maintained between 0.5 and 0.7 of the total population of points remaining. The minimum population fraction for type 0 (*MinPopFrac0*) and for type 1 (*MinPopFrac1*) are calculated in advance and then used as shown in Alg. 2. Note that the candidate list is not pruned if both population fractions are above their lower bounds.

Hyperplanes for the *pima2d* dataset at various values of *MaxDevFrac* are shown in Fig. 3. Note how the value of *MaxDevFrac* affects the placement of the hyperplanes. The results associated with *MaxDevFrac* = 0.0 are given in Table 2, and the

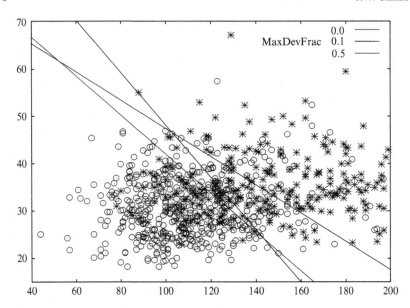

Fig. 3 Pima2d with population fraction control.

Table 2 Pima2d confusion table with population fraction control at *MaxDevFrac* = 0.0.

		Actual type				Overall	
		0	**1**	pop_z	$A_z\%$		
Nominal type	**0**	357	71	357	*83.41*	**Wrong**	202
	1	131	193	324	*59.57*	**Correct**	550
	pop_i	488	264			**Total**	752
	$A_p\%$	*73.16*	*73.11*			$A_T\%$	*73.14*

Table 3 Pima2d confusion matrix with population fraction control at *MaxDevFrac* = 0.1.

		Actual type				Overall	
		0	**1**	pop_z	$A_z\%$		
Nominal type	**0**	382	88	470	*81.28*	**Wrong**	194
	1	106	176	282	*62.41*	**Correct**	558
	pop_i	488	264			**Total**	752
	$A_p\%$	*78.28*	*66.67*			$A_T\%$	*74.20*

results for *MaxDevFrac* = 0.1 are given in Table 3. The results for *MaxDevFrac* = 0.5 are identical to those in Table 1 since this very lenient value does not place any restrictions on the selection of candidates.

The trends are clear. As *MaxDevFrac* increases, more points are classed as being of the dominant type 0. The population accuracy for type 0 increases and the type 0 zone population increases, but the type 0 zone accuracy decreases. Type 1 experiences the opposite effect: the population accuracy decreases and the zone population decreases, but the zone accuracy increases. Notice also that the overall accuracy increases. Maintaining the population fractions in a small range also tends to balance the population accuracies, remarkably so in this case when *MaxDevFrac* is 0.

3.2 Balancing the Population Accuracies

The goal of this method is to balance the population accuracies of the two types as closely as possible. Without control of this nature, the population accuracies can be quite different: in Table 1 the type 0 population accuracy is 90.57% while the type 1 population accuracy is just 52.65%.

As shown in Alg. 3, we make the reasonable assumption that removed points will be misclassified by the final hyperplane, hence the kept points at each iteration are the current best estimate of the points that will be correctly classified by the final hyperplane. The estimated final accuracy is thus easily calculated, and only points of the more accurate type are permitted to remain in the candidate list for removal and hence ultimate misclassification. Note that the candidate list is not altered if the currently estimated population accuracies are identical.

INPUT: rank-ordered list of candidate constraints and associated points.

1. If $pop_{k0}/(pop_{k0} + pop_{r1}) = pop_{k1}/(pop_{k1} + pop_{r0})$ then exit.
2. If $pop_{k0}/(pop_{k0} + pop_{r1}) > pop_{k1}/(pop_{k1} + pop_{r0})$ then eliminate type 0 points from the candidate list.
   Else eliminate type 1 points from the candidate list.

Alg. 3: Pruning the candidate list to balance the population accuracies.

The hyperplane placed by Alg. 3 for the *pima2d* dataset is identical to that shown in Fig. 3 at $MaxDevFrac = 0.0$, and the accuracy results are identical to those summarized in Table 2. As shown in Table 2, the population accuracies are very closely balanced (73.16% for type 0 vs. 73.11% for type 1), but at the cost of lower overall accuracy compared to using unadjusted candidate lists.

3.3 Balancing the Zone Accuracies

The goal of this method is to balance the zone accuracies as closely as possible. The reasonable assumption is again made that all points removed in the course of the algorithm will be misclassified by the final hyperplane. As shown in Alg. 4, the method eliminates points from the currently more accurate zone type from the list of candidates. The next point removed will then be of the least accurate type, and will end up misclassified in the more accurate zone, reducing the accuracy of that zone. If the currently estimated final zone accuracies are identical, then take the top ranked candidate, regardless of point type

The hyperplane for the *pima2d* dataset is illustrated in Fig. 4, and the accuracy results are summarized in Table 4. The zone accuracies are closely balanced (75.46% vs. 78.34%) despite the large differences in their populations. The overall accuracy is not much worse than using the original algorithm.

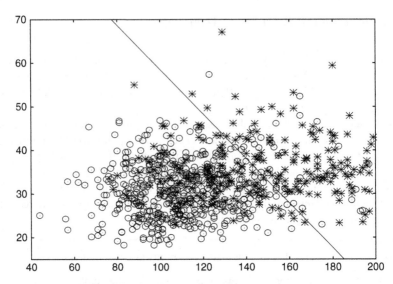

Fig. 4 Pima2d results when balancing the zone accuracies.

Table 4 Pima2d confusion matrix after balancing the zone accuracies.

		Actual type					
		0	**1**	pop_z	$A_z\%$	**Overall**	
Nominal type	**0**	449	141	595	75.46	**Wrong**	180
	1	39	123	157	78.34	**Correct**	572
	pop_i	488	264			**Total**	752
	$A_p\%$	92.01	46.59			$A_T\%$	76.06

INPUT: rank-ordered list of candidate constraints and associated points.

1. IF $pop_{k0}/(pop_{k0} + pop_{r1}) = pop_{k1}/(pop_{k1} + pop_{r0})$ then exit.
2. If $pop_{k0}/(pop_{k0} + pop_{r1}) > pop_{k1}/(pop_{k1} + pop_{r0})$ the eliminate type 0 points from the candidate list.
   Else eliminate type 1 points from the candidate list.

Alg. 4: Pruning the candidate list to balance the zone accuracies.

3.4 Favouring the Zone Accuracy of One Type

The goal here is to maintain the zone accuracy of one type above a specified threshold, which is usually quite high (e.g. 90%). This normally lowers the zone accuracy for the other type. The general effect is to slice off a small but highly accurate group of points of the favoured type. This method actually checks the correctness of the classification of each kept point at each intermediate hyperplane, as shown in Alg. 5, but assumes that removed points will be misclassified by the final hyperplane. As long as the estimated zone accuracy of the favoured type is above the threshold, then the favoured type cannot be removed (in order to keep the zone population as large as possible). There is an analogous algorithm for favouring the accuracy of type 1 points. The two versions are designated Algorithms 5/0 and 5/1.

INPUT: rank-ordered list of candidate constraints and associated points.

1. If $pop_{k00}/(pop_{k00} + pop_{r1} + pop_{k10}) \geq threshold$ then eliminate type 0 points from the candidate list.
   Else eliminate type 1 points from the candidate list.

Algorithm 5: Pruning the candidate list of favour the zone accuracy of type 0.

The hyperplanes for the *pima2d* dataset when favouring the zone accuracy of type 0 at various values of *threshold* are shown in Figure 5, and the accuracy results appear in Table 5 to Table 7. Fig. 5 shows that a threshold setting of 1.0 slices off a zone that is almost purely type 0 (accuracy of 99.09% over 110 points). However it does so at the cost of low overall accuracy (49.47%), and low type 0 population accuracy (22.34%). The trends as the threshold is lowered are clear. The type 0 zone encompasses more and more points, but the zone accuracy decreases. Meanwhile the type 0 population accuracy increases as does the overall accuracy.

This type of edge "slicing" of almost pure zones is useful in many ways. In this application, for example, it eliminates a set of people who almost certainly do not have diabetes. There is no need to subject these people to tests. Pure zones will be useful in the construction of decision trees.

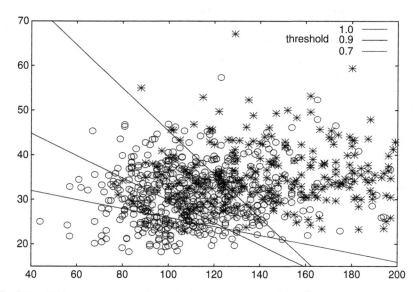

Fig. 5 Pima2d hyperplanes when favouring the zone accuracy of type 0.

Table 5 Pima2d confusion matrix when favouring type 0 zone accuracy at *threshold* = 1.0.

		Actual type				Overall	
		0	1	pop_z	$A_z\%$		
Nominal type	**0**	109	1	110	99.09	**Wrong**	380
	1	379	263	642	40.97	**Correct**	372
	pop_i	488	264			**Total**	752
	$A_p\%$	22.34	99.62			$A_T\%$	49.47

Table 6 Pima2d confusion matrix when favouring type 0 zone accuracy at *threshold* = 0.9.

		Actual type				Overall	
		0	1	pop_z	$A_z\%$		
Nominal type	**0**	182	9	191	95.29	**Wrong**	315
	1	306	255	561	45.45	**Correct**	437
	pop_i	488	264			**Total**	752
	$A_p\%$	37.30	96.59			$A_T\%$	58.11

Table 7 Pima2d confusion matrix when favouring type 0 zone accuracy at *threshold* = 0.7.

		Actual type				Overall	
		0	1	pop_z	$A_z\%$		
Nominal type	**0**	368	77	445	82.70	**Wrong**	197
	1	120	187	307	60.91	**Correct**	555
	pop_i	488	264			**Total**	752
	$A_p\%$	75.41	70.83			$A_T\%$	73.80

3.5 Degenerate Hyperplane Remedies

A degenerate separating hyperplane of the form $0x_1 + 0x_2 + \ldots = 0$ is sometimes re-turned by every hyperplane placement method. This has the effect of classifying all of the points as being of the same type and usually happens when the population of one type is much greater than the population of the other type, hence classifying all points as the majority type gives quite a good overall accuracy. When a degenerate hyperplane is detected, some remedial steps can be taken.

The most effective response is to replace the degenerate hyperplane with the hyperplane obtained by favouring the zone accuracy of the majority type, with the threshold accuracy set higher than the overall accuracy obtained by the degenerate hyperplane. This typically produces an edge slice of the type described in Section 3.4, preserving any clusters of the minority type on one side of the hyperplane. A minority cluster can eventually be isolated by other edge slices as the decision tree develops.

A similar approach is to restart the placement algorithm when a degenerate hyperplane is detected, and to disallow the removal of any minority points at all. This is an extreme version of favouring the zone accuracy of the majority type.

Table 8 Characteristics of example datasets.

dataset	comments	features	pop_0	pop_1
Iris	versicolor vs. others	4	100	50
hd_hungarian	features ignored: slope, ca, thal	10	163	98
Glass	type 2 glass vs. others	9	138	76
Pima		8	500	268

4 Examples

The flexibility of the algorithm variants is demonstrated on a small number of examples in this section. These variants are useful for datasets that are difficult to separate by a single hyperplane, or in which the two populations are mismatched in size, or when there are other special considerations. The four datasets are taken from the UCI repository [Blake and Merz 1998], as summarized in Table 8. Note that the type 1 population is smaller than the type 0 population in all cases, comprising about a third of the points in each dataset.

Controlling the population fractions (Alg. 2) gives interesting results in practice. It always produces very high total accuracies, regardless of the threshold setting. Note that the two extreme threshold settings (0 and 1) have special meanings. At a threshold of 0, Alg. 2 is equivalent to Alg. 3 which balances the population accuracies. Alg. 3 works by always removing points from the type that currently has the highest population accuracy; Alg. 2 with threshold 0 does the same. At a threshold of 1, Alg. 2 is usually equivalent to Alg. 1 since it normally imposes no conditions at all on the removal of points, so the behaviour reverts to that of Alg. 1.

The variants are quite effective in operation. A few specific results for the example datasets are summarized in Table 9. Alg. 2 is excluded from Table 9 since its most interesting results, at the threshold extremes of 0 and 1, are covered by Alg. 3 and Alg. 1 respectively. Boldface entries highlight the effect that each algorithm tries to achieve, e.g. balancing the zone accuracies for Alg. 4; pairs of results are italicized.

The results show that the specialized algorithm variants achieve their goals. Alg. 1 gives the highest total accuracy for each dataset in all of the specific statistics that are shown in Table 9. Alg. 3 always provides the most balanced population accuracies and Alg. 4 the most balanced zone accuracies. Alg. 5 always provides the highest zone accuracies. Other expected patterns can also be seen. The highest false positive rates are associated with the highest zone accuracies for type 0, and the lowest false positive rates are associated with the highest zone accuracies for type 1.

Receiver Operating Characteristic (ROC) curves [Metz 1978] are shown for the example datasets in Fig. 6. ROC curves are created for Alg. 2, for Alg. 5/0 and for Alg. 5/1 by varying the threshold parameter between 0 and 1. Algs. 1, 3 and 4 result in single points rather than curves.

Table 9 Selected statistics for example datasets.

dataset	algorithm(threshold)	fpr	A_{p1}	A_{p0}	A_{z1}	A_{z0}	A_T
Iris	1	0.170	0.840	0.830	0.712	0.912	**0.833**
	3	0.170	*0.840*	*0.830*	0.712	0.912	0.833
	4	0.060	0.340	0.940	*0.739*	*0.740*	0.740
	5/0(1.0)	0.380	1.000	0.620	0.568	**1.000**	0.747
	5/1(1.0)	0.000	0.080	1.000	**1.000**	0.685	0.693
hd_hungarian	1	0.049	0.776	0.951	0.905	0.876	**0.885**
	3	0.135	*0.878*	*0.865*	0.796	0.922	0.870
	4	0.067	0.786	0.933	*0.875*	*0.879*	0.877
	5/0(1.0)	0.540	1.000	0.460	0.527	**1.000**	0.663
	5/1(1.0)	0.006	0.531	0.994	**0.981**	0.779	0.820
Glass	1	0.087	0.645	0.913	0.803	0.824	**0.818**
	3	0.203	*0.776*	*0.797*	0.678	0.866	0.790
	4	0.072	0.579	0.928	*0.815*	*0.800*	0.804
	5/0(1.0)	0.464	0.987	0.536	0.540	**0.987**	0.696
	5/1(1.0)	0.000	0.382	1.000	**1.000**	0.746	0.780
Pima	1	0.088	0.608	0.912	0.787	0.813	**0.806**
	3	0.212	*0.784*	*0.788*	0.665	0.872	0.786
	4	0.074	0.545	0.926	*0.798*	*0.791*	0.793
	5/0(1.0)	0.708	0.996	0.292	0.430	**0.993**	0.538
	5/1(1.0)	0.002	0.168	0.998	**0.978**	0.691	0.708

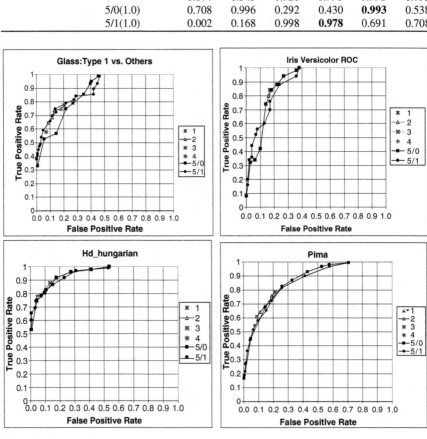

Fig. 6 ROC curves for example datasets.

A notable characteristic of Alg. 5 is the extent to which it affects the ROC curve (see Fig. 6). Alg. 5/0 bulges the ROC curve upwards in the upper right quadrant of the curve, and Alg. 5/1 bulges the ROC curve leftward in the lower left quadrant. This moves the curve towards the desirable (0,1) extreme of the ROC space in both cases. In addition, Alg. 2 tends to provide high quality results in the central portion of the curves (most visible in the *pima* results in Fig. 6). As shown by Provost and Fawcett [2001], combining the convex hulls of several ROC curves allows the construction of a single improved curve. The resulting ROC Convex Hull (ROCCH) is robust, defined as performing at least as well as the best constituent classifier under any target cost and class distributions [Provost and Fawcett 2001]. Instead of simply targeting the best overall accuracy as in the original version, the customized algorithms permit the creation of an ROCCH curve with excellent overall properties by combining the results from Algs. 2, 5/0 and 5/1.

Generally speaking, the tailored versions do not have much impact when Alg. 1 already produces the desired effect. For example, the first two results rows in Table 9 are identical because Alg. 1 already balances the population accuracies quite well. However the customizations have a great effect when the original version does not produce the desired effect, e.g. Alg. 5/1(1.0) greatly improves A_{z1} for the *iris* dataset. Achieving these special results can affect the populations in each zone though, a theme we will return to in Sec. 5.

As heuristics, the customized algorithms function very well, but cannot guarantee to provide perfect results. An example of imperfect operation is visible in Fig. 6: the downward jog for Alg. 5/0 on the left hand extreme in the *glass* dataset. In addition, the best overall accuracy is not always provided by Alg. 1; in some cases a slightly better value is provided by Alg. 2 or 5 at some particular threshold setting. This happens in the *glass* dataset where an A_T of 0.822 is given by Alg. 2(0.1) and by Alg. 5/1(0.65), versus an A_T of 0.818 given by Alg. 1.

5 Toward Better Decision Trees

Classification decision trees are created by the recursive application of hyperplane placement methods (see Rokach and Maimon [2008] for background on decision trees). The general idea motivating the algorithm variants developed here is that a greedy "best total accuracy" metric for placing hyperplanes at every node may not result in the best final decision tree. There exist numerous alternative metrics for measuring the value of a candidate separating hyperplane at a node, including recall, total accuracy, weighted relative accuracy, precision (zone accuracy), Ripper's pruning heuristic, information content, entropy, the Gini index, information gain, Laplace and m-estimates (see Fürnkranz and Flach [2003] for details on these methods). Still, the candidate hyperplanes themselves are very often produced by algorithms that emphasize total accuracy during the placement process. This is so even for methods that have a controllable parameter that results in an ROC curve from which a suitable specific point (and hence specific separating hyperplane) can be chosen.

One important feature of the maximum feasible subsystem algorithm is that the hyperplane selection metric can be specifically considered *while the hyperplane itself is calculated*. We have concentrated on relatively simple accuracy-related metrics here, such as precision, balancing population accuracies and balancing zone accuracies, but the general principle applies to *any* metric. For example, the candidate list could be pruned based on the current value of the Gini index or entropy or any other metric, resulting in a final hyperplane that tends to have a better value for that metric. Thus instead of using the metric solely as a *selection* criterion applied to a set of (mediocre) candidates, we can use the metric to directly *generate* good hyperplanes that score well on the metric.

As mentioned previously, the relative costs of misclassification can also be handled by the customization framework, by assigning weights to the elastic variables. Here again, a measurement metric can be directly incorporated in the algorithm for developing the hyperplane, rather than simply used afterwards to measure the goodness of a hyperplane developed based on some other goal.

The specific algorithm variants presented here may prove quite useful. Alg. 5 is effective in separating out very pure zones: consider Fig. 5 for example. The population of the zone so separated may be small however. For this reason new kinds of visualizations may be needed to help in deciding how to place the hyperplane. One such visualization is shown in Fig. 7 for the *pima2d* dataset from Fig. 5. Fig. 7 shows the relationship between the accuracy of the zone and the population of the zone (as a fraction of the total population). It shows that a much more accurate type 0 zone can be isolated than a type 1 zone, for any zone population size. It also shows that almost any possibility between $A_{z0} = 99.1\%$ for 14.6% of pop_T (110 points)

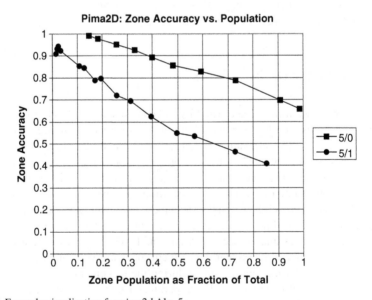

Fig. 7 Example visualization for *pima2d* Alg. 5.

and $A_{z0} = 65.7\%$ for 98.5% of pop$_T$ (741 points) can be selected, depending on the goal of the resulting decision tree.

Similarly, Algs. 3 and 4 may prove useful in specific situations. For example, when trying to subdivide a very mixed node (e.g. at a leaf node), it may be desirable to be about as sure about your type 0 predictions as about your type 1 predictions (assuming similar misclassification costs). Algs. 3 and 4 apply in this case: a new point arriving at this node in the decision tree has an approximately equal chance of being correctly classified, no matter which zone it falls into. Of course, Algs. 3 and 4 provide different separating hyperplanes, and the interpretations are different, mainly with respect to how representative the training set is of the relative frequency of the two types in the general population.

There are two ways to handle misclassification costs in Algs. 3 and 4 when they are not equal. Weighted elastic variables can be used. Another approach is to work towards balancing in terms of the relative misclassification costs. For example, if misclassifying a type 1 point is twice as costly as misclassifying a type 0 point, then remove two type 0 points for every type 1 point as the algorithm proceeds: this will balance the overall misclassification costs, either by zone or by population.

6 Conclusions

The specific algorithm variants for controlling hyperplane accuracy studied in this paper are very effective in reaching their stated goals, e.g. balancing zone accuracies etc. This demonstrates the potential that the maximum feasible subsystem classification heuristic has for customization to produce good values on a variety of other metrics. This differs from the usual approach of using the metrics to select from among a palette of possibly mediocre candidate hyperplanes. The idea here is to *produce* hyperplanes that score well on the selected metric.

There is extensive scope for further work:

- The full integration of the three avenues for customization mentioned in Sec. 2 should be explored. A special point of interest is balancing the effect of list pruning (which works towards minimizing the total number or cost of misclassification) and the figure of merit for selecting the candidate, which may work towards a different goal. Integrated goals, such as balancing zone population sizes at the same time as achieving specific population accuracies should also be investigated.
- Specific customizations to achieve good values of other metrics such as the Gini index should be developed.
- The specific accuracy-related customizations developed here can also be improved, e.g. to find the hyperplane more quickly. Modifications to Alg 5 should also be explored, e.g. to avoid pruning the candidate list at all when the current accuracy is above the target threshold.

- There may be new measures or visualizations that are useful in the development of decision trees (as opposed to the evaluation of a completed decision tree). See Fig. 7 for example.

Finally, the academic prototype software used to carry out the algorithms described herein should be developed into generally-available code. Work is already underway on this project using an open-source LP package.

The ability to find hyperplanes having good scores on a variety of metrics provides much greater flexibility in the construction of decision trees to achieve particular purposes. Experiments in decision tree construction via different policies are ongoing.

References

Amaldi E (1994) From Finding Maximum Feasible Subsystems Of Linear Systems To Feedforward Neural Network Design. Ph.D. thesis no. 1282, Département de Mathématiques, École Polytechnique Fédérale de Lausanne, Switzerland.

Amaldi E, Kann V (1995) The Complexity And Approximability Of Finding Maximum Feasible Subsystems Of Linear Relations, *Theoretical Computer Science* 147:181-210.

Bennett KP, Bredensteiner E (1997) A Parametric Optimization Method for Machine Learning, *INFORMS J. on Computing* 9:311-318.

Bennett KP, Mangasarian OL (1992) Neural Network Training via Linear Programming in Pardalos PM (ed.)Advances in Optimization and Parallel Computing, North Holland, Amsterdam, 56-67.

Blake CL, Merz CJ (1998) UCI Repository Of Machine Learning Databases. Department of Information and Computer Science, University of California, Irvine, CA. http://www.ics.uci.edu/~mlearn/MLRepository.html.

Brown G, Graves G (1975) Elastic Programming: A New Approach To Large-Scale Mixed Integer Optimisation, ORSA/TIMS conference, Las Vegas.

Chakravarti N (1994) Some Results Concerning Post-Infeasibility Analysis, European Journal of Operations Research 73:139-143.

Chinneck JW (1996) An Effective Polynomial-Time Heuristic for the Minimum-Cardinality IIS Set-Covering Problem, Annals of Mathematics and Artificial Intelligence 17:127-144.

Chinneck JW (2001) Fast Heuristics for the Maximum Feasible Subsystem Problem, INFORMS Journal on Computing 13:210-223.

Cristianini N, Shawe-Taylor J (2000) An Introduction to Support Vector Machines and Other Kernel-Based Learning Methods, Cambridge University Press.

Flach PA (2003) The Geometry of ROC Space: Understanding Machine Learning Metrics through ROC Isometrics, Proceedings of the Twentieth International Conference on Machine Learning (ICML-2003), Washington D.C.

Fürnkranz J, Flach PA (2003) An Analysis of Rule Evaluation Metrics, Proceedings of the Twentieth International Conference on Machine Learning (ICML-2003), Washington D.C.

Glover F (1990) Improved Linear Programming Models for Discriminant Analysis, Decision Sciences 21:771-785.

Metz CE (1978) Basic Principles of ROC Analysis, Seminars in Nuclear Medicine 8:283-298.

Parker MR (1995) A set covering approach to infeasibility analysis of linear programming problems and related issues. Ph.D. thesis, Dept. of Mathematics, University of Colorado at Denver, Denver, Colorado.

Provost F, Fawcett T (2001) Robust Classification for Imprecise Environments, Machine Learning 42:203-231.

Rokach L, Maimon O (2008) Data Mining with Decision Trees: Theory and Applications, World Scientific, New Jersey.

Sankaran JK (1993) A Note On Resolving Infeasibility In Linear Programs By Constraint Relaxation, Operations Research Letters 13:19-20.

Xiao, B (1993) Necessary and Sufficient Conditions of Unacceptable Solutions in LP Discriminant Analysis, Decision Sciences 24:699-712.

The Multi-Sensor Nuclear Threat Detection Problem

Dorit S. Hochbaum

Abstract One way of reducing false-positive and false-negative errors in an alerting system, is by considering inputs from multiple sources. We address here the problem of detecting nuclear threats by using multiple detectors mounted on moving vehicles in an urban area. The likelihood of false alerts diminishes when reports from several independent sources are available. However, the detectors are in different positions and therefore the significance of their reporting varies with the distance from the unknown source position. An example scenario is that of multiple taxi cabs each carrying a detector. The real-time detectors' positions are known in real time as these are continuously reported from GPS data. The level of detected risk is then reported from each detector at each position. The problem is to delineate the presence of a potentially dangerous source and its approximate location by identifying a small area that has higher than threshold concentration of reported risk. This problem of using spatially varying detector networks to identify and locate risks is modeled and formulated here. The problem is then shown to be solvable in polynomial time and with a combinatorial network flow algorithm.

Key words: Nuclear threat detection, network flow, parametric cut.

1 Introduction

We consider here a scenario in an urban environment facing potential nuclear threats such as "dirty bombs". With recent technology it has become operational and cost-effective for multiple detectors to be mounted on vehicles in public service. Sodium Iodine detectors are currently deployed on vehicles such as police cars, fire trucks, trains, buses or even taxi cabs. A scenario involving taxi cabs carrying detectors

Dorit S. Hochbaum
UC Berkeley Ca 94720 e-mail: hochbaum@ieor.berkeley.edu

J.W. Chinneck et al. (eds.), *Operations Research and Cyber-Infrastructure*, Operations Research/Computer Science Interfaces Series 47, DOI: 10.1007/978-0-387-88843-9_20, © Springer Science+Business Media, LLC 2009

in Manhattan was recently proposed by Fred Roberts (at the ARI Washington DC conference) as a problem of interest. The information transmitted by the detectors is to be used as input in a process which is to identify a "small region" with a "high concentration" of risk. We formalize and define this problem quantitatively and devise an efficient graph algorithm that solves the problem in polynomial time.

Detecting nuclear threats is a challenging problem under any circumstances. The detection task is more challenging when the relative positions of the detector and the source, if exists, are unknown. The sensitivity of the detectors is diminishing with distance from the source, thus their geographic position impacts the reliability of their reporting. Further, a detector may fail to detect correctly an existing threat (false-negative), or report an alert on the existence of a nuclear source when there is none (false-positive). The likelihood of false reports is diminished and their effect is mitigated when relying on reports from several independent sources. We are interested in reducing the likelihood of false-positive and false-negative reports on detecting nuclear threats in an urban environment. The idea is to mount detectors on every taxi cab in an environment such as New York City, or on police cars in areas where the density of taxi cabs is small. The position of each detector is known at any point in time from GPS information transmitted to a central control data processing facility.

The goal is to identify, at every period of time, a region within the area of interest, which is limited in size and with high concentration of alerts. The purpose is to delineate the presence of a potentially dangerous source and its approximate location. The detectors transmitted information, along with the geographical positioning of the collection of detectors is to be consolidated into reliable reporting on whether nuclear threat exists, and if so, its approximate position. In case this information is deemed to indicate a high enough likelihood of real danger, the detection operations shifts to a high alert state where higher sensitivity detectors and personnel with expertise will be deployed into the region of interest with the task of pinpointing, locating and disabling the source of the threat.

The alert concentration problem is quantified here as an optimization problem, combining two goals: One goal is to identify a small region; another goal is to have large number of alerts, or high concentration of alerts in the region. These two goals are potentially conflicting – focusing on a large number of alerts within an area is likely to result in the entire region; on the other hand focusing on concentration alone would result in a single block of the area containing the highest level of reported alert, thus disregarding information provided by other detectors in the adjacent area.

Overview of paper We first provide the formalism for describing the problem. We then formulate a mathematical programming model for the problem, parametrized by a weight, β, that balances the relative contribution of the two goals. We then show how the problem is solvable in polynomial time as a minimum s,t-cut problem. We further show how to solve the problem for all values of the parameter using a parametric cut procedure.

2 Notation and Preliminaries

We introduce here graph theoretic notation to be used in formulating the problem. Without loss of generality we consider the region where the detectors are deployed to be a rectangular area subdivided in grid squares. These will be small enough to contain approximately one vehicle and up to two detectors (although this assumption plays no role in the formulation). Let V be the collection of positions (blocks or pixels of the grid) in the area considered.

We construct a directed graph G with the set of nodes V corresponding to the set of blocks. For each adjacent pair of blocks, if one is within the region and the other outside, the added length to the boundary is 1. The adjacency $[i,j]$ is represented by a pair of arcs in opposite directions each of capacity 1. These arcs are referred to as the "adjacency" arcs of G, and denoted by A_a.

Let $B_1, B_2 \subset V$ be two disjoint sets of nodes in a graph $G = (V,A)$ with arc capacity u_{ij} for each $(i,j) \in A$. The capacity of the *cut* separating the two sets is $C(B_1, B_2) = \sum_{i \in B_1, j \in B_2, (i,j) \in A} u_{ij}$. Note that this quantity is not symmetric as $C(B_1, B_2)$ is in general not equal to $C(B_2, B_1)$.

Let $S \subset V$ be the blocks of a selected sub-region. We measure the *size* of the area delineated by S, by the length of its boundary, counted as the number of block sides that separate S from $\bar{S}$. The length of the boundary of a subset of grid points S is then $\sum_{i \in S, j \in \bar{S}, (i,j) \in A_a} u_{ij}$. Since the set A_a contains arcs of capacity 1, this length is equal to $C(S, \bar{S}) = |\{[i,j] | i \in S, j \in \bar{S}\}|$. Note that there is no requirement that the set S is contiguous. Indeed it can be formed of several connected components. It will be shown that a ratio formulation of the problem can always obtain a solution forming a single connected component.

Let G_{st} be a graph (V_{st}, A_{st}), where $V_{st} = V \cup \{s,t\}$ and $A_{st} = A \cup A_s \cup A_t$ in which A_s and A_t are the source-adjacent and sink-adjacent arcs respectively. A flow vector $f = \{f_{ij}\}_{(i,j) \in A_{st}}$ is said to be *feasible* if it satisfies:
(i) Flow balance constraints: for each $j \in V$, $\sum_{(i,j) \in A_{st}} f_{ij} = \sum_{(j,k) \in A_{st}} f_{jk}$ (i.e., inflow(j) = outflow(j)), and
(ii) Capacity constraints: the flow value is between the lower bound and upper bound capacity of the arc, i.e., $0 \leq f_{ij} \leq u_{ij}$.

A *maximum flow* is a feasible flow f^* that maximizes the flow out of the source (or into the sink), called the *value of the flow*. The value of the maximum flow is $\sum_{(s,i) \in A_s} f_{si}^*$. An s,t cut in G_{st} (or *cut* for short) is a partition of V_{st} to $(S \cup \{s\}, T \cup \{t\})$. The capacity of the cut is $C(S \cup \{s\}, T \cup \{t\})$. The minimum s,t cut is the cut of minimum capacity, referred to here as *min-cut*. It is well known (Ford-Fulkerson [3]) that the maximum value of the flow is equal to the capacity of the min-cut. Every algorithm known to date that solves the min-cut problem, also solves the maximum flow problem.

2.1 The Input

The information captured by a detector is a spectrum of gamma ray emissions recording the frequency at each energy level. As such this is not scalar-valued information. The analysis of the detected energies spectrum therefore presents a challenge. The analysis process is currently under development using advanced data mining techniques (by e.g. the DONUTS research group at UC Berkeley, [2]). The output of the analysis is an indication of whether the detected information indicates the presence of a nuclear threat or not.

At a given time instance, let D be the set of positions of taxis with $D^* \subseteq D$ representing the set of positions reporting alert. The set $\bar{D}^* = D \setminus D^*$ is the set of taxi positions reporting no alert.

We will consider an extension of the model to account for varying levels of alert and varying levels of no-alert. This is when the analysis of the detectors transmitted information delivers, for each alert reported by a detector at i, an alert confidence level of p_i. For each no-alert reported from position j, there is a no-alert confidence level of q_j.

3 Formulating the Objective Function

Since our objective involves multiple goals, we address these by setting a trade-off between the importance of the short boundary versus the high concentration of alerts. One way of trading these off is by minimizing a ratio function – of the length of the boundary divided by the concentration of alerts in the region. Another, is to use a weighted combination of the goals.

To formalize the goal of "small area" we define an area to be of small size if it is enclosed by a "short" boundary. The boundary of an area is then the number of edges that separate in-region from out-region, or the rectilinear length of the boundary. In the graph $G = (V, A_a)$ defined in Section 2 the length of the boundary of a set $S \subset V$ is $C(S, \bar{S})$. Prior to proceeding, we note that this definition of length needs certain tweaking. Let the set of boundary blocks of the entire area considered be denoted by B. With the definition of the set of arcs A_a, the selection of any subset of B reduces the defined size of the region. For example, if the selected region is all of V then the length of the circumference $C(V, \emptyset)$ is equal to 0. To prevent that, we add a set of arcs A_B from the boundary nodes to an imaginary point in space. This will be quantified in a manner explained later. We let the corner blocks contribute 2 to the length of the boundary, if included in the set. The length of the boundary is thus $C(S, \bar{S}) + |B \cap S|$ where we count the corner block twice in B (instead of introducing additional notation.)

Next we formalized the goal of identifying high concentration of alerts. One indication of the level of alert in an area is the number of alerts at higher than threshold level within the area. Let for now, for the sake of simplicity, assume that the inputs are in the form of alert or no-alert. Let $D \subseteq V$ be the set of position occupied by vehicles. Let $D^* \subset D$ be the set of positions reporting alerts. Part of our objective is then to identify a subregion of positions containing S so that $|D^* \cap S|$ is maximized.

Maximizing the number of alerts within the selected region is an objective that has some pitfalls. For instance, if the region considered, S, contains, in addition to the alerts, also a relatively high number of no-alerts $\bar{D}^* \cap S$, for $\bar{D}^* = D \setminus D^*$, then this should diminish the significance of the alerts in the region. The extent to which the alert significance is diminished is not obvious at this point in time and will require simulation studies, which we plan to undertake. Therefore, we add yet another minimization objective, $\min |\bar{D}^* \cap S|$. This objective is then combined with the length of the boundary objective, as $\min C(S, \bar{S}) + |B \cap S| + \alpha |\bar{D}^* \cap S|$. Although, in terms of the model, we do not restrict the value of α, it is reasonable that α should be a small value compared to the contribution of alert positions, as discussed below. If we choose to disregard the number of no-alerts in the region, then this is captured by setting $\alpha = 0$.

3.1 Ratio Function and Weighted Combination Formulations

One way of combining a maximization objective $g(x)$ with a minimization objective $f(x)$ is to minimize the ratio of the two functions $\frac{f(x)}{g(x)}$. For the alert concentration problem the ratio objective function is:

$$\min_{S \subset V} \frac{C(S, \bar{S}) + |B \cap S| + \alpha |\bar{D}^* \cap S|}{|D^* \cap S|}.$$

One advantage of using this ratio formulation is that it is guaranteed that an optimal solution will be a single connected component. This was proved in Hochbaum [5] for a general family of ratio problems. Formally, we define the concept of *additive functions*. For a set of connected components in the graph $A_1, \ldots, A_k$, $A_i \subset V$, that are pairwise disjoint, the function $f()$ is said to be additive if $f(\cup_{j=1}^{k} A_j) = \sum_{j=1}^{k} f(A_j)$. For additive ratio functions there is an optimal solution consisting of a single connected component:

Theorem 1. *[Hochbaum 2008] For additive functions f and g, there exists an optimal solution to the problem $\min \frac{f(x)}{g(x)}$ consisting of a single connected component and its complement.*

It is easy to verify that our functions here are additive, and hence the existence of a single connected component optimal solution follows.

An alternative to the ratio presentation is to minimize a function which is a linear combination of the two objectives. Using β as a weight for the relative importance of the weights, the objective function is:

$$\min_{S \subseteq V} C(S, \bar{S}) + |B \cap S| + \alpha |\bar{D}^* \cap S| - \beta |D^* \cap S|.$$

It is in comparison to β that the value of α should be small. This will reflect the perceived relative diminishing of the threat in the presence of no-alerts in the region.

The solution procedure for this linear combination problem can be used as a routine for solving the respective ratio problem. A standard technique for solving a ratio problem is to "linearize" it. The β-question for the problem $\min \frac{f(x)}{g(x)}$ is:

Is $\min \frac{f(x)}{g(x)} \leq \beta$?

This is equivalent to solving the linear version

Is $\min f(x) - \beta g(x) \leq 0$?

Therefore if we can solve the linear version of the problem for each β and the logarithm of the number of possible values of β is small enough (of polynomial size) then the ratio problem is solved by a polynomial number of calls to the linear version. Note that the reverse is not necessarily true and the ratio version and the linear version might be of different complexities (for details on these issues that reader is referred to [5].)

Here we devise an algorithm that solves the linearized problem, and for all values of β, in strongly polynomial time.

The linearized objective of the concentrated alert (CA) problem is then modified:

$$(CA) \quad \min_{S \subseteq V} C(S,\bar{S}) + |B \cap S| - \beta |D^* \cap S| + \alpha |\bar{D}^* \cap S|.$$

The problem (CA) has two parameters, β and α. We show solve the problem for all values of β provided that α is fixed, and vice versa. Each of these algorithms will be shown to be running in strongly polynomial time for all values of the parameter.

3.2 Constructing the Graph

Let the region be represented by a collection of nodes V of a directed graph where each block is represented by a node. The set of nodes is appended by a *source* dummy node s and *sink* dummy node t.

An edge represents two adjacent blocks, where the adjacency can be selected to be any form of adjacency. Here we use either the *4-neighbors* adjacency or *8-neighbors* adjacency. The weight of each edge is set to 1, and each edge $[i, j]$ is replaced by two directed arcs, (i, j) and (j, i) both of capacity 1. These arcs form the set A_a.

We connect the set of arcs A_B to the sink t with capacities of 1 except for "corner" blocks that contribute 2 to the length of the boundary. Each position that contains an alert taxi in D^* is set to be adjacent to s with a directed arc of capacity β. Each position that contains a no-alert taxi, in $\bar{D}^*$, is set to be adjacent to t with a directed arc of capacity α. We denote these sets of arcs by A_β and A_α respectively.

We therefore constructed a directed s, t graph $G_{st} = (V_{st}, A)$, where $V_{st} = V \cup \{s, t\}$ and $A = A_a \cup A_B \cup A_\beta \cup A_\alpha$. The construction of the graph is illustrated in Figure 1 where an alert position is indicated by a solid circle, and a no-alert position by a crossed circle.

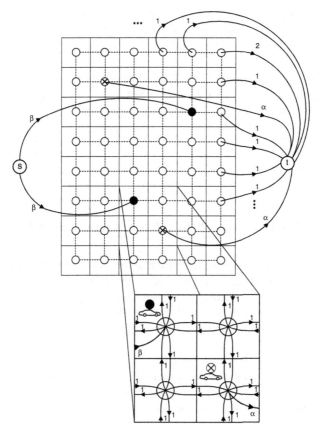

Fig. 1 The graph G_{st}.

We now have a graph $G = (V \cup \{s,t\}, A)$ with arc capacities u_{ij} for arc $(i,j) \in A$, on which we define the minimum s,t-cut problem and show that solving it provides the optimal solution to our CA problem.

4 Main Theorem

Let a cut be a partition (S,T) of V of capacity $C(S,T) = \sum_{(i,j)\in A, i\in S j\in T} u_{ij}$.

Theorem 2. *The source set of the minimum cut in the graph G_{st} is the optimal region for problem CA.*

Proof. Let $(S\cup\{s\}, T\cup\{t\})$ be a partition of $V\cup\{s,t\}$ and thus an s,t-cut in G. We compute this cut's capacity:

$$C(S \cup \{s\}, T \cup \{t\}) = |B \cap S| + |\bar{D}^* \cap S|\alpha + |D^* \cap T|\beta + \sum_{(i,j) \in A, i \in S j \in T} 1$$
$$= |B \cap S| + |\bar{D}^* \cap S|\alpha + (|D^*| - |D^* \cap S|)\beta + C(S, T)$$
$$= |D^*|\beta + |B \cap S| + C(S, T) + |\bar{D}^* \cap S|\alpha - |D^* \cap S|\beta.$$

Now the first term is a constant $|D^*|\beta$. Thus minimizing $C(S \cup \{s\}, T \cup \{t\})$ is equivalent to minimizing $|B \cap S| + C(S, T) + |\bar{D}^* \cap S|\alpha - |D^* \cap S|\beta$, which is the objective of the CA problem.

We conclude that solving the concentrated alert problem reduces to finding the minimum s, t cut in the graph G_{st}. The region we are seeking will then correspond to the source set S of the minimum cut $(S \cup \{s\}, T \cup \{t\})$.

5 The Weighted Version of the Alert Concentration Problem

The information provided by the detector may be too ambiguous to translate to a simple binary statement of the form of alert or no-alert. Instead, one defines a threshold level, and within the above-threshold alert category, one creates a function that maps the alert profile transmitted from location i to a weight value p_i that is monotone increasing with the increased confidence in the significance of the alert information.

Similarly, the below-threshold category of no-alert maps into a weight value q_i that is monotone increasing with the increased confidence in the significance of the no-alert information. The modified *weighted concentrated alert* problem is then to find a sub-region S, optimizing the function

$$\text{(WCA)} \quad \min_{S \subseteq V} C(S, \bar{S}) + |B \cap S| + \alpha \sum_{i \in \bar{D}^* \cap S} q_i - \beta \sum_{i \in D^* \cap S} p_i.$$

In order to solve this weighted problem we modify the assignments of capacities to the arcs in the graph G_{st} as follows:
For each position i in D^* we let the capacity of the arc from the source to i be, $u_{si} = \beta p_i$, and for each position i in $\bar{D}^*$ we let the capacity of the arc from i to the sink be, $u_{it} = \alpha q_i$. We call the graph with these modified arc capacities G_{st}^W. We claim that a weighted version of Theorem 2 applies:

Theorem 3. *The source set of the minimum cut in the graph G_{st}^W is the optimal region for problem WCA.*

Proof. The proof is a simple generalization of Theorem 2. We include it here for the sake of completeness.
Let $(S \cup \{s\}, T \cup \{t\})$ be, as before, an s, t-cut in G, of capacity:

$$C(S \cup \{s\}, T \cup \{t\}) = |B \cap S| + \alpha \sum_{i \in \bar{D}^* \cap S} q_i + \beta \alpha \sum_{j \in D^* \cap T} p_j + \sum_{(i,j) \in A, i \in S j \in T} 1$$
$$= |B \cap S| + \alpha \sum_{j \in \bar{D}^* \cap S} q_i + \beta (\sum_{i \in V} p_i - \sum_{j \in D^* \cap S} p_j) + C(S, T)$$
$$= \beta \sum_{i \in V} p_i + |B \cap S| + C(S, T) + \alpha \sum_{i \in \bar{D}^* \cap S} q_i - \beta \sum_{j \in \bar{D}^* \cap S} p_j.$$

Since $\beta \sum_{i \in V} p_i$ is a constant, the source set of the minimum cut is also minimizing $|B \cap S| + C(S,T) + \alpha \sum_{i \in \bar{D}^* \cap S} q_i - \beta \sum_{j \in \bar{D}^* \cap S} p_j$.

6 Solving for all Values of the Parameters

As the value of β is changing the solution changes as well. Instead of solving for each value of β we note that the source adjacent arcs are monotone increasing in β and the sink adjacent arcs's capacities are unaffected. Therefore this is a scenario of the parametric maximum flow minimum cut problem. The complexity of solving such a problem is the same as the complexity of solving for a single minimum s,t cut [4] with the push-relabel algorithm. We plan to use the parametric pseudoflow algorithm, [6], that also solves the problem in the same complexity as a single cut. The source code of the solver we use is available at [1].

Since we can find the solution for all values of β, this leads to finding the optimal solution to the respective ratio problem which corresponds to the largest value of β where the solution value is still ≤ 0.

It is possible to conduct the sensitivity on the parameter α independently from that on β. In other words, we keep β fixed and then study the effect on the solution of solving for all possible values of α.

7 Numerical Examples

Several instances of the problem were devised on a grid. In the figures below a full circle represents a detector position reporting alert and a crossed circle represents a detector position reporting no-alert. The length of the boundary was taken to be its rectilinear length. That is, the 4-neighbor adjacency was selected. The problem instances were run for $\beta = 3.99$ and $\alpha = 0.5\beta$. The reason why the value of β is just under 4 is to prevent the generation of regions consisting of singletons of alert positions.

In Figure 2 the set V is a 7×10 grid. The set of three alert positions forms the optimal solution. The optimal region is indicated by darker shade. Notice that in this example there are, on row 10, two alert positions separated by an empty position. Although these might indicate an elevated alert status for that area, the vacant grid position rules out selecting this set. The presence of vacant positions therefore should not necessarily be interpreted as diminishing the alert level. These are only the result of a random distribution of the positions.

To allow for regions to be generated even if they contain alert positions separated by a small number of empty grid points, we assign a small value of β, denoted by γ, to each vacant grid point. That means that every vacant position is interpreted as a "minor" alert position and the objective function has an extra term $-\gamma |V \setminus D|$. The modification in the graph of Figure 1 is to add arcs from source s to every

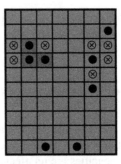

Fig. 2 The solution for a 7×10 grid.

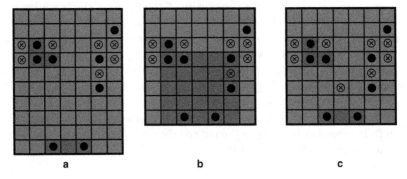

a   b   c

Fig. 3 The effect of introducing γ values to vacant grid positions.

unoccupied square in the grid with capacity γ each. Theorem 2 is easily extended for this case. In the next set of examples we set $\gamma = 0.021$.

As we see in Figure 3(a), the addition of the γ coefficient indeed changes the optimal solution, and now we have two alert regions, one of which contains an empty position. However, if the two regions are "close", and in the given configuration they are 3 rows apart, as shown in Figure 3(b), then the two regions merge into one. In Figure 3(c) one sees that adding one no-alert position within the region has the effect of separating the two regions. The determination of which values to set and when regions should be consolidated is to be determined by nuclear detection experts and the geographical parameters of the region, as well as the density of the detectors' distribution in the region.

8 Conclusions

We present here a formulation and an efficient algorithm solving the alert concentration problem. The approach presented allows to focus resources on real threats and reduce the likelihood of false-positive and false-negative alerts. We believe that each practical setting should be characterized by the density of the the vehicles carrying detectors, by the sensitivity of the detectors – in terms of distance from a source – and by the finesse of the grid. Each setting requires different values of the parameters β, γ and α. The plan for follow up research is to have these values fine-tuned by simulating the application of the procedure on simulated data. This will be done by considering the resulting size of the region generated and how it corresponds to the detectors' range.

Acknowledgements The author's research has been supported in part by CBET-0736232 and NSF award No. DMI-0620677.

References

1. B. Chandran and D. S. Hochbaum. Pseudoflow solver, accessed January 2007. http://riot.ieor.berkeley.edu/riot/Applications/Pseudoflow/maxflow.html.
2. Domestic Nuclear Threat Security initiative. http://donuts.berkeley.edu/.
3. L. R. Ford and D. R. Fulkerson. (1956). Maximal flow through a network. *Canadian Journal of Math.*, 8, 339–404.
4. Gallo G., M. D. Grigoriadis, R. E. Tarjan. (1989). A fast parametric maximum flow algorithm and applications. *SIAM J. Comput.* 18(1), 30–55.
5. D. S. Hochbaum. Polynomial time algorithms for the normalized cut problem and bi-criteria, multi-objective and ratio problems in clustering, imaging and vision grouping: Part II. 2008.
6. D. S. Hochbaum. The Pseudoflow algorithm: A new algorithm for the maximum flow problem. *Operations Research*, to appear. Extended abstract in: The pseudoflow algorithm and the pseudoflow-based simplex for the maximum flow problem. (1998). Procdeedings of IPCO98. *Lecture Notes in Computer Science*, Bixby, Boyd and Rios-Mercado (Eds.) 1412, Springer, 325–337.

Radiotherapy optimAl Design: An Academic Radiotherapy Treatment Design System

R. Acosta, W. Brick, A. Hanna, A. Holder, D. Lara, G. McQuilen, D. Nevin, P. Uhlig, and B. Salter

Abstract Optimally designing radiotherapy and radiosurgery treatments to increase the likelihood of a successful recovery from cancer is an important application of operations research. Researchers have been hindered by the lack of academic software that supports comparisons between different solution techniques on the same design problem, and this article addresses the inherent difficulties of designing and implementing an academic treatment planning system. In particular, this article details the algorithms and the software design of Radiotherapy optimAl Design (RAD), which includes a novel reduction scheme, a flexible design to support comparative research, and a new imaging construct.

Key words: Optimization, Radiotherapy, Radiosurgery, Medical Physics

R. Acosta
Stanford University, Palo Alto, CA, e-mail: `raacosta@standford.edu`

W. Brick
Trinity University, San Antonio, TX, e-mail: `William.Brick@gmail.com`

A. Hanna
St. Mary's University, San Antonio, TX, e-mail: `ahanna@stmarytx.edu`

A. Holder
Rose-Hulman Institute of Technology, Terre Haute, IN, e-mail: `holder@rose-hulman.edu`

D. Lara
Altarum Institute, San Antonio, TX, e-mail: `ronin2448@gmail.com`

G. McQuilen
The International School of the Americas, San Antonio, TX, e-mail: `gmcqui@neisd.net`

D. Nevin
Decision Strategies, Houston, TX, e-mail: `dnevin@decisionstrategies.com`

P. Uhlig
St. Mary's University, San Antonio, TX, e-mail: `mathpaul@stmarytx.edu`

B. Salter
Huntsman Cancer Institute, Salt Lake City, UT, e-mail: `Bill.Salter@hci.utah.edu`

J.W. Chinneck et al. (eds.), *Operations Research and Cyber-Infrastructure*, Operations Research/Computer Science Interfaces Series 47, DOI: 10.1007/978-0-387-88843-9_21, © Springer Science+Business Media, LLC 2009

1 Introduction

With the USA spending about 18% of its gross national product on health care, the need to efficiently manage and deliver health services has never been greater. In fact, some distinguished researchers have claimed that if we are not judicious with our resources, then our health care system will burden society with undue costs and vast disparities in availability (Bonder, 2004; Pierskalla, 2004). Developing mathematical models that allow us to study and optimize medical treatments is crucial to the overall goal of efficiently managing the health care industry. Indeed, we have already witnessed medical advances by optimizing existing medical procedures, leading to better patient care, increased probability of success, and better time management.

Much of the previous work focuses on using operations research to improve administrative decisions, but several medical procedures are now being considered. The breadth and importance of these is staggering, and the academic community is poised to not only aid managerial decisions but also improve medical procedures. A prominent example of the latter is the use of optimization to design radiotherapy treatments, which is the focus of this article.

Cancer remedies largely fall into three categories: pharmaceutical - such as chemotherapy, surgical - whose intent is to physically remove cancerous tissues, and radiobiological - which uses radiation to destroy cancerous growths. Radiotherapy is based on the fact that cancerous cells are altered by radiation in a way that prevents them from replicating with damaged DNA. When a cell is irradiated with a beam of radiation, a secondary reaction forms a free radical that damages cellular material. If the damage is not too severe, a healthy cell can likely overcome the damage and replicate normally, but if the cell is cancerous, it is unlikely that it will be able to regenerate. The differing abilities of cancerous and non-cancerous cells to repair themselves is called a therapeutic advantage, and the goal of radiotherapy is to deliver enough radiation so that cancerous cells expire but not so much as to permanently damage nearby tissues.

Radiotherapy treatments are delivered by focusing high energy beams of ionizing radiation on a patient. The goal of the design process is to select the pathways along which the radiation will pass through the anatomy and to decide the amount of dose that will be delivered along each pathway, called a *fluence value*. Bahr et al (1968a) first suggested that we optimize treatments in 1968, and since then medical physicists have developed a plethora of models to investigate the design process. Currently, commercially available planning systems optimize only the fluence value and do not additionally optimize the pathways. All of these commercially available systems rely on some form of optimization algorithm and these algorithms can range from gradient descent to simulated annealing. To date, the optimization approaches implemented clinically, typically by medical physicists working in the field of radiation oncology, have been reasonably effective but have failed to exploit the significant advances of robust operations research theory. As operations researchers have become aware of such problems, increasingly sophisticated optimization expertise has been brought to bear on the problem, leading to a growing potential for more elegant solutions.

The knowledge barrier between medical physicists, who understand the challenges and nuances of treatment design, and operations researchers, who know little about the clinical environment, is problematic. Clinical capabilities vary significantly, making what is optimal dependent on a specific clinic (treatments also depend on an individual patient). So, the separation of knowledge stems not only from the fact that the operations researchers generally know little about medical physics, but also from the fact that they typically know even less about the capabilities of a specific clinic. This lack of understanding is being overcome by several collaborations between the two communities, allowing academic advances to translate into improved patient care.

One of the most significant research hindrances is the lack of head-to-head comparisons, with the vast majority of numerical calculations being undertaken by individual research groups on patients from their associated clinic. This work describes the academic treatment system Radiotherapy optimAl Design (RAD), which is designed to use

- standard optimization software to model and solve problems,
- a database to store cases in a well-defined manner, and
- a web-based interface for visualization.

The use of standard modeling software makes it simple to alter and/or implement new models, a fact that supports head-to-head comparisons of the various models suggested in the literature. Storing problems in a database is an initial step toward creating a test bank that can be used by researchers to make head-to-head comparisons, and the web interface facilitates use. These features agree with standard OR practice in which algorithms and models are compared on the same problems and on the same machine.

The paper proceeds as follows. Subsection 1.1 gives a succinct introduction into the nature of radiotherapy and an overarching description of the technology associated with intensity modulated radiotherapy. Section 2 presents the radiation transport model that is currently implemented in RAD. This deterministic model estimates how radiation is deposited into the anatomy during treatment and provides the data used to form the optimization models. Section 3 discusses the somewhat annoying problem of dealing with the different coordinate systems that are native to the design question. A few optimization models from the literature are presented in Section 4. This section also highlights RAD's use of AMPL, which allows the optimization model to be altered and/or changed without affecting other parts of the system. Unfortunately, addressing the entire anatomy associated with a standard design problem leads to problems whose size is beyond the capability of modern solvers, and our reductions are presented in Section 5. The methods used by RAD to generate the images needed to evaluate treatments are presented in Section 6, and Section 7 discusses our software design, which includes the novel use of a database to store anatomical features. A few closing remarks are found in Section 8.

The fourth author once believed that a rudimentary version of RAD was possible within a year's effort. This was an extremely naive thought. RAD's implementation began in 1999, with the initial code being written in Matlab. The current version is written in C++ and PHP and links to AMPL, CPLEX and a MySQL database. At every turn there were numerical difficulties, software engineering obstacles, and verification problems with the radiation transport model. The current version required the concentrated effort of eight mathematics/computer science students, three Ph.Ds in mathematics/computer science, and one Ph.D in Medical Physics spread over 3 years. The details of our efforts are contained herein.

1.1 The Nature of Radiotherapy

Radiotherapy is delivered by immobilizing a patient on a horizontal table, around which a linear accelerator, capable of producing a beam of radiation, rotates. The table may be moved vertically and horizontally, which allows the central point of gantry rotation, called the *isocenter*, to be placed anywhere in the anatomy, and the table may also be rotated in a horizontal plane. The gantry is capable of rotating 360 degrees around the patient, although some positions are not allowed due to collision potential, see Figure 1.

Treatment design is typically approached in 3 phases,

1. **Beam Selection:** Select the pathways through which the radiation will pass through the anatomy.
2. **Fluence Optimization:** Decide how much radiation (fluence) to deliver along each of the selected beams to best treat the patient.
3. **Delivery Optimization:** Decide how to deliver the treatment computed in the first two phases as efficiently as possible.

The first two phases of treatment design are repeated in the clinic as follows. A designer uses sophisticated image software to visually select beams (also called pathways or angles) that appear promising. The fluence to deliver along these beams is decided by an optimization routine, and the resulting treatment is judged. If the treatment is unacceptable, the collection of beams is updated and new fluences are

Fig. 1 A standard treatment delivery system.

calculated. This trial-and-error approach can take as much as several hours per patient. Once an acceptable treatment is created, an automated routine decides how to sequence the delivery efficiently. There is an inherent disagreement between the objectives of fluence and delivery optimization since a fluence objective improves as beams are added but a delivery objective degrades. Extending the delivery time is problematic since this increases the probability of patient movement and the likelihood of an inaccurate delivery.

The initial interest in optimizing radiotherapy treatments was focused on fluence optimization, and numerous models and solution procedures have been proposed (see Bartolozzi et al, 2000; Holder, 2004; Holder and Salter, 2004; Rosen et al, 1991; Shepard et al, 1999). The variety is wide and includes linear, quadratic, mixed integer linear, mixed integer quadratic, and (non) convex global problems. Clinically relevant fluence problems are large enough to make combining the first two phases, which is trivial to express mathematically, difficult to solve, and much of the current research is directed at numerical procedures to support a combined model. One of RAD's contributions is that it is designed so that different models and solution procedures can easily be compared on the same cases, allowing head-to-head comparisons that were previously unavailable.

There are many treatment paradigms, with one of the most common being Intensity Modulated Radiotherapy (IMRT). This treatment modality is defined by the use of a multileaf collimator that is housed in the head of the gantry. The leaves of the collimator shape the beam, see Figure 2, and by adjusting the beam's shape continuously during treatment, we can modulate the delivered dose. The idea is to adjust the leaves so that different parts of the anatomy receive variable amounts of radiation. By combining several beams from multiple orientations, we hope to deliver a uniform tumoricidal dose while sparing the surrounding healthy organs and tissues.

While the treatment advantages of a collimator are apparent, the collimator significantly adds to the complexity of treatment design since it provides the ability to control small subdivisions of the beam. This is accomplished by dividing the open-field into sub-beams, whose size is determined by the collimator. For example, the collimator in Figure 2 has 32 opposing leaves that vertically divide the open-field. Although the leaves move continuously, we horizontally divide the open-field to

Fig. 2 A multileaf collimator.

approximate the continuous motion and design a treatment that has a unique value for each rectangular sub-beam. The exposure pattern formed by the sub-beams is called the fluence pattern, and an active area of research is to decide how to best adjust the collimator to achieve the fluence pattern as efficiently as possible (see Ahuja and Hamacher, 2004; Baatar and Hamacher, 2003; Boland et al, 2004).

A radiotherapy treatment is designed once at the beginning of treatment, but the total dose is delivered in multiple daily treatments called fractions. Fractionization allows normal cells the time to repair themselves while accumulating damage to tumorous tissues. The prescribed dose is typically delivered in 20 to 30 uniform treatments. Patient re-alignment is crucial, and in fact, the beam of radiation can often be focused with greater precision than a patient can be consistently re-aligned. Radiosurgery treatments differ from radiotherapy treatments in that the total intended dose is delivered all at once in one large fraction. The intent of a radiosurgery is to destroy, or ablate, tissue. Patient alignment is even more important for radiosurgeries because the large amount of radiation being delivered makes it imperative that the treatment be delivered as planned.

2 Calculating Delivered Dose

The radiation transport model that calculates how radiation energy per unit mass is deposited into the anatomy, which is called dose, is crucial to our ability to estimate the anatomical effect of external beam radiation. Obviously, if the model that describes the deposition of dose into the patient does not accurately represent the delivered (or anatomical) dose, then an optimization model that aids the design process is not meaningful.

Numerous radiation transport models have been suggested, with the "gold standard" being a stochastic model that depends on a Monte Carlo simulation. This technique estimates the random interactions between the patient's cells and the beam's photons, and although they are highly accurate, such models generally require prohibitive amounts of computational time (although this is becoming less of a concern). We instead adapt the deterministic model from Nizin and Mooij (1997) that approximates each sub-beam's dose contribution. The primary dose relies on the beam's energy and on the ratio between the radius of the sub-beam and the open-field. The way a sub-beam scatters as it travels through the anatomy depends on the radius of the sub-beam. Small radius beams have a large surface area compared to their volume, and hence, they lose a greater percentage of their photons than do larger radius sub-beams. When many contiguous sub-beams are used in conjunction, much of this scatter is gained by surrounding sub-beams, called scatter dose buildup.

The radiation transport model estimates the rate at which radiation is deposited, and we let $D_{(p,a,i)}$ be the rate at which dose point p gains radiation from sub-beam i in angle a. A few comments on the term 'dose point' are warranted. Much of the literature divides the anatomy into 3D rectangles called voxels and then considers the amount of radiation delivered to an entire voxel. This approach is well suited to other radiobiological models, but the one that we use is based on geometric distances. To calculate these distances, we represent each voxel by its center and call this a dose point. The units of $D_{(p,a,i)}$ are Grays per fluence, where one Gray is equal to 1 joule per kilogram. The triple (p,a,i) defines the depth d of dose point p along sub-beam (a,i), see Figure 3. Beams *attenuate* as they pass through the anatomy, meaning that lose energy as they pass through tissue. The maximum accumulation is not at the anatomy's surface but rather at a depth of M due to the previously mentioned dose buildup, after which the attenuation is modeled as exponential decay, $e^{-\mu(d-M)}$, where μ is an energy parameter. For a 6MV beam, the maximum dose rate is typically observed to occur at a depth of 1.5 cm. The dose rate at the surface is approximately 60% of the maximum rate at depth M, and we linearly interpolate between this value at depth 0 and the maximum rate at depth M. While this interpolation is not exact, it is reasonable and the majority of critical structures are at depths greater than M. The dose model we use is

$$
D_{(p,a,i)} = \begin{cases} \left(P_0 e^{-\mu(d-M)}(1-e^{-\gamma r}) + \frac{rd\alpha_d}{r+M} \right) \times ISF \times O, & d \geq M \\[2ex] \left(\frac{0.4d}{M} + 0.6 \right) \times \left(P_0(1-e^{-\gamma r}) + \frac{rM\alpha_M}{r+M} \right) \times ISF \times O, & 0 \leq d < M. \end{cases}
$$

The primary dose contribution for depths at least M is $P_0 e^{-\mu(d-M)}$, where P_0 is a machine-dependent constant. The factor $(1-e^{-\gamma r})$ represents the percentage of the open-field radiation present in a sub-beam, where γ is experimentally defined and r is the radius of the sub-beam. Notice that as r decreases the sub-beam's intensity falls exponentially, so extremely small sub-beams are not expected to effectively treat deep tissue malignancies. The term $(rd\alpha_d)/(r+M)$ models the scatter contributions from the surrounding sub-beams, where

$$
\alpha_d = -0.0306\ln(d) + 0.1299.
$$

Again, the contribution from scatter decreases with r (although linearly instead of exponentially).

The final two factors are the inverse square factor, ISF, and the off-axis factor, O. The inverse square factor is the square of the ratio of the distance from the gantry to the isocenter and the distance from the gantry to the dose point. Allowing $l(s,\text{isocenter})$ and $l(s,p)$ to be the distances from the source s to the isocenter and from s to the dose point p, we have

$$
ISF = \left(\frac{l(s,\text{isocenter})}{l(s,p)} \right)^2.
$$

The off-axis factor adjusts the dose contribution so that dose points near a sub-beam accumulate radiation faster than those that are farther away. This factor depends on the off axis distance o in Figure 3 and is machine and beam energy dependent, making it necessary to use a table tailored to a specific machine. Linear interpolation

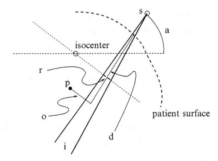

Fig. 3 The geometry of a radiobiological model.

Fig. 4 The dose contour of a single sub-beam.

is performed to determine off axis contributions for distances not listed in the table. A two dimensional image of a beam is found in Figure 4.

For distances greater than M, Nizin and Mooij (1997) report that the maximum error is 5% for clinically relevant beams when compared to Monte-Carlo models. For extremely narrow beams, which are not clinically relevant, there is a maximum error of 8%. For our purposes, this level of accuracy is sufficient.

The dose rates discussed in the previous section are arranged to form a dose matrix, denoted by A, whose rows are indexed by p and whose columns are index by (a,i). Allowing $x_{(a,i)}$ to be the fluence of sub-beam i in angle a, the cumulative dose at point p is

$$\sum_{(a,i)} D_{(p,a,i)} x_{(a,i)} = (Ax)_p,$$

where the indices of the vector x correspond to the columns of A. So, the linear map $x \mapsto Ax$ transforms a fluence pattern into anatomical dose (Gy).

Although Figure 3 depicts angle a being divided into 'flat' sub-beams, the collimator segments a beam into a 2D grid. The column widths of the grid are decided by the width of the leaves, and the row widths depend on the type of collimator. Some collimators are binary, and each leaf is either open or closed. Other collimators allow each leaf to move continuously across the column, and in this situation the rows of the grid are used to discretize the continuous motion. The subscript i

indexes through this grid at each angle, and hence, i is actually a 2D index. Similarly, the index for angles need not be restricted to a single great circle around the patient, and the index a represents an angle on a sphere around the patient.

3 Coordinate Systems

A complete foray into the authors' tribulations with the different coordinate systems is beyond the scope of this article, but a few notes are important. There are three coordinate systems that need to be aligned: 1) the coordinates for the patient images, 2) the coordinates for the dose points, and 3) the location of the gantry. The patient images are three dimensional of the form (μ, v, ζ), where each ζ represents a typical cross sectional image. The images are not necessarily evenly spaced, with images often being closer through the target. The dose points are also three dimensional of the form $p = (u, v, z)$. As discussed below, placement of these points is restricted to an underlying, evenly space grid, and hence, the z coordinate does not necessarily agree with ζ. However, each dose point needs to be linked to a tissue that is defined by an image, and we associate (u, v, z) with (u, v, ζ_z), where ζ_z is the closest ζ to z. The gantry coordinates describe the machine and not the anatomy. To link the gantry's position and rotation to the patient, we need to know the location of the isocenter within the patient and the couch angle. Gantry coordinates are calculated in polar form and translated to rectangular coordinates that are synced with the anatomy's position on the couch.

Our solution to aligning the coordinate systems is to build a three dimensional rectangle whose coordinates are fixed and whose center is always the location of the isocenter. We load the patient images into the rectangle so that they position the isocenter accordingly, and then build a three dimensional grid in the rectangle that defines where dose points are allowed to be placed. The couch angle defines a great circle around the fixed rectangle that allows us to position and rotate the gantry, which in turn allows us to track the sub-beams as they gantry moves.

4 Optimization Models

The linear operator $x \mapsto Ax$ facilitates an optimization model. For convenience, we sub-divide the rows of A into those that correspond to the target, critical structures, and normal tissue, and we let A_T, A_C, and A_N be the corresponding sub-matrices so that $A_T x$, $A_C x$ and $A_N x$ are the anatomical doses for the target, the critical structures, and the normal tissue. Physicians form a prescription by placing bounds and goals on the anatomical dose. The precise definition of a prescription depends on the definition of an optimal treatment. For example, a simple least squares model is

$$\min\{\omega_1 \|A_T x - TG\|_2 + \omega_2 \|A_C x\|_2 + \omega_3 \|A_N x\|_2 : x \geq 0\}. \tag{1}$$

The prescription for this model is the vector of goal doses for the targeted region, TG, which is commonly a scalar multiple of the vector of ones. The ω scalars weight the terms of the objective to express clinical preference. A linear model with a more complicated prescription is

$$\min\{\omega_1 \cdot \alpha + \omega_2 \cdot \beta + \omega_3 \cdot \gamma : TLB - \alpha e \leq A_T x \leq TUB, A_C x \leq CUB + \beta e,$$
$$A_N x \leq NUB + \gamma e, 0 \leq A_T x \leq TLB, \beta \geq -\|-CUB\|_\infty, \gamma \geq 0\}, \qquad (2)$$

where e is the vector of ones (length is decided by the context of its use). The prescription for this model is TLB - vector of lower bounds for the target, TUB - vector of upper bounds for the target, CUB - vector of upper bounds for the critical structures, NUB - vector of upper bounds for the normal tissues, and the weighting values ω_i, $i = 1, 2, 3$. Both (1) and (2) are fluence problems since they define an optimal treatment for a known set of angles, sub-beams and dose points. In general, a prescription is the information provided by a physician that is used to define an instance of a fluence problem. Table 1 shows the prescription information gathered by RAD. The $ABSMIN$ and $ABSMAX$ information is used in some models to define 'hard' constraints instead of the goals suggested by other bounds. For example, the model below differentiates between the goal lower bound TLB and the target's absolute minimum bound $ABSMIN_T$.

$$\min\{\|z\|_2 : ABSMIN_T \leq A_T x \leq TUB + z, A_C x \leq CUB + z, A_N x \leq NUB + z, x \geq 0\}.$$

The hard constraint $ABSMIN_T \leq A_T x$ guarantees the target will receive at least the values in $ABSMIN_T$, whereas TUB, CUB and NUB are goals parametrized by z.

Error bound parameters are commonly used in what are called dose volume constraints, which limit the volume of tissue allowed to violate a goal. For example, a mixed integer extension of (1) that limits the amount of under irradiated target is

$$\min\{\omega_1 \|A_T x - TG\|_2 + \omega_2 \|A_C x\|_2 + \omega_3 \|A_N x\|_2 :$$
$$(1 - y_p)\sum_{(a,i)} A_{(p,a,i)} x_{(a,i)} \leq TLB, \sum_{p \in T} y_p \leq \text{PERBLW} \cdot |T|, y \in \{0,1\}^{|T|}, x \geq 0\}.$$

These are notoriously difficult problems with a substantial literature (see Cho et al, 1998; Lee et al, 2003, as examples).

Once an optimization model is decided, an optimal treatment can be calculated using a host of different solvers. If the model is linear, solver options include the primal simplex method, the dual simplex method, Lemke's algorithm, and several interior point methods. Unless the optimization problem has a unique solution, it is likely that different solution algorithms will terminate with different fluence patterns (although the objective values will be the same). This phenomena has been observed in Ehrgott et al (2005), where CPLEX's dual simplex was shown to routinely design treatments with a few angles having unusually high fluences. If the model is nonlinear but smooth, typical options are gradient descent, Newton's method, and variants of quasi-Newton's methods.

Table 1 Prescription information gathered by RAD. Each of these vectors is indexed to accommodate the required number of structures.

	Notation	Description
Goals	TG	A goal dose for a target.
	TLB	A goal lower bound for a target.
	TUB	A goal upper bound for a target.
	CUB	A goal upper bound for a critical structure.
	NUB	A goal upper bound for the normal tissues.
Dose Bounds	$ABSMAX$	An absolute maximum dose allowed on any structure.
	$ABSMIN$	An absolute minimum dose allowed on the target.
Error Bounds	$PERABV$	Percent of volume allowed to violate an upper bound.
	$PERBLW$	Percent of volume allowed to violate a lower bound.

In the spirit of RAD's academic intent, one of our goals is to allow easy and seamless flexibility in how optimal treatments are defined and calculated. This is possible by using pre-established software that is designed to model and solve an optimization problem. In particular, we separate data acquisition, modeling, and solving. This differs from the philosophy behind most of the in-house systems developed by individual clinics, where modeling and solving are intertwined in a single computational effort. The mingling of the two complicates the creative process because changing either the model or the solution procedure often requires large portions of code to be rewritten, thus hindering exploration. We instead use standard software to model and solve a problem. For instance, RAD uses AMPL to model problems, which makes adjusting existing models and entering new ones simple. AMPL links to a suite of 35 solvers such as (integer) linear and (integer) quadratic models (as well as many others). RAD currently has access to CPLEX, MINOS and PCx. This approach takes advantage of the numerous research careers that have gone into developing state-of-the-art software to model and solve optimization problems, and hence, brings a substantial amount of expertise to the design of radiotherapy treatments.

There are limitations to this design approach, especially with global (non-convex) problems that are often successfully solved with simulated annealing or other heuristics. The lack of access to quality heuristics for global optimization problems is a detriment because one of the industry's primary solution methods is simulated annealing. Simulated annealing has the favorable quality that it can successfully accommodate any model, but the unfavorable quality that there is no guarantee of optimality. However, the medical physics community has learned to trust this technique because it has consistently provided quality treatments. Moreover, some of the suggested optimization models are non-convex global models. A future goal is to link RAD to global solvers like LGO, simulated annealing, and genetic algorithms. Once this is complete, a large scale study of which model and solution methodology provides the best clinical benefit is possible. Wide scale testing of different models and solution procedures has not been undertaken, but RAD has the potential to support this work. These comparisons are important because clinical desires vary from clinic to clinic and from physician to physician. This leads to the situation where the sense of optimality —i.e. the optimization model can be different from one physician to another for the same patient. It is possible, however, that the basic treatment goals pertinent to all clinics and physicians are best addressed by a single model and solver combination. If this is true, then such a combination would provide a consensus on what an optimal treatment is for a specific type of cancer and a subsequent standard of care for clinics with similar technology.

5 Problem Management

The size of a typical design problem is substantial, making them difficult to solve. Indeed, the results in Cheek et al (2004) show that storing the dose matrix can require over 600 Gigabytes of memory. For this reason, it is necessary to use reduction schemes to control the size of a problem, and this section discusses the methods introduced in RAD, several of which are designed to assist the combination of beam selection and fluence optimization.

The current practice of asking the treatment planner to select beams has the favorable quality that the underlying fluence problem only considers the selected beams, which reduces the number of columns in the dose matrix. RAD is capable of addressing a fluence problem with a large number of candidate beams by judiciously selecting sub-beams and dose points. The first reduction is to simply remove the sub-beams that do not strike the target. One naive way to remove these sub-beams is to calculate an entire dose matrix and then remove the columns whose aggregate rate to the target is below a specified threshold. RAD's approach is different, and before calculating the rates associate with a sub-beam, we search for the minimum off-axis factor over the dose points on the surface of the target. If the minimum value is too great, we classify the sub-beam as non-target-striking and are spared the calculation of this column. This technique requires two calculations that are not needed by the naive approach, that of locating the target's surface and evaluating the minimum off-axis factor. Both of these calculations only consider the target, whereas the naive approach calculates rate information for each point in the anatomy. Our numerical comparisons, even for large targets, show that RAD's approach is significantly faster.

A novel reduction introduced in RAD is to accurately define the anatomical region that will receive significant dose. For example, consider a lesion in the upper part of the cranium. The volume defined by the entire set of patient images is called the *patient volume*, and for this example it would likely encompass the head and neck. However, it is unlikely that we will need to calculate dose in the area of the neck. We have developed a technique that defines a (typically much) smaller volume within the patient where meaningful dose is likely to accumulate.

Assume that a designer considers a unique great circle around the patient by selecting a single isocenter and couch angle, represented by the pair (c, j). Further assume that beams will be selected from the collection of beams placed every 5° on this great circle. Using only the sub-beams that strike the target, we trace them through the anatomy to define a swath. A mathematical description highlights the ease with which this region can be calculated. Let B_0 be the plane defined by the gantry as it rotates around the isocenter with a fixed couch angle. B_0 is defined by the unit normal vector N and the isocenter c_0: $B_0 = \{c_0 + Nv : Nv = 0\}$. Two additional planes B_1 and B_2 are defined using the same normal vector N, so that they are parallel to B_0, but with the respectively different points,

$$c_1 = (\max\{\text{dist}(E(i), B_0) : i \in S\} + r)N$$
$$c_2 = (\min\{\text{dist}(E(i), B_0) : i \in S\} - r)N.$$

In this calculation, S is the set of all sub-beams that are target striking and E is the map from S into $\mathbb{R}^3$ so that $E(i)$ is the point where sub-beam i exits the anatomy. The distance between this point and the B_0 plane is

$$\text{dist}(E(i), B_0) = \frac{N^T E(i) - N^T c_0}{\|N\|}.$$

Note that this is the signed minimum distance between a point and a plane. Points in the direction of N have a positive distance, and points in the direction of $-N$ have a negative distance. Allowing D to be the collection of all possible dose points in the patient volume defined by the entire set of images, we define the swath for isocenter c and couch angle j to be

$$W_{(c,j)} = \{d \in D : \text{dist}(d, B_1) \leq 0\} \cap \{d \in D : \text{dist}(d, B_2) \geq 0\}.$$

This development shows that constructing the swath is computationally simple because we only need to iterate over the elements of S, which are already defined by the first reduction, calculate $\text{dist}(E(i), B_0)$, and keep the maximum and minimum elements. We additionally add any delineated critical structures that lay outside this region. The combined region is called the *treatment volume* for (c, j). If there are further isocenters and couch angles, the entire treatment volume is the union over all (c, j). Dose points are only placed within this volume for planning purposes, reducing the number of rows of the dose matrix.

The arrangement of dose points over the treatment volume is critical for two reasons: 1) the discrete representation of the anatomical dose needs to accurately estimate the true continuous anatomical dose, and 2) the size of the problem grows as dose points are added. Clinical relevance is achieved once the dose points are within 2mm of each other. Some technologies are capable of taking advantage of 0.1mm differences, and hence, require much finer grids. Our experiments show that using the treatment volume instead of the patient volume reduces the storage requirement to 10s of Gigabytes instead of 100s of Gigabytes with a grid size of 2 mm, assuming a single isocenter and couch angle. Although this is a significant reduction, solving a linear or quadratic problem with a dose matrix in the 10 Gigabyte range is impossible with CPLEX on a 32 bit PC, there are simply not enough memory addresses.

Our final reduction is a technique that iteratively builds a dose matrix for the treatment volume. The idea is to eliminate the numerous dose points in the normal tissue that are largely needed to protect against *hot spots*, which are clinically defined as a cubic centimeter of tissue receiving an unusually high dose, say 110% of the average target dose. While hot spots are not desired in any part of the anatomy, including the target, the general consensus is that hot spots should never be located outside the target. Our final reduction scheme attempts to ensure that we place normal tissue dose points so that we can monitor areas likely to have hot spots while eliminating the dose points in the normal tissue that do not influence the problem. RAD uses the following iterative procedure:

1. On the first solve we only include normal tissue dose points that are adjacent to the target, forming a *collar* around the target. This concept was used in the earliest work in the field (see Bahr et al, 1968b).
2. We segment the patient volume into $1 cm^3$ sectors.
3. We trace the sub-beams that have sufficiently high fluence values, and each sector is scored by counting the number of high fluence sub-beams that pass through it.
4. Normal tissue dose points are placed within the treatment volume for the sectors with high scores.
5. The process repeats with the added dose points until every sector receives a sufficiently small score.

This iterative procedure solves several small problems instead of one large one. On clinical examples, the initial dose matrices are normally under 1 Gigabyte, a size that is appropriate for the other software packages. We point out that RAD does not calculate the anatomical dose to each sector but rather only counts where high exposure sub-beams intersect. Just because a few high exposure sub-beams pass through a sector does not mean that this sector is a hot spot, but it does mean that it is possible. Sectors with low counts can not be hot spots because it is impossible to accumulate enough dose without several high exposure sub-beams. We find that 1 to 5 iterations completely removes hot spots outside the target. At the end of the process, the dose matrix has typically grown negligibly and remains around 1 Gigabyte in size.

The iterative procedure above reduces the number of rows of the dose matrix so dramatically and successfully that we can increase the number of beams. Although a clinic will only use a fraction of the added beams, solving for optimal fluences with many beams provides information about which beams should and should not be selected. A complete development of beam selection is not within the scope of this work, and we direct readers to Ehrgott et al (2005) for a complete development. Beam selectors are classified as *uninformed*, *weakly informed* or *informed*. An uninformed selector is one that only uses geometry, and the current clinical paradigm of selecting beams by what looks geometrically correct is an example. A weakly informed selector is guided by the dose matrix and the prescription, and an informed selector further takes advantage of an optimal fluence pattern calculated with a large set of possible beams. The premise behind an informed selector is that it begins with a large set of possible beams that are allowed to 'compete' for fluence through an optimization process. The expectation is that a beam with a high fluence is more important than a beam with a low fluence. The numerical results in Ehrgott et al (2005) demonstrate that informed selectors usually select quality beams in a timely fashion.

RAD is designed to study beam selection and fluence optimization and is well positioned to address the current research pursuit of simultaneously optimizing both fluence and beams (see Aleman et al, 2006, 2007; Lim et al, 2007). Rather than asking a user to identify beams, users are instead asked to select collections of couch angles and isocenters, which are clinically easier. RAD then places angles on each of the great circles, calculates the treatment volume, and uses the iterative procedure above to control hot spots. Beams are typically spaced at 5° increments on each of the great circles. The resulting optimal treatment is not clinically viable but is available for an informed beam selector. Of course, uninformed and weakly informed beam selectors are possible as well, but RAD provides the additional option of using an informed selector. Once beams are selected, RAD places dose points on a fine mesh (spacing no greater than 2 mm) throughout the treatment volume. Since the number of beams is small, this leads to a dose matrix that remains appropriate with our other software packages. A final optimal treatment is calculated with this matrix. Table 2 contains the expected size reductions for a $20cm^3$ region.

We conclude this section with a brief discussion about sparse matrix formats and other reductions that did not work. A straightforward approach of reducing the storage requirements of the dose matrix is to store only those values above a predefined threshold. This method requires the calculation of every possible rate coefficient over the patient volume. Our approach of defining the treatment volume preempts the majority of these calculations and is faster. That said, about 90% of the rate coefficients over the treatment volume are insignificant since each sub-beam delivers the majority of its energy to a narrow path through the treatment volume. So, a sparse matrix format over the treatment volume should further reduce our storage requirements. However, our reduction schemes allow us to forgo a sparse matrix format and store a dose matrix as a simple 2D array with double precision. This simplicity has helped us debug and validate the code.

Before arriving at the reductions above, we attempted a different method of placing dose points. The idea was to use increasingly sparse grids for the target, critical

Table 2 Approximate dose matrix sizes for a $20cm^3$ region with 3 couch angles around a single isocenter in the middle of the patient volume. A 2mm 3D grid spacing is assumed. Each swath is 1cm in width (6 dose points wide), is parallel to one of the axes, and passes through the center of the patient volume. The example assumes that 10,000 dose points in the treatment volume are not normal and that 20,000 additional dose points outside the treatment volume are needed to describe the critical structures. Each beam is assumed to have a 25×25 grid of sub-beams, of which 4 are assumed to strike the target. The final treatment has 10 angles.

Size	Number of Rows	Number of Columns	Size of A
Patient Volume	10^6	1.3×10^5	1.3×10^{11}
Sequential Solves	3.0×10^4	8.4×10^2	2.5×10^7
Final Solve	3.8×10^5	4.0×10	1.5×10^7

structures, and normal tissues. This is not a new idea, with different densities being considered in Lim et al (2002) and Morrill et al (1990). There are two problems with this approach. First, the voxels of different grids have different volumes, and our code to handle the volumes at the interface of different grids was inefficient. Second, the sparsity of the normal tissue grid had to exceed 1 cm (often 2+ cm) to accommodate the use of many angles, which is clinically unacceptable. Moreover, the sparsity did not prevent hot spots from appearing in the normal tissue. We are aware that Nomos's commercial software uses an octree technique that allows varying densities, so it is possible to use this idea successfully, although our attempt failed.

6 Solution Analysis

A treatment undergoes several evaluations once it is designed. In fact, the number of ways a treatment is judged is at the heart of this research, for if the clinicians could tell us exactly what they wanted to optimize, we could focus on optimizing that quantity. However, no evaluative tool comprehensively measures treatment quality, which naturally makes the problem multiple objective (see Hamacher and Küfer, 2002; Holder, 2001). The issue is further complicated by the fact that treatment desires are tailored to specific patients at a specific clinic. That said, there are two general evaluative tools.

A Dose Volume Histogram (DVH) is a graph that for each structure plots dose against percent volume, which allows a user to quickly evaluate how the entirety of each structure fairs. A treatment and its corresponding DVH from the commercial system Nomos are found in Figures 5 and 6. The upper most curve of the DVH corresponds to the target, which is near the brain stem. This curve starts to decrease at about 52 Gy, which indicates that 100% of the target receives at least this dose. The next highest curve represents the spinal cord, a structure whose desired upper

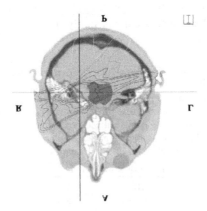

Fig. 5 The isodose contours for a clinically designed treatment.

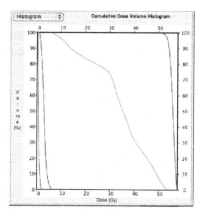

Fig. 6 The DVH for the treatment in Figure 5.

bound is 45 Gy. This curve shows that about 18% of the spinal cord is to receive a higher dose. The remaining curves are for the eye sockets and the remaining normal tissue.

Notice that a DVH curve depends on the volumetric estimate of the corresponding structure, an observation that leads to a subtle issue. Different clinics are likely to create different volumes of the normal tissue by scanning different patient volumes. This means the curve for normal tissue will vary, and in particular, the information provided by this curve diminishes as more normal tissue is included. For example, if we were treating the lesion in Figure 5, we could artificially make it appear as though less than 1% of the normal tissue receives a significant dose by including the tissue in the patient's feet. The authors of this paper are unaware of any standard, and for consistency, all of RAD's DVHs are based on the treatment volume, which is a definable and reproducible quantity that removes the dependence on the clinically defined patient volume.

A DVH visually displays the amount of a structure that violates the prescription but does not capture the spacial position of the violation. If 10% of a structure's volume violates a bound but is distributed throughout the structure, then there is likely no radiobiological concern. However, if the volume is localized, then it might be a hot spot and the treatment is questionable. To gain spatial awareness of where dose is and is not accumulated, each of the patient images is contoured with a sequence of *isodose curves*. Examples are found in Figure 5. Each of these curves contains the region receiving dose above a specified percentage of the target dose. So, a 90% isodose curve contains the tissue that receives at least $0.9 \times TG$. Isodose curves clearly indicate the spatial location of high dose regions, but they require the user to investigate each image and form a mental picture of the 3D dose. Since there are often hundreds of scans, this is a tedious process.

Rendering isodose curves proved more complicated than we had first assumed, and RAD incorporates a new approach. We build a cubic approximation of the continuous dose with a *B*-spline. Let $\delta_{(k,t)}$, $\delta_{(k+1,t)}$, $\delta_{(k,t+1)}$ and $\delta_{(k+1,t+1)}$ be the dose at four neighboring dose points on one of the patient images (recall that dose on an image is associated with the dose at the closest dose point - since we are dealing with a single image, we remove the ζ coordinate). The cubic approximation over this region is

$$S_{(k,t)}(\mu,v) = (1/36)UMQ_{(k,t)}M^T V^T, 0 \le \mu, v, \le 1,$$

where $U = [\mu^3, \mu^2, \mu, 1], V = [v^3, v^2, v, 1],$

$$M = \begin{bmatrix} -1 & 3 & -3 & 1 \\ 3 & 6 & 3 & 0 \\ -3 & 0 & 3 & 0 \\ 1 & 4 & 1 & 0 \end{bmatrix} \text{ and } Q_{(k,t)} = \begin{bmatrix} \delta_{(k-1,t-1)} & \delta_{(k-1,t)} & \delta_{(k-1,t+1)} & \delta_{(k-1,t+2)} \\ \delta_{(k,t-1)} & \delta_{(k,t)} & \delta_{(k,t+1)} & \delta_{(k,t+2)} \\ \delta_{(k+1,t-1)} & \delta_{(k+1,t)} & \delta_{(k+1,t+1)} & \delta_{(k+1,t+2)} \\ \delta_{(k+2,t-1)} & \delta_{(k+2,t)} & \delta_{(k+2,t+1)} & \delta_{(k+2,t+2)} \end{bmatrix}.$$

By design, these regional approximations combine to form a smooth approximation over the entire patient image, which is

$$S(\mu,v) = S_{(\lfloor \mu \rfloor, \lfloor v \rfloor)}(\mu - \lfloor \mu \rfloor, v - \lfloor v \rfloor),$$

where $(\mu, v) \in [1, m] \times [1, n]$. If the indexing exceeds the image, then exterior dose values are interpreted as the dose of their nearest neighbor. For example, $\delta_{(0,0)} = \delta_{(1,0)} = \delta_{(0,1)} = \delta_{(1,1)}$, of which $\delta_{(1,1)}$ is the only real dose value.

This is a traditional (uniform) B-spline, and nothing is new about continuously approximating discrete information with this technique. However, the cubic estimation allows us to draw an isodose curve by finding a level curve of $S(\mu, v)$ – i.e. the solutions to $S(\mu, v) - \alpha TG = 0$, where $0 \le \alpha \le 1$. What is new is that we use a shake-and-bake algorithm to identify the isodose curve (see Boender and et al, 1991). The idea is to start within the region of high-dose, randomly select a direction, and then find the high dose boundary along the forward and backward rays. Formally, fix α between 0 and 1 so that we are looking for the α isocontour. Let (μ_0, v_0) be a position on the patient image such that the dose $\delta_{(\mu_0,v_0)}$ is greater than αTG. Uniformly select ρ_0 in $[0, \pi)$, and along the line segment $(\mu_0, v_0) + \theta(\cos(\rho), \sin(\rho))$, find the smallest positive θ and largest negative θ such that either $S((\mu_0, v_0) + \theta(\cos(\rho_0), \sin(\rho_0))) - \alpha TG = 0$ or θ is at a bound that prevents the coordinate from leaving the patient image. This calculation renders a line segment defined by $\theta_0^{\max}$ and $\theta_0^{\min}$, and the next iteration begins with the midpoint of this segment,

$$(\mu_1, v_1) = (\mu_0, v_0) + (1/2)(\theta_0^{\max} + \theta_0^{\min})(\cos(\rho_0), \sin(\rho_0)).$$

This technique has the favorable mathematical property that if the region within the isocontour is convex, then the random sequence $(\mu_k, v_k) + \theta_k^{\max(\text{or min})}(\cos(\rho_k), \sin(\rho_k))$ converges to the uniform distribution on the isocontour (Boender and et al, 1991). Moreover, it is suspected, although not proved, that the uniformity is achieved for any connected region (Caron, 1998). An example is shown in Figure 7.

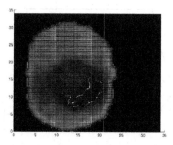

Fig. 7 A 90% isocontour rendered with the shake-and-bake algorithm.

We let (μ_0, v_0) be the location of the dose point with the maximum dose. We mention that this may or may not be the largest value of $S(\mu, v)$, and another option would be to solve $\nabla S(\mu, v) = 0$ to find its maximum value. We use Newton's Method, with a full step, to solve $S((\mu_0, v_0) + \theta(\cos(\rho_0), \sin(\rho_0))) - \alpha T G = 0$, which has favorable quadratic convergence and is simple to implement since the partials of $S(\mu, v)$ are

$$\frac{\partial}{\partial \mu} S_{(k,t)}(u, v) = (1/36) U \hat{I} M Q_{(k,t)} M^T V^T$$

and

$$\frac{\partial}{\partial v} S_{(k,t)}(u, v) = (1/36) U M Q_{(k,t)} M^T \hat{I}^T V^T,$$

where

$$\hat{I} = \begin{bmatrix} 0 & 0 & 0 \\ 1 & 0 & 0 \\ 0 & 1 & 0 \end{bmatrix}.$$

Many alternative line searches are available, such as a binary search, and such techniques may provide stability if the gradient of S is near zero. Lastly, we mention that this method renders an unordered collection of points on the isocontour, and without an order, it is not clear how to connect them. This is not a concern if enough points are rendered, for after all, every displayed curve is a collection of pixels.

7 Software Design & Structure Identification

The previous sections' discussions about the algorithms that support RAD do not address the software engineering aspects, and the authors would be remiss if they did not discuss how the different parts of RAD interlink. Some of the topics in this section are general software issues and others are specific to the design of radiotherapy treatments.

The basic idea behind our approach is to exploit a language's strengths. As Table 2 indicates, the size of the dose matrix is significant, and the code used to

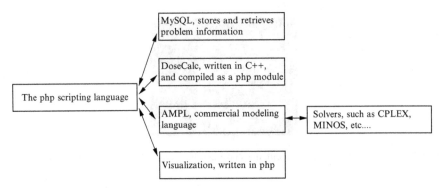

Fig. 8 The SWIG compiler links PHP to C++, which in turn allows us to pass information between DoseCalc (the parallel implementation of our radio-biological model) and other software.

calculate this matrix is written in C++. Dose matrices may be written to disc for debugging purposes or they may be kept in memory and passed directly to other applications. Reading and writing a 1 Gigabyte file from and to disc is time consuming, and the latter approach saves time, especially when everything stays in RAM. We use the SWIG compiler to link our C++ code to the scripting language PHP, which allows the dose matrix to be stored in a native PHP structure. Through the use of a bi-directional pipe, we can pass the dose matrix to other applications like AMPL and receive information when a problem is solved. Moreover, PHP gives us control of the linux command line, naturally interfaces with MySQL, and easily interfaces with the web to support the user interface. For these reasons, PHP has become the 'glue' that holds the system together, and the power of this ability should not be under estimated. Figure 8 depicts the general design of how different parts of the code interact. This is not descriptive of the flow of information through the system, which is discussed below.

Another of RAD's unique features is that it stores problems in a MySQL database. Beyond being an information repository for RAD, its intent is to become a library of problems for comparative research. The medical literature on treatment design is vast, but each paper highlights a technique on a few examples from a specific clinic, examples that can not be used by others to compare results. This is strange from a computational perspective, and RAD's database will support the numerical work necessary to fairly evaluate different algorithms and models.

A natural question about data storage is, What is a problem? In other words, what data is needed to define a problem instance. We adhere to the following structure, which is new as far as the authors can tell,

$$Problem = (Case, Prescription, Settings)$$
$$Solution = (Problem, Model, Solution Technique).$$

A Case is defined by the geometry of the patient. We parse RTOG files (a standard protocol for radiotherapy treatments) to gain a description of the structures that were delineated on the patient images. Each structure is defined by a series of

Fig. 9 An enlarged view of a kidney. The white areas are not kidney and were delineated on the patient images.

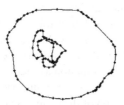

Fig. 10 The kidney was defined for this patient image by three segments: an outer segment delineating the larger volume and two inner segments that contain non-kidney tissue. The points listed in the RTOG file are indicated by small circles.

connected regions on individual patient images, with each region being defined by an ordered list of points. We construct a continuous boundary for each structure by linearly joining consecutive points on each image. We mention that other splining techniques were tested in an attempt to make the structural boundaries smooth, but none were more accurate when overlaid on the CT scan. Some structures, such as the kidney shown in Figures 9 and 10, may be described by several regions on the same slice, creating geometries that complicate the process of automatically defining the regions associated with each tissue. The regions defined by these curves may or may not be contained within each other. If the regions are disjoint, we assume they enclose the same tissue. However, if one of the regions is within the other, such as in Figure 9, we assume that the region defined by the inner curve is not part of the defined tissue. To test whether or not the regions are disjoint, we calculate a winding number. Let (μ_k, v_k) and $(\hat{\mu}_k, \hat{v}_k)$ be two lists of points on the same image for the same structure. To see whether or not the region defined by $(\hat{\mu}_k, \hat{v}_k)$ is within the region defined by (μ_k, v_k), we select a single $(\hat{\mu}_K, \hat{v}_K)$ and consider the vertical line through this point. For every directed line segment from (μ_k, v_k) to (μ_{k+1}, v_{k+1}) that passes the vertical line above (below) $(\hat{\mu}_K, \hat{v}_K)$ from right to left, we accrue 1 (-1). The signs reverses if we pass from left to right. In the event that (μ_{k+1}, v_{k+1}) lies on the vertical line, we instead consider the directed line segment from (μ_k, v_k) to (μ_{k+2}, v_{k+2}) (or an even larger index if the second point is also on the vertical line) for the calculation. Under the assumption that regions are either disjoint or nested, which is an assumption we make, this calculation returns 0 if and only if the region defined by $(\hat{\mu}_k, \hat{v}_k)$ is within the region defined by (μ_k, v_k).

Tissue information is captured with a tga image that is generated for each patient image by flooding each tissue with a unique color. For example, the three segments in Figure 10 would be linearly interpolated and the pixels within the outer region but outside the inner region would be flooded with a color unique to kidney tissue. This is possible with a PHP class that generates tga images, which are not stored but rather generated as needed from the list of points in the database (this saves storage requirements). Representative tga images for each tissue are displayed via a web interface that additionally asks the user for the prescription information for each tissue. Each dose point is associated with the closest pixel on a patient image, where ties are decided with a least index rule. Thus, the tga images are the link between the user defined prescription and the associated bounds of the optimization problem.

Another concern about tissue identification is that regions representing different tissues may intersect. Our simple solution follows that of several commercial systems, and we ask the user to rank tissues. In the case of an intersection, the dose points within the intersection are labeled as the tissue with the highest priority.

We have already defined the information available for the prescription in Table 1. The *Settings* information details the dose point grid, the location of the possible angles, and the type & sub-division of the beam. Whereas the information that comprises a Problem details what is needed to design a treatment, a Solution additionally includes the type of optimization model and the technique used to solve it -i.e. it includes how we are defining and finding optimality. Hence, a Solution is everything needed to define the anatomical dose of an optimal treatment, and with this information it is possible to render a treatment to be evaluated.

The information flow through RAD is described by the following algorithmic description.

1. **Step 1:** RTOG files are parsed by a php script that reads Case information into a MySQL database.
2. **Step 2:** Representative tga images are generated from the Case and are displayed via a web interface to gain a Prescription.
3. **Step 3:** Settings are selected to match a clinical setting.
4. **Step 4:** An optimization model and solution technique are selected.
5. **Step 5:** Using the reductions and the iterative scheme described above, RAD calculates an optimal treatment. Models are generated in AMPL and solved by the solver selected in Step 4.
6. **Step 6:** Solution information is written to the MySQL database.
7. **Step 7:** Visualization scripts written in php generate dose-volume histograms and isocontours, which are displayed through a web interface.

8 Conclusion

Orchestrating the creation of a radiotherapy design system is a significant task that lives at the application edge of operations research and computer science. This paper has discussed many of the fundamental concerns and has introduced several new tactics that allow the underlying optimization problem to be approached with standard software, even in the case of numerous possible angles. It additionally introduces a new method to draw isocontours. The system is based on an efficient and well studied radiation transport model.

Many researchers have faced the challenge of designing their own design software, which is why there are several in-house, research systems. Our goal was to detail the algorithmic and software perspectives of RAD so that others can incorporate our experience as they either begin or continue their research. In the future, the authors will initiate the process of a rigorous, detailed and wide-spread investigation into which model and solution method consistently produces quality treatments. Moreover, RAD will allow others to compare their (new) techniques to ours with the same dose model and patient information. Lastly, RAD is designed to accommodate the amalgamation of beam selection and fluence optimization, a topic that is currently receiving interest.

Acknowledgements Research supported by the Cancer Therapy & Research Center in San Antonio, TX and by the Department of Radiation Oncology, Huntsman Cancer Center, Salt Lake City, UT.

References

Ahuja R, Hamacher H (2004) Linear time network flow algorithm to minimize beam-on-time for unconstrained multileaf collimator problems in cancer radiation therapy. Tech. rep., Department of Industrial and Systems Engineering, University of Florida, revised version under review in Networks

Aleman D, Romeijn H, Dempsey J (2006) A response surface approach to beam orientation optimization in intensity modulated radiation therapy treatment planning. In: IIE Conference Proceedings

Aleman D, Romeijn H, Dempsey J (2007) A response surface approach to beam orientation optimization in intensity modulated radiation therapy treatment planning. Tech. rep., Department of Industrial Engineering, the University of Florida, to appear in IIE Transactions: Special Issue on Healthcare Applications

Baatar D, Hamacher H (2003) New LP model for multileaf collimators in radiation therapy planning. In: Proceedings of the Operations Research Peripatetic Postgraduate Programme Conference ORP^3, Lambrecht, Germany, pp 11–29

Bahr G, Kereiakes J, Horwitz H, Finney R, Galvin J, Goode K (1968a) The method of linear programming applied to radiation treatment planning. Radiology 91:686–693

Bahr GK, Kereiakes JG, Horwitz H, Finney R, Galvin J, Goode K (1968b) The method of linear programming applied to radiation treatment planning. Radiology 91:686–693

Bartolozzi F, et al (2000) Operational research techniques in medical treatment and diagnosis. a review. European Journal of Operations Research 121(3):435–466

Boender C, et al (1991) Shake-and-bake algorithms for generating uniform points on the boundary of bounded polyhedra. Operations Research 39(6)

Boland N, Hamacher H, Lenzen F (2004) Minimizing beam-on time in cancer radiation treatment using multileaf collimators. Networks 43(4):226–240

Bonder S (2004) Improving or support for healthcare delivery systems: Guidlines from military or experience. INFORMS Annual Conference, Denver, CO

Caron R (1998) Personal communications

Cheek D, Holder A, Fuss M, Salter B (2004) The relationship between the number of shots and the quality of gamma knife radiosurgeries. Optimization and Engineering 6(4):449–462

Cho P, Lee S, Marks R, Oh S, Sutlief S, Phillips M (1998) Optimization of intensity modulated beams with volume constraints using two methods: Cost function minimization and projections onto convex sets. Medical Physics 25:435–443

Ehrgott M, Holder A, Reese J (2005) Beam selection in radiotherapy design. Tech. Rep. 95, Trinity University Mathematics, San Antonio, TX

Hamacher H, Küfer KH (2002) Inverse radiation therapy planing – A multiple objective optimization approach. Discrete Applied Mathematics 118(1-2):145–161

Holder A (2001) Partitioning multiple objective optimal solutions with applications in radiotherapy design. Tech. rep., Department of Mathematics, Trinity University, San Antonio, USA

Holder A (2004) Radiotherapy treatment design and linear programming. In: Brandeau M, Sainfort F, Pierskalla W (eds) Operations Research and Health Care: A Handbook of Methods and Applications, Kluwer Academic Publishers, chap 29

Holder A, Salter B (2004) A tutorial on radiation oncology and optimization. In: Greenberg H (ed) Emerging Methodologies and Applications in Operations Research, Kluwer Academic Press, Boston, MA

Lee E, Fox T, Crocker I (2003) Integer programming applied to intensity-modulated radiation therapy treatment planning. Annals of Operations Research 119:165–181

Lim G, Choi J, Mohan R (2007) Iterative solution methods for beam angle and fluence map optimization in intensity modulated radiation therapy planning. Tech. rep., Department of Industrial Engineering, University of Houston, Houston, Texas, to appear in the Asia-Pacific Journal of Operations Research

Lim J, Ferris M, Shepard D, Wright S, Earl M (2002) An optimization framework for conformal radiation treatment planning. Tech. Rep. Optimization Technical Report 02-10, Computer Sciences Department, University of Wisconsin, Madison, Wisconsin

Morrill S, Rosen I, Lane R, Belli J (1990) The influence of dose constraint point placement on optimized radiation therapy treatment planning. International Journal of Radiation Oncology, Biology, Physics 19:129–141

Nizin P, Mooij R (1997) An approximation of centeral-axis absorbed dose in narrow photon beams. Medical Physics 24(11):1775–1780

Pierskalla W (2004) We have no choice - health care delivery must be improved: The key lies in the application of operations research. INFORMS Annual Conference, Denver, CO

Rosen I, Lane R, Morrill S, Belli J (1991) Treatment plan optimization using linear programming. Medical Physics 18(2):141–152

Shepard D, Ferris M, Olivera G, Mackie T (1999) Optimizing the delivery of radiation therapy to cancer patients. SIAM Review 41(4):721–744

Integrated Forecasting and Inventory Control for Seasonal Demand

Gokhan Metan and Aurélie Thiele

Abstract We present a data-driven forecasting technique with integrated inventory control for seasonal data, and compare it to the traditional Holt-Winters algorithm in the context of the newsvendor problem. The data-driven approach relies on (i) clustering data points reflecting a similar phase of the demand process, and (ii) computing the optimal order quantity using the critical quantile for the relevant data, i.e., data observed when the demand was in a similar phase to the one forecasted for the next time period. Results indicate that the data-driven approach achieves a 1-5% improvement in the average regret when holding and backorder costs are of the same order of magnitude. For particularly imbalanced cost structures, average regret can be improved by up to 90%. This is because traditional forecasting penalizes under- and over-shooting equally, but penalties at the inventory management level are much more severe in one case (typically, backorder) than the other (typically, holding). This suggests the data-driven approach holds much promise as a cost reduction technique.

Key words: data-driven optimization, integrated inventory control, clustering, Holt-Winters method.

1 Introduction

Forecasting and optimization have traditionally been approached as two distinct, sequential components of inventory management: the random demand is first estimated using historical data, then this forecast (either a point forecast of the future

Gokhan Metan
American Airlines, Operations Research and Decision Support Department, 4333 Amon Carter Blvd, Fort Worth TX 76155, USA e-mail: gom204@lehigh.edu

Aurélie Thiele
Lehigh University, Department of Industrial and Systems Engineering, 200 W Packer Ave, Bethlehem PA 18015, USA e-mail: aurelie.thiele@lehigh.edu

J.W. Chinneck et al. (eds.), *Operations Research and Cyber-Infrastructure*, Operations Research/Computer Science Interfaces Series 47, DOI: 10.1007/978-0-387-88843-9_22, © Springer Science+Business Media, LLC 2009

demand or a forecast of the distribution) is used as input to the optimization module. In particular, the primary objective of time series analysis is to develop mathematical models that explain past data; these models are used in making forecasting decisions where the goal is to predict the next period's observation as precisely as possible. To achieve this goal, demand model parameters are estimated or a distribution is fitted to the data using a performance metric such as Mean Square Error, which penalizes overestimating and underestimating the demand equally. In practice, however, the optimization model penalizes under- and over-predictions unequally, e.g., in inventory problems, backorder is viewed as particularly undesirable while holding inventory is less penalized. In such a setting, the decision-maker places an order in each time period based on the demand prediction coming from the forecasting model, but the prediction of the forecasting model does not take into account the nature of the penalties in the optimization process, and instead minimizes the (symmetric) error between the forecasts and the actual data points.

In this paper, we investigate the integration of the forecasting and inventory control decisions; in particular, our focus is on comparing the performance of this data-driven approach with the traditional Holt-Winters algorithm for random demand with a seasonal trend. The goal is no longer to predict future observations as accurately as possible using a problem-independent metric, but to blend the inventory control principles into the demand analysis to achieve superior performance. Data-driven operations management has been the focus of growing interest over the last few years. In an early work, van Ryzin and McGill (2000) determine the optimal protection levels in airline revenue management by combining the optimality conditions derived by Brumelle and McGill (1993) with the stochastic approximation procedure proposed in Robbins and Monro (1951); while promising, the method exhibits mixed performance in numerical studies. Godfrey and Powell (2001) present an adaptive technique based on concave piecewise linear approximations of the value function for the newsvendor problem with censored demand. More recently, Bent and van Hentenryck (2004) consider a scenario-based planning approach to the multiple vehicle routing problem with time windows and achieves significant gains by exploiting stochastic information. Bent and van Hentenryck (2005) focus on on-line stochastic scheduling where time constraints limit the opportunities for offline optimization; instead of sampling distributions, it relies on machine learning techniques and historical data. That paper also presents the idea of historical sampling, which selects a starting position in the past sequence of data, and generates a sample of pre-specified size starting from that position and selecting the next data points in a continuous fashion, without gaps. The reader is referred to Van Hentenryck and Bent (2006) for an in-depth treatment of online stochastic combinatorial optimization. Bertsimas and Thiele (2004) investigate the data-driven newsvendor problem under risk aversion, using one-sided trimming of the historical data in a tractable approach that incorporates trimming and optimization in a single linear programming problem. Data-driven management can also be applied to multi-product pricing, as demonstrated in Rusmevichientong et al (2006).

The present work adds to this growing body of literature by focusing on cyclical demand, and comparing the performance of a novel algorithm based on the *clustering* of data points (Metan and Thiele (2008)) with that of the traditional Holt-Winters approach. Cluster creation and recombination allow the decision-maker to place his order at each time period based only on the most relevant data. Because the Holt-Winters algorithm was developed for uncensored data, we only investigate the uncensored case in our comparative study. Issues related to the censored newsvendor, i.e., a newsvendor who observes sales data but not the demand, are discussed in Ding et al (2002) and Bisi and Dada (2007). To the best of our knowledge, we are the first authors to propose a clustering approach to the data-driven (seasonal) inventory management problem. As pointed out in Metan and Thiele (2008), customer behavior exhibits cyclical trends in many logistics applications where the influence of exogenous drivers is difficult to quantify accurately, which makes the approach particularly appealing. The proposed methodology captures the tradeoff between the various cost drivers and provides the decision-maker with the optimal order-up-to levels, rather than the projected demand. Results indicate that the data-driven approach achieves a 1-5% improvement in the average regret when holding and backorder costs are of the same order of magnitude. For particularly imbalanced cost structures, average regret can be improved by up to 90%. Again, this is because traditional forecasting penalizes under- and over-shooting equally, but penalties at the inventory management level are much more severe in one case (typically, backorder) than the other (typically, holding). This suggests that inventory managers could significantly benefit from implementing this approach.

The rest of the paper is organized as follows. In Section 2, we describe the methodology for integrated forecasting and inventory control in a data-driven framework. We present simulation results and compare the performance of the proposed approach with the traditional Holt-Winters algorithm in Section 3. Finally, Section 4 contains concluding remarks.

2 Integrated Data-driven Forecasting and Inventory Control

In this paper, our objective is to determine the optimal order for the newsvendor problem under cyclical demand using the integrated approach; however, the method can extended to other problem structures. The data-driven algorithm seeks to differentiate between the deterministic *seasonal effect* and the *stochastic variability* (see Figure 1) so that cycle stock and safety stock levels can be set accurately.

We use the following notation.
Cost parameters:
  c: the unit ordering cost,
  p: the unit selling price,
  s: the salvage value,
  c_u: undershoot cost ($c_u = p - c$),
  c_o: overshoot cost ($c_o = c - s$),
  α: critical ratio ($\alpha = \frac{c_u}{c_u + c_o}$).

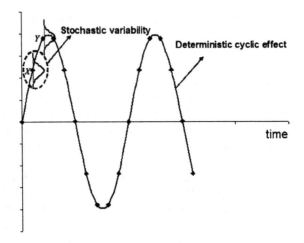

Fig. 1 Differentiation of cyclic behavior and stochastic variability.

Demand parameters and decision variable:

Q: the order quantity,

D: the demand level,

$\phi(.)$: pdf of standard normal distribution,

$\Phi(.)$: cdf of standard normal distribution,

S: the set of data points obtained from previous observations,

N: the number of historical observations in S,

d_i: the ith demand observation in set S, with $i = 1, 2, \ldots, N$,

$d_{<i>}$: the ith smallest demand in set S, with $i = 1, 2, \ldots, N$,

Additional parameters required in algorithm:

T: periodicity of time series,

C_j: list of data points assigned to cluster j, $j=1,\ldots,T$, ranked in increasing order,

m: number of data points assigned to each cluster.

The methodology that we propose here is a *dynamic and data-driven approach* that builds directly upon the historical observations and addresses seasonality by creating and recombining clusters of past demand points. Our description follows Metan and Thiele (2008) closely, although at a less technical level, since our purpose here is not to demonstrate the algorithm's absolute performance but its relative performance with respect to the Holt-Winters method. *Clustering* can be defined as grouping a set of instances into a given number of subsets, called clusters, so that instances in the same cluster share similar characteristics. Most research efforts in clustering focus on developing efficient algorithms, in particular in the context of marketing applications and customer data (Jain et al (1999)), which are beyond the scope of this paper. We only mention here the method of k-means, which was originally developed by MacQueen (1967) and is one of the simplest clustering approaches available in the literature: it partitions the data into k clusters by minimizing the sum of squared differences of objects to the centroid or mean of the cluster. The objective of minimizing total intra-cluster variability can be formulated as: $\min \sum_{i=1}^{k} \sum_{j \in S_i} |x_j - \mu_i|^2$, where there are k clusters S_i, $i = 1, 2, ..., k$ and μ_i is the mean point of all the instances x_j in S_i. This method presents similarities with the clustering approach we propose; in particular, we sort the demand and assign the data points to clusters in a manner that also attempts to minimize intra-cluster variability. A difference is that, while the k-means algorithm proceeds iteratively by updating the centroids of each cluster but keeps the same number of clusters throughout, we update the number of clusters by merging subsets as needed. Techniques for cluster aggregation/disaggregation are not discussed here; the reader is referred to Metan and Thiele (2008) for more details.

The approach consists of five main steps, as described in Algorithm 2.1. For simplicity of exposition, we assume that the periodicity of the time series is known to the master algorithm; for settings where the true periodicity is unknown, an initial period estimation subroutine can be used to initiate the master algorithm.

Algorithm 2.1 (Master algorithm for cyclical demand (Metan and Thiele) (2008))
Step 1. Sort the historical demand data in set S in ascending order to form the list $\hat{S}$.
Step 2. Create T data clusters using $\hat{S}$ (Algorithm 2.2).
repeat *(until the end of the planning horizon)*
Step 3. Detect the phase φ and the corresponding cluster C_j of the demand at the next time period ($j = 1, 2, ..., T$).
Step 4. Select the next order level using inventory control policy π defined over the set C_j.
Step 5. Assign the new demand observation to appropriate cluster C_j ($j = 1, 2, ..., T$).
    Update the phase for the next decision point ($\varphi \longleftarrow (\varphi + 1) \bmod T$)
end repeat.

The objectives of each step of the master algorithm are summarized in Table 1. In Step 1 of Algorithm 2.1 the historical data is sorted and stored in the list $\hat{S}$, which is then used by Algorithm 2.2 to create the initial clusters (Step 2). Algorithm 2.2 creates as many clusters as the periodicity of the seasonal demand function, i.e., one cluster for each phase of the seasonality, and assigns $m = \lfloor \frac{N}{T} \rfloor$ data points to each cluster, with the $N - mT$ oldest data points being discarded. (Alternatively, the last cluster could receive more points than the others.)

Table 1 Categorization of the master algorithm's steps.

Activity Category	Objective	Steps
Forecasting	Initialize forecasting method	Steps 1 & 2
	Forecast cyclic effect	Step 3
	Update forecasts	Step 5
Inventory control	Make optimal ordering decision given the forecast	Step 4

The output of Step 2 is a set of clusters $\{C_j | j = 1, 2, \ldots, T\}$ and each cluster can be thought of as a set that defines a group of possible forecasts corresponding to a given phase of the time series. The algorithm selects such a set C_j among the available sets $\{C_j | j = 1, 2, \ldots, T\}$ in Step 3, which is equivalent to defining a set of predictions rather than having a single point forecast. Then, Step 4 concludes the decision-making process by selecting the order-up-to level using inventory control policy $\pi : C_j \rightarrow \Re$. Finally, Step 5 updates cluster C_j by assigning the new observation to this set and the process repeats itself starting from Step 3.

Algorithm 2.2 (Initial clustering) *Set* $m = \lfloor \frac{N}{T} \rfloor$, $j = 1$.
repeat
    Assign observations $d_{<m(j-1)+1>}, \ldots, d_{<m(j-1)+m>}$ *to cluster* C_j,
    $j \longleftarrow j + 1$,
end repeat *when* $j = T + 1$.

Figure 2 shows the repartition of 100 data points into clusters for a cyclical demand with a periodicity of $T = 20$. Since, $m = \frac{N}{T} = \frac{100}{20} = 5$, the algorithm creates 20 clusters with 5 data points in each. The data points that lie within the boundaries of two consecutive horizontal lines in Figure 2 all belong to the same cluster.

The newsvendor problem, which is the focus of this work, has been extensively studied in the literature under a wide range of assumptions (see, e.g., Porteus (2002).) We review here properties of the optimal order when the demand D is a continuous non-negative random variable with probability density function (pdf) f and

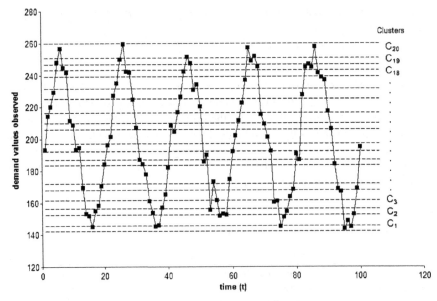

Fig. 2 Clustering the historical data for $D \sim N(200 + 50\sin(\frac{2\pi t}{20}), 7)$. (Metan and Thiele (2008))

cumulative density function (cdf) F, and there is no setup cost for placing an order. The newsvendor decides how many items to order before knowing the exact value of the demand, with the goal of maximizing his expected profit. Since the goods are perishable, no inventory can be carried over to the next time period. The classical newsvendor problem is then formulated as:

$$\max_{Q \geq 0} (p - c) Q - (c - s) E \left[\max(0, Q - D) \right],$$

The optimal solution to the classical newsvendor problem is (Porteus (2002)):

$$Q^* = F^{-1} (\alpha)$$

The value of the optimal order depends heavily on the underlying demand distribution. In practice, however, such precise knowledge is difficult to obtain, because we lack historical observations to compute meaningful estimates. This data scarcity may be due to the introduction of a new product (no historical data is available), or to the non-stationarity of the demand (historical data is then in large part irrelevant, since past demands obey different distributions than the demand in the current time period.) This motivates the *direct use* of the empirical data to guide the manager, so that the decision-making process builds upon the precise amount of information available without estimating any additional parameters.

In what follows, we focus on non-stationary demand as the main reason for scarce data. We assume that we do not have any information about the distribution of the underlying demand process, but we do have a set of historical observations at our disposal. The data-driven counterpart of the classical newsvendor problem becomes:

$$\max_{Q \geq 0} (p - c) Q - \frac{(c - s)}{N} \sum_{i=1}^{N} \max(0, Q - d_i),$$

and the optimal order Q^* is given by:

$$Q^* = d_{<j>}, \text{ with } j = \lceil \alpha N \rceil.$$

where all d_i are possible realizations of the demand at the next time period.

In the problem with seasonal demand, we define the control policy as the α-quantile of the data set C_j, rather than the whole data set (which contains data points observed for different phases of the cycle). Therefore, we restate Step 4 of the master algorithm as follows:

Step 4. Select the next order level using inventory control policy $\pi : Q^* = d_{<\lceil \alpha |C_j| \rceil>}$ *defined over the set* C_j.

3 Experimental Results

3.1 The Holt-Winters Method

We start by reviewing the traditional procedure. The Holt-Winters method is a type of exponential smoothing technique that is best suited for forecasting a time series with a linear trend and seasonality. The technique is due to Winters (1960) and the method assumes that the time series can be described by the model:

$$y_t = (\beta_0 + \beta_1 t)SN_t + \varepsilon_t,$$

where β_0, β_1, SN_t are the *permanent component* (or intercept), *trend*, and *seasonal factor*, respectively. These parameters are estimated using the historically available data and the estimates are calculated using Equations (1)-(3). Let us assume that we are at the end of period $T - 1$ and already have the estimates of the parameters β_0, β_1, SN_t (the estimates of the parameters at time $T - 1$ are denoted as $a_0(T - 1)$, $b_1(T - 1)$, and $sn_T(T - L - 1)$, respectively). In period T, we observe a new data point, y_T, and we would like to update our estimates using this new information. By using Equations (1)-(3), we can obtain the new estimates of the model (i.e., $a_0(T)$, $b_1(T)$, and $sn_T(T)$) and forecast next period's value via Equation (4). In these equations L is the periodicity of the process and α, β, γ are the smoothing constants. In Equation 4, τ is the variable that defines the number of periods from the current period in which the forecast is being made. For instance, if we are at period $T = 10$ and want to forecast the time series' value at time 12, then $\tau = 2$ and the corresponding prediction is denoted by $\hat{y}_{T+\tau}(T)$.

$$a_0(T) = \alpha \frac{y_T}{sn_T(T-L)} + (1-\alpha)[a_0(T-1) + b_1(T-1)] \tag{1}$$

$$b_1(T) = \beta[a_0(T) - a_0(T-1)] + (1-\beta)b_1(T-1) \tag{2}$$

$$sn_T(T) = \gamma \frac{y_T}{a_0(T)} + (1-\gamma)sn_T(T-L) \tag{3}$$

$$\hat{y}_{T+\tau}(T) = [a_0(T) + b_1(T)\tau]sn_{T+\tau}(T+\tau-L) \tag{4}$$

One of the difficulties with the Holt-Winters method is setting the optimal values of the smoothing constants, α, β, and γ. These constants take their values in $[0, 1]$. An appropriate combination of smoothing constants is found by minimizing a performance metric, such as Mean Square Error (MSE), over the historical data set.

3.2 Results

In this section, we implement the Holt-Winters method and the integrated data-driven forecasting technique proposed in Section 2. We compare the performances of both techniques in terms of the average regret via simulation.

Table 2 Experimental Parameters.

Exp. Set	b	T	σ	Warm-up	Simulation length
Set 1	200	10	7	200	5000
	200	20	7	200	5000
	200	100	7	1000	5000
Set 2	50	10	7	200	5000
	50	20	7	200	5000
	50	100	7	1000	5000

The underlying demand process used in the experiments is modeled as a Normally distributed demand, $N(\mu, \sigma^2)$, where $\mu = a + b\sin(\frac{2\pi}{T})$. We consider two sets of experiments as shown in Table 2. In Set 1 and Set 2 of the experiments, we consider high and moderate levels of amplitude for the seasonality (i.e., $b = 200$ as high and $b = 50$ as moderate). We use the value of 500 for the demand level (i.e., $a = 500$) and standard deviation of $\sigma = 7$. At the beginning of the simulation, we generate demand observations from the underlying demand distribution for a length of time defined by the warm-up period. This set of demand observations is used by the Holt-Winters method and the data-driven method for initializing their own parameters. We set the optimal values for the smoothing constants (i.e., α, β, γ) of the Holt-Winters method with 0.05 precision. For each experimental setting we generate 20 simulation replications with each replication having a run length of 5000 time periods, and collect the performance statistics of each method. We use the following values for the inventory cost parameters: $p = 10$ (the unit selling price); $c = 7$ (the unit purchasing cost), and $s = 5$ (the unit salvage value). Finally, different methods can be used to initialize the Holt-Winters method's initial estimates. Here, we use the one described in Bowerman and O'Connell (1979). When we examine the results of the individual simulation runs, we see that the data-driven method always outperforms the Holt-Winters method in terms of the average regret values. (Note that this version of the Holt-Winters method, which is the version traditionally used by practitioners, generates a point forecast for the demand and not a distribution.) To further strengthen our analysis, we construct the 95% paired-t confidence intervals. Table 3 summarizes the results including the 95% confidence intervals for each experiment. None of the confidence intervals given in Table 3 contains the value 0, which allows us to conclude that the average regret achieved by using the data-driven method is significantly less than the average regret achieved by Holt-Winters method with 0.95 confidence level. Also, experiments indicate that the data-driven method provides a 2-5% improvement in average regret over this version of the Holt-Winters method for the experimental setting tested. The improvement is greater in experiments with large amplitude.

We also investigate the impact of the length of the planning horizon on the performances of the methods. Figure 3 shows the average simulated regret values for both methods as a function of the simulation run length. Figure 3 suggests that the performance of both methods improves as time elapses and the rate of improvement

Table 3 Summary of results.

Experiment	Avg. Performance of Data-Driven meth.	Avg. Performance of Holt-Winters meth.	Avg. Performance Difference	95% CI
Set 1, Exp. 1	13.7645	14.418	0.6535	[0.5712, 0.7357]
Set 1, Exp. 2	13.6365	14.3975	0.761	[0.6949, 0.8270]
Set 1, Exp. 3	13.762	14.4255	0.6635	[0.6348, 0.6921]
Set 2, Exp. 1	13.739	14.29	0.551	[0.4981, 0.6038]
Set 2, Exp. 2	13.6335	14.295	0.6615	[0.6136, 0.7093]
Set 2, Exp. 3	14.1155	14.423	0.3075	[0.2124, 0.4026]

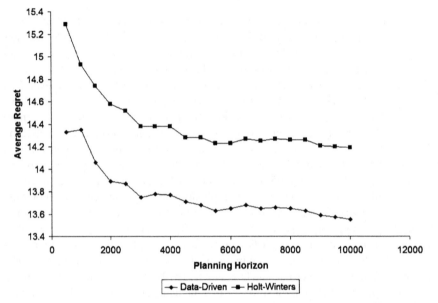

Fig. 3 Effect of planning horizon on the methods' performance (results obtained under Set 1, Experiment 3 parameter levels).

is higher early in the process as compared to the rate of improvement near the end of the planning horizon. Also, the performance of both methods stabilizes once enough time periods have elapsed.

The preliminary simulation results above indicate that the integrated data-driven forecasting and inventory control technique improves the performance of the system over the Holt-Winters method. We now perform additional experiments to answer the following questions:

1. What are the performances of both methods measured in terms of mean square error (MSE) as well as average regret?
2. What impact does a different inventory control policy $\hat{\pi}$ have on the performance of the data-driven technique?

Table 4 Experimental Parameters.

Instance	b	T	σ	Warm-up	Simulation length	p c s
I1	200	10	7	200	5000	10 7 5
I2	200	20	7	200	5000	10 7 5
I3	200	100	7	1000	5000	10 7 5
I4	200	10	7	200	5000	10 3 1
I5	200	20	7	200	5000	10 3 1
I6	200	100	7	1000	5000	10 3 1

Table 5 Experimental Results.

Instance	Holt-Winters with safety stock		Data-driven with π	
	Avg. Regret	MSE	Avg. Regret	MSE
I1	13.9425	55.2970	13.7557	53.8062
I2	13.9626	55.3469	13.5916	52.8218
I3	14.0027	54.5063	13.8555	52.8032
I4	20.0325	105.9309	19.1052	78.4688
I5	20.0450	106.0904	18.8668	78.1311
I6	19.7161	89.5257	19.6570	67.6535

3. What is the impact of the cost parameters on the relative performance of the forecasting techniques?

We investigate these issues under the same experimental conditions as above, except for the number of simulation replications (we perform 60 replications rather than 20 to obtain tighter confidence bounds), by extending the first experimental set in Table 2. The new experimental instances are shown in Table 4, in which the first three instances impose a critical ratio of $\alpha = \frac{c_u}{c_u + c_o} = 0.6$ whereas the second three instances have a critical ratio of $\alpha = \frac{c_u}{c_u + c_o} \approx 0.78$. Also, to test the impact of the inventory control policy on the system performance, we use the following alternative policy in Step 4 of the master algorithm.

Step 4. Select the next order level using inventory control policy $\widehat{\pi} : Q = \frac{\sum_{d_i \in C_j} d_i}{|C_j|}$
defined over the set C_j.

The reason for using the cluster averages as the order-up-to level policy is that it minimizes the mean-square error (MSE) and it provides neutral predictions against under- and over-shooting the demand. In other words, it provides forecasts similar to those of the Holt-Winters method since it now discards the imbalance between the cost parameters when producing the predictions.

Results of the second set of experiments are summarized in Tables 5–7 (confidence intervals in Table 7 are calculated for the average regret difference between the two methods). In Table 5, we summarize the experimental results in which we compare the performances of the data-driven method operating under the policy π and the Holt-Winters method with the safety stock, that is, a modified Holt-Winters

Table 6 Experimental Results.

Instance	Holt-Winters without safety stock		Data-driven with $\widehat{\pi}$	
	Avg. Regret	MSE	Avg. Regret	MSE
I1	14.4127	52.0754	14.1444	50.3155
I2	14.4316	52.2010	14.0038	49.3302
I3	14.4611	52.5743	14.2142	50.6321
I4	25.9762	52.0754	25.4281	50.3155
I5	25.9990	52.2010	25.1729	49.3302
I6	26.0188	52.5610	25.4555	50.2703

Table 7 Experimental results: 95% confidence interval for the average regret difference.

Instance	95% CI for the difference between Holt-Winters and Data-driven with π		95% CI for the difference between Holt-Winters and Data-driven with $\widehat{\pi}$	
	Lower bound	Upper bound	Lower bound	Upper bound
I1	0.1730	0.2007	0.2243	0.3123
I2	0.3557	0.3864	0.3860	0.4695
I3	0.0391	0.2552	0.0920	0.4018
I4	0.8257	1.0291	0.3406	0.7556
I5	1.0850	1.2716	0.6275	1.0247
I6	0.0280	0.0902	0.4388	0.6878

method where we estimate the future demand distribution rather than a point forecast. Since the Holt-Winters method provides the point estimate that minimizes the mean square error, we adjust its predictions by adding the safety stock term. This safety stock changes the order quantity by considering the imbalance between the cost parameters as well as the standard deviation of the random error term of the forecast. If $\sigma_\varepsilon = \sqrt{\text{MSE}}$ is the standard deviation of the residuals, then the safety stock for the Holt-Winters predictions can be calculated as $\text{ss} = z_\alpha \sigma_\varepsilon$, where z_α is the α-quantile of the standard Normal distribution. In Table 6, we present the results for the comparison of the data-driven method operating under the policy $\widehat{\pi}$ and the Holt-Winters method without the safety stock. Since the data-driven method operating under the policy $\widehat{\pi}$ (where the decision-maker orders an amount equal to the cluster average) does not consider the imbalance between the cost terms, it is most appropriate to compare it to the Holt-Winters method without adjusting the Holt-Winters' predictions as well.

In terms of average regret, the data-driven method (under both π and $\widehat{\pi}$ policies) performs significantly better than the Holt-Winters method (with and without safety stock, respectively). Also, the proposed method performs even better when π is used as the inventory control policy (compared to policy $\widehat{\pi}$), which is the optimal policy for the newsvendor problem. This indicates that under the problem-specific optimal control policy, the integrated forecasting and inventory control results in significantly improved performance. In terms of MSE, the data-driven method results in lower values than the Holt-Winters method; this suggests that the data-driven

Table 8 Percentage of improvement in average regret (HW with safety stock and DD with π).

	$\alpha = 0.6$			$\alpha \approx 0.78$		
I1	I2	I3	I4	I5	I6
1.34%	2.66%	1.05%	4.63%	5.88%	0.30%

Table 9 Percentage of improvement in average regret (HW without safety stock and DD with $\hat{\pi}$).

	$\alpha = 0.6$			$\alpha \approx 0.78$		
I1	I2	I3	I4	I5	I6
1.86%	2.96%	1.71%	2.11%	3.18%	2.16%

approach also has the power of closely predicting the actual observations when an appropriate policy such as $\hat{\pi}$ is used (Table 6). However, if we compare the MSE results across alternative policies, Table 6 provides lower MSE values than the corresponding MSE values given in Table 5. This observation is mainly due to the different objectives of the two policies, in which the objective of the first policy is to minimize the cost whereas the objective of the second policy is to minimize the average error between the predictions and the actual demand observations. Therefore, the first policy results in better regret values and the second policy results better MSE values.

Another performance statistics is presented in Tables 8 and 9. We observe from these results that the percentage of improvement achieved by the data-driven method over the Holt-Winters method is more significant when the integrated forecasting and inventory control policy is implemented. Also, the percentage of improvement generally increases when the imbalance between the cost parameters increases; however, when the periodicity of the demand process is large (e.g., problem instance I6), the potential improvement diminishes since it becomes more difficult to differentiate the seasonal behavior from the stochastic variability. To quantify the impact of the critical ratio on the average regret one more step further, we perform additional experiments for instance I1 for different cost parameter combinations. Figure 4 shows the percentage of improvement in the average regret values with respect to the critical ratio. We calculate the percentage of improvement by comparing the average regret values of the data-driven method ("DD") under policy π and the Holt-Winters ("HW") method without safety stock. The percentage of improvement is a convex function of the critical ratio and reaches its minimum value at 0.5, which is the point where under- and over-shooting the demand are penalized equally. Therefore, the integrated forecasting and inventory control loses its attractiveness since bare forecasting achieves the same performance. However, when the imbalance is high (in many practical applications, backorder costs are much higher than holding costs), the cost reduction becomes significant: up to 90% improvement is observed at extreme critical ratio values (Figure 4).

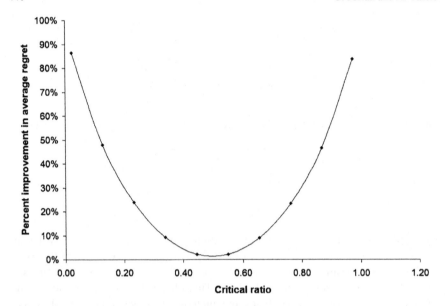

Fig. 4 Effect of imbalance between cost parameters on the percentage of improvement in average regret (results obtained using the parameter levels of instance I1).

4 Conclusions

We have compared the performance of a data-driven algorithm based on the clustering of data points to the Holt-Winters method when the demand faced by the newsvendor is seasonal, and observed the integrated forecasting-control approach achieves significant gains over the traditional method.

Acknowledgements This work is supported in part by NSF Grant DMI-0540143.

References

Bent R, van Hentenryck P (2004) Scenario-based planning for partially dynamic vehicle routing with stochastic customers. Operations Research 52(6):977–987

Bent R, van Hentenryck P (2005) Online stochastic optimization without distributions. In: Proceedings of the Fifteenth International Conference on Automated Planning and Scheduling, pp 171–180

Bertsimas D, Thiele A (2004) A data-driven approach to newsvendor problems. Tech. rep., Massachusetts Institute of Technology, Cambridge, MA

Bisi A, Dada M (2007) Dynamic learning, pricing and ordering by a censored newsvendor. Naval Research Logistics 54(4):448–461

Bowerman B, O'Connell R (1979) Forecasting & Time Series. Duxbury Press, Belmont, CA

Brumelle S, McGill J (1993) Airline seat allocation with multiple nested fare classes. Operations Research 41:127–137

Ding X, Puterman M, Bisi A (2002) The censored newsvendor and the optimal acquisition of information. Operations Research 50(3):517–527

Godfrey G, Powell W (2001) An adaptive, distribution-free algorithm for the newsvendor problem with censored demands, with applications to inventory and distribution. Management Science 47:1101–1112

Jain A, Murty M, Flynn P (1999) Data clustering: A review. ACM Computing Surveys 31:264–323

MacQueen J (1967) Some methods for classification and analysis of multivariate observations. In: Proceedings of 5th Berkeley Symposium on Mathematical Statistics and Probability, University of California Press, Berkeley, CA, vol 31, pp 264–323

Metan G, Thiele A (2008) Computational Optimization and Logistics Challenges in the Enterprise, Springer, chap A dynamic and data-driven approach to the newsvendor problem under seasonal demand. To appear

Porteus E (2002) Stochastic Inventory Theory. Stanford University Press, Palo Alto, CA

Robbins H, Monro S (1951) A stochastic approximation method. Annals of Mathematical Statistics 22:400–407

Rusmevichientong P, van Roy B, Glynn P (2006) A non-parametric approach to multi-product pricing. Operations Research 54(1):82–98

Van Hentenryck P, Bent R (2006) Online Stochastic Combinatorial Optimization. MIT Press, Cambridge, MA

van Ryzin G, McGill J (2000) Revenue management without forecasting or optimization: an adaptive algorithm for determining seat protection levels. Management Science 46:760–775

Winters P (1960) Forecasting sales by exponentially weighted moving averages. Management Science 6:324–342

A Provably Good Global Routing Algorithm in Multilayer IC and MCM Layout Designs

Mohamed Saad, Tamás Terlaky, Anthony Vannelli, and Hu Zhang

Abstract Given a multilayer routing area, we consider the global routing problem of selecting a maximum set of nets, such that every net can be routed entirely in one of the given layers without violating the physical capacity constraints. This problem is motivated by applications in multilayer IC and multichip module (MCM) layout designs. The contribution of this paper is threefold. First, we formulate the problem as an integer linear program (ILP). Second, we modify an algorithm by Garg and Könemann for packing linear programs to obtain an approximation algorithm for the global routing problem. Our algorithm provides solutions *guaranteed* to be within a certain range of the optimal value, and runs in polynomial-time even if all, possibly exponentially many, Steiner trees are considered in the formulation. Finally, we demonstrate that the complexity of our algorithm can be significantly reduced in the case of identical routing layers.

1 Introduction

Traditionally, the VLSI routing process is divided into two phases: global routing and detailed routing. Global routing is to find a routing tree for each net, and detailed routing assigns the actual tracks and vias. Advances in VLSI fabrication technology

Mohamed Saad
Department of Electrical and Computer Engineering, University of Sharjah, United Arab Emirates,
e-mail: msaad@sharjah.ac.ae

Tamás Terlaky
Department of Industrial and Systems Engineering, Lehigh University, Bethlehem, PA, USA,
e-mail: terlaky@lehigh.edu

Anthony Vannelli
College of Physical and Engineering Sciences, University of Guelph, Guelph, ON, Canada,
e-mail: vannelli@uoguelph.ca

Hu Zhang
Canadian Imperial Bank of Commerce, Toronto, ON, Canada, e-mail: hu.zhang@cibc.ca

J.W. Chinneck et al. (eds.), *Operations Research and Cyber-Infrastructure*, Operations
Research/Computer Science Interfaces Series 47, DOI: 10.1007/978-0-387-88843-9_23,
© Springer Science+Business Media, LLC 2009

have made it possible to use multiple routing layers for interconnections. A significant amount of research exists on handling multiple routing layers in the detailed routing phase. However, only limited research exists on multilayer global routing [13]. In other words, multiple routing layers have been dealt with in the detailed routing phase rather than in the global routing phase [13].

Given a *multilayer* routing area and a set of nets, we consider the *global routing* problem of selecting a maximum (weighted) subset of nets, such that every net can be routed entirely in one of the given layers without violating the physical capacity constraints. This problem is motivated by the following.

- Routing the majority of nets each in a single layer significantly reduces the number of required vias in the final layout. It is known that vias increase fabrication cost and degrade system performance [7].
- Routing the majority of nets each in a single layer greatly simplifies the detailed routing problem in multilayer IC design [7].

Two examples of the global routing problem are shown in Fig. 1 and Fig. 2. For simplicity, a single-layer routing area is assumed in both examples. It is assumed also that each channel is able to accomodate at most one routing tree. In the example of Fig. 1, two nets are given in the routing area. The vertices belonging to the first (respectively, second) net are all labeled by the number 1 (respectively, number 2). Furthermore, a solution is presented such that both nets can be successfully realized in one layer. In particular, the first net is realized by the thick solid routing tree, while the second net is realized by the dashed routing tree. However, if a third net is added as in Fig. 2, there is no feasible solution for the routing problem any more. In particular, the third net (with vertices labeled by the number 3) cannot be realized by a routing tree any more. In practical global routing instances, this feasibility problem frequently occurs. Therefore, we address in this paper the important objective of selecting a maximum (weighted) subset of nets, such that every net can be routed entirely in one of the given layers without violating the physical capacity constraints.

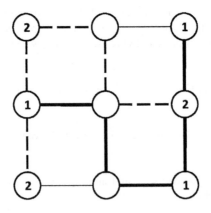

Fig. 1 A feasible routing.

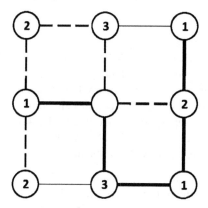

Fig. 2 An infeasible routing.

A similar multilayer topological planar routing problem was addressed in [8] and [7]. Given a number of routing layers, these studies addressed problem of choosing the maximum (weighted) subset of nets such that each net can be topologically routed entirely in one of the given layers. In particular, Cong and Liu proved in [8] that the problem is **NP**-hard. A provably good greedy algorithm for the problem was presented by Cong, Hossain and Sherwany [7]. A limitation of these studies is that they considered only planar routing, i.e., physical capacity constraints were not considered [7]. Moreover, planar routing graphs cannot handle state-of-the-art technologies properly [13].

The contribution of this paper is threefold.

- We formulate the multilayer global routing problem of selecting the maximum subset of nets such that every net can be routed entirely in one of the given layers without violating the physical capacity constraints, as an integer linear program (ILP).
- We modify an algorithm by Garg and Könemann for packing linear programs to obtain an approximation algorithm for the global routing problem. Our algorithm provides solutions *guaranteed* to be within a certain range of the optimal value, and runs in polynomial-time even if all, possibly exponentially many, Steiner trees are considered in the formulation.
- We demonstrate that the complexity of our algorithm can be significantly reduced in the case of identical routing layers.

The remainder of this paper is organized as follows. In Section 2, we model the global routing problem as an ILP. In Section 3, we present a polynomial-time approximation algorithm for the linear programming (LP-) relaxation of the problem (i.e., for the *fractional* global routing problem), and establish its performance guarantee and computational complexity. A reduced complexity algorithm is introduced, in Section 4, for the case of identical routing layers. In Section 5, we derive our overall approximation guarantee for solving the *integer* global routing problem. Section 6 concludes the paper.

2 Mathematical Model

In this section we introduce an ILP formulation for the global routing problem. Following [1], an undirected grid graph $G = (V, E)$ is constructed. In other words, a two-dimensional grid is placed over the chip. For each tile, there is a vertex $v \in V$, and two vertices corresponding to adjacent tiles are connected by an edge. In other words, each edge $e \in E$ represents a routing area between two adjacent tiles. In multilayer designs, an edge may consist of more than one layer [19]. In particular, the following are given as inputs to the problem.

- V: the set of vertices in the routing graph, $|V| = N$.
- E: the set of edges in the routing graph, $|E| = M$.
- $\mathscr{L} = \{1, 2, \ldots, L\}$: the set of available routing layers[1].
- $c_{e,l}$: the capacity of edge $e \in E$ on layer $l \in \mathscr{L}$.
- $\mathscr{I}$: the set of nets. Each net $i \in \mathscr{I}$ is defined by a subset of vertices $V_i \subseteq V$ that need to be connected. In particular, a net $i \in \mathscr{I}$ is realized by finding a Steiner tree that connects all vertices in V_i.
- $\mathscr{T}_i$: the set of all Steiner trees in G that can be used to realize net $i \in \mathscr{I}$. In other words, every tree $T \in \mathscr{T}_i$ connects the vertices in V_i. It is worth noting that $\mathscr{T}_i$ can be exponentially sized. Our algorithm, however, does not require that the sets $\mathscr{T}_i$ are explicitly given.

A net $i \in \mathscr{I}$ is realized by finding a Steiner tree $T \in \mathscr{T}_i$ that is routed entirely in one of the given layers $l \in \mathscr{L}$. The objective is to maximize the number of nets successfully realized. The design variables are $\{x_i(T, l) : i \in \mathscr{I}, T \in \mathscr{T}_i, l \in \mathscr{L}\}$, where for some $i \in \mathscr{I}$:

$$x_i(T, l) = \begin{cases} 1, & T \in \mathscr{T}_i \text{ is selected to route net } i \text{ on layer } l \in \mathscr{L}; \\ 0, & \text{otherwise.} \end{cases}$$

The global routing problem can be cast as ILP as follows:

$$\max \quad \sum_{l \in \mathscr{L}} \sum_{i \in \mathscr{I}} \sum_{T \in \mathscr{T}_i} w_i(T, l) x_i(T, l)$$

$$\text{s.t.} \quad \sum_{i \in \mathscr{I}} \sum_{T \in \mathscr{T}_i : e \in T} x_i(T, l) \leq c_{e,l}, \ \forall e, l \tag{1a}$$

$$\sum_{l \in \mathscr{L}} \sum_{T \in \mathscr{T}_i} x_i(T, l) \leq 1, \ \forall i \tag{1b}$$

$$x_i(T, l) \in \{0, 1\}, \ \forall i, T, l, \tag{1c}$$

---

[1] A routing layer considered in this paper may, in practice, be implemented as a pair of layers: one for wiring in the x direction, and the other for wiring in the y direction. The problem formulation and algorithm presented in this paper avoids the use of stacked vias between different pairs of layers. However, vias used to connect wires within any pair of layers may be required. These vias are less expensive, and may be minimized in the detailed routing phase. In the sequel, pairs of layers are simply termed "layers".

where $w_i(T,l)$ is the weight associated with the design variable $x_i(T,l)$. Although all of our results remain valid for the weighted case, to keep the discussion simple, in the rest of this paper we assume that all weights $w_i(T,l)$ are equal to one.

Equation (1a) represents the capacity constraints. It ensures that the number of nets routed over any edge e and assigned to the same layer l does not exceed the capacity $c_{e,l}$ of that edge. Equation (1b) ensures that at most one tree is chosen for every net i. Equation (1c) represents the non-negativity and integrality constraints of the variables. The objective is to maximize the number of nets successfully routed.

It is straightforward to see that the global routing problem as formulated by (1) is **NP**-hard. In fact, it contains the unsplittable maximum multicommodity flow problem as a special case. Let $\mathscr{L}$ contain only one layer, and let every net $i \in \mathscr{I}$ contain only two vertices, i.e., for every net $i \in \mathscr{I}$ let $V_i = \{s_i, d_i\}$ where $s_i, d_i \in V$. In this case $\mathscr{T}_i$ will contain only simple paths that join s_i and d_i. Under these restrictions ILP (1) will be equivalent to the following problem: Given a graph $G = (V,E)$, a capacity associated with every edge, and a set of commodities (each defined by a pair of vertices and associated with a unit demand), we seek to route a subset of the commodities of maximum total demand, such that every demand is routed along a single path and that total flow routed across any edge is bounded by its capacity. This is precisely the unsplittable maximum multicommodity flow problem, which is known to be **NP**-hard [12].

The **NP**-hardness of the global routing problem as given by (1) justifies the use of heuristics. In this paper, however, we are interested in polynomial-time approximation algorithms that have a theoretically proven worst-case performance guarantee. We start by giving an efficient algorithm to solve the linear programming (LP-) relaxation of ILP (1).

3 A Provably Good Algorithm for Fractional Global Routing

We briefly digress from the global routing problem to a more general packing problem, which is a special kind of LP. In fact the LP-relaxation of (1) is a packing problem. In this section we will design a fast approximation algorithm for the LP-relaxation of (1) based on the method in [18].

We consider the following *fractional packing problem*:

$$\begin{aligned} \max \ & c^T x \\ \text{s.t. } & Ax \leq b; \\ & x \geq 0. \end{aligned} \tag{2}$$

Here A is an $m \times n$ positive matrix, and $b \in \mathbb{R}^m$ and $c \in \mathbb{R}^n$ are positive vectors. It is worth noting that problem (1) has exponentially many variables. Therefore, it cannot be solved using many exact algorithms for LPs, e.g., standard interior point methods. The volumetric cutting plane method [2] or the ellipsoid method with separation oracle [10] may be employed, but in general they lead to large complexity. Therefore, we are interested in approximation algorithms.

The approximation algorithms for fractional packing problems (2) are well studied in [9, 14, 18, 20]. All these algorithms are based on the duality relation for LPs. However, the algorithms in [14, 20] run in a time depending on the input data, and therefore only lead to polynomial time algorithms. The algorithm in [9] is the first with a strictly polynomial time but the block problem (subproblem) is required to be polynomial time solvable. Unfortunately it is not the case as we shall show later that the block problem of LP-relaxation for (1) is **NP**-hard. Hence, we will apply the algorithm proposed in [18].

The approximation algorithm in [18] is an iterative approach. It maintains a sequence of a pair of the primal solution x and the dual solution y. At each iteration, for a pre-computed $y \in \mathbb{R}^m$, an approximate block solver $ABS(y)$ is called once that finds a column index q that:

$$(A_q)^T y / c_q \leq r \min_j (A_j)^T y / c_j,$$

where $r \geq 1$ is the approximation ratio of the block solver, which plays a role similar to the separation oracle in [10]. It is shown in [18] that their algorithm can find a $(1 - \varepsilon)/r$-approximate solution within coordination complexity (bounds on the number of iterations) of $O(m\varepsilon^{-2} \ln m)$. The approximation algorithm for fractional packing problem (2) is in Table 1.

In the algorithm, the parameters f and D are in fact the objective values of the primal and dual programs for current pair x and y. It is shown in [18] that the scaled solution $x/\log_{1+\delta}((1+\delta)/u)$ at the final iteration is a feasible solution and its corresponding objective value is at least $(1 - \varepsilon)OPT/r$, where OPT is the optimum value of (2). For the complexity, the following result holds:

Proposition 1. *[18] There exists a $(1 - \varepsilon)/r$-approximation algorithm for the packing problem (2) running in $O(m\varepsilon^{-2} \ln m)$ iterations, each iteration calling an r-approximate block solver once.*

Table 1 Approximation algorithm for fractional packing problems.

$\delta = 1 - \sqrt{1-\varepsilon}$, $u = (1+\delta)((1+\delta)m)^{-1/\delta}$, $f = 0$, $y_i = u/b_i$, $D = um$;
while $D < 1$ **do** {iteration}
$\quad$ call $ABS(y)$ to find a column index q;
$\quad p = \arg\min_i b_i/A_{i,q}$;
$\quad x_q = x_q + b_q/A_{p,q}$;
$\quad f = f + c_q b_p/A_{p,q}$;
$\quad y_i = y_i \left[1 + \delta \dfrac{b_p/A_{p,q}}{b_i/A_{i,q}}\right]$;
$\quad D = \sum\limits_{i=1}^{m} b_i y_i$;
end do

It is worth noting that the complexity of the algorithm in [18] is independent of the input data or the approximation ratio r, which is similar to the result in [11] for convex min-max resource-sharing problems.

Applying the approximation algorithm for fractional packing problems to the LP-relaxation of (1) yields the following result:

Theorem 1. *There is a $(1 - \varepsilon)/r$-approximation algorithm for the LP-relaxation of (1) with a running time $O((ML + |\mathscr{I}|)L|\mathscr{I}|\varepsilon^{-2}\beta \ln(ML + |\mathscr{I}|))$, where r and β are the ratio and the running time of the approximate minimum Steiner tree solver called as the approximate block solver, respectively.*

Proof. We just need to consider the block problem. There are two types of components in the dual vector y. The first type of components corresponding to the first set of constraints (capacity constraints) in (1) are

$$y_1, \ldots, y_M, y_{M+1}, \ldots, y_{2M}, \ldots, y_{M(L-1)+1}, \ldots, y_{ML},$$

which correspond to edge $e_i \in E$ and layer l. The remaining components $y_{ML+1}, \ldots,$ $y_{ML+|\mathscr{I}|}$ correspond to the second set of constraints in (1). It is easy to verify that the block problem of the LP-relaxation of (1) is to find a tree T such that

$$\min_i \min_l \min_{T \in \mathscr{T}_i} \left(\sum_{e \in T} y_{Ml+e} + y_{ML+i}\delta_{i,T} \right), \tag{3}$$

where the indicator variable $\delta_{i,T} = 1$ if $T \in \mathscr{T}_i$, and otherwise $\delta_{i,T} = 0$. To find the minimum, we can just search a number of $L|\mathscr{I}|$ trees to attain the following minima:

$$\min_{T \in \mathscr{T}_i} \sum_{e \in T} y_{Ml+e},$$

for all $i = 1, \ldots, |\mathscr{I}|$ and $l = 1, \ldots, L$. Then we can find the minimal objective value of (3) over all these $L|\mathscr{I}|$ trees. If we regard the first ML components of the dual vector $y_1, \ldots, y_{ML}$ as the length associated to all edges in the given graph for all layers, then $\min_{T \in \mathscr{T}_i} \sum_{e \in T} y_{Ml+e}$ is equivalent to finding a tree on the l-th layer for net i with a minimum total length. Now the block problem is in fact the minimum Steiner tree problem in graphs. With an r-approximate minimum Steiner tree solver and using the approximation algorithm for fractional packing problems in [18], we can prove the theorem. $\square$

Unfortunately, the minimum Steiner tree problem is **APX**-hard [3, 4]. The best known lower and upper bounds on the approximation ratio are $96/95 \approx 1.0105$ [6] and $1 + (\ln 3)/2 \approx 1.550$ [17], respectively. Thus, we can only use the approximation algorithm in [18] with an approximate minimum Steiner tree solver to obtain a feasible solution to the LP-relaxation of (1) to obtain an approximation algorithm with theoretical performance bounds.

4 A Reduced Complexity Algorithm for Identical Layers

In this section we consider the special case of the global routing problem where for every edge $e \in E$:

$$c_{e,1} = c_{e,2} = \ldots = c_{e,L} = c_e$$

This corresponds to the situation of all routing layers being identical. In this case, the LP-relaxation of the global routing problem will be given as follows.

$$\max \quad \sum_{l \in \mathscr{L}} \sum_{i \in \mathscr{I}} \sum_{T \in \mathscr{T}_i} x_i(T,l)$$

$$\text{s.t.} \quad \sum_{i \in \mathscr{I}} \sum_{T \in \mathscr{T}_i : e \in T} x_i(T,l) \leq c_e, \ \forall e,l \tag{4a}$$

$$\sum_{l \in \mathscr{L}} \sum_{T \in \mathscr{T}_i} x_i(T,l) \leq 1, \ \forall i \tag{4b}$$

$$0 \leq x_i(T,l) \leq 1, \ \forall i,T,l. \tag{4c}$$

Now, consider another special case of the global routing problem as given by (1), where the number of routing layers is reduced to one and the capacity of every edge e is set to $c_e \cdot L$. Let this problem be termed *single-layer problem*. It is straightforward to see that the LP-relaxation for the single-layer problem is given as follows.

$$\max \quad \sum_{i \in \mathscr{I}} \sum_{T \in \mathscr{T}_i} y_i(T)$$

$$\text{s.t.} \quad \sum_{i \in \mathscr{I}} \sum_{T \in \mathscr{T}_i : e \in T} y_i(T) \leq c_e \cdot L, \ \forall e \tag{5a}$$

$$\sum_{T \in \mathscr{T}_i} y_i(T) \leq 1, \ \forall i \tag{5b}$$

$$0 \leq y_i(T) \leq 1, \ \forall i,T. \tag{5c}$$

Recall that M and L denotes the number of edges in the routing graph and the number of routing layers, respectively. Moreover, let $|\mathscr{T}|$ and $|\mathscr{I}|$ denote the total number of Steiner trees in the graph and the total number of nets, respectively. The number of constraints in the multilayer LP (4) is $M \cdot L + |\mathscr{I}|$, while the number of constraints in the single-layer LP (5) is $M + |\mathscr{I}|$. Moreover, the number of variables in (4) is $|\mathscr{T}| \cdot L$, while the number of variables in (5) is $|\mathscr{T}|$. To give more insight, note that, in the case of ten routing layers, the single-layer LP as given by (5) has an order of magnitude less constraints and variables than the multilayer LP as given by (4). In the following theorem we establish the fact that solving LP (5) provides the same solution and objective function value as solving LP (4).

Theorem 2. *Let OPT_m denote the optimal objective function value of the multilayer LP given by (4). Also, let OPT_s denote the optimal objective function value of the single-layer LP given by (5). Then, $OPT_m = OPT_s$.*

Proof. We establish the proof by showing that $OPT_m \leq OPT_s$ and $OPT_m \geq OPT_s$.

Let $\{x_i^*(T,l) : i \in \mathscr{I}, T \in \mathscr{T}_i, l \in \mathscr{L}\}$ be an optimal solution to LP (4). Define $y_i^*(T) = \sum_{l \in \mathscr{L}} x_i^*(T,l)$ for every $i \in \mathscr{I}$ and $T \in \mathscr{T}_i$. By (4b) and (4c), for every $i \in \mathscr{I}$ and $T \in \mathscr{T}_i$, we have $0 \leq y_i^*(T) = \sum_{l \in \mathscr{L}} x_i^*(T,l) \leq 1$. Also, by (4a), for every $e \in E$, we have $\sum_{i \in \mathscr{I}} \sum_{T \in \mathscr{T}_i: e \in T} y_i^*(T) = \sum_{l \in \mathscr{L}} \sum_{i \in \mathscr{I}} \sum_{T \in \mathscr{T}_i: e \in T} x_i^*(T,l) \leq \sum_{l \in \mathscr{L}} c_e = c_e \cdot L$. Furthermore, by (4b), for every $i \in \mathscr{I}$, we have $\sum_{T \in \mathscr{T}_i} y_i^*(T) = \sum_{l \in \mathscr{L}} \sum_{T \in \mathscr{T}_i} x_i^*(T,l) <= 1$. In other words, $\{y_i^*(T) : i \in \mathscr{I}, T \in \mathscr{T}_i\}$ is a feasible solution for LP (5). Consequently,

$$\sum_{i \in \mathscr{I}} \sum_{T \in \mathscr{T}_i} y_i^*(T) \leq OPT_s. \tag{6}$$

By replacing $y_i^*(T)$ by its definition in terms of $x_i^*(T,l)$ in (6), we conclude that

$$OPT_m \leq OPT_s. \tag{7}$$

Conversely, let $\{y_i^*(T) : i \in \mathscr{I}, T \in \mathscr{T}_i\}$ be an optimal solution to LP (5). Define $x_i^*(T,l) = \frac{1}{L} \cdot y_i^*(T)$ for every for every $i \in \mathscr{I}$, $T \in \mathscr{T}_i$ and $l \in \mathscr{L}$. By (5c), for every $i \in \mathscr{I}$, $T \in \mathscr{T}_i$ and $l \in \mathscr{L}$, we have $0 \leq x_i^*(T,l) \leq 1$. Also by (5a), for every $e \in E$ and $l \in \mathscr{L}$, we have $\sum_{i \in \mathscr{I}} \sum_{T \in \mathscr{T}_i: e \in T} x_i^*(T,l) = \frac{1}{L} \cdot \sum_{i \in \mathscr{I}} \sum_{T \in \mathscr{T}_i: e \in T} y_i^*(T) \leq \frac{1}{L} \cdot c_e \cdot L = c_e$. Furthermore by (5b), for every $i \in \mathscr{I}$, we have $\sum_{l \in \mathscr{L}} \sum_{T \in \mathscr{T}_i} x_i^*(T,l) = \frac{1}{L} \cdot \sum_{l \in \mathscr{L}} \sum_{T \in \mathscr{T}_i} y_i^*(T) = \sum_{T \in \mathscr{T}_i} y_i^*(T) \leq 1$. In other words, $\{x_i^*(T,l) : i \in \mathscr{I}, T \in \mathscr{T}_i, l \in \mathscr{L}\}$ is a feasible solution for LP (4). Consequently,

$$\sum_{l \in \mathscr{L}} \sum_{i \in \mathscr{I}} \sum_{T \in \mathscr{T}_i} x_i^*(T,l) \leq OPT_m. \tag{8}$$

By replacing $x_i^*(T,l)$ by its definition in terms of $y_i^*(T)$ in (8), we conclude that

$$OPT_s \leq OPT_m. \tag{9}$$

Combining (7) and (9) completes the proof. □

Moreover, we have the following result.

Corollary 1. *Let $\{y_i^*(T) : i \in \mathscr{I}, T \in \mathscr{T}_i\}$ be an optimal solution to LP (5). Then, $\{x_i^*(T,l) : i \in \mathscr{I}, T \in \mathscr{T}_i, l \in \mathscr{L}\}$, where $x_i^*(T,l) = \frac{1}{L} \cdot y_i^*(T)$ for every $i \in \mathscr{I}$, $T \in \mathscr{T}_i$ and $l \in \mathscr{L}$, is an optimal solution to LP (4).*

Proof. Follows directly from the proof of Theorem 2. □

Furthermore, using the same argument we can show that if $y_i^*(T)$ is a ρ-approximate solution to LP (5), then $x_i^*(T,l) = \frac{1}{L} \cdot y_i^*(T)$ is a ρ-approximate solution to LP (4). Therefore, the algorithm presented in Section 3 can be used at reduced complexity to obtain a provably good solution to the single-layer LP as given by (5). This solution can then be used to obtain a solution of precisely the same quality to the multilayer LP as given by (4).

5 The Approximation Algorithm

As usual, our approximation algorithm for the global routing problem in multi-layer VLSI design is as follows: We first solve the LP-relaxation of (1) to obtain a fractional solution; Then we round the fractional solution to obtain feasible solution to (1).

By the algorithm in [18], we are able to obtain a $(1 - \varepsilon)/r$-approximate solution for the LP-relaxation of (1). Then we apply the randomized rounding in [15, 16] to generate the integer solution. Based on the scaling technique in [15, 16], for any real number v satisfying $(v e^{1-v})^c < 1/(m+1)$, where $c = \min_{e,l} c_{e,l}$ is the minimal capacity, we can obtain a bound for the integer solution by randomized rounding:

Theorem 3. *There is an approximation algorithm for the global routing problem in multilayer VLSI design such that the objective value is no less than*

$$
\begin{cases}
(1-\varepsilon)vOPT/r - (\exp(1)-1)(1-\varepsilon)v\sqrt{OPT\ln(M+1)/r}, & \text{if } OPT > r\ln(M+1); \\
(1-\varepsilon)vOPT/r - \dfrac{\exp(1)(1-\varepsilon)v\ln(M+1)}{1+\ln(r\ln(M+1)/OPT)}, & \text{otherwise,}
\end{cases}
$$

where OPT is the optimal integer solution to (1).

Another strategy to obtain an approximate solution to (1) is to directly apply the approach to find $(1 - \varepsilon)/r$-approximate solution for integer packing problems in [18]. Thus we have the following result:

Theorem 4. *If all edge capacities are not less than $(1 + \log_{1+\delta}(ML + |\mathscr{I}|))/\delta$, then there exists an algorithm that finds a $(1 - \varepsilon)/r$-approximate integer solution to the global routing problem in multilayer VLSI design (1) within $O((ML + |\mathscr{I}|)L|\mathscr{I}|\varepsilon^{-2}c_{max}\beta\ln(ML+|\mathscr{I}|))$ time, where r and β are the ratio and the running time of the approximate minimum Steiner tree solver called as the oracle, and c_{max} is the maximum edge capacity.*

Though this approach has complexity depending on the input data, i.e., it is only a pseudo polynomial time approximation algorithm, it is worth using this method for some instances as the rounding stage is avoided.

In addition, at each iteration there are only $L|\mathscr{I}|$ Steiner trees generated. Thus, there are only a polynomial number of Steiner trees generated by using the approximation algorithm for fractional packing problem in [18], though there are exponentially many variables. This is similar to the column generation technique for LPs.

Corollary 2. *The approximation algorithms for the global routing problem in multilayer VLSI design only generates at most $O((ML + |\mathscr{I}|)L|\mathscr{I}|\varepsilon^{-2}\ln(ML+|\mathscr{I}|))$ Steiner trees.*

6 Concluding Remarks

Given a multilayer routing area, this paper has addressed the problem of selecting the maximum (weighted) set of nets, such that every net can be routed entirely in one of the given routing layers without violating the physical capacity constraints. This problem is motivated by the following.

- Routing the majority of nets each in a single layer significantly reduces the number of required vias in the final layout. It is known that vias increase fabrication cost and degrade system performance [7].
- Routing the majority of nets each in a single layer greatly simplifies the detailed routing problem in multilayer IC design [7].

First, we have formulated the problem as an integer linear program (ILP). Second, we have modified an algorithm by Garg and Könemann [9] for packing linear programs to obtain a $(1 - \varepsilon)/r$ approximation algorithm for the LP-relaxation of the global routing problem, where r is the approximation ratio of solving the minimum Steiner tree problem[2]. This has led also to an algorithm for the *integer* global routing problem that provides solutions *guaranteed* to be within a certain range of the optimal solution, and runs in polynomial-time even if all, possibly exponentially many, Steiner trees are considered in the formulation. Finally, we have demonstrated that the complexity of our algorithm can be significantly reduced in the case of identical routing layers.

References

1. C. Albrecht, "Gloabal Routing by New Approximation Algorithms for Multicommodity Flow", *IEEE Transactions on Computer Aided Design of Integrated Circuits and Systems*, vol. 20, no. 5, pp. 622–632, May 2001.
2. K. M. Anstreicher,"Towards a Practical Volumetric Cutting Plane Method for Convex Programming", *SIAM Journal on Optimization*, vol. 9, pp. 190–206, 1999.
3. S. Arora, C. Lund, R. Motwani, M. Sudan and M. Szegedy, "Proof Verification and Hardness of Approximation Problems", *Journal of the Association for Computing Machinery*, vol. 45, pp. 501–555, 1998.
4. M. Bern and P. Plassmann, "The Steiner Problem with Edge Lengths 1 and 2", *Information Professing Letters*, vol. 32, pp. 171–176, 1989.
5. C.-C. Chang and J. Cong, "An Efficient Aproach to Multilayer Layer Assignment with an Application to Via Minimization", *IEEE Transactions on Computer Aided Design of Integrated Circuits and Systems*, vol. 18, no. 5, pp. 608–620, May 1999.
6. M. Chlebík and J. Chlebíková, "Approximation Hardness of the Steiner Tree Problem", *Proceedings of the 8th Scandinavian Workshop on Algorithm Theory*, SWAT 2002, LNCS 2368, pp. 170–179.
7. J. Cong, M. Hossain and N.A. Sherwani, "A Provably Good Multilayer Topological Planar Routing Algorithm in IC layout Designs", *IEEE Transactions on Computer Aided Design of Integrated Circuits and Systems*, vol. 12, no. 1, pp. 70–78, Jan. 1993.

---

[2] The best known apoproximation guarantee for the minimum Steiner tree problem is 1.55 [17].

8. J. Cong and C.L. Liu, "On the k-Layer Planar Subset and Via Minimization Problems", *IEEE Transactions on Computer Aided Design of Integrated Circuits and Systems*, vol. 10, no. 8, pp. 972–981, Aug. 1991.
9. N. Garg and J. Könemann, "Fast and Simpler Algorithms for Multicommodity Flow and Other Fractional Packing Problems", *SIAM Journal on Computing*, vol. 37, no. 2, pp. 630–652, 2007.
10. M. Grötschel, L. Lovász and A. Schrijver, "The Ellipsoid Method and Its Consequences in Combinatorial Optimization", *Combinatorica*, vol. 1, pp. 169-197, 1981.
11. K. Jansen and H. Zhang, "Approximation algorithms for general packing problems and their application to the multicast congestion problem", *Mathematical Programming*, vol. 114, no. 1, pp. 183–206, 2008.
12. J.M. Kleinberg, "Approximation Algorithms for Disjoint Paths Problems", Ph.D. Dissertation, Department of Electrical Engineering and Computer Science, Massachusetts Institute of Technology, May 1996.
13. L.-C. E. Liu and C. Sechen, "Multilayer Chip-Level Global Routing Using an Efficient Graph-Based Steiner Tree Heuristic", *IEEE Transactions on Computer Aided Design of Integrated Circuits and Systems*, vol. 18, no. 10, pp. 1442–1451, Oct. 1999.
14. S.A. Plotkin, D.B. Shmoys and E. Tardos, "Fast Approximation Algorithms for Fractional Packing and Covering Problems", *Mathematics of Operations Research*, vol. 2, pp. 257–301, 1995.
15. P. Raghavan, "Probabilistic Construction of Deterministic Algorithms: Approximating Packing Integer Programs", *Journal of Computer and System Sciences*, vol. 37, pp. 130–143, 1988.
16. P. Raghavan and C. D. Thompson, "Randomized Rounding: A Technique for Provably Good Algorithms and Algorithmic Proofs", *Combinatorica* vol. 7, no. 4, pp. 365–374, 1987.
17. G. Robins and A. Zelikovsky, "Improved Steiner Tree Approximation in Graphs", *Proceedings of the 11th Annual ACM-SIAM Symposium on Discrete Algorithms*, SODA 2000, pp. 770–779.
18. M. Saad, T. Terlaky, A. Vannelli and H. Zhang, "Packing Trees in Communication Networks", *Journal of Combinatorial Optimization*, vol. 16, no. 4, pp. 402–423, 2008.
19. J. Xiong and L. He, "Extended Global Routing With *RLC* Crosstalk Constraints", *IEEE Transactions on Very Large Scale Integration (VLSI) Systems*, vol. 13, no. 3, pp. 319–329, March 2005.
20. N.E. Young, "Randomized Rounding without Solving the Linear Program", *Proceedings of the 6th ACM-SIAM Symposium on Discrete Algorithms*, SODA 1995, pp. 170–178.

Eliminating Poisson's Spot with Linear Programming

Robert J. Vanderbei

Abstract A leading design concept for NASA's upcoming planet-finding space telescope involves placing an occulter 72,000 km in front of a 4-m telescope. The purpose of the occulter is to block the bright starlight thereby enabling the telescope to take pictures of planets orbiting the blocked star. Unfortunately, diffraction effects prevent a simple circular occulter from providing a sufficiently dark shadow—a specially shaped occulter is required. In this paper, I explain how to reduce this shape-optimization problem to a large-scale linear programming problem that can be solved with modern LP tools.

Key words: linear programming, large scale optimization, optical design, high-contrast imaging, extrasolar planets

1 Introduction

Over the last decade or so, astronomers have discovered hundreds of planets orbiting stars beyond our Sun. Such planets are called *exosolar planets*. The first such discovery (by Marcy and Butler (1998)) and most of the subsequent discoveries involved an indirect detection method called the *radial velocity* (RV) method. This method exploits the fact that in a star-planet system, both the star and the planet orbit about their common center of mass. That is, not only does the planet move in an elliptical "orbit", so does the star itself. Of course, planets are much less massive than their stars and therefore the center of mass of the system generally lies close to the center of the star itself. Nonetheless, a star with a planet orbiting it will show a sinusoidal wobble which, even if quite small, can be detected spectroscopically using clever modern techniques in spectroscopy assuming, of course, that we are not

Robert J. Vanderbei
Princeton University, Princeton NJ e-mail: rvdb@princeton.edu

J.W. Chinneck et al. (eds.), *Operations Research and Cyber-Infrastructure*, Operations Research/Computer Science Interfaces Series 47, DOI: 10.1007/978-0-387-88843-9_24, © Springer Science+Business Media, LLC 2009

viewing the star-planet system "face-on". Clearly, this technique is strongly biased toward very massive (say Jupiter sized) planets orbiting very close to their star (say closer than Mercury is to our Sun).

It should be apparent that the radial velocity method of indirect planet detection is a rather subtle method. The results should be confirmed by other means and in some cases this has been done. The most successful alternative method for planet detection is the so-called *transit method*. This method only works for star-planet systems that we "see" almost perfectly edge-on. For such systems, from our perspective here on Earth the planet orbits the star in such a manner that at times it periodically passes directly in front of the star causing the star to dim slightly, but measurably, during the "transit". The first such example, discovered by Charbonneau et al (2000) involves the star HD209458. Its planet was discovered by the radial velocity method but confirmed by detecting transits. This particular planet is 1.3 times larger than Jupiter in radius and it orbits HD209458 once every 3.5 days. During a transit event, the intensity of the starlight dips by 1.7%.

These discoveries have generated enormous interest among professional astronomers in actually detecting and even imaging Earth-like planets in Earth-like orbits around Sun-like stars. The planets detected by indirect methods tend to be much more massive than Earth and have orbits much closer to their star. Such planets would be rather uninhabitable by life-forms that have evolved here on Earth. The interest is in finding, and more specifically imaging, so-called habitable planets. This is called the *direct detection* problem. But it is a hard problem for three rather fundamental reasons:

1. **Contrast.** In visible light our Sun is 10^{10} times brighter than Earth.
2. **Angular Separation.** A planet at one Sun-Earth distance from its star viewed from a distance of 10 parsecs (32.6 light years) can appear at most 0.1 arcseconds away from the star itself.
3. **Paucity of Targets.** There are less than 100 Sun-like stars within 10 parsecs of Earth.

2 Large Space Telescope

The simplest design concept is just to build a telescope big enough to overcome the three obstacles articulated in the previous section. An Earth-like planet illuminated by a Sun-like star at a distance of about 10 parsecs will be very faint—about as faint as the dimmest objects imaged by the Hubble space telescope, which has a light-collecting mirror that is 2.4 meters in diameter. Hence, the telescope will need to be at least this big.

But, the wave nature of light makes it impossible to focus all of the starlight exactly to a point. Instead, the starlight makes a diffraction pattern that consists of a small (in diameter) concentration of light, called the *Airy disk* surrounded by an infinite sequence of rings of light, called *diffraction rings*, each ring dimmer than the one before. The complete diffraction pattern associated with a point source is called the *Airy pattern*. About 83.8% of the light falls into the Airy disk. Another 7.2% lands on the first diffraction ring, 2.8% on the second diffraction ring, etc. Mathematically, the diffraction pattern is given by the square of the magnitude of the complex electric field at the image plane and the electric field is given by

$$E(\rho,\phi) = \frac{1}{i\lambda f} \int_0^{D/2} \int_0^{2\pi} e^{\frac{i\pi}{\lambda f}(\rho^2 - 2r\rho\cos(\theta-\phi))} r \, d\theta \, dr$$

$$= \frac{2\pi}{i\lambda f} e^{\frac{i\pi\rho^2}{\lambda f}} \int_0^{D/2} J_0(2\pi r\rho/\lambda f) r \, dr$$

$$= \frac{D}{2i\rho} e^{\frac{i\pi\rho^2}{\lambda f}} J_1(\pi D\rho/\lambda f).$$

Here, (ρ,ϕ) denotes polar coordinates of a point in the image plane, (r,θ) denotes polar coordinates of a point on the telescope's light-collecting mirror, f is the focal length of the telescope, D is the *aperture* (i.e., diameter) of the mirror, and J_0 and J_1 are the 0-th and 1-st Bessel functions of the first kind. Note that the electric field can in principle depend on both ρ and ϕ but in this case it depends only on ρ because the ϕ dependence disappeared after integrating the inner integral (over θ). When the electric field is manifestly a function of only ρ, we will denote it simply by $E(\rho)$.

From the last expression we see that, except for some scale factors, the Airy pattern for a point source is given by the square of the function J_1 (see Figure 1). Of course, the scale factors are critically important—we need them to figure out how large to make the telescope. In other words, we need to figure out values for D and f that will allow us to "see" a dim planet next to a bright star. With two point sources, a star and a planet, the combined image is obtained by adding the Airy patterns from each source together, after displacing one pattern from the other by an appropriate amount. Simple geometry tells us that the physical separation of the two images in the image plane is just their angular separation on the sky (typically 0.1 arcseconds) in radians times the focal length of the telescope. For example, 0.1 arcseconds is 4.85×10^{-7} radians and so a planet separated from its star by 0.1 arcseconds as viewed from Earth will form an image a distance $\rho = 4.85 \times 10^{-7} f$ from the star's image in the image plane of a telescope of focal length f. At this value of ρ, the intensity of the starlight $I(\rho) = |E(\rho)|^2$ must be reduced by 10 orders of magnitude otherwise the starlight will overwhelm the planet light. In other words, we need

$$|E(\rho)| \le 10^{-5}|E(0)|.$$

Substituting

$$|E(\rho)| = \frac{D}{2\rho}|J_1(\pi D\rho/\lambda f)|$$

and

$$|E(0)| = \frac{2\pi}{\lambda f}\left(\frac{D}{2}\right)^2$$

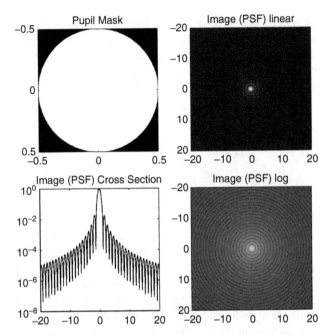

Fig. 1 The upper left figure shows that we are considering a telescope whose mirror has a circular profile (as is typical). The associated Airy pattern is shown in the two right-hand figures. The top one is shown with the usual linear scale. The bottom one is shown logarithmically stretched with everything below 10^{-10} set to black and everything above 1 set to white.

into this inequality, we get

$$\frac{D}{2\rho}|J_1\left(\pi D\rho/\lambda f\right)| \le 10^{-5} \times \frac{2\pi}{\lambda f}\left(\frac{D}{2}\right)^2$$

This inequality simplifies to

$$\frac{|J_1(u)|}{u} \le 10^{-5},$$

where $u = \pi D\rho/\lambda f$. As most programming languages (e.g., C, C++, Matlab, and Fortran) have Bessel functions built in just like the trigonometric functions, it is easy to determine that the inequality is satisfied if and only if $u \ge 1853$. Now, as mentioned before, $\rho/f = 4.85 \times 10^{-7}$. Also for visible light $\lambda \approx 5 \times 10^{-7}$ meters. Hence, we can assume that $\rho/\lambda f$ is about 1 and therefore simplify our contrast criterion to

$$\pi D \ge 1853.$$

In other words,

$$D \ge 590 \text{ meters.}$$

Of course, atmospheric turbulence is a major problem even for moderate sized telescopes. Hence, this telescope will need to be a space telescope. The Hubble space telescope (HST) has a mirror that is 2.4 meters in diameter. To image planets with a large but straight-forward telescope would require a space telescope 250 times bigger in diameter than HST. Of course, cost grows in proportion to the volume of the instrument, so one would imagine that such a telescope, if it were possible to build at all, would cost $250^3 = 16 \times 10^6$ times as much as HST. Such a large telescope will not be built in our lifetime.

3 Space Occulter

In the previous section, we saw that it is not feasible to make a simple telescope that would be capable of imaging Earth-like planets around nearby Sun-like stars. The problem is the starlight. One solution, first proposed by Spitzer (1965), is to prevent the starlight from entering the telescope in the first place. This could be done by flying a large occulting disk out in front of the telescope. If it is far enough away, one could imagine that it would block the starlight but the planet would not be blocked. Of course, as explained already the angular separation between the planet and the star is on the order of 0.1 arcseconds. Also, simple calculations about the expected brightness of the planet suggest that the telescope needs to have an aperture of at least 4 meters in order simply to get enough photons from the planet to take a picture in a reasonable time-frame. So, the occulting disk needs to be at least 4 meters in diameter. To get the planet at 0.1 arcsecond separation to be not blocked by the occulter, means that the occulter has to be positioned about 8250 kilometers in front of the telescope. But, this back-of-the-envelope calculation is based on the simple geometry of ray optics. As before, diffraction effects play a significant role. A 4 meter occulting disk at 8250 km will produce a shadow but the shadow will not be completely dark—some light will diffract into the shadow. In fact, at this small angle, lots of light will diffract into the shadow (see Figure 2). The occulter needs to be made bigger and positioned further away.

The first question to be addressed is: how much bigger and further? To answer that requires a careful diffraction analysis. The formula is similar to the one before. It differs because now there is no focusing element. Instead we have just an obstruction. Also, the disk of the occulter blocks light whereas the disk represented by the light-collecting mirror of a telescope transmits the light. Nonetheless, the formula for the downstream electric field can be explicitly written:

$$E(\rho, \phi) = 1 - \frac{1}{i\lambda z} \int_0^{D/2} \int_0^{2\pi} e^{\frac{i\pi}{\lambda z}(\rho^2 - 2r\rho\cos(\theta-\phi)+r^2)} r \, d\theta \, dr$$

$$= 1 - \frac{2\pi}{i\lambda z} e^{\frac{i\pi\rho^2}{\lambda z}} \int_0^{D/2} J_0\left(2\pi r\rho/\lambda z\right) e^{\frac{i\pi r^2}{\lambda z}} r \, dr,$$

where z is the distance between the occulting disk and the pupil of the telescope.

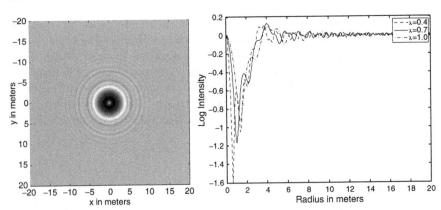

Fig. 2 A circular occulting disk 4 meters in diameter and 8250 km away gives a shadow that provides less than an order of magnitude of starlight suppression in its shadow. The left image is plotted on a linear scale. The right image shows a semilog plot of intensity as a function of radius. Note that the shadow is darkened by less than an order of magnitude. Also, note the small but bright spot at the center—this is *Poisson's spot*.

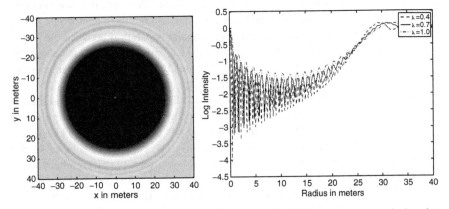

Fig. 3 A circular occulting disk 50 meters in diameter and 72,000 km away gives a shadow that provides only a few orders of magnitude of starlight suppression in its shadow. The left image is plotted on a linear scale. The right image shows a semilog plot of intensity as a function of radius. Note that the shadow is only about 2 orders of magnitude suppressed, a far cry from the 10 orders needed for planet finding. Also, note that Poisson's spot is again visible.

Figure 3 shows that even an occulter 50 meters in diameter 72000 km away does not give a dark enough shadow. Even an occulter 100 times larger and further away than that achieves only 4 orders of magnitude suppression.

4 Poisson's Spot

Note that both Figures 2 and 3 show a bright spot at the center of the shadow. One would expect that a shadow would be darkest at its center and this spot might make one think there is something wrong with the formulae used to compute the shadow. In fact, when Poisson realized in 1818 that the wave description of light would imply the existence of just such a bright spot, he used this as an argument against the theory, not well-accepted at the time, that light is a wave. But Dominique Arago verified the existence of the spot experimentally. This was one of the first, and certainly one of the most convincing, proofs that light is indeed a wave. Today, the bright spot is called either *Poisson's spot* or the *spot of Arago*.

Mathematically, it is easy to see where the spot comes from. Putting $\rho = 0$ in the formula for the electric field, the field can be computed explicitly:

$$E(0, \phi) = 1 - \frac{2\pi}{i\lambda z} \int_0^{D/2} e^{\frac{i\pi r^2}{\lambda z}} r\, dr$$

$$= 1 + \int_0^{\frac{i\pi}{\lambda z}\frac{D^2}{2}} e^u du$$

$$= e^{\frac{i\pi}{\lambda z}\frac{D^2}{2}}.$$

Since the intensity of the light is the magnitude of the electric field squared, we see that the intensity at the center is unity.

5 Apodized Space Occulter

Conventional wisdom, developed over centuries, is that unpleasant diffraction effects such as Poisson's spot can be mitigated by "softening" hard edges. This suggests replacing the disk occulter, which is assumed to be completely opaque to its outer edge, with a translucent occulter, opaque in the center but becoming progressively more transparent as one approaches the rim (Copi and Starkman (2000) were the first to propose this). Such variable transmissivity is called *apodization*. The question is: can we define an apodization that eliminates Poisson's spot and in addition guarantees a very dark shadow (10 orders of magnitude of light suppression) of at least 4 meters diameter using an apodized occulting disk that is not too large and reasonably close by (if anything flying tens of thousands of kilometers away can be considered close by)?

Let $A(r)$ denote the level of attenuation at radius r along the occulter. Then the formula for the electric field has to be modified to this formula:

$$E(\rho) = 1 - \frac{2\pi}{i\lambda z} e^{\frac{i\pi\rho^2}{\lambda z}} \int_0^{D/2} J_0\left(2\pi r\rho/\lambda z\right) e^{\frac{i\pi r^2}{\lambda z}} A(r) r\, dr,$$

We can formulate the following optimization problem:

$$\text{minimize} \quad \gamma$$

$$\text{subject to} \quad |E(\rho)| \leq \gamma, \quad \text{for } \rho \in [0,3], \lambda \in [0.4,\ 1.0] \times 10^{-6}$$

All lengths are in meters. The wavelength λ varies over visible and near infra-red wavelengths. The radius of the deep shadow is 3 meters to leave some wiggle-room for a 4 meter telescope to position itself. We have chosen the apodization function A to depend only on radius r. Hence, the electric field depends only on radius too. We have therefore written $E(\rho)$ for the electric field at radius ρ. The variables in the optimization are the suppression level γ and the apodization function A. Since the electric field E depends linearly on the apodization function A, the problem is an infinite-dimensional second-order cone-programming problem.

We can make it an infinite dimensional linear programming problem if we replace the upper bound on the magnitude of the electric field E with upper and lower bounds on the real and imaginary parts of E:

$$\text{minimize} \quad \gamma$$

$$\text{subject to} \quad -\gamma \leq \Re(E(\rho)) \leq \gamma \quad \text{for } \rho \in [0,3], \lambda \in [0.4,\ 1.0] \times 10^{-6}$$

$$\quad -\gamma \leq \Im(E(\rho)) \leq \gamma \quad \text{for } \rho \in [0,3], \lambda \in [0.4,\ 1.0] \times 10^{-6}.$$

Finally, we can discretize the set of shadow radii $[0,3]$ into 150 evenly space points, the set of occulter radii $[0,D]$ into 4000 evenly space points, and the wavelength band $[0.3, 1.1] \times 10^{-6}$ in increments of 10^{-7} and replace the integral defining E in terms of A with the appropriate Riemann sum to get a large-scale (but finite) linear programming problem:

$$\text{minimize} \quad \gamma$$

$$\text{subject to} \quad -\gamma \leq \Re(E(\rho)) \leq \gamma \quad \text{for } \rho \in [0,3], \lambda \in [0.4,\ 1.0] \times 10^{-6}$$

$$\quad -\gamma \leq \Im(E(\rho)) \leq \gamma \quad \text{for } \rho \in [0,3], \lambda \in [0.4,\ 1.0] \times 10^{-6}$$

$$\quad A'(r) \leq 0, \quad \text{for } r \in [0, D/2]$$

$$\quad -d \leq A''(r) \leq d, \quad \text{for } r \in [0, D/2].$$

For the linear programming problem, we add additional constraints to stipulate that the function A be monotonically decreasing and have a second derivative (difference) that remains between given upper and lower bounds. These additional constraints help to ensure that the solution to the discrete problem is a good approximation to the solution to the underlying infinite dimensional problem.

The linear programming problem was formulated in AMPL (Fourer et al (1993)) and solved using LOQO (Vanderbei (1999)). The AMPL model is shown in Figure 4. The linear programming problem has 4001 variables and 8645 constraints.

```
function J0;

param pi   := 4*atan(1);
param pi2  := pi/2;
param N    := 4000;          # discretization parameter at occulter plane
param M    := 150;           # discretization parameter at telescope plane
param c    := 25.0;          # overall radius of occulter
param z    := 72000e+3;      # distance from telescope to apodized occulter
param lambda {3..11};        # set of wavelengths
param rho1 := 25;            # max radius investigated at telescope's pupil plane
param rho_end := 3;          # radius below which high contrast is required

# a few convenient shorthands
param lz   {j in 3..11 by 1.0} := lambda[j]*z;
param pi2lz {j in 3..11 by 1.0} := 2*pi/lz[j];
param pilz {j in 3..11 by 1.0} := pi/lz[j];

param dr := c/N;
set Rs ordered;
let Rs := setof {j in 1..N by 1} c*(j-0.5)/N;

var A {r in Rs} >= 0, <= 1;

set Rhos ordered;
let Rhos := setof {j in 0..M} (j/M)*rho1;

var contrast >= 0;

var Ereal {j in 3..11 by 1.0, rho in Rhos} =
    1-pi2lz[j]*
    sum {r in Rs} sin(pilz[j]*(r^2+rho^2))*A[r]*J0(-pi2lz[j]*r*rho)*r*dr;
var Eimag {j in 3..11 by 1.0, rho in Rhos} =
    pi2lz[j]*
    sum {r in Rs} cos(pilz[j]*(r^2+rho^2))*A[r]*J0(-pi2lz[j]*r*rho)*r*dr;

minimize cont: contrast;

subject to main_real_neg {j in 3..11 by 1.0, rho in Rhos: rho < rho_end}:
    -contrast <= Ereal[j,rho];
subject to main_real_pos {j in 3..11 by 1.0, rho in Rhos: rho < rho_end}:
    Ereal[j,rho] <= contrast;
subject to main_imag_neg {j in 3..11 by 1.0, rho in Rhos: rho < rho_end}:
    -contrast <= Eimag[j,rho];
subject to main_imag_pos {j in 3..11 by 1.0, rho in Rhos: rho < rho_end}:
    Eimag[j,rho] <= contrast;

subject to monotone {r in Rs: r>first(Rs)}: A[prev(r)] >= A[r];
subject to smooth   {r in Rs: r>first(Rs) && r<last(Rs)}:
    -0.044 <= (A[next(r)]-2*A[r]+A[prev(r)])/dr^2 <= 0.044;

let {j in 3..11 by 1.0} lambda[j] := (j-0.5)*1e-7;

solve;

printf: "%12e, %f, %f \n", contrast^2, 2*c, z/1000;

printf {r in Rs}: "%10.7f %10.7f \n", r, A[r] > "A";
```

Fig. 4 AMPL model for optimal apodization.

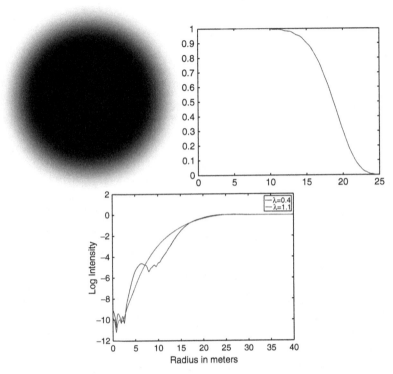

Fig. 5 An apodized circular occulting disk 50 meters in diameter and 72,000 km away gives that achieves roughly 10 orders of magnitude suppression over the entire desired band of wavelengths. The top-left image shows the apodized occulter. The top-right graph shows its attenuation as a function of radius. The bottom graph shows the intensity at the pupil plane at the two extreme wavelengths 0.4 and 1.0 microns.

Using its default stopping criteria, LOQO solves the problem in 51 iterations which takes 224 seconds on a current generation Macbook Pro. The optimal apodized occulter is shown in Figure 5.

By modern computational standards, this is not a very large linear programming problem. But, there are several issues at play here not the least of which is that this particular instance is only a discrete approximation to a much larger, in fact infinite dimensional, problem. It is of paramount importance to verify that the discretization provides a meaningful solution to the real problem. To do this, we have code that uses a spline to resample the apodization function at a finer level and then compute the electric field at the telescope pupil also at a finer level of discretization. We also need to check at wavelengths falling between the discrete set at which we have stipulated high contrast. All of these checks have been performed. It turns out that the discrete sampling of wavelengths creates the biggest errors. Hence, at times we have run the model with twice as many wavelength sample points. But, we should also bear in mind that there are many other issues. For one, we are still in the design phase and are therefore considering many different designs. This occulter becomes transparent beyond 0.075 arcseconds. Is that adequate? Do we need to be able to detect planets closer to their star than that? Is 10^{-10} a strong enough level of contrast? Is it stronger than it needs to be? These issues are still being debated by the scientists who have a feel for what is needed. Also, what about sensitivity? There will undoubtedly be manufacturing error. How precisely must the occulter be made to ensure the design level of performance? This is one of the most critical questions and will be addressed in more detail in the next section. Finally, how accurately can two

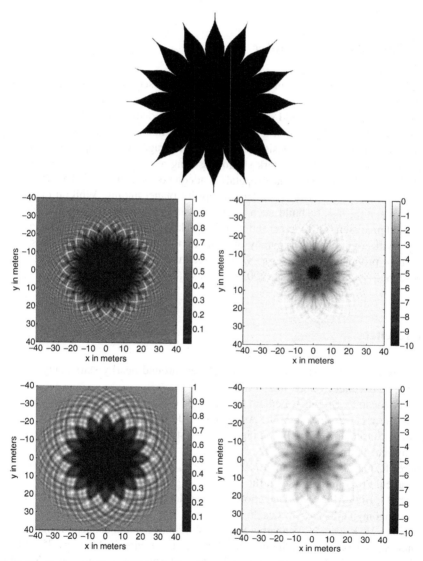

Fig. 6 The top image shows a 16-petal approximation to the optimal apodization. The second row shows the downstream shadow for $\lambda = 0.4$ microns using both a linear (on the left) and a log (on the right) stretch. The third row shows the downstream shadow for $\lambda = 1.0$ microns.

spacecraft separated by tens of thousands of kilometers be positioned with respect to each other? Can we get the telescope centered in the shadow and can we keep it there long enough to take a multi-hour exposure? These are difficult engineering questions. Optimization plays a critical role in assessing various trade-offs. We have produced a large number of scenarios for consideration. The one presented here is currently the one that seems to provide the best balance of the various trade-offs that must be considered. But, surely next month a slightly different version will be considered better.

6 Petalized Space Occulter

The apodized occulter design given in the previous section provides the starlight suppression necessary to image an Earth-like planet. But, sensitivity analyses show that it is not possible to build such an occulter with adequate precision. It is shown in Vanderbei et al (2007) that a binary, i.e. unapodized, non-circular occulter that consists of multiple petals designed so that the average level of opacity at radius r matches $A(r)$ can provide a dark shadow as long as the number of petals is large enough. Simulations show that 16 petals is adequate—see Figure 6. This is the current baseline design for the occulter concept for planet finding. While it may seem like a daunting task to build such a large occulter (50 meters tip-to-tip) with the required precision (millimeter) and fly it 72000 kilometers in front of a 4 meter telescope with a positioning accuracy of 1 meter, this design is currently considered the most promising concept for NASA's eventual Terrestrial Planet Finder space telescope—see Simmons et al (2003) and Cash (2006).

References

Cash W (2006) Detection of earth-like planets around nearby stars using a petal-shaped occulter. Nature 442:51–53

Charbonneau D, Brown T, Latham D, Mayor M (2000) Detection of planetary transits across a sun-like star. The Astrophysical Journal 529:45–48

Copi C, Starkman G (2000) The big occulting steerable satellite (boss). The Astrophysical Journal 532:581–592

Fourer R, Gay D, Kernighan B (1993) AMPL: A Modeling Language for Mathematical Programming. Scientific Press

Marcy G, Butler P (1998) Detection of extrasolar giant planets. Annual Review of Astronomy and Astrophysics 36:57–97

Simmons W, Kasdin N, Vanderbei R, Cash W (2003) System concept design for the new worlds observer. Bulletin of the American Astronomical Society 35:1205

Spitzer L (1965) The beginnings and future of space astronomy. Am Scientist 50(3):473

Vanderbei R (1999) LOQO user's manual—version 3.10. Optimization Methods and Software 12:485–514

Vanderbei R, Cady E, Kasdin N (2007) Optimal occulter design for finding extrasolar planets. Astrophysical Journal 665(1):794–798

Index